SECOND EDITION

HUMAN
RELATIONS
Behavior at Work

SECOND EDITION

HUMAN
RELATIONS
Behavior at Work

Originally called *Human Relations: Concepts and Skills*

JAMES M. HIGGINS
The Crummer School
Rollins College

RANDOM HOUSE BUSINESS DIVISION/NEW YORK

To MacIntosh and Misty, companions throughout the
long days at the word processor.

Second Edition
98765432
Copyright © 1982, 1987 by Random House, Inc.

Library of Congress Cataloging in Publication Data

Higgins, James M.
    Human relations.

    Includes indexes
    1. Personnel management.   2. Communication in
personnel management.   3. Organizational behavior.
4. Interpersonal relations.   5. Psychology,
Industrial.   I. Title.
HF5549.H474   1987   658.3′145   86-31450
ISBN 0-394-35112-6
Manufactured in the United States of America

Photo Credits
Page 3: Courtesy of Delta Airlines, Inc. Page 13: Courtesy of Western Electric.
Page 25: Courtesy of Human Edge Software Corporation. Page 49: UPI/Bettmann
Newsphotos. Page 75: Greg Davis/Sygma. Page 84: Richard Howard/Time, Inc.
Page 101: Mark Antman/The Image Works. Page 120: Random House photo by
Kathy Bendo. Pages 130 & 131: James M. Higgins. Page 135: Bob Kalman/The Image
Works. Page 163: Peter Yates. Page 191: Mark Antman/The Image Works. Page 219:
Courtesy of Elizabeth Hishon. Page 243: Tom Cheek/Stock, Boston. Page 269:
Courtesy of Photocircuits. Page 297: Peter Menzel/Stock, Boston. Page 309: Diego
Goldberg/Sygma. Page 319: Courtesy of Apple Computer. Page 343: J. P. Laffont/
Sygma. Page 371: Random House photo by Kathy Bendo. Page 393: Laimute E.
Druskis/Stock, Boston. Page 425: Courtesy of Chrysler Corporation. Page 447:
Courtesy of AT&T.

Photo on cover: Geoff Gove/The Image Bank
Cover and interior design by Dorothy Sparacino Bungert.

PREFACE

As in the previous edition, the purpose of HUMAN RELATIONS: BEHAVIOR AT WORK, second edition, is to give you the opportunity to learn both the concepts and the skills that will benefit you in practicing human relations on the job, in an organization, or in many other situations. This book provides you with very thorough and detailed text coverage of the topic presented and combines this textual coverage with cases and exercises that allow you to practice and apply what you have learned in the materials you have read. Since these concepts can be practiced and applied in your daily life, you can make personal use of this book, both now and later.

TEXT ORGANIZATION

The human relations concepts and skills presented in this book are discussed in 18 chapters organized within six major parts. Part One, "Striving Toward Positive Human Relations in Organizations," introduces the subject of human relations in organizations and discusses individual differences and perception. Part Two, "Understanding and Improving Individual Relationships," deals with motivation and performance, and with communication and its techniques. Part Three, "Understanding and Improving Group Relationships," reviews topics including intra- and intergroup dynamics, leadership, special groups (those protected by laws designed to ensure equal employment opportunity), and unions and discipline. Part Four, "Understanding and Improving Organizational Relationships," focuses on appraisal systems, job design, technology, the quality of work life, and individual values and organizational culture. Part Five, "Understanding and Improving Relationships Across Cultures," discusses international relationships. Part Six, "Understanding and Improving Yourself," discusses creativity, organizational power, politics, and conflict, and life and career planning.

AIDS TO STUDENT LEARNING

HUMAN RELATIONS: BEHAVIOR AT WORK, second edition, is a unique book. Because it combines both background concepts and the opportunity to use and apply those concepts, it employs several special features to aid the student in the learning process:

- Each chapter contains both cases and experiential exercises to use in building skills.
- Each chapter features one or more "Human Relations Happening," containing lengthy examples of topics discussed in that chapter. One "Human Relations Happening" opens each chapter in order to illustrate how the topic of the chapter applies to an actual organizational situation.

- Most chapters contain one or more "Test Yourself" sections which are used to determine your skill or knowledge level about topics in that chapter or to show you how the topics relate to you on an individual level.
- Numerous real world organizational examples are interspersed throughout the text.
- Cartoons are used to reinforce the basic points of each chapter in a fun way, and they are combined with a lively writing style and quotations to stimulate interest.

The text also features several chapters, or parts thereof, that are not often found in other human relations texts. These include:

- personality and perception
- communication skills
- organizational communication systems
- discipline handling
- appraisal systems
- organizational culture
- cross cultural relations
- creative problem solving
- power and politics
- life planning.

The text also features more comprehensive coverage of communication, motivation, and leadership; coverage of motivation and leadership models that include a pragmatic decision-making approach; and a sound review of foundational topics in organizational behavior. Other important timely topics which are discussed, in addition, are quality circles, time management, conflict management, individual values, listening, self-image, and job design and technology.

PHILOSOPHY OF THE TEXT

Essential to this book are the beliefs that

- A person with a positive self-image is more productive than a person with a negative self-image.
- Human relations is a skills process, one that can be learned. Some of these skills are easily mastered. Most are not. Acquiring skill requires practice.
- Human relations is a science and an art.
- The skills learning process is enhanced by experience and experiential learning exercises. We learn best by doing.
- Everyone in the organization is responsible for human relations, therefore everyone in the organization should have some knowledge of the process and some basic skills in the process.
- The manager is the pivotal factor in successful versus unsuccessful organizational human relations.
- Effective communication is the most critical human relations skill. Com-

munications occur in every interpersonal dynamics situation and is vital to both leadership and motivation—two primary managerial skills.

- The human relations course is moving toward more practical commentary in line with current trends in organizational needs.
- Results are more likely to occur where requirements/criteria/objectives are known in advance.
- In this decade in the United States and Canada, the managerial emphasis will be on improving human relations in a determined effort to improve productivity. Teamwork will be an integral component of management systems to be employed.
- Organizational cultures must meet the needs of the workplace.
- We desperately need more creativity in our lives and organizations.

SELF-ANALYSIS EXERCISES

A vital ingredient in learning human relations is your examination of your perspective relative to the concepts and skills being taught. Many of the aforementioned exercises provide self-analysis. The purpose of these exercises is to cause you to work on that part of the human relations process over which you have the most control—YOU! The basis for all improvement is you. It is hoped that the exercises will enable you to think in terms of self-improvement. They will help you see: what approaches you now use and which ones need improvement; what some of your basic attitudes are and their possible impacts on others; and why you may act the way you do in certain situations and whether you should change those behaviors. Finally, the exercises and the textural materials should motivate you to make positive changes in your human relations behavior, which in turn should cause positive changes in the human relations behavior in those around you.

INSTRUCTIONAL AIDS

- *Instructor's Manual.* The Instructor's Manual contains teaching suggestions, chapter synopses, definitions of key terms and concepts, answers to chapter discussion questions, discussions of cases and exercises, supplementary materials for each chapter, test banks of questions by chapter, and a list of recommended films and sources for each chapter. Transparency masters for key figures and other materials used in the text are also provided.
- Penn State University Film Library films are available to adopters.

A SPECIAL NOTE TO THE STUDENT

More than any other course you will take, this one probably has the most in it for you personally as a human being. You can only get out of it what you put in it. Remember: you don't just learn about human relations, you have to live them.

ACKNOWLEDGMENTS

No author writes alone. He or she is the product of many who have influenced him or her. Hugh Russell first introduced me to human relations in one of his courses. He has greatly affected my thinking in this area for many years. Moreover, there are countless scholars who have also influenced the content of this book. Their works are cited in the text. As in the first edition, thanks are due to Tom Clark and John Cannaday for ideas on motivation and assertiveness, respectively.

The following people have provided significant input into the final form of the text as a consequence of their reviews of both the first edition and the manuscript of the second edition.

Gerald Arffa, Indiana University—Purdue
Patricia P. Baxter, Pensacola Junior College
Patricia Capps, St. Petersburg Junior College
Mary Jane Dawe, Scottsdale Community College
Louise Everett, Hillsborough Community College
M. Roger Goodson, New Hampshire College
Robert Hammond, Lexington Technical Institute
Donald Hucker, Cypress College
E. Bruce Isaacson, Mesa College
Pat Jones, Brevard Community College
Miles LaRowe, Laramie County Community College
Robert Nixon, Pima Community College
Estella R. Pomroy, Parkersburg Community College
Steven Tilley, Gainesville Junior College

Many thanks must go to the editorial staff at Random House. Susan Badger, Acquiring Editor, guided this project throughout and provided several very good ideas for the book. Anne Mahoney, Developmental Editor, counseled and advised well over the past two years as she worked me through the manuscript process. The production process was handled well by Project Editor Elaine Rosenberg. Dorothy Bungert, the designer, and Barbara Salazar, the copy editor, are to be praised for their fine efforts. I am also grateful to Valerie Raymond, who was of invaluable assistance to me in the later stages of the project.

My wife Ellen has encouraged me throughout this process, and her tolerance for my passion for writing is to be greatly admired. I also greatly appreciate my children, Tracy and Laura, for their encouragement and tolerance.

Linda Horton, my graduate assistant, helped put the final touches on the manuscript. Susan Crabill, my secretary, met unbelievable deadlines with amazing thoroughness and with a smile. Finally, Martin Schatz, Dean of the Crummer School of Business at Rollins College, has provided the organizational culture and reward systems that make writing enjoyable.

Special thanks are due to my mother who provided me with self-confidence and love.

CONTENTS IN BRIEF

DETAILED CONTENTS

PART TWO
UNDERSTANDING AND IMPROVING INDIVIDUAL RELATIONSHIPS 47

PART THREE
UNDERSTANDING AND IMPROVING GROUP RELATIONSHIPS 161

- HUMAN RELATIONS -
HAPPENING
Are Women Lawyers
Discriminated Against at
Large Law Firms? 219

- HUMAN RELATIONS -
HAPPENING
Highlights of the GM-UAW
Settlement 243

PART FOUR
UNDERSTANDING AND IMPROVING
ORGANIZATIONAL RELATIONSHIPS 267

- HUMAN RELATIONS -
HAPPENING
Photocircuits 269

PART SIX
UNDERSTANDING AND IMPROVING YOURSELF 369

1

STRIVING TOWARD POSITIVE HUMAN RELATIONS IN ORGANIZATIONS

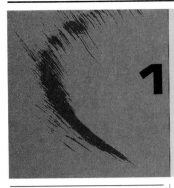

1 HUMAN RELATIONS: BEHAVIOR, WORK, AND YOU

LEARNING OBJECTIVES

When you have completed this chapter, you should be able to:
1. Define human relations and describe its history.
2. List reasons why both organizations and individuals should be concerned about human relations.
3. Explain why human relations training is necessary.
4. Describe the various types of human relations within an organization.
5. Identify the major themes in human relations in work organizations.
6. Enumerate the variables that require a positive approach to human relations in organizations.

EMPLOYEES SAY, "THANK YOU, DELTA!"

The lengthy recession and the deregulation of the airlines hit the major air carriers particularly hard in 1982. For the first time in 25 years, the acknowledged industry profit leader, Delta, had lost money—$18.4 million in the first quarter. Yet in August, true to its value system, Delta gave its 37,000 employees a healthy raise of 8.5 percent. Most employees were surprised. Having expected the worst (40,000 airline industry employees had recently lost their

"The Spirit of Delta," tied with ribbon, at the dedication ceremony

jobs), they received the best. Three flight attendants, Ginny Whitfield, Jean Owens, and Diane Carvelli, wondered if they and other employees could do something to repay the company for its good treatment of them over the years. They hit upon the idea of buying a Boeing 767 and presenting it to the company. The company was scheduled to take delivery of its first 767 in December, so the timing was right, but the amount of time available to raise the money was short.

Two weeks later, taking advantage of the company's open-door policy and a layover in Atlanta, the three discussed their plan with Robert Oppenlander, senior vice-president for finance. He told them that the plane would cost $30 million. They were relieved; they had thought it would be more. He promised to let them know quickly the company's reaction to their idea. Within a few days he reported that the company would support the project but could not sponsor the campaign: it would have to be an employee effort. In addition, the company required that no records of support be kept and that no pressure be put upon employees to contribute. The program had to be totally voluntary. It was estimated that 80 percent of the employees would have to contribute $810 each in order to purchase the plane. The company would provide an empty storeroom for the campaign's headquarters and limited assistance for such items as telephones.

The women organized a committee. Objectives and strategies were formulated. The task of raising $30 million was not easy. At first employees thought it was a joke. Raise $30 million? **Them**? Many felt it couldn't be done. But through active communication, high levels of participation, and the driving force of the wish to repay Delta for its years of positive treatment of its employees, the task was accomplished. On December 15 the employees pre-

(Continued on page 4)

sented the first 767, **The Spirit of Delta,** to the company. At that time 77 percent of the employees had pledged their share of the cost. Delta's president, Dave Garrett, was presented with a large, symbolic key to the plane. Garrett admitted, "It was one of the most emotional times in my life. I've never felt so much togetherness."

SOURCE: Linda Lawrence, "Thank You, Delta Airlines," *Reader's Digest*, November 1983, pp. 112–16.

"If you dig deeply into any problem, you will get to "people."
J. WATSON WILSON

You are about to embark on a journey that has personal meaning to you. You are about to explore the world of human relations in organizations. Human relations is a concept that everyone seems to know about, intuitively and from personal experience. But we know that the actions that people may take intuitively in their dealings with others or the approaches to interpersonal relations that they have learned through experience are not always appropriate. To make matters worse, ways of relating to others that are known to be effective are often neglected. Small wonder, then, that we need to learn more about human relations and apply more of what we learn. And since our relationships occur most frequently within the confines of organizations, and in particular in work organizations, any knowledge we can gain about behavior at work is bound to be helpful in our working lives.

"Man's life in contemporary society can be characterized largely as one of organizational memberships."
ARNOLD S. TANNENBAUM

This chapter introduces the topic of human relations in organizations, discusses the various forms of interaction that such human relations may take, identifies the central themes in the field of human relations in organizations, explores the history of the human relations movement, reviews the importance of positive organizational human relations, and points out several factors that will require organizations to take a more positive approach to human relations than they have been accustomed to taking.

HUMAN RELATIONS IN ORGANIZATIONS

The term **human relations** refers literally to all interactions of two or more people. Our primary concern here is with those interactions that occur among people within organizations, but most of the concepts and skills discussed are applicable to human relations outside an organization as well. An **organization** is a group of people who work to achieve a set of common objectives. Because it is people that achieve the organization's objectives, the relationships among those people are critical to the organization's success. Because people have personal objectives that they seek to realize, the successful organization tries not only to achieve its own objectives but to help its members achieve their objectives as well. Why? Because people are not going to help the organization to achieve its objectives if they are unable to achieve their own.

Delta Airlines is one of those rare organizations that seems to satisfy both individual and organizational needs. Delta has long been known for its approach to human relations. One Delta employee told me, "When the unions from the other airlines go on strike, what they want is what we already have."

And he didn't mean just money, although certainly that was a part of it. He meant more than working conditions, too. He meant the way in which company managers managed (their management style) and the way people treated each other within the company. He also meant the desirability of both the work and the social environment at Delta. Can you think of another company whose employees would voluntarily contribute $810 each toward its welfare? Does Delta do something different? You bet it does. That difference is what makes Delta's—or any organization's—human relations positive. And within the organization, it is the manager who has the primary responsibility to ensure that that positive difference exists.

But everyone can benefit from improved human relations. And while the manager has the formal responsibility for human relations, all must work to improve them, within the organization and elsewhere, if they are to be successful. Thus while Delta's managers are very concerned about human relations, so are all of the other employees.

Successful human relations depend on the participants' human relations skills. These skills are as beneficial outside the organization as they are within it. Have you thought about your own interpersonal skills lately? How good are they? Have you said to yourself recently, "I wish I hadn't said that," or perhaps "Now I wonder why she did that," or "If I had only . . ."? How good are the skills of those with whom you interact—your family, your friends, your boss, your co-workers, your professors? What causes some people and some organizations to manage human relations better than others? How can you improve your human relations skills? This book will help you to answer those questions.

There are **positive and negative human relations**. Positive relations improve the self-esteem and self-images of the people involved. They also leave participants feeling better about others. As a result, organizational productivity and the satisfaction of its employees are increased. Negative interpersonal activities produce negative self-images and lower one's esteem for others. Productivity and satisfaction are not normally enhanced. It is for this reason that we all must strive for positive human relations.

Many organizations are actively seeking to improve interpersonal relationships among their members because their leaders believe that positive human relations pay off in both organizational and individual terms. They want not only to make the workplace productive but to make it contribute to employees' satisfaction, and they believe that the two objectives are related.

Dana Manufacturing Company, a leader in the vehicular components market and a diversified firm with three other main business divisions, operates on the announced philosophy that

> business is 90% people and only 10% money. . . . We seek and stress people involvement, and we are responding to the involvement of our people. We listen, discuss, meet, communicate, explain, talk, argue, start task forces—try, and try again, to get involvement from everyone.[1]

Dana's corporate policy states:

> We are dedicated to the belief that our people are our most important asset.

We will encourage all of them to contribute and to grow to the limit of their desire and ability.

We believe people respond to recognition, freedom to contribute, opportunity to grow, and to fair compensation. We believe that higher pay follows job performance and endorse the practice of an above average base compensation with a high incentive potential.[2]

Dana's philosophy and policies are translated into action. Most employees own stock in the firm, most participate in relevant decisions, all are communicated with, and all have a chance to say what they feel. Dana's attitude toward its employees is translated into the major portion of its total corporate policy. And this positive attitude carries over to other corporate policies (which are presented in detail in Chapter 13). This people orientation helped Dana survive the recession of the early 1980s, which hit its industry particularly hard.

But what of the results? Dana is a leader in its industry. Its financial measurements are stronger in most performance areas than those of comparable organizations. And the available evidence indicates that it has achieved high levels of employee satisfaction.[3] This is not to say that Dana is without interpersonal problems. No organization is. But its people work them out, and they produce. Much the same approach and results can be found in such companies as 3M, Analog Services, People Express, Marriott, Hewlett-Packard, IBM, and numerous others.[4]

Human relations are of concern not only to large organizations but to smaller ones as well. The chief operating officer of a 175-employee electronics testing laboratory reports that he is concerned about human relations in his organization for two major reasons. "The bottom line is that we do a tremendous amount of interrelating with the customer," he told me. "Whatever environment we have translates to the customer very quickly. We are a custom shop. Every job is unique. Every job requires special effort and concern. The other reason is simply that our concern for our people makes a lot of lives better. I have spent a great deal of my time in an informal way, as an example and as a teacher, building the right climate here. We have to have a very open system of communication. We have constant changes to adapt to. We have to be able to communicate with a lot of different people. We do not follow normal chains of command very often. When one has a problem, one simply seeks out the best person to help solve that problem."

> *"An institution is like a tune; it is not constituted by individual sounds but by the relations between them."*
>
> Peter Drucker

Organizations and their managers should be concerned about human relations. You should be too. In the modern organization, you will be unsuccessful if you do not have sound human relations skills. Whatever other skills you may have, your skills in human relations are critical to your career. They are also critical to your success in other areas of life, because all our dealings with other human beings require sound interpersonal abilities. The evidence very strongly indicates that the people who are most successful and who derive the most satisfaction from life are for the most part highly effective in interpersonal skills.[5] In today's world, without competence in interpersonal dynamics, you may be left behind. Fortunately, interpersonal skills can be learned.

FIGURE 1.1   *Human relations in and out of the organization*

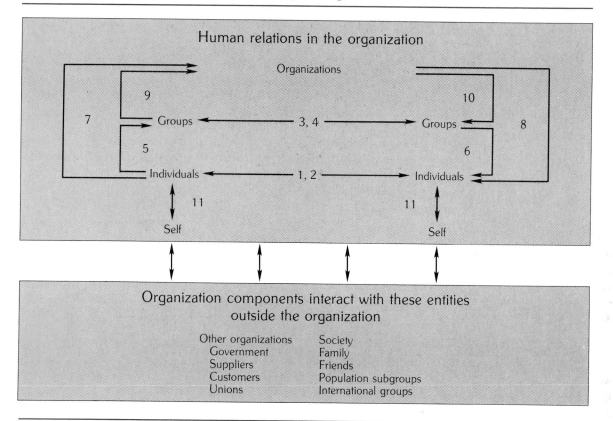

SOURCE: Adapted from Figure 1 (p. 198) in Orlando Behling. "Some Problems in the Philosophy of Science in Organizations," *Academy of Management Journal* 3, no. 1 (January 1978).

It is useful to think of types of human relations in organizations as occupying the categories indicated at the top of Figure 1.1. The numbers in the figure refer to the relationships listed below.

FORMS OF HUMAN RELATIONS

1, 2. *Individual to individual.* Individuals relate within the organization primarily as fellow subordinates, co-managers, or manager and subordinate. There are two sides to this story: Individual 1 relating to Individual 2 and Individual 2 relating to Individual 1. When one employee talks to another about anything, when a manager directs a subordinate to do a job, when friends meet and have coffee, individual-to-individual relationships are taking place.

3, 4. *Group to group.* Many groups exist within the organization. Some are designated as formal, having been created by the organization—for example, the formal work group. Others arise informally—for example, the group that goes to lunch together every day. These formal and informal groups may relate to each other in numerous ways, but at any one point there are still only two sides to this story: Group 1 relating to Group 2 and Group 2 relating to Group 1. When company softball teams compete, when accounting is unhappy with purchasing, when the personnel staff sends out memos to line managers, group-to-group relationships are taking place.

5, 6. *Individual to group and group to individual.* Employees, including managers, relate to their work group, to other formal groups, and to informal groups that may develop. In order to be a leader, for example, a manager must motivate the group to follow his or her lead. The group determines the manner in which it chooses to relate to individuals. A work group will often cause its individual members to follow the group's dictums (norms) rather than the rules and requirements of the formal organization. The individual who wishes to belong will conform.

7, 8. *Individual to organization and organization to individual.* The individual seeks certain need satisfiers from the organization. He or she is expected to behave in certain ways in order to obtain those need satisfiers. The organization seeks certain behaviors from the individual, and offers selected need satisfiers in order to elicit that behavior. When the individual works for expected pay, he or she is relating to the organization. When the organization terminates an employee, it is relating to an individual.

9, 10. *Group to organization and organization to group.* Normally work is divided among formal work groups, within which informal work groups may emerge. The manager must cope with both kinds of group. The manager is designated leader of the formal work group, but other leaders may establish themselves within the informal groups. Both formal and informal groups must interact with the organization. Normally these interactions relate to work requirements, but occasionally such issues as participation in decision making may become important. The organization's relations with the group must be considered when the organization establishes work requirements and distributes authority. Group norms may work against the organization. When the organization redesigns a work group's tasks, it is relating to a group. When a group of workers refuses to do certain tasks, it is relating to the organization.

11. *Individual to self.* Have you talked with yourself lately? Of course you have. When you do, you are communicating with yourself, are you not? We all talk to ourselves. We all mentally say things like "Now, why did I do that?"; "Way to go!"; "You can do it, just keep going"; "If I'm going to get that promotion, I have to . . ." The way you communicate with yourself has a very important bearing on the way you communicate with other people. One of the objectives of this text is to induce you to talk to yourself in ways that will help you analyze the status of your interpersonal relations skills.

Many concepts that will be discussed—leadership, for example—will involve more than one of these relationships. When you make decisions in regard to human relations, whether as an individual or as a manager, it is important to keep in mind that many relationships may be involved.

As Figure 1.1 shows, individuals and groups within an organization relate to other individuals and groups outside the organization as well as to those within it. Often these external relations have a significant bearing on the nature of relations within the organization. How much productivity, for example, can be expected from an employee who has a very sick child? Or how productive can a group of employees be when their bowling league's championship playoff commences just after work that day, and that championship is all they can think about? Or if an arbitrator requires the organization to rehire a terminated union member, human relations within that work group are likely to be strained, productivity may be lessened, motivation made more difficult. Individuals, groups, and organizations must consider the effects of such external relations when they make decisions about internal relations. For example, when General Electric's new chief executive officer (CEO), Jack Welch, decided in 1984 to restructure the company and change the portfolio of businesses the company wanted to operate, he realized that internal human relations would be significantly affected. He also knew that these consequences could hinder his efforts to make his company more competitive. He therefore took great pains to communicate the changes and the reasons for them to all the people who would be affected by them. "It's not enough that general management understands the desired changes; everyone must," he noted. "Change may be initiated top-down, but its confirmation is mostly bottom-up."[6]

THE HISTORY OF HUMAN RELATIONS

Today the term "human relations" signifies a genuine interest in the improvement of human relationships within the organization. But organizations' attitudes toward these relationships have not always been so positive. Until recently organizations often treated human beings as cogs in the organizational wheel; plenty of other cogs were available to replace those that did not fit

"Are you trying to tell me that human relations are more important than public relations?"

smoothly into the organizational machinery. And the manipulation of employees during the "human relations era" of the 1940s and 1950s gave the concept of human relations a bad image. But today human relations are receiving the attention they deserve within the organization, and these efforts are more humanistic and more positive than those of earlier years. Several historical developments have greatly affected today's organizational human relations programs. As we review the most important of these developments, you will notice that until the mid-twentieth century, most actions taken in regard to human relations flowed from the organization to the individual. Later, the importance of various group relations, of individual-to-individual relations, and of individual-to-organization relations become evident.

THE EARLY YEARS

It is impossible to say exactly when employers became concerned about human relations. Before the Industrial Revolution, the Western world did not have work organizations of any great size, and thus organizational human relations were of little concern. The few sizable government and religious organizations that existed were primarily authoritarian. Early business management practices were patterned after this authoritarian approach.[7]

But with the advent of industrialization in the latter half of the eighteenth century, the process of management was recognized as important, and with this recognition came a concern for the human factor in the production equation. Most businesses in the nineteenth century were owned by individuals. The corporation did not become a prominent form of ownership until much later. Partly because the individual owners were interested overwhelmingly in profit, they often cared little for the well-being of their workers. Many owners felt that money spent on human resources was wasted (as Figure 1.2 suggests). Human beings were in large supply; jobs were scarce. The laws of economics dictated that little needed to be done for the workers. But one owner realized the potential ability of human resource management to improve the relations between the organization and the individuals and groups within it: Robert Owen.

ROBERT OWEN

Robert Owen, a Welsh industrialist and social theorist, is recognized as the first manager-entrepreneur to comprehend the need to improve the work environment and the employee's overall situation. Owen was deeply concerned about what he saw as the evils of the industrialized society of the early nineteenth century; he also believed that profit would be increased if the employees worked shorter hours, were paid adequately, and were provided with sufficient food and housing. He did not believe that children younger than ten and a half years old should be employed in factories (a revolutionary attitude in 1813, when children were considered ready for full-time work at age nine). Owen instituted a type of performance-appraisal system, in which color-coded blocks indicated to all the level of worker and supervisory performance for the day. But alas, much of what he proposed never became reality outside of his own company, or if it did, it did so only briefly in a very few factories.[8]

FIGURE 1.2 *Factory rules in 1830*

RULES & REGULATIONS
To Be Observed By All Persons
Employed In The Factory Of
A M A S A   W H I T N E Y

FIRST : The Mill will be put into operation 10 minutes before sunrise at all seasons of the year. The gate will be shut 10 minutes past sunset from the 20th of March to the 20th of September, at 30 minutes past 8 from the 20th of September to the 20th of March. Saturdays at sunset.

SECOND : It will be required of every person employed, that they be in the room in which they are employed, at the time mentioned above for the mill to be in operation.

THIRD : Hands are not allowed to leave the factory in working hours without the consent of their Overseer. If they do, they will be liable to have their time set off.

FOURTH : Anyone who by negligence or misconduct causes damage to the machinery, or impedes the progress of the work, will be liable to make good the damage for the same.

FIFTH : Anyone employed for a certain length of time, will be expected to make up their lost time, if required, before they will be entitled to their pay.

SIXTH : Any person employed for no certain length of time, will be required to give at least 4 weeks notice of their intention to leave (sickness excepted) or forfeit 4 weeks pay, unless by particular agreement.

SEVENTH : Anyone wishing to be absent any length of time, must get permisison of the Overseer.

EIGHTH : All who have leave of absence for any length of time will be expected to return in that time; and, in case they do not return in that time and do not give satisfactory reason, they will be liable to forfeit one week's work or less, if they commence work again. If they do not, they will be considered as one who leaves without giving any notice.

NINTH : Anything tending to impede the progress of manufacturing in working hours, such as unnecessary conversation, reading, eating fruit, &c.&c., must be avoided.

TENTH : While I shall endeavor to employ a judicious Overseer, the help will follow his direction in all cases.

ELEVENTH : No smoking will be allowed in the factory, as it is considered very unsafe, and particularly specified in the Insurance.

TWELFTH : In order to forward the work, job hands will follow the above regulations as well as those otherwise employed.

THIRTEENTH : It is intended that the bell be rung 5 minutes before the gate is hoisted, so that all persons may be ready to start their machines precisely at the time mentioned.

FOURTEENTH : All persons who cause damage to the machinery, break glass out of the windows, &c., will immediately inform the Overseer of the same.

FIFTEENTH : The hands will take breakfast, from the 1st of November to the last of March, before going to work—they will take supper from the 1st of May to the last of August, 30 minutes past 5 o'clock P.M.—from the 20th of September to the 20th of March between sundown and dark—25 minutes will be allowed for breakfast, 30 minutes for dinner, and 25 minutes for supper, and no more from the time the gate is shut till started again.

SIXTEENTH : The hands will leave the Factory so that the doors may be fastened within 10 minutes from the time of leaving off work.

AMASA WHITNEY

Winchendon, Mass. July 5, 1830.

SOURCE: Samuel H. Adams, *Sunrise to Sunset* (New York: Random House, 1950).

THE UNION
MOVEMENT

The few events that benefited the individual worker between Owen's time and the early twentieth century resulted primarily from the increasing power of labor unions. The growing militancy of the union movement forced some employers to make changes in the way they treated employees. But several factors, including employers' political influence, kept unions from gaining enough power to make many changes until the 1920s and 1930s. Militancy therefore increased throughout the 1930s. After World War II, as unions gained power and recognition, they changed their strategies to emphasize negotiation.

THE HUMAN
RELATIONS ERA

The knowledge that human interactions were important to organizational success came to be known accidentally as the result of the so-called Hawthorne studies in the mid-1920s and early 1930s. This series of studies on the effects of the work environment on productivity was conducted by Elton Mayo and his associates at Western Electric's Hawthorne plant, near Chicago. The study began as a test of the effects of changes in illumination and other characteristics of the physical environment on workers' productivity. Two groups of workers doing similar tasks were examined. For one group—the "test group"—illumination was increased. The group's productivity also increased. No changes were made in the other group's environment. That group's productivity remained the same. To determine whether the increase in illumination was the cause of the increase in productivity, the researchers reduced the illumination level for the test group. Its productivity continued to increase. The researchers were amazed to find that the highest levels of productivity occurred at a level of illumination equal to that of moonlight. Replications of these and similar studies over a long period of time resulted in the same findings. Obviously, some factor other than the characteristics of the physical environment was causing the changes in productivity.

Interviews with the workers indicated that they liked the attention they were receiving and that they enjoyed higher morale and more autonomy during the study than they had had before. As a consequence of these studies—including the revised program to determine why illumination and other characteristics of the physical environment were not singly responsible for changes in productivity, as the researchers had anticipated—several unexpected discoveries were made in regard to the various combinations of group and individual relationships within the organization. First, the investigators discovered that workers had many needs beyond those satisfied by money. These needs, primarily social, were found to have a powerful impact on productivity because of the pressure of group norms on the individual. Second, the researchers discovered the existence of informal work groups and came to understand that such groups are a powerful force within the organization. Third, simple attention—the attention given the workers by the researchers—was found to be a powerful influence of behavior. Thus individual-to-individual relationships—such as the relationship of manager to subordinate—could be enhanced by an increase in the amount of recognition given. Fourth, many of the workers' needs were found to be satisfied away from the job. Motivating factors were therefore not always within the control of the organization. Fifth,

A relay assembly test room of the 1920s

high morale in a work group was shown to overcome the negative effects on productivity of certain environmental factors, such as illumination and ventilation. Sixth, the attention given the workers served to moderate the effects of the phenomenon under study. The impact of a secondary agent is now known as "the Hawthorne effect."[9]

Many managers began to use the knowledge gained in these experiments to manipulate employees. Recognition and peer pressure were used to the advantage of the manager or the organization, but not of the employee. As a result, the term "human relations" came to be associated with manipulation and for some time had a negative connotation. Now, however, the term implies the application of techniques for the benefit of all parties—nonmanagement employees as well as managers and the organization.

Until the Great Depression of the 1930s, most American citizens believed that hard work would lift anyone out of poverty. But this depression proved otherwise. Plenty of people were willing to work hard, long hours, but there were just not enough jobs to go around. People who had jobs feared to lose them, and the government supported their efforts to obtain job security and the other benefits of collective bargaining. Thus labor unions gained power, particularly in manufacturing and heavy industries. More important, the role of the federal government within the economy grew as it provided jobs and income security and regulated the relationships between employees and their employers. These interventions paved the way for further government inter-

THE DEPRESSION

vention in the labor market. Since that time, human resource management programs, and hence many aspects of human relations within the business organization—certain compensation and benefit programs, equal employment opportunity programs, safety and health programs, and freedom of information, to name a few—have become federally mandated.

THE MOVEMENT CONTINUES

The interest in human relations probably reached its peak in the 1970s at the levels of individual-to-individual and group-to-individual relations. This was the decade of the quest for self-fulfillment, of increased "sensitivity" to others. Books on self-improvement hit an all-time high in volume sales. Hundreds of books were—and still are—devoted to new and old ways of improving interpersonal communication, leadership skills, individual motivation, physical and mental fitness, stress management, and on and on. Many efforts were made to understand how to improve organizations and management. But somehow, the matter was not pressing, for the economy enjoyed a high growth rate until 1973. But as the unprecedented economic success became history and international competition increased dramatically, Americans turned elsewhere for guidance.

JAPANESE MANAGEMENT MANIA

In the early 1980s, Americans became enthralled by the management practices of the Japanese. In the years since World War II the Japanese had developed one of the world's strongest economies. And they had done so with a management system somewhat different from that used in America.

William G. Ouchi's *Theory Z* ignited an infatuation with the subject of Japanese productivity and Japanese management styles. Ouchi found that a number of very successful U.S. companies—among them Delta Airlines, IBM, Hewlett-Packard, and Xerox—resembled successful Japanese firms in several respects. He called such companies Theory Z firms. He pointed out that other firms could learn to employ many of the Theory Z management practices.[10] (Theory Z is not directly related to Theories X and Y, which are discussed in Chapter 8.) Hundreds of articles and several books followed Ouchi's important work, and the pros and cons of adopting Japanese management practices and corporate cultures came to be debated throughout the United States and Canada. The results of these debates indicate that many Japanese techniques—several of which, ironically, were introduced into Japan by American consultants but never adopted at home—can indeed be incorporated into the American scheme of management. Some modifications are necessary and several techniques cannot be used because of cultural differences, but for the most part, the major points in the Japanese system are being used with increasing frequency in organizations in the United States and Canada. Among these approaches are increased levels of employee participation in decision making, increased emphasis on the work group as a decision point, an increase in company concern for employee welfare and for the employee as an individual, the creation of a people-oriented organizational culture, increased emphasis on quality, and the adoption of a more strategic perspective. In recent years such firms as Ford, General Motors, Lockheed, and Martin Marietta have instituted "quality circles," a Japanese group participative

> *"Theory Z organizations capture the best in management methods from Japanese and American approaches. [Such an organization] is egalitarian, engages fully the participation of employees in running the company and emphasizes subtle concern in interpersonal relations. It is characterized by employee cooperation and commitment to the objectives of the company."*
> WILLIAM G. OUCHI

management technique. Even hard-charging and highly demanding PepsiCo is attempting to change its organizational management style, showing more concern for employee welfare in order to reduce burnout and turnover.[11]

Several trends that began many years ago continue today. Government continues to regulate many of the ways employers treat the people who work for them and those who apply to them for jobs. Equal employment opportunity laws and the occupational safety and health laws are but two kinds of federal legislation that affect organization-to-individual and thus many other interpersonal relationships. Unions have become powerful forces in the economy (although they are less powerful now than they were in the 1970s). The scientific investigation of management is continuing today. These investigations have enabled researchers to accumulate a large body of knowledge from which sound human relations practices are emerging. No one claims that the final word on human relations problems has been spoken. But organizations and managers know more about human relations practices today than they ever did before, and they are putting these practices to work in their organizations. Organizations and managers have begun to realize that the needs of the employee that can be satisfied on the job *must* be satisfied on the job if the organization is to elicit the individual's best performance. This is one of the major reasons that so many organizations are now committed to human resource management programs, often involving extensive training in human relations skills. Similarly, firms are going to great lengths to make employees feel secure, wanted, needed, and part of the team. All new salespeople brought to the Dallas headquarters of Mary Kay Cosmetics, for example, are welcomed by Mary Kay herself in orientation classes. She even invites them to her home, where she serves cookies she has baked herself. And while few CEO's bake cookies for employees, many have barbecues and picnics, lavish holiday parties, and other get-togethers for the same purposes.[12]

HUMAN
RELATIONS
TODAY

Published during the peak of a recession, at a time when the need to improve productivity and the quality of products and services was causing increasing concern, Thomas J. Peters and Robert H. Waterman, Jr.'s *In Search of Excellence* became the most successful management book ever written; it has probably done more to change management philosophy than any of its predecessors.[13] Two key points are made throughout this book that successful companies have a culture that is people-based and that successful managers have a management style that expresses high levels of concern for people. *In Search of Excellence* is based on research on well-known, successful companies. The book makes an important connection between this concern for people—for appropriate human relations—and productivity. It now appears that American managers will take a more serious approach to the issue of corporate culture, human relations, and behavior at work, at least partly as a result of this book.

Search was followed by *Passion for Excellence*, by Peters and Nancy J. Austin. This book, also a best-seller, provides detailed commentaries on recommended management styles—those that express this concern for people.

THE SEARCH
FOR
EXCELLENCE

THE POWER OF POSITIVE PEOPLE

Research and experience have shown that a person who has a **positive self-image** is normally more productive and more satisfied than one who has a negative self-image.[14] Much of the material in this book is based on the belief that actions taken to increase your self-image and the self-images of others will result in a more productive and happier organization and a more productive and happier you; and the opposite is also true.

Just ask yourself this question: Who are the five most successful people I know? Now ask yourself: How do these people feel about themselves—about their capabilities, their knowledge, their skills? Do they have high or low self-esteem? Unless some of these people have negative self-images that they are making great efforts to overcome, it is probable that they have very positive self-images, and that they feel competent.

Now consider yourself. How high is the level of your self-esteem? Take the Test Yourself for self-esteem and find out. How does your self-image affect your interpersonal relations?

When you are successful, how do you feel? When you are rewarded, given recognition for a job well done, how do you feel? Now compare these feelings with those you have when you are not successful and when your accomplishments are not rewarded or recognized. Are you as likely to repeat behavior that has not been recognized or rewarded as you are to repeat behavior that has won you rewards and recognition? Probably not. It is in your best interest to seek out organizations and managers who reward performance, because unfortunately, organizations spend too much time ignoring the positive and giving recognition to the negative, the ineffective, the inefficient. This type of management behavior is known as "management by exception." By recognizing poor performance, such managers ensure that it will be repeated. By failing to recognize good performance, they help ensure that it will not be repeated.

This type of management practice simply does not bring forth the kind of commitment from employees that organizations need. Furthermore, the demands of employees and of the organization's environment make these approaches simply inadequate.

> *He that respects himself is safe from others: he wears a coat of mail that none can pierce.*
> HENRY WADSWORTH LONGFELLOW

> *The unexamined life is not worth living.*
> PLATO

> *Treat people as adults. Treat them as partners; treat them with dignity; treat them with respect. Treat them—not capital spending and automation—as the primary source of productivity gains. These are the fundamental lessons from the excellent companies research.*
> THOMAS J. PETERS AND ROBERT H. WATERMAN, JR.

TEST YOURSELF

SELF-ESTEEM

How high is your self-esteem? By answering the questions on page 17 truthfully, you can get an estimate of your self-esteem level. Self-esteem is an elusive concept to measure, so we are trying here only to find a relative measure of how we feel about ourselves. In the blank space next to the number to the left of each question, place the number of the following statement that most accurately reflects your feelings:

4 The statement is always or completely true.
3 It is usually or mostly true.
2 It is occasionally or partly true.
1 It is seldom or rarely true.
0 It is never or not true.

1. _____ I get along well with most other people.
2. _____ I am growing and changing positively.
3. _____ I have good friends.
4. _____ My physical health is sound.
5. _____ I am satisfied with my physical appearance.
6. _____ I handle difficult interpersonal relations well.
7. _____ I listen to others.
8. _____ The people who count listen to what I say.
9. _____ I make good decisions.
10. _____ My life has been a good one.
11. _____ My sex life is good.
12. _____ I have a sense of humor.
13. _____ I enjoy my work (or school).
14. _____ I am happy most of the time.
15. _____ I have important objectives to accomplish in life.
16. _____ I have already accomplished a lot at this point in life.
17. _____ I am highly motivated.
18. _____ If I had my life to live over, there are only a few things I would do differently.
19. _____ I control my own destiny.
20. _____ I listen to other people, but I make up my own mind.
21. _____ I let people know what I think about an issue.
22. _____ Each day's experiences are worth the time I have traded for them.
23. _____ People seek me out as a friend.
24. _____ People seek my opinion.
25. _____ I am happy with my physical surroundings at home.
26. _____ I really wouldn't want to be anybody else.
27. _____ I feel comfortable meeting new people.
28. _____ I like doing something different.
29. _____ I handle stress well.

(Continued on page 18)

30. _____ I don't worry about things I can't change.
31. _____ I'm organized.
32. _____ I'm persistent and don't give up easily.
33. _____ I am not overly sensitive to others' opinions of me.
34. _____ I relate well to people of all cultures.
35. _____ I am flexible.
36. _____ I like to stop and smell the roses.
37. _____ I do not yield to excesses; for example, I do not eat too much, drink too much, or smoke too much.
38. _____ I'm a kind person.
39. _____ I can laugh when the joke's on me.
40. _____ People of the opposite sex find me attractive.

How high is your self esteem?

Add together all points you scored on the test. Now compare that score with the ranges of scores below. Remember that this test, like any other, makes certain assumptions. This particular questionnaire tests for many of the types of concepts and skills that are discussed in this book.

130 or better—*Excellent!* If you were really honest with yourself, then you have a positive self-concept. If you scored above 145, you may have a realistic self-image. You may in any case want to have someone else fill out the questionnaire on you as he or she thinks you should have answered.

96 to 129—*You really do like yourself, and that's good.* You recognize that you're not perfect, but you can cope with life. This is a healthy position to be in.

64 to 95—*You must feel by now that you need to change.* You can! Just how much depends on which end of the scale you are on. You see certain strengths and weaknesses. Set personal change objectives and get started.

Below 64—*You do not like yourself nearly as much as is desirable.* It could be that you are in a down moment right now. It could be that you are too tough on yourself. It could be that you really do have a very low self-image. Talking with a significant other could be a great help. Setting objectives as above would also be useful.

VARIABLES REQUIRING A POSITIVE APPROACH TO HUMAN RELATIONS

Some of the principal employee demands and other important variables that require a more concerted and positive human relations approach to management include the following:

1. The increased expectations of workers in regard to life, the nature of work, the kinds of jobs they want, and the kind of treatment they will tolerate on the job.

2. Rising levels of education among employees (which partly explain item 1).
3. The increased influence of government on the treatment of employees by employers.
4. Increased research on management practices and subsequent training of supervisors and managers, which has led to a better understanding of appropriate management behavior and practices.
5. A resurgence of the work ethic, which has resulted in the need to change worker motivation systems.
6. Increased governmental support of the nonworking population. Thus work is not the only way to satisfy needs. Employers must compete with government for the supply of employees, especially at the lowest wage and skill levels.
7. Increased attention to the satisfaction of higher-level needs. Most people in the United States and Canada do not have to worry about satisfying such basic needs as food and shelter. They seek to satisfy higher-level needs.
8. Competition and the success of other management systems, primarily those of the Japanese.
9. Changing work force demographics. There are now more white-collar than blue-collar jobs, and for the first time in history, white males make up less than half the work force. Women and minorities may have a somewhat different set of need priorities than the less numerous but still dominant white males in the work force.
10. An increasing demand by consumers for improved product quality.
11. A service orientation in the economy.
12. The movement toward a high-tech society, which requires a corresponding movement toward a high-touch society.
13. An environment in which workers' right to information related to their individual employment situations is greater than at any time in the past.

All of these factors and several others have caused management to recognize the need to improve, and a great deal of the improvement has come in human relations. Organizations and their managers are striving to make the workplace more desirable and more productive.

TIPS FOR SUCCESS
---

1. Keep in mind that your human relations skills could very well make or break your career.
2. Periodically assess your human relations skills.
3. Develop a program of self-improvement for your human relations skills.
4. Maintain positive relationships and a positive self-image.

SUMMARY
---

1. The topic of human relations is personally relevant to you; you can use what you learn about it.
2. This text focuses on human relations in organizations.
3. Human relations are critical to both individual and organizational success and survival.
4. There are eleven major categories of human relations within an organization.
5. Historically, the field of human relations has been concerned primarily with organization-to-individual relationships. But in recent years

researchers and practitioners have realized the importance of understanding and improving other types of human relations, especially relationships between individuals and among groups.

6. In recent years, American management has been confronted with challenges whose solutions commonly involve understanding and improving behavior in the organization.

7. People with positive self-images are normally more productive and more satisfied than those with negative self-images.

8. Leadership, motivation, and communication are key ingredients in the success of both individual and organizational human relations.

9. Appropriate organizational climates and cultures are necessary for organizational success and survival.

DISCUSSION QUESTIONS

1. This book is based on the belief that human relations skills can be taught. What do you think?

2. What are human relations? What are human relations skills?

3. What are the eleven categories of human relations within the organization?

4. What effect may external factors have on organizational human relations?

5. Historically, what have been the major trends in human relations within organizations?

6. What major variables require positive human relations in organizations today more than ever?

7. What is Theory Z?

APPLYING HUMAN RELATIONS SKILLS

CASE | **Centre Bank**

Mark Williams was one of five loan officers for the Evansville affiliate of Centre Bank, a twenty-three-member banking group. Mark's immediate supervisor, Larry Champion, the senior loan officer, sauntered into the loan office one afternoon as Mark was reviewing a loan application. Larry called all of the loan office employees together and announced that the loan department was going to be expanded and that the loan area would be completely remodeled, with each officer receiving his or her own office. Larry asked what their preferences were for the portion of their offices that would face the central reception area. There were three styles to choose from, and the majority would rule. They all voted.

When the votes were counted, Larry gleefully announced the results. "The winning combination is glass tops and wood bottoms. It's a good thing, too, because that's what we ordered last week. We knew you'd like it." He departed triumphantly.

Mark's eyes followed Larry from the room. His face revealed his disbelief. Lorraine, another loan officer who sat next to him, caught his eye. Her expression matched Mark's, and as they stared at each other, they began to laugh. Lorraine had been employed by Centre Bank for only two months, but she already knew through the grapevine that management "didn't really care what the employees thought about anything."

Mark moved closer to Lorraine. "Listen, if you think that's bad, you should have seen what they did to us about three months ago, just before you came to work here. The branch manager came in here and told us they were going to buy all new typewriters. So he asked all of the secretaries and all of the loan officers to research the choice. He told us to go out and talk to people with various types of typewriters and he even gave us a list of names of people to contact. So Matt, Sarah, and the rest of us went out and spent probably thirty hours each talking with more than twenty people—bosses, secretaries, everybody. It was unanimous—Exxon Qyx. You see what name is on those typewriters, don't you? IBM. After all that work, they did what they wanted to. It makes me so mad I could . . ." Mark's voice trailed off.

Lorraine nodded.

1. What is wrong with human relations in this company?
2. What can Mark and Lorraine and other subordinates do to improve their situation?
3. What different forms of communication are portrayed in this case?

"Getting to Know You, Getting to Know All about You"   EXERCISE

The purpose of this exercise is to engage in human relations. Each student will be asked to tell his or her name, place of employment, educational background, and hobbies, and why he or she is taking this course. Any other information the instructor wishes may also be revealed, for example, if married, the number of children, and so on. The instructor will also tell you about himself or herself. The purpose here is to get to know one another. For larger classes, it will be necessary to do this exercise in small groups.

Once this introduction has taken place, your instructor may ask you to do any or all of the following.

Personal strengths and weaknesses: List your two greatest personal human relations strengths and your two worst personal human relations weaknesses on a sheet of paper (without your name) and pass it in. The professor may then read random selections to the class. One of the objectives of a human relations course ought to be to help students with personal strengths and weaknesses. When some of these strengths and weaknesses are enumerated, perhaps in writing on the chalkboard, direction may be given to the course. This exercise also provides information about classmates. This is part of the disclosing process that is so important in human relations.

Listing of objectives: The class may offer suggestions as to the objectives that each would like to accomplish in taking this class. These objectives may be listed on the chalkboard. This exercise also helps to establish direction and purpose, and also reveals to others some of the inner workings of fellow students.

Perceived problems in human relations: Your professor may ask for class discussion of the greatest problems the students perceive, both within the group and in general. Again, direction and disclosure are obtained.

Learning contract: Your professor may ask you to draw up a personal contract indicating how you plan to achieve your objectives for this course. He or she may ask you to turn your contract in as an assignment, or may ask only that you keep it for yourself. This contract should state your objectives in taking this course and how you plan to achieve them.

REFERENCES

1. *The Dana Story, 1983* (Toledo, O.: Dana Corp., 1984), p. 27.

2. Ibid., p. 26.

3. The evidence inspected includes financial reports, industry surveys, internal reports and information, and discussions with employees.

4. Thomas J. Peters and Robert H. Waterman, Jr., *In Search of Excellence: Lessons from America's Best-Run Companies* (New York: Harper & Row, 1982); Jeremy Main, "A Chyimaker Who Beats the Business Cycle," *Fortune*, December 23, 1985, pp. 114–20.

5. Many sources indicate that the person who can work successfully with others will be more successful in life than the person whose working relationships with others are difficult. Both the management literature and the psychological literature indicate that successful human relations are also important to organizational success. One study with an extremely large sample size (16,000) found that high-achieving executives, about 13 percent of the total, cared about people and profits; average achievers were concerned only about profits; and low achievers were obsessed with their own security. Low achievers displayed a basic distrust of subordinates' abilities; high achievers viewed them optimistically. High achievers sought advice from underlings; low achievers didn't. High achievers were listeners; moderate achievers listened only to achievers, and low achievers avoided communications, relying on policy manuals. ("Nice Guys in High Corporate Positions Get the Best Results from Subordinates," *Wall Street Journal*, August 22, 1978, p. 1).

6. Donald E. Kane, "From Critical Steps to Cultural Change," *Executive Excellence*, November 1984, p. 12.

7. James D. Mooney and Alan C. Reiley, *The Principles of Organization* (New York: Harper & Row, 1939), chap. 2.

8. Daniel A. Wren, *The Evolution of Management Thought* (New York: Ronald Press, 1972), pp. 63–66.

9. Fritz J. Roethlisberger and William J. Dickson, *Management and the Worker* (Cambridge: Harvard University Press, 1939), pp. 15–86.

10. William Ouchi, *Theory Z: How American Business Can Meet the Japanese Challenge* (Reading, Mass: Addison-Wesley, 1981).

11. Trish Hall, "Demanding PepsiCo Is Attempting to Make Work Nicer for Managers," *Wall Street Journal*, October 23, 1984, p. 31.

12. James M. Cole, "Put On a Happy Face, You Managements!" *Wall Street Journal*, October 15, 1984, p. 30.

13. Peters and Waterman, ibid.

14. A number of studies have reported this relationship. Many of these studies, however, have been conducted by educators; relatively few are work-oriented. See, for example, Harold Sigall and Robert Gould, "The Effects of Self-Esteem and Evaluator Demandingness on Effort Expenditure," *Journal of Personality and Social Psychology* 35, no. 1 (1977): 12–20; C. D. Snyder and L. W. Ferguson, "Self-Concept and Job Satisfaction," *Psychological Reports*, 1976, pp. 38, 603–10; John G. Watson and Sam Borone, "The Self-Concepts, Personal Values, and Motivational Orientations of Black and White Managers," *Academy of Management Journal*, March 1976, pp. 36–48; Robert L. Dipboye, "A Critical Review of Korman's Self-Consistency Theory of Work Motivation and Occupational Choice," *Organizational Behavior and Human Performance*, February 1977, pp. 108–26; James F. Gavin, "Self-Esteem as a Moderator of the Relationship between Expectancies and Job Performance," *Journal of Applied Psychology*, 1973, pp. 83–88; J. Sideny Shrauger and Melanie I. Terbovic, "Self-Evaluation and Assessments of Performance by Self and Others," *Journal of Consulting and Clinical Psychology*, August 1976, pp. 564–72.

2 INDIVIDUAL DIFFERENCES AND PERCEPTION

LEARNING OBJECTIVES

When you have completed this chapter, you should be able to:
1. Discuss the major factors underlying individual differences and their effects on behavior.
2. Identify ways in which your knowledge of individual differences can be used to improve your own human relations.
3. Describe the nature of the perception process and show how it affects behavior.
4. Use your knowledge of the perception process to improve your own human relations.

PSYCHOLOGICAL SOFTWARE

Understanding what makes people tick and using that knowledge properly are critical to successful interpersonal relations. Strangely enough, some new means of honing those skills have recently been introduced by a few hi-tech companies that are offering "psychological software" for personal computers (PCs). Such software is intended generally for the business market, but much of it can be used by virtually anyone who hopes to improve his or her human relations skills.

Two of the leading firms in psych software are Human Edge Software of Palo Alto, California, and Thoughtware of Coconut Grove, Florida. Human Edge has three primary programs: sales, management, and negotiating skills. Thoughtware has two series of programs: management diagnostics and management training. The diagnostics series contains three programs: assessment of personal management skills, organizational effec-

tiveness, and personal interaction styles. The training series has seven programs, covering leadership, motivation, objective setting, improving employee performance, performance appraisal, time management, and conducting meetings. Other firms, such as Interactive Health Systems of Los Angeles and Wilson Learning of Minneapolis, have programs on a variety of subjects, such as stress, leadership, and motivation.

Many of these programs query the user and then recommend strategies for interpersonal behavior based on the user's responses. Typical of this approach is that employed in "The Management Edge," developed by Human Edge. This program asks 86 questions about the user's personality, designed to build a profile of that person. It also asks about the other person in the interaction situation and then offers advice on how to interact with that person. In this program, each manager falls into one of twelve categories, as does each other

(Continued on page 26)

person with whom the PC operator interacts. Finally the machine recommends behaviors on the basis of the categories in which the interactants fall and other situational variables that the user has described. Typical of other programs is Thoughtware's "Leading Effectively," which queries managers on solutions to various interpersonal problem situations and then allows respondents to see how a large national sample of managers responded to those same questions. Some programs can be used by several colleagues at once. Several programs use environments similar to those found in computer games. Some have accessory video disks.

Though these programs are based on scientific research, they are subject to criticism because by necessity they simplify complex situations and provide answers that may not take into consideration all of the variables in the decision situation. Some questions seem irrelevant or inappropriate, and users must learn to recognize simplistic answers. Some questions of ethics might arise. But these programs have thousands of active users, most of whom apparently believe that psychological software offers them significant help.

SOURCES: David Stipp, "Managers Are Using Personal Computers to Help Them Deal with Personnel Issues," *Wall Street Journal*, July 26, 1984; "Firm Gives Its Software the Human Edge," *Orlando Sentinel*, March 12, 1984, p. E-12; Tom Alexander, "Why Computers Can't Outthink the Experts," *Fortune*, August 20, 1984, p. 112.

What patterns of individual behavior can be identified? Why do people behave the way they do? Will people continue to behave in the future as they have behaved in the past? Much of the psychological software being developed today presumes to know the answers to these questions. Most of it attempts to help you answer these questions yourself. One thing is certain: if your behavior and the behavior of others you influence are to be productive, you need to become acquainted with the numerous patterns of human behavior and their causes. You need to be able to predict with reasonable accuracy how people will act in the future. And you must be able to use this knowledge to guide your own behavior. If you hope to be able eventually to put such knowledge to use, you should begin now to attempt to understand the fundamental differences between individuals, and in particular how these differences affect behavior. To aid you in that endeavor, this chapter introduces the topic of individual differences, viewing each fundamental characteristic briefly. It next provides a more lengthy discussion of perception, one of the vital elements of successful human relations. Every decision you or anyone else makes depends upon perception. Improving perception is therefore of vital concern to individuals, managers, and organizations.

INDIVIDUAL DIFFERENCES

As Figure 2.1 indicates, an individual's behavior depends on that individual's fundamental characteristics and the interaction of that individual with his or her environment. All of us have six **fundamental psychological charac-**

teristics: personality, needs, self-image, attitudes and values, and modes of perception and of learning. We all have two **fundamental physiological characteristics** as well: physical attributes and mental attributes.[1] When an individual interacts with his or her environment, these eight characteristics, in various states and in various combinations, define the boundaries of that individual's behavior. As Figure 2.2 suggests, these characteristics are highly interdependent. Each may cause changes in each of the others. An employee who has a negative attitude toward the boss, for example, may perceive the boss's slightest suggestion as a major criticism, and react with anger. Similarly, behavior may change each characteristic and may be changed by each. High productivity, for example, especially if it is rewarded, usually leads to an increase in self-image and a change in needs. It is these factors, especially personality, needs, and self-image, that the psychological software discussed in the opening Human Relations Happening analyzes for the user. The software then bases its recommendations in regard to the user's behavior on that analysis.

66There are only three things you need to know about human relations in organizations: People are different, people are different, people are different.99

WARREN S.
BLUMENFELD

FIGURE 2.1   *Fundamentals of individual behavior*

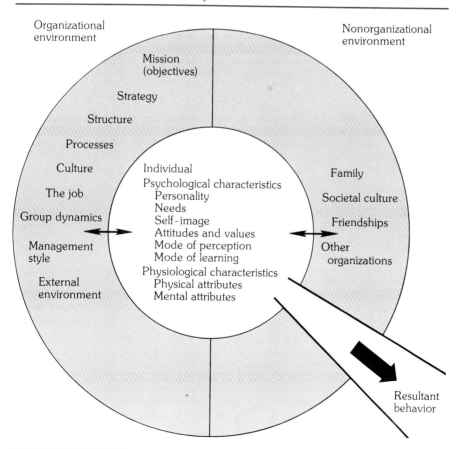

FIGURE 2.2   *Psychological factors and behavior*

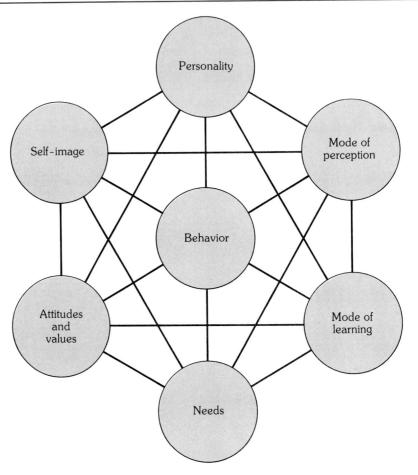

PERSONALITY: THE DIFFERENCES YOU SEE MOST CLEARLY

Each of us is born with a personality that changes and matures as we experience life. This maturing personality is the foundation of adult behavior. It's what makes us all what we are, individually and together. Virtually every event that occurs in an organization is the result of the expression of someone's personality. **Personality** is that set of relatively enduring and consistent but ever-changing behavioral patterns and related psychological and mental characteristics that distinguishes one person from another. This definition assumes that personality is concerned with the whole person, allows for change in that person, recognizes a pattern in the behavior and characteristics of each person, and assumes a uniqueness identifiable with each person.[2] We all have a personality and it continually interacts with the personalities of others. What is your personality like? Spend a moment to find out a little bit about yourself. Complete the "Test Yourself" on personality.

PERSONALITY

1. Personalities may be described in many ways. One very simple way is to choose a series of adjectives that describe you in various situations. Write the one or two words that best describe your behavior most of the time when you are:

   a. At work. _____

   b. Relaxing. _____

   c. Studying. _____

   d. Thinking. _____

   e. Making decisions. _____

   f. In disagreement with others. _____

   g. Competing with others. _____

   h. Shopping. _____

   i. Driving. _____

   j. Creating. _____

   k. With your family. _____

   l. With close friends. _____

   m. With your spouse or a close friend of the opposite sex. _____

   n. Improving your career potential. _____

   o. Spiritually involved. _____

   p. Enjoying life. _____

2. Now describe in five words or less:

   a. Your self-image. _____

   b. Your level of psychological maturity. _____

   c. How you learn. _____

   d. Your needs. _____

   e. Your most common feelings about life in general. _____

Now you have a concept of your personality. What use do you plan to make of this information?

The word *personality* is a summary construct. It is concerned with behavioral patterns and related factors—emotions, attitudes, motives (needs), interests, thoughts, moods, abilities, and so on—and their causes. The word *personality* has many meanings, each meaning largely a function of one's orientation toward the world. A psychologist examining personality, for example, might be very concerned with the behavioral patterns observed, especially as these patterns result from psychological constructs such as need for achievement and intelligence. An anthropologist, on the other hand, might view personality primarily from the point of view of the impact of culture on behavior. The biologist might be interested in the unique genetic makeup of each individual and how it contributes to behavior. Each of these professionals is concerned with personality and behavior, but each has a unique explanation of the causes of behavior and a definition of personality that differs from all the others.

Similarly, a manager in an organization is concerned with the effects of personality on an individual's work behavior. The manager wants to know how much employee *A* contributes to the organization and to the achievement of its objectives, why employee *B* acts as she does, and how employee *C*'s behavior can be changed to make him more productive. In contrast to the biologist and the anthropologist, the manager must view the individual's personality as a whole. The manager must understand first of all what the individual's personality is and secondly how to change those aspects of the individual's behavior that the organization considers undesirable. Do managers always use their knowledge of personality correctly? Most assuredly not. Few people have the training to use such knowledge well. But you can bet that managers and numerous others put their knowledge of personality to use every day. You do too. We all do, and we must. But we all need to improve our skills. We don't expect to be professional psychologists, but we should act professionally in our judgments.

You will encounter many different types of personalities in the workplace. You must learn to "work with" them all. For example, all subordinates must attempt to determine the personality of their managers. You and I and everyone else who has a boss must learn to work with that "personality." Dee Hock, president of VISA International, has a very interesting personality. He is hard driving, demanding, and possesses a definite authoritative bent (demonstrated especially early in his career). He has been extremely successful in turning VISA into a major force in the credit card industry. But coming to grips with his personality is difficult, as the following comments from some of the top executives at VISA reveal:

> Most people at VISA are seeking Dee's attention and approval.
>
> He's very intimidating to most people. There are some very bright people here who turn to putty when they see him—their minds go foggy.
>
> People are afraid of him, but no more so than they are afraid of anyone in power.
>
> Is he fair? Absolutely. Can he be brutal? Definitely.
>
> Dee manages by fear, uncertainty, and change, with fear the least important, uncertainty the most important, and change in between.
>
> I guess you'd call his the Socratic method of management. Dee will grill you when you present an idea to him, and you had best have the answers.
>
> He's almost clairvoyant. He has an uncanny feel for what people are thinking. It's a sixth sense. I guess it would really be called "street smarts."

He has an uncanny grasp of situations. He's almost always right. He's one hell
of a decent human being. He gives the impression of being gruff and
ruthless, but he's more of a pussycat.

He's brilliant, he's visionary, he's a genius, but he's one of the worst admin-
istrators that we've got at VISA.[3]

Our primary concern with personality is to understand its impact on human
relations and to use this understanding to improve behavior at work. When
we attempt to employ our knowledge of personality, we want to learn to identify
typical behavior, that is, the individual's typical personality. Then when
deviations occur, we can ask ourselves why, and we can adjust our behavior
to meet the needs of the situation. Furthermore, when someone else's behavior
is inappropriate, we can help that person behave more appropriately; we can
help ourselves behave more appropriately, too, when our own actions are out
of line.

NEEDS

Each of us has needs, many of which began at birth or even before. Unsatisfied
needs motivate people to take action to satisfy them. Organizations use this
fact to channel individual actions toward the fulfillment of organizational
needs. A manager who understands how an individual's needs are motivating
his or her behavior can relate better to that person. A manager who has an
employee with a problem of alcoholism, for example, must understand how
needs drive the alcoholic to behave in certain ways. To make use of this
knowledge the manager must be aware of an alcoholic's typical behavioral
pattern and be able to recognize that pattern when it develops. The personnel
manager called upon to design an organization's compensation package typ-

"I'm sorry, I'm not speaking to anyone tonight. My
defense mechanisms seem to be out of order."

Drawing by Joe Mirachi; © 1958 The New Yorker Magazine, Inc.

ically takes into account the wage scales for various jobs in the local area and any competitive wage scale nationally that must be considered. When she does so, she assumes that the individuals who work for her organization have needs for self-esteem, that they have placed a value on their efforts, and that they expect their pay to be in line with the pay offered for similar jobs. Mary Kay Ash, CEO of Mary Kay Cosmetics, believes that satisfying the need for self-esteem is very important. "Making people feel important is precisely what a manager is paid for—because making people feel important motivates them to do a better job."[4]

Needs are major factors in behavior. Needs appear to be arranged in some order of priority that varies with the individual, with culture, and with numerous other factors. Thus food and shelter are more basic needs than social relationships. When these basic needs have been satisfied, such higher-order needs as social relationships come to the fore. As these needs are satisfied, needs of a still higher order, such as self-esteem and self-fulfillment, become more important to the individual. People may be affected by several different needs at any one time, and determining which need is most important to any one individual is often difficult. Chapter 3 examines our needs in more detail.

THE LEARNING PROCESS

As we function in our environment, we learn from our experiences in it. For most people, psychological development accompanies physiological development. Thus, by the time they reach their early twenties, most people have acquired a fully developed personality, but one that can still grow through the learning process. A learning pattern is established and reinforced throughout life. Learning subsequently affects personality, attitudes, self-image, and perception. Learning seems to take at least two major and quite different forms. One is known as rote learning. The individual learns through repetition. Children say their ABC's and memorize the state capitals. An organization trains most employees in this manner. Thus a job is demonstrated and the new employees are then asked to repeat the job's actions until they are able to perform them well.

The other type of learning is known as cognitive learning. This is the "ah-ha experience." We experience insight as we relate two or more factors we have not related before. This insightful type of learning is considered to be of a higher level than rote learning. On the other hand, rote learning usually forms the data base for cognitive learning. Insightful learning has produced numerous inventions, including the light bulb, the computer chip, and the basic operating software for the MacIntosh personal computer.

Organizations and managers are concerned with the way people learn for several reasons. First, they need to know the best way to train and develop them for their jobs, and to do so they have to know how people learn. Second, they often want their employees to grow into increased job responsibilities. An organization that wants to benefit from such growth should provide opportunities that will permit it to occur. The provision of the right opportunities requires knowledge of the learning process. The company must also identify deficiencies in knowledge and skills before it begins the training and development process. Some companies emphasize training more than others. IBM reportedly spends over $500 million a year—about 1.25 percent of annual sales—on training and development.[5] Few other companies spend this large a percentage of their revenues on training.

Self-image plays a major role in behavior. Our view of ourselves greatly affects our personality, needs, perception, attitudes, and learning, and has a great effect on our behavior. In fact, some behavioral scientists believe that virtually all behavior is designed to support one's self-image. Thus personality, a summary description of behavior, is also a direct consequence of self-image. The importance of self-image was discussed in Chapter 1 from the perspective of positive self-esteem. People with high self-esteem are believed to perform at higher levels than people with low self-esteem. IBM believes that a positive self-image and a high level of self-esteem are so important that it establishes sales quotas at a level that can be reached by 70 to 80 percent of its sales force. The members of its sales staff thus perceive themselves as winners. Many of IBM's competitors think it desirable to set sales quotas that only a small percentage of the sales force can achieve. Thus the vast majority of their salespeople are encouraged to perceive themselves as losers.[6]

SELF-IMAGE

You and I and everyone else possess a set of attitudes about life, human relations, work, ourselves, everything. These attitudes help determine our perception, our behavior, our self-image, our needs, and the way we learn—in fact, whether or not we are even willing to learn. **Attitudes** are predispositions to react to stimuli in certain ways. Attitudes define our outlook on life. If you understand someone's attitudes, your ability to predict his or her behavior will be greatly enhanced. Each year companies spend millions of dollars to determine and alter their employees' attitudes. Each year millions of managers attempt to discern the attitudes of their subordinates, their bosses, their peers, and themselves. All of this concern for attitudes arises at least in part because attitudes drive behavior, and behavior drives profits and salaries.

ATTITUDES AND VALUES

One way in which companies attempt to determine employees' attitudes is by administering a questionnaire that lists a variety of statements related to such matters as the supervisor's management style and the way in which the company motivates its workers. Employees are asked to check the items that best reflect their own attitudes. AT&T, for example, periodically uses an attitude survey to keep in touch with its employees' needs and their commitment to the organization. Such surveys help the company to head off problems before they develop. When potential problems are spotted, the company can take action to change negative employee attitudes before they are translated into negative behavior. Organizations may also choose to change employee attitudes in order to implement new strategies. Florida Power & Light Company, for example, decided to adopt a more participative management style in an effort to increase productivity; when middle and front-line managers resisted the change, the company offered special training sessions designed to alter their negative attitudes.[7]

Just as we all have attitudes, everyone has a set of **values**—ideas about what is important, what is relevant to our concerns. When we have choices, our values greatly influence our behavior. For example, L. M. Clymer, president of Holiday Inns, resigned when the company decided to diversify into casinos.[8] He disapproved of gambling, and his values would not permit him to work for a firm that operated a casino.

TAKING ACTION ON INDIVIDUAL DIFFERENCES

Understanding and using knowledge related to individual behavior are not easy tasks. No two people are the same. Each person has a unique personality, a unique set of ever-changing needs, a unique and often quite fragile self-image. Each perceives situations according to an individualized set of internalized information, functions with a set of specific attitudes, and learns differently from every other person. Each person differs from every other in physical and mental attributes. Furthermore, situations in which one person encounters another also vary, further complicating the tasks of understanding and using our knowledge of behavior. As one of my professors once wryly observed, there are only three things you need to know about people's behavior. *"People are different, people are different, people are different."*

Yet despite all of this dissimilarity, there are *patterns* to personalities, to needs, to self-images, to attitudes, to perception, to learning, to physiological characteristics, to situations, and indeed to behavior. These patterns help us to discern why people behave as they do and to predict how people—ourselves included—will behave. We know from research, from observation, from experimentation, and from experience that people tend to act in certain ways. One of the fundamental beliefs of human relations is that most of the time most people respond to comparable or like stimuli in similar ways. This belief leads people and organizations to take certain actions in the expectation of certain outcomes. Behaviors are thus predicted on the basis of knowledge about personalities, needs, self-images, attitudes, perceptions, learning, and situations. For example, we expect people to work harder if a reward is offered, because they usually do, up to some point. We expect improved performance after disciplinary counseling because people usually improve after such a session. But we should also be able to predict that one person or another will not increase performance in response to the offer of a reward or respond favorably to counseling because of our knowledge of one or more fundamental elements of those individuals' behavior.

We should not expect our predictions to be completely accurate. It is the susceptibility of individuality to change that makes the development of one "best" approach to human relations impossible and makes successful interaction so difficult. As you interact, you must keep individuality, with its susceptibility to change, and the paradoxical similarity of individuals in perspective simultaneously. The ability to determine when someone will fail to behave according to normally predictable patterns is a very important human relations skill. Our ability to make such predictions depends to a great extent on our ability to discern other people's modes of perception.

PERCEPTION

Perception is our window to the world. Every decision, every action taken by anyone hinges on the ability to perceive. **Perception** is the process of organizing and interpreting incoming sensory information in order to define oneself and one's surroundings.[9] As Figure 2.3 indicates, behavior is a result of the perception process. We seek to interpret our situation and behave in accordance with that interpretation. As the feedback arrow between perception and behavior indicates, however, the perception process, especially the experiential data base on which it is founded—what we call the perception set—is modified by behavior, even if only slightly. Our ways of perceiving are highly interrelated with and dependent upon our other psychological characteristics. When we examine Figures 2.2 and 2.3, we find that all six elements of the factors that influence behavior are in some way determinants of the other factors. Similarly, behavior both modifies and is modified by these factors. Thus personality is both a cause and a consequence of perception. And once a self-image becomes established, future perception and hence behavior and personality will normally support this self-image, but not always. The employee who receives a very negative performance appraisal, for example, often attributes it to factors other than himself, typically the manager's dislike for him or the manager's inability to manage. Such defensive judgments may be true, but often the individual is simply interpreting incoming information (perceptions) in a way that will support his self-image.

"Perception is no mirror of reality."
LINDA DAVIDOFF

FIGURE 2.3   *Factors that influence perception*

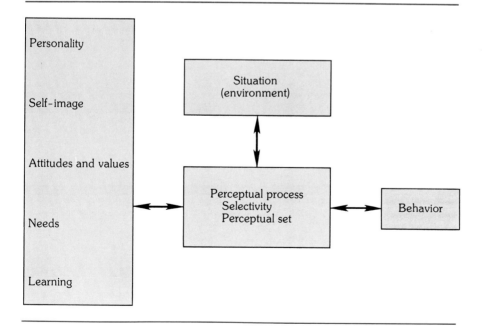

TEST YOURSELF

SELECTIVITY

Please answer the following questions. Do not look up or around you when you answer the first three questions.

1. What is the color of the room in which you are now seated?
2. If there are other people in this room, how many are within fifteen feet of you?
3. What is the wattage of the light bulbs in the fixture you are currently using?
4. What is the precise title of this textbook?
5. Within $1, how much did you pay for this textbook?

If you answered more than two of these questions correctly, you are:

a. Probably not screening enough information.
b. A trivia buff.
c. More observant than most people.
d. Lucky.

It is important to realize that the senses do not give meaning to the environment; they merely extract raw data—not information—for processing by the brain. The brain, through reference to the perceptual set, provides the meaning, the interpretation of the data that turns them into information. The senses employed in extracting information are sight, hearing, the five senses of the skin (touch, deep pressure, warmth, cold, and pain), smell, taste, and balance. (Some people might add extrasensory perception [ESP] as well.) These senses function independently. It is the brain's responsibility to coordinate their efforts and to make use of the tremendous amount of data these systems provide. The following pages discuss some components of the perceptual process and examine two common errors to which it is prone.

SELECTIVITY

The perception process is one means by which the body adapts to various and varying environments. One environment is the organization. Everywhere, but especially in organizations, people are constantly bombarded by a complex array of related and unrelated stimuli. Policies, rules, interpersonal communications, time clocks, break buzzers, ringing phones, the taste of coffee, the color of the room, the size of the machine, the smell of the raw materials, the tint of her hair, the shape of his nose, the touch of the keyboard, the feel of the plush carpet—all these and hundreds of other stimuli arrive simultaneously. Under such a barrage, the mind must screen the data provided by the sensory input mechanisms so that the mental processes can focus on the facts that the brain can adequately process and give meaning to—the most important ones. Our minds have developed a process for screening out those stimuli that provide no vital data. This process of screening stimuli according to some predetermined criterion is known as **selectivity.** Selectivity normally follows rather predictable patterns. The mind typically elects to attend only to the items that are most physically, mentally, or emotionally prominent. STOP. Now look at the Test Yourself for selectivity.

Having completed this exercise, you should now have a better realization of the importance of the selectivity function. One really should not be aware of all of these data, because in the great scheme of things they are basically unimportant. The purpose of selectivity is to unburden you of such data.

Unfortunately, the perceptual screening process does not always work to the individual's or the organization's best advantage. Valuable information may not be fully perceived or may be subconsciously ignored or suppressed. Executives, for example, typically suffer from what is known as "information overload." Managers often do not know which report to read, which figures are really critical, or what exactly they mean when they see them. Thus the university president who sees a decline in the number of students enrolled in a revitalized graduate program may not realize that because tuition has been raised and the quality of the program has improved, the institution is better off in the long term than it would be if it had more students. His mind is so fixed on the number of students that he has screened out total revenues and the implications of increased prestige for the future of the university. The design of management information systems is of critical importance. The system must screen the relevant data and provide all managers with the information that is important to them; it should not burden them with information they do not need and require them to decide whether or not it is important. By the time information reaches any level of management, all of it should be necessary. The information that the mind tends to select varies from individual to individual, and apparently according to an identifiable pattern. Awareness of this pattern can help greatly to improve human relations, as the Human Relations Happening "Testing Perceptual Styles" suggests.

HUMAN RELATIONS HAPPENING

TESTING PERCEPTUAL STYLES

In a 500-restaurant division of a major conglomerate, a division that grossed over $800 million in 1985, certain personnel development decisions, especially those related to leadership style, are based in part on the Meyers-Briggs Type Indicator (MBTI). The MBTI is designed to reveal the perceptual and judgmental processes of the person tested—the way that person both gathers (selects) and evaluates information.

The MBTI is currently administered only to the top management team, although departments may use it if they choose, and some have done so. All top managers have taken the MBTI, and each one knows or has access to the MBTI profiles of all other members of the team. People use it every day in their relations with their bosses, peers, and subordinates. One vice-president offered this description of the way he uses it: "My boss is an ESTJ [one of 16

(Continued on page 38)

perceptual types described by the MBTI]. I'm an ESFP. Because of his type, I know that I can't bring him the same information in a report that I would want myself. He simply is not a people person. He also tends to be quick to make judgments, and prefers factual information to any kind of gut feeling I may have. So I have to provide him with different information than I might have provided had it not been for the MBTI."

When the profiles of the top management group—some 30 people—were developed, it was found that about 80 percent of them were sensor-thinkers: they were highly analytical and had a narrow focus, and thus were unlikely to have a great capacity to understand the big picture or to be creative. The same vice-president commented, "This is ironic because conceptual and creative skills are critical at this level of management. So the burden falls to the few of us in top management who do have intuitive and feeling combinations to push for innovation, and to stress the need to be concerned about people. Don't get me wrong, we're a people business, but the numbers seem to stay foremost in the minds of many of our top managers as opposed to the impacts of decisions on our people. This is one reason we have an organizational development program."

This firm is not alone in its dilemma. Business managers and the schools that train them seem to stress the facts, the numbers, the short-term bottom line. As a result, our businesses tend to lack interest in the long term, in creativity, and in people. The importance of these concerns has been recognized, though, and more and more firms are addressing them.

SOURCE: Interview with a senior vice-president of the organization.

Selectivity often stifles creativity. Roger Von Oech, a creativity consultant, feels that one of the major reasons that innovation and ideas for new products are so scarce in American firms lies in a series of mental blocks that program the information we select to focus on. An anecedote that Von Oech tells about one of his consulting projects reveals just how perception can interfere in the innovation process. The client, Applied Material, is a supplier to the semiconductor industry. A promising new silicon-wafer-engraving program that it was developing seemed to be a total debacle. As a result, morale was low, defeatism took over, and the creative process was paralyzed. "Wafers had always been etched horizontally," Von Oech explains, "so I called a seminar and we played with ideas about other ways to handle wafers—vertically, merry-go-rounds, anything." Morale rose, specific ideas emerged. "The project came in months ahead of schedule," Von Oech adds. "It's now their single biggest-selling product. And the turning point, they said, was the seminar. I've done a lot of other projects with them since."[10] The single key issue was that everyone perceived that wafers had to be etched horizontally. Von Oech changed their minds by asking "Why?" He changed their perception.

PERCEPTUAL SET/ INTERPRETATION

Once pieces of information are selected, they are evaluated by reference to what is known as the **perceptual set**—an information base that includes a self-image component. Incoming stimuli are compared with learned evaluative criteria for the purposes of interpretation. When new stimuli are encountered, they are compared with similar ones stored in the information base. Reality for the individual consists of the meanings given to those stimuli. This is the process of **interpretation.** Once meanings have been assigned, the individual can and will take action on those stimuli, even if that action is merely to dismiss them as unimportant.

Vital insight into the content of the perceptual set has been provided through the efforts of neurological research. One of the major early contributors to this field was Dr. Wilder Penfield. As he performed brain surgery for focal epilepsy, Penfield would conduct an experiment: he would touch the temporal cortex of the patient's brain with a galvanic probe that emitted a weak electrical current. This surgery was always performed under local anaesthetic, so that the patient was fully conscious. As various parts of the cortex were stimulated, the patient seemed to relive past experiences. Patients gave highly detailed accounts of experiences they had not thought of for years—perceptions that had been screened out but that now were consciously reexperienced. These accounts eventually caused Penfield to conclude that probably every single event that we have ever consciously experienced is stored in our brains. Most such events slip from our memory; we forget them. When an experience is of no particular importance to us, apparently the electrical current they generate in the nervous system is too weak to sustain a memory of it. Events that the individual defines as important are more readily remembered. Most important to our understanding of the way the perceptual set is constructed is the fact that under external electrical stimulation, patients remembered not only long-forgotten events but the emotions that the events had aroused—no matter how unimportant the event, no matter how long ago it had "taken place."[11] Thus the perceptual set influences emotional as well as factual interpretations. This knowledge of perceptual set helps us to understand why a seemingly unimportant event may trigger a highly emotional reaction: the mind associates it with a similar, remembered piece of information that is highly charged with emotion.

Personality, learning, attitudes and values, needs, and self-image are all influenced by perceptual set, but at the same time they all contribute to it. The manager can use this information in any number of ways—to determine the way subordinates will react to a decision, for example, or how they will respond to low raises or a new reward system. Anyone can use such information to anticipate the behavior of others. The perceptual set of a company's president can have a monumental impact on the firm's fortunes. Steven Jobs, co-founder of Apple Computer, told an interviewer about his decision to develop the MacIntosh personal computer, with its unique software and its mouse, rather than something like IBM's PC Jr., with its more traditional operating system.

Jobs: We think the Mac will sell zillions, but we didn't build Mac for anybody else. We built it for ourselves. We were the group of people who were going to judge whether it was great or not. We weren't going to go out and do market research. We just wanted to build the best thing we could build. When you're a carpenter making a beautiful chest of drawers, you're not going to use a piece of plywood on the back, even though it faces the wall and nobody will ever see it. You'll know it's there, so you're going to use a beautiful piece of wood on the back. For you to sleep well at night, the aesthetic, the quality, has to be carried all the way through.

Interviewer: Are you saying that the people who made the PC Jr. don't have that kind of pride in the product?

Jobs: If they did, they wouldn't have turned out the PC Jr. It seems clear to me that they were designing that on the basis of market research for a specific market segment, for a specific demographic type of customer, and they hoped that if they built this, lots of people would buy them and they'd make lots of money. Those are different motivations. The people in the Mac group wanted to build the greatest computer that has ever been seen.[12]

Jobs is an entrepreneur and former computer hack, what some people might call a free spirit. His perceptual set is fundamentally different from that of most of the people who determine the thrust of IBM's product efforts. If Jobs had had more of a business background, the MacIntosh might have been driven by market needs rather than by the desires of the people who created it.

PERSONAL CHARACTERISTICS

Characteristics of the object affect perception, for example, its uniformity, its physical background, whether it is moving or not. Personal characteristics also affect perception. The personality and its needs, along with learning in the form of knowledge, have a major influence on the individual's perception. The need to maintain one's self-image has a strong impact on the content of one's perceptual set, as we have seen. A dramatic illustration of the impact of physiological needs on perception was provided by the ABC news program *20/20* some years ago. The program's investigations revealed that a large number of airline pilots were getting less sleep than they needed between flights. One plane crash that killed 70 people was reported to have been caused by the pilot's inability to process sensory information properly. Apparently he was too tired to judge altitude correctly.[13] Finally, knowledge is necessary for the proper interpretation of stimuli. The person's past learning experiences and their results provide the data base. We find organizations increasingly giving their employees opportunities to practice their skills in such areas as selling and discipline handling, because experience provides a knowledge base that permits the employees to function well when the real situation arises.

COMMON ERRORS IN PERCEPTION: STEREOTYPING AND HALO EFFECT

The two most common errors in interpersonal perceptions are stereotyping and the halo effect. Each is a function partly of the individual's characteristics and partly of the properties of the stimulus.

Stereotyping occurs when a person, probably to maintain his or her self-image, attributes a belief about a group to an individual member of that group. Given the necessity for perceptual selectivity, stereotyping is to be expected. But it poses a problem for organizational performance when the behavior it leads to is nonproductive. A manager, for example, may perceive all union members as "the enemy." Any individual may stereotype members of the opposite sex as "dingy" or "domineering." Such views can ultimately interfere with cooperation and productivity. It is appropriate to note that we engage in true stereotyping only when we ignore information that shows that the individual does not possess the characteristics that we have attributed to the group. If no such information comes our way, we may be showing prejudice but we are not stereotyping. Stereotyping plays a major role in discrimination, as we shall see in Chapter 9.

The halo effect operates in the opposite direction. The **halo effect** causes us to judge a stimulus (usually but not necessarily a person) on the basis of one or two traits that appeal to us. Those traits, in effect, cast a halo about the stimulus, so that the good feeling aroused by the favored traits are extended to the stimulus as a whole. Managers often fall victim to the halo effect. A manager who places a high value on the ability to get along with others is quite likely to judge a subordinate who gets along well with everyone as trustworthy too, even if he has no idea whether or not she is indeed trustworthy.

> *Most men, when they think they are thinking, are merely rearranging their prejudices.*
> KNUTE ROCKNE

> *After you've heard two eyewitness accounts of a motor accident, you begin to worry about history.*
> JOHN McNAB

YOUR CONCERN WITH PERCEPTION

Every behaviorial situation is perceived by everyone involved and by those who simply view the event. Each time someone engages in communication, each time someone engages in any type of behavior, people are watching, perceiving, recording, and often transmitting to others their perceptions of what occurred. Every time a manager says hello to someone, disciplines someone, praises someone, plans an event with someone; every time the organization pays someone, promotes someone, or terminates someone, perceptions of the meanings of these events are being made, edited, stored, and often retransmitted, not necessarily accurately. Every behavior of any major consequence should therefore be carefully planned in order to ensure that it has the desired effect. Unintended consequences should be avoided whenever possible.

A firm that distributed packaged cakes to supermarkets, for example, dated each package so that it would not be sold after a certain date. If a package was not sold before its expiration date, the delivery person returned it to the warehouse. The company found that far too many packages were being returned. Rules and procedures at the factory, at the warehouse, and relative to the delivery vans were investigated. All were found to be satisfactory.

A chance encounter with one of the delivery van operators uncovered the problem. A manager and a delivery person happened to fall into a lengthy conversation just before the start of the workday. It dawned on the manager that at no time did the van operator load his van. The manager investigated and discovered that vans were not being loaded daily, as was required, but weekly. Van operators had taken it upon themselves to shorten the time they spent in the warehouse by loading only once a week, despite rules requiring daily loading.

The rules in this situation were clearly perceived differently by the two parties. Management sought to have packages loaded fresh each day. Operators saw this rule as a nuisance that hindered the satisfaction of their personal needs. So they changed the rules without permission. A group problem-solving session was definitely required.[14]

None of us must lose sight of the fact that no two people are alike. If you want to communicate successfully, behave successfully, or change someone's behavior, then you must anticipate how your communications and behaviors will be perceived and try to act accordingly. You must attempt to recognize the other person's perceptual set and way of perceiving and tailor your communications and your behaviors appropriately. Yet, because no two people are totally dissimilar, you need only to modify your basic patterns to suit the specific situation.

TIPS FOR SUCCESS

1. Never forget that reality is as you perceive it.
2. Remember, you adjust your perception of reality to your self-image, your needs, your attitudes and values, your personality, and the way you learn.
3. Try to perceive the situation from the other person's perspective.
4. Find out what your preferences are in regard to perceiving and judging. Go to your school's counseling department and ask to complete the MBTI. This may be one of the most important steps you can take in an attempt to understand yourself. If you are married, have your spouse complete the test as well. Your profiles will give you a better understanding of your interpersonal communications.

5. Once a year, either through a professional or through one of the various testing books that are available, take a personality test. Find out who you are and what makes you tick. Start a program of self-improvement. Read books on the subject.
6. Systematically analyze the way you interact with others and attempt to see how your behavior is influenced by each of the six factors discussed in this chapter: needs, attitudes and values, personality, self-image, and ways of learning and perceiving.

SUMMARY

1. Behavior results from the interaction of the individual with his or her environment.
2. Personality, needs, self-image, attitudes and values, and modes of perception and of learning are the fundamental factors that define the boundaries of individual differences and similarities.
3. No two people are the same, but neither are any two people totally dissimilar.
4. It often pays to investigate determinants of personality in order to formulate a strategy to guide your interaction with someone.

5. Perception depends primarily on selectivity and perceptual set for effective interpretation.
6. Interpretation of what is perceived is often influenced by personality, self-image, needs, learning, and attitudes and values.
7. Many factors influence the perception process, including characteristics of the environment and of the individual.
8. Your knowledge of perception can be used to improve your communications and your interactions with others.

DISCUSSION QUESTIONS

1. Spend a few minutes and list:
   a. Words that characterize your personality.
   b. Your dominant needs.
   c. Major attitudes and values that guide your behavior.
   d. The nature of your self-image.

e. Unique features of your perceptual process or perceptual set.

f. The ways in which you learn.

2. Discuss ways in which factors of the organizational environment and of the nonorganizational environment may affect behavior.

3. Recall as many examples as you can of the operation of the following in your own perceptual process: selectivity, perceptual set/interpretation, properties of stimuli, and personal characteristics.

APPLYING HUMAN RELATIONS SKILLS

Organizational Relationships

CASE

Greg Tyler slouched in his chair. With his elbows propped on the chair's arms, his hands met, fingertip to fingertip; he was lost in contemplation. His thoughts returned to the incident with Alicia Clark just a few minutes previously.

Alicia was Greg's immediate superior in the advertising firm for which they both worked. She had recently been made a partner in the firm, one of the largest such firms in the area. Greg was new to the business. He had graduated from the state university, with a very high grade-point average, only six months before. He had majored in advertising. He could have gone with any of several firms, but had chosen this one because it was growing and promised rapid advancement. His first few months had been exciting. He had worked very hard on several new accounts, and had demonstrated the kind of creativity and initiative that the firm had been seeking.

He loved advertising and he worked hard. He had not always been a hard worker, primarily because he worked best at something he was interested in. In college he had worked hardly at all before he concentrated on business subjects, which he found to be much more to his liking than the literature, science, history, and basic math that had filled his first two years. He was an extremely intelligent person, and now he was highly motivated. His work took so much of his time that there was little left for the jogging and sports that he used to enjoy. He had gained eight pounds, and he wished he could spend more time getting back into shape. Yet he really liked his work.

On the other hand, he was growing tired of Alicia's way of expecting him to know what to do without any instructions. She always seemed to expect him to have everything ready before she even told him what she wanted. The situation was really impossible. They had had a blowup. His perceptions of the best ways of relating to people had changed since he'd joined the firm. Relationships didn't have much effect on grades in college, but they had a big effect on success in business. Before, he had always felt that if things didn't work out, if you didn't get along with someone, you could always find somebody else to be friends with. But you couldn't always find another organization to work for. So he knew he had to learn to get along with her; he just didn't know how.

Alicia, too, had been thinking about the blowup with Greg. He has a point, she thought, but it's sink or swim in this world. No one helped me get where I

(Continued on page 44)

am. She felt herself getting angry all over again. She pulled her slim frame from the deep leather chair with which she had rewarded herself when she was made a partner. What the heck, I'll go talk it out with him, she told herself.

1. What are the probable reasons that both Greg and Alicia acted as they did?

EXERCISE   Make a copy of the form below. Then, moving rapidly through the list, circle the letter of each adjective that describes you most of the time. You may circle as many as you like. Now have someone who knows you well complete the copy of the form with you as the subject.

1. a. appreciative
    b. autocratic
    c. adaptable
    d. absent-minded
    e. adventurous
    f. aggressive

2. a. considerate
    b. bossy
    c. alert
    d. argumentative
    e. changeable
    f. emotional

3. a. cooperative
    b. complaining
    c. clear-thinking
    d. confused
    e. cheerful
    f. dependent

4. a. forgiving
    b. demanding
    c. deliberate
    d. distractible
    e. curious
    f. excitable

5. a. friendly
    b. distrustful
    c. efficient
    d. defensive
    e. energetic
    f. fearful

6. a. generous
    b. fault-finding
    c. foresighted
    d. disorderly
    e. enthusiastic
    f. immature

7. a. honest
    b. fussy
    c. individualistic
    d. hard-headed
    e. frank
    f. impulsive

8. a. industrious
    b. intolerant
    c. intelligent
    d. preoccupied
    e. humorous
    f. impatient

9. a. patient
    b. nagging
    c. insightful
    d. rattlebrained
    e. imaginative
    f. moody

10. a praising
    b. opinionated
    c. logical
    d. suggestible
    e. interests wide
    f. rebellious

11. a. responsible
    b. prejudiced
    c. original
    d. stubborn
    e. natural
    f. self-centered

12. a. self-confident
    b. rigid
    c. planful
    d. suspicious
    e. pleasure-seeking
    f. selfish

13. a. trusting
    b. sarcastic
    c. rational
    d. superstitious
    e. spontaneous
    f. sulky

14. a. understanding
    b. self-punishing
    c. realistic
    d. unrealistic
    e. uninhibited
    f. weak

15. a. warm
    b. stern
    c. reasonable
    d. worrying
    e. zany
    f. whiny

Instructions for Scoring

On page 45 is a box containing a series of subboxes. Row 1 indicates the responses to the adjective checklist that match the positive and negative aspects of each of the three selves identified above it. Count each a you circled and place the total in the space provided in row 2 beneath the box where the letter a appears with $+1$. Similarly, count each b, c, d, e, and f you circled and place the totals in the spaces provided in row 2 under b, c, d, e, and f as they appear with either $+1$ or -1 in row 1. Now subtract the b's from the a's, the d's from the c's, and the f's from the e's and place the differences in the spaces provided in row 3. Now add the amounts in row 3 to come up with a grand total in row 4.

	Socialized self		Rational self		Natural self	
1	$+1^a$	-1^b	$+1^c$	-1^d	$+1^e$	-1^f
2						
3						
4						

Meanings

The socialized self indicates how much you have been socialized according to external influences. The rational self indicates your ability to think rationally. Your natural self includes your innate feelings and your intuition. There are positive and negative aspects of all three selves. The plus signs indicate what psychologists believe to be the positive sides of the three selves. The minus signs indicate what experts believe to be the negative sides. If your total in row 3 is a negative number, it means that you describe your own behavior as being dominated by the negative characteristics of that self. The total in row 4 averaged 17 for the 1,200-person sample used to test this checklist. It is generally believed that the higher the number, the happier (and probably healthier) the person. A score over 30 is excellent. Give this checklist to another person or to several other people who know you and have them complete it on you. Their responses will tell you whether their perceptions of you are the same as your perceptions of yourself. If they differ significantly, what does this tell you?

SOURCE: Adapted from "The Development of a Transactional Analysis Scale for the Adjective Check List," by Charles E. Schaefer, *The Journal of Psychology*, September 1976. Reprinted by permission of the Helen Dwight Reid Educational Foundation. Published by Heldref Publications, 4000 Albemarle St., N.W., Washington, D.C. 20016. Copyright © 1976.

REFERENCES

1. James L. Gibson, John M. Ivancevich, and James H. Donnelly, Jr., *Organizations: Behavior, Structure, Processes*, 4th ed. (Plano, Tex.: Business Publications, Inc., 1982), p. 47.
2. Linda L. Davidoff, *Introduction to Psychology*, 2d ed. (New York: McGraw-Hill, 1980), chap. 13.
3. J. Stewart Dougherty and Robert G. Eccles, "Visa International: The Management of Change."
4. James M. Cole, "Put on a Happy Face, You Managers!" *Wall Street Journal*, October 15, 1984, p. 471.
5. Reported to the author by an IBM official.
6. Thomas J. Peters and Robert H. Waterman, Jr., *In Search of Excellence: Lessons from America's Best-Run Companies* (New York: Harper & Row, 1982), p. 57.
7. Leonard M. Apcar, "Middle Managers and Supervisors Resist Moves to More Participatory Management," *Wall Street Journal*, September 16, 1985, p. 27.
8. "Holiday Inns Sets Its First Hotel-Casino, Prompting Clymer to Resign as President," *Wall Street Journal*, October 2, 1978, p. 16.

9. Davidoff, *Introduction to Psychology*, p. 172.

10. Quoted in Robert S. Wieder, "How to Get Great Ideas," *Success*, November 1983, pp. 29–32, 59, 60.

11. Maxwell Maltz, *Psycho-cybernetics* (New York: Pocket Books, 1960), p. 22.

12. "Steven Jobs," *Playboy*, February 1985, p. 58.

13. *20/20*, ABC TV, August 13, 1981.

14. R. S. Stainton, "Reality Is in the Eye of the Beholder," *Business Quarterly*, Summer 1984, p. 84.

2

UNDERSTANDING AND IMPROVING INDIVIDUAL RELATIONSHIPS

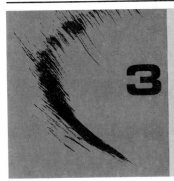

3 MOTIVATION AND PERFORMANCE: THE CYCLE BEGINS WITH NEEDS

LEARNING OBJECTIVES

When you have completed this chapter, you should be able to:
1. Define motivation.
2. List the determinants of individual motivation and performance.
3. Explain the major theories of motivation and how they relate to each other through the use of the motivation/performance cycle model.
4. Discuss the various stages of this model.
5. Explain the basic concepts embodied in each of the major theories of motivation.
6. Use your knowledge of motivation to improve your own motivation and that of others.

GRANT MANAGERS RISK PIE-IN-FACE FOR A FAILURE

NEW YORK—Managers for W. T. Grant Co. stores were hit in the face with custard pies or suffered other indignities if they didn't meet their credit quotas.

The hazing procedure was discussed by John E. Sundman, former senior vice president and treasurer of Grant, in his deposition discussing the problems besetting the chain before it went bankrupt.

It was called a Steak and Beans program and had "negative incentives, which consisted of, beside the pie-in-the-face, store managers having their ties cut in half, being forced to run around their stores backward, pushing peanuts with their noses, and not being promoted to larger stores," he said.

Asked if it also had come to his attention that a losing district manager was required to walk around a hotel lobby dressed in nothing but a diaper, Mr. Sundman answered that he had never heard of that one.

What motivates you? What does it take to cause you to do something? What does it take to get you to perform in an organization? Probably no two of you will answer these questions in exactly the same way. Yet it is reasonably certain that W. T. Grant's Steak and Beans program would motivate few of you, except maybe to quit your job. It is very unlikely that Grant elicited the best performance from its managers, unlikelier still that it maintained or strengthened commitment to the organization. It's no wonder the company went bankrupt. Contrast W. T. Grant with Delta Airlines, discussed in Chapter 1. Delta succeeded while Grant failed. Much of the difference in results is a

> *I learned the meaning of [motivation] when standing on the green and thinking, I've got to make this putt to eat dinner tonight.*
>
> JANE CRAFTER, professional golfer

consequence of employee motivation in the first case and the lack of it in the second. Perhaps most important, the difference results from the fact that one organization succeeded in influencing its employees' motivations in a positive direction while the other succeeded all too well in influencing them negatively.

Chapters 3 and 4 deal with the complex questions of how to elicit the best performance from each person in the organization while at the same time maintaining or strengthening each individual's commitment to the organization and its objectives. This chapter first reviews the individual motivation process and then discusses that process within the framework of the work organization.

INDIVIDUAL MOTIVATION

Motivation is an internal process directed at the goal of satisfying needs. You should be concerned with its causes, its direction, and its strength or persistence.[1] While our motivation is an internal process, it can be influenced by other people who know how to control our attempts to satisfy our needs and how to direct our needs (or wants). In most situations, it is unsatisfied needs that trigger the internal motivation mechanism. As Figure 3.1 indicates, the motivation process consists of essentially six steps:

1. The individual feels a need that is not being satisfied.
2. The individual searches for ways to satisfy that need, examines the alternative means available, and chooses among them, taking into consideration the likely outcome of each alternative.
3. The individual, thus motivated to take action, acts to obtain that need satisfier.
4. The individual either obtains the sought need satisfier or does not obtain it.
5. The individual reasseses the situation and evaluates the process for further action.
6. The issue of continuance then arises: will the individual continue to be motivated to satisfy this need in the same way?

An example of an individual going through this cycle twice in rapid succession occurs in the opening scene of the film *Indiana Jones and the Temple of Doom*. The good doctor is critically in need of an antidote to the poison he has just swallowed. His enemy has such an antidote. Jones considers the alternative courses of action available and decides to offer a huge diamond in exchange for the antidote. His enemy, having accepted the diamond, then refuses to provide the antidote. The doctor reassesses his situation, finds himself with his need still unsatisfied, and decides on more violent means to satisfy it. A whole series of calamities ensues, but eventually he prevails, obtains the antidote, and survives to search for fame and glory.

Our needs are usually less urgent than Dr. Jones's, but we all find ourselves in need of certain things every day. You probably need money for tuition and for textbooks. You definitely need food to eat and a place to live. What's worse, you probably need to learn how to run a personal computer in order to pass your stat course. Your needs change rapidly over time, and the means by which you are able to satisfy those needs change too.

FIGURE 3.1   *The individual motivation process*

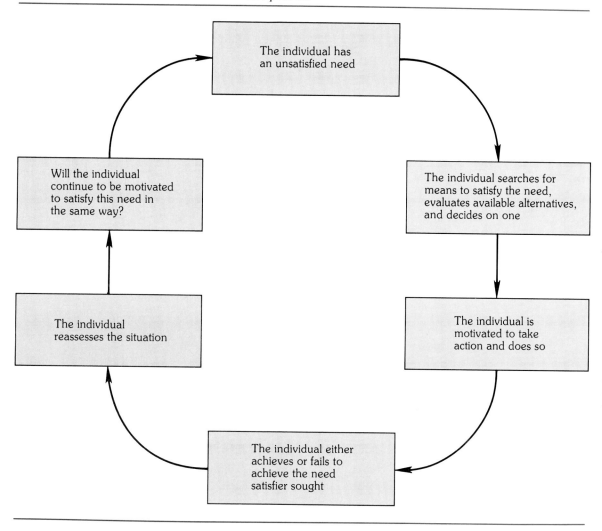

Any number of external factors influence the internal motivation process. We are all pulled in numerous directions, often simultaneously. Friends ask us out. The family seeks our presence. A fraternity or sorority asks us to pledge or not. Our spouse wants us to spend more time with the kids. The government demands that we pay our taxes. Our employer requires us to work overtime. All of these and numerous other external factors influence our internal motivation process.

These external influencers of our motivation affect it in several specific patterns. They may create needs (or wants) for us.* The work organization, for example, may create wants by offering bonuses, awards, and promotions. Assuming that such external influencers recognize our needs and are willing

INFLUENCING INDIVIDUAL MOTIVATION

*Create may be too strong a term. Actually, they merely activate latent needs.

and able to satisfy them, they may offer us the means to satisfy our needs. These means are usually offered in return for our efforts to help them to satisfy their own needs. In this exchange process they may also take actions that make it easier for us to help them achieve their objectives. For example, the organization may provide resources to work with and training for a particular job. When we can and do satisfy the organization's needs, the organization has succeeded in eliciting from us what it has sought: our performance. Having done so, it may or may not actually provide the need satisfiers it has offered. The Human Relations Happening on the Lincoln Electric Company demonstrates a successful application of the external influence process.

THE MOTIVATION/PERFORMANCE CYCLE

Motivation and performance are two of the most difficult but most important topics in the entire field of management practice. A vast amount of research has been devoted to these subjects, and from this research several major definitions and theories have emerged. The **motivation/performance cycle** presented in Figure 3.2 combines the elements of the external influence

process with those of the individual motivation process shown in Figure 3.1. The colored boxes represent the actions that external influencers may take; the white boxes represent the individual motivation process.

FIGURE 3.2   *The motivation/performance cycle*

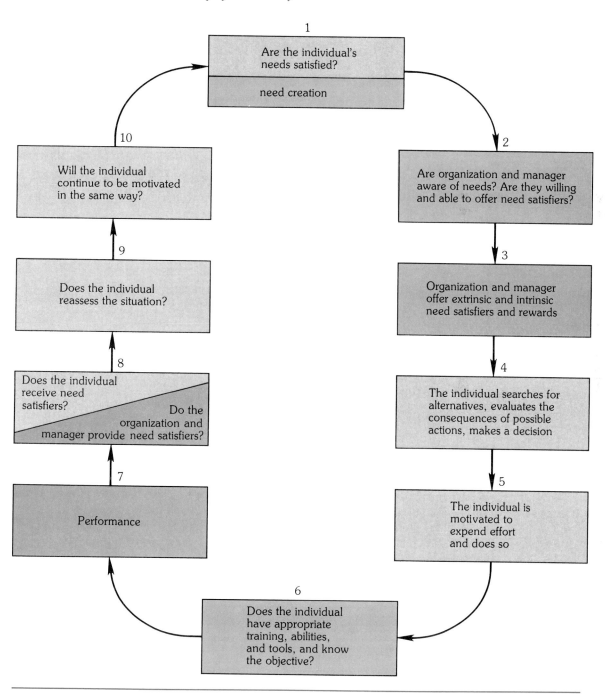

This model conceptualizes the relationship of the major theories of motivation and performance. Having erected this framework, we can now discuss a few of the classical contributions to theory in the context of the model. Rather than concentrate on the differences among the contributions, we shall emphasize how each contribution fits into the model and enhances its explanatory power. Finally, the model will be used to identify the causes of typical difficulties experienced in the motivation/performance process and to suggest potential remedies for some of those difficulties.

Figure 3.2 is concerned simultaneously with virtually all of the possible relationships portrayed in Figure 1.1, but especially with relationships between individuals, between individuals and organizations, and between the individual and the self. This motivation model is also concerned with several human relations skills, but especially, with:

1. Leadership: the making of decisions on how to treat people in order to influence their internal motivation mechanism, and the carrying out of those decisions.
2. Communication: the conveying of leadership decisions and other necessary information to the appropriate people.

The basic philosophy of this model, and indeed of this book, is that *appropriate managerial decisions on how to treat people, properly communicated and carried into action, result in motivation, performance, and productivity.*

HUMAN RELATIONS HAPPENING

LINCOLN ELECTRIC COMPANY

A classic example of the external influence process in action is provided by the pay-for-performance program of the Lincoln Electric Company of Cleveland, Ohio. The company is the premier manufacturer of arc welding equipment in the world. It paid its workers an average of more than $35,000 in compensation in 1985, about twice as much as the average Cleveland factory worker in a similar situation earned that year. How does the company pay such high wages and remain productive? It pays for performance. It uses a bonus system that about doubles the basic wage. Each worker's bonus, paid at the end of the year, depends on the worker's productivity and effective efforts to reduce costs. Workers are expected to be self-motivated, but the company is careful to select and retain only those who work hardest for the financial compensation it provides. The company seeks employees with the same basic needs: the things that money can buy. The company offers them the money that will satisfy their needs. The employees examine the situation and feel that the reward offered is worth the very hard work involved. They are motivated to perform. The company is careful to provide everything the workers need in order to perform well. The company then keeps its promise and at the end of each year rewards its workers' efforts

> with a bonus. Among employees who survive the first few months—those who respond positively to the incentives the firm offers—there is very little turnover. Employees continue to be motivated in the same way, year after year.

SOURCE: Arthur Sharplin, "Lincoln Electric, 1984," in James M. Higgins and Julian W. Vincze, *Strategic Management and Organizational Policy Text and Cases*, 3d ed. (Hinsdale, Ill.: Dryden Press, 1986), pp. 494–514.

Because motivation begins with an individual's needs, managers and organizations offer ways to satisfy those needs in order to influence employees to perform their work functions. This process has two essential components. First, unsatisfied needs motivate most people. By offering ways to satisfy those needs, including satisfaction with the job, organizations and managers are able to activate and influence the direction and strength of individual motivation. Second, the various stages in the motivation/performance process are constructed in recognition of the fact that the individual may not be motivated to work as the organization wishes regardless of his or her needs, the need satisfiers offered, or the satisfaction obtained from need satisfiers.

THE CONCEPTS UNDERLYING THE MODEL

The motivation/performance cycle model is based primarily on needs theories, instrumentality or expectancy theories of motivation, attribution theories, reinforcement theories, and consistency theories of motivation. Taken together, these theories contend that individuals have needs, and that they choose among alternative behaviors that may lead to the satisfaction of those needs. Choices are based on their perceptions of the probable outcomes of those behaviors (pay, for example) and their relative attractiveness (overtime pay versus time off). The resultant impact of the process on satisfaction and self-image helps to determine whether or not the process can be repeated with the same need satisfiers. The model therefore draws heavily on the research and integrative works of Abraham Maslow,[2] Frederick Herzberg,[3] Victor Vroom,[4] Lyman Porter and Edward Lawler,[5] John Campbell and his associates,[6] John Miner and Peter Dachler,[7] Robert Sutermeister,[8] Abraham Korman,[9] Thomas Clark,[10] H. H. Kelly and Terrence R. Mitchell,[11] B. F. Skinner,[12] and numerous others. The essence of the model can be summarized in the following proposition:

> To the extent that an individual believes that by exerting effort in a particular direction, he or she will obtain rewards or need satisfiers that will contribute significantly to the satisfaction of the individual's current needs, he or she will be motivated to exert that effort. Performance will result if certain conditions are met. And to the extent that satisfiers are given, are contingent on performance, and are attributed to the correct cause, and to the extent that the process maintains or increases the individual's self-image, the individual will probably continue through the motivation/performance cycle in the same manner as before.

This proposition describes the process through which the individual proceeds when the organization, the manager, or any other entity or individual seeks to motivate (influence) him or her to some end, known as performance. To understand the dynamics of this process, we must examine the relationships shown in the model. Please remember that motivation comes from within. Practically speaking, the leader's role is to influence others to move in a desired direction, that is, to direct motivation toward organizational objectives. The leader obtains and uses influence by following the steps outlined in Figure 3.2.

Normally we assume that human beings will react rationally to certain offered need satisfiers. The model does recognize, however, that human beings do not always react rationally; in fact, sometimes they don't even react at all. No one thinks rationally all of the time. (How rationality or the lack of it affects motivation will be explained in more detail later in this chapter and in Chapter 4.) Furthermore, only the individual who concurs with both the required objective and the required action will be motivated. Let us now examine the first three stages of the model in detail. We will examine the remaining stages in Chapter 4.

STAGE 1: INDIVIDUAL NEEDS AND THEIR CREATION

Needs, as the term is used in the motivation/performance cycle model, is quite broadly defined. Needs are not restricted to tangible items directly controlled by the formal organization. People have many and varying needs, which can be satisfied in many different ways. As the term is used here, *needs* also includes *wants*. Researchers have offered a variety of analyses of needs and their causes.

Maslow's Hierarchy Abraham Maslow has contributed greatly to our understanding of human needs. His theory was introduced in the psychological literature in 1954 and was popularized in the management literature by Douglas McGregor in 1960.[13] Maslow contended that five basic types of human needs can be distinguished, and that these types are arranged in a hierarchy, as shown in Figure 3.3.

According to **Maslow's hierarchy of needs** theory, each person starts at birth at the bottom level of the hierarchy; that is, the person's first concern is to satisfy his or her immediate *physiological needs*. Until those basic requirements for survival have been met, the individual can devote little attention to anything else. Therefore, only rewards and need satisfiers that contribute significantly to the satisfaction of those needs can have motivational value. As such needs are met, however, their importance begins to diminish, and the individual can begin to concentrate on the needs at the next higher level—*security needs*. A new set of rewards assumes increased importance and motivational value to the individual.

According to the theory, this process continues step by step as the individual gradually works his or her way up the hierarchy of needs. It is entirely possible, however, that an individual may fall back down the hierarchy through some misfortune, such as loss of a job or illness. Just ask yourself how long you can go without eating. After a few hours without food you return to the first level, at least for the moment. Of course, some people ignore certain needs.

FIGURE 3.3   *Maslow's hierarchy of needs*

SELF-ACTUAL-IZATION
Achieving one's full potential, personal growth, creative fulfillment

ESTEEM NEEDS
Self-esteem, esteem of others, status, power, autonomy, competence, prestige, recognition

SOCIAL NEEDS
Acceptance, affection, affiliation, love, interaction

SECURITY NEEDS
Stability, protection, freedom from fear, provisions for the future

PHYSIOLOGICAL NEEDS
Immediate survival, food, shelter, clothing, bodily needs

Martyrs apparently have little concern for their own safety, but they are, of course, satisfying other needs.

People seem to differ in the amount of satisfaction they require at each level. Some people seem to require more love and affection than others to satisfy their social needs. Others may have unusually great need for status, power, or esteem—esteem needs. Some artists seem to place little importance on any but self-actualization needs. It's evident that the basic needs of most people are satisfied. As individuals move up the hierarchy, organizations find it necessary to change the ways in which they attempt to influence the motivation process, as the Human Relations Happening on Honeywell suggests.

The validity and applicability of Maslow's theory have been subjected to much discussion and research. Does a hierarchy of needs really exist? Is the hierarchy the same for all people? Has Maslow correctly classified the many types of human needs, and has he arranged them correctly in his hierarchy? Does the individual always react as Maslow predicts? The net results of research are not overwhelmingly supportive of the theory, especially if the theory is interpreted rigidly. And the steps in the hierarchy are reported to vary from country to country.[14]

> *"Not even God can talk to a hungry man."*
> MOHANDAS K. GANDHI

> *"There is no clear evidence that human needs are classified in five distinct categories, or that these categories are structured in a special hierarchy. There is some evidence for the existence of possibly two types of needs, deficiency and growth needs, although this categorization is not always operative."*
> M. A. WAHBA AND
> L. G. BRIDWELL

HONEYWELL'S WINNING EDGE

The way organizations must approach human relations today differs markedly from the practices of ten to twenty years ago. People seem to have a greater need for esteem today, particularly those in certain industries. Most of their workers have worked their way up to that level of the hierarchy. Jim Renier, president of the Control Systems Division of Honeywell, has commented, "If people know you are really interested in them, they will respond. Most people want to do a good job, be recognized as intelligent and trusted workers, receive information so that they can make informed decisions, derive a sense of self-fulfillment on the job, and experience self-esteem." Honeywell, through Jim Renier, set out to create an organizational culture that satisfied people's higher-level needs. Mr. Renier feels that most people want to be productive, and that the organization must provide a climate that will enable them to be productive. To create such a climate, Honeywell introduced the "Winning Edge" program. Honeywell's management style underwent several changes designed to make it more humanistic and to increase managers' concern for the long-term aspects of managing human resources. Many participative management techniques, such as quality circles, were introduced. Honeywell is extremely pleased with its "human management," as it calls its new management program.

SOURCE: Perry Pascarella, "Management at Honeywell," *Industry Week*, July 27, 1982.

> *Man is a wanting animal and rarely reaches a state of complete satisfaction, except for a short time. As one desire is satisfied, another pops up to take its place.*
> ABRAHAM MASLOW

Alderfer's Hierarchy C. P. Alderfer, having examined Maslow's theory and the related research, proposed that the hierarchy of needs has only three levels, as indicated in Figure 3.4: existence needs, relatedness needs, and growth needs. His limited research supports this model, which does appear to be more universally appropriate than Maslow's.[15] Further, **Alderfer's hierarchy of needs** does not contain the rigid constraints of activation of higher-level needs embodied in Maslow's conceptualization. His theory also allows for need frustration and subsequent regression to lower levels.

Achievement Motivation Another major contribution to our understanding of human needs, the theory of **achievement motivation,** has been made by David C. McClelland and J. W. Atkinson.[16] They discovered that a fairly small percentage of people have an unusually high *need for achievement*, or *nAch*. Such people tend to possess a consistent set of traits:

1. They prefer to set their own goals and pursue tasks for which the probability of success is moderately high. If the probability is too high, they feel no sense of achievement when they succeed. If the probability is too low, they succeed so infrequently that their need for achievement is frustrated.
2. They prefer tasks that give them fast and objective feedback concerning their performance. Without such feedback, they cannot gauge their achievement and thereby obtain satisfaction.
3. They prefer tasks that permit their own efforts and ability to have a major influence on the outcome of the endeavor. Otherwise, they feel little sense of achievement at a successful outcome.

4. They constantly search for ways to improve their performance.

People with a high need for achievement are likely to choose such occupations as business management or entrepreneurship, sales, and professional sports (especially individual sports, such as golf or tennis). Do you think you are a person with a high nAch?

McClelland and Atkinson observed that in addition to a need for achievement, individuals also possess a *need for power* (control over others) and a *need for affiliation* (social interaction). The successful business manager is typically believed to have both a high need for achievement and a high need for power but a low need for affiliation. Apparently the successful manager in a large corporation has a slightly higher need for power than the individual entrepreneur who runs his or her own firm—and should, in McClelland's view.[17]

Though most organizations need to have a few high achievers in key positions, it is difficult to manage an organization with a very large number of such people. Since high achievers tend to operate autonomously with respect to goal selection and motivation, it can be quite difficult to obtain coordination and cooperation among them.

Most people in this world, psychologically, can be divided into two broad groups. There is that minority which is challenged by opportunity and willing to work hard to achieve something, and the majority which really does not care all that much.
DAVID C. MCCLELLAND

FIGURE 3.4   *A comparison of the Alderfer and Maslow hierarchies*

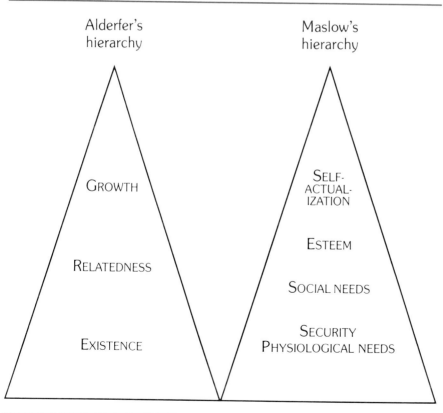

Alderfer's hierarchy

GROWTH

RELATEDNESS

EXISTENCE

Maslow's hierarchy

SELF-ACTUAL-IZATION

ESTEEM

SOCIAL NEEDS

SECURITY
PHYSIOLOGICAL NEEDS

The high achiever develops most often under the following circumstances:

1. A favorable religious/cultural environment. When the dominant belief system of the culture encourages or at least allows individuals to make money and to use it for their own ends, economic development will come about and high achievers will emerge. When the prevailing belief system opposes individual wealth and economic development, the high achiever will fail to materialize.

2. Children's stories that stress economic achievement. A society in which the stories told to or written for children stress economic achievement will have more high achievers than one whose tales for children stress other measures of success.

3. A favorable family environment. The family plays an extremely important role in the development of high achievers. High achievers are most often found in families that stress achievement and performance; give positive recognition for performance and little or no negative feedback that can damage the child's self-image; give continuous feedback; and are headed by a person whose leadership style is more democratic than authoritarian.

The need for achievement can be trained, but there is an ethical question as to whether people should change the needs of others. The Human Relations Happening on peak performers reports on one recent research project that indicates that achievement in at least one particular field can be learned. Needless to say, business organizations seek high achievers.

Objectives as Motivators   Because people are goal-striving animals, objectives may be used to direct and intensify motivation. Programs that establish objectives, then reward on their achievement, are usually very successful.

HUMAN RELATIONS HAPPENING

PEAK PERFORMERS

Since persons with a high need for achievement tend to gravitate toward positions in business organizations, much of the research on the need for achievement has been conducted in these types of organizations. One recent study by Charles A. Garfield examined the characteristics of "peak performers" in businesses. Included in the sample examined were 250 managers, salespersons, and entrepreneurs identified through a careful peer selection process; that is, they were chosen by other managers, salespersons, and entrepreneurs in their fields. Garfield and his associates conducted lengthy interviews with each of these peak performers. Distillation of the data gathered revealed that they had ten characteristics in common:

1. Foresight and the ability to carry out effective strategic planning.
2. A drive to transcend previous levels of accomplishment.
3. High levels of self-confidence and self-esteem.
4. A high need for responsibility and control.

5. High communication and salesmanship skills.
6. A tendency to engage in mental rehearsal for "critical incidents" or "key situations."
7. Little need for outside praise or recognition.
8. A willingness to take creative risks, rather than get stuck in a "comfort zone."
9. The ability to accept feedback and make self-corrections.
10. A proprietary attitude toward their ideas and products.

Garfield notes that these characteristics can be learned, and that many more persons could be peak performers if they practiced these behaviors. One interesting final observation is that few peak performers are workaholics. Garfield believes that this finding can be attributed to their tendency to become too engrossed in what they are doing to be concerned about the results. They are activity-oriented, not results-oriented.

SOURCE: Richard Trubo, "Peak Performance," *Success*, April 1983, pp. 30–33, 56.

Role Motivation   Another very interesting and related theory of human needs, **role motivation,** has been proposed by John Miner.[18] Miner's research indicates that certain individuals have a need to fulfill specific roles, and while he has focused on the characteristics of individuals who seek to fulfill the manager's role in business, there is no reason not to believe that others— teachers, politicians, doctors, lawyers, carpenters—do not feel a need to fulfill their roles as well. Most of you are probably familiar with the "professional student" role. People who have 500 credit hours, four majors, six minors, and a year to go to graduation would appear to enjoy the student's role. What role do you aspire to?

The Need for Recognition   Since the Hawthorne studies (discussed in Chapter 1), it has been evident that people feel a strong need to have their existence recognized. People want other people simply to say hello, or for that matter to say anything at all. As this need is very much a part of all of us, it can be used to influence others. Most important, it must be satisfied in a positive way in order to prevent the problems that can arise when people seek to satisfy the need for recognition in negative ways. This need is very strong, more basic than Maslow's social needs, and probably could be called a physiological need.[19]

Other Needs   Many people are highly motivated by other needs—truth, beauty, or justice, for example—or perhaps the need to contribute to society.

Personality and Needs   An individual's personality and the environment in which he or she exists are responsible for that individual's current needs and their strength. The effective leader can and does discern these needs primarily in the subordinate's behavior. Entire courses are devoted to the examination of the relationship of personality and needs. While detailed discussion of personality theory is not possible here, we can keep in mind that in our attempts to motivate others we must always consider personality and learn to adapt motivation techniques to those aspects of personality that we recognize.

Situational Factors   A starving person is more concerned about food than a person with a full stomach. A truck driver who is unemployed has a greater need for security than one who has a job. Similarly, an individual who works in a hot, humid steel foundry is less likely to seek self-actualization on the job than an executive who works in an air-conditioned office and whose job permits a great deal of autonomy. Clearly *the situation affects motivation*. One of the most relevant and most significant of the factors in the situation is the work environment. The individual's manager, peers, and job and the organization's management philosophy all create a certain climate that affects the employee's needs and responses to rewards and need satisfiers. Another relevant and significant environmental ingredient is the family. An employee whose spouse is very concerned about money will probably respond well to an offer of money as a motivator. An employee whose spouse is more concerned about having a close-knit family life may reject overtime work and its associated financial rewards. Each employee has individual feelings and values in regard to these trade-offs as well.

Need Creation   External influencers can and do facilitate and frustrate the satisfaction of needs. They may also create needs, or at least make them manifest in some way. The family, the fraternity, the church, the school, the work organization, and its managers engage in **need creation** by the demands they make on us. The family creates many of our basic psychological needs, such as the need to achieve, the need to feel guilty, the need to be dominant, the need to let others control the situation. It may even affect certain physical needs: your need for food may seem unusually compelling, for instance, if you have to wait for everyone in the family to arrive before you can sit down to eat. The work organization and its managers may require increased work effort, demand a certain level of performance, send a person to a foreign country. Such demands can activate various needs within the individual. The teacher who must grade sixty papers by Tuesday may end up needing sleep because she stayed up late to complete the task. The stock broker who sees the rewards that money can buy may feel compelled to sell more, as the Human Relations Happening on Merrill Lynch suggests. The individual who

HUMAN RELATIONS HAPPENING

Motivation 101 at Merrill Lynch

By WALL STREET JOURNAL *Staff Reporters*

How do you motivate stockbrokers? A couple of Merrill Lynch offices think they've found an answer: Show them what money can buy.

John Joyce, head of Merrill Lynch's Boston office, has taken 60 subscriptions to the Robb Report, a glossy monthly featuring articles on the interests and activities of the rich. (Merrill Lynch's Hartford office has also bought some subscriptions for the $55-a-year magazine.) The most recent issue includes a story on the comeback of big cars—one is described as "a culmination of the ultimate materialistic expression of excess"—and advertisements for gold-plated pistols and raccoon rugs and bedspreads.

"It's a great magazine," says Gerard Sullivan, a Boston sales manager who gets one of the company-paid subscriptions.

"It's nice to see what the wealthy do with their money."

Mr. Joyce thinks the magazine is just what his brokers need. "Our clients and prospects are reading this magazine," he says. "My account

executives should not only know what their clients are reading, but should also aspire themselves to be a part of the life style."

SOURCE: *The Wall Street Journal*, June 14, 1984, p. 33.

works long and stressful hours may need psychotherapy and physical fitness training. The person who is promoted may need training and development to perform adequately at the new job. Someone who is reprimanded for poor performance may need considerable consolation from his or her spouse and friends. Organizations and managers must be attuned to the needs they create and attempt to reduce the negative consequences.

Now that you know the various categories of individual needs, you may wonder how they apply to you. Why not take the Test Yourself on individual needs and find out?

TEST YOURSELF

INDIVIDUAL NEEDS

The purpose of this exercise is to gain insight into your own needs. After you have answered the following questions, they may be discussed in class with your instructor.

1. What are your current physiological needs?
2. What is your greatest security need at the moment?
3. What are your major social needs at this time?
4. What are your esteem needs at this time?
5. What are your self-actualization needs at this time?
6. What other growth needs do you have?
7. Do you have a strong need for achievement? power? affiliation?
8. What are your personal objectives for the next three years? How could an organization motivate you through these or other objectives?
9. What roles would you like to engage in that would motivate you?
10. How many times since yesterday have you done something just to get recognition?
11. How does personality affect your needs? How does the situation affect your needs?
12. What external influences affect your motivation?

NEEDS AND THE ORGANIZATION

- Tom Walters is an outstanding faculty member. He always receives excellent ratings from students. He publishes frequently in various journals. He presents papers at professional meetings. He is a member of two major campus committees. He assists local businesses with their problems. He has just completed a textbook on a subject that is a core course in most business schools. Tom has been granted fair pay raises for two years, and he enjoys his work. He has just been promoted to associate professor in record time. But Tom is leaving his current school for another one. He will receive significantly more money in his new position, but more important, he says it will provide him with "things I need." As it turns out, his dean has not once given him a positive comment about his work. He even complained when Tom started work on another book, thereby taking up the time of an already burdened secretarial staff.

- Jerri Shaw recently completed a three-day seminar on human relations. The instructor stressed the importance of providing satisfiers for the needs at the three highest levels of Maslow's hierarchy. When Jerri returned to the job, she enthusiastically set out to put into practice what she had learned. She provided her subordinates with recognition and made an effort to improve the content of their jobs. She let them help her make decisions. But when pay raises were given out at the end of the month, several subordinates complained that she should have been fighting to get them more money instead of "wasting time on this other stuff."

- Catrina Konsolvi wondered how to motivate Larry. He was her best accountant, but because of company guidelines on pay raises, she could give him only a 5 percent raise. He was already looking for another job, because he knew that he could improve his pay situation tremendously by going with another firm.

- Paul Arni was the president of a plastics extrusion plant that employed 300 people. He was 55 years old. He believed that money motivated everybody, and that was all there was to motivation. He was very fond of saying, "If they don't like it here, they can hit the door." He was sure there was nowhere else for most of them to go. Sure enough, his plant had the highest turnover rate of any in the area. After a long strike called by a union to force the firm to recognize its right to represent the firm's employees, the company filed for bankruptcy and Paul was looking for a new business.

STAGE 2: AWARENESS OF INDIVIDUAL NEEDS AND PROVISIONS OF SATISFIERS

The stories about Tom Walters, Jerri Shaw, Catrina Konsolvi, and Paul Arni are all true. What do they have in common? The external influencers—here managers or their organizations—had insufficient *awareness of needs*, or lacked *willingness* or *latitude to supply need satisfiers*. The result: diminished or negative performance, productivity, efficiency, and profits.

While many factors doubtless contributed to each unfortunate situation, in each case one unmet need or failure seems to have been paramount:

Tom Walters: recognition. Tom had not received a single positive comment on his work from any of his superiors. In fact, his dean thought Tom was too achievement-oriented and gave him little support. The dean even counseled him to slow down and not to be so eager for success. Why do you suppose he was so unwilling to satisfy Tom's obvious need for recognition?

Jerri Shaw: money. Yes, money motivates when one doesn't have it. Its absence may motivate some people to leave the organization. Jerri saw one need that she had not recognized before. Unfortunately, she failed to recognize this normally obvious need.

Catrina Konsolvi simply was not permitted to reward subordinates in the way she would have liked. What kinds of problems for the company and the manager might this situation pose?

Paul Arni: consideration for employees. Paul cares little for people, and therefore his people care little for him. Times have changed since Paul grew up. Employees no longer have to love it; they really can leave it. Was Paul guilty of not recognizing needs, unwilling to satisfy them, or lacking in the latitude to satisfy them?

How can managers and organizations know employees' needs? By knowing their employees and being concerned about their needs, not just about their own. Harold Geneen, former CEO of ITT, observes that

> managers and in particular the CEO should realize that people are not really working for him. They have their own needs for self-fulfillment. He has to help fill their needs as much as they do his.
>
> No chief executive should ever order a division or company manager to do something with which he disagrees. You can order a man *not* to do something: "Don't burn the building down." But if you order him to do something with which he disagrees, you have taken over the responsibility for that decision.
>
> He has the right to come back to you later and say, "I did what you ordered and the whole thing fell apart, and it's not my fault." Subconsciously, he was almost committed to proving that your idea would not work.[20]

Even when managers recognize their subordinates' needs and are able to satisfy them, many are unwilling to do so. Why? Insecurity, jealousy, and frequently a desire to reward ("do right by") other people who are more important to them. In any case, few managers today have the latitude to determine subordinates' pay or benefits or other need satisfiers. The union or the budget or the board of directors often makes these determinations. But most managers can provide many satisfiers—a good, healthy organizational climate, for example—and if they do not, they will have problems.

When General Motors sits down with the United Auto Workers to negotiate a new contract, it may or may not recognize union members' needs. Perhaps more important, it is often unwilling to satisfy those needs it recognizes. For example, the union invariably seeks to protect jobs. GM feels it must automate to compete with Japan; it wants to eliminate jobs, not to protect them.

How about everyday relationships with people outside the formal work organization—will understanding their needs improve your relationships with them? You bet it will. Think of some one person in your life who is important to you now—a girlfriend, a boyfriend, a spouse, a parent, a son, a daughter, a friend. How well do you interrelate with that person? If you relate well, think of the ways in which you satisfy that person's needs. If you don't relate well to that person, ask yourself first if you've ever let that person's needs guide your behavior. If not, could that be part of the reason for the less than

People at work are not so different from people in other aspects of life. They are not entirely creatures of logic. They have feelings. They like to feel important and to have their work recognized as important.

FRITZ J. ROETHLISBERGER

People react to fear, not love. They don't teach that in Sunday school, but it's true.

RICHARD M. NIXON

satisfactory relationship? Have you failed to recognize that person's needs? Are you willing and able to satisfy those needs? How about your own needs—does that person recognize them, and is he or she willing and able to satisfy them?

Now think of someone who is not particularly close to you with whom you've had an unsatisfactory encounter recently—perhaps a post office clerk, a salesperson in a store, an acquaintance. How could that negative situation stem from a lack of understanding and inability or unwillingness to satisfy the other's needs? How could you or the other person have used an understanding of needs to improve that situation?

STAGE 3: NEED SATISFIERS AND REWARDS

Once needs are determined and the manager and the organization or other external influencers are able and willing to provide appropriate need satisfiers (Stage 2), then they must offer them. The theories of **need satisfaction** state that if people have needs and are offered rewards that will help them to satisfy those needs, they will be motivated to act to acquire those satisfiers.

The Classical Approach   Historically, the classical approach to need satisfaction has been to offer incentives, primarily monetary incentives (pay and benefits), in order to activate, direct, and strengthen employee motivation. As long as employees were at the level of physiological needs, this approach worked pretty well. But as employees moved up the needs hierarchy, it began to fail. Obviously, the employees at Lincoln Electric are somehow an exception to this general experience. Perhaps the money itself, not just what it can buy, becomes a critical motivator. Thus it continues to motivate strongly at all levels of the hierarchy of needs.

The Human Relations Approach   Once employees had moved upward in the hierarchy, their needs changed. The famous Hawthorne studies led to the realization of the importance of "human relations." For a while a human relations approach to need satisfaction was popular. This approach focused on providing social need satisfaction as a means of influencing motivation. Its proponents claimed that treating employees "nicely" and making them "happy" would result in increased productivity. It did and it didn't. As Daniel Bell observed, "contented people, unlike contented cows, do not necessarily give more or better milk."[21] This approach was nevertheless popular for some time, but it has finally lost much of its appeal.

66The psychology of motivation is tremendously complex, and what has been unraveled with any degree of assurance is small indeed.99
FREDERICK HERZBERG

Frederick Herzberg   An important contribution to the understanding of human needs and employees' reactions to need satisfiers has been made by Frederick Herzberg.[22] Herzberg and his colleagues interviewed employees, asking them to describe specific incidents in their work that made them feel happy or satisfied and other incidents that made them feel unhappy or dissatisfied. He then analyzed the incidents in each category to determine the factors that seemed to cause the feelings of satisfaction or dissatisfaction. Herzberg reported that satisfaction and dissatisfaction were caused not by different degrees or levels of the same factors (such as high versus low pay), but by completely different types of factors. The factors associated with sat-

FIGURE 3.5   *Herzberg's hygiene factors and motivators*

Hygiene factors (external, extrinsic dissatisfiers)	Motivators (internal, intrinsic satisfiers)
Company policy and administration	Achievement
Methods of supervision	Recognition of achievement
Interpersonal relations with peers, superiors, and subordinates	Responsibility
Working conditions	Advancement
Compensation	Interesting work
Job security	Personal growth
Symbols of status	
Personal problems	

isfying experiences he called **motivators,** and those associated with dissatisfying experiences he called **hygiene factors** (see Figure 3.5).

The motivators relate directly to the content of the individual's job, while the hygiene factors relate to the environment in which the employee works. Herzberg contends that organizations cannot create a motivating situation by manipulating the hygiene factors alone. The most the organization can do with hygiene factors is to provide a "clean" environment, thereby minimizing the causes for dissatisfaction.

It is important to understand that motivation, as Herzberg defines it, results not simply in a minimally acceptable level of performance, which often is sufficient, but rather in increased levels of performance. In other words, according to Herzberg, the only employee who is motivated is one who performs better than he or she used to perform. Only by redesigning jobs to enhance the motivator factors, Herzberg believes, can organizations create a motivating situation. This theory has led to the concept of job enrichment, which is discussed in Chapter 12. Thousands of organizations adopted Herzberg's philosophy and the job environment approach. The best-known instance is found at Texas Instruments, which "enriched" about 30 percent of its jobs.

Herzberg's research methods and his interpretation of the data have been the subjects of considerable academic criticism. The interview technique, for example, can lead some people being interviewed to spin elaborate tales. More important is the fact that Herzberg's original hypotheses were based on samples of accountants and engineers. People in these occupations are less likely to be motivated by Herzberg's "hygiene" factors than people in other occupations because the needs met by such factors have already been satisfied. Most telling, however, is the fact that Herzberg virtually ignored respondents who reported that they were satisfied or dissatisfied in a manner contrary to the majority. Thus, while achievement is the "motivator" most often reported, it is also the fourth most frequently reported "hygiene factor." But this fact is not stressed in Herzberg's conceptual representations. Finally, Herzberg's theory disagrees with substantial evidence that money is indeed a motivator.[23] Many other theorists suggest that Herzberg's theory takes on more meaning

> *But the carrot-and-stick theory does not work at all once man has reached an adequate subsistence level and is motivated primarily by higher needs.*
> DOUGLAS MURRAY MCGREGOR

when organizational level is considered. Thus Herzberg's motivators play a more prominent role at higher organizational levels than they do at lower levels of the organization. Conversely, Herzberg's hygiene factors "motivate" more at the bottom of the management hierarchy than they do at the top of the hierarchy.

These comments are offered not in criticism of Herzberg, who has made a valuable contribution to the study of motivation, but rather to alert you to the inadequacies of this theory, which has been embraced by many practitioners, partly because of its simplicity, partly because of the persuasiveness of the argument, and partly because of managers' own experiences. While many employees are motivated by the "motivators," many are dissatisfied by these same factors and hence "dismotivated." For example, American Telephone & Telegraph, which widely adopted a program of motivation through the "motivators," discovered that many workers shun responsibility and decision making and perform more poorly when their jobs are "enriched" with these ingredients.[24] At least part of this situation can be explained by the analysis of personality, which suggests that people whose primary goal is security rather than responsibility and independence will not function well under a job enrichment program.

Some people view Herzberg's work as a unique, general, and complete theory of motivation. My own view is that Herzberg has contributed to the growing understanding of the complex process of motivation, but that his is not a complete theory of motivation. If we compare the motivation and hygiene factors identified by Herzberg with the five levels of Maslow's hierarchy of needs, it is apparent that the hygiene factors correspond to the lower level of the hierarchy and the motivators correspond to the two upper levels (see Figure 3.6). If we are willing to accept the basic validity of both theories, we can conclude that Herzberg's research indicates that the need levels that have been reached by many working people of the middle class (or above) in a developed, stable society are not so motivating as they once were. In other words, many people in that class have attained a standard of living, sense of security, and degree of social comfort that allows them to focus their attention on their esteem and self-actualization needs. This is not true, however, of most people in most societies, or even of most people in an industrialized society. For example, the fact that many older workers are concerned primarily with existence needs while many younger workers are more concerned with growth needs is based on the differences in their experiences. Cultural differences can also be identified. Most important, the relevance of these classifications is strongly associated with economic well-being and occupation. People who are suffering economically have little interest in self-actualization and job enrichment. Most people in the world, in fact, probably are not predominantly motivated by high-level need satisfiers. Thus lower-level need satisfiers are still viable alternatives. Certainly lower-level needs must be satisfied first, or is that not always true? Research and experience suggest that some people may have their higher-level needs satisfied while their lower-level needs are still unsatisfied. Nurses, schoolteachers, counselors often fall into this situation. What, then, motivates these people? In the long term can they "afford" to stay in their self-actualizing jobs?

If we review our discussion of need satisfaction so far, it is easy to see the dilemma faced by managers in formal organizations. Herzberg's very popular theory indicates that many employees in our society are seeking to satisfy esteem and self-actualization needs. The appropriate rewards for such needs are often intangible and difficult for formal organizations to provide, but individual managers can do much in this regard. To the extent that other entities can provide the appropriate rewards, however, the individual may become more committed to the objectives of those entities and less committed to the objectives of the formal organization. This makes the effort to induce motivation to achieve organizational objectives just that much more complicated and difficult.

Several researchers are currently indicating that it is the unsatisfied need, regardless of its place in the hierarchy, that motivates. Maslow noted that upward movement in the hierarchy takes place over a person's lifetime. Thus in his scheme, self-actualization occurs very late, if at all, in the lives of most people. We should note also that people's needs change, often quite rapidly.

It appears that the wise manager and organization will use need satisfiers of all types. Yet many constraints, such as job design, unions, available resources, and personalities, often keep them from doing so. Most managers and organizations, however, have at their disposal some satisfiers that will work most of the time. These are the need satisfiers on which we must focus.

FIGURE 3.6 *Maslow's need hierarchy and Herzberg's motivation-maintenance model*

Maslow's need hierarchy	Herzberg's motivation-maintenance model
Self-realization and fulfillment— self-actualization	Work itself Achievement Possibility of growth Responsibility
Esteem and status	Advancement Recognition Status
Social activity	Interpersonal relations Superior Subordinates Peers Supervision (technical)
Safety and security	Company policy and administration Job security
Physiological needs	Working conditions Salary Personal life

Need Satisfaction: A Complex Process   The individual has many changing needs, some more dominant than others. The manager and the organization have many need satisfiers that they can offer. The classical and human relations approaches and Herzberg's theory are oversimplifications of a complex process. Because of the cost and difficulty of recognizing and meeting every individual employee's ever-changing needs, most organizations offer a general package of pay and benefits in the hope of satisfying their employees' lower-level needs. They are reacting to the general classification of needs, not to the individual's specific needs. Some organizations provide appropriate satisfaction of relatedness needs by managing recognition (discussed in Chapter 6); by working to maintain good relations with various groups (discussed at length in Chapters 7, 8, 9, and 10); and by developing managers who seek to meet the needs of their employees. Too few organizations have programs designed to meet employees' growth needs. The cost of such programs is generally prohibitive, and for many jobs the task is virtually impossible. You will find, therefore, that your life in some organizations, in some jobs, will be more rich and meaningful than in others. Fortunately, increasing numbers of organizations are becoming concerned with the satisfaction of higher-level needs.

> *In contemporary society, business is the dominant institution. It is industry that has been defining the basic characteristics of the human.*
>
> FREDERICK HERZBERG

TIPS FOR SUCCESS

1. Analyze your needs periodically to see how they affect your behavior.
2. In key situations, analyze the needs of others periodically to see what makes them behave as they do. You can then use your analysis to adjust your behavior in the interest of more satisfactory relationships.
3. Recognize the various stages in the motivation/performance cycle in order to uncover your motivations and those of others.
4. In attempting to influence others, use the motivation/performance cycle as a basis for action.
5. If you are a manager, you can do any number of things to influence the individual who works for you. You can listen, give positive strokes, keep confidences, smile, be sincere, treat people fairly, make yourself available, be concerned about personal problems, develop subordinates, let people participate in decision making, look for ways to give raises and promotions, show friendship, and let others know about someone's positive performance.

SUMMARY

1. Motivation is an internal process directed at the goal of satisfying needs.
2. The individual motivation process takes place within the framework of multiple external influencers.
3. One of the most prominent external influencers is the organization, and in particular the work organization.
4. Organizations and managers seek to motivate employees to behave in ways that will help the organization achieve its objectives.
5. Employees of most organizations trade their motivated behavior for need satisfiers.
6. Motivation and performance appear to be interdependent in a cyclical process. Once the cycle is completed, external influencers must seek to influence the individual again in order to achieve their objectives.

7. There appears to be a hierarchy of needs, but strict rules for its application cannot be formulated, as the steps in the hierarchy vary with economic condition, culture, and other factors. Higher-level needs are thought to be activated only when lower-level needs have been satisfied.

8. In addition to the needs postulated in most hierarchy theories, other needs are commonly felt: needs for achievement, for power, for role enactment, to achieve objectives, for recognition, for truth and beauty, to contribute to society.

9. Once needs are identified, the individual searches for satisfiers, and the organization and its managers must offer appropriate need satisfiers in order to channel motivation.

DISCUSSION QUESTIONS

1. What is motivation? How does the individual motivation process work with you personally?
2. What are the major stages of the motivation/performance cycle?
3. What are the major hierarchy theories? What are their strengths and weaknesses, and what do they contribute to our understanding of the motivation process?
4. What role do objectives play in the motivation process?
5. Discuss the concept of achievement motivation, the three types of needs it identifies, how one comes to have a high need for achievement, and the characteristics of a person who has a high need for achievement. Discuss the characteristics of the peak performer that Garfield has identified.
6. Discuss the impact of role motivation on the overall motivation process.

7. What influence does personality have on motivation?
8. What influence might a person's environment have on the motivation process? What external factors influence your motivation? How?
9. Give an example from your own experience of an organization or manager who was not aware of individual needs, or unable to satisfy those needs, or unwilling to satisfy them. What effect did this failure have on motivation?
10. The classical, human relations, and Herzberg approaches are all incomplete. What elements would a more thorough model of need satisfiers include? Why?
11. Now think of a motivation situation and follow the motivation/performance model up to and including stage 3 in the situation of which you are thinking.

APPLYING HUMAN RELATIONS SKILLS

Walters, Aycock, and Hampton

CASE

The law firm of Walters, Aycock, and Hampton was a highly respected firm in the San Diego area. It employed more than fifty lawyers and had a large clerical staff. The key need in law firms today is to increase billing hours. Jud Casmier was promoted six months ago to a junior partnership in the firm. His immediate superior, Ben Murphy, was one of the three full partners in the firm. Ben had become concerned with Jud's recent slowdown. It seemed that since Jud had been made junior partner, his productivity had dropped, and with it his billable hours. The firm had a profit-sharing plan, and Jud was now a member of that plan, so Ben felt that Jud should have been motivated even more now than he had been previously. Ben wondered what to do.

1. What might Ben be overlooking?
2. If you were Ben Murphy, how could you employ the motivation/performance cycle model to solve this problem?
3. What would you do to solve this problem?

EXERCISE

What Do People Value at Work?

INSTRUCTIONS: Please *rank-order* the seven items below in terms of their importance to *you* as reasons to continue working. Indicate the most important reason by putting the number 1 by that item in column *A* ("Myself"). Put a 2 by the second most important, and so on until you have put a 7 by the least important (no ties, please). When you have finished ranking the items for yourself, rank them in column *B* as you think most *men* would rank them. (Think in terms of the average person rather than of individuals holding particular jobs.) Finally, rank-order the items as you think most *women* would rank them in column *C*.

	A *Myself*	B *Men*	C *Women*
1. Work keeps me from being bored.	‐‐‐	‐‐‐	‐‐‐
2. I enjoy what I do on my job.	‐‐‐	‐‐‐	‐‐‐
3. I would feel guilty if I did not contribute to society.	‐‐‐	‐‐‐	‐‐‐
4. My work is important and valuable to others.	‐‐‐	‐‐‐	‐‐‐
5. I would continue out of habit.	‐‐‐	‐‐‐	‐‐‐
6. I enjoy the company of my co-workers.	‐‐‐	‐‐‐	‐‐‐
7. I derive a major part of my identity from my job.	‐‐‐	‐‐‐	‐‐‐

SOURCE: Reprinted with permission from *Psychology Today Magazine*, copyright © 1978 (APA).

When you have completed this exercise, your instructor will tell you how 2,300 readers of *Psychology Today* responded to the questionnaire.

1. What differences do you find between your values, your estimates of those of others, and those of *Psychology Today*'s readers?
2. Can you account for those differences on the basis of various motivation theories discussed in this chapter?
3. Discuss how perception enters into those differences.

REFERENCES

1. John P. Campbell, Marvin D. Dunnette, Edward E. Lawler III, and Karl E. Weick, *Managerial Behavior, Performance, and Effectiveness* (New York: McGraw-Hill, 1970), p. 340.
2. Abraham H. Maslow, *Motivation and Personality*, 2d ed. (New York: Harper & Row, 1970).
3. Frederick Herzberg, *Work and the Nature of Man* (New York: World, 1971).
4. Victor Vroom, *Work and Motivation* (New York: Wiley, 1964).

5. Lyman W. Porter and Edward E. Lawler III, *Managerial Attitudes and Performance* (Homewood, Ill.: Richard D. Irwin, 1968).

6. Campbell et al., *Managerial Behavior, Performance, and Effectiveness.*

7. John B. Miner and H. Peter Dachler, "Personnel Attitudes and Motivation," *Annual Review of Psychology* 24 (1973): 379–401.

8. Robert A. Sutermeister, "Employee Performance and Employee Satisfaction: Which Comes First?" *California Management Review* 13, no. 4 (1971): 43–47.

9. Abraham K. Korman, "Toward an Hypothesis of Work Behavior," *Journal of Applied Psychology* 54, no. 1 (1970): 31–41.

10. See Lloyd Byars and Leslie Rue, *Management: Concepts and Applications* (Homewood, Ill.: Richard D. Irwin, 1979), p. 221.

11. Terrence R. Mitchell, *Motivation and Performance* (Chicago: Science Research Associates, 1984).

12. B. F. Skinner, *Science and Human Behavior* (New York: Free Press, 1953).

13. Maslow, *Motivation and Personality;* Douglas A. McGregor, *The Human Side of Enterprise* (New York: McGraw-Hill, 1960). Maslow's hierarchy was the first of the simple solutions to motivation embraced by many researchers and practitioners. Unfortunately, tests revealed that motivation was much more complex than this model. Maslow himself cautioned against perceiving it as universally appropriate, but others failed to heed his warning.

14. Mahmoud A. Wahba and Lawrence G. Bridwell, "Maslow Reconsidered: A Review of the Research on the Need Hierarchy Theory," *Organizational Behavior and Human Performance* 15 (1976): 212–40.

15. C. P. Alderfer, *Existence, Relatedness, and Growth* (New York: Free Press, 1972).

16. David C. McClelland, *The Achieving Society* (Princeton, N.J.: Van Nostrand, 1961); J. W. Atkinson, *An Introduction to Motivation* (New York: American Book, 1964).

17. David C. McClelland, "Power Is the Great Motivator," *Harvard Business Review*, March–April 1976, pp. 100–110.

18. John B. Miner, *Studies in Management Education* (Atlanta: Organizational Measurement Systems Press, 1975).

19. Muriel James and Dorothy Jongeward, *Born to Win* (Reading, Mass.: Addison-Wesley, 1977).

20. Harold Geneen (with Alvin Moscow), *Managing* (New York: Doubleday, 1984).

21. I have been unable to locate the source of this well-known quotation.

22. Herzberg, *Work and the Nature of Man.*

23. Robert J. House and Lawrence A. Wigdor, "Herzberg's Dual-Factor Theory of Job Satisfaction and Motivation: A Review of the Evidence and a Criticism," *Personnel Psychology* 20 (1967): 369–89.

24. Conversation with the director of training for one of the firms in the Bell System, who wishes to remain anonymous.

4 MOTIVATION AND PERFORMANCE: A COMPLEX CYCLE

KEY TERMS AND CONCEPTS

expectancy/instrumentality
    theories
equity theory
role prescription job design
performance
law of effect
dissatisfaction with the job
satisfaction through the job
    itself
self-image and motivation
theories of self-image (self-
    concept)
self-image and performance
    attribution
money as a motivator

LEARNING OBJECTIVES

When you have completed this chapter, you should be able to:

1. Identify and describe the series of events that follows the offering of need satisfiers in the motivation process, and the major themes of motivation/influence involved.
2. Recognize whether people in the motivation cycle are contemplating the rationality of their actions or not.
3. Explain the various actions necessary for performance to occur.
4. Discuss why rewards must follow performance if performance is to continue.
5. Describe the impact of motivation efforts on self-image and of self-image on motivation efforts.
6. Explain the impact of attribution on motivation.
7. Indicate why and how money is a motivator.
8. Improve your motivation and that of others.

THE JAPANESE HAVE THEIR PROBLEMS TOO

The highly touted Japanese management system has many inherent weaknesses. To function well, for example, it must run at optimum conditions at all times. It is therefore highly vulnerable to such external factors as the availability of petroleum and strikes (unknown in Japan until recently but occurring with increasing frequency). It depends heavily on the Japanese government's ability to pave the way for exports and to restrict imports. As other countries grow weary of trade deficits, this situation could change dramatically. The system is built on seniority, which will soon leave Japanese businesses and the national economy with an overabundance of social security recipients as the population ages. But the factor that is most likely to crack the Japanese economic armor is the decline of the Japanese work ethic.

Individual motivation of Japanese employees is extremely complex. It depends heavily on peer pressure to perform for the organization and for the country. It also relies on group participative decision making, which reinforces peer pressure. A major focal point is self-discipline. Workers are expected to be prepared for the job and to perform beyond the call of duty. The seniority feature in combination with lifetime employment (for men) leads workers to think strategically and usually to attempt to help the company in the long run. And finally, as success for the company was equated with success for the country during the years when Japan was rebuilding its economy after the devastation of World War II, hard work was seen as a patriotic duty that would lead to individual benefits as well. But now that success has been achieved, needs are beginning to change.

Changes in needs have resulted in a change in workers' willingness to adhere to the work ethic. The old do-or-die for company and country no longer holds everyone spellbound. Both blue-collar and white-collar workers are demonstrating this change in attitude, and the change is especially prevalent among the young male college graduates who will someday run the businesses of Japan. Many have begun to do only what they are told and not one iota more. Their attitude is in sharp contrast to that of older workers, who tend to come early and stay late. The enthusiasm of the young for after-work socializing with the

(Continued on page 76)

work group, including the reknowned quality circle, is significantly less than that of workers ten years earlier. The Japanese are becoming more like Americans. They want to leave the job and go home or to an enjoyable leisure activity. Many leave early on Fridays to go skiing for the weekend or to play golf—something unheard of a few years ago. Worse, young workers are quitting the larger companies, complaining that the work is too hard. And many of the brightest minds are seeking self-employment as entrepreneurs or jobs with smaller firms, thus reducing the stockpile of college graduates that the major Japanese firms have monopolized for years. These trends undermine the tradition of many hours of free overtime on which Japanese firms once depended to raise their productivity levels. At the same time, large firms are abandoning the traditional hierarchical, patriarchical structure in several areas, especially research and development, as the industrial base shifts from imitation of products developed elsewhere to innovation in product development. They have found that the old style of management does not bring the results it once did. Finally, Japanese workers are demanding more time off, and the six-day workweek is in the process of abandonment: 93 percent of Japanese firms now give workers at least some Saturdays off. Many Japanese attribute at least part of the decline in the work ethic to the universities, which have grown quite large, quite impersonal, and quite undisciplined.

These trends foretell a probable slowing of the Japanese economy, though not a collapse. Now that Japan has become an industrial giant, it appears that many Japanese intend to reap the rewards of their efforts rather than continue to climb the mountain.

SOURCES: "A Spark of Militancy in the Land of Loyalty," *Business Week*, September 5, 1983, pp. 96, 98; Steve Lohr, "The Japanese Challenge," *New York Times Magazine*, July 8, 1984, p. 18; Lee Smith, "Cracks in the Japanese Work Ethic," *Fortune*, May 14, 1984, pp. 162–68.

"The results of a 20-year study are in. The answer to the question 'What really motivates people?' is: Go ask your people."
VINCENT S. FLOWERS
AND CHARLES L.
HUGHES

What is happening in Japan? Why doesn't the old system function as well as it once did? Why are the traditional ways of motivating workers no longer producing the results they used to?

As Chapter 3 indicated, the determination of needs and the offering of need satisfiers in an effort to activate an individual's motivation mechanism is a much more complex process than it may at first appear to be. Japan is suffering from a common problem today: the rewards on which the organization has traditionally relied to activate employees' motivation simply are not of sufficient value to the employees to motivate them. In the United States and Canada, for example, money was once the prime motivator, but to many people in the work force today, the decline in its value has caused its effectiveness as a motivator to decline as well. Still, money will continue to motivate many people, and their numbers will increase under certain economic conditions. The shift in the power of money to motivate is only one of many factors that serve to moderate the motivation cycle. It is now becoming painfully obvious to employers that it is no longer enough to offer the standard rewards and need satisfiers that seemed to serve so well in the past. Beyond the changing needs of the individual, numerous factors cause such simplistic approaches to lose their effectiveness. This chapter examines the major factors that have been identified as in some way modifying the need-based motivation process, and reveals that the process was never quite so simple as it was once thought to be. As in Chapter 3, the stages in the motivation/performance cycle, outlined in Figure 3.2, form the basis for discussion.

THE MOTIVATION/PERFORMANCE CYCLE (MPC)

At stage 4 of the motivation/performance cycle the individual is searching for alternative ways of satisfying his or her needs, both inside and outside the organization. The search process need not involve a particularly active effort. While some people want to have a choice of alternatives, many others take the first thing that presents itself. In most work situations, people tend to take what they can get. They accept the pay they are offered, for example, with no thought of asking for more. Many people accept thankless and unsatisfying jobs, never thinking to seek out recognition or ask for more satisfying work. Once need satisfiers are offered, the rational person evaluates them before coming to a decision. But people do not always behave rationally: They may not ponder the situation at all, instead permitting learned or emotional responses to guide their behavior.

STAGE 4: THE SEARCH FOR AND EVALUATION OF ALTERNATIVES

The complexity of this process is compounded by the fact that people who search for alternatives often have several means to satisfy a particular need in addition to the satisfiers offered by the organization and its managers. And they may have multiple needs, some of which will conflict with the results the organization is seeking. The manager may expect employees to work overtime, for example, when they prefer to spend that time with their families. This preference responds to a totally different need, and apparently one of higher priority at that moment than the needs that could be satisfied by overtime pay.

At this point people who are acting rationally typically ask themselves a series of questions about the need satisfiers they are offered. These questions are derived from the concepts embodied in the **expectancy/instrumentality theories** of motivation.[1] An assumption of the instrumentality theory (and also of the **equity theory,** on which this and most other motivation models are based) is that we operate as rational human beings; that is, people examine the issues and base their decisions on the results of their examination. This rational approach is taken probably less than half of the time. The majority are letting learned or emotional responses determine what will motivate them and what will not. They don't think about what they are doing. They don't search for alternatives, or if they search, they don't evaluate those they find. They act without contemplating the consequences of their actions.

Some of this behavior will be congruent with efforts to achieve the organization's objectives. Some will not. Actions dictated by emotions often are not. Managers who wish to be successful motivators must learn to discern whether or not subordinates will ponder their future actions or will simply react in accordance with past experiences or their emotions. Such learning is acquired through both experience and formal educational development.

Evaluation of Possible Consequences   Simplified and pragmatic interpretation of the major principles of the expectancy/instrumentality approaches are contained in stages 4 and 8 of Figure 3.2. These principles are enumerated in the following sections. Those aspects of these theories related to stage 4 are described as a series of questions that one asks oneself in response to a particular motivation situation. The first three questions are based on expectancy theory; the fourth is based on equity theory.

1. Is the reward contingent on my doing the job (performance), and if it is, can I do the job (perform)?

As long as we feel that a reward is contingent on performance, we will probably not attempt to do the work unless we think we can do it well. If the reward does not seem to be contingent on performance, then we may go ahead and try to do the job, since effort alone seems to be enough to bring us the offered reward.

2. If I do the job, will I get the reward?

Having satisfied ourselves that the reward is contingent on our performance and that we can do the job, we are operating rationally if we then assess the probability that we will receive the reward if we do perform successfully. If we think we have a good chance of getting the reward, we may go ahead and try, but if the probability of receiving the reward seems small, we are unlikely to expend any effort. Organizations, for example, commonly offer bonuses and prizes to salespeople during major sales campaigns. If the sales force consists of a thousand people and only one prize is offered, most salespeople are much less likely to strive to make enough sales to win the prize than they would be if only twenty people were competing for it. Even worse, if employees see no reward, they are not likely to be motivated at all, as the Human Relations Happening "Why Invent?" suggests. The key? When they ask "What's in it for me?" the answer should not be "Nothing."

3. If I get the reward, what's it worth to me?

To the extent that we consider the reward worthwhile, in terms of our current and future needs, we will be motivated to expend our effort. But if the reward is not worth the mental or physical effort we must expend to get it, we will not be motivated to expend our effort. Consider a salesman in our hypothetical sales contest. If the prize is a trip to Hawaii, he may be ecstatic at the thought of winning it if he has never been to Hawaii, but if he has already won the same prize last year and the year before, then the offered reward will be less motivating. Frankly, he is tired of pineapple juice and sunshine. But he might jump at a chance to go snow skiing.

As you discovered in Chapter 3, the relative value of money is reduced as financial needs are satisfied. Further, additional money shrinks substantially in real value as we move into the higher income tax bracket and as our Social

Security tax rises with our income. Thus time for leisure becomes a prime consideration when we weigh the value of offered need satisfiers. Many business and public nonprofit organizations are experiencing severe shortages of applicants for managerial positions. More and more prospective managers are opting for additional leisure time in place of the headaches and ulcers often associated with managing. Obviously, in these situations, the perceived after-tax rewards are insufficient to motivate some employees. The opening Human Relations Happening on Japan further shows what happens when workers ask such questions and get negative answers. A major recession, however, could quickly change an employee's perception of the value of money, as did the 1986 reduction of federal income tax rates.

Two subtle but extremely significant aspects of this process deserve comment.

First, the answers to all three of these questions depend on our perceptions. It is only our perception of our own situation that is relevant to the determination of our level of motivation. No one else's perception of this situation is pertinent to what you or I will do. This notion helps to explain why so many managers have difficulty understanding and remedying an apparent lack of motivation in their subordinates. The manager simply does not perceive the subordinate's situation in the same way that the subordinate does.

> *"What's in it for me?"*
> EVERYBODY

HUMAN RELATIONS HAPPENING

WHY INVENT?

The average American company does not reward its employees for their inventions; the most they can expect is continued remuneration for their continuing jobs. Most companies require employees to sign a waiver of their rights to any inventions they may make during their tenure with the company. A few companies do provide some financial rewards, but seldom more than a few hundred dollars. Neal Orkin suggests that companies and individuals would both benefit if the company paid for inventions. He cites reductions in the growth rate of gross national product and an approximate 50 percent decrease in the number of patents issued in proportion to the population between 1970 and 1980 as indicators of a serious problem in the U.S. economy: too few new ideas. He feels that the solution lies in legislation. Western European countries and Japan have laws governing payments to inventors by their companies. Such payments are typically required in Western Europe, their amounts determined by a mandatory negotiation process. Orkin cites the voluntary Japanese law as a good example of how such payments stimulate applications for patents. Statistics show a 300 percent increase in patent applications in Japan during the first ten years the law was in force. He also cites the high level of creativity in the video game industry, where inventors of games virtually always share in the profits from their games.

SOURCE: Neal Orkin, "Rewarding Employee Invention: Time for Change," *Harvard Business Review*, January–February 1984, pp. 56–57.

The second subtle factor is the interrelationship of all three questions. Only if we answer yes to all three are we going to be motivated to expend effort. Thus if we think the answer to any of the three questions is "no" or "probably not" or "not much," we are not likely to be motivated. Your answers to the "Test Yourself" questions should give you insight into this process of assessing the reward situation.

4. Will the rewards be equitably distributed?

One of the major causes of the absence of motivation is the employee's perception of the inequity of the offered rewards. Research on the equity theory has confirmed the idea that employees compare their inputs and outcomes with those of other employees, especially with those of people who perform the same job[2] (see Figure 4.1). In the military, for example, a commissioned officer, such as a captain, and a noncommissioned officer, perhaps a technical sergeant, occasionally perform essentially the same duties, especially in such staff departments as personnel, accounting, and supply. Yet their pay and associated benefits, both financial and social, are quite different. In such cases the captain clearly receives greater rewards and more need satisfiers than the sergeant. Even appeals to professionalism cannot eliminate the inevitable demotivating effect of such inequity. The result is that the sergeant will tend to reduce his inputs in order to make his input/outcome (I/O) ratio more nearly equal to the captain's.

In business the equity moderator more commonly is a matter of seniority. A worker with one year of seniority, for example, may receive $6.50 an hour while a worker with twenty years' seniority receives $8.50 an hour for the same work, simply because the older employee has been with the firm longer. Again, the employee who receives less tends to lower his or her inputs in order to make the I/O ratios more nearly equal. Some employers, such as

---

TEST YOURSELF

THE EVALUATION PROCESS

Think of a course that you are taking now. Then think of the actions that you must take to earn a good grade in that course. Now answer the questions below.

1. Can you do the work?
2. What's the reward?
3. If you do the work, will you get the reward?
4. What's the reward worth to you?

5. Are you therefore motivated to take the necessary action?

Upon what information, experiences, and so on did you base your decision? Past courses with the same professor? current classroom events? current grade experience? the professor's reputation?

Now do you have a better understanding of stage 4 of the comprehensive motivation/performance cycle model?

FIGURE 4.1   *The equity theory*

Worker 1 compares		
his/her inputs	to	other workers' inputs
his/her outcomes		other workers' outcomes

General Motors, have historically attempted to eliminate the equity problem by paying all employees equally within many job classifications. Seniority is then used to determine the order of layoffs and recalls, but not compensation. Even GM, however, has changed its approach in order to become more competitive. Like many other employers, it now uses a two-tier pay system in some plants. In this system newly hired employees receive substantially less pay for certain work than do more senior employees. GM has been successful in the two-tier approach where others, such as Hughes Aircraft, LTV, and American Airlines, have failed. Most firms find reduced morale and productivity under the two-tier system. Many are abandoning it. GM's success is apparently due to its work with the union to convince employees that their jobs could not exist if two-tier pay were eliminated.[3]

Inputs may be both physical (such as labor) and psychological (such as perceived effort). Outcomes may also be either physical (such as money) or psychological (such as the perceived importance of the job). Employees may vary the mixture of inputs and outcomes in many ways in their efforts to make the I/O ratios more nearly equal, but by far the most common method is to reduce inputs.[4] One of the major issues in pay equity today is that of "comparable worth." The evidence indicates that women are paid significantly less than men in comparable jobs. Many organizations, especially in the public sector—the state of Minnesota, for example—have voluntarily adopted comparable worth programs in an attempt to equalize pay for comparable jobs. The state of Washington has been sued for failure to offer comparable pay for jobs of comparable worth.[5] Evidence suggests that where pay equity has not been established, knowledgeable women will perform below par. What do you think will happen?

Some people feel overcompensated for their inputs. This situation is much rarer than that of perceived inadequacy of outcomes. In this rare situation, the individual may increase inputs or decline to accept so much outcome in order to achieve equity.

Have you ever suffered any inequities? What did you do to make your I/O ratio more nearly equal to those with whom you compared yourself? Have you even felt that your ratio was too high in comparison with those of other people? What did you do then?

Aspects of the Evaluation Process   Several aspects of this questioning process deserve mention. First, we will base our estimates of our personal competence to do the job, the contingency of rewards on performance, the probability of receiving rewards, and the value and equity of rewards on our own experiences. We constantly (though perhaps not consciously) monitor the relations between our efforts and the rewards they bring us. Students, for

"You've got to want to do this to be here."
CHIEF PETTY OFFICER JAMES SCALY, U.S. NAVY, on the stressful conditions of submarine duty

example, are often alarmed to learn that a lot of effort did not lead to the grade (reward) they had anticipated. This information is processed and stored for future reference—when they study for future tests, for example, or select future courses and instructors. Also, as we receive rewards and need satisfiers over a period of time, the nature or strength of our needs changes. The process is dynamic and virtually every variable must be continuously adjusted to accommodate our recent experience. But often an organization cannot adjust, at least not so rapidly as it would like. Managers can and should observe these changes in estimates and in needs and act accordingly whenever they can. GM's adoption of the two-tier wage system, noted earlier, is a good example of adjustment to changing conditions.

In the short run, most organizations make no attempt to link rewards directly to performance within the most obvious rewards/compensation system. People who work for an hourly wage or who are on a straight salary may perceive that they are being compensated for their time rather than for their performance. Even in the long run, raises in pay are often more clearly related to seniority (a reward at least partly for loyalty) than to performance. Bonuses and profit-sharing plans are often based on overall company performance, so that most individuals feel that their individual job performance has a negligible impact on the rewards they receive. Not that there are no effective incentive payment plans in existence. The Lincoln Electric Company, profiled in Chapter 3, and others such as Nucor Steel demonstrate that pay-for-performance plans can be extremely effective. Their use is limited, however, by the difficulties of administering them, the opposition of labor unions, and other opposing forces. Even some other types of formal rewards, such as promotions, are sometimes perceived to be more closely related to seniority, nepotism, favoritism, or discrimination than to individual performance.

Since organizations have difficulty in balancing effort, performance, and rewards, they sometimes compress the system by relating rewards to effort. In other words, the reward goes to the individual who makes the greatest effort, without regard for performance. As appealing as this approach may be, it creates a serious danger. Individuals, and eventually the entire organization, can become activity-oriented.[6] People soon realize that it is more important to look busy than to accomplish anything. They begin to create unnecessary work for themselves and for others. Though such an environment can be quite secure for some individuals, it will become extremely frustrating for the high achiever. Furthermore, the organization and its financial contributors suffer greatly. Many government employees spend a significant amount of time and a substantial amount of money engaging in activities that accomplish little that taxpayers want accomplished. Unfortunately, this version of the process is often aggravated by the practice of rewarding people for their time, without regard for either their efforts or their performance. When former president Jimmy Carter attempted to install a pay-for-performance program for top federal executives, they rose up in arms. The bureaucrats won. Government is not the only guilty organization. Far too often businesses fall victim to such activity (or nonactivity) traps.

Look around at the people with whom you work (or think back to those

"The specific outcomes attained by a person are dependent not only on the choices that he makes but also on events which are beyond his control."
VICTOR H. VROOM

with whom you have worked). Does everyone contribute to the achievement of the organization's objectives? Or do some people contribute little more than their time? What do you contribute?

In summary, depending on the perceived value of offered rewards and need satisfiers in conjunction with types of needs, the perceived probability that these rewards will be received, the perceived effort necessary to secure these rewards, the perceived relationship between rewards and performance, and the perceived equity of the offerings, the individual may be motivated—provided that the individual is contemplating all of this information and evaluating the consequences of his or her actions.

Failure to Consider the Consequences   If one is not consciously thinking when rewards are offered, if one is reacting without thinking through the consequences of one's actions, one will respond in accordance with learned patterns or with emotions. Familiar sayings that the individual accepts as true—"Hard work will be rewarded"; "Money is what life is all about"; "If a thing is worth doing at all, it's worth doing well"; "Finish what you start"; "Do just enough to get by"; "You're nothing but a lazy bum"—play important roles in some people's motivation. Others may react to offered need satisfiers (or their absence) emotionally. They are not thinking, nor are they behaving as they have been taught to behave. Rather they are letting their feelings determine their actions. Such people normally will not ask themselves all four of the questions enumerated above. They may in fact ask themselves none of those questions. Most people probably react without questioning what is happening more often than they contemplate the consequences of their actions.

This tendency has an obvious impact on motivation. In order to motivate people, the organization, and especially the manager, must learn to identify and anticipate the way people are likely to react to offered need satisfiers. People do shift from one state to another, so the problem does not have an easy solution. Most organizational influence systems were designed around someone's learned perception of how to activate individual motivation processes; for example, the belief that money motivates (and it does motivate most people). Any influence system that addresses only one viewpoint, only one set of learned reactions or emotions, is doomed to failure, because not all people operate from the same set of perceptions, and each individual's set of perceptions shifts over time. If organizations and managers are to employ their knowledge of human relations successfully, they must learn to recognize the most common individual reactions to offered need satisfiers and take advantage of them. At the same time they must be prepared to cope with individual exceptions. The Human Relations Happening "The Hot 100" reveals that some firms understand the principle of multiple motivation in a group of people.

If all has gone well up to this point, the individual will be motivated to expend mental or physical effort and will do so. All does not need to have gone perfectly up to this point for most people to be motivated. If the rewards that are offered are generally sufficient to evoke affirmative responses to the four

STAGE 5: MOTIVATION AND ACTION

HUMAN RELATIONS HAPPENING

THE HOT 100

A few years ago, Diamond International, a manufacturer of paper egg cartons, faced serious problems: the recession, stiff competition, and lack of job security for its employees. David Boyle, personnel director at Diamond's plant in Palmer, Massachusetts, had to tackle the job of motivating the troubled employees. Today productivity is up 16.5 percent, quality-related errors are down 40 percent, time lost to industrial accidents is down 44 percent, and workers' grievances have declined by 72 percent.

Mr. Boyle created a simple incentive system that he called the 100 Club. Above-average performance is recognized by a point system. For example, 25 points are awarded to employees who show perfect attendance in a given year, and 20 points to workers who have no industrial accidents during the year. The points are totaled each year and a record is sent to each employee. Employees who accumulate 100 points receive a jacket with the company's logo and a patch signifying membership in the 100 Club. Workers can receive additional rewards by accumulating more points.

Diamond workers with coveted jackets.

Diamond International's management asserts that this motivational technique is designed to give recognition to the good employees rather than to the problem workers. The 100 Club incentive plan has generated goodwill and optimism among the workers. Surveys conducted before and after the plan was instituted showed a large increase in workers' perception of management's recognition of their contributions. The firm's labor relations problems have decreased; workers have even declined a wage hike because of their concern about industry competition.

Although money will always be a motivator of performance, Diamond International's creative plan demonstrates that other factors can also satisfy workers and serve as incentives.

SOURCE: "Hot 100," *Time*, July 4, 1983, p. 46.

questions or to fit in with the individual's learned behaviors or feelings (and perhaps a little of each), then the individual will be motivated to expend effort, at least some minimal amount of effort. Just how much effort is the critical question.

Moderator variables again enter into the cycle. At this point the moderators include (1) individual abilities and characteristics that can be developed into skills; (2) the individual's knowledge or ignorance of what is expected and the objectives of those expectations; (3) the training necessary to enable the employee to develop the necessary skills; and (4) the technology, job design, and tools required for the job.

If the individual lacks the skills, the knowledge of what is expected (role prescription and objectives), or the technology to perform the task, then regardless of effort, performance will be inadequate.

Skills and Training: Selection Is Motivation   The term *skill* means proficiency in the performance or execution of a task. Skill requires two things: first, the individual must have some basic abilities or characteristics with which to function; and second, the individual must have had the necessary training to develop those abilities or characteristics to the point of proficiency. The personnel function of the organization plays an extremely important role in ensuring that these two criteria are satisfied. The personnel function is assigned the task of selecting individuals with the proper skills or with the abilities or characteristics that can be developed into skills. The personnel function may provide the training to enable employees to obtain or maintain the required skills. Have you ever muddled your way through a situation in which you did not really know what you were doing? What were the performance results? Probably not very good. Unfortunately, far too many employees, including managers, know far too little about what they are doing. Progressive firms, such as Sentry Insurance, perceive that training and development is a career-long effort. Each of their development programs is tied to the increasing skill demands of a career progressing from supervisory to middle-management to executive positions.[7]

Objectives and Role Prescription   Think of a job you have had in which you knew what was expected of you. Now think of one in which you were uncertain as to what was expected of you. In which situation did you perform best? As the saying goes, if you don't know where you're going, any road will get you there. The unfortunate truth is that you usually don't get where you should have gotten. Surveys reveal that much of the time, managers and their subordinates disagree as to just what the subordinate's objectives are.[8] Is it any wonder, then, that the team accomplishes less than it could? This point will not be belabored here. Management by objectives, results, and rewards, a management system that ensures that subordinates and their managers agree on objectives, is discussed in Chapter 11. But honestly, if you don't know where you're going, how are you going to get where your manager and organization want you to get to? Objectives are the destination of the **role prescription,** those actions one should take to reach the organization's objectives. Objectives are the ends sought.

Technology, Job Design, and Tools   Technology, the applied science used in organizations, plays an important role in economic success and in virtually every performance area today. Technology often leads to a competitive advantage. Technology often leads to superior job design. Technology often leads

STAGE 6:
SKILLS, ROLE
PRESCRIPTION,
AND JOB
REQUIREMENTS

"As for the practical feasibility of goal setting as a means of improving employee performance, the research shows goal-setting programs to be effective over an extended period in a variety of organizations, at both managerial and nonmanagerial levels."

GARY P. LATHAM AND
GARY A. YUKL

to the development of the best tools. The Japanese apparently understand how to combine technology, job design, and tools far better than any of their international competitors.

If the sequence of tasks one is given is incorrect (the **job design,** which leads to the role prescription), if the anticipated results (objectives) could be accomplished more readily and more efficiently with another set of tasks, then performance will be deficient. Perhaps the most famous example of the latter situation comes from Texas Instruments (TI). In one of TI's job-enrichment programs, its employees reduced the assembly time on a particular piece of equipment from more than 100 hours to less than 40 hours by redesigning the task sequence and the nature of the tasks.[9] Virtually no new skills were necessary, only a redesign effort. This enrichment process was especially motivating because it allowed for participation, and, most important for the purposes of this discussion, the redesign program also caused effort and performance to have a more satisfactory relationship because the job was accomplished more efficiently, an important performance measurement.

A good friend of mine showed me a slogan taped to the wall over his desk not long ago. It read, "We have done so much for so long with so little that now they expect us to do the impossible with nothing!" The frustrations expressed in that statement are often shared by those who do not have the proper tools—equipment, budget, and everything else necessary to do the job. All else being equal, a writer who has the use of a word processor is simply going to be more productive than a writer who does not have such a machine available. A carpenter with an electric saw is going to cut more boards than one who has only a hand saw. A company with a computer should sell more products more cheaply than one without.

STAGE 7: PERFORMANCE

At last, performance. Yes, Virginia, there is performance at the end of the management rainbow. If all has gone relatively well up to this point, **performance,** the desired results, should be forthcoming.

Yet even when performance is obtained, problems often arise. First, if performance has not been defined in advance—that is, if objectives are lacking—how will you, your manager, and the organization know when performance has been achieved?

Second, for many types of jobs, performance is very difficult to measure objectively. This is especially true for indirect labor—a personnel staff person, for example. In large public service organizations, objectives are often ill defined or not defined at all. They should be, but in reality, this leaves the evaluator with a problem. Just how do you evaluate the performance of a college professor, for example? Is the performance measured by student evaluations, by the accumulation of knowledge in students' minds, by students' successes? Or just exactly how? Well, one thing is sure, what can be measured is the number of hours the professor spends in his or her office. Therefore, some professors who spend a significant amount of time in their offices, whether or not they accomplish anything there (or elsewhere), may be viewed by their dean as having a high level of performance (an activity approach to the measurement of performance).

66I'm usually motivated by somebody saying, 'You can't do that.'99
     F. Lee Bailey

In large and complex organizations, a multitude of factors other than effort impinge on an individual's performance. Several factors that affect performance are simply beyond the individual's control. These factors include the performance of others and the changing external environment—the economy, for example. Consider a salesperson for a manufacturer of office supplies, whose performance over time would seem to be directly related to his or her own efforts. Typically, however, the salesperson depends on other elements of the organization to produce and deliver on schedule the goods that he or she sells, to maintain an acceptable level of quality, and to provide any necessary customer service after delivery. To the extent that these other organizational elements fail to perform, the salesperson's own performance will probably suffer. If a supplier fails to deliver goods by the time the salesperson has promised delivery to a customer, the sale may well be lost. A general decline in the level of business activity in the particular industry or the region could also be very detrimental to the salesperson's performance, despite his or her effort or ability.

But if we assume that the individual has performed, and if we assume only some degree of efficiency in the application of the process to this point in the model, there next arises the question as to whether or not the individual will continue to be motivated, and if so, how.

If the rewards and need satisfiers offered are not forthcoming, future performance will seldom be forthcoming either. The history of human enterprise is replete with examples of organizations that failed to reward performance and thereafter failed to receive it again.

Once performance has occurred, the organization and manager normally issue need satisfiers. Woe unto those who don't! One firm promised its workers huge raises if they would just vote the union down. The employees kept their part of the bargain; the bosses did not keep theirs. The union won the next organizing campaign.

STAGE 8: PROVISION OF NEED SATISFIERS AND REWARDS

Most of the time, rewards will be distributed among the eligible employees. The employees then may or may not ask themselves versions of the questions they asked at stage 4: Was the reward contingent on performance? Was the reward worth the effort? Were the rewards equitably distributed? If the answers to all of these questions are sufficiently positive, the employees are likely to be motivated in the same manner again. Or if some of them react according to learned behaviors or emotions, they may or may not continue to be motivated in the same manner again. Sometimes personality and satisfaction or dissatisfaction with the process, with the job, with life in general may determine whether or not a person will continue to be motivated as he or she has been motivated in the past.

STAGE 9: REASSESSING THE SITUATION

The last stage of the model questions how the cycle will be continued or renewed. Depending on what has happened previously, the individual may or may not be motivated in the same way again. Four principal variables are

STAGE 10: CONTINUED MOTIVATION

understood to play important roles at this stage of the cycle: the law of effect, satisfaction or dissatisfaction with the process, attribution of causes for successes and failures, and the impact of the process on the individual's self-image.

The Law of Effect and Behavior Modification Principles   Edward L. Thorndike, an early researcher of the learning process, postulated the **law of effect,** which states that we tend to repeat behavior for which we have been rewarded and tend not to repeat behavior for which we are not rewarded or for which we have been punished.[10] The famous behavior modification principles of B. F. Skinner, which were based partly on Thorndike's efforts, reinforce this position.[11] People most definitely do tend to repeat behavior that has brought them a reward and to discontinue behavior that has resulted in no reward or in punishment. Thus, if the motivation/performance cycle has been followed appropriately up to this point, the employee should tend to continue to perform for the organization. But again the process may be disrupted. Three key factors—satisfaction and dissatisfaction with the process; personality variables, especially self-image factors; and attribution tendencies—often cause the law of effect to become the law of ineffect.

Satisfaction/Dissatisfaction with the Process   Satisfaction has been the focus of more speculation and disagreement in recent years than any other single topic related to motivation and performance. There is little doubt that satisfaction, motivation, and performance are related, but which causes which is not yet clear. The research evidence suggests that satisfaction is more often the *result* of performance achieved as a consequence of motivation than it is the *cause* of the motivation that leads to performance.[12] The evidence also suggests, however, that individuals who are not satisfied, who experience overall **dissatisfaction with the job,** will not be motivated, at least not enough to achieve more than a barely acceptable level of effort and performance. Furthermore, one's general satisfaction with life is reflected in one's satisfaction with a job. The manager's efforts to provide job satisfaction in hopes of influencing an employee who is dissatisfied with life will be wasted. This is one reason that counseling (to help employees with their personal problems) and assertiveness (in stating the manager's and organization's positions) are critical skills.

Job satisfaction has been more narrowly defined in recent years than it was in the past. Many people believe that the only way to trigger motivation is to abide by Herzberg's contentions regarding intrinsic job satisfiers (see Chapter 3). Thus **satisfaction through the job itself**—achievement, rewarding work, advancement, recognition, increased decision making (together known as job enrichment)—is proposed as the primary means of motivation. The research evidence indicates that this type of motivation is limited in its appeal, but is effective with many people.

What does all this mean to the average manager? to the organization trying to influence its employees? to the average individual trying to influence someone else? to you? First, dissatisfaction needs to be kept to a minimum. On this point, research is in agreement with Herzberg, but there is disagreement as to the factors that lead to dissatisfaction. As we saw in Chapter 3, virtually

"By God, I'm so pleased with the way you handled that lousy, thankless job I gave you, Frawley, that I'm going to give you another one."

all need satisfiers will cause dissatisfaction in some people. This is another reason the manager must be alert to individual needs and situations. Most people can achieve basic levels of motivation if the dissatisfiers are eliminated. Thus the average worker will usually do an average job if you eliminate the dissatisfiers.

Much of what was traditionally thought to provide satisfaction (before Herzberg) still does for many people. Traditional reward systems are still effective in influencing many people.[13] Higher motivation levels can be reached by traditional motivation systems—*if* rewards are related to performance. Salespersons still sell more to make more money when commissions are related to sales, for example. Some rewards, however, can be intrinsic.

Thus, for some people, Herzberg's "motivators" need to be included in the job itself if they are to be motivated to reach their fullest potentials and to maintain their commitment to the organization. The people motivated by Herzberg's factors appear to be those whose lower-level needs have been satisfied.

When overall job satisfaction is not related to performance, performance is not likely to recur. This is a partial explanation of the fact that the "happy" employee is not necessarily a productive one. If satisfaction does not follow performance, as the result of either reward tied to performance or satisfaction in the job itself, then there is no reason to assume that performance will ever occur.

Apparently overall job satisfaction does not result in motivation unless either of two conditions are met: either positively perceived rewards must be related to performance or satisfaction must be designed into the job itself. Neither guarantees motivation; each only increases the probability that it will occur. Charles Greene's research has indicated that rewards for performance are more likely than job satisfaction to cause performance in the future.[14]

John Naisbitt and Patricia Aburdene suggest that in the future, most organizations will have to use different structural and motivational systems than those they currently employ. Among the causal factors they cite are the needs of employees in an information society and the values of baby boomers, who will make up most of the work force in the coming years (54 percent by 1990).[15] These systems will be more participative and will provide for more satisfaction. Many companies are already moving in that direction. For example, W. L. Gore and Associates, Inc. (the maker of Gore-Tex, a military and sport material that keeps out water but allows the body to breathe), has no bosses, no organization chart, and two principal objectives: to make money and to have fun. It manages through "commitment, not authority" and through work teams. The system works well, even though the firm employs 4,000 people, and provides high levels of intensive satisfaction to its employees.[16]

Personality and Motivation   Authors and practitioners generally agree on the nature of the motivation performance process up to this stage of our model. The third part of stage 10 is an area that is relatively new. Substantive research to verify the influence of personality on motivation and performance is lacking. Much of what is included in this section is derived from the conceptual literature. It is difficult to test the relationship between **self-image and motivation** because of the difficulty of operationalizing the concept of self-image. I point this out not to cause you to doubt the propositions I am about to discuss, but rather to cause you to see them as tentative, ideas that are rational but still largely unsupported by research evidence.

The influence of personality on motivation and performance is immense, and in fact can enter into the process at any point in the model. Entire books have been devoted to the subject. The following three propositions summarize these perceived impacts:

1. If the motivation process has maintained the individual's self-image, he or she will probably be motivated by the same motivators again.
   a. Under such conditions, performance levels will be maintained.
2. If the motivation process has lowered the self-image of the individual, he or she is not likely to continue to be motivated by the same motivators.
   a. Under such conditions, performance will decrease.
3. If the motivation process has enhanced the individual's self-image, he or she may or may not be motivated by the same need satisfiers again.
   a. Performance may or may not continue at present levels.

b. If the employee's level of aspiration rises (self-image significantly improves), job enrichment and higher-level need satisfiers will be necessary to motivate this person again.

Principal Managerial Theories of Self-Image   Several **theories of self-image** (or **self-concept**) have been proposed. All focus on essentially the same elements. Transactional analysis, Richard DeCharms' "pawns" and "origins,"[17] Abraham Korman's competency theory,[18] and Maxwell Maltz's psycho-cybernetics[19] all focus on a primary stated or underlying contention that motivation, performance, perhaps all behavior, is a function of self-image.

Very few management studies have tested the validity of this contention in a practical job-related sense. Studies in the field of education have repeatedly shown that academic achievement and related surrogates are highly correlated with participants' self-image.[20] Only a limited number of studies have examined the relationship between self-image and productivity in actual work situations, but they, too, have largely supported this contention.[21]

Transactional Analysis   Transactional analysis (TA) has seven basic focal concepts, two of which are the life script and the life position. Both of these concepts portray a central belief that our control of our own destiny is a function of the way we feel about ourselves and others, and that these feelings, acquired at a very early age, dominate our actions throughout our lives. People can change their views about themselves and others, but their feelings about them normally remain essentially the same.

DeCharms' Pawns and Origins   Richard DeCharms depicts two major types of individuals: pawns, who feel controlled by external events, and origins, who feel that they can control their own destiny. The ability to control one's life is at the heart of this theory, as it is of the other theories reviewed here.

Korman's Competency Theory   Korman's competency theory proposes three types of persons with respect to feelings of competence: the chronically competent person, who feels competent in most situations; the task competent, who feels competent only in certain tasks; and the socially competent, who feels competent only with certain people—a particular work group, for example. Korman's theory can be extended to say that performance in a variety of tasks and social relationships is a function of the person's feeling of competence, an aspect of self-image.

> *Lord, grant that I may always desire more than I can accomplish.*
> MICHELANGELO

Psycho-Cybernetics   In his book *Psycho-Cybernetics* Maxwell Maltz proposes that if you think you can, you can. But if you think you can't, you never will because you just said so. Substantial observational and empirical research is offered throughout this book and numerous others to support this view. This and related theories propose that our motivation, productivity, and much else are significantly related to our self-image. This concept has intuitive appeal, and some limited research appears to support the basic idea.

Self-Image and Performance   Some very limited research, most of it based on observations and interviews, indicates that an individual whose self-image is lowered by a work process will suffer demotivation.[22] Much of the leadership research confirms this proposition without stating it directly. For example, highly authoritarian or degrading leadership actions are normally considered to be correlated with reduced levels of motivation and productivity. A substantial number of research studies (mostly in educational settings) indicate that a person with a low self-image will perform less well in a variety of tasks than a person whose self-image is higher. Transactional analysis lends a considerable amount of knowledge research on the relationship between **self-image and performance.** TA theory and research indicate that recognition (which can be given in many ways—pay raises, bonuses, vacations, time off, compliments, awards, etc.) is critical to the maintenance of performance.[23]

Carl Rogers has suggested that maintaining the self-image is almost as important as maintaining life itself, that the basic human drive for self-enhancement includes the elimination of "control by external forces."[24] Certainly this is true of some people. And many people will go to great lengths—will lie, for example—to maintain their self-image and the image that others have of them. Self-image is critical to most of us. That is why the traditional authoritarian motivation approaches do not work well in the long run. In the long run most employees will seek a situation in which they can maintain or improve their self-image. Some employees, however, will seek a place that confirms their low self-image, and they fit into an authoritarian situation quite well. The central thrust of this text is the belief that *self-images should be enhanced or maintained for two key purposes: individuals are happier and healthier when they feel good about themselves, and they are more productive as well.* Perfusion Services, Inc., a health-care firm, attempts to build self-images and reinforce behavior by providing a raise in every paycheck. Employee raises, given twice a year on the basis of merit, are divided into pay periods. Thus employees receive a certain amount of the raise in each paycheck.[25]

Think of a work situation in which you found that you felt better about yourself when the task was completed. Did you feel that you could go on to bigger and better things? Well, an enhanced self-image has a similar effect on many people: they are no longer motivated by the same reward systems that satisfied them before. What apparently happens is that the individual moves up in Maslow's or Alderfer's hierarchy. Of course, people who are already operating in the area of self-actualization must then enrich their jobs, become involved in many different activities. But for most people, enhanced self-image means a continuance of motivation in the same manner as has operated in the past; at least, that is what I propose here.

Eliza Doolittle of Bernard Shaw's *Pygmalion* and the musical *My Fair Lady* is a classic example of a person who could no longer be motivated in the same way after her self-image had been enhanced. Once Henry Higgins had transformed her into a lady, she refused to return to her previous role of guttersnipe. Her self-image was much too positive to allow that to happen!

Attribution Tendencies   The way we perceive the causes of events, especially successes and failures, has a significant bearing on our future behavior—our reactions to those perceptions. Also important is whether or not we are observing someone else's situation or our own. Various reviews of the way people attribute events to causes reveal that most personal successes are attributed to internal factors and most personal failures are attributed to external factors. In short, we tend to assume responsibility for our successes but are likely to blame other people and external factors for our failures. These **attribution** tendencies appear to operate in concert with our motivation to protect our self-image. Unfortunately, the connections between attribution and motivation and between attribution and subsequent behavior are not clear.[26]

Attribution behaviors should, however, trigger concern for individual needs (and personalities) and for their effect on the individual's other behavior, such as reactions to a performance appraisal. It is evident that the ability of satisfiers to continue to motivate an individual will depend greatly on whether the individual has attributed related, especially recent, events in the motivation/performance cycle to internal or external factors. The manager must at least be minimally conscious of the way an employee is likely to attribute success and failure.

This managerial perspective points to another issue: the observer, here the potential managerial influencer, tends to attribute failures to the other individual's characteristics rather than to the situation. Hence, if a sales agent fails to fulfill a quota, the sales manager is more likely to attribute the failure to some defect in the sales agent and ignore situational circumstance, such as an economically depressed territory. A plant manager may similarly see a work group's increased productivity as resulting from a new process rather than from the group's efforts.[27] Managers must be attuned to attribution tendencies in themselves and in others.

THE ROLE OF THE MANAGER IN MOTIVATION

The manager is the linking mechanism between the organization and the individual. Within any organization the manager is responsible for influencing people so that organizational objectives will be met, yet he or she must work within the constraints of the organization's need-satisfaction system. The manager's role in motivation is critical. As we shall see in Chapter 8, the leader/manager has a wide range of choices of behaviors. Choosing the appropriate behaviors, offering the correct need satisfiers, and communicating these choices are really what influence and management are all about.

> *When I was young, I thought that money was the most important thing in life; now that I am old, I know that it is.*
> OSCAR WILDE

DOES MONEY MOTIVATE?

Does money motivate you?

From what has been said up to this point, it should be obvious that money is still a motivator. It motivates most employees to perform at satisfactory levels and many to perform at superior levels, *when it is used properly*. Money motivates in almost mysterious ways. First of all, for most people it is not a motivator for its own sake, but rather for what can be bought with it. With money a person can usually purchase goods and services that do satisfy lower-level needs—physiological needs. If money can be provided for future contingencies through savings, pension plans, and insurance, it will help to satisfy security needs. And money can help to satisfy social needs as well. For example, it can help you engage in activities that win friendships. Do you have enough money for that date this weekend?

When we consider **money as a motivator,** though, it may at first be difficult to see how money can contribute significantly to the satisfaction of needs at the upper levels of the need hierarchy. In reality, money can satisfy higher-level needs, by serving as a tangible symbol of an intangible reward. For example, a person who seeks to satisfy esteem needs may value a raise in salary as a symbol of increased status. The symbolic value may be more important than the increased buying power represented by the raise. And for the individual with a high need for achievement, money can serve as an objective measure of performance. Commissions for the salesperson, prize money for the professional athlete, and profit for the entrepreneur can provide the feedback desired by high achievers. In such cases, the money itself may not be as important as the satisfaction of earning it. Our society tends to look more favorably on the person who makes a great deal of money than on one who makes little. Would you like to become a millionaire? Why?

To the person who seeks self-actualization, money is probably a symbol of achievement. Becoming all that one is capable of becoming includes the financial demonstration of achievement.

There is a problem, however, in relying on money as a reward at the upper levels of the need hierarchy. The problem is that larger and larger quantities of money are generally required to yield the same degree of satisfaction as one progresses up the hierarchy. For an individual who seeks to satisfy physiological needs, $100 may have great motivational value, but for an executive who is primarily concerned with the need for esteem or self-actualization, thousands of dollars may be required to yield the same level of motivation, especially if a high level of performance is sought and not just an adequate level of performance.

Money motivates more effectively in the short run than over the long term. It is too seldom linked to performance, so its reinforcement potential is often reduced. Money induces higher performance levels in those who value it, and not all do. But in refuting Herzberg's contention that money does not motivate (as he defines the term), Robert J. House and Lawrence A. Wigdor found that 95 percent of the research up to that time (1967) indicated that money was indeed a motivator.[28] More recently, the Conference Board found in a survey of over 500 companies that 82 percent perceived their compensation-for-performance programs to be successful. Any problems they encountered related to administration of the programs, not to the concept of pay for performance. It should be pointed out that these programs covered mostly management positions. Compensation based on performance is at the heart of successful financial motivation programs such as those used by Lincoln Electric, Cummins Diesel, and Nucor Steel.[29] Additional support is found in numerous research studies of the effects of incentive systems, which show productivity gains of from 15 to 35 percent when incentive systems are introduced.[30] Some firms have been quite clever in their uses of money to influence motivation, as the Human Relations Happening indicated.

The major problem with all of these programs is of course administration. It is of critical importance to be able to set measurable standards, to identify contributions, and to appraise performance accurately. Furthermore, because of problems with managerial leniency or severity, group accomplishments, employee expectations, communication of the relationship of compensation to performance, and a host of other difficulties, the pay-for-performance approach is used primarily for sales and management personnel. John D. McMillan and Thomas E. Shea have provided guidelines for effective incentive plans.[31]

One thing is certain: more and more companies are moving toward pay systems based on performance, especially in highly competitive industries. With reduced levels of inflation, firms find it increasingly difficult to pass on across-the-board pay raises to customers through price increases. Some firms—the Bank of America is one—give no raises at all to their lowest-performing employees, who then move on. Such firms withhold raises from the lowest-performing to 30 percent of their employees. The raises distributed to the remainder are based on measured productivity.[32]

Please recall, however, that money motivates within the constraints of the situation—current needs, their strength, and the environment. Money is not so forceful a motivator when the economy is strong as it is during a recession or in a period of high inflation. Some personalities would not fit well in a company such as Lincoln Electric. They are not "money motivated." A host of other variables intervene. Nonetheless, the evidence is strong that when compensation is directly related to performance, it can be an effective motivator. We should always be alert, however, to the other factors that motivate.

> *Self-esteem is not only the right of every employee but an absolute necessity for a highly productive employee.*
>
> JAMES RENIER

TIPS FOR SUCCESS

The following tips for success are posed as questions you can use whenever you must influence someone or understand someone's motivation, including your own. Normally a manager would use this approach only to solve problems, not each and every time a decision was to be made about offering someone a need satisfier, such as a pay raise. A periodic review of the motivation process for all of the people you must motivate, however, is logically necessary as part of effective human relations. The questions below are phrased within the general context of a manager's perception of a subordinate's job situation. But these questions are relevant in virtually any situation.

1. What are the needs of this person?
2. Have I overlooked any needs? How can I determine if I have overlooked any? If I have, how can I determine what they are? Am I willing to satisfy those needs? If not, why not? Can I satisfy them? If not, why not? What are the implications?
3. Now I need to offer need satisfiers. What choices do I have available? What need satisfiers are available outside the normal reward system?
4. Will this person react to the need satisfiers I offer on the basis of past learned behaviors or emotions? Are the need satisfiers I offer contingent on performance? Are they likely to induce effort? Are they of sufficient value to this person to induce effort? Are they equitably distributed? What other questions may she be asking herself as the result of learned reactions or feelings? What should I do as a result of the answers to those questions?
5. Has she been motivated to expend mental and physical effort? Is this effort at least adequate? If not, why not?
6. Does she have sufficient training and ability

to do the job? to do the job well? Does she know what series of tasks are required? Does she know the end result desired? Can I make the proper technology and tools available to her? Is the job well designed?

7. Did the desired performance result? If not, why not? How do I know?

8. If I have not issued the need satisfiers I offered, why not? (And the explanation had better be good.)

9. Does this person perceive these need satisfiers as contingent on performance, of value, equitably distributed?

10. Will she continue to be motivated in the same way because the organization and I have re-warded her for her efforts/performance? If not, what must I do to motivate her?

11. Will she continue to be motivated in the same way because she is satisfied with the overall job situation, with this process, or with the job itself? If not, what must I do to motivate her?

12. Will he continue to be motivated in the same way because his self-image has been enhanced or maintained by this process, by the overall situation, or by the job itself? If not, why not? What are the effects of attribution? What must I do now? By my leadership style have I made this process as likely as possible to maintain or enhance his self-image?

SUMMARY

1. Once need satisfiers have been searched for and discovered by the individual and offered by the organization, the individual may evaluate the alternatives, consider the consequences of possible actions, and decide how to satisfy his or her needs.

2. Individuals who consider the consequences of their actions ask themselves a series of questions: Can I do the job and is the reward contingent on performance? If I do the job, will I get the reward? If I get the reward, what's it worth to me? Will rewards be equitably distributed?

3. In 60 to 70 percent of cases, people do not actively search for satisfiers, do not evaluate or consider, but rather act in emotional or learned ways.

4. Managers and organizations must be attuned to the ways in which employees will react to the need satisfiers they may offer.

5. If all has gone well to this point, the employee is motivated and will take action.

6. If action is to be translated into performance, the employee must have a satisfactory level of skill, which depends on innate abilities and training; a satisfactory knowledge of objectives and of the job itself; and the proper technology, job design, and tools.

7. If the above requirements are met, performance results.

8. Need satisfiers that have been offered should be given. When they are withheld, the consequences are usually negative.

9. Once rewards have been issued, employees ask themselves essentially the same set of questions they asked earlier: Did I do the job? How well? Were the rewards contingent on performance? Did I get the reward? If not, why not? Was the reward worth my effort? Were the rewards equitably distributed? The answers to these questions will affect the employee's continuance in the cycle.

10. At least four viable explanations for continuance or noncontinuance of the motivation/performance cycle have been offered: the law of effect, satisfaction or dissatisfaction with the process, the effect of the process on the employee's self-image, and the factors to which the employee attributes success or failure.

DISCUSSION QUESTIONS

1. Can you think of times when you have reacted to offered need satisfiers on the basis of learned behaviors or feelings? What was the impact of these learned behaviors or emotions on your reaction to offered need satisfiers?

2. Name three situations in which you have seen the questions asked in stage 4 of the model considered by someone who was the subject of someone else's motivation efforts. What effects did these considerations have on the motivation process?

3. What problems may arise between motivation and performance? How can they be prevented?

4. What happens when rewards are given? not given?

5. In what ways do the law of effect and satisfaction or dissatisfaction with the process and the job itself affect self-image, and consequently the cyclical nature of the motivation/performance process?

6. What is the role of the manager in the motivation/performance process?

7. How does attribution affect continuance of the motivation/performance process?

APPLYING HUMAN RELATIONS SKILLS

Indiana Steel

CASE

Marion Tyler is the works manager for Indiana Steel's Vincennes plant, and he has a problem. The absenteeism rate among hourly workers is increasing rapidly. Under the existing union contract, workers must accept overtime work if it is offered. But they are now balking at overtime. The result has been a considerable amount of "sickness" among the employees.

The Vincennes plant is modern and in the past has been productive. It employs about 200 first-line workers and about 30 managerial or staff employees. The entry wage is $9.50 plus $3.50 in benefits an hour. The work is hard and hot (especially in summer). But the average worker receives $13.00 an hour plus $4.50 in benefits. Needless to say, there are plenty of applicants for jobs in the plant, but there is also a substantial turnover.

Marion does not understand the cause of the problem and has only some very basic ideas as to what he wants to do about it. Having thought about this problem for some time, he approached the plant personnel director, Wally Leach.

"Wally, what can we do about this absenteeism problem?" Marion asked. "Why don't they want to work overtime? They get time and a half! Why, I can remember when I worked for straight-time overtime."

"Well, I think we need to look at the possible causes and then determine some appropriate disciplinary actions, or better yet, enforce the ones we have on the books now," Wally replied.

"O.K., O.K., so what's the problem?" Marion was impatient for an answer.

"Well, I'm not sure I know the exact cause of the problem, but let me tell you about a conversation I heard the other day. A bunch of the workers were having a little bull session the other day just outside the main building, by 'A' deck. Lester Condit said he figured he made very little after taxes and Social Security and all that other stuff was taken out and he'd rather go fishin' than work overtime. You know, boss, to a man they agreed with him," Wally added.

"So, so . . ." responded Marion anxiously.

"So I think what is happening is this.. . ."

(The events described in this case are true. The names have been changed.)

1. Work through the motivation/performance cycle model using the information given

in this case. What is wrong? How can the works manager correct the problems he has—or can he?

2. What national events might once again make money a motivator for most people in our society?

EXERCISE

Motivation is based on the satisfaction of needs. Motivation is also based on the fact that various moderators affect the needs/need satisfiers process. Much of this process is at least partly a function of the particular job in question.

In this exercise, students are asked to form groups of from three to six persons. Each group is to complete the following table, indicating how the members feel that each stage in the model would be affected by each of the jobs named in the table.

Stage	First-line manufac-turing employee position	Middle-level management position	Staff accountant position
1			
2			
3			
4			
5			
6			
7			
8			
9			
10			

REFERENCES

1. Victor H. Vroom, *Work and Motivation* (New York: Wiley, 1965); Terrence R. Mitchell, "Expectancy Models of Job Satisfaction, Occupational Preference, and Effort: A Theoretical, Methodological, and Empirical Appraisal," *Psychological Bulletin* 79 (1974): 1053–75.

2. J. Stacy Adams, "Toward an Understanding of Inequity," *Journal of Abnormal and Social Psychology*, November 1963, pp. 422–36; Paul S. Goodman and A. Freedman, "An Examination of Adams' Theory of Inequity," *Administrative Science Quarterly*, December 1971, pp. 271–88; M. R. Carrell and J. E. Dettrich, "Equity Theory: The Recent Literature, Methodological Considerations, and New Directions," *Academy of Management Review*, April 1978, pp. 202–10.

3. "Two-Tier Pay Stirs Backlash among Workers," *U.S. News and World Report*, September 23, 1985, p. 61; David Wessel, "Two-Tier Pay Spreads, but the Pioneer Firms Encounter Problems," *Wall Street Journal*, October 1985, p. 1.

4. Adams, "Toward an Understanding"; Goodman and Friedman, "Examination"; Carrell and Dietrich, "Equity Theory."

5. Cathy Trost, "Pay Equity, Born in Public Sector, Emerges as an Issue in Private Firms," *Wall Street Journal*, July 8, 1985, p. 15.

6. This reference to activity orientation appears in deference to George Odiorne, who many times and in many places has so accurately described this phenomenon.

7. Chris Lee, "Sentry Insurance: Training from the Ground Up," *Training*, January 1984, pp. 66–68.

8. Several experiments have been conducted to ascertain the correlation between subordinates'

and managers' perceptions of the required results. Subordinates' perceptions differ from those of their managers about 30 percent of the time.

9. M. Scott Myers and Earl D. Week, Jr., "Behavioral Change Agents: A Case Study," *Management of Personnel Quarterly* 6 (Fall 1967): 16.

10. Edward L. Thorndike, *Animal Intelligence: Experimental Studies* (New York: Hafner, 1965 [1911]).

11. B. F. Skinner, *Science and Human Behavior* (New York: Free Press, 1953).

12. Lyman W. Porter and Edward E. Lawler III, *Managerial Attitudes and Performance* (Homewood, Ill.: Richard D. Irwin, 1968). This relationship is also discussed in Donald P. Schwab and Larry L. Cummings, "Theories of Performance and Satisfaction," *Industrial Relations* 9, no. 4 (1970): 408–30.

13. Robert J. House and Lawrence A. Wigdor, "Herzberg's Dual-Factor Theory of Job Satisfaction and Motivation: A Review of the Evidence and Criticism," *Personnel Psychology* 20 (1967): 369–89.

14. Charles N. Greene, "The Satisfaction-Performance Controversy," *Business Horizons*, October 1972, pp. 31–41.

15. John Naisbitt and Patricia Aburdene, *Re-Inventing the Corporation* (New York: Warner, 1985), chap. 1.

16. "The Un-Manager," *Inc.*, August 1982, pp. 34–40.

17. Richard DeCharms, *Personal Causation* (Reading, Mass.: Addison-Wesley, 1968).

18. Abraham K. Korman, "Toward an Hypothesis of Work Behavior," *Journal of Applied Psychology* 54, no. 1 (1970): 31–41.

19. Maxwell Maltz, *Psycho-cybernetics: The New Way to a Successful Life* (Englewood Cliffs, N.J.: Prentice-Hall, 1960).

20. A search of the ERIC system revealed more than 100 articles dealing with one or another facet of this relationship. People with high self-images consistently outperformed others on achievement tests.

21. Most of the studies were designed to investigate something else and have contributed to our knowledge of this relationship inadvertently. For example and brief review, see Rick Jacobs and Trudy Solomon, "Strategies for Enhancing the Prediction of Job Performance from Job Satisfaction," *Journal of Applied Psychology*, September 1977, pp. 53–57; for a longer review of the associated concepts and a list of references, see Robert L. Dipboye, "A Critical Review of Korman's Self-Consistency Theory of Work Motivation and Occupational Choice," *Organizational Behavior and Human Performance*, February 1977, pp. 108–26.

22. Korman, "Toward an Hypothesis," and Dipboye, "Critical Review," contain reference lists, as do many educationally oriented studies.

23. Dorothy Jongeward, *Everybody Wins* (Reading, Mass.: Addison-Wesley, 1975).

24. Carl R. Rogers, *A Theory of Therapy, Personality, and Interpersonal Relationships* (New York: McGraw-Hill, 1959), p. 196.

25. E. Wojalm, "A Raise in Every Paycheck," *Inc.*, February 1984, pp. 110, 111.

26. Harold H. Kelley and John L. Michela, "Attribution Theory and Research," *Annual Review of Psychology*, 1980, pp. 457–501.

27. Ibid.

28. House and Wigdor, "Herzberg's Dual-Factor Theory."

29. "Pay-for-Performance Plans Found Successful," *Wall Street Journal*, June 12, 1984, p. 2; also see Robert W. Braid, "The Power of Pay," *Management World*, April/May 1984, pp. 44–45; Edward E. Lawler III, "Whatever Happened to Incentive Pay?" *New Management*, 1984, pp. 37–41.

30. William Baldwin, "This Is the Answer," *Forbes*, July 5, 1982, p. 38; Frank Barnes, "Nucor Steel," in *Strategic Management and Organizational Policy*, James M. Higgins and Julian W. Vinze, 3d ed. (New York: Dryden Press, 1986); and Ed Leefeldt, "Profit-Sharing Plans Reward Productivity," *Wall Street Journal*, November 5, 1984, p. 35.

31. John D. McMillan and Thomas E. Shea, "Why Many Management Incentive Plans Don't Work—and How to Develop Ones That Do," *Management Review*, November 1983, pp. 47–49.

32. Carrie Dolan, "Many Companies Now Base Workers' Raises on Their Productivity," *Wall Street Journal*, November 15, 1985, pp. 1, 18.

5 COMMUNICATION: GETTING THE MESSAGE

KEY TERMS AND CONCEPTS

communication
functions of communication
ideation
encoding
transmission
receiving
decoding
noise
feedback
verbal communication
nonverbal communication
oral communication
paralanguage
language
listening
written communication
body language
proxemics
chronemics
status symbols
touching
clothing and appearance as
    means of communication
aesthetic forms of communi-
    cation
overload
structural approaches
informational approaches

LEARNING OBJECTIVES

When you have completed this chapter, you should be able to:
1. Describe the functions of communication in the organization.
2. Explain how you should communicate.
3. Determine whether the results of communication are positive or negative.
4. Discuss the various forms of verbal and nonverbal communication and paralanguage.
5. Identify the problems involved in communicating effectively, and explain how one copes with those problems.
6. Explain how listening skills can be developed.
7. Improve your communications.

REPORTS GIVE COPS CRASH COURSE IN TRAGICOMEDY

BY PATRICK JENKINS

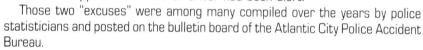

Not every highway collision is an accident: Some actually are caused.

For instance, one motorist told police, "The indirect cause of this accident was a little guy in a small car with a big mouth."

But in another instance, both parties were blameless.

Or were they?

"No one was to blame for the accident," a motorist told police after his collision, "but it never would have happened if the other driver had been alert."

Those two "excuses" were among many compiled over the years by police statisticians and posted on the bulletin board of the Atlantic City Police Accident Bureau.

They were culled from numerous reports filled out by unfortunate motorists involved in accidents.

One stunned motorist initially told police he wasn't injured, but later amended that. "When I removed my hat, I found that I had a fractured skull."

While most of the reasons, causes or excuses for accidents were mundane, some made it into the twilight zone.

"The other car collided with mine without giving warning of its intention," reported one driver, while another said, "The accident happened when the right door of a car came around the corner without giving a signal."

The second driver didn't see fit to talk about the rest of the car.

Maybe it was the "... invisible car that came out of nowhere, struck my vehicle and vanished," that another motorist complained to police about.

Some of the reasons seemed to fall into categories, such as a motorist's familiarity with his surroundings.

One puzzled police by explaining, "Coming home, I drove into the wrong house and collided with a tree I don't have."

Another reported, "I was backing my car out of the driveway in the usual manner when it was struck by the other car in the same place it had been struck several times before."

And by some reports, the accidents seemed the result of sheer determination.

"The guy was all over the road. I had to swerve several times before I hit *(Continued on page 102)* him," reported one motorist. Another said, "The accident occurred when I was attempting to bring my car out of a skid by steering it into the other vehicle."

At least one motorist might have been well-advised to check his constitutional rights before filing his accident report.

"I pulled away from the side of the road, glanced over at my mother-in-law and headed over the embankment," he wrote.

And, of course, some people are never to blame. One reported that his car was legally parked when it backed into the other vehicle, while another tried desperately to avoid the telephone pole that was bent on smashing into the front of his car.

But by far the biggest bane of all for motorists is pedestrians.

"A pedestrian hit me and went under my car," reported one incensed driver.

"To avoid hitting the bumper of the car in front, I struck the pedestrian," proudly proclaimed another.

Yet a third, seemingly congratulating himself on a job well done, said, "The pedestrian didn't know which way to go, so I ran him over."

A fourth, apparently more observant than some others, wrote, "I saw this slow-moving, sad-faced old gentleman as he bounced off the hood of my car."

SOURCE: *The Star-Ledger*, Newark, N.J., November 15, 1981, sec. 1, p. 48.

We rule men with words.
NAPOLEON BONAPARTE

Communication is the transfer of information from one communicator to another through the use of symbols. For communication to be complete, both parties must understand what has been transferred. It is impossible to name any human relations activity that does not involve communication. The understanding and proper use of communication are therefore essential to successful human relations. Unfortunately, the accident reports quoted in the Human Relations Happening above are indicative of a common problem. Most of us are more ineffective at communications than we would like to admit. Few of us actively practice the skill; we just engage in it. Most of us seem to take it for granted that we know how to communicate; all too often, nothing could be further from the truth.

Effective communication is just as critical a skill within the organization as it is in private life. The average manager spends 50 to 70 percent of his or her time communicating in some way.[1] Professionals, staff, and first-line employees often communicate as much as or more than managers do. The coordination that is required to achieve organizational objectives depends on effective communication. Yet few organization members really know how to communicate effectively. Perhaps that is why many organizations fail to achieve their objectives.

Sam Walton, CEO and owner of Wal-Mart, is so convinced of the importance of communication to the achievement of objectives that he personally visits the managers of each of the company's 750-odd stores at least once a year. At the company's annual meeting, he can call every manager by name and recall details of each store's operations. His concern for communication reflects his concern for people.[2]

Communication is a two-way process. As we saw in Chapter 1, communication in organizations involves three major communicators—individuals, groups, and the organization—in eleven combinations, including communication with oneself. These possibilities are shown in Figure 1.1.

This chapter first briefly examines the functions of communication and then explores the basic communication process by means of a two-communicator model. The various verbal and nonverbal forms of communication are then explored. You may be surprised to discover just how many ways of communicating exist and how they complement or detract from one another. It is just as important to know the meanings conveyed by finger pointing as it is the words that may accompany the gesture. Finally, the common problems associated with effective communication are noted and some solutions to these problems are suggested.

THE FUNCTIONS OF COMMUNICATION

William G. Scott and Terrence R. Mitchell have identified four major functions of communication within the organization: the emotive, motivation, information, and control functions.[3] A communication normally involves at least one of these functions, and often more than one.

THE EMOTIVE FUNCTION

It is people who communicate, even when one of the communicators is a group or organization. People have emotions. They express these emotions to others through communication. The emotive function is oriented toward feelings. Within the organizational framework, the objective of this type of communication is an increasing acceptance of organizational roles. But informally, satisfaction, dissatisfaction, happiness, bitterness, the entire range of human emotions may be expressed. When a member of the opposite sex looks at you with interest, emotions are probably being communicated.

Holiday Inns, Inc., is so concerned with the emotional side of its customer service business that it requires the managers of its hotels to train their employees in the handling of upset customers. A standardized program for dealing with various emotional issues is incorporated in its comprehensive customer satisfaction program, known as "The First Concern."[4]

THE MOTIVATION FUNCTION

Motivation, in this context, is **influence,** the ability or process of affecting the behavior of others. Communications concerned with motivation are designed to elicit commitment to the organization's objectives. Virtually all of motivation (influence) approaches detailed in Chapters 3 and 4, plus the leadership approaches you will read about in Chapter 8, are entailed in this type of communication. Leaders lead; that is, they make choices among ways to treat people in order to trigger their followers' internal motivation mechanisms. They do so through communication of these choices, in both words and actions. Most of the major activities of leaders, especially those activities concerned with the implementation of plans, require communication. Instructing, rewarding, disciplining, informing subordinates about objectives, defining roles—all require communication. Outside the organization, we all engage in efforts to influence others, to activate their internal motivation. We do so by communicating.

THE INFORMATION FUNCTION

"The only means by which one person can influence another is by the behaviors he performs—that is, the communicative exchanges between people provide the sole method by which influence or effects can be achieved."

B. AUBREY FISHER

Decision making depends on information. The organizational objective of this communication function is to provide the information necessary for decision making. The information involved is often technical. Financial information, for example, is the technical information necessary to make capital budgeting decisions. Much of the communication involved in the information function takes place through the organization's formal management information system. Any time you wish to make a decision about anything, you need information—what movie to go to, when the plane arrives, where the lecture is to be given. You learn these bits of information through communication.

THE CONTROL FUNCTION

"I have never been able to understand why it is that just because I am unintelligible, nobody understands me."

MILTON MAYER

Reports, policies, plans, and so forth function to control the behaviors of the organization's members. They define roles; clarify duties, authority, and responsibilities; and provide organization structure (defined as jobs and the authority to do them). By routinizing organizational activity, by providing a means of checking for achievement of objectives, these types of communication further the mission of the organization. In other contexts, with friends, parents, spouses, children, bankers, waiters, just about anyone whose behavior you wish to influence, your efforts take the form of communication.

THE COMMUNICATION PROCESS

The communication process, shown in Figure 5.1, begins when the sender—a person, a group, an organization—has a thought, feeling, idea, or concept that the sender wishes to share with another entity, the receiver. This message must be encoded in a form that the receiver can easily recognize. Transmission may be verbal or nonverbal. Communications may be transmitted in person, in print, in memos, on television—by any medium. The message is received through the various senses—hearing, sight, feeling, touch, smell—and by intuition. Once the message has been transmitted, it must be decoded by the receiver. The receiver transforms the message into thought and (ideally) understands or finds its meaning. Are you understanding this message? If not, is it you or I—the receiver or the sender—that is at fault? Or is the message being interfered with by some external factor (noise) or by some internal factor pertaining to the sender or receiver or both? Such factors as personality, role, status, perception, and self-image have an impact on the process. They affect the sender's ideation, encoding, and transmission of the message, and they have an equal impact on the way the receiver receives, decodes, understands, and acts on that message. Finally, if communication is to be effective, the

FIGURE 5.1   *A basic model of communication*

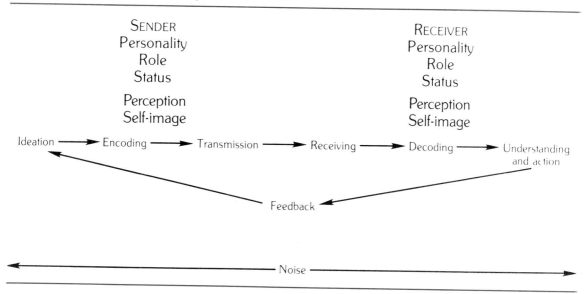

sender must receive feedback from the receiver during or after the communication process.

IDEATION

The conception of an idea or a thought is known as **ideation**. Ideation is the first step in the communication process. Ideation encompasses all that occurs before the idea is encoded, that is, before it is placed in an understandable language for transmission. Consider an individual who has developed a new product, a social group that has established norms of acceptable behavior, an organization that has established rules and procedures for achieving its objectives. The conceptions of the product, the norms, the rules—all occur as part of the ideation process. Before the product developer, the group, or the organization can convey a message, it must have formulated an idea.

> *"It is a luxury to be understood."*
> RALPH WALDO EMERSON

ENCODING

The person, group, or organization that wishes to communicate must place the message in some transmittable language, either verbal or nonverbal. Verbal languages include not only oral encodings but written language and silence as well. Nonverbal languages may be as simple as body movements or as complex as a work of art that conveys many messages in a language all its own. The essence of **encoding** is to choose symbols that others will understand. The individual's personality, the personality of group members, and the personalities of organizational members who are given the task of encoding messages greatly affect the encoding process and the subsequent content of the message. Each person has his or her own perception of what a message should accomplish and how it should be symbolized, that is, encoded. Perception also plays a major role in decoding. Encoding requires the careful selection of the appropriate verbal or nonverbal symbols to convey the exact idea that was originally conceived.

If you have ever had to write rules, directives, policies, procedures, or the like for others to follow, you know the difficulty involved in the encoding process. Many times communications must be written and rewritten, practiced and repracticed until the message is exactly as we would like it to be. And even then we sometimes fail to communicate. (Believe me, if I am not communicating, it's not because this book hasn't gone through several drafts.) The difficulties of the encoding process become clear when one tries to follow the instructions for the assembly of such things as bicycles, lawn mowers, barbeque grills, and fertilizer spreaders. If you have never tried to understand these directions, if you have never tried to put one of these pieces of equipment together, you should. It's quite an experience! The manufacturer's encoding often leaves a lot to be desired. Some incorrect encodings were seen in the Human Relations Happening on pages 101–102. Some obvious miscodings appear in the Human Relations Happening "Say What You Mean."

TRANSMISSION   Once the sender has determined the content of the message, it then undergoes **transmission** across one or more of the available channels (corresponding to the senses) and through some medium. If the channel is the spoken word, the medium is the air through which the sound waves pass. Other media include body movements, the written word, television, radio, an artist's paint— anything through which a message is transmitted. To what senses did each

HUMAN RELATIONS HAPPENING

SAY WHAT YOU MEAN

It is said that back in the 1940s, the following message was prominently displayed at the front of the main chemistry lecture hall at a major university.

"The English language is your most versatile scientific instrument. Learn to use it with precision."

In the intervening years, the teaching of proper grammar in the public elementary and high schools fell into disfavor. The inevitable result is that manuscripts submitted to us are often full of grammatical errors, which their authors probably do not even recognize (and often would not care about if they did).

We regard this state of affairs as deplorable, and we want to do something about it. For many years we have tried to correct the grammar of papers that we publish. This is toilsome at best, and sometimes entails rather substantial rephrasing. It would obviously be preferable to have authors use correct grammar in the first place. The problem is how to get them to do it.

One fairly effective way is to provide examples of what not to do; it is particularly helpful if the examples are humorous. We have recently seen several lists of grammatical examples of this type. A few weeks ago we found taped to a colleague's office door the most complete one we have seen. (He tells us it was passed out in a class at Dartmouth—not in English—at the time a term paper was assigned.) We reproduce it here in the hope that it will have some effect.

1. Make sure each pronoun agrees with their antecedent.
2. Just between you and I, the case of pronouns is important.
3. Watch out for irregular verbs which have crope into English.
4. Verbs has to agree in number with their subjects.
5. Don't use no double negatives.
6. Being bad grammar, a writer should not use dangling modifiers.
7. Join clauses good like a conjunction should.
8. A writer must not shift your point of view.
9. About sentence fragments.
10. Don't use run-on sentences you got to punctuate them.
11. In letters essays and reports use commas to separate items in series.
12. Don't use commas, which are not necessary.
13. Parenthetical words however should be enclosed in commas.
14. Its important to use apostrophes right in everybodys writing.
15. Don't abbrev.
16. Check to see if you any words out.
17. In the case of a report, check to see that jargonwise, it's A-OK.
18. As far as incomplete constructions, they are wrong.
19. About repetition, the repetition of a word might be real effective repetition.—take, for instance the repetition of Abraham Lincoln.
20. In my opinion, I think that an author when he is writing should definitely not get into the habit of making use of too many unnecessary words that he does not really need in order to put his message across.
21. Use parallel construction not only to be concise but also clarify.
22. It behooves us all to avoid archaic expressions.
23. Mixed metaphors are a pain in the neck and ought to be weeded out.
24. Consult the dictionery to avoid mispelings.
25. To ignorantly split an infinitive is a practice to religiously avoid.
26. Last but not least, lay off clichés.

George L. Trigg

SOURCE: "Grammar," *Physical Review Letters*, March 19, 1979, pp. 747–48. Reprinted by permission of George L. Trigg.

of these media appeal? Over what channels were such messages transmitted? Selections of channels and media are important. Each has certain advantages over the others. Some may be used in certain situations but not in others. For example, organizations that communicate internal information to employees via television have found this medium to be superior in many ways to company newspapers, but not all can afford television, so some must use newspapers. Speed of message delivery, cost, effectiveness, and availability are important considerations when a channel and a medium must be chosen. After all, a picture is worth a thousand words—or is it?

Oral communication most often flows from individual to individual, but it may flow from individual to group or from organization to group. A leader who talks to a group of followers may be speaking as an individual; but if the leader is speaking on behalf of an organization, the organization may be said to be communicating with the group. Once the transmission is under way, the message is no longer under the sender's control. It is now up to the receiver to receive the message, decode it, and extract its meaning. Feedback from receiver to sender may cause the sender to restate the message in order to improve the receiver's understanding.

Walter St. John, director of educational services and management development of National Food Associates, cautions that selection of the medium is of critical importance to the success of the attempted communication. He suggests the following guidelines based on what he has found to be effective:

1. Important messages should be shared, both orally and in writing.
2. Face-to-face communication is usually best; don't rely too heavily on written communication.
3. Provide for feedback.
4. Use a variety of media.
5. Customize the medium.
6. Be sure you understand the message and follow up.
7. Be cautious about using cost as a criterion.[5]

RECEIVING

The process of **receiving** a message is more complex than one might assume. The various senses must work in combination to detect the message and subsequently report it to the brain, where the perceptual set will be consulted and meaning will be given to the perceived message. Ideally, understanding and action will result. Numerous factors affect the receiving process, including the degree to which the senses and brain are already engaged in other activities, the individual's sensory and extrasensory capabilities, one's current physical and mental capacities (a cold may interfere with hearing). External noise also affects the receiving process. The ability to listen is a critical skill that is discussed later in more detail.

66A word or stone once launched cannot be recalled.99
SPANISH PROVERB

DECODING

The sensory information that arrives from the sender must undergo **decoding**—interpretation—by the receiver. Messages that are received are interpreted in light of all the factors that affect the perceptual process: selectivity, stereotyping, the receiver's self-image, needs and personality, and all the others discussed in Chapter 2. If the sender is sending two contradictory messages at once, the task of decoding is compounded. Interpretation of sensory inputs depends greatly on perception. Interpretation of other visual messages, or of written messages, sounds, smells, or emotional cues, often depends on individual perceptions, which can alter meanings significantly. This is one reason that encoding must be carefully done.

UNDERSTANDING AND ACTION

If all has gone well to this point, the receiver understands the message. But all does not always go well. In fact, it is impossible for understanding ever to be perfect because of the unique nature of the two communicators, no two of whom share identical perceptions of the same event. So we settle for a satisfactory level of understanding, which most of the time is sufficient. We should always be concerned that the message is understood and acted upon. The receiver must be motivated to take *action*.

66Don't talk unless you can improve the silence.99
VERMONT PROVERB

NOISE

Communication is subject to noise at any stage of the process. **Noise** is any factor that interferes with communication. During ideation, noise may take the form of unclear conceptualization. During encoding, an unfortunate choice of symbols—for example, the use of slang to communicate with someone who does not understand it—will result in noise. If the message is garbled during transmission, as when a television signal breaks up, the result is noise. If a word, a symbol, or an event has a different meaning for the receiver than for the sender, their differing perceptions will cause noise during the decoding process. If the receiver does not link all parts of the message as the sender intended, the resulting noise will interfere with understanding. Many of these problems have to do with word meanings and individual personalities. The common problems or barriers to communication are discussed in more detail later in this chapter.

"Perfect understanding between human beings is impossible. Grasp that concept. . . . Perfect understanding between you and the other people with whom you live and work is simply impossible. You will never understand me the way that I understand me."
JAMES W. NEWMAN

Feedback consists of a message sent by the receiver to the sender in the course of the communication process. A frown on the receiver's face as the sender is talking, for example, may be interpreted as disagreement or incomprehension and so may cause the sender to alter the message. Such return messages facilitate understanding and increase the potential for appropriate action.

FEEDBACK

FORMS OF COMMUNICATION

There are two major forms of communication: verbal and nonverbal. **Verbal communication** may take the form of either speech (oral communication) or writing. **Nonverbal communication** consists of body language and the use of time, space, touch, clothing, appearance, and aesthetic elements to convey a message.

Verbal communications are transmitted by means of two primary channels, hearing (for oral communication) and sight (for written communication). Oral communication frequently involves other channels as well; for example, we see another communicator's body movements, facial expression, eye contact, gestures, and so on. But written communication usually depends solely on what is on that piece of paper. No other clues, such as voice tones, can be given or received to help us encode or decode the message. Feeling, smell, hearing, and touch normally do not come into play.

VERBAL COMMUNICATION

"The tongue is the deadliest of blunt instruments."
SHANNON FICE

Oral Communication   We probably spend more time in **oral communication**, speaking and listening, than we do in any other activity except perhaps sleeping. Speech involves language and **paralanguage**—voice tone, inflection, speed, volume, silence—in ideation, encoding, and transmission of messages. Variation of any or all of these elements may give the message an entirely different meaning.

Language   **Language**—communication by manipulation of recognizable symbols—varies by country, culture, social class, age, sex, and other factors. Even when two people have all these factors in common, they may not agree on the meanings of all words. There are always slang and colloquial definitions as well. No two persons have exactly the same perceptions of a word's meaning because no two persons have identical life experiences on which to base their definitions. If we are to be effective speakers, we must learn the language and we must learn to use it well. We must be alert to subtle differences in meanings and in sentence construction that could have significance. The Human Relations Happening "Say What You Mean" offers some horrible examples of ill-chosen constructions.

Voice Tone and Inflection   Voice tone is that quality of voice which gives us some indication of the speaker's attitude. We characterize voice tones in many ways; for example, we speak of an assertive tone, a bashful tone, an aggressive tone, an angry tone, a passive tone, an embarrassed tone, a nervous tone, and so forth. Inflection adds to our knowledge of attitudes. Inflection is a change in tone. We normally change tone by changing pitch—from high to low or vice versa. Tone and inflection are vital elements of effective communication, especially for managers. A tentative tone on the part of a manager who must reprimand a disruptive employee may render the communication effort ineffective.

Speed and Volume   Rapid communication is appropriate for some messages and not for others. Important points are normally better made slowly. Less important items can be moved over quickly. Speed also indicates attitude. Nervous people usually talk more rapidly than those who are confident. Thus varying the speed of your speech and paying attention to the speed of others' words can assist your communication efforts. Volume can be employed to stress certain points. Sometimes high volume shows the importance of a subject. Sometimes you can capture your listener's attention most effectively by whispering your most important points. Unvarying volume or speed becomes monotonous; both are better varied throughout a conversation or presentation if understanding is to be achieved.

Silence   Silence communicates. Pauses, nonresponse, blank stares—all communicate. If you pause just before you want to make your point, you tend to attract the listener's attention. If you pause before you speak, you seem to lend importance to what you are about to say. If you do not respond to someone, you may communicate disagreement or lack of respect. What else may failure to respond indicate? How else does silence communicate?

Listening   **Listening**, the other half of the oral communication process, involves reception and decoding.

LISTENING

Listening is not just hearing; it's more than that. Effective listening involves the interpretation and the understanding and action phases of communication. Effective listening requires hard work and self-discipline. And you cannot become an effective listener overnight. To do so requires patience, practice, and persistence. Studies suggest that we spend as much as 80 percent of our time in communication and 45 percent of that time listening. As a student, you probably spend 60 to 70 percent of your classtime listening, so learning how to listen is very important. Unfortunately, most of us are inefficient listeners. Controlled research studies reveal that most people cannot recall more than half of what they have heard within a few minutes of having heard it.[6] Because of poor listening, you and everyone else engage in activities that are unproductive. The cost of poor listening to an organization or to a country is staggering. The cost to you may be staggering as well. The good news is that effective listening can be learned.

If you want to listen effectively, you must be motivated to listen. *You* must want to listen. You must be concerned about others. People like to be listened to. Don't you? If you want others to listen to you, it seems reasonable to assume that you will have to listen to them. The following is an example of how not to listen:

A husband comes home from a long day at work. *Monday Night Football* is on, and he can hardly wait. He has been thinking about the game all the way home from work. He becomes engrossed in the game. His wife comes in and sits down next to him. The ritual they normally go through requires that he say something.

After the "How are you's?" and "Fine, dear's," the conversation goes something like this:

HE: What did you do today, dear?
SHE: Robbed a bank.
HE: That's nice. What else did you do?

This is a true story. Yes, she was playing a game in order to make a point. Next she said, "You never listen to anything I say!" She was right; he did not listen to her, at least not when football was on the idiot screen.

Why might you want to listen?

You might just solve the problem.

You might get promoted.

You might get a raise.

You might make a sale.

You might make a friend.

You might keep a friend.

You might get that job you wanted.

You might find that other people will listen to you.

These seem like pretty good reasons for listening. Mike McCormack, the extremely successful professional sports agent, feels strongly about the importance of listening. He claims that if he listens for the first few minutes he spends with a new acquaintance, he can learn enough about that person's personality to enable him to formulate a strategy for working and negotiating with that person.[7]

The Sperry Corporation became concerned about communication among its members and with its various constituents. It was concerned that its customers' needs were not being heard, that inefficient listening was lowering productivity and might be having a negative effect on its climate and culture. Sperry's top managers decided to solve the problems they had observed. They did something about listening: they started their now-famous listening program. How good a listener are you? Test yourself and find out. The "Test Yourself" questions on page 112 are part of the Sperry program.

> *"Listening is just as active as talking, although most people believe the primary responsibility for good communications rests with the speaker. But think how much better we could communicate if both the listener and the speaker took at least 51% of the responsibility for successful communications!"*
> SPERRY CORPORATION

TEST YOURSELF

LISTENING

As a listener, how often do you find yourself engaging in these 10 bad listening habits? First, check the appropriate columns. Then tabulate your score using the key below.

Listening habit	Frequency					Score
	Almost always	Usually	Some-times	Seldom	Almost never	
1. Calling the subject uninteresting						
2. Criticizing the speaker's delivery or mannerisms						
3. Getting *over*-stimulated by something the speaker says						
4. Listening primarily for facts						
5. Trying to outline everything						
6. Faking attention to the speaker						
7. Allowing interfering distractions						
8. Avoiding difficult material						
9. Letting emotion-laden words arouse personal antagonism						
10. Wasting the advantage of thought speed (daydreaming)						

Total
score

Key:
For every "Almost always" checked, give yourself a score of **2**
For every "Usually" checked, give yourself a score of **4**
For every "Sometimes" checked, give yourself a score of **6**
For every "Seldom" checked, give yourself a score of **8**
For every "Almost never" checked, give yourself a score of **10**

The average score is 62. Of course the best way to find out just how good a listener you are is to have someone who knows you well rate you on these items.

SOURCE: "Your Personal Listening Profile," Sperry Corporation, 1980, p. 7. Reprinted with permission.

TABLE 5.1   Ten Keys to Effective Listening

These keys are a positive guideline to better listening. In fact, they're at the heart of developing better listening habits that could last a lifetime.

KEYS TO EFFECTIVE LISTENING	THE BAD LISTENER	THE GOOD LISTENER
1. Find areas of interest	Tunes out dry subjects	Opportunitizes; asks "What's in it for me?"
2. Judge content, not delivery	Tunes out if delivery is poor	Judges content, skips over delivery errors
3. Hold your fire	Tends to enter into argument	Doesn't judge until comprehension is complete
4. Listen for ideas	Listens for facts	Listens for central themes
5. Be flexible	Takes intensive notes, using only one system	Takes fewer notes. Uses 4–5 different systems, depending on speaker
6. Work at listening	Shows no energy output. Fakes attention.	Works hard, exhibits active body state
7. Resist distractions	Is easily distracted	Fights or avoids distractions, tolerates bad habits, knows how to concentrate
8. Exercise your mind	Resists difficult expository material; seeks light, recreational material	Uses heavier material as exercise for the mind
9. Keep your mind open	Reacts to emotional words	Interprets color words; does not get hung up on them
10. Capitalize on the fact that *thought* is faster than *speech*	Tends to daydream with slow speakers	Challenges, anticipates, mentally summarizes, weighs the evidence, listens between the lines to tone of voice

SOURCE: "Your Personal Listening Profile," Sperry Corporation, 1980, p. 9. Reprinted by permission. Courtesy of Sperry Corporation.

Now that you've tested yourself on your listening skills, you are undoubtedly wondering what you can do to improve them. The keys to effective listening found in Table 5.1 (also part of the Sperry listening program) provide some keen insights into what it takes to be an effective listener. If you will follow the prescribed actions, your listening will improve, but remember: patience, practice, persistence.

> *If there is any secret of success, it lies in the ability to get the other person's point of view and see things from his angle as well as from your own.*
> HENRY FORD

Written Communication   Because of the absence of tone, inflection, speed, volume, and silence, the effectiveness of **written communication** is almost totally a function of the words chosen and the structuring of sentences and paragraphs. Writers, like speakers, communicate to their audiences. No matter how simple an idea may seem to you, it may not be so simple to the people for whom you are writing. One way to test the effectiveness of a written communication is to ask yourself: If I knew nothing about what I have just written, would I understand it?

Written communications pose serious problems for organizations today. The widespread decline in the ability to use language effectively and to write it understandably has led many organizations to conduct special classes to teach their people how to communicate. People who have been trained in such specialties as engineering and accounting often have difficulty communicating in any language other than that of mathematics. They, too, are often trained in communication by the organizations that employ them.

NONVERBAL COMMUNICATION

While written communications stand alone, oral communications are often accompanied by nonverbal forms of communication, such as body language. Many types of nonverbal communication, however, also stand alone. We need to be aware of these forms of communication if we are to function fully in our world.

Have you ever been talking with a member of the opposite sex, someone you really wanted to get to know well, and had the feeling that the two of you were not really seeking the same objective? Have you heard all of the right words and even the right voice tones, but detected something in the person's expression, his or her way of standing, the glance at someone else, that told you all was not going as well as you would like? Perhaps it was the yawn, perhaps it was the physical distance between the two of you, but something was not right. We all learn to read the subtleties in other persons' body language, but few of us are as aware of this nonverbal form of communication as we should be. Body language has very significant meanings in various organizational transactions. In addition to body language (primarily facial expressions, eye contact, hand gestures, and body postures), the physical distance between people (proxemics) and their attitudes toward time (chronemics) are important types of nonverbal communication. Status symbols, touching, and clothing also communicate quite clearly their intended messages. Other forms of nonverbal communication include the visual arts and music.

Body Language   In interactions between people, body language may take various forms and have various meanings. There are no easy definitions that are applicable to all types of body language in all situations. But if you know people fairly well, you should be able to detect the meanings of their **body language**—their various facial expressions, postures, and gestures, and use or avoidance of eye contact. Holiday Inns, Inc., instructs its employees in the reading of body language to improve customer satisfaction.

Some gestures have commonly accepted meanings within most cultures, but the meanings of many gestures vary from culture to culture. For example, the gesture that we commonly use to indicate "Come here"—hand upright, palm inward, fingers curled—means "Good-bye" in many countries of Latin America. (See Chapter 14.) Table 5.2 lists common body actions and their generally accepted meanings in most parts of the United States and Canada. The meanings of body language are very much affected by culture. Hence, when we communicate with people of other cultures, even of subcultures within our own country, confusion may result.

Body language is more readily interpreted when its four major components—facial expressions, eye contact, gestures, and body postures—occur in combination. For example, when someone stands with arms crossed, lips

"Your face, my thane, is as a book where men may read strange matters."

Macbeth, Act I

TABLE 5.2 Commonly Accepted Interpretations of Various Forms of Body Language in the United States

BODY LANGUAGE	INTERPRETATION
Facial expressions	
Frown	Displeasure, unhappiness
Smile	Friendliness, happiness
Raised eyebrows	Disbelief, amazement
Narrowed eyes, pursed lips	Anger
Eye contact	
Glancing	Interest
Steady	Active listening, interest, seduction
Gestures	
Pointing finger	Authority, displeasure, lecturing
Folded arms	Not open to change, preparing to speak
Arms at side	Open to suggestions, relaxed
Hands uplifted outward	Disbelief, puzzlement, uncertainty
Body postures	
Fidgeting, doodling	Boredom
Hands on hips	Anger, defensiveness
Shrugging shoulders	Indifference
Squared stance or shoulders	Problem solving, concerned, listening
Fidgeting, biting lip, shifting, jingling money	Nervousness
Sitting on edge of chair	Listening, great interest
Slouching in chair	Boredom, lack of interest

pursed, and eyes narrowed, maintains steady eye contact, and leans forward toward you, what message is being conveyed? Body language is also best interpreted within the context of the situation: who is involved, what has just happened, what is about to happen?

If you want to see just how important body language can be, tune in to your favorite television show, turn off the sound, and see if you can determine the plot of the story. It is less difficult than you might think, because the verbal and the nonverbal messages usually reinforce each other.

Body language provides clues to the real meaning of a speaker's words. As Norman Sigband has noted, when nonverbal messages conflict with verbal messages, most of the time you should probably believe the nonverbal ones.[8] Some teachers often receive clear body-language messages: yawns, slouching, closed eyes, nodding heads. What do these messages mean?

The Use of Space Think of organizations to which you have belonged. What was the meaning of a corner office in comparison with an office along a corridor? What was the meaning of a large office in comparison with a smaller one, an office with a window in comparison with one without a window? These are some of the ways space can be used to convey messages about status.

Think of conversations you have recently had. How close did you stand to each person? Why did you stand closer to some people than you did to others? Who sits at the head of the table at important organization meetings? Why should you stand up when you want someone who is already standing to view you as an equal? These questions are related to the use of space to define territory.

Proxemics is the study of the language of space. Look around you right now. What uses of space do you see? If someone moved the furniture, would someone else be very upset? Must everything be in its place or is your current environment less structured?

We are territorial animals. We all try to lay claim to territory and to defend it against unwanted intrusion. Our territory may range from many acres of land to the foot or two of space with which we try to surround ourselves in a crowd. We allow some people to be closer to us than others. Edward T. Hall distinguishes four interpersonal space zones: intimate distance, from physical contact to eighteen inches; personal distance, from eighteen inches to four feet; social-consultative distance, from four to eight feet; and public distance, from eight to twelve feet on out.[9] The amount of space between two people reveals quite accurately the degree of intimacy of their conversation, their status, and the respect they accord each other. The intimacy involved decreases as the space between them increases. But a distance that indicates intimacy to us would not necessarily indicate intimacy to an Arab, who is likely to seek much closer contact with other people than most of us prefer. The use of space varies by country, sex, and certain cultural factors.

Companies communicate their respect and concern for their employees by their use of space. The larger, more nicely appointed offices, and those on the upper floors, usually go to top managers. I shall never forget my first job experience, with a large, multinational aerospace firm. Three hundred professionals, virtually all college graduates, were sitting behind three hundred identical gray metal desks in one enormous room—nothing but people as far as the eye could see. This company's use of space told me that it didn't have much concern for people—and it didn't.

During the 1970s many companies adopted the open office concept, with partitions and open doorways. Such offices were designed to save costs and promote "an open atmosphere for communication." Westinghouse's Turbine Generator Division adopted this concept expressly to encourage openness.[10] But now many companies see productivity declining, as "open" also means "noisy." Xerox, for one, has reversed its position and is moving toward more traditional settings. It found that noise was not the only problem; so was lack of privacy.[11]

As a student, you, too, should be interested in space—not only for the obvious reason of learning to use it to communicate and to understand what others are communicating, but also because space is related to grades. Abne Eisenberg has shown that the classroom space occupied by students is directly correlated with participation in discussions. The students who sit in the middle of the row at the front of the room participate more than do those in other seating positions.[12] If you were taking a course such as business policy, which required a high degree of participation, you might raise your grade by sitting in one of those seats.

Even communities communicate by their use of space. Those housing developments, cities, and towns that incorporate large green belts into their plans communicate a much higher regard for human beings than do those that cram as many people as possible into the available space.

If you want to test just how important space can be, invade someone's space, move the furniture, stand when the others are sitting, occupy the power position at the table. All of these violations of someone else's territory will show you just how important space can be. Space can be used to manipulate others. One plant manager constantly violated other people's territory and intimidated them by doing so. He would always stand right up next to someone when he spoke. He usually got his way, partly because of his use of space. This is not to suggest that you should manipulate others, only to show you just how important an awareness of space can be to you. If others invade your space, what can you do to counteract the invasion?

The Use of Time   When was the last time you were late for an appointment with your boss? What happened? Or have you been late to a meeting lately? You probably received several dirty looks (eye-contact, body-language statements). Or maybe you missed an airplane or a date or a sales contract because you were late. All of these events reveal the importance of your use of time. The study of the use of time, **chronemics**, can be of great use to you in your studies, your career, and your life.

Most of our interest in time in this chapter is focused on arrivals and departures, and how time is structured during meetings. (Chapter 16 discusses more comprehensively your uses of time.) People communicate disrespect, lack of concern, and lack of interest when they are late. The chronically late person also communicates a lack of organization in his or her life.

In the United States, Canada, and parts of Western Europe, "time is money." The more efficiently you use your time, presumably the more money you can make. But in other parts of the world, other uses of time are more important. Norman Sigband notes that in Ethiopia, for example, lower-level bureaucrats take a disproportionately long time to make simple decisions in order to enhance their apparent importance in the eyes of the people who are waiting for those decisions.[13] And an American manufacturing firm recently found that the Japanese like to have documents all signed and sealed when they are ready to leave, even if the final negotiations are not complete. The firm expected to meet again with the Japanese firm, but the Japanese had allocated only a certain amount of time to the negotiations. That was it. Either the deal was made or it was not, but no more time could be spent on it.[14]

Time seems to take on more importance as one grows older, because then there seems to be so little of it.

What practical message can you learn from these uses of time? Watch your arrivals and departures and those of other people. Watch what you communicate by your use of time. Be alert to cultural meanings of time. Use your time wisely.

Status Symbols   Many employers use **status symbols** as a reward system. Organizations use many status symbols, and they can become almost as important as life itself to some people, probably because status symbols enhance

*"Could you go over that once again, Gene? Just in
case any of us don't understand it."*

their self-image and the esteem in which others hold them. Common organizational status symbols include the size, location, and furnishings of offices,
first-class versus tourist air fare, titles (wouldn't you rather be a maintenance
engineer than a janitor?), reserved parking spaces, executive lunchrooms and
bathrooms, country club memberships, private chauffeurs, one's name on
one's door, and so forth. William L. Gore and Associates has a unique practice
of designating all employees as associates. This title fits the democratic style
of the firm, where everyone is viewed essentially as an equal. This approach
works despite the fact the firm employs more than 4,000 people.[15] Think of
organizations you have worked for. How important were such status symbols?
How were they used? What were first-line employees' perceptions of such
things?

Status symbols also play important roles outside of the organization: the
type of car you drive, the social organizations to which you belong, the kind
of home and neighborhood you live in, the size of your salary, the schools
you attend, the vacations you take, the clothes you wear.

None of these ideas is new to you. But have you thought how each of these things has been used to communicate something? Think of your own experiences. How have you used these things to communicate? Why did you use them to communicate in that way?

Touching   **Touching** and avoidance of touching play important roles in communication. A handshake, a backslap, a tender touch on the arm or body, holding hands, an embrace—all convey messages. In some organizations, touching is strictly forbidden; in others it is not. What is your organization's climate with respect to touching? What does it mean with respect to your organization's concern for people?

Clothing and Appearance as Means of Communication   "Clothes make the man," the old saying goes—and the woman, too. What impact does clothing have? Several current books stress the importance of **clothing and appearance as means of communication**, and claim that they have a great impact on one's success in the business world. (And they probably do.) For years the rule in many firms was that men could wear suits of any color as long as they were gray or black. Now navy blue appears to be the color of power and prestige. Look at what you are wearing. What messages are you conveying? If you want to make sure you don't get a white-collar job, just go to a job interview dressed in jeans and a T-shirt and see what happens. What message does such an appearance convey? Your clothing is only part of your appearance; your hair, your teeth, even your weight convey messages. Dirty or unkempt hair, yellow teeth, or extreme obesity convey various messages to others. What do they mean to you? What about the appearance of one's office, desk, home, study area—what messages do they convey? Such messages can be very important, as the Human Relations Happening on clutter (page 120) makes clear.

Aesthetic Forms of Communication   Art, poetry, music, dance, religious symbols, some plays and movies are **aesthetic forms of communication**. The symbols used may not be commonly recognizable, and they may not even be thought of as communication, but of course they are. And the message communicated by the symbol may vary with the context. When Emily Dickinson writes, "Hope is the thing with feathers," the image she evokes conveys a message quite different from that of another "thing with feathers," the Black Swan of the ballet *Swan Lake*.

COMMON BARRIERS TO COMMUNICATION

Many problems may interfere with a smooth transmission of thought from one communicator to another. Many of these problems stem from the characteristics of the sender and receiver. Many stem from the nature of the organization. Many stem simply from our culture.

Language limits virtually all communication. The symbols chosen are abstractions of thoughts, feelings, concepts. It is impossible to communicate every   LANGUAGE LIMITATIONS

HUMAN RELATIONS HAPPENING

TO CLUTTER OR NOT TO CLUTTER, THAT IS THE QUESTION

Harold S. Geneen, former chief executive of ITT for seventeen years, proclaims: "It is practically impossible for a top manager, or even a middle manager, to be doing the work that he should be doing and at the same time have a clean desk." Geneen dictated his own letters and wrote his own speeches, thus conveying clearly that he was the boss. He did not want to give the impression that others came to him with prepared decisions that he simply checked off. He wanted people to know that he made the decisions. Geneen feels that people on the firing line must have information at their fingertips. If the information they need is to be available when they need it, their desks are going to be cluttered.

Cliff Yudell, author and consultant, suggests that your desk may be whispering something behind your back. Yudell maintains that your desk may be sending subliminal messages about you to others, messages about your work habits, your personality, your level of authority. The size of the desk, its formal or informal nature (glass means you have nothing to hide), its location, its level of clutter, all signal something to those who enter your office.

Ross Webber, formerly a professor at the Wharton School of the University of Pennsylvania, comments, "I'd say that the view of the perfectly clean desk as a sign of an organized person is pretty much nonsense, but

piles of papers and a messy desktop can interfere with communication." Efficient managers communicate a real sense of tranquillity. They're not looking over papers and there are no piles between them and the visitors.

John Lee, time management expert, suggests that what you want is a desk where paper flows from one point to another. Clutter is inefficient, he charges. You want to be able to take action on what's on your desk.

So should you clutter or shouldn't you?

SOURCES: Harold S. Geneen, "In Praise of Cluttered Desks," *Fortune*, October 15, 1985, pp. 89–98; Cliff Yudell, "What Your Desk May Whisper behind Your Back," *Florida Trend*, July, 1982, pp. 113–18.

single sensed aspect of life, or even the most important ones. Rather, our languages enable us to communicate the aspects we perceive to be most important. Because the words we use are abstractions, other people may not interpret them the same way we do.

If we form good speaking and listening habits, our efforts at communication are likely to be effective. Few of us know how to speak properly in every situation, and most of us are simply not good listeners. Speaking too quickly or too slowly, failure to use the appropriate tone of voice, failure to make eye contact, and so forth are bound to lead to ineffective communication. Similarly, a person who does not listen well (see also Chapter 6) is just not going to be of much assistance in the communication process.

SPEAKING AND LISTENING HABITS

Physical and social differences can create barriers to effective communication. For example, barriers may be erected between managerial employees and first-line employees, between men and women, between blacks and whites, between the people in the plant and those in the home office 500 miles away. Meanings can be misinterpreted when such factors cause noise in the process. Even if interpretation is accurate, these problems may still interfere with understanding.

PHYSICAL AND SOCIAL DIFFERENCES

Communication must be well timed. It does little good to tell people that they are in over their heads when they are going down for the third time. "The British are coming!" would hardly have been remembered if Paul Revere had made his midnight ride at 6:00 A.M. Such managerial communications as instructions to change product lines, to set up new operations, or to delay payments must be issued when the need arises.

TIMING

Avoidance of wordiness is especially important in written communications, but it must be considered in oral communications as well. The receiver can grasp the meaning of a message much more quickly and accurately if the sender keeps the message simple. Remember the KISS technique: Keep It Simple, Stupid. Companies can do much to improve communication by keeping down wordiness. Loew's, Inc., has gone so far as to eliminate written memos in an attempt to make messages more meaningful and to reduce bureaucracy.[16]

WORDINESS

Personality plays an important role in communication. Each individual behaves in a unique manner. These behaviors stem from attitudes developed by experience. These attitudes help to give meaning to reality through the perceptual process. Perception is the process of using experience to give meaning to sensory inputs. The meaning we give these inputs determines how we "see" the situation, given our storehouse of experiences and our current emotions. No other person shares the set of experiences that you have lived through. Since our experiences give meaning to current reality, no two of us can ever see something in exactly the same way. But fortunately, most of us who share relatively similar backgrounds do see things in approximately the same way. This similarity of outlook makes communication possible. But enough differences remain to require us to be attuned to others' perceptions. Empathy is fundamental to an understanding of these differing perceptions.

CHARACTERISTICS OF THE SENDER AND RECEIVER: PERSONALITY, ROLE, STATUS, PERCEPTION, SELF-IMAGE

Two other sender/receiver characteristics that greatly influence the communication process are the individuals' roles and statuses. Because someone is fulfilling the role of mother, she may communicate in a certain way, either as sender or as receiver. She may send authoritative messages to little children in certain instances, but may listen nurturingly under other circumstances. The doctor sends certain communications because of the role he plays in life; so do the lawyer, the dentist, the accountant, the carpenter, the engineer, the manager, the subordinate, the friend, the child, the parent, the professor, the student. These roles affect virtually all stages of the communication process. Status, too, affects communication. Differences in status create barriers. When sender and receiver do not have the same status, their perceptions differ. We must remain alert to and adjust for the consequences of these factors in our communications.

Sometimes we hear or see what we want to, rather than what is really there. Correct interpretation becomes difficult and often impossible. A good part of life and therefore a good part of communication is involved in protecting our self-image. Thus not only may we hear what we want to hear, but our own messages may be distorted to protect our self-image. This is one reason that maintaining or raising the subordinate's self-image is a vital managerial activity.

While hearing what we want to hear implies an intentionally personal interpretation, unintentional perceptual problems also lead to problems in interpretation. When we speak with someone whose mother tongue is not English, and when we realize that some words have as many as fifteen or twenty different definitions, the difficulty of accurate interpretation becomes all too obvious. Then when we consider all of the other variable factors involved in verbal and nonverbal communication, we must realize that we are lucky to get half of the message right.

OVERLOAD

Information **overload** often boggles the mind. Today's managers are frequently swamped by too much information. We must constantly guard against paper for paper's sake. The objective of any information system should be to provide that which is needed and usable.

COPING WITH BARRIERS TO COMMUNICATION

Make no mistake about it: coping with barriers to communication requires hard work. We human beings have a well-programmed tendency to do things the way we have always done them. To overcome ineffective behavior, we must practice effective behavior. Improvement of communication requires practice of proper communication. We must give thought to the need to take appropriate actions, we must decide what the appropriate actions are in various situations, and we must then practice these behaviors so that when a difficult situation occurs, we can handle it well. First we must decide that we want to.

This may sound like going to the doctor and saying, "Doctor, it hurts when I do this," and the doctor replies, "So don't do that." The truth is that if anything you have been doing hurts your communication, then indeed you should stop doing that. Role playing can give you experience in handling

are jobs and authority. Structural approaches improve communication either by changing the nature of job content, by creating new or different jobs, by changing the way jobs are grouped, or by altering the amount of authority distribution within the organization. Improved communication systems usually call for increased delegation of authority, power equalization, and participation by subordinates in the decision-making processes of the organization. Much of the structural approach is implemented through the use of the various personnel practices.

There are numerous ways in which structure can be altered. Chapters 12 and 13 address two of the most important of these approaches, participation and organizational culture. Chapter 11 discusses appraisal systems and management by objectives, results, and rewards. Here we shall briefly review several less comprehensive programs that have been instituted in an effort to improve organizational communication.

STRUCTURAL APPROACHES

Junior Boards Some firms, such as McCormick, employ what are known as junior boards.[18] These boards function to advise top management, but unless a major strategic issue is involved, they usually decide the matter at hand. The boards are composed of junior members of management and, in some firms, first-line employees. Typical matters that might come before these boards include work hours, desired benefit programs, pay raises, and materials acquisitions. Such boards have proved successful in developing managers and in freeing communication. Increased productivity and increased job satisfaction usually result.

Employee Action Programs, Action Lines, Counseling Monsanto calls them employee action programs;[19] General American Insurance terms them action lines;[20] and many firms call them counseling programs. What are they? They are attempts to help employees solve problems both related and unrelated to the job. Many firms employ psychologists both full- and part-time to counsel employees on their problems. General American's action line focuses primarily on job-related problems; Monsanto's EAP focuses on personal problems; many other firms fall between these two ends of a continuum of concern for people's needs.

Grievance Procedures Does your organization have grievance procedures? Are these procedures perceived as being fair? How effective are they in solving employees' complaints? If they are not effective, what do employees do as a result? The odds are they decrease their productivity somehow—by absenteeism, shoddy work, tardiness, balking at orders, and more. That's why improving grievance procedures is so vital from the corporate viewpoint.

Communication Audits Organizations should analyze their communication systems periodically to determine their effectiveness and efficiency. How would you go about auditing an organization's communication system? Howard H. Greenbaum suggests that several approaches can be employed. Usually some kind of questionnaire is administered to employees. Portions of the questionnaire are designed to elicit perceptual responses. Other portions may be designed to test for the amount of information that has been disseminated or to identify the real communication networks within the organization, beyond those that the formal organization recognizes.[21] Analysis of variations between formal and actual communication networks can indicate power centers and potential communication problems, and can help to determine who is not receiving sufficient communication.

Attitude Surveys   Surveys, questionnaires, and interviews with employees have recently grown in popularity as a way of keeping tabs on employees' needs and perceptions of the organization and potential problem areas. Frederick Starke and Thomas Ferratt propose that organizations develop a "behavioral information system" (BIS), partly based on surveys. The BIS would enable management to remain aware, at least periodically, of employees' perceptions of major factors within the organization.[22] IBM has added another step to its attitude survey program. When survey results indicate negative or marginal attitudes among a particular manager's subordinates, the manager is encouraged to use IGP—"instrumented group process." This process involves manager and subordinates in open communication for the purpose of revealing the manager's weaknesses, building subordinates' confidence, and reducing their fears. In limited use to date, this program has proved quite successful.[23]

Deep Sensing   Several firms, among them Government Employee Insurance Company (GEICO), the Leeds & Northrup division of Lockheed Corporation, and Northern Natural Gas, hold no-holds-barred discussions with employees. Employees are encouraged to vent their feelings. They find out why things are done the way they are, and if managers don't know, they had better find out soon. While managers run the risk of being asked questions they can't answer, they may be better off in the long run. Employees do not expect a perfect manager, just an honest one.[24]

Ombudsmen   Have you ever worked for an organization where there was no one to turn to with questions or complaints? Then you know why so many organizations have created a position or department to handle employee questions, complaints, and problems. Usually the person in this position, often called an ombudsman, reports directly to the head of the organization, keeping communications with employees confidential. The ombudsman must have the capability to motivate the line functions to take action on employee problems; otherwise this function will simply become a dead end and employees will cease to use it.

Discussion Sessions   The General American Life Insurance Company holds what it calls RAPP sessions.[25] Other firms use different names. Most such sessions involve the same dynamics: manager and subordinate(s) sit down and discuss complaints, problems, viewpoints, objectives, results, potential problems, and so forth. Managers must listen if they are to learn what is happening. One Hertz area manager indicated that every Friday afternoon he and his staff sat down together "over a couple of brews" to "clear the air."

Open-Door Policies Managers who keep "open doors" indicate to their subordinates that they are available to listen to problems, complaints, and so forth at any time. The open door indicates a willingness to establish communication and an atmosphere of trust. Managers may have open doors as official policy, but unfortunately many managers do not make the commitment that this practice requires. Many subordinates are reluctant to take advantage of the open door because they hesitate to bypass other managers in the chain of command. Only if the organization's climate is one of trust can such problems be overcome.

Suggestion Programs Suggestion programs can make significant contributions to the organization. They provide a channel for employees to contribute their ideas. After all, who knows the job better than the person who does it? But suggestion programs do have their problems. After a while, all of the practical suggestions seem to have been offered, and when further suggestions are not accepted, some problems may arise. Overall, though, such programs can be effective.

Blue Cross/Blue Shield (BC/BS) of North Carolina is just one of many firms that asks employees how the organization can cut costs, improve effectiveness and efficiency, raise morale, improve job satisfaction, improve organizational climate, improve working conditions. BC/BS of North Carolina assigns each suggestion a number, and the suggestor remains anonymous until the suggestion has been acted on. Monetary rewards are given to people whose suggestions save the company money.

The informational approaches attempt to improve organizational communication primarily by disseminating information. Occasionally new jobs are created within the organization in this process, but usually already established positions merely expand their informational functions. Several means of disseminating information beyond those ordinarily included in a firm's information distribution system are available: periodic meetings with employees, television broadcasts, in-house publications (including newsletters, bulletin boards, and magazines), athletic programs, company manuals, and periodic performance reviews.

INFORMATIONAL APPROACHES

Periodic Meetings with Employees Whether such meetings are held daily, weekly, monthly, quarterly, semiannually, or annually, meetings between managers and employees in which employees are given a chance to learn what the organization is all about and what it is accomplishing and what it hopes to accomplish are extremely important. Employees, and lower-level managers especially, often feel that they are the "last to know." The management that keeps its employees informed about the organization's situation can expect more interested, dedicated, concerned, and loyal employees.

Pitney-Bowes, an international manufacturer of office equipment, stresses informative, open communication with its employees. Its belief is that "informed employees are the best employees." It stresses employee inputs into the system. Each month all employees meet with their supervisors to discuss problems and policies. The process of discussion moves upward in the organization through elected representatives until all problems are resolved.[26]

Television Broadcasts   One of the problems associated with relaying information to employees is that not all employees may receive the same words at the same time. And when newspapers and newsletters are distributed, not all may read the same meanings into the words. One way to alleviate such problems (but not to eliminate them totally) is to broadcast information to employees on television.

TV can also be used to reduce the costs and fatigue of travel. Ford Motor Company, for example, has eliminated the need for its sales force to gather in one place for its national sales meeting by installing TV broadcasting and reception equipment at thirty sites around the country. Atlantic Richfield and TRW are among hundreds of other national firms that now conduct conferences by television.[27]

Publications and Bulletin Boards   Management can make employees feel that they are important simply by putting their names in print. This form of recognition is relatively inexpensive but has proved to be effective for many firms. In large organizations, the key seems to be in personalizing the medium used. Employees do want to know about the company as a whole, but they most especially want to know about their plant, their office, their friends, their acquaintances, and most important, on occasion, themselves.

The Marlin Firearms Company employs what it designates as news centers. These are bulletin boards located throughout the organization which carry such items as enlarged pictures with texts, motivational messages, and company announcements. Special efforts are made to make these notices pleasing to the eye and informative. The news centers might post information on benefit plans or perhaps a comparison of Marlin benefits with the benefits offered by other employers.[28]

Athletic Programs   Believe it or not, organizational athletic programs communicate quite positive messages to employees. Such programs say, "We are a team. We need to stick together. The organization cares for your health and friendship activities. The company that plays together stays together. This is just one more benefit of belonging to the organization. This is something to do in your spare time that is safe and fun."

Organizational Rules, Regulations, Policies, Procedures, Memos   Any form of written communication with employees obviously communicates. But just what does it communicate? If it is poorly written, if it is written in "bureaucratese" that is not understandable by the average employee, if it communicates a lack of concern, then the employee is not likely to be concerned for the organization that transmitted the message.

One soft-drink bottler's retirement program was so complex that even its company lawyer had difficulty making out its meaning. Most employees could not comprehend its meaning and wondered if the company wasn't trying to pull a fast one. Finally, after realizing the effect on morale, the firm ordered a simple interpretation of the program to be written. After much difficulty, one that could be understood by virtually all employees was completed, distributed, and explained. No one thinks the company is trying to pull a fast one any more.

TIPS FOR SUCCESS

1. Listen.
2. Watch the body language.
3. Choose your medium carefully.
4. Load your mouth before you shoot it.

5. KISS.
6. Remember that everything you do communicates.
7. Give and ask for feedback.

SUMMARY

1. Communication takes place in virtually every human interaction.
2. If you can communicate effectively, you will be well along the road toward sound human relations.
3. Communication consists of seven major steps: ideation, encoding, transmission, receiving, decoding, understanding and action, and feedback.
4. Communication has four major functions: to express emotions, to activate motivation, to inform, and to control.
5. Communication may be verbal or nonverbal. Verbal communication consists of oral and written words. Nonverbal communication (paralanguage) consists of body language, the use of space, the use of time, status symbols, touching, clothing and appearance, and aesthetics.
6. Paralanguage greatly affects the meanings of oral communication.
7. Listening is of critical importance to successful oral communication.

8. Among the barriers to communication are language limitations, poor speaking and listening habits, physical and social differences, timing, and wordiness.
9. Organizational communication can be formal or informal, and can be directed from top to bottom, from bottom to top, from side to side, or diagonally.
10. Organizations may take both structural and informational approaches in their efforts to improve communication.
11. Structural approaches include junior boards, employee action programs, grievance procedures, communication audits, attitude surveys, deep sensing, ombudsmen, discussion sessions, open-door policies, and suggestion programs.
12. Information approaches include periodic meetings with employees, television broadcasts, publications and bulletin boards, athletic programs, and organizational rules and other written communications.

DISCUSSION QUESTIONS

1. What are the four major functions of communication? Give examples of each.
2. Think of a recent communication you have had with someone. Follow the communication process through each of its steps.
3. Give examples of various types of verbal and nonverbal communication.

4. How many different ways can you say "Hmm" by varying tone, inflection, speed, and volume?
5. How many different meanings can you give to the statement "You should not have done that" by varying tone, inflection, speed, volume, and the use of silence?

6. Communicate the following in as many ways as possible: happiness, sadness, anger, displeasure, joy.

7. Give examples of the use of nonverbal forms of communication within an organization.

8. Discuss the impact of personality on perception, and of personality and perception on communication.

9. How can the individual overcome barriers to communication?

APPLYING HUMAN RELATIONS SKILLS

CASE

The Ways of Communicating

Mary glanced toward the colorful partition that screened the desk of Paul, her boss. He had not yet appeared that morning. Mary leaned forward and spoke softly to Martha, at the next desk. "You know, Paul has been looking very upset lately."

"Yes, I know," Martha replied. "He seems to have something on his mind besides work." She grinned knowingly.

Mary's voice cracked slightly as she said, "Yeah, I bet it's that new girl he's been dating." They both laughed cynically.

Just then Paul, dressed in an unusually neat manner, appeared in the doorway of the office. He moved swiftly to his desk, gathered some papers together, and almost ran from the office. He was late, and he looked it.

"He's always late," Martha commented, as she nudged Mary.

A grin spread across Mary's face as she nodded in agreement, and she spoke loudly this time, so that everyone could hear her. "I'll bet he gets chewed out by Mr. Mulligan today."

1. How many different ways of communicating are portrayed in this case?
2. How could this organization's communications be improved?

EXERCISE

Nonverbal Communication

Match each picture below with the emotional state it may express by placing the number of the picture next to the appropriate descriptive term beneath.

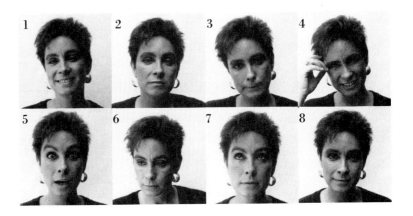

_____ Surprise   _____ Contempt

_____ Disgust   _____ Contemplation

_____ Admiration   _____ Happiness

_____ Anger   _____ Puzzlement

Match each picture below with the verbal message it may express by placing the number of the picture next to the appropriate verbal message beneath.

_____ Who knows, who cares?

_____ Stop!

_____ Are you kidding me? (angrily, disgustedly).

_____ If I've told you once, I've told you a thousand times.

_____ That's a good boy.

_____ Gee, I wish I knew, but I feel so uncertain.

_____ There must be an answer. I'm determined to find it.

_____ You're funny.

REFERENCES

1. William V. Haney, _Communication and Interpersonal Relations_ (Homewood, Ill.: Richard D. Irwin, 1979), p. 3.

2. Thomas J. Peters and Robert H. Waterman, Jr., _In Search of Excellence_ (New York: Harper & Row, 1982), pp. 246–47.

3. William G. Scott and Terrence R. Mitchell, _Organization Theory: A Structural Behavioral Analysis_ (Homewood, Ill.: Richard D. Irwin, 1979), p. 3.

4. Holiday Inns of America, Inc., _First Concern_ (Memphis, Tenn., 1985).

5. Walter St. John, "In-House Communications Guidelines," _Personnel Journal_, November 1981, pp. 872–78.

6. "Your Personal Listening Profile," Sperry Corporation, pp. 4–5.

7. Mark McCormack, _What They Don't Teach You at the Harvard Business School_ (New York: Bantam, 1984), p. 13.

8. Norman B. Sigband, _Communication for Management and Business_ (Glenview, Ill.: Scott, Foresman, 1969), p. 19.

9. Edward T. Hall, _The Hidden Dimension_ (New York: Doubleday, 1968).

10. Discussion with the senior vice-president for that division.

11. Timothy K. Smith, "Open Offices, the Idea of the 70's, Are Up against the Wall in the 80's," _Wall Street Journal_, September 26, 1985, p. 38.

12. Abne M. Eisenberg, *Understanding Communication in Business and the Professions* (New York: Macmillan, 1978), p. 392.
13. Sigband, *Communication*, p. 354.
14. Related to me by a vice-president of the American firm. This seems to be a version of the clever Japanese habit of making Americans wait until the last moment to talk business on a business trip.
15. "The Un-Manager," *Inc.*, August 1982, pp. 34–40.
16. Chris Lee, "Training at Loew's Corp.: If It's Not Broken . . . ," *Training*, April 1985, p. 43.
17. Peters and Waterman, *In Search of Excellence*, pp. 237–38.
18. "Miniboards Give Spice Maker Zest," *Business Week*, May 10, 1969, pp. 174–76.
19. Hank Houser, former Monsanto personnel official (currently with Auburn University at Montgomery, Alabama), personal communication.
20. Also called "listening posts." See John R. Hundley, "Listening Posts," *Personnel*, July–August 1976, pp. 39–43.
21. Howard H. Greenbaum, "The Audit of Organizational Communication," *Academy of Management Journal*, December 1974, pp. 739–54; Harrell Allen, "Communication Networks: The Hidden Organizational Chart," *Personnel Administrator*, September 1976, pp. 31–35.
22. Frederick A. Starke and Thomas W. Ferratt, "Behavioral Information Systems," *Journal of Systems Management*, March 1976, pp. 26–30.
23. Louis A. Mischkind, "No-Nonsense Surveys Improve Employee Morale," *Personnel Journal*, November 1983, pp. 906–14.
24. "Deep Sensing: A Pipeline to Employee Morale," *Business Week*, January 29, 1979, pp. 124, 126, 128.
25. Hundley, "Listening Posts."
26. Fred T. Allen, "Winning and Holding Employee Loyalty," *Nation's Business*, April 1977, pp. 40–44.
27. "Business' New Communication Tools," *Dun's Review*, February 1981, pp. 80–82.
28. "An Effective Way to Get Employees on Your Side," *Nation's Business*, July 1977, pp. 38–39.

6 INCREASING YOUR COMMUNICATION SKILLS

LEARNING OBJECTIVES

When you have completed this chapter, you should be able to:

1. Determine who owns the problems in a given interpersonal situation.
2. Determine when there is no problem.
3. Choose appropriate assertive action when you own the problem.
4. Identify appropriate action when someone else owns the problem.
5. Act assertively.
6. Listen actively.
7. Describe communications as a series of transactions.
8. Explain how strokes affect communication.
9. Identify someone's preference for either auditory, visual, or kinesic communication forms.
10. Improve your communication.

TEACHERS GET TOUGH IN PASADENA

Like many public school districts, Pasadena, California, found itself with a severe classroom discipline problem. Teachers reported that they were spending 29 percent of their time disciplining problem students.

After trying several alternatives, the school system decided to train its teachers in assertiveness. Over the course of two days, teachers received instruction in basic behavior modification through assertiveness training, some common-sense approaches to its use, and a pep talk. Teachers were instructed in

some situation-specific techniques to discipline students, such as writing students' names on the chalkboard when they misbehaved. This and other techniques discussed proved to be extremely useful.

The results of the program were dramatic: the amount of classroom time spent on discipline fell from the earlier high of 29 percent to only 8 percent.

SOURCE: Arthur Liebow, "Lee Center Teaches Teachers How to Get Tough," *Newsweek*, July 10, 1978, p. 69.

Do you want to improve your interpersonal effectiveness? Do you want to influence others? Do you want to make things happen? Communication is the key. We observed some basic communication concepts and skills in Chapter 5. This chapter continues the discussion of communication skills, focusing on four individual communication techniques that will enable you to improve your interpersonal effectiveness: assertiveness, active listening, transactional analysis, and neurolinguistic programming. The Human Relations Happening on school discipline in Pasadena reveals the power of such techniques to alter behavior. Each of these techniques in its own way can produce dramatic results for you.

> "There are three possible approaches to the conduct of interpersonal relations. The first is to consider myself only and ride roughshed over others. . . . The second . . . is always to put others before oneself. . . . The third approach is the golden mean. . . . The individual places himself first, but takes others into account."
>
> JOSEPH WOLPE, M.D.

TABLE 6.1   Attitudes and Skills Associated with Successful Problem Solving, by Ownership of Problem

OWNER OF PROBLEM	ACCEPTABILITY OF OTHER PERSON'S BEHAVIOR	SKILL NEEDED
Other person	Acceptable	Active listening
You	Not acceptable	Assertiveness
No one (no problem)	Acceptable	No action necessary

PROBLEM, PROBLEM, WHO'S GOT THE PROBLEM?

"Above all, as an assertive person you can learn to negotiate mutually satisfactory solutions to a variety of interpersonal problems...."
Sharon Anthony and
Gordon H. Bower

The choice between assertiveness and active listening depends primarily on a concept introduced by Thomas Gordon: **ownership of the problem.**[1] If you own the problem, you should choose to be assertive. If someone else involved in the situation owns the problem, you should choose to employ active listening. (See Table 6.1.)

How do you determine who owns the problem? A general rule of thumb may be applied whether you are a manager, a subordinate, a friend, a relative—no matter what your situation:

1. You own the problem if whatever occurs interferes with your efforts to satisfy your needs. If your boss won't give you a raise and you need more money, you own the problem.
2. Someone else owns the problem if whatever occurs does not interfere with your efforts to satisfy your needs but does interfere with another person's efforts to satisfy his or her needs. If a co-worker is about to be disciplined for failure to adhere to company policies and this action in no way interferes with your ability to satisfy your needs, the co-worker owns the problem.
3. There is no problem if no one's needs are not satisfied.

No action is necessary if there is no problem, that is, if no one's needs are not being satisfied. If you can accept the other person's behavior, then either the other person owns the problem or there is none. If you cannot accept the other person's behavior, then you own the problem.

Test your understanding of who owns the problem by taking the quiz in the box below. If you answer at least nine of the ten problems correctly, you may proceed. If not, go back and read this section again.

TEST YOURSELF

WHO OWNS THE PROBLEM?

Instructions: Read each of the statements below. Place a *Y* in the blank to the right of the statement if you own the problem. Place an *N* in the blank to the right of the statement if there is no problem. Place an *O* in the blank to the right of the statement if the other person owns the problem.

1. You are at home, studying diligently some papers your boss gave you to prepare for tomorrow's sales meeting. Your children keep interrupting your efforts. _____
2. A friend comes to you and wants to talk about her boyfriend. You have time, and you have a strong feeling that she needs your help. _____
3. You feel like playing tennis, but your mother wants you to cut the grass. She insists that you cut the grass *now*. You are fourteen years old. _____
4. Several people at work give a party and you are invited. It should be fun. _____
5. You are a manager whose secretary is going through a divorce. Her work has become erratic, she is often late, and today she is absent. _____
6. You and several friends begin discussing politics. For some reason they do not like your candidate. You feel very strongly that they are wrong, but you decide to forget it.
7. You are helping a church group distribute food to needy orphans. You see one of the other volunteers stuff a box of candy into her purse. You feel stealing is wrong. _____
8. You are late to work and your boss accuses you of being late intentionally. He is very upset and punishment seems certain. _____
9. Your most productive subordinate is having problems with her husband. He is an alcoholic and you are concerned for her safety. So far nothing has happened. _____
10. You just cannot make ends meet on your current salary, but your boss refuses to give you a raise. _____

*Answers may be found on p. 159.

ASSERTIVENESS AND ALTERNATIVE BEHAVIORS

One of the most critical aspects of interpersonal relations is the impact those relations have on the self-images of the people involved in them. When self-images are maintained or enhanced, people are usually happier and more productive. When self-images are lowered, people are usually less happy and less productive. Assertiveness is an interpersonal skill that allows all parties to maintain or enhance their self-images.

> *Between people, as among nations, respect for each other's rights ensures peace.*
> BENITO JUÁREZ

In the late 1960s Arnold Lazarus published the first paper on what has come to be known as **assertiveness**. To be assertive is to stand up for one's rights without attacking the rights of others. Lazarus suggested that people who do not stand up for their rights, and who therefore have "little freedom, feel uncomfortable and afraid, and in hunger for freedom, will sometimes turn vicious with inappropriate outbursts." If, on the other hand, we stand up for our rights in a manner we respect, our self-esteem is elevated and our self-concept is supported.[2] Although we will not always get what we want, assertive behavior should lead to a high success rate in interpersonal relations. When things don't work out, we may feel disappointed, but we will not feel irrationally hostile. Relationships should improve and we and others will feel valued.[3] Hundreds of major organizations, such as Trans World Airlines, Ford Motor Company, and the U.S. government, have trained their managers and other employees in the uses of assertiveness, in order to provide a more positive organizational culture and to help their employees cope with their everyday world.

RIGHT

What rights do you feel that all people have? According to various authors, we all have a right:

1. To be our own final judge.
2. Not to justify our behavior.
3. To refuse to solve other people's problems.
4. To change our minds.
5. To make mistakes and be responsible for the consequences.
6. To say, "I don't know."
7. To ask someone else to change his or her behavior.
8. To be illogical.
9. To say, "I don't understand."
10. To say, "I don't care."
11. To say no.
12. Not to have to win every argument.
13. To tell someone of our needs.
14. Not to need everyone to like us.
15. To have our say (to be independent).
16. To do anything as long as it hurts no one, including ourselves.
17. To be competently managed.[4]

Which of these rights do you believe people should have? Which do you feel that you have personally?

Rights may vary from individual to individual on the basis of personal value systems and the situation. Not all rights may be attainable in every situation. Practically speaking, to say no to the boss after he has decided what he wants you to do may involve excessive risk. And in some countries, especially those with authoritarian governments, asserting one's rights is simply not possible. In most situations in North America and Western Europe, however, most of these rights are attainable by most people.

ALTERNATIVE BEHAVIORS

Assertiveness is just one type of behavior that has an impact on self-image. Authorities on assertiveness identify four major types of behavior: nonassertive or passive behavior, assertiveness, aggression, and passive-aggressive behavior. Figure 6.1 portrays the relationships among these four behaviors as a continuum from nonassertion to aggression, with assertiveness at the midpoint and with passive-aggressive behavior as a fourth behavior pattern, displayed by a person who is alternately aggressive and passive, depending on the situation. Table 6.2 lists the major characteristics of nonassertive, assertive, and aggressive behavior.

FIGURE 6.1   *The four types of behaviors*

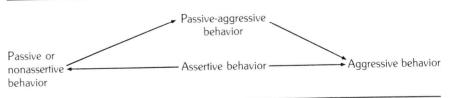

TABLE 6.2   Characteristics and Feelings Associated with Nonassertive, Assertive, and Aggressive Behavior

	NONASSERTIVE BEHAVIOR	ASSERTIVE BEHAVIOR	AGGRESSIVE BEHAVIOR
Social or cultural prescription	Self-denial; sacrifice; quiet; softness; submission to others; "not making waves"; "staying in your place"	Honesty; forthrightness; firmness; courage; directness; caring; respect for others; equality in relationships	Strength; "cool"; ambition; "macho"; drive; self-serving; hardness; toughness; lack of regard for others
Emotional response	Emotional pain; failure to gain your goals; loneliness; physical ailments (headaches, etc.); low self-confidence; low self-respect	Good feeling; accomplishment of your goals; closeness (in long run— sometimes distance at first); confidence; self-respect; affection; "I did all I could"	Guilt; loneliness; accomplishment of your goals; distance from others; power; confidence; low self-respect
Emotional response of others	Scorn; derision; lack of respect; pity; triumph; disregard; "turning off"	Good feeling; friendliness; affection; cooperation; respect; closeness; openness; *or sometimes* fear; withdrawal; *or sometimes* anger, dislike	Fear; withdrawal; submission; avoidance *or* anger; disrespect; dislike; hostility *or* firmness; assertion; resistance
Primary intent	To deny yourself; avoid risks; stay out of trouble; put yourself down; avoid hurting others; avoid hurting yourself; be liked; hide your anger	To express yourself; reach out; gain your goals; show respect for others; be honest and direct; stand up for your rights; express friendship or affection; show your anger	To express yourself; dominate; set others straight; win; do it your way; gain your goals; disregard others
Interpretation by others	You are a pushover; you don't believe in your ideas; you don't know what you're talking about	You are confident; you are friendly; you are honest; you know your feelings; you respect yourself and others; you care	You want to hurt others; you are thoughtless and rude; you are mean; you have no feelings; you are pompous
Behavior	Downcast eyes; soft voice; hesitation; helpless gestures; denial of the situation's importance; slumped posture; "Anything you want is OK with me," *or* avoidance of the situation altogether	Direct eye contact; conversational voice level; fluent speech; firm gestures; erect posture; *I* messages; honesty; positive statements; direct response to the situation	Glaring; loud voice; fluent/fast speech; confrontation; threatening gestures; intimidating posture; dishonesty; impersonal messages

(Continued on page 140)

TABLE 6.2   *(Continued)*

	NONASSERTIVE BEHAVIOR	ASSERTIVE BEHAVIOR	AGGRESSIVE BEHAVIOR
Behavioral response of others	No eye contact; not listening; being pushy; making unreasonable requests; taking advantage of you; disagreeing; denying your requests; head shaking; manipulation	Making eye contact; interested conversation; open posture and gestures; listening; forthright comments; agreeing or disagreeing; *or sometimes* giving in; *or sometimes* aggression	Backing away; hesitating; agreeing; closed posture; accepting; giving in; looking away or down; head nodding *or* counteraggression; glaring; hostile remarks; loud voice; threats; violence *or* direct eye contact; firm posture and gestures; forthright comments

SOURCE: Adapted from Robert E. Alberti and Michael L. Emmons, *Your Perfect Right: A Guide to Assertive Behavior*, 3d ed. Copyright © 1978. Used by permission of Impact Publishers, Inc., San Luis Obispo, California.

> **"**Assertiveness is based upon two fundamental assumptions: (1) Individuals are more likely to obtain what they desire by letting others know clearly what they think, feel and want; and (2) Individuals are more likely to establish climates of cooperation rather than confrontation by respecting the rights, needs, and priorities of others. **"**
>
> JACK E. HURLBURT AND
> DORIS HURLBURT

Thomas and Doreen Theobald propose that when people are confronted with a problem, they choose either flight/fight behavior or assertion. According to the Theobalds, you cannot be assertive and employ either flight or fight behavior. To take flight is passive while to fight is aggressive. You must make a choice neither to fight nor to flee.[5] When you have analyzed the factors involved in these choices, you can modify your own behavior toward appropriate assertiveness. For the manager, for the individual, the conscious choice of assertion versus passivity or aggression can mean the difference between high productivity and low productivity, between success and failure. Walt Disney Productions believes so strongly in the assertive approach to management that it teaches it to all of its managers. One of Disney's upper-middle managers has reported that he found the training especially helpful in handling temperamental actors. Others have found it useful in working with other members of the cast. (All of Disney's employees are called "members of the cast.")[6]

Assertive Behavior   When we employ **assertiveness**, we express our wants, ideas, and feelings in direct and appropriate ways that respect the rights and dignity of others. Our basic intent is to communicate rather than to dominate or manipulate. Assertive behavior promotes confidence in oneself and respect for others.

> **"**The effects of continuous passivity are insidious, cumulative, and ultimately devastating. Continued passivity erodes one's self-confidence and causes depression or a general sense of worthlessness. **"**
>
> JACK E. HURLBURT AND
> DORIS HURLBURT

Passive or Nonassertive Behavior   **Passive behavior** is used by people who wish to escape their problems and do not consider it appropriate to express their wants, ideas, and feelings. They hope to please other people rather than themselves. Passive people are often anxious, disappointed in themselves, and highly resentful of others. This type of behavior encourages feelings of guilt or superiority, and other people usually respond with irritation, pity, or disgust.[7] The body language of the nonassertive person includes an ingratiating voice, a hand covering the mouth, and averted eyes. In an organizational environment, the passive manager is often called a "nice guy." Your basic "doormat" personality is a person whose behavior is predominantly passive. The classic example is the submissive wife who feels tremendous guilt and despair when she can no longer stifle her personal needs. She may explode some day in violent anger, or she may just be miserable for the rest of her life. But most of the people around her will be miserable, too, if she has her way. Do you know anyone like that?

Patricia Jakubowski and Arthur Lange emphasize fear as the prime motivator of passive behavior: fear of displeasing others, fear of rejection, fear of retaliation, fear of a lover's moodiness, fear of losing a job, fear of being badmouthed, fear of hurting others, fear of being hurt, fear of feeling guilty, and fear of transgressing the rights of others.[8]

There are advantages and disadvantages to passive behavior. The primary disadvantages are "loss of self-respect, increased anxiety, and resentment"; the advantage is that you can manipulate people through this behavior.[9]

Aggressive Behavior   At the other extreme is the person who must win at the expense of others. Whereas the passive person lets others win, or wins only by default, the aggressive person must win at all costs, as long as the costs are someone else's. The intent of this person is to dominate and control others. Such people are often embarrassed later. **Aggressive behavior** creates hurt and humiliation in other people, who are likely to retaliate with angry and vengeful behavior.[10] Aggressive behavior is usually caused by a lack of self-confidence, a feeling of vulnerability and powerlessness in a threatening situation. Overreaction results in an attempt to protect oneself from the per-

"In his mysterious way, God has given each of us different talents, Ridgeway. It just so happens that mine is intimidating people."

ceived threat. There are distinct mind-sets associated with this behavior pattern:

> I must win to be OK. If I don't come on strong, I won't be listened to. The world is hostile and I must be aggressive in order to make it. To compromise is to lose. I must make an impact. I must get my way. Aggression is the only way to get through to some people. I must prove that I'm right and they're wrong. The world must be fair; it's intolerable when people mistreat me.[11]

Even though this person acts as though he were coming from a positive self-image, he has a constant nagging feeling that he is not OK, so he keeps trying to prove that he is OK by beating or controlling others. Many managers are characterized by this type of behavior. One plant manager I knew would remove his safety helmet and throw it up against the wall when he wanted his subordinates to listen. He often shouted verbal abuses at them. He argued with everybody. Needless to say, his was not a productive plant.

Passive-Aggressive Behavior   There is another type of behavior that alternates between aggression and passivity. Such people often behave aggressively toward some people, perhaps those below them in the organizational hierarchy, and passively toward others, often those managers above them in the organizational hierarchy. This is just one example of **passive-aggressive behavior.** (The definition of *passive-aggressive* in much of the assertiveness literature is a simplification of the more complex personality pattern identified by the same term in the psychological literature.) As the term is used here, the passive-aggressive person is one who acts passively during problem situations, but later, perhaps in just a few seconds, will do something to show his or her dissatisfaction with the situation. It is usually an indirect action, such as slamming a door. Such people express their displeasure while avoiding the danger of a confrontation. The passive-aggressive personality is very difficult to work for. And even though such people may normally react to management and subordinates as we have seen, they may at times appear rational and willing to work with subordinates. The critical word is *appear*. Often such people are merely feigning interest in order to gain time to carry out their own plans.

ASSERTIVENESS TECHNIQUES

Several assertive techniques or models have been devised. If you want to act assertive, act as the assertive person would, as indicated in Table 6.2. Beyond that, you might wish to consider using the following models when they are applicable: (1) the mixed-feelings statement, (2) empathic assertion, (3) confrontive assertion, and (4) "I"-language assertion.

The Mixed-Feelings Statement   When you make a **mixed-feelings statement,** you express first your positive feelings, then your negative feelings. You might, after expressing the positive feelings, give the receiver a chance to comment before expressing the negative feelings. Defenses are not nearly so likely to be activated or the other person's self-image lowered by negative statements when they are preceded by positive statements. Here is an example of a mixed-feelings statement: "Karen, you have made great improvements since you've been here! I want to commend you on your efforts. We still seem to be a little bit behind our competitors, though. Do you have any suggestions as to how your unit can pick up the slack?" Karen might reply: "I'm pleased that you've noticed my efforts, but I'm disappointed that you still think they're not enough."

The Empathic Assertion   The **empathic assertion** is one of the most useful of the assertive techniques. In this model, you give empathic recognition during the initial part of the statement. Your words normally reflect your understanding of the other person's feelings and situation. Then you state your own position, usually starting with the word "I." A connecting word such as "but" or "however" usually adds significant emphasis to the assertion of your position.[12] Here is an example of an empathic assertion: "I can see that you're unhappy about having to fill out these forms, and that we're not going to reach an understanding now. Why don't we get back together later, when you feel that we can resolve the issue?"

The Confrontive Assertion   The **confrontive assertion** has three parts:

1. Objectively describing what the other person said would be done.
2. Describing what the other person actually did do.
3. Expressing what you want (feedback may be solicited as part of this position).[13]

The confrontive assertion is particularly helpful when you have a recurring problem. It can be used most effectively when the other person has agreed to change his or her behavior but has failed to do so. One must be careful not to let one's words or nonverbal behavior (body language) appear to be aggressive. As in all problem-solving techniques, the emphasis here is on behavior—the discrepancy, the performance—not on the personality of the behavior. Here is an example of the confrontive assertion:

"I thought we had agreed on how you would work this machine. But I see you're still doing it the old way. As we discussed, it's very important that you do the job the correct way. Why aren't you doing it the correct way?"

The I-Language Assertion   The **I-language assertion** involves a four-part situation:

1. You objectively describe the other person's behavior or the situation that interferes with you.
2. You describe how the other person's behavior or the situation concretely affects your life, in terms of additional time, money, effort, whatever.
3. You describe your own feelings.
4. You describe what you want the other person to do—provide an explanation, change behavior, apologize, offer suggestions for solving the problem—and give his or her reaction to what you have said.

Here is an example of the I-language assertion: "You know when you turn in reports that are not completely filled in, our work load here is doubled on a per unit basis. This upsets our clerks tremendously and it upsets me, too. I'd appreciate it very much if you'd please complete the reports before you turn them in. I know it's easy to forget, but they must eventually be completed."[14]

BEING ASSERTIVE

Most assertions avoid the use of the word *you* but stress the word *I*. Of all assertions, the empathic is probably the easiest on the feelings of the other person. If someone refuses to change after you have made an assertive statement, then that person has determined the consequences that will follow. This is especially important if you are a manager. When you are disciplining employees, trying to change their behavior in a more favorable direction, assertiveness is more effective than aggressive or passive behavior. If you state your position calmly and reasonably, then the choice of what happens is theirs, not yours. Assertiveness is extremely important if you want to discipline someone who might perceive your behavior as an attack or unfair action. You may need to make such people say in their own words that the option is theirs. Assertiveness is just as important if you are in a nonmanagerial position, attempting to get your boss, co-workers, friends, or family to cooperate. You need to make certain that they understand that the choice is theirs. The Human Relations Happening "Using Assertiveness" illustrates a successful application of assertive behavior.

Being assertive does involve certain risks. If you become more assertive in a relationship that has gone along in a certain way for several years, you are going to find that the other person will have to change as well if the relationship is to continue. The other person may regard your assertiveness as aggressiveness, especially if that person operates primarily from an aggressive position.

HUMAN RELATIONS HAPPENING

USING ASSERTIVENESS

Anne is the head nurse in the surgical wing of a large metropolitan hospital. Approximately fifty nurses report to her through her five assistants. Anne has had training in assertiveness, active listening, and the process of problem identification. She describes a recent experience in which she used assertiveness to good effect:

About three weeks ago, Marcy, one of my assistants, refused to come in on an emergency basis to supervise one of the night sections. Since I am responsible for the wing, and no one else was available, I had to come in, though ordinarily it would have been my assistant's responsibility. The result was a sixteen-hour shift for me. Marcy had been receiving radiation treatments for breast cancer, and they had left her sick quite frequently. But there was no indication that she was sick at this time, except perhaps psychologically. Her prognosis was not good, but she was not considered terminal. Although she was able to function normally in most situations, she simply had had a bad temper since her treatments had begun. She had become difficult to work with. I recognized that this was obviously the result of her treatments, but still, I had to have a supervisor working for me who would be there when I needed her.

The next day I called her into my office and we had a heart-to-heart chat. I knew that I owned the problem, because she was simply not performing as she should have been. She disobeyed an order. She put me on the spot. However, I wanted to listen to her problems to see if I could help her, and in helping her, alleviate my own problem as well.

First, I listened to her. She was very disheartened by the progress of her treatments. Her tumor was smaller but there was some concern over future growth. She had a spell of crying. I tried to console her. We talked about her fears. She knows, of course, the probability of more serious trouble. Naturally, she was worried. We then talked about my situation as manager and the trouble she had left me in. I used an *I*-language assertion on her at first, in order to make her aware of her impact on others. According to policy, I had to suspend her for one day for refusing to obey an order of this nature, but with pay—that, too, is our policy. We let employees think about their behavior on that day off. She has caused me no problems since then, and seems to be adjusting better to her personal situation. She is not yet in remission, but the doctors are hopeful. She understands that she must be here unless she is sick. She apologized, and we have spoken since about her personal situation on two other occasions, with me again providing active listening. She lives alone, and basically needed someone to listen to her. We all seem to get so busy that we sometimes simply forget to supply that helping hand that others need. Basically, I solved my problem, and she has worked on hers, and seems to be solving it.

WHEN MILD ASSERTIVENESS TECHNIQUES DON'T WORK

Like all human relations techniques, assertiveness techniques do not work every time. Additional techniques that you may wish to try include the "broken record," the contract option, silence, and walking away.

Broken Record   Persistence is a major virtue in people who wish to be assertive. If all else fails, say it calmly, again and again and again and again, until the other person gives in. This is known as the **broken record** technique. For example:

Manager: Jean, I think you and I need to look at your area to see if we can improve it some.

Jean: I don't see anything wrong with it.

Manager: There are some problems with control, and you and I need to look at them.

Jean: There isn't any problem that I'm aware of.

Manager: I understand, but the report shows you're making some errors. Let's look and see.

Jean: OK.[15]

The Contract Option   Jakubowski and Lange propose that you make a statement in the form of a contract. When you choose the **contract option,**

you inform the other person what the final terms will be and give him a chance to change his behavior before those terms are carried out.[16] For example:

"You've been disobeying the rules by coming in late after every break period. I'm disappointed that our last discussion didn't change the situation. You promised to do better, but nothing has changed. According to the company's rules, you will receive a one-day suspension the next time you are late. Is that understood?" (Depending on the person, you may even want to have him repeat his options, and his understanding that the choice is his.)

If the person does not change his behavior, then he has decided the consequences of his behavior. For this option to be effective, you must be able to carry out what you indicate you will carry out. And you must carry it out. When you choose this option you must be careful that your body language does not indicate aggression. If the other person perceives you to be threatening him and believes that you are relying on fear, then he may not respond as you would like. The results are going to be passive, passive-aggressive, or aggressive behavior, none of which is as productive as assertive behavior.[17]

Silence or Walking Away   If you detect that another person is trying to manipulate you, you can assert your displeasure by silence or walking away from the situation. This is a weaker course of action than an assertive statement, however. When another person is trying to outtalk you and will not stop to listen, this may be your only choice unless you want to enter into a shouting match.

ACTIVE LISTENING

The biggest block to personal communication is man's inability to listen intelligently, understandingly, and skillfully to another person. This deficiency in the modern world is widespread and appalling.
CARL ROGERS

If you were a supervisor, how would you help a subordinate who came to you with a personal problem—her child, say, has dropped out of school? How could you develop her own problem-solving skills so that she could be less dependent on you and others? One technique that could be of great assistance in this situation is active listening, also referred to as effective listening or nondirective counseling. Active listening is appropriate primarily when the other person owns the problem, though you may also find it helpful in combination with other techniques, such as assertiveness, when you have a problem of your own to solve. But usually the active listening approach is used only when you are acting as a sounding board for someone else.

When you engage in **active listening,** you give feedback on both the content and the feelings that you hear expressed in another person's communications to you. Engaging in both of these activities, not just one or the other, is what makes active listening unique. You tell what you hear the other person saying: what the problem is, how the other person feels about it. You do not want to solve the problem for the other person; you want to help the person find his or her own solution. When you engage in active listening, you are a listener and you are a sounding board. You can be satisfied with the solution the other person finds. You do not have to try to solve the problem yourself. If you want other people to develop, then you must let them do so. Active listening allows the other person to develop. But you are not passive. You are actively listening and thus actively providing feedback. You are counseling.

Active listening requires concentration. To be effective, you must at least appear to be concerned, and you will find that you cannot appear to be concerned for very long unless you truly are.

Active listening can be thought of as a five-step process. Each succeeding step is more active than the previous one. Active listening should begin when you perceive that the other person has a problem.[18]

1. Door Openers   When other people indicate to you that they have a problem, usually you will need to open the door to them so they will feel free to talk with you. You need to let them know that you are receptive to them, that you are interested in their problems. Such **door openers** might include:

> "Tell me about it."
> "Would you like to talk about it?"
> "Boy, it sounds like you have a problem." (Followed by silence.)
> "Sounds to me like something is wrong."
> "And you feel that you have been wronged?"

2. Silence   You can communicate interest and concern through silence that is accompanied by appropriate nonverbal behavior: erect body, eye contact, nodding of the head. This is commonly known as **passive listening,** but it is not really passive. Your nonverbal behavior contributes greatly to the other person's feeling that you are concerned. And in your role as counselor, you encourage the other person to speak simply by your silence.

3. Acknowledgment Responses   *Acknowledgment responses* consist of brief verbal expressions that communicate your understanding, acceptance, and empathy. Such responses might include: "Oh? . . . I see. . . . Mm-hmm? . . . Yes, I see you are. . . . Really? . . . Yes, of course. . . . How about that!" "That's interesting!"

4. Content or Feeling Feedback   Many listeners feed back either content ("You did it in five minutes?") or feelings ("You seem to be pretty shaken up about what happened"). But **feedback** of both is most desirable.

5. Active Listening   By feeding back both content and feeling, you help both yourself and the other person to understand the situation:

> "And so she makes you mad when she makes so much noise?"
> "Are you saying that you feel he's unfair when he asks you to do the extra work? Or is it something else that really bothers you?"
> "You say what she did doesn't bother you, but you seem very anxious." (Nonverbal communication is fed back here.)

Active listening is also useful when you have a problem you need to solve. By listening actively to feedback from other people, you can get fresh viewpoints and perhaps even new information that will help you solve the problem.

The aim of any communication process that is to be used to enhance the self-image of others is to create a climate that is supportive, not defensive. Read the Human Relations Happening titled "The Winning Touchdown." Notice how the manager recognizes whose the problem is, and how he keeps it from becoming his, and how he helps the other person solve his own problem by active listening.

HUMAN RELATIONS HAPPENING

THE WINNING TOUCHDOWN

Larry Bizetti appeared in the doorway of Michael Quentin's office. Larry had worked for Michael for almost two years now, and they had become friends. Larry appeared tired and worried. Uncharacteristically, he asked if he could close the door. "Sure," Michael replied.

"I have a problem, and I wondered if we could discuss it," Larry said.

"It sounds ominous," Michael replied.

"Mike, as you know, the football season is well under way. Little Larry's been doing very well in Junior League. But there have been several accidents, broken bones and so forth. This morning Marge says she wants Larry to quit football. She's afraid he'll get hurt. I told her we'd talk about it when I got home."

There was a moment of silence.

Michael wanted to avoid suggesting a solution, since Larry had not really asked for one—at least, not yet. Finally he said, "It sounds as if you're very concerned, very worried because Marge wants to take Larry out of football."

"Worried is hardly the word for it. Frantic is more like it."

They both laughed. Larry continued:

"I thought maybe you'd have some ideas about what to do."

"You're not sure what to do, is that it?"

"Right. I thought about trying to show her how important it is to the boy, but of course she already knows that, and she knows it's really just as important to me, maybe more so. And I thought about trying to convince her that there really isn't any danger, but of course there *is* some limited amount of danger. And I thought maybe she'd calm down today."

"You've thought about a couple of approaches, and you think maybe she might listen to them better tonight, is that it?"

"Yeah, she's usually pretty reasonable, but sometimes, when she gets her mind made up, she just won't change it."

"And you're afraid this is going to be one of those times."

"Yeah, I guess I am, though of course I won't know till I try. She usually listens to reason. And she might even have a point, though I don't think the situation is that serious."

"You're very much afraid she won't listen to reason, but she usually does, and you feel that reason is on your side?"

"Yes, I do. You know, I think she *will* listen, and we can talk this out. Thanks, Mike, for listening!"

"Any time. That's what friends are for."

No one can afford to assume other people's problems. The instant you give a solution, the problem is yours, not theirs. And people do not grow if they do not solve their own problems. Their self-image is not enhanced if someone else steps in with a solution. Some people will accept the solution you suggest, and then if it fails they turn around and say, "You got me into this" or "It's not my fault, I did what you said."

TRANSACTIONAL ANALYSIS

A very useful system for improving your ability to communicate is **transactional analysis (TA)**. More than a communication analysis system, TA provides a way to analyze personality, behavior, and motivation. From the TA perspective, much of behavior and much of internal motivation result from the desire to give and receive recognition, or "strokes." The consequences of the strokes one gives may be positive, negative, or discounted. Positive strokes leave you feeling better about yourself. Negative strokes leave you feeling worse about yourself. Discounts also leave you feeling worse about yourself, but they are more complex than negative strokes; they make you feel that you received no positive recognition when you felt you deserved some, or that you received less positive recognition than you deserved.

In TA, personalities are seen as having three major parts, or ego states: the Parent (P), the decision-making Adult (A), and the Child (C). The Parent and Child have the subdivisions seen in Figure 6.2: Critical Parent and Nurturing Parent; Natural Child, Adaptive Child, and Little Professor. Table 6.3 indicates the major characteristics of each of the six primary ego states.

> *" I contradict myself. I am large. I contain multitudes. "*
> WALT WHITMAN

FIGURE 6.2   *Ego states*

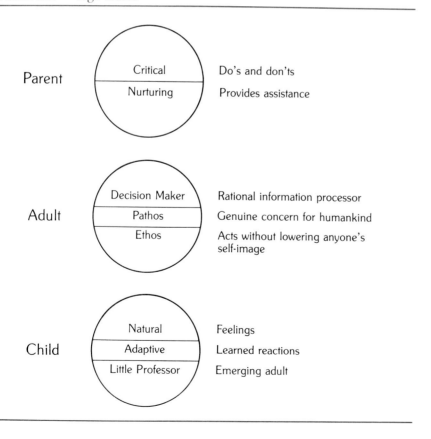

TABLE 6.3 Behaviors Associated with Parent, Adult, and Child Ego States

	CRITICAL PARENT	NURTURING PARENT	ADULT	NATURAL CHILD	ADAPTIVE CHILD	LITTLE PROFESSOR
VOICE TONES	Condescending, criticizing, putting down or accusing, insistent, tongue-clicking, sighing, harsh, indignant, commanding, judgmental.	Solicitous, comforting, caring, soothing.	Matter-of-fact, even, calm, relaxed, assertive, deliberative.	Rising, high-pitched, usually noisy, sullen, cheerful, protesting.	Whining, shrieking with rage, begging, contrite, supplicating, complaining.	Deliberative, thoughtful, assertive.
VOCABU-LARY CLUES	Don't tell me. You should. You ought. Shocking. Nonsense. Lazy. Poor thing. Everyone knows that. You should never. The only way. I can't understand why in the world you would ever. It is extremely important. Do it. You never. Be cool. You always. You disappoint me.	Poor thing. What's wrong? Are you OK? Can I help? Don't worry. Everything will be OK. I'll protect you.	Aha, I see. How? What? When? Where? Why? Who? What's the probability? Is it possible? Is it probable? In what way? I speak only for myself and not others. I see your point. I recognize. How do you feel about?	Oh, boy. I'm mad at you. Hey, great. I wish. I dunno. Gee, crazy. Rats. Wow.	It always happens to me. I guess I'm just unlucky. I never seem to win at anything. That's not fair. Everybody else does it. Come on, let's. I won't. It's not my fault.	They just don't understand me. That's it! Why? My hunch is. What happens if we try this?
PHYSICAL POS-TURES	Stroking chin, puffed up, super-correct, very proper. Superior attitudes: talking behind hand, throwing hands in air.	Open arms protecting from a fall or hurt, pat on back, arm around shoulder.	Relaxed, attentive, eye contact, listening with openness, squared-up posture. Adult listening is identified with continual movement of face, eyes, and body.	Playful, excited, running, dancing, jumping up and down, head cocked.	Withdrawn and retreating, beat down, overburdened, self-conscious, teasing, agitated, tantrum behavior.	Pacing. Deep in thought, squared posture.

FACIAL EXPRES-SIONS	Frowns, worried or disapproving looks, taut lips, jutting chin, stern gaze.	Concerned, supportive, encouraging, warm, happy.	Alert eyes, paying close attention. Slightly tilted head, regular eye contact. Confident appearance.	Excitement, surprise, eyes shining, body tense, mouth open.	Forlorn face, downcast eyes, quivering lip or chin, tic, pouting, whining, moist eyes, red face.	Eyes twinkling. Excitement. Thoughtful. Moist eyes. Alert. Raised eyebrows.
GESTURES	Pointing index finger or pencil, tapping foot, arms folded across chest, hands on hips, striking table with fist, shaking fist. Looking down over rim of glasses.	Reaching for, hugging, holding, protecting, and shielding from harm.	Leaning forward in chair, eye-to-eye contact, listening with openness.	Hugging, laughter, limbs moving freely, playful, scowling.	Wringing hands, withdrawing into corner, raising hand for permission, stooped shoulders, hung head.	Hand on chin as in thought. Snapping of fingers. Stopping cold in his tracks.
EXPRES-SIONS OF MENTAL PRO-CESSES	Closure to new data, automatic judgments based on archaic material.	Support and concern.	Data gathering, sensitivity, openness, and thinking.	Aroused feelings suggesting that the Child has been hooked.	Complying, complaining, and expectation-meeting, or withdrawing and expectation-avoiding. Procrastinating.	New ideas. New thoughts. Intuition. Manipulation.

SOURCE: Adaptation based on these TA sources: Eric Berne, *Games People Play* (New York: Ballantine Books, 1973); Muriel James and Dorothy Jongeward, *Born to Win* (Reading, Mass.: Addison-Wesley, 1977); Charles Albano, *TA on the Job* (New York: Perennial [Harper & Row], 1976); Dudley Bennet, *TA and the Manager* (New York: AMACOM, 1976); Thomas A. Harris, *I'm OK, You're OK* (New York: Avon, 1973).

One of these ego states dominates a person's interpersonal behavior at any moment in time.

TA is based on the belief that people develop the specific characteristics of these ego states because of the strokes they receive and the manner in which the strokes are given. Because people become accustomed to either giving or receiving certain strokes in certain ways in their developmental years, they give or seek out the same strokes in later years. They follow patterns of behavior that allow them to continue to get and give the same strokes in the same ways. This is how dominant ego states develop.

TA has an important bearing on communication skills because all communication occurs between ego states. Thus, once you learn to recognize the communicating ego state in yourself and in others, and to identify the ones you typically address when you communicate and the ones you should address and how, then you will be able to communicate more productively. The basis of interpersonal communication is the "transaction"—the transmission of a message from one person to another and the return transmission of a feedback message, as shown in Figure 6.3. When you have analyzed the various types of transactions, the ego states involved, and the patterns of your transactions and those of others, you will have taken a giant step toward improving your communication ability.[19]

Patterns tend to emerge in transactions. In organizations where managers make most of the decisions, managers tend to communicate most often from their Critical Parent, directing their messages to the Natural or Adaptive Child in their subordinates. Subordinates typically go along and reply from their Child ego state. In organizations where decision making is encouraged at all levels, managers and subordinates most often relate at the level of Adult to Adult.

The space available here does not allow for a detailed description of the various rules that operate in TA, but generally speaking, decision making must involve the Adult in order to be effective; there is a time and a place for all ego states; you get what you stroke—if you give positive strokes, you get back positive strokes, but if you give negative strokes, you'll get back

FIGURE 6.3   *Transactions*

		First speaker	Second speaker
1.	"Hello, how are you?"	P	P
2.	"Fine, thanks, and how are you?"	A⟷A	
		C	C
1.	"Harry, you've got to do better. You're just not going to make it here if you don't."	P	P
		A	A
2.	"I will, boss, I will."	C	C

negative strokes; various types of transactions provide for satisfactory communication or halt it, encourage productive communication or discourage it. One must also be aware that people collect strokes that they have strong feelings about ("stamps"); they eventually cash in their stamps in either positive or negative ways. People spend their time in identifiable patterns, and these patterns become very important in terms of motivation and productivity. The way people spend their time is greatly affected by strokes. (Chapter 11 explores a particular time-spending pattern known as psychological game playing.)

NEUROLINGUISTIC PROGRAMMING

We have five primary senses: we see, we hear, we feel, we smell, we taste. But sight, sound, and touch are of greater importance to most of us than taste and smell. Furthermore, most individuals develop a **preference** for one of the three dominant senses as a means of **representing** incoming stimuli and of describing those stimuli and their other life experiences to other people. They therefore interpret reality in either a visual way, a kinesic way (feel), or an auditory way. This is not to say that they do not use the other representation systems, only that people tend to use one system much more often than another. Table 6.4 indicates how people might express themselves and interpret reality in view of their preference for one of these three senses. As you can see, the visual person makes statements such as the one I just made, "As you can see." (I am a visual person.) The person with an auditory preference might have said, "This table tells you . . ." and the kinesic person

TABLE 6.4   Typical Kinesthetic, Visual, and Auditory Statements

MEANING	KINESTHETIC STATEMENT	VISUAL STATEMENT	AUDITORY STATEMENT
I (don't) understand you.	What you're saying feels (doesn't feel) right to me.	I (don't) see what you are saying.	I (don't) hear you clearly.
I want to communicate something to you.	I want you to be in touch with something.	I want to show you (a picture of) something.	I want you to listen carefully to what I say to you.
Describe more of your present experience to me.	Put me in touch with what you're feeling now.	Show me a clear picture of what you see at this point in time.	Tell me in more detail what you're saying.
I like my experience of you and me at this point in time.	This feels really good to me. I feel really good about what we're doing.	This looks really bright and clear to me.	This sounds really good to me.
Do you understand what I'm saying?	Does what I'm putting you in touch with feel right to you?	Do you see what I'm showing you?	Does what I'm saying sound right to you?

SOURCE: Adapted from Richard Bandler and John Grinder, *Frogs into Princes: Neuro-linguistic Programming* (Moab, Utah: Real People Press, 1979), p. 15.

might have said, "You can get a feel for. . . ." People tend to depend on their preferences in their communications and in the way they perceive sensory inputs.

Our representation systems govern not only our verbal communications but our nonverbal ones as well, especially those we convey with our eyes. Visual people, for example, tend to look up when they are thinking; they are attempting to see what they are thinking about. Auditory people tend to look ahead as they listen to their thoughts. Kinesic people look down, to improve their feel of the situation. People of all persuasions also look left or right, depending on whether they are remembering past experiences or constructing new thoughts, and on whether they are right-handed or left-handed.[20]

Regardless of representation preference, most people look upward when they are processing data visually, ahead or downward when they process data auditorily, downward when they process data kinesically. So what? you ask. Richard Bandler and John Grinder have found that successful communication depends on the use of the same representation system by the sender and the receiver. If people are not using the same system, their communications are likely to be not only ineffective but counterproductive. The person who says, "I feel this way . . ." and hears in response "I can see what you're saying" often feels as if the other person had not understood a word she had said. These two people may make repeated attempts to communicate, but the messages are just not going to be truly effective until one of them begins to use the other's representation system. One way to improve communication, then, is to listen to the words that other people use, watch their eyes for visual cues, and begin to build rapport with them by switching to their representation system. The numerous proponents of this course of action suggest that it works in sales, with your boss, with your spouse, with your parents, with anyone— not always, but often.

Building upon this knowledge, Bandler and Grinder have found that successful communicators in fact put themselves not only into the other person's representation system but into the same overall frame of reference as well. In what is known as **mirror imaging,** one begins to assume the same body postures and facial expressions and to use the same gestures and eye movements as the other person. These actions contribute to the establishment of a much more solid rapport than might otherwise have been achieved. Mirror imaging—or *pacing*, as it is also called—includes such nonverbal forms of communication as breathing rate and voice tempo. Even the syntax of one's sentences can be modified to pace the other through the communication process. The effectiveness of this approach depends in large measure on the inducement of a semihypnotic trance in the other person. If you move your arm in a gentle swaying motion at the same rate at which the other person is breathing, for example, you will facilitate rapport. The other person will become more at ease and thus more receptive to your communications.[21]

Neurolinguistics—mirror imaging or pacing and the related use of knowledge in regard to representation systems—is not a highly refined science. It is rather a system that seems to work for many people who have practiced it. You should recognize that people do not use only one representation system at all times, that identifying someone's dominant system is not always easy, and that this approach may not work for you. But you will never know until you give it a try. Be careful about the behaviors you choose to mirror. You wouldn't want to mirror aggression, for example. Furthermore, my own experience indicates that if you become too concerned about mirroring images, you may lose sight of what your objectives were in the first place. Nonetheless, some salesmen have reported success in using this approach with customers.

TIPS FOR SUCCESS

1. Be assertive, not passive or aggressive.
2. Know when to use each type of assertion.
3. Listen actively.
4. Recognize ego states and act accordingly.
5. Give positive strokes.
6. Watch body language.
7. Discover other people's preferences in representation systems and learn to relate to them accordingly.

SUMMARY

1. To be used effectively as communication strategies, assertiveness and active listening require that one first determine who owns the problem.
2. One identifies the owner of the problem by determining whose needs are not being satisfied.
3. Assertiveness is called for when one's own needs are not being met.
4. Active listening is called for when the other person's needs are not being met.
5. Assertiveness is based on the rights of individuals.
6. There are four major types of behaviors: assertive, aggressive, passive, and passive-aggressive. Assertive behaviors are believed to be the most productive in the long term.
7. There are several major assertiveness techniques, each of which is most useful in selected situations: mixed-feelings statement, empathic assertion, confrontive assertion, *I*-language assertion, broken record, contract option, and silence or walking away.
8. Assertiveness entails certain risks.
9. Active listening involves the feeding back of both content and feelings to the other person.
10. Active listening is used to develop other people's problem-solving skills, to help them solve their own problems, not to solve their problems for them.
11. Transactional analysis (TA) is based on an analysis of the ego state from which a communication comes and the ego state to which it is directed.
12. TA recognizes six primary ego states: Adult, Nurturing Parent, Critical Parent, Natural Child, Adaptive Child, and Little Professor.
13. The strokes one receives, according to TA, have a major influence on one's personal development as well as on one's current situation.
14. Knowledge of neurolinguistic programming and mirror imaging can be used to increase the effectiveness of communications.

DISCUSSION QUESTIONS

1. How do you know who owns the problem?
2. If neither your needs nor the needs of the other person are being satisfied, who owns the problem?

3. What rights do you believe you have? Do you agree with Thomas Paine's doctrine? (See p. 138.) Why, or why not?

4. What are the various assertive options? How would you use each one?

5. What risks do you run by being assertive?

6. What is meant by feeding back content and feeling in active listening?

7. How should you use transactional analysis?

8. What is your dominant ego state? What is your dominant representational style?

9. How are assertiveness, active listening, transactional analysis, and neurolinguistic programming related? How might each contribute to the creation of an open, trusting, productive, and satisfying environment?

APPLYING HUMAN RELATIONS SKILLS

CASE | **The Promotion**

Carrie was elated by the offer of a promotion to a management position; she was currently a systems analyst. The new job would bring a 45 percent increase in salary. But there was one hitch: she would have to move away from Austin, though not too far away—only to Houston. She looked forward to telling her good news to her husband, Doug. They had always agreed that if either of them were offered a substantial career opportunity outside of Austin, the other would seek a job in the new location. She just knew that Doug would be happy for her.

Carrie and Doug had no children yet, and no plans for any. She was the cheerier, more optimistic of the two. He tended to be quiet and pensive. A microelectronics engineer, he had been with the same firm for almost five years, two of them before he met Carrie. He liked his job and his hard work had recently won him a promotion to associate engineer. He had responded with increased enthusiasm for his work. Management didn't interest him.

Carrie arrived home that day before Doug did. She waited impatiently for him to arrive. Finally, at 6:30, exhausted by the day's efforts, he dragged himself through the front door. She was stunned by his lack of enthusiasm at her announcement.

He tried to sound interested, but inwardly he winced at the thought of moving to Houston. He enjoyed the intellectual atmosphere that surrounded Austin's university and high-tech firms. She assured him that Houston wasn't much different. She was sure he could easily find another job that paid as well as his current one, even better, and they could be happy there. If the job he got in Houston paid no more than he was making now, she would be making about 20 percent more than he did. To Doug, money was not the issue, but he said very little about his unhappiness at the prospect of giving up his job to satisfy her needs.

At work the next day, Friday, Carrie worried that Doug might blow her chance for the promotion. It would be a good idea, she thought, to ask her boss and his wife to dinner the next evening. They accepted.

Doug anticipated an unpleasant Saturday evening. He didn't like Harvey, though Teresa seemed pleasant enough (and totally mismatched with Harvey). Doug was not to be disappointed.

At dinner Harvey talked about the opportunity that Carrie was being offered. The company was growing, the dollars were there. There could be big things in store for her. Doug nodded. The evening progressed much as Doug had expected. Harvey was Mr. Sunshine, full of himself. Carrie smiled and laughed. Teresa was pleasant. But Doug did not care that Harvey and Teresa had loved Houston when they lived there.

It was a cold moment when Harvey and Teresa finally said good night and Carrie and Doug were left alone with their thoughts and needs. They looked at each other apprehensively. Then Doug announced, "I'm not going."

1. Why did this incident occur?
2. How could either active listening or assertiveness—or both—by either Carrie or Doug have changed the outcome of this incident?
3. If you were Doug, what would you have said and when would you have been assertive?
4. If you were Carrie, what would you have said and when would you have used active listening?
5. Describe the patterns of ego states that you see in this case. Describe the pattern of strokes that you see.

Assertiveness Quiz

Test your understanding of assertive, nonassertive, and aggressive behaviors by analyzing the situations and responses below. If you believe the response to the given situation is assertive, place a + in the blank to the right; if you believe it is nonassertive or passive, place a 0 in the blank to the right; if you think it is aggressive, place a − in the blank to the right. The answers may be found on page 159.

EXERCISE

(Scale: Assertive, +; nonassertive, 0; aggressive, −)

Situation	Response	
1. You would like a raise.	"Do you feel that, ah, you could see your way clear to giving me a raise?"	_____
2. A subordinate has been talking on the phone to a friend for twenty minutes.	"I thought you had some work to get out!"	_____
3. A committee of which you are a member has arranged to meet Thursdays at 3:00. The time is convenient for other people but not for you.	"Well, I guess it's OK. I'm not going to be able to attend very often, but it fits everyone else's schedule."	_____
4. Your secretary tells you she plans to take college courses at night and get a degree. You want to discourage her, fearing she will no longer be satisfied to be your secretary.	"Are you sure you want to do that? That's a very heavy load to carry when you're working full-time. I think you're trying to do too much."	_____

(Continued on page 158)

(Scale: Assertive, $+$; nonassertive, 0; aggressive, $-$) *Continued*

Situation	Response	
5. Two clerical workers in your office have been taking long coffee breaks. The work has been piling up. Others have been complaining about their long absences from their desks. You are their supervisor.	"I know how easy it is for time to slip by when you're relaxing and talking to your friends. But your work is piling up, and I would like you to stay within the twenty-minute break time."	_____
6. In a conversation, a man says suddenly, "What is it that these minorities want, anyway?"	"Fairness and equality."	_____
7. A young man just hired from a prominent business school as the new department manager is told by the woman supervisor with twenty years' experience, "That doesn't follow company procedure."	"We're going to be changing more than one thing around here. You may have to learn some new ways of doing things."	_____
8. At a meeting one person often interrupts you when you are speaking.	"Excuse me, I would like to finish my statement."	_____

SOURCE: Adapted from Arthur J. Lange and Patricia Jakubowski, *Responsible Assertiveness Behavior* (Champaign, Ill.: Research Press, 1976), pp. 41–52.

REFERENCES

1. Thomas Gordon, *Leadership Effectiveness Training* (New York: Peter H. Wyden, 1977), pp. 27–48, 93.
2. Arnold A. Lazarus, "On Assertive Behavior: A Brief Note," *Behavior Therapy* 4, no. 5 (October 1973): 697–99.
3. Patricia Jakubowski and Arthur J. Lange, *The Assertiveness Option* (Champaign, Ill.: Research Press, 1977), pp. 8, 9.
4. The first 16 rights are formulated by Thomas Theobald and Doreen Theobald, "TA as a Model for Assertiveness Training," *Transactional Analysis Journal*, January 1979, p. 25; Arthur J. Lange and Patricia Jakubowski, *Responsible Assertiveness Behavior* (Champaign, Ill.: Research Press, 1976), pp. 55, 56; and Herbert Fensterheim and Jean Baer, *Don't Say Yes When You Want to Say No* (New York: David McKay, 1975), p. 35. James Velt, a former student, suggested the final right.
5. Theobald and Theobald, "TA as a Model."
6. Related by the manager to the author.
7. Jakubowski and Lange, *Assertiveness Option*, pp. 12, 13.
8. Ibid., pp. 51–64.
9. Manual J. Smith, *When I Say No, I Feel Guilty* (New York: Dial, 1975), pp. 67–69.
10. Jakubowski and Lange, *Assertiveness Option*, pp. 12–13.
11. Ibid., pp. 69–70.
12. Ibid., pp. 161–63.
13. Ibid., pp. 163–65.
14. Ibid., pp. 165–68.
15. Smith, *When I Say No*, pp. 67–69.
16. Jakubowski and Lange, *Assertiveness Option*, p. 251.
17. Sharon Anthony Bower and Gordon H. Bower, *Asserting Yourself* (Reading, Mass.: Addison-Wesley, 1976), chap. 2.
18. Gordon, *Leadership Effectiveness Training*, chap. 2.
19. Eric Berne, *Games People Play* (New York:

Ballantine Books, 1973); Thomas A. Harris, *I'm OK, You're OK* (New York: Avon, 1973), chap. 3; Muriel James and Dorothy Jongeward, *Born to Win: Transactional Analysis with Gestalt Experiments* (Reading, Mass.: Addison-Wesley, 1977), chaps. 1 and 4; Eric Berne, *What Do You Say After You Say Hello?* (New York: Bantam, 1973).

20. Richard Bandler and John Grinder, *Frogs into Princes: Neurolinguistic Programming* (Moab, Utah: Real People Press, 1979), chap. 1.
21. John Grinder and Richard Bandler, *The Structure of Magic II* (Palo Alto, Calif.: Science and Behavior Books, 1976), p. 15.

Answers to Box and Table

Box Example *(pp. 136–137)*

1. Y
2. O
3. Y
4. N
5. Y
6. N
7. Y, but only if your values tell you that the other person is wrong and that you should speak up when someone steals.
8. Y
9. O, but Y soon, in all probability.
10. Y

Table Quiz *(pp. 157–158)*

1. O
2. −
3. O
4. −
5. +
6. +
7. −
8. +

3

UNDERSTANDING AND IMPROVING GROUP RELATIONSHIPS

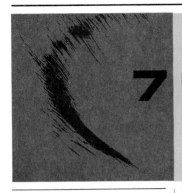

7 GROUP DYNAMICS

LEARNING OBJECTIVES

When you have completed this chapter, you should be able to:
1. Understand why groups form, the types of groups that form, and their formal and informal roles in organizations.
2. Describe the stages of group development, the functioning of groups, and some of their more important characteristics.
3. Identify individual roles in the group.
4. Manage a committee.
5. Describe the proper functioning of a quality circle.
6. Describe the informal organization.

QUALITY AT FORD MOTOR COMPANY

A virtual miracle is taking place at Ford Motor Company. In 86 of its 91 plants, Ford employees at all levels meet weekly in groups with their supervisors to deal with problems connected with production, quality, and the work environment. Ford now has to be the most participative major manufacturer in the United States. Ford has even gone so far as to install buttons that permit workers to stop the production line—an innovation that some people suggest must be causing Henry Ford to roll over in his grave. What caused this

turnaround in management style at Ford? The quest for quality.

Facing tremendous competition, especially from the quality-conscious Japanese, Ford leaders recognized that action had to be taken to improve the Ford product. The answer was "employee involvement" (EI). David A. Curson, chairman of UAW Local 898 at Ford's Rawsonville, Michigan, plant, comments, "It's democracy in the workplace. It makes the people more aware of their own self-worth and intelligence, and it makes them better union members."

Quality has indeed improved at Ford: surveys of car buyers indicate a 55 percent drop in "things that go wrong" from 1980 to 1984. Ford's advertisements, based on similar buyer surveys, proclaim that Ford is the number one quality car made in America.

The main thrust of Ford's program is trust and cooperation—between the company and the union, between the company and its workers, between supervisors and subordinates, between work group members. Work group cohesiveness is viewed as especially important. Quality circles have been established, and team building is employed to make these and all work groups more effective.

Source: "What's Creating an Industrial Miracle at Ford?" *Business Week*, July 30, 1984, pp. 80, 81; "Awakening of a Sleeping Giant . . . Ford's Employee Involvement Program," *Management Review*, June 1981, pp. 15–21.

TABLE 7.1   The Dynamics of Formal and Informal Groups

TYPES OF GROUPS	STAGES OF GROUP DEVELOPMENT	MEANS OF FUNCTIONING	POSITIVE RESULTS
Formal	Mutual acceptance	Roles	Effectiveness
Task	Decision making	Structures	Efficiency
Command	Motivation	Norms	Motivation
Informal	Control	Cohesiveness	Trust
Friendship		Size	Employee
Interest		Leadership	satisfaction
		Decision making	

"There's strength in numbers."
ANONYMOUS

What is it about groups that makes them do the things they do? What is it about leaders that makes them do the things they do when they must work with groups? Why are some groups more effective than others? Why are groups so important to organizations and to individuals? Why, when Ford needed to improve productivity and quality, did it turn to its work groups as a basis for change? (See the Human Relations Happening on p. 163.)

This chapter examines groups, both formal and informal; why they are formed; their stages of development; how they function; and the positive results of groups. Table 7.1 shows these four aspects of groups. Next the individual–group interface is examined. The latter portion of the chapter focuses on what managers can do to work well with groups, especially how the manager can best manage two specific groups: the quality circle, such as those used by Ford Motor Company, and the committee, misused in almost every organization. The primary relationships examined in this chapter are individual-to-group and group-to-individual interactions.

WHY EXAMINE GROUPS?

Much of work is accomplished through group activity. Tasks are often assigned to groups, and groups naturally develop to satisfy individual needs. Groups dominate life both at and away from work. The family is a group. Friends meet in groups. A fraternity is a group. Athletic teams are groups.

Within the organization, groups often make decisions. Groups establish norms and influence their members to adhere to those norms. Sometimes the group's norms conflict with the organization's objectives. Some informal groups may countermand formal organizational authority.

Both formal and informal groups have leaders. One of the leader's primary tasks is to provide task leadership for the formal group. Leaders have followers; otherwise they would not be leaders. Sometimes managers find themselves without followers because they are not really leaders, just managers.

Many people believe that groups make better decisions than their individual members would normally arrive at alone. Yet a group probably does not arrive at any better decisions than a superior individual would have made independently. In recent years considerable attention has been focused on the organization of work activity in groups as opposed to individual specialization, partly because of the supposed advantages of synergy—combined action—in decision making. The culture of organizations depends greatly on groups, and on leaders' ability to discern the proper combinations of behaviors that will cause groups to follow them. Ford, GM, Chrysler, Lockheed, Martin Marietta, Hyatt, Honeywell, Foremost-McKesson, and thousands of other organizations have turned to groups as a major means of changing their culture in order to improve productivity.

There are two primary groups within any organization: the formal and the informal. The manager must ascertain the right combination of actions to cause the two to work in harmony.

FORMAL AND INFORMAL GROUPS

T. M. Mills suggests that a **group** consists of "two or more persons who come into contact for a purpose and who consider the contact meaningful."[1] The group, then, has a purpose, it has interaction, it has meaning. The **formal group** consists of individuals who work together, either on a series of tasks (the **task group**) or simply because of authority distribution within the organization (the **command group**).[2] These groups are designated as formal groups because each comes together as the result of the formal organization's structuring process. (Structure is the creation of jobs and the distribution of authority to accomplish those jobs.) An example of the task group is the team that assembles any of various product units in a manufacturing plant. An example of the command group is the faculty of a university school of business. Very little, if any, of the faculty's primary work function—teaching—is performed in a group, yet its members are grouped together for purposes of authority.

An **informal group** is any group that is not formally organized. Informal groups play important roles in most organizations. We are by nature gregarious, and informal groups satisfy our social needs. Informal groups also arise for other reasons. What might some possible reasons be? What informal groups do you belong to? Table 7.2 summarizes the purposes, structures, and processes of formally and informally organized groups. Note that when the organizations of formal and informal groups do not match well, the consequences can be serious. Table 7.2 indicates the similarities of formal and informal groups and the differences between them. The process of the formal group, for example, revolves primarily around tasks, whereas the process of the informal group revolves primarily around interactions. Organizations are very concerned about informal groups because they often serve as alternative need satisfiers and sources of power for employees who might otherwise look to the formal organization for the satisfaction of their needs.

All groups form for the purpose of satisfying needs of some kind. Formal groups are formed to satisfy the needs of the formal organization. Informal groups are formed to satisfy the needs of organization members that are not being satisfied by the formal group. Physical proximity also contributes to group development.

TABLE 7.2   The Purposes, Structures, and Processes of Formally and Informally
Organized Groups

	PURPOSE	STRUCTURE	PROCESS
Formal organization	Adequate financial return for effort, investment, and risk	Jobs, positions, organizational units; formal roles, relations, and rules; designated authority and accountability	Tasks, procedures, work-flow sequences, formal organizational policies
Informal organization	Satisfaction of personal, social, and psychological needs	Personal influence or power based on interpersonal and group skills, friendships, cliques, likes and dislikes, and ability to use job processes to advantage	Interpersonal processes, group processes, intergroup processes
Possible consequences of serious mismatch	Low productivity, low profitability, may fail	Management and supervision have authority but lack power to make things happen the way they should and lack respect of workers. Low productivity, low profitability, may fail.	Formal processes misused to satisfy personal needs. Production wasteful, inefficient; everything bogged down in red tape. Buck passing, finger pointing, game playing. Low productivity, low profitability, may fail.

SOURCE: From *Organizational Team Building* by Earl J. Ends and Curtis W. Page. Copyright ©
1977. Reprinted by permission of Winthrop Publishers, Inc., Cambridge, Massachusetts.

THE FORMATION OF FORMAL GROUPS

Formal groups are formed, at least conceptually, for the purpose of accomplishing the organization's mission, or more specifically the organizational subunits' portions of that mission, known as objectives. The objective may be to win a football championship, to put together the most efficient hamburger products operation (an objective of Wendy's), or to have the most productive sewing line in the shirt industry (an objective of Arrow Shirts). All organizational objectives are eventually parceled out to groups or individuals to accomplish. The logical grouping of these tasks and the distribution of authority to accomplish them are the bases of organization structure. Think of your own work organization. How is it structured? What roles do groups play? Most organizations are structured according to jobs (horizontal structure) and authority to do those jobs (vertical structure). Jobs are typically grouped together in departments. Departments may be organized according to process (the economic functions of production, marketing, finance, personnel) or task specialization (such as cost accounting versus auditing); product line or major business segment (such as minicomputers versus mainframe hardware computers); geographic area (section of the country, state, city, and the like); client (such as the Coca-Cola account versus the Bank of America account); or size (commonly used in the military, which organizes its members into platoons of 10, companies of 100, and so on). As Figure 7.1 indicates, the large organization usually employs a mixture of these horizontal structures.

FIGURE 7.1 *Typical multidepartmental organization*

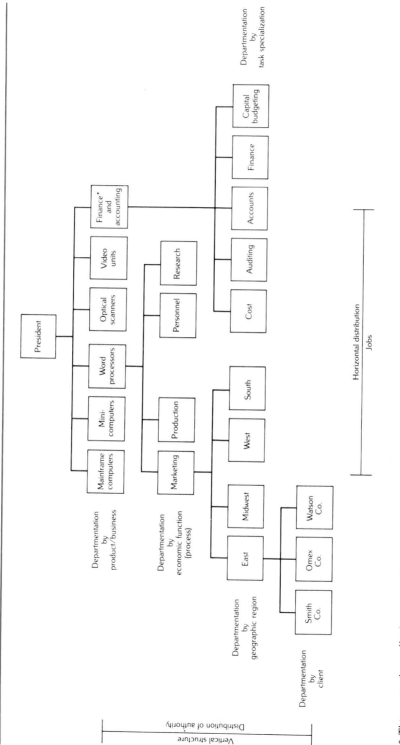

* *This particular staff job is normally centralized, that is, operating divisions do not usually have their own finance department.*

The principle of span of control usually groups similar tasks or jobs at any organizational level in a manageable size, usually five to nine persons, but the number may vary according to any number of factors. Authority is then distributed to managers, to work groups, and to individuals to accomplish their jobs. When decision power over elements of the job are included in the position, the employee is said to participate. In this instance authority is decentralized and delegated.

The Linking Pin   The manager of each work unit, whether it be an office, an assembly line, a team, a plant, or an economic or product division, is a **linking pin** that connects at least three groups: the group the manager heads, the group of peer managers of other groups in the same division of the organization, and the group of managers one step above in the organizational hierarchy (see Figure 7.2).[3] Modern organization theory (the theory of organization structuring) tells us that organizations are formed of groups—groups of managers and those who are managed. This linking pin function, then, is critical to the success of the organization because it links the groups that make up the organization.

The linking pin manager is primarily responsible for implementation. This process requires coordination and communication of organizational objectives, which come from above in the hierarchy, with individual objectives, which come from below. Influence is also an essential task. Coordination with peer managers facilitates this process. Early in the history of management practices, horizontal coordination was not viewed as essential, but in today's modern management situation, it is viewed as vital. At Honeywell, for example, the work team has become the central focus of a "total employee involvement program" in which work groups determine their own courses of action in regard to numerous work decisions. Leadership is viewed as central to the success

FIGURE 7.2   *Linking pins between lower- and upper-level groups in an organization*

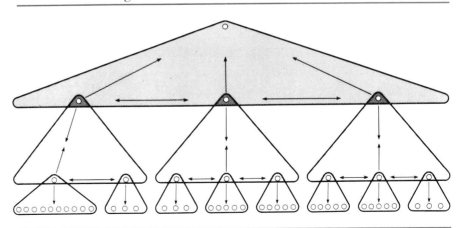

SOURCE: Rensis Likert, *New Patterns of Management* (New York: McGraw-Hill, 1961), pp. 114–15. Reprinted by permission.

"Jay, I'd like you to retract that crack about Bill's being a fiscal illiterate so that we may proceed with our board meeting."

Drawing by Opie; © 1980 by The New Yorker Magazine, Inc.

of such programs. To that end, managers are expected to exhibit competence in interpersonal relations. (See the Human Relations Happening on Honeywell.) Thus they are expected to be linking pins, "linking management with employees, employees with management, and employees with each other."[4]

HUMAN RELATIONS HAPPENING

GROUP LEADERSHIP AT HONEYWELL

Honeywell's views of group leadership have been summarized as follows:

Leadership should be the ability of those leading work units (managers, supervisors, engineers, technical support, and group leaders) to create an atmosphere of acceptance, openness, and trust that will properly motivate members of the work units.

Interpersonal competence should be the ability to relate to people in a considerate and effective way.

This means that the leader:

1. Cares.
   a. Gives positive feedback for a good job.
   b. Shows confidence in employees.
   c. Is fair and objective, not vindictive.
   d. Practices what is preached; does not ask for something that he or she would not be willing to do.
   e. Has a down-to-earth, person-to-person approach; acts as part of a team.
   f. Is compassionate and understanding; creates an atmosphere of acceptance and trust.
2. Skillfully communicates.
   a. *Listens actively.*
   b. Clarifies priorities.
   c. Is available.
   d. Links management with employees, employees with management, and employees with each other. Communicates effectively to all people on all shifts through all levels of the organization.
   e. Provides feedback for both good and bad work.
   f. Talks openly and gives straight answers about what is happening.
3. Guides, inspires.
   a. Encourages advancement.
   b. Gives direction to the work unit.
   c. Is proud of, loyal to, and supportive of employees.

   d. Has a sense of vision—a dream that is blended with employees' dreams.
   e. Projects a positive attitude.
   f. Is courageous.
   g. Sets a good example; is friendly, not moody.
   h. Enjoys his or her work.
   i. Keeps promises; plows through red tape.

Administrative competence should be the ability to achieve organizational goals within the bounds of our business constraints and policies and procedures. This means that the leader:

1. Understands his or her job.
2. Understands employees' jobs.
   a. Utilizes people's skills effectively.
   b. Is concerned with employees' work and the workflow.
   c. Stands up for and shows confidence in employees.
3. Takes immediate action.
   a. Does not ignore problems.
   b. Follows up on promises.
   c. Gets tough when necessary.
   d. Takes action to remove poor performers.
   e. Assures that next in command knows role and has authority to act.
   f. Provides proper human resources for all shifts and all levels of the organization.

SOURCE: William L. VanHorn and William D. Stimmett, "The Ideal Work Environment: Total Employee Involvement," *S.A.M. Advanced Management Journal*, Autumn 1984, pp. 43–45.

THE FORMATION OF INFORMAL GROUPS

Informal groups form for one primary reason: to satisfy employee needs that the organization or manager does not satisfy. The organization and the manager must satisfy as many of the needs of subordinates as is practical. Needs they do not satisfy will be satisfied elsewhere. Obviously the organization and manager cannot satisfy all needs of all subordinates, but they should satisfy those they are capable of satisfying efficiently. Otherwise, one of the informal groups that arise will undoubtedly be counterproductive to the aims of the organization and the manager. Not all informal groups are negative from the organizational viewpoint. **Friendship groups**—groups that satisfy social needs—naturally arise in the course of human interactions within and among work locations. **Interest groups**—those formed on the basis of any common interest, from bowling to international relations—can also further the organization's interests. But when major need satisfiers are not provided, informal groups of employees have a way of becoming formal groups that make demands instead of requests—unions. Referring first to the Maslow hierarchy and then to the other needs outlined in Chapter 3, let us examine how the informal organization can provide need satisfiers.

Physiological Needs   Unions, which are formal groups that develop out of informal groups, have become powerful for two or three basic reasons. One is that they give employees the opportunity to obtain more compensation and benefits than they could usually hope to get if they approached the organization individually. There is strength in numbers and there is strength in collective bargaining. Are you familiar with a union? Has it provided increased satisfaction of the physiological needs of its members? Did informal gripes become formalized in union demands? Groups may also offer the individual the opportunity for additional income when compensation is based on group rather than individual performance. Professional athletes in championship playoff games are compensated on the basis of their membership in the winning or losing team, and some business firms have established group compensation plans. Such Japanese firms as Toyota base their compensation programs on group performance, not individual performance. Certain types of groups, partnerships and joint ventures in particular, may also offer their members a better chance to succeed economically than they might individually.

Safety or Security Needs   There is safety as well as strength in numbers. A second major reason that unions have been successful in organizing employees is their ability to counteract poor supervision and inappropriate management rules and policies. Organized labor strives to prevent arbitrary action by management. Sometimes nonperforming employees are protected by union policies, but the positive intent is to protect the employee from the unjust actions of managers. If you examine most unions, you will find that they started as informal groups that arose in response to individual needs that were not being satisfied.

Social Needs   We are by nature social animals. Most people enjoy being with others. Employees, regardless of position or rank within an organization, seek to talk with, eat lunch with, take breaks with, and enjoy after-work activities with others. Much mechanized work and much clerical work prohibit significant interaction with others. Such jobs foster a phenomenon known as **worker alienation**. When workers are alienated, they do not identify with the formal organization or with their work. Common indications of alienation include absenteeism, high turnover rates, reduced productivity, and reduced quality of work. Unions have also been organized to campaign against the work systems that cause such feelings of isolation. The organization can counter alienation by emphasizing company-related group activities. By pro-

"All for one, one for all."
ALEXANDER DUMAS

viding bowling teams, softball leagues, and quality circles (work-related groups that meet periodically to improve quality), the organization can do much to satisfy social needs and prevent absenteeism.

Esteem Needs   All groups need leaders, and in every group one individual tends to be dominant. The leaders of informal groups tend to have a high level of self-esteem and to enjoy the esteem of others. Simply belonging to a group may raise self-esteem, too. Members of the in-group almost automatically have higher self-esteem than people to whom membership has been denied. If you are the member of a winning or successful team, you share in the team's success.

In the workplace, membership in the lunch group, the bridge group, or the league-leading basketball team may bring self- and social esteem. The organization can satisfy the need for esteem, but this is a very difficult task when the job itself is largely monotonous and dull and is accorded little social value. Still, the organization must try. Again the approaches noted in earlier chapters are applicable. Some problems, however, appear insurmountable.

Self-actualization   Belonging to a group may increase one's self-actualization in several ways—by providing the opportunity to lead, for example, or by providing fulfillment through group accomplishment. Quality circles are especially important in this regard.

Very few jobs are designed to provide self-actualization, although job enrichment at least offers an opportunity to satisfy this need in many organizations. Given the increased need levels of today's employees, organizations must consider self-actualization needs, or again employees may seek to satisfy those needs through a group that may act against the organization. Have you joined any groups in order to achieve self-actualization?

Power   Informal groups help to satisfy the need for power, for control over others, especially for the leader. We noted earlier that a leader emerges in every group. Control of the group provides the leader with power. Unfortunately, too many managers have a great need for power over the members of the formal work group. Because they are unwilling to share that power, counterproductive informal work groups and leaders may emerge. Decision-making work teams help provide their members with control over their individual situations. General Motors has recognized the importance of this need, and for this and other reasons plans to provide the members of the teams that produce its new Saturn car with substantial power over work design, machinery purchases, and all variable costs.[5]

Role Fulfillment   Informal groups give many people the chance to play out roles that they enjoy. The leader gets to lead, the followers get to follow. The person who organizes a poker-playing group of co-workers gets to play poker, and so do the other members of the group. By playing on antiorganizational sentiments, some individuals fulfill their need to be troublemakers. Other roles will be discussed later in this chapter.

Truth, Beauty, and Justice   By forming groups that visit art museums, read and criticize each other's poetry, or support the local ballet, people are able to satisfy aesthetic needs they might not otherwise be able to satisfy.

The people who formed Amnesty International, first informally, then formally, undoubtedly were attempting to achieve objectives they felt were extremely important, doing a job that had to be done. Have you joined any groups in an effort to achieve aesthetic satisfaction or justice? What were they?

Bernard Bass has proposed four **stages of group development**: mutual acceptance, decision making, motivation, and control.[6] Formal and informal groups go through the same stages. Let us take a typical work situation and see how an informal group may develop through these stages.

THE STAGES OF GROUP DEVELOPMENT

Mutual Acceptance   The new midwestern office of Transatlantic Publications had recently opened. One publisher, three editors, and twelve staff members had been assembled. The staff consisted of five production people, three secretaries, two assistant editors, and two artists. The editors and publisher were on the road about 50 percent of the time, so the twelve staff members really were the only ones who had frequent contact with each other. Soon an informal friendship group had formed among two of the production people, one of the artists, and two of the secretaries—all women. The two assistant editors, one man and one woman, and the two senior production people, one man and one woman, also formed a friendship group. Each group began to go to lunch together, and seemed to share many similar interests.

Decision Making   The all-female group soon learned that if they worked together, they could make each other's jobs a lot easier. The two secretaries passed on information quickly to the production people, who in turn were careful to give immediate feedback to the secretaries. The artist and the production people worked closely together and reached many joint decisions, which were forwarded to senior production personnel, assistant editors, and editors.

Motivation   Partly because the work was rewarding and exciting, partly because the people involved were eager to do well in their new jobs, the group quickly became efficient and motivated. Work was a continual subject, and everyone seemed eager to make sure that Transatlantic's books were the best.

Control   Fortunately, the publisher assisted them in their efforts. She reasoned that if she rewarded her staff for successful efforts, their continued motivation would lead to expanding sales and increased profits. Soon the informal group began to raise its norms. Members encouraged each other to higher levels of productivity.

As for conforming outwardly, and living your own life inwardly, I do not think much of that.
HENRY DAVID THOREAU

HOW GROUPS FUNCTION

All groups, whether formal or informal, form and function in the same basic ways. Group members fill two primary roles: task and maintenance roles. Certain individual roles must be carried out as well. Groups have definite structures and norms. Their effectiveness is influenced by the degree of conformity they require or encourage, their cohesiveness, their size, their leadership, and their decision processes.

ROLES

Task Roles   **Task roles** relate to the task that the formal group is assigned or that the informal group has determined to undertake. These are problem-solving roles, decision-making roles, solution-seeking roles. Kenneth Benne and Paul Sheats have identified twelve task roles, among them roles concerned with offering new ideas, gathering information, giving opinions, coordination, refining problems and solutions, energizing, and record keeping.[7] It is assumed that in the typical pyramidal organization these roles are performed by the manager, but in reality, especially in a democratic/participative management situation, any group member may assume one or more of these roles. In GM's Saturn project, for example, "work teams will perform these functions on a fully participative basis. They will operate without foremen."[8] In the informal group, these roles are often filled by members as well as by leaders.

Earlier we noted the importance of the manager as a linking pin. Much of the manager's success as a linking pin depends on his or her ability to perform most of these roles successfully. As Chapters 1 through 9 emphasize, leaders should facilitate problem solving and task completion. They establish the "right climate." They help members to satisfy their individual needs, within reason. They represent the group, its values, and its objectives when the group interacts with other groups. But most important, as the roles identified above suggest, they are also responsible for moving the organization forward, for achieving organizational objectives. The same comments apply to informal leaders. They, too, facilitate, represent, establish climates, and help their groups to achieve their objectives.

Think of a group to which you belong, formal or informal. How does the leader perform these roles? Is he or she a good leader?

Building and Maintenance Roles   If a group is not to dissolve, its members must take actions that support and maintain it. Benne and Sheats identify seven major **building and maintenance roles**: roles devoted to encouraging members, mediating differences, compromising, communicating, setting standards, observing, and following passively.[9]

Some of these roles are often performed by the manager. Some are not. Obviously no one can be all things to all people. Thus leaders need to draw others into performing some of these roles, but they also must be aware of the way these roles affect their own leadership actions. Leaders must be prepared to recognize who is naturally performing these roles and use these persons and their abilities. Think of a group to which you belong. Who most often performs these roles?

Individual Roles   Most groups have some members who are playing **individual roles** in the group setting, in an effort to satisfy their own needs rather than those of the group as a whole. Benne and Sheats identify the following as typical individual roles: aggressor/attacker, blocker and resister, recognition seeker, self-confessor, playboy, dominator, help seeker, and special interest pleader.[10] Think of a group to which you belong. Who fills these roles?

If you will take a few minutes to reflect on groups to which you have belonged, you will identify people who fill several roles in each of the three major categories in the group. When you are a leader, you must make certain that group roles are carried out and that individual roles are minimized, because they contribute nothing to the group's purposes. You must learn to guard against individuals who would undermine group efforts.

J. L. Moreno has developed an approach to the structure of groups known as **sociometry**.[11] Figure 7.3 identifies group structure as consisting of a leader, a primary group, a fringe group, and an out-group.

GROUP STRUCTURE

The formal group leader/manager will usually not be a major informal group leader. After all, there are many informal groups based on many interests and friendships. It is not likely that any one leader/manager could be the leader of many informal groups, nor should any manager try to be. Again, all that is necessary is to be alert to these groups and their potential meanings for the formal group.

The primary group, also popularly known as the in-group, consists of the group members of highest status—active members, members accorded all of the group's rights and responsibilities. In Figure 7.3, A, B, C, D, E, and F are members of the primary group.

The fringe or secondary group consists of people who have lesser status and fewer group privileges, but who still have greater acceptance than people whom the group does not recognize at all. G, H, I, and J are members of the fringe group.

FIGURE 7.3   *Group sociometry*

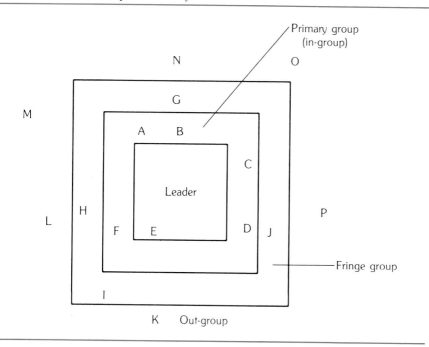

The out-group consists of people who have no membership, no privileges, and no interests in the group under discussion. These people may belong to many other groups, but not to this one.

Communication tends to be highest among members of the primary group. These people are on friendly but more distant terms with members of the fringe group. They do not communicate at all with the out-group. In the work organization, the manager must ensure communication among all group members and must also take steps to forestall or at least to minimize the exclusion of an out-group.

Overlapping Group Structures   Because of the communication among primary- and secondary-group members, and because a secondary member of one group may be a primary member of another group and vice versa, an interesting phenomenon develops—**the grapevine**, so named because its tendrils seem to reach everywhere at random. Figure 7.4 depicts the grapevine as it might function in a typical organization.

Much has been said and written about the grapevine. Just what is it? Technically, it is the communication pattern that develops among the members

FIGURE 7.4   *The grapevine*

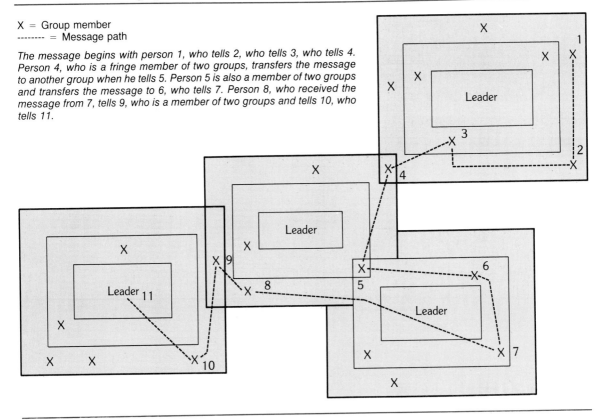

X = Group member
-------- = Message path

The message begins with person 1, who tells 2, who tells 3, who tells 4. Person 4, who is a fringe member of two groups, transfers the message to another group when he tells 5. Person 5 is also a member of two groups and transfers the message to 6, who tells 7. Person 8, who received the message from 7, tells 9, who is a member of two groups and tells 10, who tells 11.

of interacting informal groups within a formal organization. Practically speaking, it is the path of communication within the organization which exists outside the formal channels. Some people say such communication needs to be kept to a minimum. Some say managers should use it to their advantage. We do know that it is generally accurate and often faster than formal channels.

Keith Davis has examined the organizational grapevine for over thirty years. "With the rapidity of a burning powder train," Davis asserts, "information flows out of the woodwork, past the manager's door and the janitor's mop closet, through steel walls or construction-glass partitions." The messages are often "symbolic expressions of feelings." For example, if a rumor says the boss may quit, and he or she is not going to, it may very well be that the employees wish it were true. Among Davis's findings:

1. Grapevines are accurate 75 percent to 95 percent of the time.
2. There are only a few sources that supply the entire informal network.
3. Admittedly, the grapevine does have some dramatic failures in accuracy.
4. The grapevine actually is a psychological reflection of employee interest in the organization or its members.
5. Levels of activity in the informal network parallel those in the formal network.
6. Troublemakers sometimes use the grapevine. All negative rumors, whether started by troublemakers or not, are best handled by truth, told directly by management to employees early in the situation in question.

Davis concludes that wise managers "feed, water, cultivate the grapevine" because it "cannot be abolished, rubbed out, hidden under a basket, chopped down, tied up or stopped. It is as hard to kill as the mythical glass snake which, when struck, broke into fragments and grew a new snake out of each piece."[12]

GROUP NORMS

Formal groups have standards and informal groups have norms. **Group norms** are required types or levels of performance or behavior. If you have ever worked on a construction project, you know very well the meaning of group norms. While your employer may have wanted you to work at a certain pace, it is most likely that the informal group of your co-workers wanted you to work at a significantly slower pace. And they do have a way of enforcing their norms, don't they? The odds are that you soon learned to slow down and take life a little easier. This practice is common in other industries as well as construction, but in construction, the total amount of work available has a definite limit. Thus the faster you work, the more quickly you are out of work. The informal group's motto seems to be: "Only fools work themselves out of a job."

Another classic example of group norms was seen on television during a truckers' strike. One union member had not gotten the word that the union members had not yet approved the new contract. He was not supposed to report for work, but he did. Three or four of the picketers took it upon themselves to yank him literally from his truck.

Group norms, or standards of performance and other conduct, are followed in varying degrees by various members. But any norm that is particularly important to the group will usually be adhered to very strictly. Otherwise, the deviant member may be subjected to disciplinary action by the other members or by the leader. Depending on the nature of the group, such disciplinary actions can range from a reprimand to a bullet.

GROUPTHINK: THE PROBLEM OF CONFORMITY

Because we need to belong to groups and because groups exercise control over their members, people often conform to rigid and sometimes irrational behavior requirements. When self-esteem becomes extremely dependent on the group, when individualism is not highly regarded, group members will behave in quite similar ways. The designer jeans phenomenon is a classic example of conformity. You're just not "in" if your jeans don't bear a particular label. At the workplace, the informal group may establish productivity norms below (occasionally even above) company standards. To belong, and sometimes for reasons of safety, people usually adhere to these norms.

Groupthink, according to Irving Janis, is a phenomenon that arises when "concurrence seeking becomes so dumb that in a cohesive 'in' group it tends to override realistic appraisal and alternative courses of action."[13] To simplify a bit, we might say that one apple spoils the whole barrel. Groups that are extremely cohesive tend to seek complete unanimity of opinion. The groupthink phenomenon can become detrimental to decision making. Janis cites Watergate as a prime example of groupthink: the leader, in this case Richard Nixon, was surrounded by yes-men who did not challenge his assumptions and therefore did not act creatively or consider alternative courses of action. Janis identifies seven symptoms of groupthink:

1. Illusions of invulnerability by the group.
2. Collective rationalization by the group.
3. Unquestioned belief in the group's morality.
4. Stereotyping of the enemy as evil.
5. Exertion of direct pressure on deviate members of the group.
6. Self-censorship of deviate behavior by individual group members.
7. An illusion of unanimity among group members.

The dangers of groupthink can be minimized by team building, organizational development, management development, education of leaders and group members, and encouragement of an organizational culture that honors and rewards original thinking. We want groups to be cohesive, but we don't want them to be so cohesive that individual members, including the leader, lose their identity. Nor do we want members of groups to become so wedded to group norms that they fail in their roles as decision makers—fail to see proper objectives, viable alternatives, or their own biases in evaluating alternatives.

If an organization is to be effective, it must work through group norms, not against them. Organizational managers must make certain that the organization's objectives are congruent with group norms and vice versa. Ideally, the work group embraces the organization's objectives and makes them its own. The U.S. Marine Corps is outstandingly successful in inculcating this attitude. The welfare of the Corps is far more important to its members than the welfare of any individual; at the same time, the Corps encourages its members to care for the welfare of each individual Marine. By applying group norms, the Corps capitalizes on the group process rather than resisting it.

Cohesiveness is the tendency of group members to wish to maintain their membership in the group rather than to leave it. The cohesiveness of group members is usually positively correlated with their productivity and satisfaction when the group is in agreement with formal organizational objectives. Thus if cohesiveness can be created within the group, its members' productivity and satisfaction will usually increase. How does the leader promote cohesiveness, and how can members contribute to the process? By carrying out the task, and building and maintenance roles, and by following proper individual and group human relations leadership behaviors. Sometimes groups may become cohesive in opposition to the manager or the organization. In such cases, the organization's objectives are seldom achieved, at least not efficiently.

COHESIVENESS

Groups of any size can function, but the optimum **group size** appears to be between five and twelve members. Various studies find various sizes to be optimum, and different situations call for groups of different sizes.

GROUP SIZE

The larger the group, the greater the opportunities for interaction (an important function of groups), the more inputs into decision making (necessary for the operation of the synergy noted earlier), and the greater the possibilities for division of labor. At the same time, the larger the group, the less each individual's chance to contribute to discussion. Subgroups may emerge within large groups, each subgroup attempting to achieve its own goals rather than those of the group as a whole. Communication becomes more difficult as the size of the group increases, and openness among members appears to diminish. Recognition is difficult to distribute equally to everyone in a large group.

The optimum group size is a membership just large enough to serve the group's function. That size is determined by an examination of the major contingency variables. But realistically, a group much larger than twelve persons becomes difficult to manage. Unless groups are self-managing, the advantages of maintaining a multitude of small groups may be counterbalanced by the costs of paying a multitude of managers to head them.

Leadership is the process of deciding how employees are to be treated and of putting those decisions into practice for the purpose of influencing employees to work toward the accomplishment of organizational objectives. Leaders have a wide range of behaviors to choose from in their efforts to influence employee motivation. In the basic influence process the manager assesses the needs of the individual or of the group, offers appropriate satisfiers, and rewards performance. The actions that individual managers can take to satisfy needs, both their own and their subordinates', may be placed in four basic categories: those that are task-oriented, aimed at achieving organizational or group ob-

LEADERSHIP

Groups and individual factors are merely different aspects of the same phenomena in constant interaction with each other.

KURT LEWIN

jectives; those that are designed to forge or strengthen relationships between manager and subordinates; the allocation or control of rewards, either intrinsic or extrinsic; and actions designed to facilitate or hinder the participation of subordinates in decision making. In the course of these four forms of behavior, the manager's attitude may cause the relationship with the subordinate to be positive or negative. The leadership role is explored in greater detail in Chapter 8.

THE DECISION PROCESS

Groups may arrive at decisions in many ways. The most satisfactory **group decision process** is characterized by a large number of inputs from each individual member, upon which other members may build. Group decision making is often superior to individual decision making in the quantity and quality of the decisions reached. If two heads are better than one, ten may be better still: a group will approach a problem from a multitude of angles, generate far more ideas than one person is likely to arrive at alone, and be able to elaborate on a solution suggested by any of its members. So, at least, many people believe. Yet there is little evidence to assume that decisions made by groups are necessarily better than those made by individuals—especially by superior individuals.

THE RESULTS OF GROUP ACTIVITY

Proper group functioning leads to effectiveness and efficiency (which together equal productivity), motivation, trust, and the members' satisfaction.

Groups can be effective, or they can choose to be counterproductive. Only if the manager functions properly, so that the group can then function properly, are organizational objectives likely to be achieved. Even if objectives are reached, the efficiency with which they are reached has to be considered. If you must choose between effectiveness and efficiency, it is better to be effective, but it is ultimately best to be both—and be productive. Only where group synergism is found will productivity be achieved.

Membership in a group helps to motivate individuals if they are led and rewarded properly. Trust develops when the leader's and members' behaviors are appropriate. Employee satisfaction does not necessarily contribute to effectiveness and efficiency, trust, and motivation, but it usually does. Appropriate leadership choices promote all of these positive results of group membership. The leader's role is explored in Chapter 8.

The results of group activities are related to the reasons for the group's formation, though not always directly, since the formal and informal reasons are not always the same, and the objectives for which a group was formed are not always achieved. How well do you understand groups? Answer the questions on "You and Groups" and find out. They are designed to encourage you to recognize in yourselves some qualities you may have and other qualities it may be desirable for you to develop.

Your knowledge of groups can be used appropriately, or it can be misused. Earlier we saw a positive example from the book publishing industry; in another case, at a newspaper, a manager attempted to use the group to make himself look better. He knew that the organizational climate survey (a questionnaire that included a large section on each manager) would be administered to all employees in a few weeks. He seemed to sense that he might not fare well. Since top management was concerned about each manager's rating (subordinates' ratings of their managers were summarized in a total for each manager), he felt he should take action to ensure that his rating was high. He wanted a cohesive group standing behind him.

He began to bring in doughnuts for his department each morning. Suddenly he was everyone's buddy. But alas, he became too zealous and too obvious. He failed to understand how groups really work. The group became cohesive, all right—not behind him but in opposition to him. His climate survey results were very negative. He retaliated against the group, but not for long. Through the grapevine, the group managed to get him transferred to a nonmanagement position within a few months.

TEST YOURSELF

YOU AND GROUPS

Below are matched pairs of questions, the first requiring a yes or no answer, the second asking you to analyze your answer. Check the response, either yes or no, that most closely matches your perception of your personal situation. Then read the b question in each set of numbered questions and think about your own abilities and characteristics relative to group membership.

1.a. Do you feel comfortable in working with a group?   Yes_____ No_____
b. Consider the likelihood that you will work in a group in almost any job that you will ever have. If your answer is no, what does your answer indicate? If your answer is yes, what does this indicate?

2.a. In any group to which you belonged in the past, did the members feel a strong sense of belonging?   Yes_____ No_____
b. What did the leader do to create this sense of belonging? Could you create such a sense of belonging in a group now?

3.a. If you were the leader of a work group, could you make the environment warm and relaxed?   Yes_____ No_____
b. What would you do to achieve this result?

4.a. Think of a group to which you have belonged. Was the leader interested in you personally, as an individual?   Yes_____ No_____
b. If your answer is yes, what did the leader do to convince you of his or her personal interest? If the answer is no, what should the leader have done to create a feeling of personal interest?

5.a. Think of a group to which you belonged. Was it able to arrive at satisfactory solutions to problems?   Yes_____ No_____
b. Why, or why not?

6.a. Were rewards given out for participation in groups to which you belonged?   Yes_____ No_____
b. If yes, what were those rewards and how were they distributed?

QUALITY CIRCLES

Quality circles represent an application of the group process to problem solving in industrial and other settings. The groups known as quality circles (QC's), according to Laurie Fitzgerald and Joseph Murphy, "consist of three to twelve employees who perform the same work or share the same work area and function and meet on a regular basis, normally one hour per week on company time, in order to apply specific techniques and tools learned in extensive training to problems affecting their work and work area; subsequently they present solutions and recommendations to their management for the authorization of these solutions."[14] In order to be successful, quality circles seem to have four basic prerequisites. First, management must sincerely want to help each employee reach the maximum of his or her potential. Second, employees must participate voluntarily, not under compulsion. Third, a structured process must be developed for problem solving, and employees must be provided with the tools, techniques, and training that will enable them to contribute to solutions to problems. Fourth, management must provide the time and space that the program requires and support the ideas that emerge from it.[15] One company's guidelines for quality circles are seen in the Human Relations Happening on page 183.

Quality circles (QC's) were first instituted in the United States by the Lockheed Space and Missile Unit in Sunnyvale, California, in 1974. Since then the concept has spread rapidly. Most of the *Fortune* 500 firms have investigated quality circles and a large number have tried them, typically with good results. Thousands of other firms are using them as well. Quality circles are usually introduced only in selected areas of a firm; they are not typically found throughout the organization. Experience has taught us that they work extremely well in manufacturing situations. They are less effective in service areas, though there, too, some effective quality circles have been developed. Historically, they have more than paid for themselves; but payback figures are not always positive.[16]

The American quality circle is not exactly like its Japanese counterpart. In Japan the groups meet on their own time, whereas in the United States they are paid for their time. Foremen head their quality circles in Japan, but American firms often bring in an outside facilitator to begin the circle and manage it for the first several months. "The role of the facilitator is to promote and help implement the QC program; train QC members; guide their initial meetings; solve any problems that may arise; and serve as liaison between the group and staff personnel controlling resources needed by the group."[17] After a time the foreman or someone else who is elected to the position may lead the quality circle. Finally, U.S. firms create a quality circle infrastructure within the administrative system to provide support for the program, because it may meet with resistance among employees; Japanese firms do not encounter such problems.

Quality circles work for a variety of reasons. They tend to improve the person-job relationships of those who become involved in them. They are a form of job enrichment; that is, individuals are given more decision power.

HUMAN RELATIONS HAPPENING

STATEMENT ON QUALITY CIRCLES BY MORTON CHEMICAL COMPANY

Definition

A Quality Circle is a team of people, who do similar work, meeting regularly to discuss and solve problems related to their work.

Organization

A. Circle Members
1. Are volunteers.
2. Are free to join, not to join, or to drop out of a circle.
3. Identify, analyze, and solve problems related to their work.
4. Can accept or refuse problems submitted from any source.
5. Present potential solutions of problems to management for approval.
6. Will not discuss during meetings the following:
   a. Salaries and benefits.
   b. Hiring and firing policies.
   c. Formulating new products.
   d. Personalities.
7. Strive to improve communications between all employees.
8. Meet once a week for one hour and are paid for one hour overtime.

B. Circle Leaders
1. Are chosen by the circle members.
2. Train circle members in Quality Circle techniques.
3. Work with the facilitator to maintain continuity of the Quality Circles Program.
4. Are responsible for the operation of the circle.

C. Facilitator
1. Is a volunteer approved by the Steering Committee.
2. Is responsible for the Quality Circle Program.
3. Trains leaders and members in problem-solving techniques.
4. Maintains records.
5. Interfaces between circles, the Steering Committee, and other individuals and groups within the company.

D. Steering Committee
1. Will be supportive of the Quality Circles Program.
2. Will provide guidance and direction to the Quality Circles.
3. Will attend circle meetings and management presentations if requested.
4. Will implement solutions to problems recommended by quality circle when feasible and practical.

E. Goals
1. To allow circle members to recommend solutions to problems in their work environment.
2. To improve communications between all employees at all levels.
3. To improve employee knowledge of Polyset manufacture, control, and end use.
4. To create an atmosphere of trust, understanding, and mutual respect among all employees of the Electrical/Electronic Materials Group.
5. To improve quality, productivity, and working conditions by finding solutions to problems affecting our group.

SOURCE: Frank M. Gryna, Jr., "Quality Circles: A Team Approach to Problem Solving" (New York: AMACOM, 1981), pp. 51–52.

The individual is taught new problem-solving skills and provided with various decision-making tools. They promote teamwork, and thus to some extent they satisfy the individual's need to belong to a group. They also provide a mechanism for communication—up, down, and side to side. Last but perhaps most important, they provide for a way of improving self-esteem. American workers tend to believe that they are underused and undervalued. QC's give workers an opportunity to show that they can perform work at higher levels than a typical manufacturing job calls for. But some failures have been reported. QC's may fail because they are introduced in the wrong context, because training in their operations may be poor, or because the technique may be ill applied. Often managers expect so much in the short term that their expectations may fail to materialize. Firms may also encounter resistance to the QC program among managers (who fear that they are losing their authority) as well as among employees and possibly their unions. Finally, quality circles may fail if they are unable to improve aspects of jobs with which workers are dissatisfied.[18]

Like any other management fad, quality circles tend to be adopted with enthusiasm and dropped if they fail to live up to expectations. One must recognize that some cultures simply will not support quality circles. One must also recognize that the Hawthorne effect (see Chapter 1) may be responsible for some of the success of these programs. Finally, one must realize that over time any technique tends to lose its effectiveness if it is not revised to accommodate changing conditions. Toyota Auto Body of Japan, for example, found in the late 1970s that its major quality circle program was losing momentum and failing to get the kind of results it had provided earlier. Recognizing inherent problems, Toyota revitalized the program by making quality circles responsible for new areas, such as customer complaints.[19]

MANAGING A COMMITTEE

One formal group seems to cause more problems than just about any other—the committee. Many unkind words have been said about committees: "A camel is a horse designed by a committee"; "If you want to keep something from being done, assign it to a committee"; "A committee is a group of the unfit appointed by the unwilling to do the unnecessary"; "A committee is a body that keeps minutes and wastes hours."[20]

Unfortunately, the historical results of committees have not always been positive. Much of the wasted time and effort and the poor results of committees seem to stem from the absence of proper leadership. The committee leader needs to be task-oriented, and needs also to perform certain of the building or maintenance roles noted earlier. If you must run a committee meeting, the major points to remember are the following:[21]

1. Make certain that everyone's attendance, or the meeting itself, is really necessary. How many meetings do you go to that are not really necessary? If you work in a large bureaucracy, the chances are the answer is "Far too

many." Most managers attend many meetings. The person who initiates the meeting needs to ascertain whether or not the presence of those invited is necessary. Again group size is important. No more than ten to twelve persons should be in a committee meeting, and preferably fewer.

2. Make certain that all people who are necessary are in attendance. This is the converse of rule 1. Are there any other persons who can contribute to the solution of the problem at hand who have not been invited?

3. Provide information and an agenda. Attendees should be provided with the information necessary to function in the meeting, and with an agenda of proposed courses of action. These processes enable participants to be prepared for action and to schedule other events during the day. The problem, as the leader sees it, should be defined. The agenda should be circulated two to three days in advance of the meeting. Any sooner, and some people are likely to forget it or lose it.

4. Prepare opening questions. The committee's leader should have opening questions prepared in advance of the meeting. These questions are to be used to focus the meeting on the problems at hand, either to identify them or to seek solutions.

5. Be punctual; start and end meetings on time. Identify in the minutes of the meeting the people who arrive late or leave early. This practice will curb those bad habits. If meetings tend to drag out, schedule them shortly before lunch or quitting time. People will tend not to waste other people's time when their own is at stake.

6. Be a facilitator, not a boss. Silence the vociferous and draw out the silent. Clarify, listen, pay attention to details, be aware of the obstructive roles individuals may play and keep those role-playing actions from harming the committee's efforts. Anthony Jay suggests that the weak must be protected, that a clash of ideas should be encouraged, that the most senior persons should be addressed last.[22]

7. Close on a note of action. The meeting should end with specific results identified, with actions to be taken clearly spelled out and proper responsibilities and authorities distributed.

8. Following the meeting, minutes containing pertinent information should be distributed to all persons concerned. Important points to include are all agenda items discussed, people who were absent or tardy or who left early, the length of the meeting, the time and date of the meeting, and the schedule for the next meeting.

The next time you are in charge of a meeting, use these suggestions to make your committee's work more effective.

TIPS FOR SUCCESS

1. Remember, there is always a group of importance to you in virtually any situation. Learn about it. Learn how it functions.

2. Groups often control their members' behavior. Be alert to this in groups you belong to.

3. Know the formal and informal power structure.

4. Use the grapevine.

5. Learn who satisfy what roles in groups you belong to.

6. Learn to work well in groups.

SUMMARY

1. Groups form to satisfy needs. Formal groups form to satisfy the needs of the formal organization. Informal groups form to satisfy needs that the organization is not satisfying.

2. The organization's structure results from the grouping of jobs and the distribution of authority. Managers become important linking pins in this structure, linking various authority levels and job groups.

3. All groups, whether formal or informal, go through approximately the same stages of development and have essentially the same functions. The stages of development include mutual acceptance, decision making, motivation, and control.

4. Groups function in accordance with the task and maintenance roles that must be played and the individual roles that people choose to play, their structure (as identified by sociometry), the norms that define acceptable group conduct, their cohesiveness, and their size.

5. Proper group functioning leads to effectiveness and efficiency (which together equal productivity), motivation, trust, and the members' satisfaction.

6. Quality circles represent an application of the group process to problem solving in industrial and other settings.

DISCUSSION QUESTIONS

1. Think of groups to which you belong or have belonged. Trace these groups through each of the parts of the model presented in Table 7.1.

2. "Rate busters" are high achievers who go beyond the group's productivity norms or the formal organization's standards in the workplace. What sanctions can you think of that the group might impose against such persons in various work situations—for example, construction (carpenters, electricians, bricklayers), manufacturing (sewing-machine operators, tool and die makers, welders), clerical work (accounts payable clerks, secretaries), and professional activities (accountants, lawyers, college teachers)?

3. Think of a recent committee meeting you have attended. Evaluate the leader's performance as a facilitator. Then evaluate the effectiveness with which various members carried out the task and maintenance roles. What were the results of this meeting? How good were these results?

4. Explain how the informal group leader can help or hinder the formal group leader/manager. What can the formal group leader do to ensure the informal group leader's assistance?

5. If you were the leader of a formal work group and the informal group seemed always to countermand your directives, what strategies could you follow to change the situation?

6. Demonstrate your knowledge of group processes by showing how the group dynamics shown in Table 7.1 operate in quality circles.

APPLYING HUMAN RELATIONS SKILLS

CASE ┃ **The Blue-Gray Phenomenon**
┃ Louisa Manchester had just been appointed a supervisor in her company's new
┃ plant. She had always lived in Buffalo, but now the company wanted her to

move to north Florida. Who could refuse? The winters had been just too much. So she moved to the new plant along with seven other Buffalo supervisors—one other woman and six men.

The new plant had a total of sixteen supervisors, ten on day shift, six on nights. The eight old supervisors were to show the eight new ones the ropes. Louisa soon found the area to her liking, but not the people. The local supervisors seemed too easygoing to her. They were not much concerned with productivity. A lot of the others said they were "dumb rednecks." She would not go that far, but they were slow. The plant manager was a Yankee and his popularity was not very high among the workers. The top managers said all of the right words, but somehow no front-line workers seemed to believe them. The company seemed sterile to them.

Louisa had been taught to manage by exception—not to socialize with her workers on the job, but to participate in the get-togethers the company sponsored to ensure that a team spirit was developed. Her workers wanted to talk to her and each other. Louisa's work group was as productive as any other, but when she needed them to do favors for her, when she needed them to come through— for example, to work voluntary overtime—they would not. She just did not know what to do.

1. What assumptions have Louisa and the other Yankees made here that may have led to their problems?
2. What could Louisa do to improve her work group's attitudes toward her?

NASA Exercise in Group Problem Solving

EXERCISE

You are a member of a space crew originally scheduled to rendezvous with a mother ship on the lighted surface of the moon. Due to mechanical difficulties, however, your ship was forced to land at a spot some 200 miles from the rendezvous point. During landing, much of the equipment aboard was damaged, and, because survival depends on reaching the mother ship, the most critical items available must be chosen for the 200-mile trip. On the next page are listed the fifteen items left intact and undamaged after the landing. Your task is to rank them in terms of their importance to your crew in reaching the rendezvous point. In the first column (step 1) place the number *1* by the most important item, the number *2* by the second most important, and so on, through number *15*, the least important. You have fifteen minutes to complete this phase of the exercise.

After the individual rankings are completed, participants should be formed into groups having four to seven members. Each group should then rank the fifteen items as a team. This group ranking should be a general consensus after a discussion of the issues, not just the average of each individual ranking. While it is unlikely that everyone will agree exactly on the group ranking, an effort should be made to reach at least a decision that everyone can live with. It is important to treat differences of opinion as a means of gathering more information and clarifying issues and as an incentive to force the group to seek better alternatives. The group ranking should be listed in the second column (step 2). The third phase of the exercise consists of the instructor's providing the expert's rankings, which should be entered in the third column (step 3). Each participant should compute the difference between the individual ranking (step 1) and the expert's ranking (step 4), and between the group ranking (step 2) and the expert's ranking (step 5). Then add the two "difference" columns—the smaller the score, the closer the ranking is to the view of the experts. The difference is in absolute values, not in pluses or minuses. Now compare columns 4 and 5. Who did better—the individual or the group? (There may be an observer to this process.)

NASA TALLY SHEET

Items	Step 1: Your individual ranking	Step 2: Your team's ranking	Step 3: Survival experts' ranking	Step 4: Difference between steps 1 & 3	Step 5: Difference between steps 2 & 3
Box of matches					
Food concentrate					
50 feet of nylon rope					
Parachute silk					
Portable heating unit					
Two .45 calibre pistols					
One case dehydrated Pet milk					
Two 100-lb. tanks of oxygen					
Stellar map (of the moon's constellation)					
Life raft					
Magnetic compass					
5 gallons of water					
Signal flares					
First aid kit containing injection needles					
Solar-powered FM receiver-transmitter					
TOTAL (The lower the score the better)				Your score	Team score

REFERENCES

1. T. M. Mills, *The Sociology of Small Groups* (Englewood Cliffs, N.J.: Prentice-Hall, 1967), p. 2.

2. James L. Gibson, John M. Ivancevich, and James H. Donnelly identify two types of task group: the problem-solving group and the training group (*Organizations: Behavior, Structure, and Processes* [Dallas: Business Publications, 1979], pp. 142–43). As the latter seems to be a special case of a task group—that is, a problem-solving group—no such distinction is made here, though some differences do exist.

3. Rensis Likert, *New Patterns of Management* (New York: McGraw-Hill, 1961), p. 114.

4. William L. Van Horn and William D. Steinmett, "The Ideal Work Environment: Total Employee Involvement," *SAM Advanced Management Journal*, Autumn 1984, p. 43.

5. "How Power Will Be Balanced on Saturn's Shop Floor," *Business Week*, August 5, 1985, pp. 65–68.

6. Bernard Bass, *Organizational Psychology* (Boston: Allyn & Bacon, 1965), pp. 197–98.

7. Kenneth D. Benne and Paul Sheats, "Functional Roles of Group Members," *Journal of Social Issues* 4, no. 2 (1948): 43.

8. "How Power Will Be Balanced," p. 66.

9. Ibid., pp. 43–44.

10. Ibid., pp. 45–46.

11. J. L. Moreno, *Foundations of Sociometry*, Sociometry Monographs no. 4 (Boston: Beacon, 1943).

12. Keith Davis, "Cut Those Rumors Down to Size," *Supervisory Management*, June 1975, pp. 2–6; "The Care and Cultivation of the Corporate Grapevine," *Dun's Review*, July 1973, pp. 44–47; and "Management Communication and the Grapevine," *Harvard Business Review*, September–October 1953, pp. 43–49.

13. Irving Janis, *Victims of Groupthink: A Psychological Study of Policy Decisions and Fiascos* (Boston: Houghton-Mifflin, 1972), p. 45.

14. Laurie Fitzgerald and Joseph Murphy, *Installing Quality Circles: A Strategic Approach* (San Diego, CA.: University Associates, 1982), p. 3.

15. Walt Thompson, "The Organization Ready for Quality Circles," *Training and Development Journal*, December 1982, p. 116.

16. Robert Wood, Frank Hull, and Koya Azuni, "Evaluating Quality Circles: The American Application," *California Management Review*, Fall 1983, p. 43.

17. Ibid., p. 40.

18. Ibid., pp. 44–49.

19. George Munchus, "Employer–Employee-Based Quality Circles in Japan: Human Resource Policy Applications for American Firms," *Academy of Management Review*, April 1983, p. 257.

20. Ralph L. Woods, *The Modern Handbook of Humor* (New York: McGraw-Hill, 1967), p. 8.

21. Anthony Jay, "How to Run a Meeting," *Harvard Business Review*, March–April 1976, pp. 43–57; Louis A. Allen, "Making Better Use of Committees," *Management Record*, December 1955, pp. 466–69, 493; George M. Price, "How to Be a Better Meeting Chairman," *Harvard Business Review*, January–February 1969, pp. 98–108; Allen C. Filley, "Committee Management Guidelines from Social Science Research," *California Management Review*, Fall 1970, pp. 13–21.

22. Anthony Jay, "How to Run a Meeting," *Harvard Business Review*, March/April 1976, pp. 43–57.

8 LEADERSHIP

LEARNING OBJECTIVES

When you have completed this chapter, you should be able to:
1. Define leadership.
2. Describe the leadership TRRAP process.
3. Explain how various theories and research have contributed to our understanding of this process.
4. Make leadership choices on the basis of the leadership TRRAP model.

IF EVER A COMPANY NEEDED A LEADER

If ever a company needed a leader, Bethlehem Steel did during the period that Donald H. Trautlein was chairman. But apparently that leadership simply failed to materialize. When Trautlein assumed the chairman's position in 1980, he inherited a company with antiquated plant and equipment, high labor costs, and declining profits. Substantial and increasing competition from imported steel added to the problem. He faced a situation with almost insurmountable odds, but still there was hope. He resigned in May 1986, under tremendous

pressure from a board of directors that had seen the company lose $1.94 billion since 1982, $1.4 billion of that coming in 1982, but with no profits since.

Trautlein was a number's man. He knew little about steel making. He seldom talked to his plant personnel or to his customers. He spent a considerable amount of time lobbying for import quotas in Washington. He had a hard time making decisions. He vacillated from one strategic position to another. He failed to take the advice of numerous consultants, advice that turned out to be correct. When he did act, he acted too late. When selling assets to raise cash, for example, he did so after other steel firms had already sold theirs, devaluing what Bethlehem would ultimately receive. Finally, he alienated his subordinates by accepting pay increases while cutting their salaries. He forced out many senior managers, many of whom justifiably could be removed from the payroll, but often replaced them with lawyers and finance types who knew nothing about steel. He changed management styles at Bethlehem, decentralizing—something that proved very confusing to managers not used to this approach.

But perhaps most telling was the morale issue. Approximately 60 percent of the white collar work force was eliminated. Those who remained had seen their salaries cut in three of the four previous years. When they found out that Trautlein and a few top lieutenants had received substantial raises and lucrative golden parachutes in the event of a takeover, morale hit rock bottom. His subsequent top management retreat, aimed at improving the company's future,

(Continued on page 192)

had the opposite effect. He angrily rebuked subordinates when they claimed that repeated pay cuts had hurt staff morale. "That's your problem," he is reported to have said.

SOURCE: J. Ernest Beazley and Carol Hymowitz, "Steel Target: Critics Fault Trautlein for Failure to Revive an Ailing Bethlehem," *The Wall Street Journal*, May 27, 1986, pp. 1, 20.

"The new leader . . . is one who commits people to action, who converts followers into leaders, and who may convert leaders into agents of change."
WARREN BENNIS AND
BURT NANUS

Everyone agrees that leadership is essential to organizational success. Unfortunately, leadership is an ambiguous concept. Business, government, and academia do not agree on a definition, but all agree that a **leader** is a person who has followers. Leaders have followers because they take certain actions, behave in certain ways. For our purposes, **leadership** is the process of choosing among alternative ways to treat people in order to influence them and of translating those choices into actions. Those choices and the actions based on them influence others to follow the leader—or to refuse to follow. If you look around and no one is following you, then you are not a leader. You have not made the right choices. You have not taken the right actions. Within the organization we are especially concerned about managers as leaders. Think of managers you have had. Which ones did you follow? Which ones did you perform best for? Was Donald Trautlein a leader? Why?

Without followers, managers have nothing to manage. All work organizations need people to carry out their work. Most successful managers are leaders who practice sound human relations and influence others to carry out the organization's work. A manager who has no followers soon finds that the work of the organization is just not getting done. Some managers, of course, try to do it all themselves. But that's not managing—that's drudgery.

This chapter pursues the basic issues of organizational leadership: how it is defined, the factors that affect its success, the major leadership theories, and the practical approaches that you can take to improve your leadership ability. There are many different approaches to leadership, ranging from the study of traits and behaviors that successful leaders share to the behaviors that successful leaders should follow in very specific situations. This chapter concludes with a situational behavior-choice model of leadership, which suggests that in any given situation, leadership choices should be based on consideration of certain major factors. The primary relationships examined in this chapter are individual-to-individual and individual-to-group interactions. Interactions between the organization on the one hand and the individual and the group on the other take place through the manager.

LEADERSHIP, POWER, AND INFLUENCE

The ability to influence other people is the most important quality of leadership. One may influence others in many ways, but all forms of influence are based on some type of power, the ability to control others. By exerting power, the leader influences motivation, as we saw in Chapters 3 and 4. Managers ordinarily have more sources of power than do leaders outside of formal organizations, but managers still must be accepted by their followers if they are to be effective.

Managers have power because of their positions in the organization. Chester Barnard recognized that unless followers accept a manager's power, the manager will have no influence.[1] It is not uncommon, for example, for athletes to break training and go into town for a few beers or a date. They simply refuse to recognize the power of their coaches. Workers often go on strike rather than accept the power of their bosses. Students sometimes question the power of their professors and refuse unreasonable homework demands. When subordinates do not accept the power of someone in a superior position, that person has no influence.

It has been suggested that the only successful leadership is that which is dictated by the followers, in which case the followers become the leaders, and vice versa. Thus if the leader fulfills certain expectations of the subordinates, the subordinates will reciprocate with performance and esteem for the leader.[2] The more conventional view is that leaders lead and followers follow. There is an element of truth in both views. The successful leader realizes these truths. Leaders must accept responsibility for their power and influence if they are to continue to lead. In order to keep their followers, leaders must accept those followers as human beings with needs that must be satisfied. Did Donald Trautlein of Bethlehem Steel do this?

Power comes to people for various reasons. John R. P. French and Bertram Raven have identified five forms of power:[3]

> *"Something is happening to our country. We aren't producing leaders like we used to. A new chief executive officer today, exhausted by the climb to the peak, falls down on the mountaintop and goes to sleep."*
> ROBERT TOWNSEND
> *Former president of Avis*

1. **Legitimate power,** usually called *authority*, comes from a person's position in the organization. The leader who depends on this type of power for success will suffer in the long run because ordinarily people will follow a leader only as long as their needs are reasonably well satisfied.
2. **Reward power** depends on the leader's ability to control rewards given to other people. Studies have shown that when leaders are no longer able to satisfy their followers' needs, the followers cease to follow.[4]
3. **Coercive power** depends on the ability to punish others. Fear is a motivator, but it does not motivate very many people very well for very long. The Nazi work camps produced less and less even though the punishment meted out to the people in them became greater and greater. The thinking adult does not respond to fear in the same manner as the child. Leaders who expect their followers to submit to their authority like children will find themselves in trouble when they face assertive subordinates.
4. **Expert power** depends on special skill or knowledge. Think of someone who is very good at what he or she does. Does this person have followers because of this skill? In most circumstances the answer will be yes.
5. **Referent power** depends on appeal, magnetism, charisma. John F. Kennedy and Martin Luther King, Jr., had this kind of power. Can you think of ways in which both of these men also used the other types of power they commanded?

THE MANAGER AS A LEADER

There are many types of leaders—leaders on the athletic field, political leaders, informal group leaders, club leaders, fraternity leaders, and so forth. Our concern is primarily with the manager as a leader. The successful manager is an organizational leader whose followers are subordinates and, to a limited extent, peers. All leaders share certain behaviors, but managers differ from other kinds of leaders in two primary respects. First, they perform many management functions in addition to leadership, such as planning, organizing, staffing, communicating, and decision making. Leaders are concerned primarily with results; managers must also be concerned with the efficiency of results. Second, in their concern for the organization's objectives, managers must not lose sight of their followers' objectives or their own. Leaders obtain their power from their followers; managers obtain theirs from the authority of the organization. Managers who seek to be leaders cannot forget either of these sources of power, or they are in trouble. The president of the United States has the tough job of being both a manager of an organization with a trillion-dollar budget and the leader not only of its employees but of the remainder of the nation's citizens. All presidents seek to make changes, but none can forget that his power is shared with Congress and derives from the electorate. He must communicate his visions so that they become our visions.

Think of a manager you have had who was independent of his or her followers, or whose own career interests received more attention than either the organization or the followers. How well and how long did you follow this person?

Managers determine the success of the organization through their leadership behavior. Unfortunately, these leaders of our work organizations do not seem to be performing as well as we would like. A recent poll of the nonmanagerial work force indicates that:

1. Less than 25 percent claim that they are working to their fullest potential.
2. Fully 50 percent report that they put no more effort into their jobs than they are required to.
3. Fully 75 percent believe they could be more effective than they are.
4. Nearly 60 percent say they "do not work as hard as they used to."[5]

The two most important points for all managers to remember are that, first, they have choices as to the way they treat their subordinates (and other people within and without the organization), and second, it is the way these choices are put into practice that determines the success or failure of the organization and of the manager. The proper choices and actions result in followers and productivity. The wrong choices and actions result in lack of cooperation, of followers, and of productivity. Managers may fail to be rewarded. They may also find that in extreme cases they may be punished from below, as the Human Relations Happening "Sweet Revenge" suggests. Managers can select the appropriate way to treat subordinates only after they have taken into consideration all of the major factors in the situation. Unfortunately, most leadership behavior is reactive, based either on learned authoritarian or emotional responses or on current examples, including the organization's policies and rules. Because much leadership behavior is learned from inappropriate role models—bad examples—leadership development and training are not only necessary but vital to the success of the organization.

HUMAN RELATIONS HAPPENING

SWEET REVENGE

Sometimes merely outlasting an intolerable boss isn't enough. When retaliation is called for, some people rise to the occasion by finding creative ways to get even. In the following examples, all names and identifying characteristics have been changed to protect the innocent and the guilty.

It was a small newspaper, and the man who ran the copy department was even smaller. He found fault with everyone's work, making his taste and biases the only criteria allowed. When an opening developed in the copy department of a large metropolitan paper nearby, he applied for the job, as did one of his staff. The happiness she felt in getting the job was doubled by the satisfaction she got walking in to her boss, giving her two weeks' notice and watching his face as she told him why she was leaving.

After years of sadistic bossing, Mr. Torquemada finally agreed to move his rack and whips to another firm. His grateful employees threw a festive going-away party, well publicized throughout the firm, to which he was cordially not invited.

The chem lab was headed by a sneak named Smith. He even wore crepe-soled shoes to deaden his footsteps as he eased up behind people to see what they were doing . . . until one imaginative woman showed him the danger of his ways. Out of the corner of her eye, she saw him coming, picked up an expensive flask, and started carefully measuring a solution into it. When Smith peered over her shoulder, she jumped, shrieked, and let the flask slip from her hand. As it smashed on the floor, she exclaimed sweetly, "Oh, Mr. Smith. You startled me so."

This boss took his cue from Mt. St. Helens. He would bumble along sullenly for a while, then suddenly erupt with a series of loud, public chewings-out of his staff before subsiding to recharge his bile. One of his favorite victims started sending him anonymous get-well cards after each outburst. This didn't improve his behavior, but it did annoy him mightily.

The man had a sharp tongue and kept it honed pointing out people's mistakes, preferably in public. He also felt he could do anything better than anyone else. So it wasn't hard to talk him into joining the office softball team for a game against the league's strongest club. As befitted his rank, he was inserted in the lineup as shortstop and cleanup hitter. Seeing him stagger around under pop flies, field hard grounders with his shins, and flail away futilely at the plate gave his troops—the office turned out en masse for the game—fond memories to help them through future tongue-lashings.

SOURCE: Jack C. Horn, "Sweet Revenge," *Psychology Today*, January 1984, p. 48.

THEORIES OF LEADERSHIP

Many theories about what makes for successful leadership have been proposed. There are approaches based on traits, abilities, or characteristics; behavioral theories, which suggest that successful leaders act in certain ways; contingency or situational theories, which propose that leadership actions should result from consideration of major variables in the situation; and theories that combine various features of all the other theories. We shall review these theories for the insight they shed on current human relations practices.

TRAIT APPROACHES

Leadership was not examined in depth until the 1940s. At that time, as earlier, leadership was approached from the perspective of traits. According to the **trait theories**, successful leaders have certain traits in common. Much of the research was directed toward inherited physical and mental traits, but eventually intellectual, personal, emotional, social, and other traits were examined. The leadership trait studies focused not only on managers but on political and religious leaders as well.[6] Apparently the trait approach came into existence partly because of the continuing dominance of certain families in power situations, such as the Hapsburgs, a family that ruled much of Europe for several centuries, and the Roosevelts, who dominated American politics and government for nearly fifty years. People noted common traits in these families and assumed that all leaders possessed them. But when the various family traits were examined and compared, few common characteristics were found. Most authorities agree that the trait approach is at best weak, but that some common traits are usually found in leaders. In general, a minimal level of intelligence, a positive self-image, a high level of motivation, and interpersonal skills characterize successful leaders. But even these traits or characteristics are not endorsed by everyone as representative of successful leaders, and they are not effective in all leadership situations.

The trait approach, though of limited applicability, contributes to our understanding of leadership by pointing out the need to consider the characteristics we ourselves exhibit in our leadership choices and actions. One of the most important such characteristics is the leader's predisposition to treat people in certain ways. Douglas McGregor's Theory X and Theory Y deal with these predispositions.

THEORY X AND THEORY Y

Douglas McGregor postulated that managers hold certain assumptions about human nature, which help to explain why they behave in certains ways. McGregor proposed that two contradictory sets of assumptions are held about human nature, which he labeled Theory X and Theory Y, and that managers tend to behave toward employees according to one or the other of these theories. Two assumptions are common to both theories:

1. Management is responsible for organizing the elements of productive enterprise—money, materials, equipment, people—in the interest of economic ends.

2. Management is a process of directing people's efforts, motivating them, controlling their actions, and modifying their behavior to fit the needs of the organization.

The assumptions of **Theory X** are:

3. Without the active intervention of management, people would be passive, even resistant to organizational needs. They must therefore be persuaded, rewarded, punished, controlled; their activities must be directed. This is management's task in managing subordinate managers or workers. We often sum it up by saying that management consists of getting things done through people.

Behind this conventional theory there are several additional beliefs, less explicit but widespread:

4. Most people are by nature indolent; they work as little as possible.
5. They lack ambition, dislike responsibility, prefer to be led.
6. They are inherently self-centered, indifferent to organizational needs.
7. They are by nature resistant to change.
8. They are gullible, not very bright, the ready dupes of charlatans and demagogues.

The assumptions of **Theory Y** (in addition to 1 and 2 above) are as follows:

3. People are *not* by nature passive or resistant to organizational needs. They have become so as a result of experience in organizations.
4. The motivation, the potential for development, the capacity for assuming responsibility, the readiness to direct behavior toward organizational goals are all present in people. Management does not put them there. It is a responsibility of management to make it possible for people to recognize and develop these human characteristics for themselves.
5. The essential task of management is to arrange organizational conditions and methods of operation so that people can achieve their own goals by directing *their own* efforts toward organizational objectives.[7]

There are two varieties of Theory X, the "hard" and the "soft." Hard Theory X managers use coercion, threats, close supervision, and tight control. Soft Theory X managers are permissive, focus on satisfying people's demands, attempt to achieve harmony. Both hold the same assumptions but react in different ways.

Theory Y managers create opportunities, release potentials, remove obstacles, encourage growth, provide guidance. But Theory Y managers do not abdicate management. Rather, they practice "management by objectives," as opposed to "management by control." Do you see that the assumptions one holds about people generally lead to a certain kind of behavior? Do you see the need to change some of those assumptions? How about your own assumptions and behavior—do they need changing? Not all people fit the assumptions of Theory Y, but most people probably do. McGregor made a tremendous contribution to leadership theory. His theories link assumptions to action. His contribution was made during the 1960s and antedates some

*"You idiot! Don't you know how to act when
I'm using Theory Y on you?"*

Art by Al Hormel.

of the work we shall be examining on leadership behavior and contingency theories.

One major employer who agrees with the Theory Y approach and urges others to follow it is Donald Burr, founder and chairman of People Express airline. In his organization everyone is a manager; people rotate among jobs, managerial and nonmanagerial (except for pilot positions, of course). Burr himself occasionally takes his turn as a flight attendant. He gives his people large amounts of authority to perform their tasks. He says other companies fail to follow his practices because their managers "think humankind is lazy and bestial and won't do anything unless you beat them to death. We live with a 'boss' structure. But we've proved that if you give people space, room and freedom, you can get trustworthy behavior."[8]

**BEHAVIOR
APPROACHES**

Historically, after the failure of the trait approach to discover common traits that could predict leadership success, a number of studies were carried out in the 1950s and 1960s in attempts to identify the **leadership behaviors** in which successful leaders engaged. Thus attention shifted from what leaders were like to what they did. Noteworthy studies were performed at both Ohio State University and the University of Michigan.

The Ohio State and Michigan Leadership Studies A series of studies at Ohio State University indicated that two behavior dimensions proved significant in successful leadership:

1. *Consideration:* behavior indicative of friendship, mutual trust, respect, and warmth.
2. *Initiating structure:* behavior that organizes and defines relationships or roles, and establishes well-defined patterns of organization, channels of communication, and ways of getting jobs done.

Studies conducted at the University of Michigan revealed two similar concepts of leadership style which correlated with effectiveness:

1. *Employee orientation:* the human relations aspects of the leader's job, with the employees considered as human beings of intrinsic importance, with individuality and personal needs.
2. *Production orientation:* stress on production and the technical aspects of the job, with employees viewed as means of getting the work done.[9]

As you can see, these are quite similar conceptualizations. More recently they have been referred to as relationship and task orientations, but the underlying behaviors remain essentially the same. What these studies and others revealed was that successful leaders (success is defined in terms of productivity and employee satisfaction) engaged not in one or the other, but in both behaviors in varying degrees. Thus to be successful most of the time the leader must behave in a manner consistent with task orientation (initiating structure and concern for productivity) and also in a manner consistent with relationship orientation (consideration and concern for people).

Soujanen's Authority and Participation Model The second behavioral model is **Soujanen's authority and participation model**. It examines participation in decision making. Waino W. Soujanen hypothesized that:

1. Organizations may be classified as either crisis-oriented, routine-oriented, or knowledge-oriented.
2. Within each classification are several possible alternative leadership behaviors, which may be charted as bell-shaped curves (see Figure 8.1).
3. The mean or average leadership behavior shifts from authoritarian to participative as the nature of the organization (crisis-, routine-, or knowledge-oriented) changes.[10]

Thus in a crisis-oriented organization—an army, for example—there is an overall style of authoritarianism, but within an army some limited number of individuals or groups (staff officers) are allowed to participate in management decisions. Similarly, in routine organizations, such as the majority of business organizations, a middle-of-the-road, perhaps "consultative" approach is taken with respect to most of the employees. Many are treated more authoritatively or more democratically than this mean treatment. Finally, in the knowledge-oriented organization, the majority *should* be treated in a democratic manner, but some few, perhaps maintenance engineers, would be treated more authoritatively.[11]

Soujanen's approach was important because it suggested a practical dispersion of manager power styles and because he recognized that no single approach is universally appropriate. His model contributes to our understand-

FIGURE 8.1   *Authority and participation model*

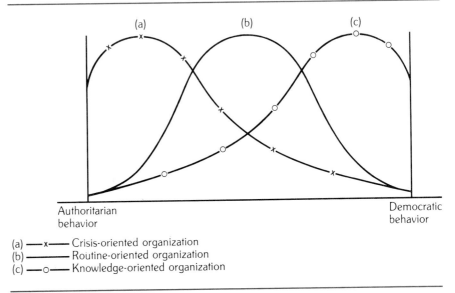

SOURCE: From *The Dynamics of Management* by Waino Soujanen. Copyright © 1966 by Holt, Rinehart and Winston. Reprinted by permission of Holt, Rinehart and Winston.

ing of leadership primarily through identification of the organizational structure and climate constraints on leadership choices.

Such approaches, which viewed leadership choices as points on a continuum, were advanced in their time (the 1960s) but were inadequate in that they did not offer specific guidance to managers attempting to choose a style appropriate in any given situation.

The Managerial Grid   The third behavioral theory, the **Managerial Grid,**® contributes a great deal to our understanding of leadership because it portrays the leadership choice situation as having many possible styles.

Robert Blake and Jane Mouton developed a model that, like most leadership models, focused on the task or relationship orientations uncovered in the Ohio State and Michigan leadership-behavior studies. But instead of showing leadership choices as points on a continuum, as Soujanen did, Blake and Mouton created a grid, based on managers' concern for both people (relationships) and production (tasks).[12] Figure 8.2 shows each of these concerns as one of the two axes of the grid, so that concerns for both people and productivity are combined in various management styles.

Like other behavioral theories, the Managerial Grid® proposes that there is a best way to manage people, the way used by the 9,9 manager, who has 9 units of concern for productivity (tasks) and 9 for people (relationships). Four other major styles are indicated: the 1,1, the 9,1, the 1,9, and the 5,5. Typical characteristics of these five styles are presented in Figure 8.3. The grid is often used in organizational development (OD) programs, which are programs of planned change that focus on organizational culture and climate (see Chapter 12). Managerial style is measured by means of a questionnaire, and managers are then located on the grid—for example, as a 3,6. After training, managers are then repositioned on the grid. The desired objective is 9,9.

The Managerial Grid® provides no indication when some other style might be more appropriate than 9,9—9,1, for example. According to this theory, 9,9 is always and everywhere best, and managers should strive to come as close to it as they can. If they develop high levels of concern for both production and people, their concerns will be translated into behavior.[13]

FIGURE 8.2   *The Managerial Grid®*

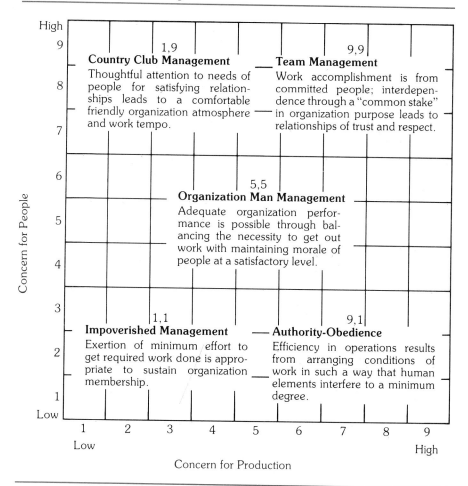

SOURCE: Robert R. Blake and Jane S. Mouton, *The Managerial Grid III* (Houston: Gulf Publishing Company, copyright © 1985), p. 12. Reproduced by permission.

FIGURE 8.3   *The major Managerial Grid® styles*

1,1 Impoverished management, often referred to as laissez faire leadership. Leaders in this position have little concern for people or productivity, avoid taking sides, and stay out of conflicts. They do just enough to get by.

1,9 Country club management. Managers in this position have great concern for people and little concern for production. They try to avoid conflicts and concentrate on being well liked. To them the task is less important than good interpersonal relations. Their goal is to keep people happy. (This is a soft Theory X approach and not a sound human relations approach.)

9,1 Authority obedience. Managers in this position have great concern for production and little concern for people. They desire tight control in order to get tasks done efficiently. They consider creativity and human relations to be unnecessary.

5,5 Organization man management, often termed middle-of-the-road leadership. Leaders in this position have medium concern for people and production. They attempt to balance their concern for both people and production, but are not committed to either.

9,9 Team management. This style of leadership is considered to be ideal. Such managers have great concern for both people and production. They work to motivate employees to reach their highest levels of accomplishment. They are flexible and responsive to change, and they understand the need to change.

SOURCE: Robert R. Blake and Jane S. Mouton, *The Managerial Grid III* (Houston: Gulf Publishing Company, copyright © 1985), chaps. 1–7. Reproduced by permission.

CONTINGENCY APPROACHES

"Never tell people 'how' to do things. Tell them 'what' to do and they will surprise you with their ingenuity."
GEORGE SMITH PATTON

Contingency theories propose that for any given situation there is a best way to manage. Contingency theories go beyond the situational approaches, which observe that all factors must be considered when leadership decisions are to be made. Contingency theories attempt to isolate those key factors that must be considered, and to indicate how to manage given the conditions of those key factors. Three such theories will be reviewed here: those developed by Robert Tannenbaum and Warren H. Schmidt, by Fred Fiedler, and by Paul Hersey and Kenneth Blanchard.

Tannenbaum and Schmidt's Continuum of Leadership Behavior   The first of these contingency models was **Tannenbaum and Schmidt's continuum of leadership behavior**.[14] Their model presents seven alternative ways in which managers can approach decision making. The manager has a choice among the behaviors shown in Figure 8.4. The actions shown at the left side of the continuum are boss-centered and authoritarian. The behaviors at the right side of the continuum are employee-centered and participative. The behaviors between the two extremes are gradations from authoritarian to participative approaches. The manager's choices, according to Robert Tannenbaum and Warren Schmidt, depend on three factors:

1. Forces in the manager: the manager's value system, confidence in subordinates, leadership inclinations, and feelings of security in an uncertain situation.

2. Forces in the subordinate: expectations, needs for independence, readiness to assume decision-making responsibility, tolerance for ambiguity in task definition, interest in the problem, ability to understand and identify with the goals of the organization, knowledge and experience to deal with the problem.
3. Forces in the situation: type of organization, group effectiveness, the problem itself (the task), and the pressure of time.

This model was extremely important because it was the first to frame leadership in terms of behavior choices. Much later, however, research by Jerome Franklin indicated that elements of point 3 of Tannenbaum and Schmidt's model, organizational structure and climate, are more important factors than that model indicates. Leaders must function in accordance with the "rules of the game" set forth by their organizations.[15]

Fiedler's Contingency Model In **Fiedler's contingency model**, leadership is effective when the leader's style is appropriate to the situation, as determined by three principal factors: the relations between leader and followers, the structure of the task, and the power inherent in the leader's position. These three factors enable the manager to influence (motivate) subordinates. After analyzing these three factors by means of selected instruments developed by Fred Fiedler, the manager would choose between task and

FIGURE 8.4   *Continuum of leadership behavior*

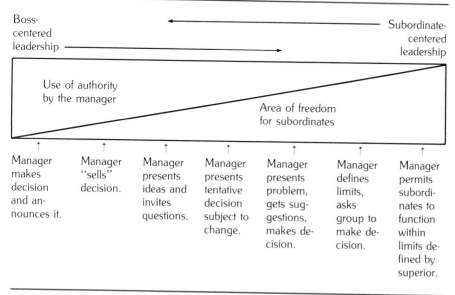

"Anyone can hold the helm while the sea is calm."
PUBLIUS

relationship leadership styles. These three variables are more precisely defined as follows:

1. Leader–member relations: the nature of the interpersonal relationship between the leader and the follower, expressed in terms of good through poor, with qualifying modifiers attached as necessary. Obviously the leader's personality and the personalities of subordinates play important roles in this variable.
2. Task structure: the nature of the subordinate's task, described as "structured" or "unstructured," associated with the amount of creative freedom allowed the subordinate to accomplish the task.
3. Position power: the degree to which the position itself enables the leader to get the group members to comply with and accept his or her direction and leadership.[16]

Fiedler and his associates have compared productivity with the two leadership styles and combinations of the three prime variables. As Table 8.1 shows, the leader who has good relations with members, a structured task, and strong position power should use a directive (task-oriented) management style, because that is the style associated with high productivity under those conditions. Other combinations of "favorable" and "unfavorable" conditions call for the management styles indicated in the rest of the table. Put simplistically, when things are going your way as manager, you can be task-oriented. When they are not, people orientation is necessary, according to this theory.

Fiedler's work, too, has contributed a great deal to leadership theory because it identifies some specific situational factors and the behaviors appropriate when these factors occur in certain combinations. As Robert Vecchio has indicated, however, not all of the variables in most managerial situations have been addressed by this research and subsequent theory, and Fiedler's methodology is fundamentally weak in several respects.[17] Thus his theory is a milestone on the way to an integrated theory, but it does not represent the goal we are seeking.

TABLE 8.1 Leadership Styles Associated with High Productivity in Eight Conditions Characterized by Varying Combinations of Leader–Member Relations, Task Structure, and Position Power

CONDITION	LEADER–MEMBER RELATIONS	TASK STRUCTURE	POSITION POWER	LEADERSHIP STYLE
1	Good	Structured	Strong	Task-oriented
2	Good	Structured	Weak	Task-oriented
3	Good	Unstructured	Strong	Task-oriented
4	Good	Unstructured	Weak	Employee-oriented
5	Moderately poor	Structured	Strong	Employee-oriented
6	Moderately poor	Structured	Weak	Employee-oriented
7	Moderately poor	Unstructured	Strong	Employee-oriented
8	Moderately poor	Unstructured	Weak	Task-oriented

SOURCE: Adapted from Fred E. Fiedler, *A Theory of Leadership Effectiveness*, copyright © 1967 by McGraw-Hill, Inc. Used with the permission of McGraw-Hill Book Company.

The Hersey-Blanchard Contingency Theory   Like most of the behavioral and contingency theories, the **Hersey-Blanchard contingency (life-cycle) theory** is based on task and relationship behaviors.[18] Each of these dimensions of leadership behavior is represented on an axis of a two-dimensional grid (see Figure 8.5).

The underlying assumption of this model is that the most important factor in determining appropriate leadership behavior is the subordinate's level of maturity. The manager should match his or her style to this maturity level. Maturity has two components: (1) job skill and knowledge and (2) psychological maturity.

The grid is broken into four quadrants, each quadrant representing a leadership style. The curvilinear subordinate's maturity line enables the manager to know when to use the styles indicated by the grid. The name may be a little misleading; the maturity line does not represent the actual maturity of a subordinate, but rather the amount or degree of task and relationship behaviors in which a manager should engage given his or her perception of the subordinate's maturity.

For purposes of illustration, assume that a single subordinate begins with a low level of maturity. The manager looks to the subordinate's maturity line to determine what his or her style should be. As the subordinate's maturity

FIGURE 8.5   *The Hersey-Blanchard contingency model of leadership behavior*

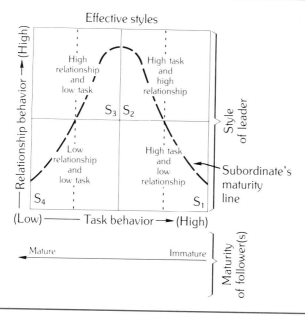

Source: From Paul Hersey and Kenneth R. Blanchard, *Management of Organizational Behavior: Utilizing Human Resources*, 4th edition. © 1982, p. 200. Reprinted by permission of Prentice-Hall, Inc., Englewood Cliffs, New Jersey.

increases (or if it begins at a relatively high level), the emphasis shifts from a high-task, low-relationship orientation to one of high task and high relationship. As the subordinate further matures, the style shifts to one of low task and high relationship. Finally, as the subordinate reaches full maturity, the style shifts to low relationship and low task. At this maturity point, the subordinate should be able to manage him- or herself. The intuitive appeal of this approach is great, and it seems to work in many areas. Bear Bryant, former football coach of Alabama, recognized the increasing maturity of the incoming players over the years, and adapted his management style to include more relationship behavior.[19]

There are numerous variations of task and relationship within each style. Ordinarily the changes in task or relationship orientation occur incrementally.

A questionnaire, the Leader Effectiveness and Adaptability Description (LEAD), is administered to managers to determine, first, their most commonly used style; second, the range of this style; and third, the leader's adaptability to the situation—that is, will the leader indeed use the proper style, or continue to use the style he or she is accustomed to using? A tridimensional grid network is then used to show when certain styles are appropriate and when they are not. Little empirical evidence exists as to the validity of this theory, but its intuitive appeal is great. Furthermore, virtually all theories of motivation and leadership can be at least partially explained by this model. To apply this approach, the leader needs considerable skill in diagnosing the maturity levels of subordinates. But this is true of virtually all leadership models. The value of this model lies in its recognition of the importance of the manager's adaptation to the subordinate's personality. Some minimal amount of recognition (relationship behavior) is required by virtually everyone, and managers should take this need into account, whether they use the model or not. Most employees will not be productive without some minimal recognition.

This approach successfully identifies an important variable in successful leadership: the match between the characteristics of the manager/leader and those of the subordinate. Many organizations, including Holiday (Inns) Corporation and Xerox Corporation, have adopted this approach. But, like all other leadership approaches to date, it leaves out several important variables that need to be considered.

THE TRRAP MODEL

Drawing upon the leadership approaches presented thus far in this chapter and the works of several others—David Bowers and Stanley Seashore, Basil S. Georgeopoulos, Gerald M. Mahoney and Nyel W. Jones, and Robert House[20]—and on the research on motivation, groups, culture, structuring, and climate discussed elsewhere in this text, I have developed a situational model of leadership incorporating the major points of these models.

The TRRAP model of leadership (see Figure 8.6) is based on the belief that leadership is a process of choosing among alternative ways to treat people, especially subordinates, and the translation of those choices into action. The leader must choose the appropriate degrees of *task*, *reward*, and *relationship* behaviors to employ or emphasize, the appropriate *attitude* to display, and

FIGURE 8.6   *The TRRAP model of leadership*

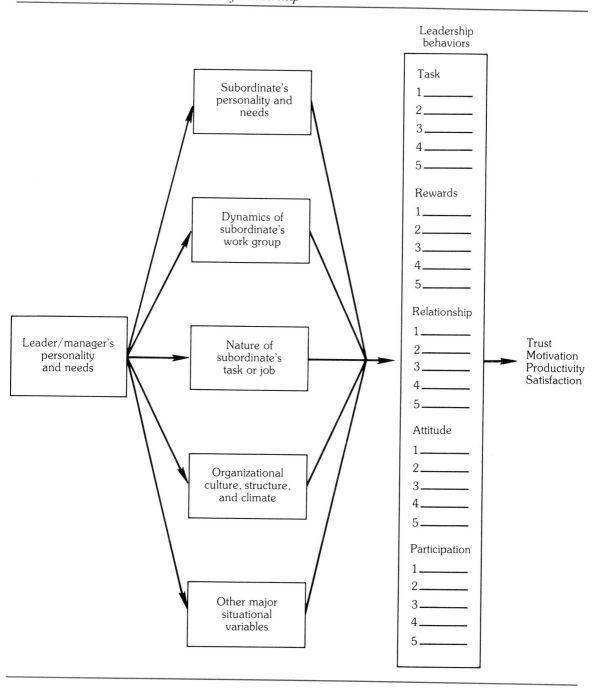

FIGURE 8.7   *The TRRAP leadership profile possibilities*

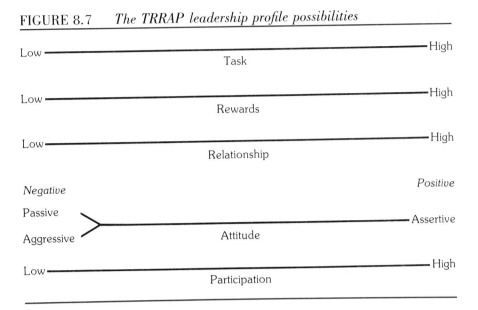

the amount of *participation* in decision making to accord subordinates. Choices in each of these areas occupy various positions on a continuum, as Figure 8.7 suggests. It is the consistent combination of task orientation, reward orientation, relationship orientation, attitude, and participation orientation that determines each leader's personal style of leadership. Table 8.2 provides examples of each of these behaviors. This model increases the number of choices from the traditional two, task and relationship, to five—TRRAP—in order to give recognition to the importance of rewards, attitudes, and participation; to distinguish between task behavior and reward behavior and between relationship behavior and participation behavior; and to recognize the effect of attitude on all of these behaviors.[21]

These choices should be made only after the major factors that affect the particular situation have been considered. Within any particular leadership situation, the choices made will depend on:

The personality of the leader or manager, especially his or her needs.

The personalities of the subordinates, especially their needs.

The dynamics of the group.

The particular task or job in which the leader or manager wants to influence the subordinate's performance.

The organization's culture, structure, and climate.

Other major situational variables.

According to this model, the overall context of the situation provides an environment within which the manager must function. The manager's choices and rational or learned responses must be adapted to the environment created by the personalities of the people involved in the situation; the dynamics of

TABLE 8.2   Behaviors Associated with the Elements of the TRRAP Model

TASK	REWARD	RELATIONSHIP	ATTITUDE	PARTICIPATION
Assigning objectives	Giving raises	Communicating openly	Acting passively	Deciding jointly
Making certain subordinates know how to do their jobs	Providing recognition	Being friendly	Being submissive	Delegating responsibility
	Giving praise	Supporting subordinates with top management when they're right	Not saying what you think	Implementing quality control
Periodically reviewing and discussing others' performances	Patting people on the back		Not making waves	Using job enrichment
	Being equitable		Acting assertively	Asking for others' opinions
Emphasizing objectives	Giving promotions	Attending to others' personal needs (family, illness, birthdays, etc.)	Showing impatience	Using others' inputs in making choices
Planning	Providing incentives		Respecting others	Letting others make decisions
Organizing resources	Publicly reporting successes	Building trust	Acting honestly	
Creating structure	Tying rewards to performance	Working well with groups	Confronting others	
Providing direction to achieve goals	Tying rewards to objectives	Listening to others	Acting aggressively	
Knowing how to do subordinates' jobs well enough to correct performance		Providing ego support	Showing contempt	
		Representing values of group	Showing indifference	
Developing subordinates' job skills		Working with informal group leader	Being deceitful	

the subordinate's work group; the nature of the task or job; the culture, structure, and climate of the organization; and all other major factors that affect the situation.

Knowing just how much task, reward, relationship, and participation behaviors to use and what attitude to take while using them is critical to a manager's success.

The TRRAP model of leadership is based primarily on the following concepts:

1. Managers have choices in leadership behaviors. These choices are contingent on several factors.
2. The behaviors from which the leader may choose are many, but several have been shown to be appropriate most of the time.
3. The leader's personality and needs affect the choice process, and these factors need to be taken into account.
4. Probably the single most important factor to be considered in making these choices is the subordinate's or other person's personality and needs.
5. Several studies have pointed to the need to include the group's dynamics

within the process, since a leader, after all, leads a group, not just individuals.

6. The task or job of the subordinate is important to the leader's choice of behavior. Some tasks require closer supervision than others, for example.

7. Organizational culture, structure, and climate play important roles in the process, since any manager's decisions must be made within the structure of the guidelines, rules, procedures, policies, and authority distributions of the organization.

8. Other variables may enter into the process: time, for example. The leader who has only a limited time to make a critical decision will probably find that a participative style is not a viable alternative, for example.

9. In the long run, those behaviors that increase or maintain subordinates' self-images are the types of behaviors in which managers should engage. In the short run, negative leadership behaviors will be effective, but the long-term consequences may be disastrous.

10. When the appropriate behaviors are chosen, motivation, productivity, satisfaction, and trust result.

11. Trust is an important ingredient in this process, and is highly correlated with continued performance.[22]

12. Managers have five primary choices: task, reward, relationship, attitude, and degrees of participation—TRRAP.

One final note: The assumption throughout has been that both productivity and employee satisfaction are the criteria by which leadership is to be judged. This is not always the case. When organizations or followers desire managers who meet other criteria—yes-men, for example, or people who can be counted on not to rock the boat—much of what has been said in this chapter has less meaning than it should.

At the end of this chapter is a fairly long case that requires you to work your way through the TRRAP model. Your instructor has a prepared solution to this case, which he or she will share with you after you have worked through the model yourself. By now you must realize that short of an actual situation, there are no right answers, only better ones. The answers to this case are prepared with this concept in mind.

It is my belief, and that of many others, that the successful manager today must be a complete leader/manager. The complete leader/manager realizes that there are few, if any, cookbook solutions. The complete leader/manager practices not just one or two but all of the relevant managerial skills, especially those presented in this book, and the management functions that are usually discussed in an introductory management course.

--- **TIPS FOR SUCCESS** ---

1. Be a leader as well as a manager.
2. Analyze the situation, then make your choices.
3. *Most* of the time, a management style of Hi Task, Hi Rewards, Hi Relationship, a Positive Attitude, and Medium to Hi Participation is what you want.

SUMMARY

1. Leadership is the process of choosing among alternative ways to treat people in order to influence them and of translating those choices into actions.
2. Leaders are concerned primarily with results; managers must also be concerned with the efficiency of results (productivity). Leaders receive their power from their followers, managers from the authority of the organization.
3. There are five kinds of power: legitimate, reward, coercive, expert, and referent power.
4. A limited number of traits are shared by managerial leaders: at least a minimal level of intelligence, a positive self-image, a high level of motivation, and sound interpersonal skills.

5. Existing contingency models point in helpful directions, but none is totally predictive of appropriate managerial leadership behavior.
6. Certain managerial behaviors seem to lead to successful managerial leadership most of the time: high task, reward, and relationship behaviors, a positive and assertive attitude, and high levels of participation. Such behaviors usually result in a successful long-term management style.
7. However, all leadership choices should in fact be tailored to the situation.

DISCUSSION QUESTIONS

1. What do you think it takes to be a good leader?
2. Do you feel that it is practical to work through the TRRAP model? When, and when not?
3. Review each of the major theories presented in the text, their contributions to leadership theory, their apparent weaknesses, and how each fits the TRRAP model.

4. Think of the best managers you have worked for. Think of the worst. How did they differ? What did the best managers do that the worst managers did not do?

APPLYING HUMAN RELATIONS SKILLS

Grant Taylor

CASE

When Grant Taylor received his BBA degree in accounting from the University of Florida, he went to work for a small but growing national firm in St. Pete. He soon received his Master of Accountancy degree at the University of South Florida. He became a senior auditor five years later, and after ten years with the firm he became a junior partner. The firm had six junior partners, three senior partners, and a managing senior partner. As a junior partner, he was responsible for the work of four senior auditors, nine supervisors, approximately thirty-five staff accountants, and eight clerical staff.

At 34, Grant was the youngest partner in the firm. He was described by his friends in the firm as "aggressive, hard-working, and quick-tempered." Grant had grown up in a lower-middle-income family. He had earned an academic scholarship to Florida, worked hard in school, and had little patience with students who couldn't do as well. He was a classic Theory X manager. He believed the worst about people, and his beliefs became self-fulfilling prophecies.

Under Grant's guidance, the profit for the tax section grew with sales, but profits as a percentage of sales declined. Grant knew it and so did everyone else. His secretary finally told him that it was the way he treated people. He asked her what she meant, and she told him in no uncertain terms. She also gave him a book on human relations from a course she was taking. He read it. He realized then that maybe he needed to change, but he wasn't convinced yet that his behavior had anything to do with the firm's problem.

The four senior auditors who worked for Grant were Bill Salters, 35; Mike Samuels, 42; Kate Alonzo, 25; and Walt Ellis, 38. Bill Salters had been more or less the informal group leader when he, Grant, Mike, and Walt had been senior auditors together. He somewhat resented Grant's promotion, because he was older and had more experience than Grant. Grant had overheard some of Bill's gripes to others and wondered what impact this negativism was having on his own effectiveness. Bill was still the informal leader.

Mike Samuels was competent, but not a go-getter. He was perfectly happy to remain a senior auditor. He had no designs on a partnership, and he intended to retire at the mandatory age of fifty-five. Kate Alonzo had been Grant's replacement. She was a hard-charging accountant. Everyone knew she was going to be a partner. It was rumored that she was going to be moved to the consulting division, but no one had confirmed that. Walt Ellis was, in Grant's mind, questionable material for the senior position. Grant felt that he just was not getting the most from his people. And while profits on all jobs had slipped since Grant had taken over as junior partner, it was Walt's projects that had slipped the most. He had already chewed out Walt for his performance, but it had not seemed to help much. Walt was an amiable person, and liked to socialize on and off the job. Walt's wife had a very good job and they seemed to have few money problems. Walt was self-confident but seemed to Grant to have reached his "comfort zone."

Walt was somehow politically linked to one of the senior partners, but no one seemed to know exactly how. They did play golf together a lot, but Grant thought that surely something as simple as that would not be important. Staff members seldom saw one another except at former meetings. Friendships did develop on audits because of the large amount of travel involved and the amount of time spent in motels and restaurants.

It happened that just after Grant finished the human relations book, the firm started team training at the top management level. A couple of times the managing partner made a special effort to emphasize what the management consultant had to say, and he always seemed to look directly at Grant. Grant had not failed to notice this. Grant's own immediate superior was easygoing. He expected you to manage your own areas without much supervision. Objectives were set and he expected you to meet them.

Grant began to try to change his way of treating people, but it wasn't easy. He had always been a name caller, and he still was occasionally. But he did progress. Still, profits remained at best stable, and sales were not increasing.

The firm had just completed a new mission/objectives/plans position paper for the next five years, and as part of this position paper, the partners began to emphasize both profits and expanded sales. Profits in accounting are based on working harder *and* smarter. Many times junior accountants do not report all of their hours because they are supposed to stay within budget if they want to get ahead. Sales are increased mostly by personal selling, even though CPA firms are now allowed to advertise their services. Most junior accountants complained about having to do all of the extra work associated with marketing the firm— giving free speeches or talks, teaching courses at colleges, and the like. And the senior accountants didn't like to bend clients' ears either, because they were usually marketing services over which they had no control and which were usually much less bottom-line-provable than their own accounting services. Senior auditors did not like to make presentations to prospective new clients either, because they knew their performance was evaluated primarily on making project budgets and keeping current clients happy. During the winter months most of the firm's staff, including the partners, worked 55 to 60 hours a week, and no one, regardless of impact on his or her career, was going to move to build the client list then. Turnover among junior staff members was 20 percent a year. After four years, only 20 percent of those hired in a group would remain with the firm.

Junior staff accountants performed the basic legwork, and were seldom in the home office. Occasionally, in a small firm, they would perform an entire audit by themselves, but mostly they saw only parts of the big picture. Supervisors managed small audits or major portions of large audits. They planned them, made staff assignments, and saw more of the big picture. Senior auditors were often responsible for several audits at one time, but had little direct contact with top managers in client firms. Partners handled these relationships while seniors met with comparable client accounting staff.

CPA firms are in the mature stage of their product's life cycle. Many firms are diversifying into related services usually performed by various management consultants, such as computer services, statistical and engineering services, even management development. The accounting staffs of most firms viewed such actions with suspicion. They were not sure if it was ethical to be auditing work done by part of their own firm, or if they should recommend such services to their clients.

One Saturday morning just after the last team-training session, Grant's boss entered Grant's office. He seemed to Grant to be in a more serious mood than usual. It didn't take long for Pete to get to the heart of the matter.

The managing partner wanted progress immediately in raising the profit percentage and total sales. Pete showed him the target numbers. They were larger than Grant had expected. "I don't have to tell you that you need to perform on this one," Pete said as he left the room.

Grant knew indeed that he had to. It was up or out in this firm. He preferred to move up.

He reached for the book on human relations which his secretary had given him. He remembered a chart somewhere. There it was—the leadership TRRAP model. He decided to try to approach his senior staff, maybe even all of his staff. He needed their help. He decided to try to think about what he was doing instead of just reacting, because that didn't seem to help much.

FIGURE 8.8   *Grant Taylor's problem*

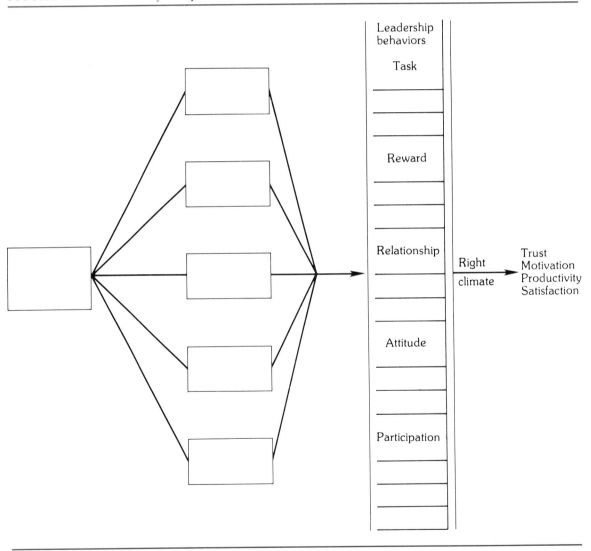

1. Complete Figure 8.8 as follows: Within the boxes to the left of the figure, write in the relevant factors that will affect Grant's decision on how to elicit the best efforts of Walt Ellis, to influence his subordinates, to increase sales, and to cut costs. Then in the spaces under "Leadership behaviors" tell what specific actions he should take, even what specific words he should say to achieve these ends within each of the five categories.

2. If you were Grant, what suggestions would you make or what actions might you take to help the seniors and the supervisors motivate the first-line staff accountants to increase their marketing efforts? Please answer in terms of Figure 3.1, referring to MPC stage and specific actions.

REFERENCES

1. Chester I. Barnard, *The Functions of the Executive* (Cambridge: Harvard University Press, 1938), pp. 160–75.
2. Jeffrey C. Barrow, "The Variables of Leadership: A Review and Conceptual Framework," *Academy of Management Review*, April 1977, pp. 233–34.
3. John R. P. French and Bertram H. Raven, "The Bases of Social Power," in *Studies in Social Power*, ed. Dorwin Cartwright (Ann Arbor: University of Michigan Press, 1959).
4. Daniel C. Pelz, "Influence: Key to Effective Leadership in the First Line Supervisor," *Personnel*, 1952, pp. 209–17.
5. Daniel Yankelovich and Associates, *Work and Human Values* (New York: Public Agenda Foundation, 1983), pp. 6–7.
6. William H. Hendrix, *Contingency Approaches to Leadership: A Review and Synthesis* (Brooks Air Force Base, Tex.: Air Force Systems Command, June 1976), contains a good history of the related research efforts, as does Daniel A. Wren, *The Evolution of Management Thought* (New York: Ronald Press, 1972).
7. Douglas A. McGregor, *The Human Side of Enterprise* (New York: McGraw-Hill, 1960), pp. 33–57.
8. "Seven Who Succeeded," *Business Week*, January 7, 1985, pp. 40–41.
9. J. C. Taylor, "An Empirical Examination of a Four-Factor Theory of Leadership Using Smallest Space Analysis," *Organizational Behavior and Human Performance* 6 (1971): 249–66.
10. Waino W. Soujanen, *The Dynamics of Management* (New York: Holt, Rinehart and Winston, 1966).
11. Ibid., pp. 102–11.
12. Robert R. Blake and Jane S. Mouton, *The New Managerial Grid* (Houston: Gulf, 1978).
13. Ibid., chap. 7.
14. Robert Tannenbaum and Warren H. Schmidt, "How to Choose a Leadership Pattern," *Harvard Business Review* 36 (1958): 95–101.
15. Jerome L. Franklin, "Down the Organization: Influence Processes across Levels of Hierarchy," *Administrative Science Quarterly*, June 1975, pp. 153–65.
16. Fred E. Fiedler, *A Theory of Leadership Effectiveness* (New York: McGraw-Hill, 1967), pp. 10–37.
17. Robert Vecchio, "An Empirical Examination of Fiedler's Model," *Organizational Behavior and Human Performance*, June 1977, pp. 180–206.
18. Paul Hersey and Kenneth R. Blanchard, *Management of Organizational Behavior: Utilizing Human Resources* (Englewood Cliffs, N.J.: Prentice-Hall, 1977).
19. "Football's Supercoach," *Time*, September 29, 1980, pp. 70–77.
20. David G. Bowers and Stanley E. Seashore, "Predicting Organizational Effectiveness with a Four-Factor Theory of Leadership," *Administrative Science Quarterly* 11 (1966): 238–63.
21. Basil S. Georgeopoulos, Gerald M. Mahoney, and Nyel W. Jones, "A Path-Goal Approach to Productivity," *Journal of Applied Psychology*,

1957, pp. 345–52; Robert House, "A Path-Goal Theory of Leader Effectiveness," *Administrative Science Quarterly*, 1971, pp. 321–38; James M. Higgins, "The Leadership TRRAP," forthcoming.

22. William V. Haney, *Communication and Interpersonal Relations: Text and Cases* (Homewood, Ill.: Irwin-Dorsey, 1979), pp. 12–15.

9 EQUAL EMPLOYMENT OPPORTUNITY

KEY TERMS AND CONCEPTS

Civil Rights Act of 1964
Title VII
Equal Employment Opportunity Commission (EEOC)
affirmative action program (AAP)
prejudice
discrimination
comparable worth
selection criteria
performance criteria
reverse discrimination
sexual harassment
age discrimination
significant emotional events

LEARNING OBJECTIVES

When you have completed this chapter, you should be able to:

1. Identify the major groups that are protected by federal laws.
2. Identify the characteristics that make those groups unique and discuss ways in which managers must adapt their behavior to these characteristics and the laws.
3. Describe the basic problems for the manager and the organization caused by federal, state, and local laws and regulations that require special treatment for members of certain groups.
4. Explain the key provisions of the major federal equal employment opportunity laws.
5. Understand the equal employment opportunity laws sufficiently so that you can recognize a related potential problem when you make human relations decisions.

ARE WOMEN LAWYERS DISCRIMINATED AGAINST AT LARGE LAW FIRMS?

At a weekend outing held in North Carolina this past summer by the prestigious Atlanta law firm of King & Spalding, a group of lawyers decided it would be fun to stage a "wet T-shirt" contest featuring the firm's women summer associates.

But cooler heads prevailed. The lawyers had to content themselves with a more old-fashioned, and not quite so revealing, bathing suit competition. As he bestowed first prize on a third-year law student from Harvard University, one of the firm's partners said, "She has the body we'd like to see more of."

Elizabeth Hishon

Lawyers at King & Spalding dismiss the incident as an example of the rollicking good times that characterize the firm's social events and contribute to an unusually high esprit de corps among the firm's lawyers.

But some participants in the impromptu bathing suit event say that they felt humiliated and that they didn't protest only because they were candidates for year-round jobs with the firm. They say they were stunned that the contest occurred, because King & Spalding was the defendant in a sex-discrimination suit. . . .

Whether such attitudes do amount to sex discrimination at King & Spalding remains to be decided. But women lawyers elsewhere say they help explain why women are leaving the large, competitive law firms for smaller firms and corporations where the absence of drastic "up or out" partnership policies reduces pressure to conform to masculine norms.

King & Spalding denies any sex discrimination, and it recently argued before the Supreme Court that Title VII's ban against discrimination in employment doesn't apply to law-firm partnerships because partners aren't employees. The 39-year-old [Elizabeth] Hishon [who is suing the firm] is the odds-on favorite to win this point. If she does, trial on the sex-discrimination charge will proceed in a lower court.

Mrs. Hishon's circumstances are far from unique. Women are entering law school in record numbers, and they seem to face few if any barriers to being hired for entry-level positions as associates. But gaining access to partnership ranks, where virtually all a firm's power is wielded and where profits are

(Continued on page 220)

219

distributed, is another matter. Women apparently are being passed over for partnership at a rate far greater than men.

Of the 26 women in Mrs. Hishon's class at Columbia Law School, 10 of whom went to large law firms immediately upon graduation, only one today is a partner in a law firm comparable in size and stature to King & Spalding. At least four of her women classmates were also passed over for partnerships. The others either abandoned the quest or were encouraged to leave before the decision was formally announced. By comparison, about 20% of Mrs. Hishon's male classmates are partners in highly competitive law firms like King & Spalding; 50% are partners in law firms of any sort, compared with 11.5% of the women.

Elizabeth Hishon was one of seven associates hired in 1972, and she was the first woman hired as a regular associate. A graduate of both Columbia Law School and Wellesley College, she was promised that she would be considered for partnership on the same basis as her male peers. At her request, she was assigned to the firm's real estate department. . . .

But women lawyers who have worked at the firm say, in some cases vehemently, that the firm's intangible criteria for partnership are the essence of sex discrimination. . . .

Mrs. Brown and Mrs. Varner [partners in the firm] cite their own success as the best evidence that women can and do succeed at King & Spalding. Other women say that Mrs. Varner's success is particularly impressive. She was the first woman associate in the department of litigation, traditionally perceived as a difficult area for women, and her promotion to partnership was championed by Mr. Attridge, who called her not "sugar" or "honey" but "sis."

No one, including Mrs. Hishon, suggests that King & Spalding made these women partners because of the sex-discrimination suit. If anything, other women at the firm fear that Mrs. Brown and Mrs. Varner are so outstanding that they have set standards other women will have difficulty matching.

Privately, Mrs. Brown and Mrs. Varner have advised other women in the firm that they must prove themselves in ways that men don't have to.

SOURCE: James B. Stuart, "Fairness Issue: Are Women Lawyers Discriminated Against at Large Law Firms?" *The Wall Street Journal*, December 20, 1983, pp. 1, 10.

"I have a dream."
MARTIN LUTHER KING, JR.

The events outlined in the Human Relations Happening above suggest a disappointing lack of progress in the way women—and all people who are not white and male—are treated by many employers. And while much progress has been made in efforts to ensure equal employment opportunity, thousands of people in the United States, Canada, and elsewhere face these and similar problems every day.

Discrimination is not so open and widespread today as it was twenty years ago, but problems still exist. Many people are still discriminated against in employment decisions on the basis of sex, race, color, religion, national origin, pregnancy, age, mental or physical impairment, and veteran status, even though such discrimination is illegal, and even though most organizations subscribe to equal employment opportunity. This chapter discusses situations of this type, situations that will confront you in the workplace as either a manager, a professional, a first-line employee, or a member of the staff. You may be discriminated against. You may even find yourself discriminating against someone else. You will learn what you should and should not do in order to comply with the law.

Throughout this book, the fact that each individual differs from every other individual has been stressed. The law recognizes and emphasizes this fact, but paradoxically may require you to take special actions on behalf of members of certain groups, even though no member of any group acts the same way or possesses precisely the same characteristics as any other member of that group. From both a managerial and an individual perspective, you must learn to cope with this situation.

This chapter examines individual-to-group behaviors (leadership), individual-to-individual relationships, and organization-to-individual relationships. These behaviors must be considered within the environment created by organizational equal employment opportunity programs. We shall begin with a very brief review of federal laws relating to employment situations. (State and local laws usually parallel federal laws.) We shall then consider selected groups and some problems that may arise in working with them and some solutions to those problems. The information presented in earlier chapters is still applicable, but some fine-tuning may be necessary in certain situations.

EQUAL EMPLOYMENT OPPORTUNITY LAWS

In the United States and Canada, laws protect certain groups of people from discrimination in employment situations. The Canadian laws approximately parallel those of the United States. In the United States, the early 1960s were marked by an indecisive Congress. Despite the pleas of racial minorities for equality in housing, public accommodations, voting, employment, and education, Congress turned a deaf ear, possibly fearing a white backlash at the polls if any actions were taken.

In any event, at least partly in response to massive public demonstrations, Congress finally passed the **Civil Rights Act of 1964.** This act, the cornerstone of federal civil rights law, addressed each of the major civil rights issues, but its primary thrust was in the areas of public accommodations (use by minorities of restaurants, hotels and motels, and other public facilities) and equal employment opportunity. It is the equal employment opportunity section of this law that concerns us most here. **Title VII** of this act made it illegal to base employment decisions on race, color, religion, sex, or national origin. The law was written quite vaguely, and the definition of its terms was left largely to the administrative agency created to enforce it, the **Equal Employment Opportunity Commission (EEOC),** and to the courts, which in time were required to interpret the EEOC's definitions. In 1972 this law was broadened to include governments and educational institutions, which until

"No women are on the fast track to the chief executive's job at any Fortune 500 corporation. That's incongruous given the number of years women have been working in management . . . and tough for management to deal with."

SUSAN FRAKER

that time had not been included in the act's provisions. Then virtually every employer with fifteen or more employees became governed by the law.

What does the law effectively require? It demands that an organization and its managers, when performing the personnel functions—planning, recruiting and attracting, selecting, orienting, compensating and otherwise rewarding, developing, evaluating, and providing safety for its employees—make no decisions on the basis of race, color, religion, sex, or national origin.

The EEOC was originally dependent on the Justice Department for its clout. But in the 1972 revision, the EEOC gained the right to sue in its own name. A 1978 revision outlawed the use of the fact of pregnancy as a determinant of personnel decisions. Because its staff and budget are limited, the EEOC relies primarily on voluntary compliance and court actions against the most visible large employers, hoping to scare other employers into compliance. The EEOC has managed to win significant discrimination cases against the U.S. steel industry, American Telephone & Telegraph, and numerous other defendants. But as one expert has reported, except for the largest firms, banks, and government bodies, many organizations ignore equal employment opportunity, saying, "Catch me if you can," or making only token efforts at compliance.[1] Numerous statistical studies indicate that though much discrimination is still practiced, significant strides toward its elimination have been made.

Other major U.S. statutes and orders that prohibit discrimination in employment practices include:

- The Equal Pay Act of 1963, which prohibits discrimination in compensation on the basis of sex.
- The Age Discrimination in Employment Act of 1967, which prohibits discrimination in employment against people between the ages of 40 and 70.
- Executive orders that prohibit discrimination in employment on the basis of race, color, sex, religion, or national origin by contractors and subcontractors of the federal government, or by the federal government itself.
- The Rehabilitation Act of 1973 and Executive Order on the Handicapped of 1974, which prohibit discrimination in employment against the mentally and physically handicapped by contractors and subcontractors of the federal government.
- The Veterans' Discrimination Act of 1974, which prohibits discrimination in employment against veterans of the Vietnam War.
- The Pregnancy Act of 1978, an amendment to Title VII, which equates pregnancy with other medical situations for the purposes of the allocation of benefits.

These laws and executive orders are enforced primarily by the U.S. Department of Labor or the agencies that are parties to federal contracts, such as the Department of Agriculture, the Department of Defense, and the U.S. Treasury. From 1963 to 1975 the precise actions that employers had to take to comply with these new laws were essentially unknown. But between 1976 and 1980, much of the confusion abated, although some federal agencies still have differing compliance and reporting requirements and have issued conflicting directives. The task of satisfying varying and often contradictory federal guidelines has not been easy. For that reason, President Jimmy Carter proposed the establishment of an equal employment opportunity agency to oversee the entire federal enforcement program.[2] The proposed agency has not been established, but the EEOC has assumed the role of a superagency and other enforcement efforts have been restructured.

In all but the smallest organizations, the equal employment opportunity (EEO) program is formulated and administered by the personnel department. But effective implementation of this program depends on all employees, especially managers. The organization may establish an EEO program or **affirmative action program (AAP)** (a more active approach than an EEO program), but managers and other employees must live with it. The AAP requires that an organization determine its racial and sexual compositions and compare these ratios with those of the available persons in the population of the appropriate recruitment area. On the basis of these numbers, action must be taken to obtain the proper percentages according to a complex calculation process.[3] Compliance is difficult, but difficulty is no excuse for noncompliance.

PREJUDICE AND DISCRIMINATION

Federal EEO laws attempt to eliminate discrimination, not prejudice. What is the difference? **Prejudice** is an attitude; **discrimination** is an action. The law prohibits discriminatory actions. Presumably such actions are based on certain prejudices, but regardless of cause, they are illegal. Prejudice is formed before the facts are known, and sometimes continue even after the facts are known. Even though many of "those people"—be they white, black, yellow, red, male, female, Norwegian, Polish, Irish, Negro, Caucasian, or whatever—may act in a certain way, the essence of prejudice is to believe that all of "those people" act "that way" or are "that way." Prejudice is not allowing for the fact that every individual differs from every other individual. Discrimination, then, is taking action as a matter of course against some of "those people" on the basis of those beliefs.

> *Prejudgments become prejudices only if they are not reversible when exposed to new knowledge.*
> GORDON W. ALLPORT

If you choose to be prejudiced, you can, but as an employer, or as a manager or staff person representing an employer, you cannot discriminate in employment situations on the basis of race, color, religion, sex, national origin, pregnancy, age, mental or physical handicap, or veteran status. You can of course choose to discriminate if you think you will not get caught, or if you do not care about fairness. But discrimination is inconsistent with a positive approach to human relations.

The essence of good human relations has been stated over and over as helping create a positive self-image in others, of being assertive, not aggressive. No matter which group you belong to, no matter which group's members you are working with, from the human relations viewpoint the problem is the same. Positive human relations means carrying out positively oriented behavior with people whose backgrounds are not the same as yours. Empathy is a vital part of working with people who belong to other groups.

There are no federal laws protecting many other people against whom discrimination is common—homosexuals, for example, and the overweight. And significant prejudice often exists within an organization dominated by one of the protected groups. The EEOC, for example, was in the past primarily a black organization that reportedly discriminated against whites, Spanish-speaking Americans, and Jews.[4] Some organizations have gained reputations for being closed to all but members of certain groups: if you are not Catholic, or Jewish, or WASP, you simply do not get promoted to the top. Others will not hire people who are not members of "the group." But since the largest employing organizations are dominated by white male managements, it is these organizations that have received most federal, state, and local attention with respect to discriminatory personnel practices.

Historically, most discrimination has occurred in five areas of employment practice:

1. *Recruitment:* failure to recruit actively in minority residential areas, in minority media, in minority schools. (Women and selected demographic groups are defined here as minorities.)
2. *Selection:* artificially high selection standards or selection standards that bear no significant relationship to performance on the job.
   A high school diploma has often been used to keep racial minorities from qualifying for jobs that really do not require a high school diploma. Any selection standard (known as a criterion) must bear a statistically significant or demonstrable relationship to job content or performance if it is to be legally acceptable. Criteria that prevent a large number of members of minority groups from being selected are viewed with suspicion.
3. *Compensation:* equal pay for equal work is required, yet in most organizations disparities exist.
   A common ploy has been to use differing titles for jobs that are essentially the same, and to base rates of pay on the titles of jobs rather than on their content. This has been a common means of rationalizing the practice of paying women less than men. **Comparable worth** is a dominant compensation issue. The concept holds that jobs that are typically held by men and those that are typically held by women can be evaluated for like elements and a market wage determined. Striking secretaries at Yale threatened to bring the university to a standstill over the issue. Female workers in Washington State won a discrimination suit that could cost the state over $1 billion in back pay and increased wages.[5]
4. *Upward mobility systems:* selection of people to be transferred, trained, and promoted as well as those to be hired.
   Criteria are an integral part of this problem. High school diplomas have again been used in the past to keep many members of racial minorities from receiving promotions for which they were otherwise qualified. Women have often been discriminated against because, well, you know, "women just don't have the aggressiveness it takes to make it." (Let them try being assertive and see how quickly they become "bitchy" and "abrasive.")
5. *Evaluation:* performance appraisals, terminations, and disciplinary actions.

Minorities must attend to these problems as well. They must be attuned to the need to "fit in," as the following story suggests:

Fleming Golden, a 34-year-old black manufacturing manager at International Business Machines Corp., recalls the incident that helped teach him how to climb the corporate ladder.

It happened in 1976, when he was with IBM's corporate staff in Armonk, N.Y. "I was always a flashy dresser," he says. "I had lots of orange and green suits. Then one day, an older, white guy took me aside and said, 'Hey, don't get offended, but it's about those suits you wear. They just don't blend in at IBM.' "

So Mr. Golden switched to pin stripes. "One day my boss mentioned that he liked the suit I was wearing. I got the message."

Mr. Golden understood that the message was less about his clothes than about the delicate line that he must walk between being black, or different, and being perceived as a "team player" in a white corporate culture. Having reached middle management by his technical skills, he learned that the selection for top management is more subjective.

Since then, "I've shown in a lot of ways that I function as a member of the team. I've established enough contacts so that I'll achieve my goals," he says confidently.[6]

> *Stereotypes are not beliefs in a vacuum. They are reinforced by the behavior of both prejudiced people and their targets.*
>
> MARK SNYDER

RULES OF CONDUCT

What can you do as a manager, as a staff person, or as a nonmanagerial first-line employee to prevent yourself and your organization from violating the law in these common problem areas? First, you need to become familiar with the law. All organizations should provide training in these laws, but they do not always do so. Below are some rules of conduct related to discrimination which you need to follow if you have responsibilities in these problem areas.

Recruitment   If you have responsibilities for recruitment, you need to examine your AAP and determine how many more members of protected groups you need for each kind of job. Then you need to determine how actively to recruit them. This may mean placing advertisements in minority media, establishing contacts in minority residential areas, making recruiting trips to minority secondary schools and colleges, even teaching courses in minority schools. Recruiting at women's colleges, for example, will produce more female applicants than recruiting exclusively at coeducational institutions. Advertisements for most job openings cannot specify the sex or age of desired applicants.

Selection   Three common problems occur during the selection process: (1) determining the selection criteria, the basis for hiring the one individual from the pool of applicants who will do the job; (2) the questions asked on the application blank; and (3) the questions asked during the selection interview, if one is given.

Most of you will not have responsibility for establishing **selection criteria,** the standards for selecting someone for a job. So this discussion is brief, at least in relation to its complexity. If you do have such responsibility, whatever criteria you choose should have some logical and preferably statistical relationship to job content or to performance on the job. For example, it is reasonable to test a prospective typist to see how well he or she can type, but to test applicants' ability to write English or to solve mathematical problems is not reasonable if the jobs for which they are applying do not require those skills. Unless you can show a clear statistical relationship between the qualifications you want in a person, the means you use to measure those specifications, and performance on the job (usually accomplished through some kind of test), then you had better reconsider the use of those qualifications and tests. The difficulty of establishing statistical relationships has led many employers to establish "hear thunder, see lightning" tests. In other words, if you can hear and see, you have successfully passed the selection test for many jobs. If several applicants pass this test, then "first come, first served" may be the critical criterion.

Establishing selection criteria and tests to measure potential performance is a highly sophisticated process for some jobs. Most large employers leave this process to the experts in the personnel or human resource department. Smaller organizations often just hope for the best, since they can seldom afford to validate (prove statistically or otherwise) all tests or all criteria.

Most of you will not have responsibility for designing application blanks. Again, the personnel department usually handles this. But if you should happen to be involved in this process, the questions that can be asked follow approximately the same rules as those that can be asked in a selection interview.

The federal government prohibits the asking of very few questions. You cannot ask if an employee has been arrested or how many times. You can ask about convictions if they might be related to the job. You cannot ask women questions that you do not ask men. Other than that, you can ask just about any question you want to, *but* you had better be certain that what you ask is related to the job for which the person is applying. Furthermore, you had better be able to show that asking a particular question did not result in discrimination. (Some state laws do prohibit certain questions, however.) The exercise at the end of the chapter indicates those question areas that are viewed with suspicion by federal enforcement agencies.

Compensation   If the work involved in two jobs is substantially the same, regardless of the jobs' titles, then the pay should be the same. Men and women are frequently paid differing amounts for essentially the same type and amount of work. If you have responsibility for anyone's pay, you need to make certain that this does not occur in your organization.

"If one more person engages me in a conversation about jazz, I think I'll scream. Not all blacks like jazz and I happen to be one who doesn't."
BLACK CORPORATE
VICE-PRESIDENT

Upward Mobility Systems   If you are involved in the process of choosing people to be transferred, given training, or promoted, you need to make certain that your selection criteria—that is, the bases on which you decide who is to be transferred, trained, or promoted—are related (again preferably statistically) to performance on the job. Artificially high criteria are the ones that federal enforcement agencies most carefully scrutinize. If the new job or new job situation or training does not require the skill or other qualification on which you base your decision, you are on shaky ground in using that requirement. A primary concern of federal EEO enforcement agencies today is upward mobility for women, blacks, Spanish-speaki g Americans, American Indians, Asian-Americans, and the mentally and physically handicapped.

Evaluation (Especially Discipline)   Employees are evaluated for raises, promotions, transfers, training, and discipline, usually on the basis of a performance appraisal system. The single most important aspect of performance evaluation is the establishment of objectives—that is, **performance criteria**—in advance of appraisal, and making certain that these criteria are communicated and understood by the employee. This process is discussed in more detail in Chapter 11. If you are involved in this process, either as a manager or as a peer-group evaluator, you need to adhere to this "in advance and understood" requirement. Next, proper counseling and performance appraisal interviewing techniques should be employed. Such techniques involve the general methods of motivating, communicating, leadership, problem solving, assertiveness, and active listening noted in Chapters 2 through 8.

Discipline will be reviewed in Chapter 10. The techniques used here are much the same, no matter whom you are disciplining. Because of the potential legal difficulties involved in disciplining a member of a protected group, however, you must be certain to document all actions taken. If necessary, have a witness present, and it is recommended that you have the person being disciplined sign the disciplinary counseling statement. It is especially important that all relevant information be gathered and carefully analyzed before action is taken. This does not mean that you cannot discipline people in the protected groups, only that you must be certain that discipline is warranted and that you have "covered your answers" (CYA) in case of trouble. Termination is the ultimate form of discipline, and it requires extremely careful documentation. One must be very careful in discharging people over 40 years of age, for example, because they could claim age discrimination.

Layoffs must also be carefully considered. The laws here are complex and unfortunately often contradictory. A unionized company must follow the guidelines of the National Labor Relations Board, which call for seniority systems to be implemented; but a company that bases layoffs on seniority may be considered discriminatory by the EEOC, because the people with the most seniority tend to be overwhelmingly white and male. Relevant case law (actual legal cases and their results) is best consulted in this situation.

Reverse Discrimination   In the late 1970s, **reverse discrimination** became an important issue. In the case of *Webber* v. *Kaiser*, the U.S. Supreme Court upheld the right of employers to give preferential treatment to members of certain protected groups. This issue has still not been definitively clarified, but for a while the general rule of thumb seemed to be to give preferential treatment in order to satisfy AAP requirements. A black male personnel director for a large national bank told me, "If a white guy does that, we fire him. If a black guy does that, because of the law, we have to give him two warnings; then we can fire him." However, a more recent Supreme Court ruling, *Firefighters* v. *Stotts*, though limited in its scope, suggests that reverse discrimination is inappropriate. (See the Human Relations Happening on p. 228.)

HUMAN RELATIONS HAPPENING

FIREFIGHTERS V. STOTTS

When blacks protested against discrimination in employment practices, the city of Memphis agreed in 1980 to an affirmative action plan approved by a federal judge. The cornerstone of the plan was the hiring of a large number of black firefighters (50 percent of all new employees) until two-fifths of all firefighters were black. But in 1981, Memphis, like most U.S. cities, encountered highly unfavorable economic conditions, and consequently cut its budget substantially. A large number of firefighters would be laid off (72 whites and 8 blacks), the city announced, in accordance with the existing seniority plan. But a federal district court ruled that the city could not use its seniority plan if the effect was to reduce the proportion of blacks in the firefighting force. Consequently, three whites lost their jobs to blacks with less seniority. Although the layoff lasted only one month, the firefighters and their union pressed an appeal against the court's decision. Eventually, on June 12, 1984,

the U.S. Supreme Court held that the lower court and the appeals court that upheld the lower court's decision had erred. Justice Byron White, writing for the Court's majority, declared, "Mere membership in the disadvantaged class is insufficient to warrant a seniority award." When seniority and affirmative action plans are in opposition, White said, only "those who have been actual victims of illegal discrimination" can win a job-bias claim.

This decision is likely to have a significant impact. Many civil rights leaders claim that the decision set back civil rights in the United States by twenty years. Legal scholars point out, however, that the decision is a narrow one, and that it is unlikely to affect mainstream efforts to reduce discrimination, though it does reinforce the perception that people in organizational management positions need not be as concerned with affirmative action as they once were.

SOURCE: "Seniority vs. Minorities—Impact of Court Ruling," *Business Week*, June 25, 1984, pp. 22–23; Louis P. Britt III, "Affirmative Action: Is There Life after Stotts?" *Personnel Administrator*, September 1984.

EMPLOYER ACTIONS TO HELP MINORITY GROUPS

66A woman has to be twice as good as a man to go half as far.99
FANNIE HURST

Employers have instituted many programs in attempts to remedy the problems generated by cultural differences among the members of the various groups they employ. Such programs have been aimed primarily at integrating blacks and Spanish-speaking people into the work force. Employers have organized programs of sensitivity training for supervisors and other managers to help them to overcome their and other employees' differing cultural perspectives; provided training in basic English and mathematics, in which many minorities failed to receive adequate instruction in the public schools; offered indoctrination courses to familiarize minorities with typical organization work rules, which may differ from the rules they have been accustomed to following; instituted work-simplification programs, which make tasks easier to accomplish; offered incentives to trainees to provide immediate reinforcement of the behaviors that lead to work accomplishment; reduced reliance on tests and increased validation of the tests used; offered flexible work hours to accommodate employees with family or other responsibilities; provided on-site day-care centers for employees' children; and helped to form car pools, posted bus schedules, even provided company buses for employees.

Many employers go beyond the requirements of EEO legislation to help minority groups to achieve their objectives. Sometimes external pressures have resulted in significant company efforts. Nine months of negotiation between the National Association for the Advancement of Colored People (NAACP) and McDonald's restaurants resulted in McDonald's agreement to funnel approximately $110 million into the black community over five years by actively seeking blacks to buy and manage franchises, establishing at least 100 new black-owned restaurants, increasing the number of blacks promoted, actively seeking black vendors, and using black-owned construction companies.[7]

The most important factor to remember is that people are different. The world would be a dull place if everybody were the same. Within the limits of the work we do, we can make changes to help one another.

WOMEN IN THE WORK FORCE

More and more women are entering the work force. In 1985, 53.5 percent of all women over age 16 worked. Those figures have risen rapidly. As equal employment opportunity comes closer to reality, more and more women move from the low-paying, low-skilled jobs to which women have historically been relegated (or from the low-paying, high-skilled jobs of teaching and nursing) into higher-paying professional and managerial positions. Why do women

> *"Why can't a woman be more like a man?"*
> GEORGE BERNARD
> SHAW *Pygmalion*

> *"Why should a woman be more like a man?"*
> CAROL GILLIGAN

"IN SEEKING A FEMALE EXECUTIVE TO JOIN OUR MANAGEMENT TEAM, MS. WHITSOCK, WE'VE REACHED UNANIMOUS AGREEMENT THAT YOU'RE OUR MAN."

From *The Wall Street Journal*—Permission, Cartoon Features Syndicate

work? Mostly because they must. Married women who work do so largely because a single salary is no longer enough for the average working family. (That women "don't have to work" is just one of the myths about women. What are some of the others? See "Myths about Women.") Some women, of course, work because they enjoy work and are bored with "domestic engineering." Single women work to support themselves and their families. In 1980, a Bureau of Labor Statistics survey reported that 7 out of 10 women worked out of economic necessity. So the old adage that women don't really need to be paid the same as a man is invalid.[8]

How can women be better integrated into the work force and what can men (whatever their color or ethnicity) do to relate better to the increasing number of women managers and professionals they encounter? Well, to dismiss the differences between the sexes is difficult. Some people believe it is appropriate to try; others say such attempts are unrealistic. Certainly there are differences,

---

MYTHS ABOUT WOMEN

Women have been the victims of several prejudicial beliefs that do not survive close examination. George Biles and Holly Pryatel have listed some of these myths and provided information that reveals their inaccuracy.

Myth 1: Women are poor economic risks because they are often sick and quit work when they have children. Actually, there is no statistically significant difference in the number of days of absenteeism of men and of women. Historically women did leave the work force to have children, but this trend is changing, and women who quit work to care for their children are now reentering the work force once the children reach school age; many mothers do not stop working at all.

Myth 2: Women do not make good managers because they are too emotional. Female managers do not bear out this belief, and in fact many women are calmer than many men.

Myth 3: Women have a low commitment to the world of work. Men actually job-hop more than women. Women's perceived lack of commitment may result from the fact that they usually have had access only to the most mundane jobs.

Myth 4: Women lack education and experience. Women actually have higher education levels than men, on the average. Their major problem has been upward mobility—again a problem of stereotyping.

Myth 5: Women are not interested in certain phases of business. This may be partly true, as a result of socialization processes—but these processes are changing.

Myth 6: Women should be banned from certain organizational groups because of their disruptive influence. Experience has shown that this problem exists only in the mind.

Myth 7: Man is the prototypical worker. Women do suffer from this myth, but there are almost as many working women as men.

Myth 8: Women lack the motivation to achieve. Not so. Women do achieve when they are given the opportunity to do so.

SOURCE: George E. Biles and Holly A. Pryatel, "Myths, Management, and Women," *Personnel Journal*, October 1978, pp. 572–78; and Women's Bureau, Employment Standards Administration, U.S. Department of Labor, *Role of Women* (Washington, D.C., 1975). Reprinted with permission of *Personnel Journal*, Costa Mesa, CA; all rights reserved.

but a large part of those differences is cultural, and in any case they are irrelevant to competence on the job. Except for a limited number of jobs, such as wetnurse, exotic dancer, and restroom attendant, the federal government recognizes no job for which sex is a bona fide occupational qualification. So the sex of an applicant or employee must not be considered in decisions on hiring and promotion. Women and men want and deserve the same kind of treatment: we all want fairness. We all want to be recognized as individuals, with individual talents, strengths, and weaknesses.

Sexual harassment is a problem that women do not like to talk about, but one with which most women in the work force are well acquainted. Patricia Somers and Judith Clementson-Mohr defined sexual harassment as "unsolicited non-reciprocal male behavior that asserts a woman's sex role over her function as a worker." Such behavior may include verbal abuse, sexist remarks, patting or pinching, leering, demands for sexual favors in return for personnel actions, physical assault, and rape. While some women may take suggestive comments in stride, continued sexual harassment, including demands for sexual favors as a condition of employment, is intolerable. Several surveys have revealed that at least 80 percent of working women have experienced some form of sexual harassment.[9] Retaliation is common against those who complain. Thus many women's livelihoods are threatened by these actions. Many women report that they resort to such tactics as "avoiding working with men," "being careful how I dress," and "pretending not to notice." (See the Human Relations Happening "The Truth Is Stranger.") Several recent lawsuits indicate that women are becoming more assertive in their responses to harassment, as they should be. The future will apparently hold a more assertive female work force, one less intimidated by this kind of treatment.[10] Sexual harassment has also been committed by women against men and by homosexuals against heterosexuals. Neither of these forms of harassment seems to occur frequently, but both are certainly significant to the people harassed. Religious, ethnic, and racial harassment is also of concern. All forms of harassment are offensive and are subject to legal action.

SEXUAL AND OTHER KINDS OF HARASSMENT

HUMAN RELATIONS HAPPENING

THE TRUTH IS STRANGER

The stories of women who have been sexually exploited on the job are astounding. Here are a few:

- In the *Redbook* survey, a typist described the area behind the file cabinets as "grope alley."

- An employee in the EEO Department of the Environmental Protection Agency was fired after refusing to have sex with her boss. She sued and settled out of court.

- *Ms.* reports the case of an executive secretary in her late forties who was continually

(Continued on page 232)

subjected to detailed descriptions of her boss's extramarital affairs. When he began to accompany these recitals with pats to her buttocks and requests for oral sex, she left. However, he gave her unwarranted poor work references and wouldn't support her claim for unemployment benefits.

- Harragan tells of a woman who complained to the company personnel manager about sexual advances from her boss. His reaction was to grab her breast.
- In 1976, a leading female jockey retired early, calling the track a "hooker's paradise." Said she, "If you don't cooperate sexually, you don't get the mounts—it's that simple."
- A professor who left her job because of sexual assault by the chairman of the department was offered two jobs. One of them was available only because the previous employee left due to sexual harassment. She said, "The abuse is incredible. They are just going to sexually abuse us until we drop out of the competition."

- Farley interviewed a woman who was forced to submit to intercourse to keep her job. She said, "You could just see the pattern. The less skill the woman had, the less essential her job, so the heavier the hassle; hence the range was anywhere from 'yes, I've seen it happen' . . . to 'yes, I've given in.' Of the eight women who started when I did, they all have quit."
- A female police officer in Washington, D.C. reported coercion for better assignments. She said, "You've got to make love to get a day off or make love to get a good beat."

SOURCE: Patricia A. Somers and Judith Clementson-Mohr, "Sexual Extortion in the Work Place." Reprinted from the April 1979 issue of *Personnel Administrator*, 30 Park Drive, Berea, OH 44017, $26 per year.

WHAT CAN WOMEN DO?

Women can take any number of positive actions to enhance their own career situations. Attendance at skills training seminars for women is rapidly increasing. The subjects covered include assertiveness, public speaking, dress and appearance, and fundamental management skills.

Dress, appearance, and speaking voice (an assertive tone of voice) are important factors in career success. Women who wish to succeed in business are now being advised to dress in a manner that is businesslike but not masculine. The skirted suit with a blouse is currently the most popular attire for the female executive or professional, although many such women seem to be returning to the wearing of dresses. Women as well as men must learn to be assertive, and to recognize any tendency they may have to assume the traditional female role of the passive supporter. This is not to suggest that women become gruff, only that people who are adaptively meek usually do not go very far up the corporate ladder. As one female executive has said, "Now I holler back to clear the air instead of hiding under my desk."[11]

Another tactic that women can employ is establishing an "old girls' network." Men have had an "old boys' network" for years, but until recently women have failed to initiate such a system—partly, of course, because few women reached the top of their organizations. But now those who do reach positions of authority have a responsibility to sponsor others for promotions, career-assisting transfers, and choice assignments.

Fight off stereotypes. Women are confronted daily with numerous stereotypes related to their attitudes, their employment longevity, their personalities, their physical abilities. Table 9.1 gives insight into the problems that women face in this regard. How do you overcome these stereotypes? You assert yourself. You create successes and others will follow.

A woman faces many problems in pursuing a career, especially if she has children. There are value decisions to be made here. The choice is not clearly between home and work, but some compromises frequently must be made. But as one female executive noted, "It's not how much time, it's the type of time you spend with your kids."[12] Unfortunately, some men still cannot accept their wives' success—or be interested in work that does not involve them. The issue of whose job is more important has ended more than a few marriages. And more than a few women have been beaten by their husbands over the work issue.

There are many negative factors that women must contend with. For example, most women are not as competitive on team events as they are individually. Since much work is accomplished in teams, this factor works against them. But becoming team players is something that women do well. So the problem can be overcome. Women also tend to be channeled differently from men at early ages. Women are usually better students, so whatever field they enter, this should be to their advantage. Parents who wish their children to excel in certain areas should program them at an early age. Tell your daughter she can grow up to be a doctor if she wants to; she doesn't have to be a nurse. Tell her she can grow up to be an electrical engineer, not a domestic one. Remember, a parent's words are remembered forever. These are just a few hints, and this section barely brushes the surface of the subject. Numerous books have dealt with these issues. The important point here is that women should acquire the necessary work skills and the necessary human relations skills—just as men should.

TABLE 9.1 How to Tell a Businessman from a Businesswoman

MAN	WOMAN
A businessman is aggressive.	A businesswoman is pushy.
He is careful about details.	She's picky.
He loses his temper because he's so involved in his job.	She's bitchy.
He's depressed (or hung over), so everyone tiptoes past his office.	She's moody, so it must be her time of the month.
He follows through.	She doesn't know when to quit.
He's firm.	She's stubborn.
He makes wise judgments.	She reveals her prejudices.
He is a man of the world.	She's been around.
He isn't afraid to say what he thinks.	She's opinionated.
He exercises authority.	She's tyrannical.
He's discreet.	She's secretive.
He's a stern taskmaster.	She's difficult to work for.

> *Most hierarchies were established by men who now monopolize the upper levels, thus depriving women of their rightful share of opportunities to achieve incompetence.*
> LAURENCE J. PETER

SOURCE: Robert M. Fulmer, *Practical Human Relations.* Copyright © 1977 by Richard D. Irwin. Reprinted by permission.

With 53 percent of the U.S. population composed of women, they can hardly be called a minority. But they are treated as one in most organizations. Women are usually paid less than men for the work they do, but women have increased as a percentage of the work force and will continue to do so. The stereotypes exist, and only time and dedication can remove them. But the success stories of those women who have been mobile and competent and who have played out their executive roles well should spur others to success. The future looks bright for the assertive, competent woman, despite the prejudices that remain.

RELIGIOUS MINORITIES

In the United States and Canada, the two groups that encounter the most problems in the workplace because of their religious practices are those of the Jewish faith and the Mormons. These problems occur primarily because their religious days of worship and holidays differ from those commonly celebrated by the majority of people in the work force. The law protects all persons from discriminatory employment practices due to religion. Employers must make reasonable accommodations for the religious practices of others. However, when an organization exists primarily to serve people of a specific religion—for example, a Jewish or Catholic educational institution—that institution has the right to exclude employees of other faiths.

OLDER WORKERS

66In our society, turning 40 for a man is a marker event in itself. By custom, as if he were merchandise on a rack, he will be looked over by his employers and silently marked up or down, recategorized by his insurers, labeled by his competitors.99
GAIL SHEEHY

Discrimination based on age is one of the most difficult for the victimized individual to prove. While most of the early federal antidiscrimination efforts focused on discrimination based on race, sex, national origin, and color, recently increased attention has been paid to discrimination against people between the ages of 40 and 70.

Age discrimination is very much related to problems of performance appraisal and the evaluation of workers' contributions to the organization. Older workers usually make higher salaries than younger employees, simply because they have been employed long enough to have achieved seniority and to have collected more raises. They usually cost the organization more in terms of benefits—employers' social security taxes are based on employees' salaries, as are contributions to pension funds, and longer-term employees usually receive longer vacations. Thus, if performance is not evaluated appropriately, if performance criteria are not properly established, employers often tend to eliminate the older worker in favor of a young worker who is perceived to be less costly and more energetic. The issues are often complex. In 1985, for example, the U.S. Supreme Court found TWA guilty of age discrimination because it terminated pilots at age 60. Federal law bars them from piloting commercial aircraft after 60 but permits them to remain as flight engineers. TWA chose to terminate them instead.[13]

If you are in a position in which you must relate to older workers, this relationship does not require skills very different from those regarded as appropriate for relating to other groups. Empathy is essential—let's face it, we will all be old someday. The most important skill is simply understanding the differences between the experiences of the old and the young. Older people have experienced most of what there is to experience, and their need hierarchy is likely to differ from a younger person's, as we saw in Chapter 3. Their need hierarchy is almost the inverse of the younger person's. Morris Massey suggests that major cultural developments, such as the Great Depression, World War II, the Vietnam War, and television, have profound effects on the value orientations and motivations of the people whose childhoods they have dominated. Even after people have reached maturity, other facets of their personalities may be greatly affected by such developments, which Massey terms **significant emotional events**. The needs of an entire age group are functionally dependent in many ways on these "events."[14] Obviously, other variables enter into dominant values and needs, such as the statements made about these events by authority figures, but Massey's argument is a good one. You should not be surprised that the need for security dominates the value hierarchies of people over 60. Many of these people literally faced starvation. Nor should you be surprised that many of their children couldn't care less about security. They are sick and tired of hearing about how tough it was then.

As with women, certain myths exist about older employees. Overcoming them is primarily a function of observing and absorbing factual information. Some of the myths are these:[15]

MYTHS ABOUT OLDER WORKERS

1. Older workers stay sick longer than younger ones. Actually the frequency of sickness is slightly less for older workers than for younger ones, though the duration of illness is slightly greater.
2. Mental capabilities decline with age. Actually, they do not decline appreciably as long as people have goals toward which they can work.
3. Older workers cost the employer more. Probably not if the older workers' experience, work ethic, and low rates of tardiness and absenteeism are included in the calculation. Some employers seek out older employees for these reasons.[16]

Eventually everyone faces the life crisis of retirement, and indeed it is a crisis for many people. Most authorities today believe that without some objectives to work toward, death is hastened by retirement. As one of the researchers told me, studies of U.S. Air Force retirees reveal that for those who do not engage in second careers, death comes within an average of seven years, whether the individual retired after twenty or thirty years of service. This means that individuals who retire are dying in their late forties or fifties. Those who engage in second careers live much longer. I believe similar results can be found in civilian industry. In 1980 there were 25 million retired persons and 50 million people over age 50 in the United States. If these people are to enjoy their "golden years," employers, private and public, need to provide

PREPARING OLDER WORKERS FOR RETIREMENT

preretirement counseling. William Glueck indicates that such programs should include counseling on the following points:

- Developing a healthy attitude toward retirement: focusing on provisions society has made to help retired persons, and on the positive effects of staying healthy and active.

- Enjoyable uses of leisure time: showing potential retirees the many enjoyable ways that they can spend their time.

- Work during retirement: revealing the many ways in which retirees can have a second career, or can work part-time.

- Money matters: retirees are especially concerned about this issue.

- Relocation: should retirees and their families stay where they are or move? And if they should move, where?

- Other subjects: retirees need to know their rights—under Medicare, for example—and be introduced to such publications as *Harvest Years* and *Modern Maturity*. Wills should be prepared and other necessary adjustment actions taken.[17]

NEW PROBLEMS WITH RETIREMENT

While the Age Discrimination in Employment Act (ADEA) allows employees to continue to work until age 70 (some states have laws barring a mandatory retirement age), most employees, especially salaried ones, continue to retire at 65 or younger. Surveys show that historically, early retirement, not later, is the choice of those who have a choice, and that most employers and employees prefer this trend to continue.[18] There are changes in the offing, however, which may make this choice unpleasant and undesirable: an increase in mandatory retirement age under Social Security from 65 to 68 or 70; and any increase in the rate of inflation leaves the retiree without a second career walking a dangerous financial tightrope. Such developments could cause people to remain employed longer.

In the past, an individual could often come close to making his or her current salary when Social Security and other pensions were added together, especially if the retiree earned some limited amount of income (to stay within the limit beyond which Social Security benefits were reduced). When the age at which full Social Security retirement benefits are paid is raised, the option to retire before that age will be substantially reduced. When Social Security was first formed and the retirement age was established as 65, few people lived that long. But now most people do, and they live longer once they retire. Funding problems have already forced Social Security to roll back the eligibility age to 67 in the year 2003, and these retirees will have longer to live than those who were eligible when Social Security first started. My own guess is that we'll soon see Social Security eligibility rolled back to age 70 in order to cut budget deficits.

THE MENTALLY AND PHYSICALLY HANDICAPPED

Federal laws and executive orders protect the mentally and physically handicapped from discrimination in employment practices. The actual rules that must be followed are still being determined. Generally, the employer must make a "reasonable accommodation" to the physically or mentally handicapped individual. The important question is: What is "reasonable"?

These laws and executive orders apply only to the federal government and to its first- and second-tier contractors and subcontractors. When obvious mental and physical handicaps are encountered, employers seem to be responding well. Ray Bressler has shown, for example, that little if any discrimination exists against physically handicapped individuals in the U.S. government.[19] But most employers are less comfortable about considering such conditions as diabetes and heart conditions as handicaps that have no effect on a worker's ability to perform. The obvious costs of extending the laws to cover such conditions would be tremendous. As with other discrimination laws, the courts will determine what ultimately is to be covered by the law.

TIPS FOR SUCCESS

1. Don't discriminate.

2. Be familiar enough with what you should do legally that you don't unknowingly discriminate.

3. Remember, people are different.

4. Cover your answers.

5. Be empathetic.

SUMMARY

1. With very few exceptions, federal law prohibits employers from basing employment decisions on race, sex, color, religion, national origin, age, pregnancy, mental or physical handicap, or veteran status.

2. In general, the behaviors expected of managers and other employees with respect to members of the groups covered by these laws are fairly well defined.

3. No person can be denied opportunity for employment or advancement on the basis of any of the characteristics covered by these laws.

4. Prejudice is an attitude; discrimination is an action. The law cannot eliminate prejudice, but it can and does prohibit discrimination.

5. Historically, most discrimination has occurred in five areas of employment practice: recruitment, selection, equality of compensation, upward mobility systems, and evaluation.

6. Employers have instituted many programs to recruit members of minority groups and integrate them into the work force.

7. All forms of harassment—sexual, racial, religious, ethnic—are offensive, and all are subject to legal action.

DISCUSSION QUESTIONS

1. What are the major federal laws and executive orders and whom do they protect?

2. What is meant by "employment practices"? What are they?

3. Have you recently interacted with any members of the protected groups on the job? What

are your perceptions of their work competence? Are you prejudiced?

4. How do you feel about working with people who are different from yourself? Why do you feel that way?

5. To what characteristics of each of the protected

groups must managers give special thought before they interact with those persons?

6. What are the behaviors that managers should follow in interacting with members of each of the protected groups?

7. What can women do to improve their own career possibilities?

8. If you are not a member of a minority group, pretend that you are. Pick any group. Describe your feelings about not being hired after applying for ten jobs, all of which you felt you were qualified to fill.

APPLYING HUMAN RELATIONS SKILLS

CASES

Lunchtime Madness

Carolyn Spears, a recent law school graduate, joined a large law firm in Philadelphia. She soon began to invite clients to lunch. Most of her clients were men. Many of them made passes at her, and she was not sure how to cope with them. She wanted very much to remain professional, to advance her career, yet to retain the clients.

1. What do you recommend that she do in such situations?

EEOC Investigation

Winston Morehead was the personnel manager for a large retail store in San Francisco. Early one Monday morning he received a call from a representative of the local office of the EEOC. The representative indicated that his organization had received more than eight complaints in the last year about racial discrimination against Asian-Americans. As a result, the EEOC would be investigating Winston's firm. A mutually convenient date for the opening of the investigation was agreed upon, and the EEOC representative hung up.

Winston was shocked. He had taken sufficient actions, he thought, to provide every opportunity for the hiring of minorities of all types. The EEOC representative had said that upward mobility was the principal concern. Winston checked his figures and found that indeed there were no Asian-Americans above the entry level. He wondered how he could have let this situation slip past him.

1. What types of actions should Winston have taken earlier to prevent this investigation?

2. What can he do now to limit the damage done to his organization by this investigation? Be aware that if the EEOC decides to investigate a firm, it investigates every facet of employment practices for all protected groups.

Developing Nonsexist Attitudes at Work

Marsha Simpkins had been given the unenviable task of designing an EEO training and development program for her 1,000-person bank for the purpose of reducing sexist attitudes among male employees. She had sufficient funding to do a good job. Basic training in the law had already been given, but attitudes had not sufficiently changed, especially with regard to moving women into top management.

1. If you were Marsha, what types of skills and knowledge would you try to impart to your managers and others? Why?

Lawful or Unlawful?

With the exceptions of the questions noted in the text, virtually any question can be asked in a preemployment or prepromotion interview—but you had better be prepared to defend your judgment in asking any question. The basic ground rules are that if the information sought cannot be shown to be (1) related to the job, (2) a bona fide occupational qualification, or (3) in the interest of national defense, you are in trouble.

The best interview is one that is structured, one that seeks the same types of information from each applicant. Some limited variation may be permissible in order to enable some applicants to give more in-depth responses to certain questions. Scoring of interviews for each applicant is recommended.

Do you think you know how to word questions in an interview? The following questions and requests frequently show up on job application forms and in interviews. Circle L if you feel the question is lawful, U if you feel the question is unlawful.

EXERCISE

1. What is your maiden name? L U
2. What was your previous married name? L U
3. Have you ever worked under another name? L U
4. What is your title—Mr., Miss, Mrs., or Ms.? L U
5. What is your marital status? L U
6. What is your birthplace? L U
7. What is the birthplace of parents, spouse, or other relatives? L U
8. Submit proof of age (birth certificate or baptismal record). L U
9. What is your religious denomination or affiliation? (or church, parish, pastor or religious holidays observed). L U
10. Are you available for Saturday or Sunday work? L U
11. Are you a citizen of the U.S.? L U
12. Are you a naturalized citizen? L U
13. On what date were you granted citizenship? L U
14. Submit naturalization papers or first papers. L U
15. List past work experience. L U
16. List organizations, clubs, societies, and lodges to which you belong. L U
17. What is your wife's maiden name? L U
18. Submit names of persons willing to provide professional and/or character references. L U
19. Supply names of three relatives other than father, husband or wife, or minor-age dependent children. L U
20. What relative can we notify in case of accident or emergency (name and address)? L U

21. What foreign languages can you read, write, or speak? L U
22. How did you acquire the ability to read, write, or speak a foreign language? L U
23. Have you ever been arrested for any crime? If so, stipulate when and where. L U
24. List names of dependent children under the age of 18. L U
25. What arrangements have you made for the care of minor children? L U
26. What is the lowest salary you would accept? L U
27. What is your height and weight? L U
28. Have you ever had your wages garnished? L U
29. Have you ever been refused a fidelity bond? L U
30. Do you own a home? Car? Have charge accounts? L U
31. What kind of work does your spouse do? L U
32. Attach a photograph to the application form. L U
33. Please submit a photograph (optional). L U

Reproduced from an article entitled, "The 1.5 Million Dollar Interview," by Dr. Suzanne H. Cook, published in the December 1977 issue of *Management World*, with permission from the Administrative Management Society, Willow Grove, PA 19090. ©1977.

The class will discuss why each of these questions is either lawful or unlawful.

Except for questions 11, 15, 18, and 21, the questions could reasonably be construed to be discriminatory unless the employer had a very good and statistically valid reason for asking them.

Your instructor has information to assist in this discussion.

REFERENCES

1. Quoted from a national EEO management consultant who wishes to remain anonymous.
2. Philip Springer, "Roundup—Merged Antibias Authority May Mean More Uniform Enforcement," *Personnel*, July–August 1978, pp. 45–46.
3. James M. Higgins, "The Complicated Process of Establishing Goals for Equal Employment," *Personnel Journal*, December 1975, pp. 631–37.
4. D. Rabinowitz, "Bias in the Government's Anti-Bias Agency," *Fortune*, December 1976, pp. 138–42.
5. Linda Chavez, "Pay Equity Is Unfair to Women," *Fortune*, March 4, 1985, pp. 161–63.
6. Robert S. Greenberger, "Up the Ladder: Many Black Managers Hope to Enter Ranks of Top Management," *Wall Street Journal*, June 15, 1981, p. 1.
7. "McDonald's Agrees to Seek Out More Black Owners, Managers," *Orlando Sentinel*, February 17, 1985, p. A-6.
8. See, for example, Reid T. Reynolds, "All About Working Women," *American Demographics*, January 1980, pp. 40–41.
9. See Patricia A. Somers and Judith Clementson-Mohr, "Sexual Extortion in the Work Place," *Personnel Administrator*, April 1979, pp. 23–28.
10. Barbara Hayler, "Sexual Harassment Reported among Illinois Employees," *New York Times*, March 9, 1980, p. 42.
11. "Teaching Women How to Manage Their Careers," *Business Week*, May 28, 1979, pp. 148, 150.
12. Robert M. Fulmer, *Practical Human Relations* (Homewood, Ill.: Richard D. Irwin, 1977), p. 449.
13. Stephen Wermiel, "High Court Rules TWA Discriminated against Pilots on the Basis of Their Age," *Wall Street Journal*, January 9, 1985, p. 5.
14. Morris Massey, *You Are What You Were When* (Farmington, Mich.: Magnetic Video Corp.).
15. Benson Rosen and Thomas H. Jerdee, "Too

Old or Not Too Old," *Harvard Business Review*, November–December 1977, pp. 97–106; Glen Elder, "Age Differentiations and the Life Course," *Annual Review of Sociology*, 1975, pp. 165–90; "Aging and the Twilight Years," *Psychology Today*, March 1974, pp. 35–40; Robert Fjerstad, "Is It Economical to Hire the Over Forty-Five Worker?" *Personnel Administration*, March–April 1965, pp. 22–32; A. C. Laufer and W. M. Fowler, "Work Potential of the Aging," *Personnel Administration*, February 1971, pp. 20–25.

16. "Keeping Informed," *Management Review*, March 1978, p. 4.

17. William F. Glueck, *Personnel: A Diagnostic Approach* (Dallas: Business Publications, 1978), pp. 541–42.

18. Alfred P. Diotte and Douglas M. Soat, "Employee Attitudes toward Retirement," *Personnel Administrator*, February 1979, p. 27; *The Employment and Training Report of the President* (Washington, D.C.: U.S. Department of Labor and U.S. Department of Health, Education, and Welfare, 1978); Sara E. Rix, "Rethinking Retirement-Age Policy in the United States and Canada," *Personnel Journal*, November 1979, pp. 781–82.

19. Raymond B. Bressler and A. Wayne Lacy, "An Analysis of the Relative Job Progression of the Perceptibly Physically Handicapped," *Academy of Management Journal*, March 1980, pp. 132–43.

10 UNIONS AND DISCIPLINE

LEARNING OBJECTIVES

When you have completed this chapter, you should be able to:
1. Identify the conditions that lead to a successful unionization campaign.
2. Identify the problems involved in managing relations with unions.
3. Develop a plan of action to cope with these problems.
4. Recognize what the nonunion employee can do to improve relations with union members.
5. Describe the problems faced by unions in the 1980s and their strategies for overcoming them.
6. Describe the progressive disciplinary process.
7. Discuss the "hot-stove" rule.
8. Describe the actions required to administer discipline to persons in each of the four traditional disciplinary problem groups.

HIGHLIGHTS OF THE GM-UAW SETTLEMENT

Wages:

■ 2.25% average base-wage increase in the first year. Included in base rate.

■ 2.25% average increases in second and third years. Paid in lump sums, not included in base rate.

■ Cost-of-living allowances continued with 1967 as base year. Only $2.39 an hour of the $3.04 in allowances accumulated since 1979 will be included in base wage rate for calculation of certain benefits.

■ To help defray cost of fringe benefits, one cent an hour of the

COLA allowances to be kept by GM for first nine quarters of new pact and two cents for next two quarters.

■ Profit-sharing program essentially unchanged.

■ $180 "special payment" upon ratification.

Pensions:

■ Current retirees to get $1 a month for each year of seniority. Lump-sum payment of $200 in second and third years.

■ Pensions for workers retiring in the future after 30 years to rise to maximum of $1,025 a month in first year from $935 a month, $1,115 in second year, and $1,205 in third year.

■ Some workers retiring earlier than 30 years to be eligible for up to $55,000 lump-sum payment depending on seniority.

Job Security:

■ $1 billion program lasting up to six years to cover workers with more than one year's seniority who are laid off because of technological advances, transfer of work to an outside supplier, or negotiated productivity improvements. Covered workers to be placed in a "bank" for new jobs at GM or elsewhere or for retraining. GM to pay covered workers wages and benefits.

■ GM statement of intention to keep its "Saturn" small-car project in the U.S.

■ GM promise to consult with union on "outsourcing."

SOURCE: *The Wall Street Journal,* September 24, 1984, p. 3. Reprinted by permission of *The Wall Street Journal.* © Dow Jones & Company, Inc. 1984. All Rights Reserved.

When organizations and managers fail to satisfy the needs of their employees, they face problems with their employees. In such situations, employees tend to look to unions for help. Unions thereby serve a useful function for dissatisfied employees. And despite the organization's best efforts, some employees will engage in behavior that requires disciplinary action. Every manager must be prepared to cope with the difficulties posed by union activities and by problem employees.

Unions pose problems for most organizations whose workers they represent. A union represents a concentration of power in opposition to the organization's authority—a nonvoluntary participatory form of management. Unions are a threat to the nonunionized organization. They often require the special attention of management and of fellow workers who are not members of the union. Union members must also learn a certain code of behavior, which varies from union to union and from organization to organization.

UNIONS IN A CONSERVATIVE CLIMATE

"There is considerable evidence that labor stands lower in public regard than business, and in some cases it is held in even lower esteem than government or politics."
DANIEL SELIGMAN

Recent years have not been kind to the unions. They have lost ground on all fronts: in membership, in receptivity to their objectives by the society at large, in financial and political strength. As Figure 10.1 suggests, they have lost much of the power they achieved in the thirty years from 1945 to 1975. The need for increased productivity, caused largely by competition from abroad, has led many U.S. firms, especially those in critically affected industries, to seek and gain concessions from the unions in exchange for the continued employment of their members. Virtually all firms in the steel and auto industries have suffered from competition by the Japanese, and firms in many other industries have moved some of their operations overseas, primarily to Asia, Mexico, and the Caribbean islands, where wage rates are far below those commanded by U.S. and Canadian workers. That unions are undergoing complex changes in the face of complex problems is indicated by the highlights of the GM-UAW settlement described in the Human Relations Happening on pp. 247–248. This contract emphasized job security, not the usual financial benefits. Given the potential for increased Japanese competition after the elimination of voluntary export quotas for autos, union members could be forced to make further concessions in order to retain their jobs.

Some observers have suggested that the United States is entering a period "beyond unions." They propose that a growing web of laws and court rulings have done much and will continue to do much to promote the interests of employees, thus making unions less necessary than they once were. Even the employer's right to fire at will, for example, is being questioned.[1] Unions are in fact in competition with government to supply many need satisfiers. Though in recent years the government has reduced its efforts to enforce federal laws and regulations governing conditions in the workplace, the power of unions continues to decline. Nonetheless, many workers remain unionized, and the unions are increasing their efforts, often successfully, to organize workers in fields that have never been unionized in the past. The UAW, for example, has conducted successful campaigns among staff workers at some colleges and universities.

FIGURE 10.1   *Percent of nonfarm work force organized in the United States*

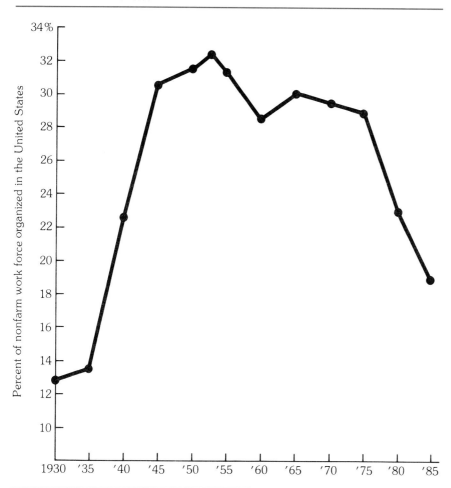

SOURCE: U.S. Department of Labor.

A **union** is a collection of individuals joined together for mutual benefit. Here we shall view them as employees joined together by common interests that do not typically coincide with those of their employers. Unions seem to exist for two primary reasons: first and most important, unions exist because employers have failed to provide need satisfiers of some type for their employees. Second, if a large union makes a particular organization its target, if it commits enough resources and is willing to wait, it can unionize virtually any organization. Because unions exist, employers must learn to live with them, or learn how to prevent their own organizations from being unionized. Employees must learn to live with them as well, as members or nonmembers.

Historically, unions have come into existence because of intolerable working conditions, improper supervision, low pay and benefits, and the desire of

WHY UNIONS EXIST

"Employees don't vote for labor unions; they vote as a protest against management."
STEPHEN J. CABOT

employees for job security. Matthew Goodfellow, in studying successful union elections, discovered that the following five factors are common causes of successful union organizing campaigns:

1. Asleep at the switch: Management failed to heed the early warning signals of a union movement.
2. Appointing a committee: Time is of the essence, and so is labor relations experience. Committees usually have neither.
3. Concentrating on money and benefits: In 54 percent of cases, money and benefits were the center of attention, but were not the problem. Money is important, but more important to unionizing efforts are neglect of employees, lack of recognition, poor supervision, the ignoring of seniority, and the lack of proper grievance procedures.
4. Industry blind spots: Far too many executives treat their employees like cogs in a wheel. They are not. Cogs do not unionize. Employees do.
5. Headquarters vs. branch plants: When one plant is already unionized, the union has a wedge in another plant. Also, corporate headquarters is often so distant from the plants that it fails to see what is going on.[2]

During the late 1970s, unions began to suffer a decline in their ability to win organizing campaigns and to defeat decertification campaigns (the process by which employees decide they do not want a union). Much of this failure to secure new members and retain old ones is the result of the work of antiunion consultants, people who specialize in keeping unions from organizing a company's employees or in decertifying a union once it has organized them.[3] In 1970 unions won an average 55.2 percent of organizing and decertifying elections; that percentage slipped to 51.1 in 1973, to 48.1 in 1976, to 45.0 in 1979. In 1984, unions won only 46 percent of certification elections and only 34 percent of decertification elections.[4] Antiunion consultants sometimes advise clients to resort to illegal tactics, such as firing pro-union employees, but for the most part they simply show employers how to recognize when a union may be attempting to organize the firm, what steps to take to defeat the union, and how to decertify an existing union. In most cases they simply show employers how to become more sensitive and responsive to the needs of their employees.

> *The worst crime against working people is a company which fails to operate at a profit.*
> SAMUEL GOMPERS

Unions have recently focused their organizing campaigns in the southern United States, an area that has the lowest percentage of unionized workers in the country.[5] Unions have also targeted white-collar workers and even managers as prospective members, since most unionizable blue-collar workers have been unionized. White-collar workers now outnumber blue-collar workers, so if unions are to survive as powerful forces in the economy, they must organize these workers. Unions scored substantial success in organizing government employees during the 1970s. Professional and government workers— for example, schoolteachers and nurses—were organized in large numbers in the 1970s. The 1980s, though, have proved less fertile.

UNIONIZATION CAMPAIGNS

Organizations and managers need to be aware of the possibilities of unionization and must be prepared to take the necessary actions to thwart an organizing attempt. Many managers have awakened one morning to discover that their employees were seeking a union recognition election. They were, as Goodfellow observes, "asleep at the switch." Positive human relations can do much to overcome such attempts.

Some experts suggest that by using employee organizational climate surveys, the employing organization can stay attuned to employees' attitudes. Charles Hughes, a labor relations consultant, suggests that a 50 percent or lower rate of support for management forewarns of fertile ground for possible union organizing efforts. He also suggests that wage rates be kept 5 to 10 percent above the rates common in the local area and that management have a written commitment to sound human relations.[6] Obviously, participation in some management decisions, a fair and formal grievance system, preestablished standards of performance, fair and consistent discipline, fair and consistent evaluation, and other sound human relations policies will help to keep employees from wanting a union.

The two most critical elements in **preventing unionization** are (1) adequate compensation and benefits and (2) concern for and responsiveness to the other needs of employees. In short, managers must make the right leadership choices and communicate these choices properly—especially during the recognition campaign. Avoiding unionization is no accident. Organizations must work to create and sustain their employees' loyalty. Union Carbide has beaten union organizing efforts four times in nine years. Its program includes all of the essentials noted above, plus an experimental incentive system based on value added during production and a job redesign program for employees.[7] Other firms have promised their employees the world; then when the company failed to deliver, the employees voted the union in.[8]

Many firms go to great lengths to prevent unionization. They have what amount to intelligence systems that report on any potential union activity. Their vengeance is usually swift. For an example of such programs, see the Human Relations Happening "An Inside View." It is interesting to note that the firm in this story is one that has developed job enrichment for approximately 40 percent of its employees and is often highly touted for its humanism.

HUMAN RELATIONS HAPPENING

AN INSIDE VIEW

The security is seamless, presumably to prevent the leak of trade secrets to competitors. Everyone, even the mail robot, wears an identification badge. Ceilings are studded with watchful cameras. "It's like 1984," says one worker as he waits for a machine in the lobby to read his badge and unlock the entrance.

Texas Instruments (TI) is an attractive union target: the third largest nonunion company in the United States, second only to IBM and Kodak. Labor unions have tried repeatedly and unsuccessfully to organize the company. Even the Teamsters, notorious for their shrewdness, call it a hopeless cause.

(Continued on page 248)

Beth Nissen, a reporter for the *Wall Street Journal* (though TI did not know that), became a member of the assembly line at a TI plant. During her first hour of orientation, TI trainers made it quite clear that unions were to be avoided. She found that many personnel policies at TI were aimed at preventing unionism.

The workers' life seemed to center around breaks. No one else mentioned a union, so Beth did. "Don't you mess with unions, girl," her supervisor warned her. "That's the one thing that'll put you out the door faster'n what you come in. . . . They'll put you somewhere you can't make no trouble."

Beth persisted, and her co-workers avoided her. Beth decided that fear was one of the key motivators in the TI program to remain nonunion. She tested the TI system. She reported to her supervisor (falsely) that she had been approached by someone in the parking lot to sign a union card. She feigned interest in union activity.

TI questioned her supervisor. Other workers informed her, "If TI finds out you're for the union, they won't fire you for union activity, but they'll sure find something else they can fire you for."

"TI is very careful," one union organizer has said. "They terminate people right and left, but they don't tag them for union activity." TI has a high rate of turnover, a clear deterrent to organizing campaigns.

Just before the Independence Day celebration, Beth was called into the office of the chief of security. He charged her with a "very serious offense"—falsifying her application by omitting the fact that she was a college graduate. He had her sign a statement to that effect. He told her that the company had contacted her references. She knew they had not.

The next day Beth was terminated by the plant personnel director. He denied that it was for her union activity. He said it was for her falsification of records.

On her way out of the plant, one employee said, "You see how it works? They got you fair and square. Probably all of us here got something to hide."

Summarized from Beth Nissen, "An Inside View: At Texas Instruments, If You're Pro-Union, Firm May Be Anti-You." Reprinted by permission of *The Wall Street Journal,* © Dow Jones & Company, Inc. 1978. All Rights Reserved.

All nonunion firms need to remain aware of the **early warning signals** of a unionization attempt. Such signals may include a sudden absence of idle chatter among the workers, especially when their supervisor draws near; employees gathering in groups other than those they usually gather in; the appearance of strangers near the company grounds and in lounges and restaurants frequented by employees; the hiding of pieces of paper as the supervisor approaches; and not infrequently, reports from employees who have been contacted by the union but are not interested in it. Employers need to be aware of possible unionization attempts. Strategies for defeating unionization must be carefully calculated. As Figure 10.2 indicates, private-sector employers are prohibited from engaging in certain actions by the National Labor Relations Act (the Wagner Act). Some of these actions might occur before the recognition campaign, some during the campaign, some after the union is recognized, and some during all three stages. Figure 10.2 also indicates that private-sector unions are prohibited from taking certain actions.

FIGURE 10.2   *Employees' rights under the Wagner Act and employers'*
                rights under the Taft-Hartley Act

Under the terms of the National Labor Relations Act (the Wagner Act), employers are forbidden:

To interfere with, restrain, or coerce employees in the exercise of their rights to join unions and bargain collectively.

To dominate or interfere with the formation or administration of any labor organization or to contribute financial or other support to it.

To encourage or discourage membership in any labor organization by discrimination in regard to hire or tenure or any term or condition of employment.

To discharge or otherwise discriminate against an employee for filing charges or giving testimony under the act.

To refuse to bargain collectively with the representatives of the employees.

Under the terms of the Taft-Hartley Act, unions are forbidden:

To coerce employees in the exercise of their rights or to coerce employers in the selection of their representatives for purposes of collective bargaining or adjustment of grievances.

To cause an employer under a union shop agreement to discriminate against employees denied admission to the union or expelled from the union for reasons other than nonpayment of dues and initiation fees.

To refuse to bargain collectively.

To engage in a jurisdictional strike or secondary boycott.

To charge excessive or discriminatory initiation fees to employees covered by a union shop agreement.

To cause an employer "in the nature of an exaction" to pay for services not performed.

These provisions give the employer some protection. Do you feel that the Texas Instruments program to monitor union sympathizers, as described in "An Inside View," is legal?

Employers who have become accustomed to making all of their own decisions find that the union seeks to share the decision-making power. Most of unions' concerns in the United States and Canada are with personnel-related policies and actions, although some minor sentiment seems to exist for moving employee unions into the strategic decision process and into decision making in other operational areas, such as job design.

Unions are structured much like companies, with presidents and staffs, at both local and national levels. The union's shop steward represents the union at the worker level and enjoys a role somewhat similar to that of the organization's first-line supervisor or foreman. Depending on the union, the law, and the contract negotiated, the local union is usually subordinated to the will of the national union. Several large national unions exist. The American Federation of Labor and the Congress of Industrial Organizations (AFL-CIO) are the largest, while the Teamsters, the United Auto Workers, and the National Education Association are among the larger independent unions not associated with the AFL-CIO. Nonteaching government employees are repre-

**IMPROVING
ORGANIZATIONAL
RELATIONS
WITH UNIONS
AND THEIR
MEMBERS**

"Samuel Gompers once put the matter succinctly. When asked what the labor movement wanted, he answered, 'More.' The answer is still 'More.'"
GEORGE MEANY

sented by several unions, of which the Federal Employees Union and the State, County, and Municipal Employees Union are the two largest. The right of workers in the private sector to join unions is guaranteed by the National Labor Relations Act. The right of public employees to join unions is generally guaranteed by the governing body, for example, the city of Atlanta or the state of Colorado.

Once a union is recognized, a collective bargaining agreement must be reached between the employer and the union (which represents the employees). The agreement spells out the conditions of employment. The areas with which the collective bargaining agreement is most commonly concerned are compensation and working conditions, employee security, union security, contract duration, and remaining management rights.

The unionized organization and its managers must be careful to abide by the terms of the collective bargaining agreement, and to document all actions concerning employees more carefully than a nonunionized organization usually does. The organization needs to train its employees, especially its supervisory and managerial personnel, to conform with the requirements of the union contract. One mistake can cost an organization and its managers thousands of dollars in settlement, but more important, it can cause bitter feelings, work stoppages, sabotage, work slowdowns, and a demoralized supervisory staff. If ever a group of people needed human relations training, it is the first-level supervisors in most organizations. Many of these people were once line employees and union members themselves. Now that they are members of management, their perspectives on employment issues are required to change. Unfortunately, many new and old supervisors let this power go to their heads. The old joke "Yesterday I couldn't even spell supervizer and today I are one" conveys quite appropriately the dismaying qualities of the job. Supervision is complex, and with the legal entanglements involving federal laws for unions, EEO, and safety and health, as well as company rules and procedures, it is no wonder that so many supervisors perceive themselves as underpaid.[9] In any event, one of the most critical issues that leads to unionism is discipline. As the consultant Charles Hughes observes, a hard discipline program will not necessarily cause problems, but an inconsistent one will.[10] Again, transactional analysis, assertiveness, active listening, and other communication techniques described in Chapters 5 and 6 are appropriate in any situation. The treatment of employees is, after all, the essence of leadership and motivation. In addition, because of the normal management–labor relations, managers must become good at negotiating, learning and following rules, remaining calm, resolving conflicts, and holding their own against antimanagement sentiment.

As Matthew Goodfellow's study of successful organizing campaigns indicates, there are identifiable differences between the management practices of firms that become organized and those of firms that do not. Differences can also be identified between the management styles commonly found in unionized companies whose workers engage in strikes and those of firms that are free of labor strife. Table 10.1 compares management practices in five pivotal areas in 28 unionized plants that were struck and 28 others that were not

TABLE 10.1   Management Practices in Five Issue Areas in 28 Struck and 28 Nonstruck Plants

ISSUE	STRUCK PLANTS	NONSTRUCK PLANTS
Handling of grievances	Follow letter of the law "File a grievance" 498 grievances in 3 months Time to arbitration: 126.5 days No informal meetings	Work to solve problem before grievance occurs 43 grievances in 3 months Time to arbitration: 46 days Informal problem-solving meetings
Treatment of third shift[a]	Many complaints (65) about shortages of materials, tools, maintenance personnel, problems with foremen, lack of personnel representation, scarcity of visits from top management	Few complaints (16)
Overtime	Mandatory overtime	More flexible overtime plus actions to mitigate its negative effects
Seniority	Promotions, layoffs, recalls based strictly on seniority	Seniority observed, as required by contract, but union and management often agree on additional criteria, such as trial period of performance for senior person
Disciplinary methods	Foremen have considerable power over termination	Foremen generally have no power over termination Informal problem solving encouraged

[a]As the third shift is considered the most difficult, the number of complaints registered by third-shift workers is considered a good indication of morale in the plant.

SOURCE: Woodruff Imberman, "Who Strikes and Why," *Harvard Business Review*, November–December 1983, pp. 18–28.

struck. As you can see, the dominant management style in the plants that endured strikes is more rigid and less flexible in its task orientation, less relationship-oriented, less participative, less prone to reward for results, and generally more aggressive in attitude than the management style found in plants whose workers did not strike. An additional factor contributing to labor problems uncovered by this study is the impact that a multiple-plant structure has on management style: 24 of the 28 striking plants were members of multiple-plant organizations, while only 3 of the 28 nonstriking plants were members of such organizations. The study showed that the top managers of multiple-plant operations typically manage by statistical control reports, which do not lend themselves to identifying potential labor problems. The top managers of the nonstriking plants, on the other hand, attempted to find out what was troubling their employees and sought ways to alleviate the difficulties.

Managers of multiple plants were more prone to work strictly through union leaders, while the managers of nonstriking plants worked both through union leaders and directly with the rank and file.[11] Organizations that find themselves unionized need to take appropriate human relations actions to prevent strikes and other confrontations with their workers.

Participative management programs, whether they consist of teams, quality circles, or even discussion groups, seem to improve relations between management and union members. When organizational members are given a voice in what happens to them on the job, more positive relations seem to develop. Ford Motor Company reports significant success with the quality circles and team projects it has initiated in its efforts to improve quality (discussed in the Human Relations Happening at the beginning of Chapter 7). The Human Relations Happening "Giving Workers a Voice" highlights one such program.

IMPROVING
INTERPERSONAL
RELATIONS
WITH UNIONS
AND UNION
MEMBERS

In only twenty-two states and half of another (Louisiana) does a nonmanagerial employee of a business firm have the right to decline union membership if the employees of the organization are represented by a union. In public employment situations, employees are not required to join a union. What does this mean to you? If you should find yourself compelled to join a union, you will have to learn to live with the union system. If you are not required to join a union, you may still be subjected to tremendous peer pressures to join. Such pressures sometimes even take the form of violence. If you have an option, consider the **reasons for joining a union:**

HUMAN RELATIONS HAPPENING

GIVING WORKERS A VOICE

The Management of the Ford Motor Company's Sharonville Plant has high praise for the plant's employee involvement (EI) program. Under this employee-management participation program, 80 teams of employees, composed of 20 percent of the blue-collar work force and 30 percent of the white-collar work force, meet together weekly to resolve problems in production. The program has been in force since 1980, and in the opinion of both Ford's management and UAW leaders, it has been a complete success.

The number of grievances filed at the Sharonville plant, for example, has been reduced to one-tenth of the number filed before the EI program was started. Ford claims that product quality has improved 55 percent and estimates that for every $1 it puts into the program, Ford gets $5 out.

Ford's EI program is not without its problems. Many blue-collar workers refuse to participate, and some who do are not fully committed to it. The program is time-consuming and not inexpensive.

Such companies as GM, Xerox, and Citicorp have also instituted some form of employee participation program. A 1982 survey by the New York Stock Exchange indicated that 41 percent of companies with more than 500 employees had worker-management participation programs of some kind. Yet other statistics indicate that only 25 percent of all

> worker-management participation programs last more than five years. The high rate of attrition among such programs is apparently due to management's unwillingness to make changes in the power relation between management and labor.

SOURCE: William Sherrin, "Giving Workers a Voice of Their Own," *New York Times Magazine,* December 2, 1984.

1. Better wages and improved working conditions. While these benefits do not always result from union membership, they often do. Depending on the employer, union members may be treated better than nonunion employees, or vice versa.
2. You may obtain more power than you would have as an individual. There is power in numbers. That is another reason why unions exist. Regardless of the issue, a group probably stands a better chance of reaching its goals against a countervailing power—the employing organization—than a single employee does.
3. There is also safety in numbers. As a member of a union, you have some protection against the abuses of power that some managers commit.
4. You may gain or retain friendships. Yoy may avoid peer pressures. It is not uncommon for lifelong friends to split over the issue of joining a union.
5. Unions provide a voice for their membership in state and federal governments. Your opinions, your needs, your wants and desires can be heard.

And while you might not consider joining for this reason, it is probable that union membership increases the positive self-image of many members because it satisfies power, social, and monetary needs.

Some **reasons for not joining a union** include:

1. If you have a high need for achievement, if you are an exceptional performer, then the union may not be for you. Most unions prefer to disregard differences in performance, lumping the ineffective with the effective. Lowered productivity is often a result of unionization.
2. You may be opposed to unions in principle. Unions are held in low esteem by most managers and professionals. The abuses of the worker protection system practiced by some unions have contributed greatly to this attitude.
3. Union membership may limit your opportunities for advancement in the organization. "Once a union member, always a union member" is the perception of many employers and their managers.
4. Union membership, especially in the South, often follows racial lines. Typically southern unions are predominantly white or predominantly black. Many recent unionization efforts have focused on low-paid black workers' continuing distrust of a mostly white management. Unfortunately, some employers have responded by hiring fewer blacks in order to avoid unionization.

If you are not a member of a union that represents some employees of your organization, what kinds of problems may you expect to encounter? Primarily social pressures and such comments as "You're not carrying your fair share"; "We won the contract for you. You reap the benefits, but you don't help"; "Be part of the team"; "You're all by yourself. What happens if you cross management?" You need to be aware of the power sources within the organization. Legally the union must represent you, whether you join it or not, as long as you are a member of the bargaining unit. But for all practical purposes, it may not.

THE FUTURE OF UNIONS

The future of unions is clouded. Improved working conditions and benefits for most workers, combined with management's concern and responsiveness to employees' needs, may further the decline already suffered by unions, which have seen their memberships decrease as a percentage of the total work force in recent years. The increasing use of advanced technology and the shift to a service economy have eliminated many of the more undesirable tasks and horrendous working conditions that fostered the earlier growth of unions. Furthermore, unions do not have a good image among many of the groups they must organize—the white-collar workers, who now make up 64 percent of the work force—if they are to continue to be a viable force in the economy. With the aid of consultants, employers have refined their strategies to defeat organizing efforts, and these sophisticated strategies pose additional problems for unions. Unions have found themselves pressured on many fronts. Thus while the concessions made by automobile and steel firms had largely stopped by 1984, givebacks still continued in some industries. After the deregulation of the airlines, for example, such nonunion airlines as People Express put so much competitive pressure on unionized firms that the employees of several major carriers, most notably Eastern Airlines, had to agree to substantial cuts in pay and benefits. Some airlines used other strategies. Continental Airlines broke the backs of its unions by filing for bankruptcy and then hiring a nonunion work force after reorganization. Others sought two-tier wage systems in order to be more price-competitive, a tactic that saved American Airlines over $100 million a year.[12]

Some of the problems that unions face can be seen in the strategies employed by the Ingersoll Rand Company. Between June 1981 and the end of 1985, this company has managed to reduce the union membership of its work force from 60 percent to 30 percent. The company has resorted to a variety of tactics: moving plants, dropping product lines, and winning workers' votes for decertification of the union. Similar strategies by numerous employers have helped reduce organized labor's share of the manufacturing work force from 32.2 percent in May 1980 to 26.5 percent in September 1984.[13] To cope with these and a myriad of other problems, unions have attempted new strategies.

The Bricklayers' Union, for example, has found membership plunging, to just a little over 100,000 in 1985, down one-third since the 1970s. Cheaper building materials and stiff competition from nonunion shops have jeopardized the union's future. Jack Joyce, the union's youthful (49) leader, has a $65 million plan to rejuvenate the union: he intends to fund a $7.5 million membership drive, and he wants $20 million for a joint union-employer marketing campaign, $20 million to help the industry introduce new products, and $20 million for training centers for new members. The major question is how to raise the money. The membership can fund only a small portion of the total, so Joyce is relying on employer contributions to a great extent. He feels that if he can demonstrate that employers and the union will benefit, employers will contribute. Only time will tell.[14]

Organizing practices have had to change as well. The National Union of Hospital and Health Care Employees has changed with the times. Representing the (largely black) workers at the bottom of the wage scale in the hospital industry, the union has pretty much stopped distributing tapes of Martin Luther King's speeches and moved to surveys of workers' needs in order to determine the issues that most concern its members. The union now targets firms instead of responding to workers' pleas for "causes."[15] Other unions are moving to organize the white-collar and pink-collar employees who now make up the largest segment of the nonunion work force. Nurses, office employees, clerks are all targeted for unionization campaigns. Unions often find the going rough, as such workers have traditionally shunned unions, which they tend to associate with manual labor. The increasing participation of women in union organizing activities, however, has helped union efforts to organize female employees.[16]

Another strategy being used by unions is to invest their pension funds in projects that will help their members. For example, a $9.1 million loan commitment by a foundation formed by union pension plans spurred the building of the Minnesota World Trade Center. It is estimated that this project created 450 new jobs in the building trades. A related strategy is the attempt to control the investment policies of pension fund trustees, generally through union-owned or -controlled life insurance and lending institutions.[17] Unions are also seeking mergers with other unions in an attempt to retain their power. Such mergers cut overhead costs and release funds for organizing activities.[18]

Public employee unions have been plowing money into political action committees in an attempt to thwart the cutting of members' pay and benefits.[19] But most unions, traditionally dependent on their ties to the Democratic party for political clout, see little chance of finding a solution to their problems in the political area in today's conservative climate.

The economic climate, too, has caused unions to change their demands in an effort to protect their members. Job security has become the number one concern in union contract negotiations. Battered by competition, many employers have taken substantial cost-cutting measures, most of which involve the elimination of jobs. Unions cannot continue to lose members and expect to make much headway against employers. Their power bases have suffered significant erosion. In an effort to stem the decline, the unions and their members are willing to make concessions on work rules and to attempt to increase productivity in order to meet competition and hence save their jobs.[20]

Can unions survive? Certainly. Will they prosper? Probably not in the immediate future. But there will always be employers who fail to be concerned about their employees and to respond to their needs. Such firms provide fertile ground for unionization efforts.

DISCIPLINE

One of the most distressing problems a manager has to face is the need to discipline employees. Until recently business and government did not really attempt to educate managers in proper disciplinary actions. But they are coming increasingly to realize that managers do not necessarily know how to manage simply because they are given the title of manager. Organizations now realize that certain skills must be taught, among them how to administer discipline. Discipline is a critical skill in the manager's repertoire because of its repercussions.

Here is a convenient checklist of questions that managers should ask themselves before beginning a disciplinary action:

1. Do you have all of the facts? Do you have documentation to support the facts you do have?
2. Did the employee know the rule?
3. Was the employee capable of following the rule?
4. Was the rule fair and consistently applied?
5. Have you checked the employee's history for past offenses (within the legal limits, that is)?
6. Are you calm? Hasty, angry actions almost always result in problems for the manager.
7. Have you planned what you are going to say and do?
8. Are you either alone with the employee or in the company of the shop steward, if necessary? (Do not discipline in front of peers.)
9. Remember to take a problem-solving orientation.

Here are some rules for conducting a disciplinary interview:

1. Calm the subordinate's emotions.
2. Get to the point.
3. Find out whose problem it is; make sure you know.
4. Recognize your own and the other person's personality states.
5. Stay adult; be rational.
6. Avoid communication blocks.
7. Use active listening and assertiveness as necessary.
8. Keep the discussion focused on the subordinate's behavior.
9. Go easy on the subordinate's feelings. Do not engage in name calling.
10. Set up a program of improvement or a probationary period, with a definite timetable.
11. If you determine that discipline is necessary, make sure the measures you take are consistent with past practices.
12. End on as positive a note as possible.

Remember to introduce the action with a statement about having a problem to solve. Say something to calm the subordinate's emotions but do not praise. Then deliver the negative—the disciplinary interview core, the problem solving, the action. Follow up with a positive, for example, a statement of your belief that the employee will do better.

Discipline is usually perceived as a negative form of action, as punishment that managers must mete out to employees who violate the organization's rules or policies or who are not functioning at the level at which you have reason to believe they are capable of functioning.

I believe that discipline is different from punishment. Discipline should be as self-administered as possible, and it should damage the individual's self-image as little as possible.[21] Disciplinary action should occur in conjunction with a problem-solving approach in which the manager engages with the subordinate. When disciplinary actions are necessary, they should result from the employee's understanding of the options. It should be the employee's choice that the disciplinary action be taken. The employee must be allowed to choose between doing what is right and what is wrong, knowing the consequences of inappropriate behaviors in advance. If the employee chooses to take a course of action as a result of which the indicated disciplinary action will automatically occur, then the choice of receiving discipline is his. Most important, the responsibility for the discipline is his, not the manager's. Douglas McGregor's **"hot-stove rule"** is valuable in this regard; see Figure 10.3.

FIGURE 10.3   *McGregor's hot-stove rule*

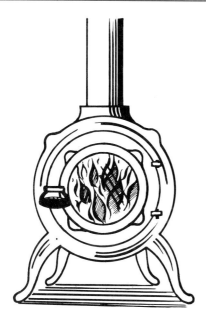

Douglas McGregor is generally credited with drawing an analogy between proper disciplinary rules, procedures, and enforcement and a hot stove, now known as the "hot-stove rule":

1. When one touches the stove, the reaction (the burn) is *immediate*. There is no question about cause and effect.
2. The person has had a *warning*. The stove is hot, and everyone knows what happens when you touch a hot stove: you get burned.
3. The discipline is *consistent*. Every time someone touches the stove, he or she gets burned.
4. The result is *impersonal*. The burn occurs not because of who the person is and not because of what the manager thinks of the person, but because of what he or she did. The person touched the stove. The stove burns everyone who touches it impartially.

(While everyone seems to agree that McGregor is responsible for this analogy, I have been unable to find a specific reference to it.)

FOUR CATEGORIES OF DISCIPLINARY PROBLEMS

John Ivancevich and William Glueck have identified four categories of disciplinary problems:

1. Alcoholic- and drug-addicted employees: employees whose drinking or drug abuse interferes with their performance on the job.
2. Ineffective employees: individuals who have motivational problems, whose performances fall below their capabilities.
3. Participants in illegal acts: employees who steal from the company or in some other way break the law.
4. Rule violators: individuals who have been counseled but continue to engage in behaviors that have been identified as undesirable.[22]

Traditionally, discipline has been viewed as requiring a progressive series of actions and a fairly traditional series of questions to be asked by the manager before he or she engages in a disciplinary counseling session.

A TRADITIONAL PROGRESSIVE DISCIPLINARY PROGRAM

Step 1. Verbal warning: The manager talks with the subordinate about his or her problem.

Step 2. Written warning: The manager presents a written warning notice to the employee, detailing the undesirable behavior. It has become necessary in many situations, especially in unionized organizations, to have the employee sign this notice or to have a witness present.

Step 3. A one-day suspension: If the undesirable behavior is repeated after the written warning, a one-day absence without pay is usually prescribed.

Step 4. A three-day suspension: If the undesirable behavior still continues, the employee is suspended for three days without pay.

"... That's right! He no longer works here. He flunked his URINALYSIS TEST."

Jim Berry, NEA, Inc.

Step 5. Termination: If the employee's behavior has still not improved, the employee is terminated.

It is not always necessary to complete all steps of this pattern. Some offenses require differing disciplinary actions. For example, if Trudy carries company-owned items home with her, she should be terminated at once if it is proved that she has stolen. Breaking the law is an offense that normally results in termination. But for chronic absentees, for employees who have poor work performance, who are insubordinate, who have personal problems that interfere with work (such as financial or marital problems), who do not seem to be doing quite as much as they could, progressive disciplinary actions, combined with active listening and assertive techniques, are advisable. The techniques of transactional analysis are helpful here.

On the basis of contingency theory, especially individual personality variables, it is apparent that each and every individual should be considered differently, and that each treatment should be designed to meet the needs of that person and the unique situation. Right? Wrong! (At least most of the time.) Why? For two primary reasons: First, federal statutes (equal employment opportunity laws and labor laws) require that equal disciplinary actions be given for equal offenses, regardless of the personalities of the people involved. Thus the offense, not the motive, determines the disciplinary action. Second, the treatment you accord one employee is observed by every other employee. If you are not consistent in your treatment of employees, you will be viewed as unfair, inconsistent, playing favorites, and discriminatory, no matter how sound your reasoning may be. So even though no two people are ever exactly the same, you may have to pretend they are. There are times, however, when individual differences should be considered. An old-timer with no previous offenses obviously should be given a second chance. *But* be careful that you do not break the law, and that you do not set an unbreakable precedent. Anticipate the reactions of others. Remember the "hot stove."

A drug is any substance that, when introduced into the body, induces significant changes in mental or physical functioning. In recent years many business organizations have treated alcoholism and other forms of drug addiction more as illnesses than as disciplinary problems. While such problems are not yet required by law to be treated in this way, there is a movement in that direction, especially in the courts. But until addicted employees learn to rid themselves of their addiction, disciplinary problems in this area are probably inevitable. Here are a few indications of drug use on the job:

ADDICTIVE HEALTH PROBLEMS

- In Louisiana, trained dogs sniff at an oil company's helicopter pads.
- In California's Silicon Valley, cocaine dries in computer plants' microwave ovens.
- In the Chicago Board of Trade Building, brokers sell cocaine.
- At a Virginia nuclear power plant, security officers are dismissed for off-duty use of marijuana.

- In the Department of Justice mailroom, employees are arrested for the use and sale of illicit drugs.
- In an Alabama pizza manufacturing plant, funny little brown leaves end up on pizzas.
- In Miami, a company announces it is moving corporate headquarters to avoid rampant drug use by employees.[23]

ALCOHOLISM

Alcoholism and other forms of drug addiction pose a tremendous problem for employers, and for fellow employees and managers. It has been estimated that in 1986 there were at least 11 million alcoholics in the United States. Many more people, perhaps as many as 30 million, are adversely affected by alcohol. Thus, while other forms of drug addiction have received considerably more attention, alcoholism remains the number one drug problem. Over half of all fatal automobile accidents are caused by drunk drivers. Some 23,000 people die in auto accidents each year as a result of alcohol. Business losses attributable to alcohol are enormous, perhaps as much as $10 billion per year. Health costs related to alcoholism are staggering, perhaps another $10 billion per year.

Perhaps because drinking alcohol is so socially acceptable, people are often unaware that they have become alcoholics. Theories on the subject abound. Some people believe, for example, that only certain persons are physically susceptible to alcohol addition, perhaps because of some genetic factor. Others believe that alcoholism is caused by stress, and certainly many people begin drinking to relax in times of tension. Others view alcoholism as a result of vitamin deficiency—a situation that is self-perpetuating, as alcoholics eat little or nothing when they are drinking. Peer pressure also plays an active role. Here are some facts about alcoholics that you might find interesting:

- 50 percent of alcoholics are women.
- 50 percent have completed or attended college.
- 25 percent are white-collar workers.
- 30 percent are manual workers.
- 45 percent are from the professional and managerial ranks.[24]

ADDICTION TO OTHER DRUGS

The use of drugs other than alcohol, especially marijuana and cocaine, is an increasingly common problem for employers. Drug sales were estimated to total $100 billion in the United States in 1985. The strength of marijuana is increasing, and so is the number of users. Use of marijuana by employees in routine manufacturing and clerical positions is common. It appears that managerial and professional employees are using cocaine in increasing numbers.

The evidence indicates quite clearly that many managers and professional employees are also addicted to other drugs, especially tranquillizers. Furthermore, the use of cocaine is increasing in all segments of the U.S. population.[25] Newer drugs seem to be continually replacing others in popularity. Crack is so cheap, even kids can afford it. The use of heroin has decreased in recent years as "safer" drugs have taken its place.

TEST YOURSELF

ARE YOU DRINKING TOO MUCH?

The following questions were prepared by Alcoholics Anonymous as guidelines for evaluating people's drinking habits. If you answer yes to four or more questions, says AA, "chances are you have a serious drinking problem or may have one in the future."

1. Have you ever tried to stop drinking for a week or longer only to fall short of your goal?

2. Do you resent the advice of others who try to get you to stop drinking?

3. Have you ever tried to control your drinking by switching from one alcoholic beverage to another?

4. Have you ever taken a morning drink during the past year?

5. Do you envy people who drink without getting into trouble?

6. Has your drinking problem become progressively more serious during the past year?

7. Has your drinking created problems at home?

8. At social affairs where drinking is limited, do you try to obtain extra drinks?

9. Despite evidence to the contrary, have you continued to assert that you can stop drinking on your own whenever you wish?

10. During the past year, have you missed time from work as a result of drinking?

11. Have your ever blacked out during your drinking?

12. Have you ever felt you could do more with your life if you did not drink?

"What Industry Is Doing about 10 Million Alcoholic Workers." Reprinted from *U.S. News & World Report*. Copyright 1976, U.S. News & World Report, Inc.

What causes drug addiction? Much the same things that lead to alcoholism. While there is now strong evidence that a tendency to addiction to various substances is inherited, clearly peer pressure, stress, lack of a positive self-image, the desire to escape an unpleasant life situation, a traumatic childhood, and the inability to get along with others are contributive factors.

Signs of Drug Addiction   The **signs of drug addiction** are approximately the same whether the addiction is to alcohol or to some other drug, with the obvious exception of the smell of alcohol on someone's breath. What are these signs?

1. Continually glassy eyes.
2. Reduced productivity.
3. Inability to concentrate.
4. Spaced-out looks and actions.
5. Increased absenteeism, especially on Mondays, and increased tardiness.
6. Apathy, indifference, emotionlessness.
7. Chronic breaking of rules, disregard of responsibility for one's own behavior.
8. Suspiciousness, guilt; appearance of hiding something.

9. Aggressive or strange behavior.
10. Forgetfulness, memory lapses, failure to complete work on time.

When these signs appear fairly suddenly and become more noticeable over time, one may suspect some form of drug addiction. Fellow employees or managers are less likely to be aware of family problems, but when they are combined with the other indicators, such problems also indicate the possibility of drug addiction.

COPING WITH ADDICTED EMPLOYEES

As a fellow employee, you are limited in what you can do to help an alcoholic or drug-addicted worker. The most and the least you can do is to show concern and to urge the person to seek professional help. There is little any individual can do to cure alcoholism or prevent others from becoming alcoholics or drug addicts. These are diseases and must be treated by professionals. What you can do is watch for signs that others are becoming involved with drugs of any kind. You can choose to ignore them or report them to the organization. Reporting the individual to the organization is usually a productive form of action, but peer pressure or the fear of some retaliatory action by the drug addict may prevent you from doing so.

The manager's role is to show concern, but also to act responsibly—toward the organization and toward the alcoholic's or drug addict's fellow employees. A person who abuses alcohol or other drugs is often responsible in some way for the safety or job performance of other people. In manufacturing plants, for example, the equipment used may be dangerous; one slip by an alcoholic could be fatal to someone else. Managers must be attuned to such situations. In one real situation, a purchasing agent for a large national retail chain was usually drunk by noon, and after lunch would sign anything put in front of him. All of the sellers knew it. Although a contract is not enforceable if either party had diminished mental capacity at the time it was signed, all contracts were honored until the problem was discovered. Store managers often had to unload goods of such inferior quality that they were almost unmarketable. As the purchasing agent noted, "It was nothing for me to blow $50,000 a day in bad purchases."[26] The organization's role in solving drug-addiction problems has been well defined by now. Most knowledgeable and concerned organizations attempt to treat the problem as a disease. Alcoholics frequently relapse more than once, and so do people addicted to other substances, but it is helpful to remember that most such people do conquer their addiction eventually. Those that don't conquer it are conquered by it. Consultant Peter Bensinger suggests that organizations need to have drug policies and communicate them to employees. The policy and education in regard to it must be reinforced. He cites Commonwealth Edison's policy as a very good one. Its first two provisions are:

1. The illegal use, sale, or possession of narcotics, drugs, or controlled substances while on the job or on company property is a dischargeable offense. Any illegal substances will be turned over to the appropriate law enforcement agency and may result in criminal prosecution.
2. Off-the-job illegal drug use which could adversely affect an employee's job performance or which could jeopardize the safety of other employees, the

public, or company equipment is proper cause for administrative or disciplinary action up to, and including, termination of employment.

Additional provisions cover off-the-job drug-related arrests, drugs covered by the policy, and drug rehabilitation programs.[27]

William Glueck suggests that managers can best deal with alcoholism or drug addiction by taking the following steps:

1. The manager documents the fact that a subordinate's alcoholism or drug addiction affects his or her work.
2. The manager extends an offer to help.
3. The manager requires the employee to participate in some form of professionally administered rehabilitation program.
4. The consequence of failure to participate in rehabilitation is termination, and the employee is made to understand that this is the consequence.[28]

TIPS FOR SUCCESS

1. Recognize the need for unions.
2. Recognize that unions have certain advantages and disadvantages to members and to employers.
3. Be prepared for changing labor relations.
4. Know how to discipline properly.
5. Be alert to the consequences of drugs in the workplace.
6. Know how to help, what actions to take, with respect to co-workers with alcohol or other drug problems.

SUMMARY

1. A union represents a concentration of power in opposition to the organization's authority.
2. Management must make certain that it provides adequate need satisfiers if it seeks not to be unionized.
3. During a unionization campaign the organization must be alert to the factors that tend to result in unionization: (a) failure to heed warning signals; (b) appointing a committee; (c) concentrating on money and benefits to the exclusion of improvement in management practices; (d) treating employees like cogs in a wheel; and (e) failure of corporate headquarters to be aware of developments in branch plants.
4. Collective bargaining agreements are most commonly concerned with compensation and working conditions, employee security, union security, contract duration, and remaining management rights.
5. Managers and organizations should put human relations skills into practice in order to avoid strikes and other confrontations with unions.
6. With the erosion of union strength since the 1970s, unions are seeking to organize white-collar and pink-collar employees and are concentrating on job security to protect their members.
7. Disciplinary actions should be approached from a problem-solving perspective.
8. According to the "hot stove" rule, discipline should be as automatic, immediate, consistent, and impersonal as the consequences of touching a hot stove.
9. The offense, not the motive, determines the disciplinary action.
10. Managers must be alert to signs of alcoholism and addiction to other drugs and act responsibly to help the addict and to protect the organization and its other employees.

DISCUSSION QUESTIONS

1. What is the situation facing unions today?
2. What can the organization, the individual manager, and the individual employee do to relate better to employees who are members of unions?
3. What is the probable future of unions?
4. What strategies are unions using in their attempts to regain their power and increase their membership?
5. What should a manager do before beginning a disciplinary action?
6. What steps should a manager follow in a disciplinary interview?
7. In what ways is proper discipline like a hot stove?
8. Describe how you might discipline a person in each of the four categories of problem employees.

APPLYING HUMAN RELATIONS SKILLS

CASES

Georgia Southern Railway

Wendell Martins, the accounts payable manager for Georgia Southern Railway, was discussing with Fred Voight, the accounts receivable manager, a problem he was having with one of his employees. "Fred, Videlia Watson has just six months left until retirement. And do you know what she's doing?" He did not wait for an answer. "She's writing out her orders in the morning in pencil and tracing over them in the afternoon in ink. I talked with her, and she says it would take me six months to fire her, so I can go ahead and try. She says the union would never let her be fired in less time. I just don't know what to do!"

"I know, Wendell, it's a real problem. Everybody knows about it, and you're not going to come out well no matter what you do. But let me suggest this to you. . . ."

(Yes, this is a true story.)

1. Actually, Wendell could fire her in a matter of days for failure to do her job, but the case could be drawn out and Wendell might lose. What can Wendell do in this situation?

EXERCISE

Now that you have read the chapter, it's time to test your skills against those of the other members of the class. Your instructor will ask each of you to write a paragraph describing a situation—a real-life situation that you have experienced or witnessed. Describe the situation as accurately as you can but change the names. The situation should involve two persons: one who must choose an appropriate disciplinary action and one whom the first person seeks to discipline. The two people can be manager and subordinate, teacher and student, parent and child—any two people who interact with each other in a situation in which one has authority over the other.

These situations may be role-played in class for practice or for grades. Each student should bring in three typed copies of the situation, one for the instructor and one for each role player. Roles will be exchanged until every student has played the roles of both a discipliner and a person being disciplined. Depending on the size of the class, all roles may be played in front of the class or in subgroups. Your objectives are to practice your human relations skills and to increase your ability to empathize.

When you grade the exercise, attention must be paid to both verbal and nonverbal messages, how well the discipliner recognized who owned the problem, how well the discipliner employed empathy or self-disclosure if either would have helped the situation, and how well either assertiveness or active listening was used. Assign a score from 1 to 4, using the form that follows. The instructor will also grade the players.

Typical situations include the following:

1. A subordinate is constantly late
2. A subordinate's performance is not up to standard.
3. You must review a poor performance appraisal with a subordinate.
4. You must counsel someone with a drug-related problem.
5. You have evidence that someone has been stealing.

Your submissions will of course contain much more detail.

How effective was this person at:	Excellent	Good	Average	Poor
1. Calming the emotions				
2. Getting to the point				
3. Staying adult (thinking)				
4. Using active listening				
5. Being assertive				
6. Staying on behavior				
7. Going easy on feelings				
8. Establishing improvement schedule				
9. Answering questions				
10. Dealing with the situation				
Total number of checks				
Multiply by	4	3	2	1
To get total of				
Grand total				

REFERENCES

1. Thomas J. Condon and Richard H. Wolff, "Procedures That Safeguard Your Right to Fire," *Harvard Business Review*, November–December 1985, pp. 16–18; "Why It's Harder to Fire Workers These Days," *U.S. News & World Report*, June 4, 1984, pp. 96–97.

2. Matthew Goodfellow, "How to Lose an NLRB Election," *Personnel Administrator*, September 1976, pp. 40–45.

3. "Taking Aim at Union Busters," *Business Week*, November 12, 1979, pp. 98–102; "A New Breed of Anti-Union Experts," *U.S. News & World Re-*

port, January 30, 1978, pp. 82–83; "Labor Fights Back against Union Busters," *U.S. News & World Report*, December 10, 1979, pp. 96–98.

4. U.S. Department of Labor.

5. "No Welcome Mat for Unions in the Sunbelt," *Business Week*, May 17, 1976, pp. 108–9.

6. Thomas M. Rohan, "Would a Union Look Good to Your Managers?" *Management Review*, June 1976, pp. 52–55.

7. Ibid., p. 53.

8. As related by an arbitrator.

9. William F. Glueck, *Personnel: A Diagnostic Approach* (Dallas: Business Publications, 1978), pp. 663–64.

10. Rohan, "Would a Union Look Good?" p. 53.

11. Woodruff Imberman, "Who Strikes and Why," *Harvard Business Review*, November–December 1983, pp. 18–28.

12. Irwin Ross, "Employers Win Big in the Move to Two-Tier Contracts," *Fortune*, April 29, 1985, pp. 82–92; "Dealing with Unions: A Tale of Two Comeback Airlines," *U.S. News & World Report*, November 4, 1985, p. 78.

13. David Wessel, "Tough Employer: Fighting Off Unions, Ingersoll-Rand Uses Wide Range of Tactics," *Wall Street Journal*, June 13, 1985, pp. 1, 22.

14. "How Jack Joyce Is Rebuilding the Bricklayers' Morale," *Business Week*, September 9, 1985, pp. 73–74.

15. Richard Koenig, "Hard Labor: Hospital-Union Chief Finds That Organizing Requires New Tactics," *Wall Street Journal*, August 27, 1985, pp. 1, 24.

16. Cathy Trost, "Three Labor Activists Lead a Growing Drive to Sign Up Women," *Wall Street Journal*, January 29, 1985, pp. 1, 16.

17. "When Unions Link Pension Funds, Jobs," *U.S. News & World Report*, May 13, 1985, pp. 73–74.

18. Gregory Strichonchuk, "With Ranks Thinning, Unions Seek Mergers to Retain Their Clout," *Wall Street Journal*, January 18, 1985, pp. 1, 19.

19. Brooks Jackson and Leonard M. Apcar, "Public Worker Unions Plow Money into PAC's to Thwart Efforts to Cut Members' Pay, Benefits," *Wall Street Journal*, January 1985, p. 64.

20. Dale D. Buss and Melinda Grenier Guiles, "GM Pact Has Job Security Gains but Isn't Assured of Ratification," *Wall Street Journal*, September 24, 1984, p. 31; "Stumbling toward an Auto Settlement," *Business Week*, October 1, 1984, pp. 36–37; Leonard Apcar and Cathy Trost, "Realizing Their Power Has Eroded, Unions Try Hard to Change," *Wall Street Journal*, February 21, 1985, pp. 1, 26.

21. John Huberman, "Discipline, Not Punishment," *Harvard Business Review*, July–August 1964, pp. 62–68.

22. Glueck, *Personnel*, pp. 498–506.

23. Peter B. Bensinger, "Drugs in the Workplace," *Harvard Business Review*, November/December 1982, p. 48.

24. Gopal C. Pati, "The Employer's Role in Alcohol Assistance," *Personnel Journal*, July 1983, p. 568; Steven H. Applebaum, "A Human Resources Counseling Model: The Alcoholic Employee," *Personnel Administrator*, August 1982, p. 35.

25. Steven Flax, "The Executive Addict," *Fortune*, June 24, 1985, pp. 24–31.

26. Related to me at a seminar sponsored by the government of the city in which I was then living. At that time my informant worked for the state and lectured on how to spot alcoholics, how to treat them, and in general how to develop a rehabilitation program for alcoholics.

27. Bensinger, "Drugs in the Workplace," p. 50.

28. Glueck, *Personnel*, pp. 708–9.

UNDERSTANDING AND IMPROVING ORGANIZATIONAL RELATIONSHIPS

11 APPRAISAL SYSTEMS

LEARNING OBJECTIVES

When you have completed this chapter, you should be able to:
1. Understand the various roles of appraisal systems in the organization.
2. Describe the major evaluation systems, the primary evaluators, and the major problems involved in appraising performance.
3. Choose who, what, when, where, why, and how to appraise.
4. Give a satisfactory performance evaluation.
5. Describe MBORR as a system and as a philosophy.
6. Understand the problems involved in MBORR and the proper implementation of the system.

PHOTOCIRCUITS

Most companies use some performance appraisal system to evaluate the work of managers and other employees. Ordinarily, managers evaluate their subordinates. But at Photocircuits, a New York manufacturer of printed circuit boards with 800 employees, the performance of managers, including that of first-line supervisors, is reviewed by their subordinates.

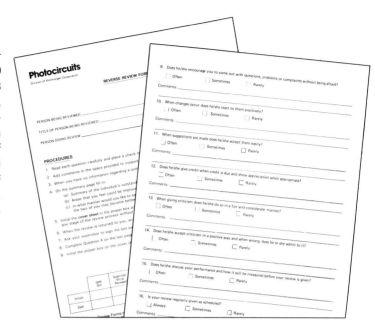

Subordinates at Photocircuits first fill out a questionnaire designed to measure their immediate superiors' attitudes, performance, and relations with colleagues. Some typical questions include:

- Does your manager show interest in you as an individual?
- Is he a good listener who tries to understand your point of view?
- Does he make sure that you receive the training you need?
- Is he fair and explicit in his assignments at work?
- Does he provide challenge in your job?
- Does he accept suggestions easily?
- Does he give criticism in a fair and considerate manner?

On a separate sheet, subordinates also summarize their supervisors' strong points and those that need improvement. The subordinate and the manager then meet to discuss the appraisal. After the discussion, both must sign the appraisal, and one copy goes to the manager's superior.

At first, many employees had difficulty expressing criticism of their bosses, and their first evaluations tended to be uniformly glowing. But the company encouraged honest appraisals of everyone, starting with President John Endee, who was told by one subordinate that he was "too aggressive" and that he "frightened people." "This sort of program doesn't work in a climate of fear," says Endee. "It requires a lot of sensitivity on the part of a manager to encourage a subordinate's honesty."

The fear can work both ways. Some managers were fearful of being evaluated by the people they supervised. But, as Endee explains, "only managers who

(Continued on page 270)

lack self-confidence in their abilities are afraid of criticism. After all, criticism of management occurs in any organization. Employees constantly criticize their boss—behind his back. The manager who has a problem—who needs to improve his behavior or attitude—will be made aware of this by the very people who can help him most." Asked whether the reverse review policy might be a deterrent in recruiting new managers, Endee replied, "I hope so. Anyone unwilling to be evaluated, by anyone, would not work out well here."

SOURCE: Berkeley Rice, "Reversing Performance Reviews," *Psychology Today*, March 1984, p. 80.

> *Purpose is the unifying principle around which human energy clusters in the organization.*
> ROBERT R. BLAKE AND JANE S. MOUTON

Organizations exist to carry out their missions. Objectives and related plans are established so that those missions may be accomplished. The organization designs its jobs to fulfill those objectives and to carry out those plans. People then perform within the definitions of their jobs to achieve their portion of total objectives and the broader plans of action. At some point the organization and its managers must ascertain whether or not its objectives are being achieved. Budgets, profits, financial statements, and numerous other measuring devices are used to evaluate organizational performance. The performance evaluation indicates the degree to which the individual has been successful at achieving his or her proportionate share of total organizational objectives.

Performance appraisal is one of the most complex of the tasks that must be undertaken in the organization. It is one of the most critical elements in ensuring individual performance, and it will do so if it is performed correctly. But unfortunately it often isn't. And no matter how it is carried out, it seems to conjure up negative feelings in both the rater and the ratee. Raters recall their earlier experiences of rating subordinates, and few find the process enjoyable. Ratees recall their own experiences of being appraised, beginning with the first report card in grade school, and find the process equally stressful. No one likes to have his ego stomped on, yet people do want to know where they stand. Could you be a manager at Photocircuits and be appraised by subordinates?

> *The most important task in human resource management, performance appraisal, most often is accomplished blindly.*
> MARK R. EDWARDS AND J. RUTH SPROULL

If you will reexamine the motivation/performance cycle model in Chapter 3 (Figure 3.2), you will see that failure to define objectives and role prescriptions properly and other violations of stage 6 of the model clearly have a negative effect on performance, even though the individual may be highly motivated. This chapter addresses the issue of how the organization, through its performance planning and control systems—primarily individual performance evaluations—helps to ensure that motivated behavior leads to performance.

PERFORMANCE EVALUATION

An organization employs numerous planning and control systems. At the heart of most organizational performance planning and control systems is the individual performance evaluation. **Performance evaluation** is the practice of determining whether or not an employee is performing his or her job effectively and efficiently. Performance may be evaluated either formally or informally, but it is always evaluated, whether the organization develops a formal appraisal system or not. Formal, scientifically designed evaluations are most effective. The best evaluations follow the classic control-function steps of comparing results against standards and then taking necessary actions. Appraisals are not ends unto themselves, but one step in a complicated process. The control process involves several steps in regard to performance evaluation:

1. Performance is defined. The process of defining performance begins with job design. A job has certain contents, which are enumerated in a **job description**. Performance areas are defined. These definitions are known as criteria. Standards are established. **Standards** are levels of expected performance on each criterion, expressed in specific amounts. (Ideally, all of these steps in the process are taken; in practice, some are often ignored. Consider the difficulties of writing a job description for the chairman of General Motors.) Appropriate weights must then be assigned to the various criteria. Measurement procedures must be agreed upon. (Unfortunately, many organizations defer this task until after step 2.)

The U.S. Office of Personnel Management defines performance standards for federal agencies as "the expressed measures of the level of achievement established by management for the duties and responsibilities of a position or a group of positions. . . . [they] may include, but are not limited to, elements [measurement factors] such as quantity, quality, and timeliness. The federal agency must then translate this definition into a performance appraisal system and form." Figure 11.1, showing performance elements and standards for one job, indicates the approach most agencies take.

2. The jobholder functions in the job. The exact nature of the jobholder's behavior on the job depends on numerous factors, such as individual needs and personalities, individual abilities and skills, job knowledge, and knowledge of expected results.
3. The jobholder's performance is evaluated. The person who is assigned to evaluate the jobholder's performance, usually the person at the next higher level of management, goes through the evaluation process at set time intervals. Such people must be trained in the task in order to perform their roles properly. Other evaluators may include the employee himself, peers, and others within and without the normal chain of command. Performance is measured and compared against the standards established earlier. Ordinarily some type of standardized form or format is used.
4. The evaluation interview is held. The evaluation is discussed with the employee. When evaluation is informal, this step is often skipped.
5. Necessary corrective and preventive actions are taken.
6. The evaluation is linked to the organization's reward system (sometimes).

Part of the proper design of an evaluation system is the degree to which performance is rewarded. (See Figure 3.2, page 53, stages 8, 9, and 10.) Note that numerous situational moderating variables intervene. Among these variables are personality factors of the people involved (their perceptions, expectations, and ego needs, their interrelationships); the availability of re-

FIGURE 11.1 *Job performance elements and standards devised by a federal agency*

TITLE Quality Assurance Director		GRADE AND SERIES GS-1910-14

Performance Element	Performance Standards	
	Fully Satisfactory	Outstanding
1. Program Management a. Ensure effective planning and review of program. b. Ensure that contracts are monitored. c. Make management visits to field. d. Report progress/status to superior.	All review schedules prepared six mos. in advance. Scheduled reviews are accomplished with less than a 15 percent backlog at the end of each quarter. Reports contain accomplishments and a list of what is to be done. The reports reach the superior no later than the seventh working day after the end of the quarter and contain fewer than two or three errors.	No quarter has a backlog greater than five percent. Ninety percent of visits result in contractors improving their work significantly.
2. Material Deficiency Reports a. Maintain control on in/out reports. b. Review in/out reports. c. Ensure corrective action is completed.	A log is kept listing all incoming reports and the offices responsible for handling them. Reports are reviewed to determine nature of complaint. All outgoing reports reviewed for completeness, accuracy and corrective action to be taken. Corrective action is tracked until it is finished.	Final corrective action is taken within 10 days of the close of investigation.
3. Employee Development a. Maintains organization's statistics on training and its benefits. b. Ensures training needs are met. c. Discusses and arranges training with Training Office.	Maintains a work force of at least 80 percent fully trained employees. Keeps abreast of training needs by continually assessing the workers' effectiveness. Plans employee training to disrupt work as little as possible.	Maintains a work force of at least 95 percent fully trained employees. Meets top two training needs fully during the period.
4. Performance Appraisal a. Assists/trains subordinate supervisors in performance appraisal for both GM and GS employees. b. Maintains a performance appraisal program. c. Operates Incentive Awards Program.	Instructs at least 95 percent of subordinate supervisors in appraisal techniques for GS and GM employees. The final performance appraisal of all employees results in fewer than 10 percent complaints because of lack of understanding of procedures. Eighty-five percent of appraisals on time. Properly documents bases for awards and effectively rewards exceptional workers.	All supervisors trained. All appraisals on time. As a result of appraisal program, 25 percent of individuals appraised improve their productivity significantly.
5. Staff Utilization a. Plans staff assignments to handle workload. b. Adjusts schedule as needed. c. Develops procedures for maximum efficiency.	Places all employees to take best advantage of their skills. Uses effectiveness measures (such as those found in the Labor and Performance Effectiveness Reporting System report) to keep organization within 85 percent effectiveness. Staff is assigned or reassigned to fill critical positions within 30 days.	Keeps the organization averaging 95 percent efficiency yearly according to the effectiveness measures for staff utilization. Staff is assigned or reassigned to fill critical positions within 20 days.

These are actual standards developed by a component of the Department of Defense. Note that not every major work activity under a performance element must have a corresponding standard as this system. The standard refers to the performance element, not to each separate work activity listed.

INSTRUCTIONS

Fully Satisfactory   **Qualitative** should indicate aspects of each performance element (product/service/major work activity) significant in determining level of achievement. Sample: "Activities performed are in full conformance with legal and program requirements: include all relevant participants: full display of cooperative agricultural research program interests in group deliberation: all reports meet time and contact requirements."

Quantitative should indicate (where appropriate) amounts, times and proportions of the aspects of each performance element. Sample: "No complaints from review staff indicating failure to comply with legal requirements: the following organizations must at least be contacted ___

Report deadlines must be met within three days. Maintain research cooperation at current level. *i.e.*, 16-20 new projects a year."

Outstanding   **Qualitative.** Sample: "A significant increase in the number of new initiatives given current level of resources which indicates clear progress toward meeting agency goal."

Quantitative. Sample: "Twenty-five or more new initiatives."

SOURCE: Robert G. Pajer, "Performance Appraisal: A New Era for Federal Government Managers," *Personnel Administration*, March 1984, p. 83.

sources; the time required to perform the evaluation and its affect on the manager's perception of the desirability of this process; the overall organizational climate and structure; the purposes for whch the evaluation is intended; and the way in which the manager conducts the evaluation. Recognizing these complicating factors, let us then begin to review the performance evaluation process.

Performance is evaluated for five primary reasons, all of which ultimately should increase productivity.

WHY WE
EVALUATE
PERFORMANCE

It appears that attempting to achieve the perfect system is the same as pursuing the Holy Grail.
ROBERT L. TAYLOR AND
ROBERT A. ZAWACKI

Control   Performance, the achievement of results, contributes to the accomplishment of the organization's mission. The organization must check to make sure that the jobholder's performance is contributing to the accomplishment of its mission. Performance appraisals indicate who should be rewarded, disciplined, counseled, or terminated. Failure to perform to standards is a reason to dismiss the jobholder. In highly competitive situations, as in some certified public accounting firms, the system may be used to weed out people who may actually be performing very well—just not well enough.

Development   Analysis of an employee's performance should contribute to the employee's development, especially if personal strengths and weaknesses and future objectives are taken into consideration in the process. At the undergraduate level, colleges and universities use the appraisal process primarily to develop their faculty, especially assistant professors, many of whom have never taught or written professionally before. At the graduate level, the process is used largely for professional development, to set objectives in three primary areas: teaching, publishing, and community service.

Motivation   Formal evaluations typically suggest that rewards (largely extrinsic, such as pay increases or promotions) may be warranted. Vital recognition also is given. Without formal evaluation, the chance that the organization will recognize individual efforts is small. Whether or not financial rewards should be tied to performance appraisals is often heatedly debated. Martin Marietta, the nation's largest defense contractor, uses two basic appraisal forms, one for exempt (usually salaried) and another for nonexempt (usually hourly) employees. ("Exempt" employees are exempt from the regulations of the Fair Employment Practices Commission, as they are considered part of management.) At one time the firm converted the individual's evaluation to a percentile score. An employee who had been informed of her score could look at a corresponding table and know with certainty what her raise was going to be and how long it would be before she received it. Martin still ties rewards to performance but in a less definitive way that gives managers more leeway over the amount and timing of financial rewards.[1] Conversely, a large health-care system believes that performance should be separated from financial incentives, partly because the budgets that provide incentives are tied to circumstances beyond the organization's control. This firm wants to focus on the appraisal as a developmental tool and feels that tying rewards to the process distorts its ability to do so.[2]

"It's publish or perish, and he hasn't published."

Drawing by Richter; © 1966 The New Yorker Magazine, Inc. Used with permission.

Communication Periodic performance evaluations force managers and their subordinates to communicate about important matters, such as objectives and expected and actual performance. Feedback is essential for future performance. For one company I served as a consultant, I recommended that a performance appraisal system be used for two primary reasons: control (discipline) and communication. With large spans of control, managers seldom provided feedback to employees. I felt that an appraisal system would provide the necessary feedback at least twice a year. The firm's union contract prohibited the tying of financial incentives to performance and little development was possible.

Employment Planning and Selection Just as organizations select individuals for initial employment, they must also select for promotions, demotions, and transfers. Evaluations provide information on skills and abilities. Such information can be computerized and entered in an employment planning data base. The U.S. Air Force, for example, maintains a computerized file of skills, abilities, and evaluations of all personnel in order to match people with job openings. When skills and abilities are found to be wanting, training should be supplied, but it is unlikely to be found to be necessary in the absence of performance evaluations.

Because one form or one system is typically used to perform all of these evaluation functions, the results are usually less helpful than the organization had hoped. One objective usually has to give way to another. Control, for example, should be exercised at the time an undesirable behavior is observed, not just six months later, when an evaluation is performed. Exercise of the control function of a performance appraisal serves primarily to provide documentation. When the developmental function of the process is linked to rewards or disciplinary actions, it tends to be ignored because of the rewarding or threatening aspects of the surrounding circumstances. Pay is based only partly on performance; such factors as seniority and market demand also figure in the determination of pay levels. Many people believe that pay should not be tied to devices designed to evaluate employees with a view to promotion. Indeed, most experts believe that promotions should not be awarded for the same reasons that pay raises are given, that is, superior performance in the current job: promotions, they say, should be given for predicted superior performance in a future job. Finally, too often no evaluations are given at all. How, then, do employees know where they stand?

The solutions to these problems obviously vary, but the use of several types of evaluations is recommended when the costs involved do not outweigh the benefits. Many employers rely on the **assessment center,** a multicriteria, job-related, skills-testing selection system, to select personnel for promotions.[3] Other evaluations are used to control and motivate. Similarly, numerous organizational communication systems are used to decrease dependency on the appraisal system for this function. Finally, some organizations have developed multifaceted, complex instruments in their attempts to accomplish several objectives at once. Zayre's managerial performance appraisal, for instance, is 17 pages long.[4]

RESULTS OF PERFORMANCE APPRAISAL

There are seven possible evaluators:[5]

1. The immediate supervisor. The person who most commonly evaluates an employee's performance is the employee's supervisor. This person is most likely to know the objectives, behavior, and performance results of the subordinate and is in a good position to evaluate them.
2. A supervisor at a higher level of management. Managers higher up in the chain of command than the immediate superior occasionally evaluate performance for purposes of pay and promotion (not for control) or when they have had an opportunity to work with particular employees or observe the results of their efforts. The U.S. Armed Forces uses this approach. In such an environment it pays to make oneself visible to one's superiors.
3. Peers. The peer group has proved to be a good predictor of suitability for promotion. Peers are in a very good position to observe performance and to

THE EVALUATORS

evaluate results. At Westinghouse's Turbine Generator Division, peer evaluation has been used in top management.[6] Japanese firms use peer pressure to encourage higher performance.

4. Subordinates. Subordinates can provide valuable insights into a manager's performance. The Human Relations Happening on Photocircuits indicates that appraisal by subordinates can be very effective if an appropriate climate is established.

5. Field reviewers. People external to the immediate chain of command—a human resources (personnel) specialist, for example, or a consultant—may evaluate an employee. This type of review provides the objectivity that is often lacking in evaluations by people who work closely with the individual being appraised.

6. The individual employee. Self-evaluation is an excellent technique for development, but it is highly dependent on one's self-perception and therefore is subject to all of the problems noted in Chapter 2. In combination with evaluation by a second party, however, it can be an excellent method of evaluation.

7. A combination of evaluators. One of the most successful systems of performance evaluation combines evaluations by the manager and the subordinate. Each arrives at an independent evaluation and then the two arrive at a joint evaluation. More and more organizations seem to be adopting this method, which increases the subordinate's acceptance of the final result. Historically, most subordinates have tended to be more critical of themselves than their bosses are.[7]

SYSTEMS OF EVALUATION

Several systems of evaluation are in use. Most involve some form of report to be completed by the evaluator.

Graphic Rating Scale   For years the **graphic rating scale** has been one of the most widely used methods of rating performance, and it still is.[8] As Figure 11.2 indicates, the graphic or trait rating scale employs a series of relevant employee characteristics that the evaluator is asked to rate according to a graduated system. Such forms are typically used for lower-paid first-line jobs, but they have often been used for managerial and staff positions throughout the chain of command. Figure 11.3 shows a trait rating scale that has been designed to provide more specific benchmarks of behavior and to eliminate as many evaluation problems as possible. Without yet knowing the various problems related to this type of appraisal, can you see why the form in Figure 11.3 is a marked improvement over that in Figure 11.2? The standard-based scale shown in Figure 11.1 also provides a stronger basis for evaluation because of its more specific description of expected results.

Forced Distribution   There are three types of **forced distribution** system. The simple ranking method requires the evaluator to rank all the employees being rated in terms of relative performance. If there are twenty people in the evaluation group, for example, the evaluator ranks them from 1 to 20. The paired comparison system has evaluators pair each person in the evaluation group with each other person in the group. In a three-person group, for example, *A* is paired with *B* and *C*, *B* with *A* and *C*, *C* with *A* and *B*. If

Figure 11.2   *Typical graphic rating scale*

Name _____ Dept. _____ Date _____				
	Outstanding	Good	Satisfactory	Fair	Unsatisfactory

	Outstanding	Good	Satisfactory	Fair	Unsatisfactory
Quantity of work Amount or volume of work	☐	☐	☐	☐	☐
Quality of work Thoroughness, neatness, effectiveness and accuracy	☐	☐	☐	☐	☐
Knowledge of job Clear understanding of job and related techniques	☐	☐	☐	☐	☐
Personal qualities Personality, appearance, sociability	☐	☐	☐	☐	☐
Ability to work with others Ability and willingness to work in a group or with supervisors and subordinates toward common goals	☐	☐	☐	☐	☐
Degree of supervision required Can work independently	☐	☐	☐	☐	☐
Initiative Seeking increased responsibilities; self starting	☐	☐	☐	☐	☐

A is better than *B* and *C* and *C* is better than *B*, then *A* is ranked number 1, *C* is 2, and *B* is 3. This method allows managers to make a more objective judgment then the simple ranking system permits. In the percentile system, the evaluator is forced to distribute a certain percentage of employees in each of the available rating positions, such as top third, middle third, and bottom third. These systems help to reduce the problems that arise when everyone is given a high rating. A difficulty is that such distributions among elite, professional, or high-achieving employees cause considerable morale problems. Such persons may be much better performers than 95 percent of the work force, but their superior performance will not be revealed by this type of appraisal. In highly mobile organizations, individuals may fare less well than lesser performers because at one point they were rated in the middle or

Figure 11.3 *Improved graphic trait rating scale*

EMPLOYEE EVALUATION

Name ____________________ Position ____________________

Department ____________________ Date of Test Review ____________________

INSTRUCTIONS Consider the employee on the job now being performed. Check the circles under each major category which most nearly expresses your judgement of each quality. Now summarize these by checking the appropriate square above the circles. The usefulness of this appraisal to you and your subordinate depends on the care and accuracy you use in completing it.

Consider the employee's performance since the last appraisal and show by a check whether he/she has gone back, remained stationary or gone ahead in each of the qualities listed to the left.

						Has im-proved	Little or no change	Has gone back
QUANTITY OF WORK	EXCELLENT	GOOD	ACCEPTABLE	UNACCEPTABLE	MUST SHOW IMMEDIATE IMPROVEMENT			
Efficiency (consistently averages)	120 & above	101 to 119	92 to 100	85 to 91	84 & below	COMMENTS		
QUALITY OF WORK (OVERALL)	EXCELLENT	GOOD	FAIR	POOR	UNACCEPTABLE			
Appearance of work	Outstanding	Above average	Satisfactory	Below average	Unacceptable	COMMENTS		
Amount of repair	Never gets repair	Seldom	Occasional	Frequently	Excessive			
COOPERATIVENESS	EXCELLENT	GOOD	FAIR	POOR	UNACCEPTABLE			
With Supervisor	Goes out of way to cooperate	Always courteous	Usually courteous	Sometimes difficult	Frequently unpleasant	COMMENTS		
With other employees	Goes out of way to help others	Will help others	Cooperates	Sometimes not cooperative	Frequently uncooperative			
Accepts change in assignment	Goes ahead with best effort	Accepts with good effort	Accepts fair effort	Complains/low effort	Refuses			
Does repair	Very promptly	Usually prompt	When necessary	At own convenience	Must be asked repeatedly			
With mechanics	Always cooperates	Usually cooperates		Sometimes causes problems	Often causes problems			
DEPENDABILITY	EXCELLENT	GOOD	FAIR	POOR	UNACCEPTABLE			
Attendance	0–2 days/year	3–5 days/year	6–8 days/year	9–10 days/year	11 or above	COMMENTS		
Tardiness	Always on time daily	1 day/month	2 day/month	3 day/month	4 or more/month			
Stays at job until quitting time	Works till bell rings	Usually works till bell rings		Quits, but stays with machine	Leaves machine			
Returns from break on time	Working when bell rings	Always at machine when bell rings	Usually at machine	Late occasionally	Usually late			
Takes unscheduled breaks	Never	Very seldom	Some occasionally	Some daily	Many daily			
SAFETY	SATISFACTORY		PARTLY SATISFACTORY		UNSATISFACTORY			
Coke bottles in work areas	Does not				Does	COMMENTS		
Smoking in work areas	Does not				Does			
Wears appropriate clothing/footwear	Does				Does not			
COMPLIANCE WITH GENERAL RULES	EXCELLENT	GOOD	ACCEPTABLE	POOR	UNACCEPTABLE			
Keeps accurate coupon sheet	Always	Seldom Inaccurate	Occasionally inaccurate	Often inaccurate	Usually inaccurate	COMMENTS		
Initials coupon stubs	Always	Seldom Misses	Occasionally misses	Frequently misses	Rarely initials			
Talks during work time (excessively)	Never	Seldom	Occasionally	Frequently	Constantly			
Personal hygiene	Excellent	Good	Fair	Needs Improving	Must improve			
Checking for someone else	Never		Occasionally		Daily			
Housekeeping/machine cleaning	Excellent	Good	Fair	Poor	Unacceptable			

EMPLOYER COMMENTS ____________________

EMPLOYEE ____________________

SUPERVISOR ____________________

REVIEWER ____________________

bottom third of a work unit that was much more outstanding than other units. Thus someone who is ultimately worthless to the firm may be promoted above one of these people on the basis of a rating in the top third or top 10 percent despite a lesser performance. In 1979 the U.S. Air Force abandoned the percentile system after using it for six months for their officers in addition to their standard graphic rating scale and essay approaches. Why? Because officers at the Pentagon and training bases who had been hand-picked for their superiority over the average officer found themselves at a tremendous disadvantage. They complained long and hard, and top management decided to abandon the new system. Parts of AT&T tried this same approach in the early 1980s and abandoned it for similar reasons.[9]

Forced Choice   The evaluator is given a series of sets of descriptive statements and asked to choose one from among each set that best describes the person being evaluated. These series of **forced choice** statements are expensive to develop but are very valuable in eliminating evaluator-related problems, such as personal bias, because the evaluator does not know what the standards are. Typically these psychology-based appraisal instruments are scored by the personnel department, which computes an evaluation score and rating for the person evaluated. The Trust Company of Georgia (now part of Sun-Trust) at one time used this form of appraisal but abandoned it partly because raters began to learn the "right" responses.[10]

Essay   The evaluator writes a short **essay** in response to each of a series of questions regarding the employee's performance. Typically, these questions deal with outstanding contributions or the indentification of major strengths and weaknesses. Evaluators may be asked to report on the promotability of the individual or on the need for training. In systems where evaluators tend to rate all candidates high on the standardized forms, it is the essay part of the appraisal that determines the person's career success. This has certainly been the case in the military, where all personnel receive very high ratings on the rating scales.

Critical Incident Report   Evaluators keep a notebook in which they record **critical incidents** in which each person being evaluated has been effective or ineffective. Such incidents are recorded as they occur, so that recent incidents will not tend to overshadow earlier incidents in the evaluator's mind. Typically such incidents are categorized according to type of occurrence. The problem with this system is that too often evaluators record the negative and neglect the positive. Furthermore, as the manager of a major exposition center discovered when he reviewed the record being kept by one of his managers, these notebooks can contain almost silly cover-your-answer comments.[11] If such records were challenged in court as violations of employees' rights, they could pose serious problems for the organization. Managers need to be alert to performance issues and ignore petty ones.

Checklists   Lists of descriptive terms with equal or weighted values are prepared. Evaluators then check off those descriptions that fit the person being evaluated. If a description does not fit, the evaluator simply does not check that item. The major advantage of the **checklist** system is that it is cheap and easy to administer. Grocery store chains often employ this type of form to evaluate their checkout personnel.

Objectives-Based Systems   Management by objectives (MBO) and **behaviorally anchored rating scales (BARS)** involve criterion-based approaches to performance in the areas of planning and control. **MBO** programs are composed for the most part of objectives and plans specified for a period of time. **BARS** consist of descriptions of behavioral expectations associated with jobs for which MBO is not quite so applicable. Both of these programs are discussed in greater detail later in this chapter. Well over half of the *Fortune* 500 companies use **objectives-based systems** of some sort.[12]

William J. Kearney has suggested that BARS can be employed to clarify role prescriptions—what it is that employees are to do. Figure 11.4 shows two examples of BARS. A BARS is nothing more than a performance continuum, with extremely good performance at one end, extremely poor performance at the other, and intermediate levels of performance in between. When employees are perceived as motivated but uncertain as to what exactly they are to do, a BARS provides a means of making them aware of their roles. Kearney cautions that since these are behavioral descriptions, they depend on observations for their accuracy; that is, the person who establishes the contents of the BARS must have observed various behaviors and graded them before placing them on the scale.[13] It appears that expert opinion as to the kinds of behavior that lead to the desired objective represents an improvement over the subjective opinions that constitute appraisal when objectives are difficult to define specifically. The organization that uses a BARS is likely to be better off than one that pays little attention to the various behaviors that add up to job performance.

PROBLEMS WITH EVALUATORS AND FORMS

"It's your last performance that counts."
        LEN DAWSON

Some problems commonly arise with regard to evaluators and the forms they use.

Halo Effect   The halo effect is said to occur when the evaluator gives the various factors being appraised the same ratings when he or she is not truly familiar with the employee's performance in regard to all of the factors. If the evaluator knows that the employee is producing a satisfactory quantity of work, for example, but knows nothing about the employee's performance with respect to quality, the evaluator may nonetheless rate the subordinate satisfactory on quality as well, assuming that good performance in one area probably indicates good performance in another.

Central Tendency   Some raters always evaluate ratees at the middle levels. This **central tendency** distorts the ratings of others and defeats the purpose of the system. This practice used to be very common in the U.S. Civil Service because high or low ratings had to be explained in detailed reports. Managers rated everyone in the middle range because they did not want to take the time to justify high and low ratings.

Figure 11.4   BARS *designed to reduce average customer checkout time*

Behaviorally anchored rating scale for the performance dimension 1a: Organization of Checkstand

Extremely good performance 7	
	By knowing the price of items, this checker would be expected to look for mismarked and unmarked items.
Good performance 6	You can expect this checker to be aware of items that constantly fluctuate in price.
	You can expect this checker to know the various sizes of cans.
Slightly good performance 5	When in doubt, this checker would ask the other clerk if the item is taxable.
	This checker can be expected to verify with another checker a discrepancy between the shelf and the marked price before ringing up that item.
Neither poor nor good performance 4	When operating the "Quick Check," this checker can be expected to check out a customer with 15 items.
Slightly poor performance 3	You could expect this checker to ask the customer the price of an item that he does not know.
	In the daily course of personal relationships, this checker may be expected to linger in long conversations with a customer or another checker.
Poor performance 2	In order to take a break, this checker can be expected to block off the checkstand with people in line.
Extremely poor performance 1	

Behaviorally anchored rating scale for the performance dimension 1b: Knowledge and Judgment

Extremely good performance 7	This checker would organize the order when checking it out by placing all soft goods like bread, cake, etc., to one side of counter; all meats, produce, frozen foods to the other side, thereby leaving the center of the counter for canned foods, boxed goods, etc.
Good performance 6	
	When checking, this checker would separate strawberries, bananas, cookies, cakes and breads, etc.
Slightly good performance 5	You can expect this checker to grab more than one item at a time from the cart to the counter.
Neither poor nor good performance 4	After bagging the order, and customer is still writing a check, you can expect this checker to proceed to the next order if it is a small order.
Slightly poor performance 3	This checker may be expected to put wet merchandise on the top of the counter.
	This checker can be expected to lay milk and by-product cartons on their sides on the counter top.
Poor performance 2	This checker can be expected to damage fragile merchandise like soft goods, eggs and light bulbs on the counter top.
Extremely poor performance 1	

NOTE: BARS go beyond the typical MBO action planning of identifying activities (means) to achieve goals (ends) and specify within these activities the job-specific behaviors that are known to result in more or less effective performance (goal achievement).

SOURCE: William J. Kearney, "Behaviorally Anchored Rating Scales—MBO's Missing Ingredient," *Personnel Journal*, January 1979, p. 23; adapted from Lawrence Fogli, Charles L. Hulin, and Milton R. Blood, "Development of First-Level Job Criteria," *Journal of Applied Psychology* 55 (February 1971): 3–8. Copyright 1971 by The American Psychological Association. Reprinted by permission of the publisher and author.

High and Low Tendencies Some raters always evaluate ratees higher or lower than other raters do. Students know this phenomenon well. Many seek out the "easy A" professor, who is apparently guilty of **high tendency.** Most certainly try to avoid the professor who flunks half of his students every term and thus is guilty of **low tendency.** In an effort to avoid such problems, some organizations rate the raters.

Meanings of Terms One of the perceptual problems involved in performance appraisal concerns the meanings of the terms used on the various forms, whether they designate the factors being rated, such as "quality of work," or the descriptions of performance, such as "outstanding." The meanings of all words lie in our perceptual set, our experiences, our situation. Thus no two human beings will interpret a word in precisely the same way. This problem helps explain the central tendency, and why one manager may rate a person as excellent while another rates the same person as only average.

> *"We judge ourselves by what we feel capable of doing, but others judge us by what we have already done."*
> HENRY WADSWORTH LONGFELLOW

Rater Skill Some raters are trained in proper techniques or have learned them over time. Others simply muddle through. How would you like to have a muddler muddling your career? Most organizations provide rater training, some more than others. GTE, for example, has an extensive program designed to make certain that employees receive a satisfactory performance appraisal.

Recency-Primary Effect One of the facts of human memory is that we usually remember more recent events better than occurrences in the more distant past. Hence the recent event is primary in our minds. As a result, evaluators tend to base their appraisals on recent performance and to overlook earlier performance, especially if hard facts are lacking. Thus a recent failure or success may bias the appraisal in one direction or the other. Ratees who are aware of this **recency-primary effect** can perform at a low level during most of the rating period and still receive a positive appraisal by raising their performance level the last few weeks before the evaluation. A list of critical incidents recorded throughout the appraisal period helps the rater to keep from being influenced by the recency-primary effect.

Personal Biases Honest, unintentional perceptual differences and intentional discrimination may occur. Studies have shown repeatedly that evaluators' personal values, beliefs, likes and dislikes, and so forth tend to color their ratings: an employee who demonstrates similar values is rated highly while a person with different beliefs is given a more negative rating. In addition, both men and women tend to evaluate men more highly than women, and people tend to rate members of their own race higher than those of other races.[14] The person who plays golf with the boss is likely to receive a more enthusiastic performance appraisal than the person who has no social contact with the boss. Religious affiliations often influence ratings as well.

Weighting of Criteria Any factor that is evaluated has some weight attached to it, that is, an indication of its relative importance. When no weights are indicated, the form makes weights equal by default. Thus quantity and quality may be considered equal to cooperation.

TEST YOURSELF

Problems with Evaluations

Look back at Figures 11.2 and 11.4. Which of the problems listed below might arise with each of the forms shown in the figures?

Problem	Fig. 11.2 Basic rating scale	Fig. 11.4 BARS rating scale
Halo effect		
Central tendency		
High or low tendency		
Meanings of terms		
Rater skill		
Recency-primary effect		
Personal biases		
Weighting of criteria		

The Test Yourself for this chapter asks you to look back to Figures 11.2 and 11.4. To which of the problems we have reviewed might each of these evaluation forms lead? Training of evaluators and insistance on sound criteria in the form itself can reduce the incidence of biased evaluations. The more highly defined the objectives and the descriptions of acceptable performance, the less likely that bias will enter into the evaluation. Rating raters also helps.

PROBLEMS WITH EMPLOYEES BEING EVALUATED

The people being rated often find flaws in the system, and often cause problems for raters. If a performance rating system is to be effective, the people being rated must understand the system, be responsive to it, and view it as an equitable measure of their performance. Employees' understanding of the system is usually increased if they are trained in the process and know what to expect. Understanding and responsiveness to the evaluation are increased when employees help to design the system or engage in self-evaluation. One of the most favored appraisal systems in use today requires the manager and the subordinate to rate the subordinate independently. Then the two sit down and reach mutual agreement as to the subordinate's rating. But regardless of procedures and involvement, virtually no responsiveness may be forthcoming from certain workers. Among those who typically resist all forms of evaluation are the very insecure who have low self-images and those who are not strongly oriented toward work or the job and do not share in the work ethic. Further-

> *There's no right way to do it. It's like walking up to someone and saying, 'Here's what I think of your baby.'*
> BERKELEY RICE

more, when employees expect ratings much higher than those they receive, they may displace responsibility upon the rater or the organization and so may make no effort to change their behavior. Finally, the way the rater and the ratee typically interact will greatly affect the value of the rating process. If the employee dislikes or distrusts the evaluator, any rating the evaluator gives is unlikely to have much effect.

ADMINISTRATIVE ISSUES

Several **administrative issues** must be addressed with respect to the appraisal process.

To Evaluate or Not to Evaluate?   Some organizations do not formally evaluate their employees. Many formally evaluate only a portion of their employees, but virtually all persons are evaluated for performance control in one way or another. Formal evaluation of all personnel seems to be appropriate if the costs of the process do not outweight its benefits. Because the evaluation process is costly, especially in terms of lost work hours and administrative time, employees at the low end of the pay scale are frequently not evaluated; or if they are, the cheaper and quicker forms of evaluation—checklists and the very basic graphic rating scale—are used. Such methods may be supplemented from time to time by critical incident reports or forced distributions.

It would seem to be imprudent to make formal evaluation of management and staff periodically. Yet many organizations do not. The failure to appraise performance and, more fundamentally, the failure to set firm performance criteria are among the major pitfalls of many organizations. Performance criteria are the guides to human behavior in the organization, and without them the organization's human relations are not sufficently related to its mission.

When and How Often to Evaluate?   Many firms perform evaluations on anniversary dates, such as birthdays or employment anniversaries. Others evaluate the entire firm all at once. The latter approach probably leads to more problems than it solves, as managers are pressed for time and may rush just to get the job done. It makes the most sense to schedule appraisals in accordance with the individual's "time-span capacity"—the time required to see the fruition of the person's efforts—or with the completion of a task cycle, such as a project, a year, or some other convenient operating period.

Should Pay and Performance Be Linked?   A major concern is whether or not the appraisal should be directly related to pay raises or other financial rewards. The answer is complex and dependent on several factors. Conceptually, the answer is most certainly yes. If you will refer to the motivation/performance cycle model in Chapter 3 (Figure 3.2), you will observe that blocks 8, 9, and 10 are very much concerned with the distribution of rewards. The research is conclusive in indicating that rewarded performance is continued and that performance that is not rewarded is less likely to be continued. Thus it seems that the organization must adequately link the individual's performance to the organization's reward system if it expects that individual to continue to perform as it wishes. The rewards given need not always take the form of money, but it is essential that some kind of recognition be given to those who perform well. Often, however, performance and rewards are not linked, and so rewards do not depend on the appraisal system. When employees' performance affects their pay very little, as in the case of workers at the lowest end of the pay scale, unionized workers, and highly paid executives, it would seem best to separate pay raises from appraisals by a considerable period of time, a month to six months. When employees' performance affects their pay, however, the two should obviously be linked. You will recall that Martin Marietta has provided some employees with tables that convert scores from a highly quantified and detailed performance appraisal into exact dollar amounts. Yet budget cycles and other factors cause many organizations not to link appraisals with rewards.

What Should Be Evaluated?   Performance should be evaluated, of course, but there's the rub. What is performance? High levels of quantity and quality of output are desired, but what else? And what does *output* really mean? Defining output for the majority of jobs is easy. But many jobs have ill-defined outputs, especially in the service areas, such as accounting, personnel management, and most jobs in nonprofit organizations. The job's design and the assignment of objectives is of critical importance to evaluation. Typically, personality factors—initiative, cooperation, dependability, and need for supervision—are often considered in both white-collar and blue-collar job evaluations. This is surprising, as these factors are difficult to rate.

How to Ensure Legality?   The guidelines issued by the Equal Employment Opportunity Commission require that the performance appraisal measure the performance of the individual in relation to the job, normally in terms of either obvious contents or scientifically established contents—what are referred to as "job-related criteria." Further examination of EEOC guidelines reveals that performance standards must be made clear to the individual in advance of performance. Employees must understand the standards against which they are being evaluated. Subjectivity should be minimal or nil. Persons being rated should understand the policies and purposes of the appraisal. Raters must have observed the behavior they evaluate. Finally, privacy legislation in fifteen states requires the organization to grant employees access to their own performance appraisals.[15] These guidelines pose problems in regard to some types of criteria. Personality factors, for example, are more difficult to defend legally than measures of quantity and quality.

Who Should Be Evaluated?   Should the evaluation focus on the individual or on the individual in conjunction with the group? Much of an organization's work is performed in groups, yet virtually all performance appraisal systems examine only individual performance. As the emphasis on teamwork increases, it seems likely that more appraisal systems will analyze group performance rather than individual performance alone. At Ford Motor Company, for example, quality circles are evaluated periodically, because they are such an integral part of the production process.[16] Group appraisals should serve to supply additional information, not as substitutes for individual appraisals.

"The annual report of our achievments and potential has a large impact on our sense of worth and accomplishment."
ROBERT L. TAYLOR AND
ROBERT A. ZAWACKI

INTERPERSONAL
COMMUNICATION
IN THE
APPRAISAL
PROCESS

Effective appraisal requires the fundamental skills of active listening and assertiveness. One should be empathetic, open, positive, and aware of the factors that are influencing the other person's behavior. Leadership behaviors are as relevant to appraisal as they are to everyday relations. In fact, if everyday relations are not appropriate, it is not likely that appraisal will be successful. The process should be one of renewal, not destruction.

Two interviews or counseling sessions commence and end the process: the objectives-setting interview and the performance-appraisal interview. Good communication skills are critical to the success of both interviews.

The Objectives-Setting Interview   The establishment of performance standards by the rater and the ratee is critical to the success of an appraisal. The ratee must be made aware of how he is to be evaluated and against what criteria his performance is measured. The **objectives-setting interview,** or the session in which the superior identifies criteria and standards for the subordinate, is therefore of great importance. Usually such interviews combine an appraisal of past performance with the setting of future objectives. Allen E. Slusher and Henry P. Sims have developed three helpful checklists for use in conjunction with an MBORR program (to be discussed below) but with slight modification they may be used in any appraisal process.[17] These checklists, shown in Figure 11.5, focus on the "how" of the setting of objectives. Naturally this session creates anxiety and apprehension for both subordinate and superior, but preparation can help to reduce such tension. Slusher and Sims suggest that this interview gives the subordinate a chance to meet three critical personal needs:

1. To find out about the superior's priorities.
2. To negotiate the priorities for his or her own job.
3. To influence his or her career development.

The interview provides the superior with opportunities, too:

1. To tell the subordinate where help is needed.
2. To obtain valuable feedback.
3. To enhance the subordinate's commitment and motivation.

Figure 11.5 suggests what both superior and subordinate should do before, during, and after the interview.

The Appraisal Interview   The **appraisal interview** communicates the employee's strengths and weaknesses. It can be an excruciating process or it can be a process that benefits the organization, the superior, and the subordinate. Joseph Cangemi and Jeffrey Claypool suggest that the **complimentary interview** is a means to provide some rewards to the outstanding performer.[18] They note that the typical appraisal interview tends to dwell on the negative, on what the employee did not do. And since most employees function acceptably, many have a better than acceptable level of performance, and a few are truly outstanding, more time should be spent in emphasizing the positive rather than calling attention to the negative. (Sound familiar? See Chapter 6.) These authors feel that recognition is the most frustrated need of

FIGURE 11.5   *Three checklists for the objectives-setting interview*

Checklist 1—Before the interview

What the subordinate should do

Develop preliminary objectives that have a clear performance standard and completion deadline.

Provide the superior with a copy of the preliminary objectives prior to the interview.

Prepare supporting data for each objective.

Decide what resources and coordination will be necessary.

List questions and problems for discussion with the superior.

What the superior should do

Decide whether each preliminary objective represents a priority need.

Check for technical completeness of objectives. Is there a clear performance standard, completion deadline, and method of checking results?

Judge whether performance standards are realistic (not too easy, not too difficult).

Decide if the subordinate has sufficient authority in the objective area.

Specify any required personnel coordination needed to achieve an objective.

Determine if needed resources can be provided.

Note whether foreseeable contingencies should be recognized.

Consider the extent of personal support that the subordinate will require for improved performance.

Examine the subordinate's other job responsibilities to see if any are being neglected.

Determine whether additional objectives are appropriate.

Insure that there are neither too few nor too many objectives in total.

Checklist 2—During the interview

What the superior should do

Select a convenient interview location and stress the meeting's importance. Be prompt and allocate sufficient time for an uninterrupted discussion.

Begin with small talk to set the subordinate at ease; tailor the approach to the individual.

Request that the subordinate explain each objective. Provide ample opportunity for developing insight into the objectives. Listen with interest and understanding.

Ask questions based on prior preparation and new information. Encourage subordinate to respond and ask his own questions.

Ask how superior can help subordinate do an even better job. Take notes on agreed support.

Avoid placing the subordinate in a defensive position. Keep advice to a minimum. Avoid clashes over personality differences, weaknesses, and past mistakes; avoid arguments.

Provide positive comments whenever possible. Be open about ideas. Seek self-awareness and mutual understanding. Help him gain insight into his behavior and its conse-

quences. Concentrate on anticipated performance. Future improvement should be the focus.

See that final objectives meet technical requirements (clear performance standard, completion deadline, and method of checking).

Remember that setting objectives is a joint process. Compromise when possible. Be willing to change viewpoints.

Be willing to resolve serious controversies (in the final analysis, there must be a boss).

What the subordinate should do

Present objectives vigorously.

Be thorough and confident in discussing each objective.

Accentuate the positive by emphasizing what should be done.

Listen carefully to the superior's responses, both positive and negative. They are important indications of his priorities and perception of career development.

Insist on final agreement. Do not leave questions hanging in the air. Use the opportunity to bring differences out into the open and resolve them.

Checklist 3—After the interview

What the subordinate should do

Set up a method for regularly reviewing progress toward objectives.

Renegotiate objectives when major changes occur.

Let the superior know when progress is lagging.

Let the superior know when a lack of coordination or resources requires action.

What the superior should do

Maintain a historical and current file on each subordinate's objectives.

Develop checks and reminders for using with each subordinate to insure continuous progress.

In a timely and informal way, let subordinates know that he is interested in week-to-week progress (however, avoid nagging).

SOURCE: From Allen E. Slusher and Henry P. Sims. Jr., "Commitment through MBO Interviews." *Business Horizons*, April 1975. p. 10. Adapted with permission.

employees, and that a complimentary interview helps to alleviate this frustration.

A complimentary interview can help to achieve several objectives:

1. Employee promotions: identification of employees eligible for promotion (emphasizes strengths).
2. Employee transfer: identification of employees who may be able to do other jobs (emphasizes strengths).
3. Employee improvement: brings out employees' strong points so that they can be developed, with a view toward promotion; employees want to know how to improve.
4. Employee training: helps employees to maximize effort and performance.
5. Need satisfaction: provides recognition of employees' strengths; employees who receive such recognition develop self-confidence and respect for their company.
6. Improved morale: creates a good relationship between employees and management.

These objectives are consistent with the positive approach to human relations, which emphasizes the encouragement of the positive self-image that appears to be critical to organizational productivity and profits.

Cangemi and Claypool point out that the complimentary interview should involve several people: the employee, his or her supervisor, the plant or division manager, the personnel manager, and even (or especially) the employee's family. The employee and the supervisor are the only participants in the actual interview, but through the various communications media available, the entire organization and the family unit can become a part of this positive process. The company newspaper, for example, can be used to highlight employees who have received outstanding appraisals. Managerial time is of course an expense of this process, and its use must be carefully weighed against the benefits to be derived from it. Another interesting approach is that used by EBASCO. This firm formally assesses potentials in its appraisal process, in order to help both the individual and the company to prepare for future situations.[19]

MANAGEMENT BY OBJECTIVES, RESULTS, AND REWARDS: A CONTINUUM OF MANAGEMENT SYSTEMS

"If you want activity, you get activity. If you want results, you get results."
GEORGE ODIORNE

We discussed MBO briefly earlier in the chapter. You may also have heard of management by results (MBR) and management by compensation (MBC). Management by objectives, results, and rewards (MBORR) combines the more operationally important features of each of these systems. The resultant system/philosophy described here is more functional than the independent parts from which it is derived. MBORR is the most advanced stage of a management process that began in General Motors as MBR (results). The original concept, popularized by George Odiorne as MBO (objectives), has since been criticized for its lack of emphasis on results and compensation.[20]

The objectives-based system is an often misunderstood, often misused, and often controversial management approach. No two implementations of the system are ever identical, and authorities on the subject often disagree as to what the proper components of this system should be. Realistically, objectives-based programs should vary in content according to any number of situational variables, especially the intentions with which the system is designed and implemented.

The organization that uses the MBORR approach sets objectives, reviews performance results in relation to those objectives, and rewards employees in accordance with those results. In its most rudimentary form MBORR is a planning/control/communications system linking organizational objectives to individual objectives. In its most complex form, it is a managment philosophy embodying virtually every major concept of positive human relations discussed thus far in this text. Between these two extremes, many versions can be found, each devised to respond to a particular situation.

MBORR is based in the following beliefs:

1. Organizations exist for specific reasons.
2. These reasons, known as missions, can be subdivided into reasons of more limited scope, known as objectives.
3. Every organizational activity (job) should contribute to the achievement of those objectives.
4. Every individual who engages in activity for the organization should do so only to achieve those objectives.
5. Any activity (and therefore job) that does not lead to the achievement of the organization's objectives should be eliminated.
6. The more specific and better understood the objective, the more likely it is to be achieved.
7. People by nature strive to achieve objectives.
8. Results must be measured and rewarded if the objectives established are to be useful.

Figure 11.6 shows how elements of an organization's mission, here to make a profit, may be allocated throughout the organization until each individual employee is given some portion of that major mission to accomplish.

Even in its rudimentary form, MBORR is an important technique for planning, control, and communications. The basic MBORR process occurs as follows:

THE STEPS IN THE MBORR PROCESS

1. Objectives for the organization are established.
2. These objectives are parceled out to all managers in the chain of command, and in some organizations to all employees. Each objective is agreed to by manager and subordinate. Varying degrees of participation in the setting of objectives are possible.
3. Manager and subordinate develop and agree to plans of action to achieve the stated objectives. Again, the degree of participation in formulating plans may vary.
4. The action plans are carried out through implementation processes.
5. Progress toward these preestablished objectives is measured periodically. Standard control procedures are followed in evaluating results.
6. Rewards are given. The basic steps of the motivation/performance cycle must be followed. Performance that is not rewarded in some way is not likely to continue.

FIGURE 11.6   *Typical distribution of objectives throughout an organization*

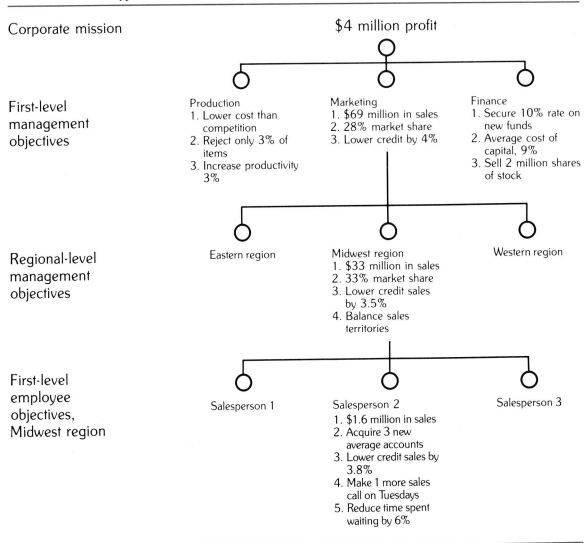

The manager and his or her superior meet to negotiate the manager's objectives and plans. Once agreement is reached, the process shifts to the next lower level of management, and it continues until objectives have been distributed and plans formulated at the supervisory level. The process usually stops here, because the technique is seldom useful for first-line positions.

MBORR tends to produce the following positive results:

1. Both quantity and quality of performance are improved.
2. Communications and understanding are improved.
3. Job satisfaction is improved.

4. Individual growth is enhanced.
5. Role prescription is clarified.

It also tends to produce some negative results:

1. Managers tend to become more critical.
2. Managers may use MBORR objectives as a whip to drive subordinates.
3. The establishment of objectives entails all sorts of problems: objectives may be set too high or too low, they may not be accepted, they may be inflexible, they may be difficult to set for nonquantifiable areas.
4. The process may overemphasize short-run objectives to the neglect of long-term goals.
5. The process seems to lose its effect over time.
6. Monetary rewards are sometimes so small in relation to the effort required that they fail to maintain performance.
7. The process often takes too much time.
8. Group dynamics are usually not taken into consideration.
9. Objectives may be set without regard for individual physical and mental limitations.
10. Goals established tend to become maximums even when they could be exceeded.

The negative results reported here far outnumber the positive effects, and at least twenty more could be listed. However, the situations in which the technique's effectiveness have been studied have varied widely, so that the findings also vary. More important, many researchers have reported that the technique's implementation, not the technique itself, was the problem. It appears that when an appropriate implementation procedure is followed and top management is involved and concerned, MBORR is effective.

TIPS FOR SUCCESS

1. Take performance appraisals very seriously.
2. Manage your performance appraisal as you would your career, because the two are often closely connected.
3. Make sure of your performance, that people are aware of your performance, and that it is recognized.
4. Be alert to the problems involved in performance appraisals, whether you are giving them or receiving them. Take actions to compensate for any deficiencies that might result.
5. Carefully evaluate the evaluator and the criteria by which your performance is evaluated. Make sure you know what is expected of you.
6. Be alert to the politics involved in the situation.

SUMMARY

1. The performance appraisal is one of the most critical elements in the planning and control of performance. Through planning and organizing functions, objectives are established, and jobs are designed to achieve those objectives.
2. The performance appraisal is a device to control, develop, motivate, communicate with, and select employees; it is designed to ensure that employees' behavior on the job furthers the accomplishment of the organizational mission.
3. There are seven possible evaluators: the im-

mediate supervisor, a supervisor at a higher level of management, peers, subordinates, field reviewers (persons external to the chain of command), the individual employee, and a combination of these evaluators.

4. The major systems of appraisal include the graphic or trait rating scale, forced distribution, forced choice, essay, critical incident report, checklists, and objectives-based systems (MBO and BARS).

5. Each of these systems is subject to several major problems, among them the halo effect, central tendency, high and low tendencies, meanings of terms, rater skill, the recency-primacy effect, personal biases, and the weighting of criteria.

6. The elimination of these problems depends heavily on training of raters and an emphasis on specific criteria in the appraisal system.

7. Several administrative issues must be addressed with respect to the appraisal process: Should employees' performance be formally evaluated? When and how often should it be evaluated? Should pay be linked to performance? What should be evaluated? How to ensure legality? Finally, who should be evaluated?

8. The process should be one of renewal, not destruction.

9. Two interviews or counseling sessions begin and end the appraisal process: the objectives-setting interview establishes the standards by which the employee's performance will be judged; the appraisal interview communicates the employee's strengths and weaknesses. A complimentary interview, by emphasizing the positive rather than the negative, recognizes the employee's contributions to the organization's efforts to achieve its objectives.

10. Management by objectives, results, and rewards (MBORR) is an advanced management system by which the organization sets objectives, reviews performance results in relation to those objectives, and rewards employees in accordance with those results.

DISCUSSION QUESTIONS

1. Describe a performance evaluation that you have had in terms of the major concepts of this chapter: the reasons it was given; who evaluated you and why others did not; problems you encountered with your evaluator, with the instrument, and with the evaluation process; and how the interview was handled.

2. Identify the major pros and cons of linking rewards to performance appraisals.

3. Discuss the major administrative issues of performance appraisal in relation to the appraisal discussed in your response to the first question above.

4. Describe the key factors involved in giving a satisfactory performance appraisal interview.

5. Describe MBORR as both a philosophy and a system of management. What are its strengths and weaknesses?

APPLYING HUMAN RELATIONS SKILLS

CASE | **A Performance Appraisal?**

Jack Barton had been with the Massachusetts Software Company for a little over five years. He had been promoted to the position of documentation manager just about a year before the impending meeting with his immediate superior, Arnold Little. Arnold, executive vice-president for administration, had been hired from another software firm two years ago. He was responsible for coordinating the efforts of those at the top level of management. He was essentially a chief operating officer, while the president was the chief executive officer. Arnold prided himself on his ability to lead. He was not, however, as good at leading people as he thought he was. While he could be inspirational at times, he lacked many basic management skills. He was an emotional leader, not a managerial one. Alas, it was Jack's misfortune to be confronted by Arnold's managerial deficiencies this day.

"Jack, we're here to discuss your job performance. As you probably know, we always perform a job evaluation on the anniversary of everyone's hiring date." Arnold fidgeted in his seat for a minute, stared out the window, then finally gathered himself together and continued: "Jack, I'm just not sure that you're doing the kind of job you should be doing. In fact, I'm very concerned about your performance."

Jack was taken aback by this announcement, but he composed himself quickly. "What are you basing your evaluation on? What specifically is wrong with my performance?"

"Well, to begin with, Jack, the quality of the documentation coming from your group is just atrocious. You can't expect us to sell quality service when we don't get quality from your department." Arnold paused, obviously mulling over other thoughts.

"What else?" asked Jack.

"Well, that's basically it. You know you don't really lead your people well, either. I mean, you do get out the work, but your people aren't as enthusiastic about their work as they ought to be." Arnold seemed to be unsure of his own statement.

Sensing Arnold's uncertainty, Jack asked, "Why do you say that? We get along fine in our group." Indeed, Jack was right, they did get along well. He was well liked, respected, listened to, and considered by one and all to be a good person to work for, though very demanding in his productivity requirements.

"It's just this feeling I get from talking to people," Arnold said. "But let's not talk about that, let's get back to the quality issue. Our sales staff sells the high quality of our work, so we have to have high quality. Documentation enables us to sell our software so that any moron can use it. You have to do better."

"Well, Arnold," Jack replied steadily, "I have two things to say. First, when I took this job, you told me that all I had to do was get the work out. The kinks could be ironed out later. Yeah, we've had a lot of problems, I admit it, but you have to look at what we have to work with. You can't say that our efforts are bad, they're not. They're just not quite as good as we'd like them to be. But the programmers give us so little time. If we had more lead time, I think a lot of things would go better for us. Secondly, if I may be candid, one of the major problems here, it seems to me, is that no one seems to know exactly what's expected. Your directions to me were very vague, I felt."

"Your're supposed to find out what your job is all about. The other guys know," Arnold retorted.

"Maybe, maybe not. Just yesterday, a bunch of us managers got together and found out that none of us is exactly certain what specifically you want us to accomplish." Jack was trying not to show his anger.

"Look, Jack, are you telling me I don't do my job right?" Arnold made no effort to conceal his anger.

"No, but I am saying that all of us could do better if we knew what we were supposed to be doing."

1. What major errors in performance evaluation do you see in this situation?
2. What was really being evaluated, if anything?
3. How should Arnold have handled this evaluation, from beginning to end?

EXERCISE

The Complimentary Interview

This is a role-playing situation. Students will join in groups of threes. One person will be the observer, one the manager, and one the subordinate. Group members will shift positions until each has had a chance to role-play the two acting parts and to be the observer.

The subordinate's performance may be assumed to be either superior, average, or substandard. Each situation should be role-played, employing the complimentary interview to the fullest extent possible. The observer is to judge the manager's and the subordinate manager's performance and preparation.

REFERENCES

1. Author's discussion with several Martin Marietta employees.
2. Author's discussion with a top manager in that firm.
3. Marilee S. Niehoff, "Assessment Centers: Decision-Making Information from Non-Test-Based Methods," *Small Group Behavior*, August 1983, pp. 353–358.
4. "Keeping Informed: Performance Appraisals Reappraised," *Management Review*, November 1983, p. 5.
5. John M. Ivancevich and William G. Glueck, *Fundamentals of Personnel* (Dallas: Business Publications, 1984), pp. 248, 249.
6. Author's discussion with a senior vice-president in the division.
7. Author's opinion.
8. Robert L. Taylor and Robert A. Zawacki, "Trends in Performance Appraisal: Guidelines for Managers," *Personnel Administrator*, March 1984, pp. 71–81.
9. Author's discussion with AT&T personnel.
10. Author's discussion with a former personnel director for the Trust Company of Georgia.
11. Author's discussion with the civic center manager.

12. Estimated from Taylor and Zawacki, "Trends in Performance Appraisal."
13. William J. Kearney, "Behaviorally Anchored Rating Scales—MBO's Missing Ingredient," *Personnel Journal*, January 1979, p. 23.
14. Berkeley Rice, "Performance Review: The Job Nobody Likes," *Psychology Today*, September 1985, pp. 30–36.
15. Ronald G. Wells, "Guidelines for Effective and Defensible Performance Appraisal Systems," *Personnel Journal*, October, 1982, p. 781.
16. "What's Creating an Industrial Miracle at Ford?" *Business Week*, July 30, 1984, pp. 80–81.
17. Allen E. Slusher and Henry P. Sims, Jr., "Commitment through MBO Interviews," *Business Horizons*, April 1975, pp. 5–12.
18. Joseph Cangemi and Jeffrey Claypool, "Complimentary Interviews: A System for Rewarding Outstanding Employees," *Personnel Journal*, April 1977, pp. 192–94.
19. Andrew O. Manzini, "Why EBASCO Assesses Potential Instead of Past Performance," *Management Review*, September 1984, p. 29.
20. For a history of MBO, see George S. Odiorne, "MBO: A Backward Glance," *Business Horizons*, October 1978, pp. 14–24; for a critique of its

results and compensation aspects, see Thomas H. Patten, Jr., "Linking Financial Rewards to Employee Performance: The Roles of OD and MBO," *Human Resource Management*, Winter 1976, pp. 2–17; Robert W. Hollmann, "Applying MBO Research to Practice," *Human Resource Management*, Winter 1976, pp. 28–36; and William H. Mobley, "The Link between MBO and Merit Compensation," *Personnel Journal*, June 1974, pp. 423–27.

12 JOB DESIGN, TECHNOLOGY, AND THE QUALITY OF WORK LIFE

LEARNING OBJECTIVES

When you have completed this chapter, you should be able to:
1. Describe the importance of work in relation to the satisfaction of individual needs.
2. List and define the primary job dimensions.
3. Identify the elements of job enlargement and job enrichment.
4. Improve the design of an individual job.
5. Determine the factors that most influence the consequences of job design.
6. Describe how and why job enrichment works, and why it doesn't always succeed.
7. Trace the changing impacts of technology (including robotics and competition) on jobs and jobholders.

A JOB YOU COULD LEARN TO HATE

We usually think of assembly lines or clerical positions when we talk about people who are dissatisfied with their jobs. But even the most seemingly glamorous jobs, such as that of acquisitions analyst for the highly respected and prestigious Wall Street firm of Morgan Stanley, has its limitations. When Elaine Ide Wood joined the firm, she knew the going would be tough, but she thought she would love it. "I felt tremendous," the Harvard MBA commented. "It was the ultimate in a high-powered, fast-learning job on Wall Steet, and to me, Wall Street was the heartbeat of business." But after being with Morgan Stanley less than two months, she quit, distressed by the seemingly endless work load. "I want to work 50 hours a week. Sixty hours is fine, and 70 or 80 is okay when there's a project. But working 90 or 100 hours a week just isn't the way I wanted to live my life."

There seems to be something about the work that one must do in some of these jobs that bothers the jobholders. One 27-year-old manager of a $7 billion money fund reported that the job was dull and monotonous. He quit. "Whether it was $1 million or $100 million, the procedure was still the same. . . . Except for the tension, a baboon could do what I was doing."

What makes for a good job, an exciting job? Why do so many people feel that their jobs are not satisfying? What does it take to make you excited about a job?

Source: Amanda Bennett, "Some Business Grads Learn to Hate Their Glamorous Wall Street Jobs," *The Wall Street Journal*, December 18, 1985, p. 31.

During your life you will spend more time at work than at any other activity, including sleep. You will spend more time at work than interacting with your family, at leisure, at church, eating, drinking, or satisfying any of your other needs. Thus choosing an occupation and the organization in which you'll practice it are critical to your future satisfaction in life. Work provides us not only with our income but also with a measure of our self-esteem and our social status. It can provide us with a chance to engage in roles that are fulfilling, such as that of a professional or a manager in a chosen field; it can give us a chance to achieve our objectives, to accomplish, to gain power, to control

"I ride the bus, the Michigan Boulevard bus in Chicago, and I look at people's faces. . . . They're tired. They're beaten. There's a fatigue. It isn't the satisfying tiredness of a day well spent, but the fatigue of another day killed."

STUDS TERKEL

our destiny. It can give us a chance to grow as human beings. Nothing else can satisfy so many needs.

The reality, unfortunately, is that for most people work at best satisfies only physiological, security, and social needs. Many, perhaps most, jobs fail to provide higher-level need satisfiers, those usually intrinsic to the job itself. But even satisfying jobs, those that satisfy most of our work-related needs, are not enough, because we have other priorities in our lives besides work. As the Human Relations Happening on page 297 makes clear, even a glamorous job at a highly respected, highly profitable New York investment banking firm can be less fulfilling than one might expect. Working 100 hours a week seems almost impossible; after all, there are only 168 hours in a week. That leaves only a little more than nine hours a day to sleep, eat, and take care of all personal business. A $70,000 per year salary hardly seems worthwhile when that equates to working two $35,000-a-year jobs at 40 hours a week plus giving each employer 10 hours of free overtime per week. Many people are beginning to realize that a job is just one element in their lives. The job and its design are also being seen more clearly as the consequences of several factors: such organizational factors as leadership and group dynamics; such environmental factors as the economy, society, government; and such personal factors as individual needs and perceptions.

This chapter first explores the design of a job, its components, and how and why organizations and managers seek to incorporate certain components in jobs. We shall then examine the impact of technology on job design. We shall also review the related topic of the quality of work life (QWL). QWL is specifically concerned with the satisfaction of the individual needs of organizational members on the job. To the extent that such satisfaction increases productivity or at least maintains it at no additional cost, the organization will ordinarily attempt to satisfy as many of those needs as it can. Much of the focus of the QWL movement in recent years has been directed at job design because it offers much promise for improving QWL. Surveys continually report dissatisfaction with work among all levels of employees, including managers. Many people express dissatisfaction with their jobs from time to time, but many dissatisfied workers are dissatisfied most of the time not just at work.[1] Surveys also reveal that dissatisfaction with work is increasing in the U.S. work force.[2] Job design and resultant satisfaction or dissatisfaction are of critical importance to the organization because the way jobs are designed has a significant impact on the jobholder's behavior. One of the probable causes of the low growth rate of productivity in American industry is job dissatisfaction.

JOB DESIGN

Figure 12.1 shows a **contingency model of job design.** The ultimate outcomes of a job are a function of four major factors:

1. Organizational factors: mission, strategy, overall structure, leadership style, management systems, culture, group dynamics.

FIGURE 12.1   *Job design and performance determinants*

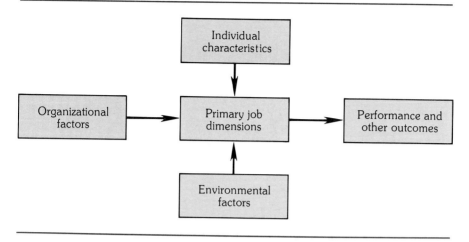

2. Environmental factors: the economy, the market, society, government, unions, technology.
3. Individual characteristics: personality, needs, self image, attitudes and values, modes of perception and learning, motivation, aspirations.
4. The primary job dimensions: the elements that constitute a job.

THE PRIMARY STRUCTURAL ELEMENTS

A job's **primary structural elements** are its horizontal and vertical components. A job has tasks (horizontal component) and the authority (vertical component) to perform those tasks.

At the individual job level, the horizontal component is referred to as having **range**—the variation and number of tasks in a single job. The vertical component is described as having various levels of **depth**—the amount of decision-making authority available to the holder of that position. A typical manufacturing assembly-line job has little or no range or depth. The job of company president, conversely, has high levels of both. A college professor's job usually has limited range but great depth. A middle manager's job often has great range but little depth.

These structural elements may be further analyzed in terms of their various component dimensions. Five core job dimensions and three additional dimensions are significant.

The **core job dimensions** are defined as follows:

Task variety: the degree to which a job requires employees to perform a wide range of operations or to use a variety of equipment or procedures in their work.

Task identity: the extent to which employees do an entire or whole piece of work and can clearly identify the results of their efforts.

Task significance: the extent to which employees perceive a substantial impact on others as the result of their job efforts.

66 . . . work has a greater effect than any other technique of living in binding the individual more closely to reality; in his work he is at least securely attached to a part of reality, the human community. 99
SIGMUND FREUD

Autonomy: the extent to which employees have a major say in scheduling their work, selecting the equipment they will use, and deciding on procedures to be followed.

Feedback: the degree to which employees receive information in the course of their work which reveals how well they are performing the job.[3]

The Anheuser-Busch aluminum can top plant in Gainesville, Florida, made special efforts to design jobs in decision-making teams in order to satisfy needs, and thus to increase satisfaction, and thus to increase performance. Team members were cross-trained to function at a large number of tasks; teams were able to complete an entire product unit, were given continuous control reports on their performance, and were allowed considerable autonomy in several decision areas. Productivity results have been satisfactory, but the plant is still too new to permit the project's success or failure to be determined.[4]

The additional job dimensions are defined as follows:

Interpersonal relations: the extent to which the individual engages in meaningful human interactions on the job with peers, subordinates, and superiors.

Authority and responsibility for goal setting: the degree of authority and responsibility delegated to and inherent in the position; of special interest is the amount of latitude an individual has in setting objectives.

Communication patterns: the formal and informal communications associated with the job.

These factors influence both the design of the job and the eventual outcomes of the jobholder's efforts—the consequences of the work to the organization, the individual, and society.

Together these eight factors are what a job is all about. When a personnel specialist, a manager, or any other person attempts to design a job, these factors are the materials that are available from which to create that job. If you want to create a secretarial position, a coaching position, an assembly-line worker's position, a teaching position, a nursing position, an accounting position, or any other, this is all that you have to work with. A job can have more or less variety, more or less identity, more or less significance, more or less autonomy, more or less feedback, more or fewer interpersonal relations, more or less authority and responsibility to set goals and make plans, and more or fewer satisfactory communications. It is up to the designer of the job to ensure that proper levels of each of these factors are designed into that job. How important are these factors to you? Take the "Test Yourself" and find out.

Over time the jobholder can attempt to add to or subtract from these factors. When they are combined in the proper proportions, they can satisfy the needs of the jobholder at the same time that they fulfill the objectives of the job and of the organization. Jobholders who fail to find the need satisfiers they seek in their jobs may move on to other jobs. The major thrust of the quality-of-work-life effort in recent years has been to increase the satisfaction that workers

In order that people may be happy in their work, these three things are needed: They must be fit for it. They must not do too much of it. And they must have a sense of success in it.
JOHN RUSKIN

Motivators are concerned with using people well and, when combined with a good hygiene program, with treating people well. The result will be motivated performance.
FREDERICK HERZBERG

TEST YOURSELF

PRIMARY JOB DIMENSIONS

How important are the various primary job dimensions to you? What do you want in a job? In the space provided below, rank the eight dimensions in accordance with their importance, from 1 (the most important) to 8 (the least important).

Dimension	Rank
Task variety	____
Task identity	____
Task significance	____
Autonomy	____
Feedback	____
Interpersonal relationships	____
Authority and responsibility for goal setting	____
Communication patterns	____

Now ask yourself why you ranked these items the way you did. What do your rankings tell you about your own needs?

What other factors would you add? Have those factors ever influenced your choice of job? In what way?

derive from their jobs. Programs that have been introduced to improve individual job design include job enlargement, job enrichment, job rotation, improvement of the sociotechnical match, quality control circles, and other types of work team arrangements. The primary targets of these efforts have been the structural elements of specialization of labor and delegation of authority.

Specialization of Labor   Historically, the principle of specialization of labor has resulted in a narrowing of the range of most jobs, and their depth has often been quite limited as well. In this century, Frederick W. Taylor has been the foremost proponent of the idea that any work task should be made so simple and repetitive that almost any individual can perform it successfully.[5] He and other experts of the scientific management era (the early twentieth century) argued that such specialization makes for the most efficient and effective job design. Jobholders whose tasks are highly specialized quickly attain high levels of performance. By eliminating the need to make decisions, specialization leads to further increases in efficiency. Up to a point, these experts have been proved correct. But not all jobs can be highly specialized. Perhaps more important, not all jobholders—in fact, not many of today's jobholders—remain maximally productive at highly specialized tasks for long.

"Perhaps the most prominent single element of modern scientific management is the task idea. . . . The task is always so regulated that the man who is well-suited to his job will thrive while working at this rate during a long term of years and grow happier and more prosperous, instead of being overworked."

FREDERICK W. TAYLOR

Highly specialized jobs usually provide little variety, little identity, little significance, low levels of autonomy and feedback, limited interpersonal relations, limited authority and responsibility to set goals, and a small amount of communication with others. Such specialized jobs are not limited to manufacturing; they are found in the professions as well. A junior accountant, for example, may simply add numbers all day, and there is certainly nothing exciting about that; a middle-level manager may make virtually no decisions because rules and policies spell out what must be done. Such highly specialized jobs typically result in dissatisfaction, disinterest, and alienation from the organization among employees who have higher-level needs—an increasing percentage of the population. The consequences for the organization are low morale, high rates of absenteeism and turnover, increased training costs, reduced efficiency and effectiveness, and consequently declining productivity. One of the major questions confronting work organizations everywhere today is how to make the job more productive by making it more satisfying. Many organizations are attempting to expand the range of their jobs in the hope of reducing job dissatisfaction and, more to the point, of consequently increasing productivity. This process, known as job enlargement, is discussed in greater detail later in this chapter.

Delegation of Authority   The amount of authority delegated to any job position reflects the organization's overall management philosophy. Just how much authority a job should have is a vital issue in job design. The natural tendency of the specialization of labor is to reduce the depth of the individual job as well as its range. When the need to think is eliminated, the chance of error is reduced, the jobholder naturally takes less time to perform the task, and thus theoretically productivity is increased. But because the individual becomes dissatisfied, productivity typically declines fairly soon. Thus severely restricted delegation of authority appears to be less desirable than it was once thought to be. Organizations are therefore attempting to expand the depth of many jobs, in the belief that such actions will increase productivity. This process, known as job enrichment, is discussed in greater detail in later paragraphs.

JOB REDESIGN PROGRAMS

"Without work, life goes rotten. But when work is soulless, life stifles and dies."
ALBERT CAMUS

Many organizations are concerned with the **quality of work life (QWL)**. This term has come to cover any number of programs aimed at increasing the satisfaction of individual needs in the workplace. Richard E. Walton suggests that the quality of work life should be assessed according to the following eight criteria:

1. Adequate and fair compensation.
2. Safe and healthy working conditions.
3. Immediate opportunity to use and develop human capacities.
4. Future opportunity for continued growth and security.
5. Social integration in the work organization.
6. Employee rights to privacy, speech, equity, and due process.

7. A balance between one's role as worker and the rest of one's life.
8. A socially responsible work organization.[6]

Of these eight criteria, numbers 2, 3, 4, 5, and 7 are directly concerned with job design. It is no coincidence that much of what can be done to improve the quality of work life revolves around the design of individual jobs. The content of the job and the amount of authority attached to it must eventually be matched with the needs, personality, and other individual characteristics of that job's occupant. It is here that QWL takes on its full meaning. Many companies have adopted QWL programs, among them General Motors, Westinghouse, General Electric, and Volvo. Most such programs focus primarily on job enlargement and job enrichment, but may include job rotation, the sociotechnological interface, and quality circles (discussed in Chapter 7). It is important to note that most such programs today are based on the concept of work teams. TRW, for example, has eliminated the supervisory position in its plant in Lawrence, Kansas. Antonomous work teams run the plant; a few former managers stayed on as advisers to the teams, but they are advisers only. Similarly, M&M/Mars recently opened a new plant in Waco, Texas, which is run by self-managing work teams. The Skippy Peanut Butter plant in Little Rock, Arkansas, has no fixed jobs, no job descriptions, no inspectors, no supervisors. A general manager, a human resources manager, and a quality assurance manager act as advisers to the 100 or so employees who in concert make the decisions. Numerous other such programs are in operation.[7]

Frederick Herzberg was the first person to advocate that firms increase the depth and range of their jobs as a means of motivating their employees. Remember that by "motivating" he means influencing employees to do more on the job or to do a better job than they have been doing, not simply influencing them to do a satisfactory job. As we saw in Chapter 3, Herzberg views motivation (as he defines it) primarily as a consequence of satisfiers intrinsic to the job. Such factors as a sense of achievement, recognition, advancement, and growth are motivators. Hygiene factors—factors used to attempt to influence people which are extrinsic to the job itself, such as salary, relationships with other workers, and company policy—do not, in his opinion, motivate.

To Herzberg, job enrichment is the loading of a job with intrinsic satisfiers. The key to successful job enrichment, in his view, is to allow the individual to develop, to use her abilities, to want to do the job. He proposes that a "good" job, one that is enriched, contains the following eight ingredients:

JOB ENLARGEMENT AND JOB ENRICHMENT

> *If I kick my dog . . . , he will move. And when I want him to move again what must I do? I must kick him again . . . . It is only when [a person] has his own generator that we can talk about motivation. He then needs no outside stimulation. He wants to do it.*
> FREDERICK HERZBERG

1. Direct feedback. Information about a person's performance should be made available directly to that person in a timely and nonevaluative manner. Such feedback is best delivered by the result itself, not through the supervisor.
2. Client relationship. The employee who is responsible to someone who is a client for his output, either within or outside of the organization, is more likely to be motivated. There must be someone who depends on him.
3. New learning. The employee must have an opportunity to grow psychologically.

4. Scheduling. One should have the opportunity to schedule one's own work.
5. Unique expertise. The employee should have a unit of work with which she can identify and which to her is significant.
6. Control over resources. The worker should have control over those factors that affect the costs of her outputs.
7. Direct communications authority. A worker should be able to talk with the person who is able to solve a problem, whoever that may be, rather than be forced to run through a lengthy chain of command.
8. Personal accountability. People with meaningful jobs should be held accountable for their performance. They want to be.[8]

Other researchers built upon Herzberg's efforts to develop new theories of job enrichment. The large number of viewpoints has resulted in some confusion as to just what *job enrichment* means. Furthermore, another term, *job enlargement*, has been used to describe some of what Herzberg and others have labeled "enrichment."

Kae H. Chung and Monica Ross reviewed the major versions of job enlargement and job enrichment to identify their common elements. Their efforts give us a better understanding of the differences between these two concepts and their similarities. Job enlargement "involves reversing the work simplification or specialization process somewhat." In their view, **job enlargement** embodies five basic concepts, any one or several of which can constitute enlargement:

1. Task variety: doing more and different tasks.
2. A meaningful work module: by working on the complete unit of work, the employee gains an appreciation of his contribution to the entire product or project.
3. Performance feedback: performance feedback is increased when a larger number of tasks involved in producing a more complete work unit are performed.
4. Ability utilization: satisfaction (and therefore, according to Herzberg, motivation) is increased where the work unit is enlarged to permit the use of a wider variety of skills and abilities.
5. Worker-paced control: when work activity is no longer paced by a machine, the employee's desire to control some part of her environment is satisfied; again, motivation results.[9]

Chung and Ross define **job enrichment** (often called *vertical job loading*) as provision for nonmanagerial employees to perform functions previously restricted to managerial and supervisory personnel (in essence, decision making). They view job enrichment as including:

1. Employee participation: employees participate in the decision process (but only at the level of the job, not at the management level, as with worker councils, junior boards, etc.); thus they feel personally responsible for carrying out their tasks.
2. Goal internalization: workers set goals for their own jobs.
3. Autonomy: workers need a high degree of control over the means they will use to achieve objectives they have set; thus they evaluate their own performance, take risks, and learn from their mistakes.

> *The authoritarian organizational hierarchy contains key factors which are counterproductive to the quality of life within and outside the organization.*
> CHRIS ARGYRIS

4. Group management: as most employees whose jobs are appropriate for enrichment work in groups, assignments and job redesign are often subject to team consensus.[10]

One often hears job enlargement concepts referred to as "job enrichment," and practically speaking, it makes little difference what you call these techniques, as long as you understand what they are. Most authorities on the subject would probably agree that job enlargement is less motivating than job enrichment, in the Herzbergian sense, but that job enlargement does reduce boredom, and so in that sense encourages employees to perform at a minimally satisfactory level. Firms often pursue both paths. For example, Sometown, Inc., a fairly large, privately held manufacturing firm, redesigned its accounting department so that its junior accountants became product accountants. These employees had historically been glorified bookkeepers, but after their jobs were redesigned they became part of the information management team. Now they were management accountants, and they also assumed responsibility for managing at least two clerical subordinates. Both range and depth were increased. Task identity, feedback, and limited autonomy were provided.[11]

Job enrichment requires a different management philosophy from the kind that most organizations seem to have. It requires more delegation of authority than most firms are willing to countenance, and it requires democratic rather than authoritarian behavior. As we have noted, the management profession tends to attract people who have a great need for power, a need to control others. Job enrichment is not compatible with this type of personality. (Could your current or a past boss implement job enrichment, given his or her personality?) Furthermore, in the United States and Canada, unions have generally opposed job enrichment/enlargement programs, or at best have failed to support them, though this situation is changing.[12] European unions, in contrast, have supported enrichment and participation programs. Finally, as several researchers have observed, job enrichment is not for everyone.[13] Workers who are motivated by lower-level need satisfiers, who do not want responsibility, who do not share middle-class attitudes toward work (that it should be fulfilling, for example), who want to do just enough to get by— such workers are not going to adapt well to job enrichment or enlargement. And, most important, the motivation/performance cycle model (Chapters 3 and 4) predicts that workers who find themselves doing increased amounts of work with no corresponding increase in extrinsic rewards are not likely to be satisfied and hence will not be motivated.

People are different, and management simply cannot embrace any single technique and expect it to work for everyone. But job enrichment will work for many people. It seems important, though, to keep Herzberg's "maintenance" factors at acceptable levels, because otherwise people will be dissatisfied and hence demotivated. Further, not every job can be enriched, at least not in a manner that pays off at the bottom line. Trade-offs are involved in virtually every situation: costs must be weighed against benefits. Absenteeism and turnover may be reduced by job enlargement or enrichment, but productivity may decline when jobs become less specialized. Workers may be discontented for any number of reasons. The problem may not be the job at

> *There's a lot of variety in the paint shop. You clip on the color hose, bleed out the old color, and squirt. Clip, bleed, squirt, think; clip, bleed, squirt, yawn; clip, bleed, squirt, scratch your nose.*
>
> Young worker at GM's Lordstown plant, as told to Barbara Garson

all. Managers must attempt to uncover other possible problems. When Bernard J. White analyzed the responses of 1,500 workers who were asked to rank various factors, both internal and external to the job, according to their importance, he concluded that employers could ignore neither maintenance factors nor satisfiers, but had to pay attention to both.[14]

Job enrichment, then, is just one more tool that you can use if you are a manager, or an arrangement that you can request as a subordinate, to improve human relations. It is a form of participative management that functions primarily at the level of the individual employee and that of the immediate supervisor.

JOB ROTATION

Job rotation moves an employee from one job to another. In that sense, it is a type of job enlargement. It is most effective as a training device. Bank management training programs typically call for job rotation. Such programs, often lasting as long as two years, give trainees an opportunity to learn how all major bank functions contribute to the accomplishment of the bank's mission. The individual who completes a job rotation program is presumed to be prepared to manage one part of the total system. Job rotation can be effective as a means of improving job design. Job rotation programs improve the quality of work life. Some rotation programs, however, enlarge nothing but frustration: now the employee has multiple dull, boring jobs instead of one.

IMPROVING THE SOCIO-TECHNOLOGICAL INTERFACE

Not only individual jobs are redesigned; sometimes the entire organization is redesigned in an effort to improve the quality of work life, job satisfaction, and productivity. At the center of such activities, commonly called organizational development (OD), is an effort to improve the interface between a person and the technological processes used in that person's job. An organization that undertakes OD makes every effort to enrich all of its jobs. Numerous other processes are often encompassed by OD, including several that we have already examined or will examine—climate surveys, leadership training, transactional analysis, assertiveness training, team building, and management by objectives, results, and rewards. One of the best-known examples of an OD intervention is that of the Swedish firm Volvo. Volvo completely redesigned the auto assembly process in a new factory, allowing semiautonomous work teams virtually to manage themselves. Understanding the **sociotechnological interface** issue requires first an understanding of how technology affects job design and job performance.

TECHNOLOGY

One of the major factors that have required organizations to provide new ways for individuals to relate to their jobs is technology. No other factor has had such a dramatic effect on job design, with the possible exception of specialization. Technology affects everyone's job, whether one is a manager, a service worker, or an operations employee.

Technology can be defined narrowly, as "the manufacturing, as distinct from administrative or distributive, processes employed by manufacturing firms to convert inputs into outputs."[15] Or, more appropriately for our purposes, as "the types and patterns of activity, equipment and material, and knowledge or experience used to perform tasks."[16] Or as "the combination of resources, knowledge, and techniques that creates a product or service output for an organization."[17] Or finally as "tools in a general sense, including machines, but also including such intellectual tools as computer languages and contemporary analytical and mathematical techniques. That is, . . . the organization of knowledge for the achievement of practical purposes."[18] The broader definitions seem the most satisfactory, but for the purposes of our discussion the second definition, focusing on equipment or knowledge, is most appropriate.

Two principal technological developments are reshaping the future of work. First, **robots** have been introduced into manufacturing facilities at an increasing rate. Robots are so cost-effective in such contexts that it would be possible to replace virtually every factory-floor worker by a machine. When Apple Computer decided to build the MacIntosh, for example, the firm wanted to employ as few human beings as possible in its manufacture in order to ensure quality as well as efficiency. As few as 300 people turn out some 80,000 MacIntoshes a month. Most of these people are quality control and distribution personnel; they are not involved in the actual manufacturing process.[19] Many jobs that were once held by humans in other manufacturing facilities, automobile plants, and steel mills are performed completely by robots now. Some factories already operate virtually without human beings, as the Human Relations Happening "Factory Toils into Night without People" indicates.

The second major event that is reshaping the future of work is office automation, specifically the personal computer (PC). While there are pros and cons to the explosive proliferation of this device, it is evident that the future holds increased automation for the office and increased use of personal computer. Organizations and individuals must be prepared to cope with these two changes in technology which are so greatly affecting the nature of work.

> *". . . whenever new technology is introduced into society, there must be a counter-balancing human response—that is, high touch—or the technology is rejected. The more high tech, the more high touch."*
>
> JOHN NAISBITT

Robots are a form of change. As such they meet with resistance. Because they often result in severe specialization of labor for the humans they do not replace, they may lead to increased boredom, a feeling of meaningless or selflessness. Among employees who must deal with their introduction, robots create fear—fear of losing their jobs, fear of their effects on social relationships, fear of the unknown. Some of their fears are well founded. Between 1980 and 1982, for example, two million manufacturing jobs were wiped out.[20] One study of the introduction of robots into a forging and machine metal alloy plant employing some 1,000 nonunion workers suggests quite simply that the situation must be handled like any other change. Employers must take actions to reduce fears; to anticipate workers' reactions, values, and beliefs, and the robots' effects on their activities and interactions; to involve

THE HUMAN SIDE OF ROBOTICS

HUMAN RELATIONS HAPPENING

Factory Toils into Night without People

ASSOCIATED PRESS

LOUISVILLE, Ky.—From midnight to 8 A.M., not a single person can be found in Mazak Corp.'s plant in northern Kentucky.

But in those eight hours, a totally automated third shift in the machine shop casts machines to be used in Ford Motor Co. engines and General Electric Co. appliances.

"We turn out the lights and go home, and let the machines do the work," said Fenton Kohler, vice president of the operation, which claims to be the world's largest automated factory.

"If there's a problem, the machines try and figure it out themselves. If not, the machine will shut down for the night."

The Florence plant is the first in the United States for Mazak. Its production accounts for 40 percent of the company's U.S. sales and is just one example in Kentucky of how American manufacturers are using automation and robotics.

"If we didn't automate, we wouldn't be able to compete in the world market," Kohler said. "We're the world innovator in unmanned systems. We're showing that American industry can be competitive again. If American industry doesn't automate, the trade deficit is just going to grow."

The arguments for increased automation and the use of robotics are growing, with most companies saying they can manufacture a higher quality, cheaper product with automation. Most pledge to automate without ordering mass layoffs.

"There have been no big layoffs, just mainly attrition or early retirement, that I am aware of," said Dick Edwards, a professor at the University of Kentucky who teaches an introductory course in automation and robotics in the school of engineering.

In Campbellsville, the only time a human is needed on the assembly line at the $50 million Batesville Casket Co. is when one of the robots needs rewiring or reprogramming. The rest of the time, a staff of robots welds, sands, finishes, paints and sews the interior materials for the caskets.

"We feel [that] to maintain leadership, it is important to mechanize to be more efficient and cost effective," said Bob Smith, vice president of investor relations at Hillenbrand Industries, which owns Batesville Casket. "If we don't, someone else—the Japanese—will beat us to the punch with cheaper products."

In Lexington, International Business Machines Corp. initiated an expensive worker retraining program—it cost $10 million in 1983–84—when it began to automate its typewriter assembly line with robots. Division manager Ed Lassetter said workers are getting new jobs and none of the plant's 6,000 employees is being laid off, although some have been encouraged to accept transfers to other IBM plants.

SOURCE: *Orlando Sentinel*, December 22, 1985, p. F-10. Reprinted with permission of The Associated Press.

the workers in the introduction of the new technology; and to provide demonstrations of how the robots will work. Organizations must also solicit feedback from workers to make sure that the message about the robots has been received. If robots have caused boredom, organizations should make provisions for increased participation in decision making. They should also train backup operators, because otherwise the robot will be essentially worthless when the operator is absent. Finally, organizations should attempt to counteract the

Robot welding machines are taking over one of the most difficult and dangerous jobs in building a car, and doing it with more accuracy.

breaking of social relationships by providing alternative ways for affected individuals to relate to each other.[21]

The people who are most enthusiastic about robots and their potential are managers. John Opal, chairman of IBM, comments, "Look at history, every time we have had technological change some people argued that we should stop the change and preserve the jobs. What actually happened was more jobs were created than destroyed. Right now the software industry is growing like gang busters and that's highly labor-intensive." Others argue that failure to become efficient, to automate, to robotize will lead to our dethronement as the most powerful industrial nation. David Packer, former chairman of Hewlett-Packard, argued, "We have no choice but to automate because foreign competitors are doing so."[22]

Millions of unionized workers are absolutely horrified at the thought of the future that robotization seems to promise them. Most fear that high-paying, middle-class blue-collar jobs will disappear from the scene. One of the great fears of many union leaders and economic forecasters is that the technological changes taking place during our transition to a service and information economy will result in an economy with a two-tier wage base: a large number of low-paying service jobs at the bottom and a large number of high-paying technology-related jobs at the top, with virtually no middle class.[23]

Regardless of the expectations of the people involved, it is evident that the move toward robotization will continue. It's also clear that when the competitive situation can be properly explained to union officials, they will support robotization. A General Electric plant in Erie, Pennsylvania, for example, found the competitive position of its product eroding. Its competitors were primarily low-cost, efficient firms in Japan, Korea, and Taiwan. Rather than move their own business offshore, GE strategists decided that they could remain in Erie if they could robotize. Faced with the prospect of some jobs or no jobs at all, the union recognized that in order to preserve its position and the jobs of many of its workers, it had to accept robotization and in fact even support it. Thus while the firm eliminated 3,000 jobs as a consequence of the decision to robotize, 7,500 jobs were saved. Of the jobs saved, 3,200 were held by workers represented by the United Electrical Workers. GE also invested some $6.5 million to retrain workers to handle the new technology.[24]

The move to robotics has not been as swift, however, as many people felt it would be in the early 1980s. General Electric, which established a division to manufacture and market robots, eliminated most of the division in 1985 because the market for robots simply did not exist at that time.[25] It seems that robots are not cost-effective in some situations. Briggs & Stratton, for example, finds that human beings are every bit as productive as robots if they are properly managed. Briggs & Stratton relies on quality circles and other quality-control measurements combined with a management-by-walking-around approach to achieve its ends. Its success is based partly on the belief that human beings can contribute valuable ideas for improvement, something that robots obviously cannot do. The firm points out that robots cannot engage in quality circles, they cannot make suggestions, they cannot improve the process, and while they may never be absent, they can break down. The Human Relations Happening "Where Robots Can't Yet Compete" details Briggs & Stratton's approach.

HUMAN RELATIONS HAPPENING

WHERE ROBOTS CAN'T YET COMPETE

The plant looks like the industrial exhibit at the Smithsonian Institution come to life, so old is much of its machinery. But in a world being engulfed by computerized automation, Briggs & Stratton Corp.'s maverick Wauwatosa, Wisconsin, factory towers as a stronghold of human skill, agility—and high productivity.

Briggs & Stratton is the world's leading and lowest-cost producer of small engines. The company has been consistently profitable; in its last fiscal year it totted up a net of $39.4 million on sales of $636 million. On last year's Fortune 500, it ranked 442nd in sales but 167th in total return to investors.

The company's secret technology is the most flexible of all manufacturing systems: the human being. "We find that people are best at doing the work that needs dexterity and a lot of repetition," says Laverne J. Socks, Briggs & Stratton's executive vice president for manufacturing. "We will consider automation wherever possible, practical, economical. But if you are talking about one of those unmanned factories, you'll never see our operation all automated like that."

Part of the reason is that the firm's principal products, small air-cooled engines used mainly in lawn mowers and garden tractors, do not readily lend themselves to automation—at least in assembly. While it is true that Fanuc Ltd. in Japan assembles electric motors with robots, internal combusion engines are more complicated. Even the small one- and two-cylinder Briggs & Stratton engines have as many as 500 parts.

But Briggs & Stratton has also achieved robotlike productivity by astute management of its factory. It minimizes the number of managers, and those managers, as Socks puts it, "communicate with the workers constantly—on the floor." Quality control is bolstered through employee participation. Housekeeping awards are issued to keep the plant clean.

The mainstay of this policy is a piecework incentive system, and visitors invariably marvel at the intensity of the work force. Workers don't linger over coffee breaks (there's only one a day, of six minutes' duration). Says one impressed visitor: "They even run to and from the bathrooms." Sixty percent are on either group or individual incentive pay; some workers earn as much as $30,000 a year. The union, local 232 of the Allied Industrial Workers, has no problem with piecework. "The people have a preference for the incentive plans," says a union official.

It remains to seen, though, how long the people at Briggs & Stratton can hold out against the new machines. There's nothing in theory to stop others—the Japanese, for instance—from redesigning engines for easier automatic assembly.

SOURCE: *Fortune*, February 21, 1983, p. 64. © 1983 Time Inc. All rights reserved.

Nineteen billion dollars' worth of nonengineering personal computers were sold in 1986 in the United States.[26] Such firms as Travelers' Insurance Company have placed PC's on many if not most managers' desks.[27] And while most of the problems that have accompanied the introduction of robots are duplicated in the introduction of personal computers, PC's have many more admirers. Most managers and professionals feel very positive toward the PC. They say it makes their jobs more exciting, allows them to make more decisions, provides them with tools for analysis. The PC allows them to make not only more decisions but better ones. It frees them from the drudgery of number-crunching and lets them engage in the more pleasurable task of analyzing what those numbers mean. It allows them to take on more tasks.

Software is changing office routines in an amazing way. The more complex word processing software allows secretaries to accomplish much more work, 50 to 100 percent more in many cases. Various other types of software allow them to manage their schedules and their bosses' schedules as well.[28]

PC's and other computers also enable the organization to take certain actions that an employee may regard as negative. From the corporate view, flattening the pyramidal structure is a desirable thing to do. Jobs can be eliminated, decision time can be reduced. An advanced information system that incorporates sophisticated combinations of word processing, mail systems, video equipment, and high-speed communication devices has permitted Hercules, Inc., to squeeze the number of levels of management from twelve to six or

COMPUTERS AND THE INFORMATION SOCIETY

"I still miss the days when we just read the
letters and made a list."

From *The Wall Street Journal*—Permission, Cartoon Features Syndicate.

seven. Hercules trimmed 1,800 jobs, about 7 percent of its work force, with
the introduction of its electronic devices, for a saving of hundreds of millions
of dollars. Cost-cutting in secretarial positions has saved Hercules an additional $3 to 6 million a year. Numerous other firms have taken similar steps.
While these actions please stockholders and management, they do not please
those who have been let go as a consequence. As we shall see in Chapter
13, the movement toward the lean, mean organization leaves many casualties
in its wake, especially among middle management and people who used to
summarize or routinely analyze data. These chores are done by computer
now.[29] Other downside factors for the individual employee include boredom
and work schedules reminiscent of the sweatshops of a bygone era. Many
workers at Blue Shield of Massachusetts who sit all day in front of video
display terminals (VDT's), feel under extreme pressure to perform. They even
hesitate to go to the bathroom because their pay is based on their productivity,
which is calculated by their computers. They complain of eyestrain, headaches, and backaches, and they are concerned about the possible effects of
microwave radiation emanating from the machines.[30]

Another problem associated with computers is their ability to keep extremely close watch on individuals, at a time when workers are seeking more
freedom and less control. The word processors used by members of typing
pools, for example, create reports showing the number of pages each individual
produced in a day, even the number of keystrokes made in a minute. Supervisors of telephone operators can read reports that indicate the number of
calls an operator handled on any given day. Computer terminals in manufacturing facilities can tell managers who is ahead and who is behind at what

machines. Even trucks may be monitored by computers to make sure that truckers do not exceed speed limits.[31]

Personal computers are affecting the lives of managers in significant ways. Not only are many managers' jobs being eliminated by computers, but the manager who sits in front of the terminal must now know how to use it and the software associated with it. Some managers are afraid of computers. Take a not too untypical banker, who, after saying that computers have not changed his life, then tells you that he has an IBM PC at his right hand, an Apple Lisa behind him for sending memos, and another IBM PC at home. He uses the machines to analyze various reports coming in to him. He uses various software packages to look at capital investment projects, to draw up budgets, and to design compensation programs for the 1,600 people under his supervision. Finally, the computer allows him to do more work at home. Other than that, it really hasn't affected his life much.[32]

Work at Home   One of the major consequences of the proliferation of computers is that it has permitted many people to do much of their work at home. Individuals whose work consists largely of analysis of data can receive, analyze, and transmit data with home computers. Insurance processors, financial analysts, and so on can thus use the time otherwise wasted in commuting to an office to accomplish other objectives. Working at home reduces their personal out-of-pocket expenses, gives them more time with their families, allows flexible work hours, and gives them freedom to dress as they wish. While telecommuters report many positive effects of working at home, however, they also report some unexpected strains and stresses. Interestingly enough, many of them gain weight because of the proximity of the refrigerator. Probably more pressing problems for most people are isolation and loneliness, concerns about visibility for political and promotional purposes, the lack of someone to discuss ideas with, and the potential for exploitation by management. One computer programmer indicates that he really couldn't get a feel for the exact situation unless he was involved in a face-to-face conversation with the person he was servicing. Working at home didn't seem to help his productivity very much. Nonetheless, I think we should expect to see more workers working at home on computers, despite opposition from organized labor.[33]

TIPS FOR SUCCESS

1. Find a job you enjoy doing.
2. Be willing to do a job you don't like: for the money, for the experience, for exposure, but not forever—not even for a long time.
3. Seek to improve your job when you can. If you are a manager, seek to improve the jobs of others when you can.
4. When and if you are asked to design a job, take care to build in the key job dimensions in a satisfactory way.
5. Make friends with computers. Your future depends on it.
6. Consider the possibilities of working at home.

SUMMARY

1. Any job has two primary structural elements: task contents and authority.
2. These two elements are based on five core dimensions—task variety, task identity, task significance, autonomy, and feedback—and three additional dimensions: interpersonal relations, authority and responsibility for goal setting, and communication patterns.
3. Historically, job design efforts have been aimed at increasingly narrow specialization of labor, which often runs counter to the goal of providing satisfactory amounts of the core job dimensions and of the other three job dimensions.
4. Quality of work life programs generally focus on job design.

5. Job enlargement aims at increasing the range of a job.
6. Job enrichment aims at increasing the depth of a job.
7. Job rotation, sociotechnological interfacing, and the use of groups, including quality circles and teams of various types, are additional ways of improving job design.
8. For our purposes, technology is broadly defined as the equipment used to perform a task or the knowledge required to perform a task.
9. Robots are replacing human beings in many manufacturing operations.
10. Computers will dominate our future world.

DISCUSSION QUESTIONS

1. Analyze your human relations professor's job in terms of the eight component dimensions, and the issues of depth and range. Do you consider the level of each of these factors satisfactory, unsatisfactory, in between?
2. Discuss the pros and cons of job enrichment, job enlargement, job rotation, sociotechnological interfacing, and team building, including quality circles.
3. Discuss the ways in which technological developments, in particular computers, have affected your life, your human relations.

4. Discuss the ways in which technological developments, in particular computers, have affected an organization with which you are familiar, perhaps your current college or university.
5. Describe how an organization should go about the introduction of robotics.
6. Describe how technology may be expected to affect you and your work organization in the future.

APPLYING HUMAN RELATIONS SKILLS

CASE | **The Bots**

Firms involved in the manufacturing of steel specialty products had taken a beating from international competition. Vince Patello was convinced that robots could help his firm. He anticipated that as much as 20 percent of the work force could be eliminated if he acquired three robots, each of which could do the work of several workers, and do it more accurately. So he took the plunge and purchased three robots. It did not take long for the word to travel around the plant that robots—or bots, as they soon came to be called—were going to be arriving. Fear began to grip the work force. Productivity declined. Vince began to draw up a plan of action to overcome the difficulties he was having.

1. What should Vince do at this point to smooth the way for the introduction of the robots?

This is a field exercise. Contact an organization in your area that will allow you to observe and talk to people at work. Organizations may at first be reluctant to cooperate. If so, you will find them more willing to cooperate if you assure them that the information you gather will not be used in any negative way. You might even be able to show them some ways of improving jobs, and this factor could be mentioned. In making your arrangements, please remember that you represent your school, and that regardless of the structure of their jobs, all employees should be treated with interest, concern, and respect.

The objective here is to analyze a job according to the Chung and Ross dimensions noted in the text and to determine what could be incorporated in a particular job in order to enlarge or enrich it. It would be very useful if several students could study managerial jobs while several others were examining nonmanagerial positions. Comparisons can be made regarding the need for enlargement or enrichment in classes of jobs.

For this exercise, please complete a job content profile for each position. You can do this by observing employees in action, and if necessary questioning them about their duties. After you have completed the profile, ask employees how they like their jobs, and what they would do to make their jobs more productive and more satisfying if they could. When all students have completed this project, job content profiles and a summary of employees' comments should be brought to class. A discussion on how each job could be redesigned, enlarged, or enriched should ensue.

Job Content Profile

Organization _____   Job title _____

Enlargement possibilities	High	5	4	3	2	1	Low
Task variety		5	4	3	2	1	
Meaningful work module		5	4	3	2	1	
Performance feedback		5	4	3	2	1	
Ability utilization		5	4	3	2	1	
Worker-paced control		5	4	3	2	1	
Enrichment possibilities	High	5	4	3	2	1	Low
Employee participation		5	4	3	2	1	
Goal internalization		5	4	3	2	1	
Autonomy		5	4	3	2	1	
Group management		5	4	3	2	1	

REFERENCES

1. Janet P. Near, C. Ann Smith, Robert W. Rice, and Raymond G. Hunt, "A Comparison of Work and Nonwork Predictors of Life Satisfaction," *Academy of Management Journal*, March 1984, pp 184–190.
2. C. N. Weaver, "Job Satisfaction in the United States in the 1970s," *Journal of Applied Psychology*, Vol. 65, 1980, pp. 364–67.
3. J. R. Hackman and G. R. Oldham, *Work Redesign* (Reading, Mass.: Addison-Wesley, 1980), pp. 77–80.
4. Author's discussion with research personnel involved in this project.
5. Frederick W. Taylor, *Scientific Management* (New York: Harper & Row, 1947).
6. Richard E. Walton, "Quality of Work Life: What Is It?" *Sloan Management Review*, Fall 1973, pp. 11–21.
7. Lawrence Miller, "The Impact of Unity: Tearing Down the Barriers between Management and Labor Leads to Increased Productivity and Greater Profits," *Management Review*, May 1984, pp. 8–15.
8. Frederick Herzberg, "The Wise Old Turk," *Harvard Business Review*, September–October 1974, pp. 70–80.
9. Kae H. Chung and Monica F. Ross, "Differences in Motivational Properties between Job Enlargement and Job Enrichment," *Academy of Management Review*, January 1977, pp. 113–22.
10. Ibid.
11. Richard M. Roderick, "Redesigning an Accounting Department for Corporate and Personal Goals," *Management Accounting*, February 1984, pp. 56–60.
12. Miller, "Impact of Unity."
13. See William T. Rutherford and James M. Higgins, "Democracy at Work or Only Away from Work," *Atlanta Economic Review*, November–December 1974, p. 8; William E. Reif and Fred Luthans, "Does Job Enrichment Really Pay Off?" *California Management Review*, Fall 1972, pp. 30–37.
14. Bernard J. White, "The Criteria for Job Satisfaction: Is Interesting Work Most Important?" *Monthly Labor Review*, May 1977, pp. 30–35.
15. Pradip M. Khandwalla, "Mass Output Orientation of Operations Technology and Organizational Structure," *Administrative Science Quarterly*, March 1974, p. 74.
16. David F. Gillespie and Dennis S. Mileti, "Technology and the Study of Organizations: An Overview and Appraisal," *Academy of Management Review*, January 1977, p. 8.
17. John R. Schermerhorn, Jr., James G. Hunt, and Richard N. Osborn, *Managing Organizational Behavior* (New York: Wiley, 1982), p. 334.
18. E. Mesthene, *Technological Change: Its Impact on Man and Society* (Cambridge: Harvard University Press, 1970).
19. Victor Lazzano, "The Automated Apple Orchard," *Discover*, September 1985, pp. 80–81.
20. "Hi-Tech: Blessing Occurs," *U.S. News and World Report*, January 16, 1984, p. 38.
21. Linda Argote, Paul S. Goodman, and David Schkade, "The Human Side of Robotics: How Workers React to a Robot," *Sloan Management Review*, Spring 1983, pp. 31–41.
22. "Hi-Tech," p. 38.
23. Ibid., p. 43.
24. Ibid., p. 42.
25. Sharman Stein, "Star Fades for Robotics Industry," *Orlando Sentinel*, March 26, 1984, pp. E1, E6, and author's discussion with officials at the GE robotics plant in Plymouth, Florida.
26. John W. Wilson, "Computers: When Will the Slump End?" *Business Week*, April 21, 1986, p. 61.
27. Dennis Kneale, "Computer Caution: Liking of PC's Is Coming, but Plenty of Obstacles Remain," *Wall Street Journal*, January 28, 1986, pp 1, 22.
28. Linda M. Watkins, "Software Gives Fed-Up Secretaries New Ways of Managing Their Bosses," *Wall Street Journal*, October 10, 1984, p. 35.
29. "Office Automation Restructures Business," *Business Week*, October 8, 1984, pp. 118, 125.
30. "As Computers Change the Nature of Work Some Jobs Lose Savor," *Wall Street Journal*, May 6, 1983.
31. Michael W. Miller, "Computers Keep an Eye

on Workers and See If They Perform Well," *Wall Street Journal*, June 3, 1985, pp. 1, 16.

32. "Computer Nut: How Personal Computers Change Managers' Lives," *Fortune*, September 3, 1984, p. 38.

33. Timothy K. Smith, "Electronic Control of Households Arrives with as Many Problems as Advantages," *Wall Street Journal*, November 11, 1985, p. 27; Robert Johnson, "Rush to Cottage Computer Work Falters Despite Advent of New Technology," *Wall Street Journal*, June 29, 1983, pp. 37, 42.

13 INDIVIDUAL VALUES AND ORGANIZATIONAL CULTURE

LEARNING OBJECTIVES

When you have completed this chapter, you should be able to:
1. Describe your values.
2. Define organizational culture and describe the culture of a particular organization.
3. Identify the characteristics of the new American corporate culture.
4. Identify principal individual values.
5. Indicate how individual values may be reconciled with organizational values.
6. Explain how cultural values within an organization may be changed.
7. Define organizational development and describe the role of the change agent.

CHANGING THE CULTURE AT APPLE COMPUTER

When John Sculley assumed the chief executive's position at Apple Computer in 1983, most people were writing Apple's obituaries. IBM had entered the market and in less than two years had become the number 1 seller in the personal computer field. The market previously had been dominated largely by Apple Computer and Commodore. Until Sculley's arrival, Apple had been managed largely as an entrepreneurial adventure since its start in 1977 by Steven Jobs and Stephen Wozniack. In 1983 the company appeared to be floundering. After seven years of unprecedented growth, its old products were showing their age, and new products recently introduced had failed miserably. Apple seemed to be wilting under IBM's tremendous financial clout and its ability to penetrate a market and hold it.

Sculley realized that if Apple was to survive, he had to turn an entrepreneurial firm into a more professionally managed organization. This meant changing the organization's culture, that system of shared values which dictates what an organization and its members do. In the beginning he altered few jobs, but he knew that eventually he would have to make major changes in management and in various staff positions. He began by changing the organization's marketing strategy, focusing on the products, making sure the organization had an appropriate product structure. To do this he combined product lines into two mainstream lines. This meant restructuring the organization on the basis of product lines. He weeded out some positions in the organization that he felt were unnecessary, combining some of their duties. He sought to become heavily automated in the manufacture of any new product line. Sculley also decentralized certain functions—manufacturing, finance, and marketing in particular. He introduced professional management systems into the Apple organization—an organization that up to this time had basically been run from Steven Jobs' hip pocket. Sculley suspended the company's generous profit-sharing program, a move with a major psychological impact. He increased accountability at the top by having fifteen division general managers report to him directly. Recognizing that the company was essentially selling a consumer product, he increased the advertising budget from $2 to $80 million to retain and maintain market share. Most important, he changed Apple's management style, orienting it more directly toward the achievement of objectives.

Continued on page 320

He instilled a new set of values in the organization, at the same time attempting to maintain the creative culture that Jobs had encouraged. He wanted people to learn that Apple was in a competitive industry and that IBM was a powerful foe who could in fact defeat Apple. Apple's employees had always tended to believe that no one could beat them at making PC's because they had been the first in the field and had been very successful in selling their products. Sculley worked hard and long to convince them that Apple was vulnerable to IBM's power. But he also realized that he had himself to assimilate some of the culture that he found at Apple when he arrived. He seldom wears a tie these days, and his work schedule matches the work ethic pervasive at Apple, where 90-hour weeks are common. He likes to add the personal touch, as when he distributed tickets to *Indiana Jones and the Temple of Doom* with everybody's paycheck one week. Sculley sees himself as a coach rather than as a forceful leader. A confirmed tinkerer, he has immersed himself in the Apple culture, a culture he has been busy changing.

Adapted from Joel Dreyfuss, "John Sculley Rises in the West," *Fortune*, July 9, 1984, pp. 180–84.

66 *There is a growing suspicion that the more relevant criterion of organizational effectiveness is not, as it used to be, that of efficiency, but rather that of adaptability to changes in the environment.* 99
DENNIS W. ORGAN

John Sculley had a set of personal values when he assumed the CEO's position at Apple Computer. Steven Jobs, who hired him, and every other individual in that organization had their own sets of personal values. These values were reflected in an organizational culture of shared values. John Sculley immediately set about to change those values. He did not want to change the culture too much, for fear of lowering the company's creativity level, but he did want to change many of the shared values at Apple in order to make the firm more competitive with IBM and other computer firms. Since the publication of *In Search of Excellence* and other books on corporate culture, we have begun to realize that the more consistent individual values are with organizational values and with one another, the more productive the organization and its members will be.[1]

Individuals should seek out organizations whose values match their own; otherwise, they must accommodate themselves to the organization's values. Similarly, organizations must seek out individuals whose values match those reflected in the organizational culture. Many organizations are finding that increasing numbers of employees do not share their values and thus are having to make accommodations of their own.

One of the major causes of such mismatches has been the rise in people's expectations in regard to their careers, their futures, their salaries, the type of job they wish to have. Many people are no longer willing to tolerate jobs that offer no excitement or challenge. Organizations therefore have been seeking to give increased responsibility to their members. As organizations' cultures change, the individuals currently working within those cultures must also change their values. Organizational cultures often change as a consequence of a change in strategy, structure, management system, leadership style, collective skills, or staff membership.[2] Before we discuss shared values, let us examine first the individual's values.

PERSONAL VALUES

Values, as we saw in Chapter 2, are ideas about what is important, what is relevant to our concerns. Our **personal values** are an extremely important part of our lives—such an important part, in fact, that they enter into every decision we make, though we often fail to realize what they are. We tend also to misjudge the values of others. Values seem to form a hierarchical structure, their individual importance ranging from slight to enormous. Thus when a choice is to be made, we choose as we do because we value one belief more than another.[3] The individual who subscribes to the Protestant work ethic is much more likely to fit into IBM, for example, than one who is less committed to the job; a person who has a strong need for achievement is much more likely to be an entrepreneur than one who is more concerned about raising his family than about raising his income.

Values influence the way individuals perform in an organization. One would naturally expect that they would, and research confirms that they do. The most generally accepted typology of personal values lists theoretical, economic, aesthetic, social, political, and religious value orientations. William D. Guth and Renato Tagiuri define the six value orientations as follows:

PERSONAL VALUES OF MANAGERS

1. The *theoretical* person is interested primarily in the discovery of truth, in the systematic ordering of knowledge. In pursuing this goal such people typically take a cognitive approach, looking for identities and differences, with relative disregard for the beauty or utility of objectives, seeking only to observe and to reason. Their interests are empirical, critical, and rational. They are intellectuals. Scientists and philosophers are often of this type (but they are not, as we shall see, the only ones).
2. The *economic* person is oriented primarily toward what is useful. Such people are interested in the practical affairs of the business world; in the production, marketing, and consumption of goods; in the use of economic resources; and in the accumulation of tangible wealth They are thoroughly practical and fit well into the world of American business.
3. *Aesthetic* persons find their chief interest in the artistic aspects of life, though they need not be creative artists. They value form and harmony. They view experience in terms of grace, symmetry, and harmony. Each single event is savored for its own sake.
4. The essential value for *social* persons is love of people—the altruistic or philanthropic aspect of love. They tend to be kind, sympathetic, and unselfish. They find people who have strong theoretical, economic, and aesthetic orientations rather cold. They regard love as the most important component of human relationships. In its purest form the social orientation is selfless and approaches the religious attitude.
5. *Political* people are characteristically oriented toward power—not neces-

sarily in politics, but in any area in which they function. Most leaders have a strong power orientation. Competition plays a large role in all of life, and many writers have regarded power as the most universal motive.

6. The *religious* person is one "whose mental structure is permanently directed to the creation of the highest and absolutely satisfying value experience." The dominant value for such people is unity. They seek to relate themselves to the universe in a meaningful way and have a mystical orientation.[4]

The idea that personal values may have important consequences to the organization is supported by evidence presented by Guth and Tagiuri in 1965.[5] They identified numerous ways in which values may affect the decisions made by top managers. A questionnaire they developed revealed that of the values held by American managers, the most important were economic, though theoretical and political values were close seconds (see Table 13.1). As you can see, these values contrast significantly with those expressed by scientists and research analysts.

Values affect not only the type of work that people pursue but also the decisions they make in their jobs. When Walter Lowrie was chief executive officer of Martin Marietta's Aerospace Division in Orlando, Florida, for example, he concluded that the organization would have to change its entire cultural value orientation if it was to survive. In the future, he felt sure, the aerospace industry was going to be based on fixed-price contracts rather than the cost-plus contracts that were then standard. Thus the organization had to become more quality-oriented and more efficient. Lowrie's value orientation led him to believe that an increase in efficiency would follow an increase in participation and concern for employees. So in 1983 he launched what he thought would be a five-to-six-year program to change the culture at Martin Marietta Aerospace to the end of being more price-competitive.[6]

Studies conducted by Martin T. Farris on the personal values of 226 purchasing managers and by D. W. England on the values of 1,072 managers found that these managers' values significantly affected their decisions and problem-solving processes, at least in part because their values affected their

TABLE 13.1   Mean Scores on Personal Value Orientations among American Scientists, Research Analysts, and Business Executives (Number of Points Scored out of a Possible 60 in Each Category)

Value orientation	Scientists	Research analysts	Business executives
Theoretical	51	49	44
Economic	41	44	45
Aesthetic	38	37	35
Social	34	32	33
Political	41	42	44
Religious	35	36	39

Source: Adapted from William D. Guth and Renato Tagiuri, "Personal Values and Corporate Strategy," *Harvard Business Review*, September–October 1965, pp. 123–32.

TABLE 13.2   Mean Scores on Personal Values Orientations among American ($n = 60$) and Egyptian ($n = 46$) Managerial Groups (Number of Points Scored out of a Possible 60 in Each Category)

AMERICAN GROUP			EGYPTIAN GROUP		
Personal Value Orientation	Mean Score	Rank	Personal Value Orientation	Mean Score	Rank
Economic	46.62	1	Theoretical	44.90	1
Political	43.62	2	Religions	42.39	2
Theoretical	43.42	3	Economic	41.26	3
Religions	37.76	4	Social	40.27	4
Aesthetic	36.87	5	Political	39.10	5
Social	32.73	6	Aesthetic	33.14	6

SOURCE: Adapted from Hamed A. Badr, Edmund R. Gray, and Ben L. Kedia, "Personal Values and Managerial Decision Making: Evidence from Two Cultures," *International Management Review* 3 (1982): 69. Reprinted with special permission from *International Management*. Copyright ©. McGraw-Hill Publications Company. All rights reserved.

perceptions of the problems they faced. England's study indicated that personal values operated at the levels of both corporate strategy and day-to-day decisions. Other studies have shown that the value orientations of Americans tend to differ from those of people in other countries. Table 13.2 indicates the differences found between American and Egyptian managers. Similar studies have been conducted among English, Japanese, and Korean managers. In most cases the rankings of the six value orientations differ from those of American managers, and in virtually all cases the strength scores for the orientations differ.[7]

We hold many values at the same time. Our minds must be able to sort through the priorities attached to those values at any given moment, and we must be able to overcome our emotions as we do so. What are your values? What do you value most? Take the "Test Yourself" on personal values and find out.

TEST YOURSELF

PERSONAL VALUES

In the blank next to each statement below, place a number from 1 to 5. 1 = strongly agree; 2 = agree; 3 = no opinion; 4 = disagree; 5 = strongly disagree.

_____ 1. I believe in God.

_____ 2. I believe in moderation in all things.

Excess of any kind—in eating, relaxing, drinking, working—should be avoided.

_____ 3. Thou shalt not steal, or cheat on tests, or plagiarize on term papers.

_____ 4. My body is a temple; therefore I should take care of it.

Continued on page 324

_____ 5. Life is sacred; therefore killing or tormenting human beings or animals of any kind is wrong.

_____ 6. You should protect your friends.

_____ 7. One is justified in lying if necessary to keep from getting in trouble with one's parents or boss or spouse or friends.

_____ 8. Democracy is the best form of government.

_____ 9. The rights and feelings of others should be respected. I should be assertive, not aggressive or passive.

_____10. My rights and feelings should be respected. I should be assertive, not passive or aggressive.

_____11. As our population ages, we must do more to take care of our older citizens.

_____12. One should abstain from drugs and alcohol because they pose a danger not only to the body but to the mind.

_____13. Capital punishment is murder.

_____14. All people should be treated as equals, regardless of race, sex, color, religion, national origin, age, mental or physical capacity or veteran status.

_____15. A manager's job is to make decisions.

Look at the statements that trigger responses of 1 or 5. Now look at the other responses. What are some of your strongest values? What values are of comparatively little importance to you?

Having seen the importance of personal values to decision making in organizations, you may wonder whether an organization's climate can have an equal effect on one's personal values. Before we consider how an individual's values are integrated into an organization, and how organizations thus affect individual values, let us explore the set of values that determines an organization's culture.

ORGANIZATIONAL CULTURE: SHARED VALUES

> "Understanding one individual's behavior is challenging in and of itself; understanding a group that's made up of different individuals and comprehending the many relationships among those individuals is even more complex. Imagine, then, the mind-boggling complexity of a large organization, made up of thousands of individuals and hundreds of work groups with myriad relationships among these individuals and groups."
>
> DAVID A. NADLER AND MICHAEL L. TUSHMAN

An organization has an intangible quality that distinguishes it from all other organizations. This quality is the **organizational culture,** the set of values that defines its beliefs and norms of behavior. The organization's culture shapes its management style and system, its objectives, policies, strategies, and structure. It provides the direction, meaning, and energy that move the organization toward success or failure.

Much of our interest in organizational culture comes from our fascination with Japanese companies and their very successful management styles and systems. Japanese businesses have profited enormously from their cultures, perhaps more than most organizations, certainly more than most American organizations. The culture of a Japanese organization is what moves its members to extremely high levels of productivity. Japanese organizations engage in an elaborate and ongoing process of adapting and channeling personal values prevalent among Japanese to serve the company's objectives. The management of their cultures is one of the primary means by which organizations can successfully adapt to their futures. The Human Relations Happening on Johnson & Johnson reveals a major corporation's efforts to change its culture to recapture lost efficiency and effectiveness.

HUMAN RELATIONS HAPPENING

CULTURAL CHANGE AT JOHNSON & JOHNSON

In 1983, Johnson & Johnson, the Band-Aid firm, moved from the old, undistinguished brick building that had been its home since the 1890s into a sleek, modernistic aluminum-and-glass building designed by the noted architect I. M. Pei. The move was symbolic of changes inside the firm as well. Chairman James E. Burke and President David R. Clare have determined that J&J's future lies in high tech. Long dominant in consumer products, Johnson & Johnson is facing internal changes in its management system and in the values on which that system is based. J&J is a collection of 170 companies, each of whose top managers has always enjoyed broad autonomy. There are barely 750 people on the corporate headquarters staff, and only one layer of management separates division presidents from the fourteen-member executive committee to which they all report. While J&J enjoyed an average annual growth rate of 13 percent from 1973 to 1983 and netted $489 million on $6 billion in sales in 1983, its ventures into high tech have not been uniformly rewarding. It has had to take write-offs on a couple of its investments, including TechniCare Corp., a high-tech medical company, which lost $110 million in six years and still seems to be far from finding its way out of the woods.

Johnson & Johnson has always considered that its first responsibility is not to shareholders or employees but to "the doctors, nurses, patients, mothers, and all others who use their products." This is not just a highminded statement that was made and then forgotten. Johnson & Johnson has always lived by that statement. But its consumer orientation was adopted when the firm was narrowly focused on consumer products—items that were sold, used, and disposed of. Its high-tech firms are making items that are sold, used, and reused and reused and reused, and they weren't quite prepared for that. They found they didn't know how to make the products appropriately. They overengineered them, and they were unable to tap their customers' needs as well as they had done in the consumer-oriented past. As a consequence, top management took a more active role in some of J&J's high-tech businesses. This change in management behavior has not been lost on the firm's employees. They have noticed that the corporate culture seems to be changing, and they wonder whether the company's historic decentralization is to give way to a centralized command structure. Many wonder as well whether the diverse organizational cultures of the consumer-product firms can in fact be merged with the kind of corporate culture that seems to be necessary to survive in high tech.

"The Protestant work ethic isn't cutting it, so we're switching to Shinto."

From *The Wall Street Journal*—permission, Cartoon Features Syndicate.

SOURCE: Adapted from "Changing a Corporate Culture," *Business Week*, May 14, 1984, pp. 130–38.

The nature of an organization's culture is revealed in four of its artifacts: its myths and sagas; its language systems and metaphors; its symbolism, ceremony, and rituals; and its identifiable value systems and behavior norms.[8]

Corporate myths and sagas, like all such tales, tell us about heroes: pioneers among people and products, past triumphs and failures, and the like. These stories shape the attitudes and values of new employees and continue to mold those of older employees. They help keep the company's people oriented to the organizational culture. One CEO of a 10,000-member corporation, for example, was fond of gambling, especially at poker. On corporate sales trips to major clients he typically took five or six of his top executives with him on the company plane. He often held the plane in a parking area until his thirst for poker was slaked. For several hours, always on the return trip, the plane and its other occupants would be made to wait until he had either won or lost $10,000, $15,000, or $20,000 in a poker game. Other executives tolerated his behavior but did not look forward to major sales trips. The new CEO liked to tell this story to his new managers, always with tongue in cheek, in an effort to disparage such behavior and to encourage a more congenial approach.[9] In a more positive vein the many stories told by WalMart employees about Sam Walton, the firm's principal owner, portray him as having tremendous energy and vision, and praise his management style. One of the stories often told about him concerns his occasional practice of startling his top managers at Saturday-morning staff meetings by jumping on the seat of his chair and shouting "Who's number one?" It is generally believed that people who seek to remain employed by the firm get the answer correct.[10] Such stories add to the leadership image of the man and help to propel the organization.

The language system and metaphors used in an organization often indicate the values it holds. Many organizations concentrate on scientific or technical terms, while others couch their communications in competitive terms: they "fight the competitive battle" and seek to "capture market shares."[11] Some customer-oriented firms do everything in the name of customer relations. For Rich's department store in Atlanta, for instance, "the customer is always right."

The symbols, ceremonies, and rituals of an organization—its logos, its flag, its slogans—convey the significance it attaches to certain ideas or events. Special award ceremonies are held to identify individual or group actions that the organization regards as important. The way a firm celebrates a corporate triumph tells us much about the values of that organization. In Silicon Valley, for instance, corporate celebrations can be especially exciting in their themes and the way they are carried out. Versitek, a Xerox subsidiary that makes computer printers, has a rather flamboyant president, Ren Zaphiropoulos, and an apparently equally imaginative director of corporate communications, Robert Murray. Murray notes that when they decided to announce the achievement of certain financial objectives to employees with a special profit-sharing program, they went all out. "We hired an elephant and the Stanford University marching band. It was quite a job to get 800 employees in a building without letting them know what was going on. We got them inside and the VP's announced this year's highlights and then got to the profit sharing. 'We can't say how big the numbers are,' one said, 'so let's see how big they really are.'

Then we slid open the door and in marched the band and the elephant. It was fairly impressive."[12] When Apple Computer decided to make a hard pitch for its upcoming battle against IBM at its 1984 sales meeting, it held the meeting in Hawaii with a *M*A*S*H* theme. The 700 people flown to the meeting were greeted by hosts and hostesses serving drinks in *M*A*S*H* costumes; flowers rained from helicopters hovering overhead, bearing the top people of the company dressed in surgical scrub suits. John Sculley, Apple's president, spoke to the group in front of a large TV screen so that the people in the rear could see his image as he explained how Apple's success with the MacIntosh would overcome the Big Brotherism of IBM.[13] Arthur Anderson, one of the big CPA firms, trains its accountants in an old college west of Chicago where the walls are of cinder block and the chairs of hard black plastic. The message is "It's all hard work at Arthur Anderson and we're going to be cost cutters and we're not going to have any excesses, we're professionals, we're accountants, we're number counters, we're no nonsense and we would be offended by frills."[14]

Company slogans also play an important role. Ford's "Quality is job 1" is part of a concerted effort to change the culture of Ford. That effort has made Ford a much more dynamic force in the marketplace and has enabled the firm to improve the quality of its cars.[15]

Value systems are reflected in strategy, structure, style, systems, policies, rules, procedures, and so on. The recent trend toward a "lean and mean" organization structure, with middle management and staff reduced in size and scope in an effort to cut costs and decentralize, has had a strong impact on the cultures of the firms that have taken that route. The many corporate mergers in the mid-1980s—Chevron gobbled up Gulf, GE acquired RCA—have eliminated many layers of management in the acquired firms. Other corporations have become lean in the move known as de-diversification; for example, Gulf & Western and IT&T, typical conglomerates of the 1960s and '70s, have sold off many of their units to become more narrowly focused in the number and types of businesses they own.[16]

What values do companies espouse? IBM has guided its entire organization by a three-part corporate credo originated by its founder, Thomas Watson, Sr.: "1. Respect for the individual, caring about the basic rights of each person in the organization and not just when it is convenient or expedient to do so. 2. Customer service—giving the best customer service of any company in the world, not some of the time but all of the time. 3. Excellence—believing that all jobs and products should be performed in a superior way." These articles of corporate faith are everywhere at IBM: in manuals, on the walls, in notebooks, in memos, in discussions among employees. Numerous other organizations have also issued statements about what is important to them. Three such statements are seen in Figure 13.1.

Managing an organization's culture is no easy task; even determining its elements is difficult. If you ask people to describe the culture of their organization, they are often hard pressed to do so, at least in those terms. But they can tell you what the key values are, what is important to the organization, how the organization's strategy, structure, systems, style, policies, rules, and procedures fit together to form a cohesive (or not so cohesive) whole.

FIGURE 13.1 *What's important around here*

Dana's 40 Thoughts

Remember our purpose—to earn money for our shareholders and increase the value of their investment.

Recognize people as our most important asset.

Promote from within.

Remember—people respond to recognition.

Share the rewards.

Provide stability of income and employment.

Decentralize.

Provide autonomy.

Encourage enterpreneurship.

Use corporate committees, task forces.

Push responsibility down.

Involve everyone.

Make every employee a manager.

Control only what's important.

Promote identity with Dana.

Make all Dana people shareholders.

Simplify.

Use little paper.

Keep no files.

Communicate fully.

Let people set goals and judge their performance.

Let people decide, where possible.

Discourage conformity.

Be professional.

Break organizational barriers.

Develop pride.

Insist on high ethical standards.

Focus on markets.

Utilize assets fully.

Contain investment—buy, don't make.

Balance plants, products, markets.

Keep facilities under 500 people.

Stabilize production.

Develop proprietary products.

Anticipate market needs.

Control cash.

Deliver reliably.

Help people grow.

Let Dana people know first.

Do what's best for all of Dana.

Dana Corp., Toledo, Ohio, manufactures automobile and industrial equipment components.

ROLM's Goals

To make a profit.

To grow.

To offer quality products and customer support.

To create a great place to work.

"Great Place to Work" means:

1. Work should be a challenging, stimulating and enjoyable experience.

2. The workplace should be pleasant.

3. ROLM should have an environment where every employee can enhance one's self-image through achievement, creativity and constructive feedback.

Therefore, every employee should have:

1. Equal opportunity to grow and be promoted.

2. Treatment as an individual.

3. Personal privacy respected.

4. Encouragement and assistance to succeed.

5. Opportunity to be creative.

6. Evaluations based on job performance only.

Employee's responsibilities include:

1. Being honest

2. Being helpful toward others to enhance teamwork.

3. Performing to the best of his or her abilities.

4. Helping to make ROLM a great place to work.

5. Understanding and supporting ROLM's goals.

ROLM Corp., Santa Clara, California, manufactures computerized telephone exchanges.

Trust at Quad/Graphics

The Trust of Teamwork. Employees trust that together they will do better than as individuals apart.

The Trust of Responsibility. Employers trust that each will carry his/her share of the load.

The Trust of Productivity. Customers trust that work will be produced to the most competitive levels of pricing, quality and innovation.

The Trust of Management. Shareholders, customers and employees trust that the company will make decisive judgments for the long-term rather than the short-term goals or today's profit.

The Trust of Think-Small. We all trust in each other. We regard each other as persons of equal rank; we respect the dignity of the individual by recognizing not only the individual accomplishments, but the feelings and needs of the individual and family as well; and we all share the same goals and purposes in life.

Quad/Graphics, Inc., Pewaukee, Wisconsin, prints magazines and catalogs.

SOURCE: R. Levering, M. Moskowitz, and Katz. *The Best Companies to Work for in America,* © 1984 (Reading, Mass.: Addison-Wesley, 1984). Reprinted with permission.

If a corporation's culture is the shared understanding of how the organization does things, then the individual who expects to get ahead had better learn and accept the way things are done around there. If the three-piece suit is the norm, then a sport coat and a sweater are simply unacceptable. If the Procter & Gamble way is to rewrite memos and return them to the sender until the individual learns to do them right, with few guidelines to what "right" is except through the editorial process, the individual must learn to adjust to this form of instruction.[17] If every male employee of IBM who makes more than $30,000 a year wears a gray suit, white shirt, dark tie, and wingtip shoes, and you are a man who makes more than $30,000 a year at IBM, then you had better be wearing that uniform.

How does the organization go about fitting employees into the company culture? Richard Pascale, who has examined hundreds of corporate cultures, suggests that they do so through a seven-step process that he calls the "seven steps of socialization":[18]

Step 1: "The company subjects candidates for employment to a selection process so rigorous that it often seemed designed to discourage individuals rather than encourage them to take the job." Numerous selection devices are used. The candidate typically goes through a series of interviews, perhaps two or three in the field before being flown to corporate headquarters for a final interview. During the interviews the company discussses the pros and cons of the job in an effort to provide a realistic preview of what the candidate can expect. The way Procter & Gamble hires people for entry-level positions is typical of the process. Its interviews are conducted not by personnel people but by front-line managers and staff members trained in the recruiting process and armed with well-thought-out evaluation instruments. Morgan Stanley, the New York investment banking house, candidly tells candidates that new recruits sometimes work 100 hours a week, and encourages them to discuss the demands of the job with their spouses or significant others. Thus candidates whose families are going to object to such long hours should eliminate themselves from consideration.

Step 2: "The company subjects the newly hired individual to experiences calculated to induce humility and to make him question his prior behavior, beliefs, and values. By lessening the recruit's comfort with himself the company hopes to promote openness toward its own norms and values." IBM and Morgan Guaranty Trust, for example, socialize their new recruits with programs that keep them working to the point of exhaustion. Teamwork is encouraged and fostered by seemingly insurmountable problem solving. At Xerox, one recruit reported, such programs turn new recruits into "Xeroids."[19]

Step 3: "The companies send the newly humbled recruits into the trenches, pushing them to master one of the disciplines at the core of the company's business. The newcomer's promotions are tied to how he does in that business." At IBM, Morgan Stanley, McKinsey & Company, Delta Airlines, and other firms, newcomers must work their way up through the organization. Trainees start at the bottom; there is very little upper-level hiring, as such positions are usually filled by promotion from within.

THE MERGING OF PERSONAL AND ORGANIZATIONAL VALUES

"Companies start with a white cloth and dye it in the colors they like."
NORITAKE KOBAYASHI

Step 4: "At every stage of the new manager's career the company measures the operating results he has achieved and rewards him accordingly." Evaluation systems also include punishment mechanisms. At IBM, for example, an individual who has stepped out of bounds—say by handling subordinates too harshly—will be shipped off to a nebulous position in some geographically undesirable location or perhaps at a dead-end headquarters job until he or she shapes up.

Step 5: "All along the way the company promotes adherence to its transcendent values, those overarching purposes that rise way above the day-to-day imperative to make a buck." People who go to work for Delta Airlines, for example, are told over and over again that they are members of "the Delta family." Everyone will make sacrifices at Delta to keep the "family" intact and healthy. Executives take pay cuts, workers accept reduced hours in order to avoid layoffs, but the "family" survives.

Step 6: "The company constantly harps on watershed events in the organization's history that reaffirm the importance of the firm's culture. Folklore reinforces a code of conduct—how we do things around here." Before deregulation, AT&T's folklore centered on heroic efforts to keep the phones working during emergencies. Such tales encouraged newcomers to make heroic efforts for the company.

Step 7: "The company supplies promising individuals role models. These models are consistent—each exemplary manager displays the same traits." Sometimes role models work in ways that may be perceived as negative in the long term. At many of the Bell systems the aggressive, hard-charging individual who sought fast promotion was punished, because the corporate culture decreed that promotion came only after a long apprenticeship. The role models waited a long time to get to their positions; the new recruit would have to wait too.

The importance of the organizational cultures can perhaps be seen most clearly in its absence. A former executive of Atari explained:

> You can't imagine how much time and energy around here went into politics. You had to determine who was on first base this month in order to figure out how to obtain what you needed to get the job done. There were no rules, no clear values. Two of the men at the top stood for diametrically opposite things. The bosses were constantly changing. All of this meant that you never had time to develop a routine way for getting things done at the interface between your job and the next guy's. Without rules for working with another, a lot of people got hurt, got burned out, and were never taught the Atari way of doing things because there wasn't an Atari way.[20]

Long-term employees are finding it increasingly difficult to absorb the changes that are being made in the cultures of many organizations in an effort to make them more competitive. The Human Relations Happening on page 331 reveals the changes made in General Electric's corporate culture to keep the firm strategically sound.

“The issue is not whether or not the control of society by business is good or bad for mankind. The important issue is this: will the dominant institution take leadership in advancing the many areas it influences?”

FREDERICK HERZBERG

HUMAN RELATIONS HAPPENING

CHANGING CORPORATE CULTURE AT GE

When Jack Welch took over the reins from Reg Jones as chairman and CEO of General Electric in 1981, GE was an extremely successful company, widely diversified and a market leader in many areas. But Welch saw that the firm was heading into an economy in which growth would be slower and competition keener. He determined to make the company "mean and agile." To do so he would have not only to cut costs but to make a real change in the corporate culture. He identified four primary actions that he would have to take if his efforts were to be successful:

1. He had to articulate the changes he desired.
2. He had to make changes in GE's strategy, structure, systems, style, policies, rules, and procedures, but especially its structure.
3. He had to communicate broadly and deeply (everyone had to know about the changes and the reasons for them).
4. He had to establish role and behavior models.

What was it specifically that needed to be changed? Eighteen aspects of the firm's operations were addressed, among them growth rate, capacity, diversification, market share, subsidizing of weak businesses, portfolio mix, management style, structure, layers of management, outlook toward environment, strategic planning, and overall climate. Among other things, Welch de-diversified, stopped subsidizing weak businesses and therefore removed them from the business portfolio, changed the way in which individuals are treated, eliminated several layers of management, decentralized, pushed strategic planning down in the organization, and changed the roles of corporate officers to make them facilitators rather than regulators.

After five years the program finally seemed to be succeeding. GE was better prepared to face the future than it had been before. But they were five rough years—years of clashes between unhappy managers, turnover, problems. Most observers seemed to think the results were worth the agony.

SOURCE: GE company magazine.

Lawrence M. Miller has identified eight primary principles that he believes will lay the foundation for a new competitive American corporate culture:

1. The purpose principle: work is a way of satisfying one's own needs.
2. The excellence principle: excellence results from the provision of opportunities to meet unsatisfied needs.
3. The consensus principle: ideas must be shared; managers should lead not into battle but in the process of bringing ideas together.
4. The entity principle: the individual must be involved in the work and decision making of the organization.
5. The performance principle: rewards must be given in accordance with the value of performance, not simply for effort or time.
6. The empiricism principle: statistics and other numbers must be seen as

THE DIRECTION OF CHANGE

"Certainly in any particular culture an individual's conscious motivational content will usually be extremely different from the conscious motivational content of an individual in another society."

ABRAHAM H. MASLOW

means to be used toward ends; corporate behavior must be based on those numbers. People must be better problem solvers.

7. The intimacy principle: feelings and emotions, needs and thoughts must be expressed so that individuals learn to trust each other and the organization.

8. The integrity principle: integrity is the foundation on which all other values rest.[21]

Whether or not these eight principles become the cornerstones of the American corporate culture of the future remains to be seen. Certainly several of them are already being adopted by many organizations. Whether or not these principles come to guide the organization of the future, it is obvious that the cultures of most American organizations are changing. They have to; they have no choice. Their workers' needs and expectations are changing, their environments are changing, their competition is changing. They, too, must change if they are to survive these challenges.

ORGANIZATIONAL CLIMATE

"We are in the process of reinventing the American Corporate culture."
JOHN NAISBITT

At the heart of the question of matching the individual's values and the organization's culture is the issue of organizational climate. **Organizational climate** is the sum of employees' perceptions of the desirability of the organization's work and social environment. Just as temperature and humidity levels measure the climates of Greenland and the Mohave Desert, such factors as communication channels, motivation techniques, and the degree of subordinates' participation in decision making are measures of the climate within an organization. And to a great extent the organization's climate determines its people's acceptance of its values. Another term for *climate* in this sense is **morale**. Morale is the sum of individual satisfactions within the organization. Climate is a major part of culture.

As Figure 13.2 indicates, the climate in which any group of employees works is determined primarily by the actions of their managers, especially with respect to their treatment of people—their strategies, systems, and management style. It is also a function of the actions of other employees, as individuals and as groups, and of certain environmental factors. Unless an organization is very small, it is likely to have many climates, each associated with a particular manager's leadership actions and his or her interactions with subordinates. Top management's leadership philosophy, however—its expressed decisions about how people are to be treated within the organization and the subsequent leadership actions that constitute a leadership style—prescribes an overall climate in any organization. These actions define boundaries within which subordinate managers and other employees may function. Climate may vary within the organization from work group to work group in accordance with the other factors noted in Figure 13.2, but especially the actions of the leader.

"An army's effectiveness depends on its size, training, experience, and morale . . . and morale is worth more than all the other factors combined."
NAPOLEON BONAPARTE

The organizational climate affects employees' work and the satisfaction they derive from it. An unpleasant climate tends to reduce both productivity and job satisfaction. The converse is apparently true also: a good climate tends to increase productivity and job satisfaction.

FIGURE 13.2   *The principal determinants of organizational climate*

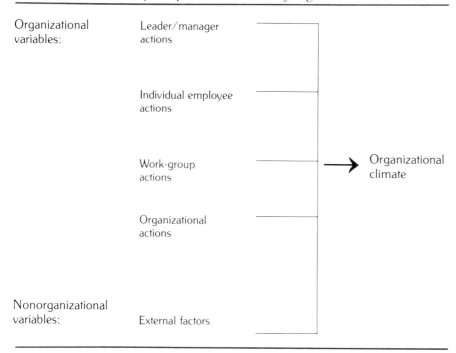

Organizational
variables:

Leader/manager
actions

Individual employee
actions

Work-group
actions

Organizational
climate

Organizational
actions

Nonorganizational
variables:

External factors

The leader should periodically examine the organization's climate to make certain that it is a comfortable one. More and more organizations are surveying their employees and monitoring the indicators of climate—productivity, absenteeism, turnover, and product quality—in order to learn when actions must be taken to improve their climates.

When you examine Figure 13.2, you can see the importance of the TRRAP process described in Chapter 8. Leaders must influence subordinates so that the organization's objectives may be achieved. Their behavior choices are affected by individual, group, job, organizational, and external constraints and events. The results of proper decisions are productivity, satisfaction, and trust. Leadership, then, becomes in large part a matter of developing the right climate. While Chapter 8's TRRAP model of behavior choice suggests that leaders should base their decisions on the key factors in the situation, we have seen in this chapter that individuals, groups, organizations, and external factors sometimes moderate the results of leaders' decisions, however they are made.

Organizations tend to attract similar types of people both in managerial categories and in line and staff positions. Organizational climates and cultures therefore tend to perpetuate themselves. When the climate and culture no longer match the demands of the situation, leaders must change them to make them more appropriate. When employees, for example, either individually or in groups, refuse to continue to accept an authoritarian management approach, managers must change either their management style or their employees, or suffer the consequences.

I believe that in most business and nonprofit organizations, if the right leadership choices are made, and if they are communicated properly in words and deeds, a climate will exist which will be both motivating and satisfying, resulting in employee productivity and satisfaction. As we have seen, satisfied employees are not necessarily motivated. What is needed is a climate that accomplishes both objectives, not just one.

MEASURING ORGANIZATIONAL CLIMATE

Every organization needs to assess its climate periodically. Several **systems for measuring organizational climate** have been developed, including those of Rensis Likert, Keith Davis, George Litwin and Robert Stringer, Garlie Forehand and B. Von Haller Gilmer, and Andrew W. Halpin and D. B. Crofts.[22] The best known of these systems and the one most applicable in many situations is that of Rensis Likert.

The Likert System   Rensis Likert has stated that four types of climate can be found in organizations: the exploitive authoritative, the benevolent authoritative, the consultative, and the participative group, referred to respectively as Systems 1, 2, 3, and 4. Likert believes that System 4 is preferable in most situations, and that the actions associated with this climate constitute a better management style than those that make up the other systems.

Likert and his associates at the Center for Social Research at the University of Michigan developed a questionnaire that asks employees to indicate which of four prepared responses best describes their organization. Questions are grouped by major climate component area: motivation, communication, interaction-influence processes, decision making, goal setting, control, and performance.[23] Figure 13.3 is a shortened version of this questionnaire. Each answer circled under System 1 scores 1 point, each one circled under System 2 scores 2 points, each one circled under System 3 scores 3 points, and each one circled under System 4 scores 4 points. The total scores for each component factor—motivation, communication, and the rest—are added to yield subtotal scores. These subtotals are divided by the number of questions in each subcomponent section. The result is a score between 1 and 4 for each climate subcomponent. The six subtotal scores are then added together and divided by the total number of questions, 19. The computed average again is between 1 and 4.

According to the proponents of this approach, the higher the score, the better the management style, allowing for some contingency considerations, of course. The national average is about 2.4, but obviously scores will vary within the same organization and between organizations, especially among industries. Organizations or subunits of organizations at the extreme lower end of the continuum—less than 2 for the total or any subtotal—need to be concerned about raising their totals. Likert has shown quite dramatically in two General Motors plants in the same town that raising these scores significantly increases productivity and satisfaction.[24] In fact, virtually all of the proponents of changing climate to improve productivity and job satisfaction

FIGURE 13.3 Likert's four styles of management

		SYSTEM 1 Exploitive Authoritative	SYSTEM 2 Benevolent Authoritative	SYSTEM 3 Consultative	SYSTEM 4 Participative Group
Leadership	How much confidence is shown in subordinates?	None	Condescending	Substantial	Complete
	How free do they feel to talk to superiors about job?	Not at all	Not very	Rather free	Fully free
	Are subordinates' ideas sought and used, if worthy?	Seldom	Sometimes	Usually	Always
Motivation	Is predominant use made of 1 fear, 2 threats, 3 punishment, 4 rewards, 5 involvement?	1, 2, 3, occasionally 4	4, some 3	4, some 3 and 5	5, 4, based on group set goals
	Where is responsibility felt for achieving organization's goals?	Mostly at top	Top and middle	Fairly general	At all levels
Communication	How much communication is aimed at achieving organization's objectives?	Very little	Little	Quite a bit	A great deal
	What is the direction of information flow?	Downward	Mostly downward	Down and up	Down, up and sideways
	How is downward communication accepted?	With suspicion	Possibly with suspicion	With caution	With an open mind
	How accurate is upward communication?	Often wrong	Censored for the boss	Limited accuracy	Accurate
	How well do superiors know problems faced by subordinates?	Know little	Some knowledge	Quite well	Very well
Decisions	At what level are decisions formally made?	Mostly at top	Policy at top, some delegation	Broad policy at top, more delegation	Throughout but well integrated
	What is the origin of technical and professional knowledge used in decision making?	Top management	Upper and middle	To a certain extent, throughout	To a great extent, throughout
	Are subordinates involved in decisions related to their work?	Not at all	Occasionally consulted	Generally consulted	Fully involved
	What does decision-making process contribute to motivation?	Nothing; often weakens it	Relatively little	Some contribution	Substantial contribution
Objectives	How are organizational goals established?	Orders issued	Orders, some comment invited	After discussion, by orders	By group action (except in crisis)
	How much covert resistance to goals is present?	Strong resistance	Moderate resistance	Some resistance at times	Little or none
Control	How concentrated are review and control functions?	Highly at top	Relatively highly at top	Moderate delegation to lower levels	Quite widely shared
	Is there an informal organization resisting the formal one?	Yes	Usually	Sometimes	No—same goal as formal
	What are cost, productivity, and other control data used for?	Policing, punishment	Reward and punishment	Reward, some self-guidance	Self-guidance, problem solving

SOURCE: From "The Corporation as a Creative Environment," by D. Fabun in *Human Organization: Its Management and Values* by Rensis Likert. © 1967, McGraw-Hill, Inc. Used with permission of McGraw-Hill Book Company.

believe that a shift toward increased participation, represented by Likert's System 4, is desirable.

The Likert system is a highly group-oriented approach. It clearly implies that group participative approaches are the best. For most situations, such a team approach is very functional. But not all people work in groups. Furthermore, high levels of achievement, especially economic achievement, are not necessarily a function of groups. People with high need for achievement are often stifled in group situations. Consideration for individual achievement must be built into any climate. Furthermore, it is clear that a highly participative approach cannot be used in every situation—for example, when subordinates are not capable of participating, or when time does not allow for participation. Given these and perhaps a few other limitations, System 4 is nonetheless highly appropriate in most situations. Each system, however, could be appropriate in some situations.

ORGANIZATIONAL DEVELOPMENT

Organizational development, a system of managing and changing organizational culture, offers the means to overcome many of the challenges that organizations will face in the future—the need to increase productivity, for example, and to reduce employee's dissatisfaction with the work process. For this reason, it is expected to be widely employed as firms seek solutions to critical problems.

In a widely accepted perspective on **organizational development (OD)**, Wendell French and Cecil Bell describe it as "a long-range effort to improve an organization's problem-solving and renewal processes, particularly through a more effective and collaborative management of organizational culture with special emphasis on the culture of formal work teams, with the assistance of a change agent, or catalyst, and the use of the theory and technology of applied behavioral science, including action reasearch."[25] Just what does OD mean in practical terms?

Long-Range Effort   Most organizational development efforts require at least two to five years for completion of the two initial stages of diagnosis and action. Maintenance of the program goes on indefinitely. As noted previously, Martin Marietta Aerospace, for example, recognized in 1984 that to become more cost-effective the firm would have to change its organizational culture, and expected it would take three to five years to do so.[26] The reason that OD programs—or interventions, as they are sometimes called—take so long is that usually a great many variables have to be considered, great quantities of data must be processed and analyzed, and a variety of techniques are employed during the action phases. The diagnostic techniques may include surveys, Managerial Grid® exercises (see Chapter 8), and job diagnoses. The action techniques include such efforts as job enrichment (see Chapter 12), MBORR (see Chapter 11), transactional analysis (see Chapter 6), participative management (see Chapter 8), and team sensitivity training exercises.

Improving Problem-Solving and Renewal Processes   OD is intended to improve decision making by transforming it into a synergistic process. Thus each decision made is intended to benefit all of the people who will be affected by it—individuals and groups as well as the organization. The total impact of a decision on the organization and its members is considered, not merely its effect on a single group or department. This effort involves the incorporation of lower-level personnel in the decision process (participative management). In fact, increasing participation is a major part of most OD interventions. Subordinates seem to be less and less willing to accept the authoritarian, nonparticipative management style. Thus leaders are becoming more participative at least partly in response to their subordinates' demands.

Management of Organizational Culture   In a survey performed by the Social Research Center of the University of Michigan, 1,500 workers from a cross section of employment situations ranked interesting work and personal authority ahead of pay and job security as important job-related needs.[27] In view of numerous earlier surveys reporting similar findings, it becomes obvious that as employees have experienced needs at the upper levels of the needs hierarchy, traditional methods of organizing and managing work have been challenged. As the nature of the worker has changed, there has been an increasing demand for organizations to change their climates and cultures. Worker participation, worker access to management, and worker-management communication programs are more appropriate now than ever before.

"Change is a way of life in today's organizations."
DONALD F. HARVEY
AND DONALD R. BROWN

Organizational development aims at increasing teamwork among members of formal work groups. To that end, positive human relations techniques, including many of the techniques discussed throughout this text, are employed to improve the relations among group members and between and among groups, and between groups and the organization. Relations between and among individuals, groups, and organizations are also taken into consideration, but the focus is primarily on the formal work group as it relates to its own members, to other groups, and to the organization. An increasing number of interventions, however, focus on other aspects of the organization's culture, such as the values of competition. In 1985 Du Pont, recognizing that it had grown fat and averse to risk, began a planned program of change, focusing not on work groups but rather on changing the values of the organization. In an effort to become lean and mean, it pushed decision making down in the structure, reorganized to eliminate much of the fat, and pushed innovation.[28]

Change Agent or Catalyst   The **change agent** is a consultant, usually but not necessarily external to the organization. Some other phenomenon, a catalyst, perhaps a decline in productivity or profits, often triggers the initiation of a change program. One factor that makes OD unique in the management consulting field is the fact that the consultant, rather than providing a plan of action and then going on to another assignment, remains with the program to help implement the appropriate changes.

Applied Behavioral Science and Action Research   Contrary to some consulting operations and many management decisions, OD relies on behavioral science theory and research studies. OD employs what is known. The OD change agent uses diagnostic and action methods and techniques that have proved successful in similar situations, that research has shown to be beneficial, and that theory indicates would be appropriate.

The OD change agent carries out research within the organization to determine what actions should be taken and to maintain the OD program. In the interventions I have conducted, for example, I have administered questionnaires and interviewed employees to find out what sort of culture the organization has. The results of these surveys indicate the appropriate techniques to use to change that culture.

TIPS FOR SUCCESS

1. Identify your values.
2. Identify the values of the organizations to which you belong.
3. Determine the match between your values and those of the organizations to which you belong or are thinking of joining. In job interviews, find out as much as you can about the real values of the organization.
4. Find out what counts in these organizations.
5. One way to determine an organization's culture is to talk with its employees.

SUMMARY

1. Much of our behavior depends on our personal values.
2. Six dominant value orientations have been identified: theoretical, economic, aesthetic, social, political, and religious. The value orientations prominent among American managers tend to differ from those of scientists and research analysts and from those of managers in other countries.
3. An organization's culture consists of its shared values.
4. The nature of an organization's culture is revealed in its myths and sagas, its language systems and metaphors, its symbolism, ceremonies, and rituals, and its identifiable value systems and behavioral norms.
5. Companies with strong cultures seem to go through a series of seven distinct steps to inculcate those cultures: (1) a rigorous selection process, (2) provision of experiences designed to make new recruits question their own values, (3) immediate immersion of recruits in the company's business, (4) a system of rewards and punishments based on performance, (5) constant promulgation of the company's values, (6) reinforcement of its values by folklore, and (7) provision of role models.
6. Organizational cultures are changing in response to competitive pressures and their member's changing needs.
7. Leadership is in large part a matter of developing the right climate.
8. Organizational development (OD) is a system of managing and changing organizational culture for the purpose of improving the organization's decision making, with emphasis on participative managment.
9. An OD intervention is conducted by a catalyst or change agent, usually an external consultant, who relies on behavioral science theory and research studies to indicate the appropriate measures to take in each situation.

DISCUSSION QUESTIONS
---

1. Describe the culture of an organization to which you belong.
2. Describe your values.
3. Describe the match between 1 and 2 above.
4. Describe the myths and sagas of an organization to which you have belonged. Describe its language systems and metaphors, its symbolism, ceremonies, and rituals, and its identifiable value systems and behavioral norms. (You may use your educational institution if you wish.)
5. How does an organization's culture differ from its climate?
6. What difficulties might one encounter in administering a climate survey in an organization?

APPLYING HUMAN RELATIONS SKILLS

The Unprofitable Acquisition

CASE

Wellesly Industries, an industrial conglomerate, purchased Space Systems Technology in 1977 for $200 million. Space Systems was an extremely profitable company involved in all phases of electronics, including minicomputers, its most profitable line. Most of Space Systems' products were the results of the efforts of 63 engineers, mathematicians, and physicists. Willard Simenski, the firm's founder, had always believed in "letting them do their own thing." In one interview with a business magazine reporter, he indicated that he "just tried to stay out of their way and let them have free rein over product development." Willard ran the marketing and production end of the enterprise.

But Willard's health was failing and he decided to retire, so he sold his stock to Wellesly Industries. Marvin Wellesly had made plenty of money by applying tight controls to his acquired firms. Within six months after his acquisition of Space Systems, his own management team had completely reshaped the operating rules for the elite 63. There was no more coming and going at their leisure. There was no more fraternization between the staff and management. There were no more office parties. There were no more bonuses. People would do their jobs, period.

By the end of 1980, Space Systems was losing money. It had failed to introduce three new products on time. By the end of 1980, the elite 63 were only 22. The other 41 had found employment elsewhere. Marvin Wellesly wondered what had happened.

(Yes, this is a true story.)

1. What happened to this company's culture, and why?

Complete the questionnaire in Figure 13.3 in respect to your work group, the work organization to which you currently belong, or one to which you have belonged. Discuss the results in class.

EXERCISE

REFERENCES

1. Thomas J. Peters and Robert H. Waterman, Jr., *In Search of Excellence* (New York: Harper & Row, 1982); Lawrence M. Miller, *American Spirit: Visions of a New Corporate Culture* (New York: Morrow, 1984).

2. McKinsey's famous seven S's include shared values as well as these six items, with leadership as a citation from Robert H. Waterman, Jr., "The Seven Elements of Strategic Fit," *Journal of Business Strategy*, Winter 1982, pp. 69–73.

3. Hamed A. Badr, Edmund R. Gray, and Ben L. Kedia, "Personal Values and Managerial Decision Making: Evidence from Two Cultures," *International Management Review*, 3 (1982), pp. 65–73.

4. William D. Guth and Renato Tagiuri, "Personal Values and Corporate Strategy," *Harvard Business Review*, September–October 1965, pp. 125–26.

5. Ibid.

6. Author's discussion with top executives at Martin Marietta.

7. Martin T. Farriss, "Purchasing Reciprocity and Anti-Trust," *Journal of Purchasing* (February 1973), pp. 15–27; George W. England, "Personal Value Systems of American Managers," *Academy of Management Journal*, 10 (1976), p. 54.

8. Terence Deal and Allen Kennedy, *Corporate Cultures* (Reading, Mass.: Addison Wesley, 1982).

9. Author's discussion with chief executive officer.

10. Tom Peters, speech to the American Hospital Association, 1983.

11. Terence Deal and Allen Kennedy, *Corporate Cultures*.

12. Walter Kechel III, "Celebrating a Corporate Triumph," *Fortune*, August 20, 1984, p. 259.

13. Ibid.

14. Mary Williams Walsh, "Company Built Retreats Reflect Firm's Cultures and Personalities," *Wall Street Journal*, August 16, 1984, p. 27.

15. Ford television advertisement, June 1986.

16. "Shifting Strategies: Surge in Restructuring is Profoundly Altering Much of the U.S. Industry," *Wall Street Journal*, August 12, 1985, p. 1.

17. Nancy Kaible, "Recruitment of Socialization at Procter & Gamble: A Case" (Palo Alto: Stanford University Press, 1984).

18. Richard Pascale, "Fitting New Employees into the Company Culture," *Fortune*, May 28, 1984, pp. 28–42.

19. Author's discussion with recent trainee.

20. Pascale, "Fitting New Employees," p. 40.

21. Miller, *American Spirit*, pp. 15–18.

22. Rensis Likert, *New Patterns of Management* (New York: McGraw-Hill, 1961); Keith Davis, *Human Behavior at Work*, 5th ed. (New York: McGraw-Hill, 1977); George H. Litwin and Robert A Stringer, Jr., *Motivation and Organizational Climate* (Boston: Division of Research, Graduate School of Business Administration, Harvard University, 1968); Garlie A. Forehand and B. Von Haller Gilmer, "Environmental Variation and Studies of Organizational Behavior," *Psychological Bulletin*, December 1964, pp. 361–82; Andrew W. Halpin and D. B. Crofts, *The Organizational Climate of Schools* (Washington, D.C.: U.S. Department of Health, Education, and Welfare, July 1962).

23. Likert, *New Patterns of Management*. Over the years, various versions of this questionnaire have appeared.

24. William K. Dowling, "System 4 Builds Performance and Profits," *Organizational Dynamics*, Winter 1975, pp. 23–38.

25. Wendell L. French and Cecil H. Bell, Jr., *Organizational Development: Behavioral Science Interventions for Organization Improvement* (Englewood Cliffs, N.J.: Prentice-Hall, 1973), p. 15.

26. Discussion by the author with top management at Martin Marietta.

27. Charles N. Weaver, "Job Satisfaction in the United States in the 1970s," *Journal of Applied Psychology*, Vol. 65, 1980, pp. 364–67.

28. Alix M. Freedman, "Giant Overhaul: Du Pont Trims Costs, Bureaucracy to Bolster Competitive Position," *Wall Street Journal*, September 25, 1985, pp. 1, 19.

5

UNDERSTANDING AND IMPROVING RELATIONSHIPS ACROSS CULTURES

14 CROSS-CULTURAL HUMAN RELATIONS

LEARNING OBJECTIVES

When you have completed this chapter, you should be able to:
1. Identify basic differences in international human relations.
2. Describe some of the major problems encountered by people who seek to do business in foreign countries.
3. Recognize common problems you might have if you worked in a foreign country.
4. Describe how the individual and the organization can cope with international business operations and international human relations.

PEOPLE REALLY ARE DIFFERENT

Some amazing oversights have occurred in the international business arena. Astute, even spectacularly successful companies have made colossal blunders. Here are a few international marketing mistakes, all based on misunderstandings of human relations:

A U.S. manufacturer of razor blades began to sell its products in England, marketing them in drugstores and grocery stores, just as it had done in the United States. The blades did not sell. Why? Because at the time that this sales campaign was initiated, the British bought their razor blades in hardware stores.

A U.S. fried-chicken fast-food organization, whose colors are red and white, was an instant hit in Japan. They quickly moved forward to Hong Kong. But to their dismay, they flopped. Why? Because the Chinese expect to be served towels with their meals.

A U.S. cereal manufacturer established a cereal line in Brazil. But they did not sell any cereal. Why? Because cereals were not part of the diet of the Brazilians, at least not for breakfast.

Not to let one mistake keep them from making another, a different division of the same firm launched a massive campaign to sell a gelatin dessert to the Brazilians. Funny thing was, only 3 percent of the people in Brazil had refrigerators.

A U.S. automobile manufacturer introduced its new car line into a Spanish-speaking country. Sales failed to materialize. Investigation into why sales lagged produced this startling discovery: the car's name, in Spanish, meant "no go."

We could go on, but you get the point.

Vous venez d'être témoin de certaines fautes classiques dans le domaine du marketing international. Pourquoi celà est-il arrivé? Parce que les personnes qui ont pris ces décisions supposaient que les peuples des autres pays réagiraient comme les Américains.*

You have just experienced culture shock. Unless you are fluent in French,

*I thank Pat Lancaster for translating this paragraph.

you probably did not know what the above paragraph stated. What it said was: "You have just witnessed some classic international business marketing goofs. Why did they occur? Because the people who made those decisions assumed that people in other countries would react like Americans."

If you want to be successful in **cross-cultural human relations,** you must be aware of the basic differences between cultures, and you must behave in accordance with, or at least with consideration of, the requirements of the culture with which you are dealing. This chapter focuses on what individuals and organizations can do to improve international cross-cultural relations, but many of the basic issues raised here apply also to the cross-cultural situations noted in Chapter 9. Those situations should be easier to deal with than relations with people in other countries because the language spoken by the subculture is similar to yours, though not identical, and so are most major mores, social values, and other **cultural universals.** (See Table 14.1.)

Have you ever been outside the country in which you now live? How did the country you visited differ from your own? Even Canadians who come to the United States and U.S. citizens who go to Canada may notice some slight variations in culture. And within Canada, two primary cultures exist, one

TABLE 14.1   Cultural Universals

age grading	food taboos	music
athletic sports	funeral rites	mythology
body adornment	games	numerals
calendar	gestures	obstetrics
cleanliness training	gift giving	penal sanctions
community organization	government	personal names
cooking	greetings	population policy
cooperative labor	hair styles	postnatal care
cosmology	hospitality	pregnancy usages
courtship	housing hygiene	property rights
dancing	incest taboos	propitiation of
decorative art	inheritance rules	supernatural
divination	joking	beings
division of labor	kin groups	puberty customs
dream interpretation	kinship nomenclature	religious rituals
education	language	residence rules
eschatology	law	sexual restrictions
ethics	luck superstitions	soul concepts
ethnobotany	magic	status differentiation
etiquette	marriage	surgery
faith healing	mealtimes	tool making
family	medicine	trade
feasting	modesty concerning	visiting
fire making	natural functions	weaning
folklore	mourning	weather control

SOURCE: George P. Murdock, "The Common Denominator of Cultures," in *The Science of Man in the World Crisis,* ed. Ralph Linton (New York: Columbia University Press, 1945), pp. 123–42. Reprinted by permission.

derived from England, the other from France. Persons from either of those countries who visit Mexico, Central America, the Caribbean, South America, Europe, Asia, or Africa are bound to encounter many more problems in international human relations. For people from other lands who visit and work in the United States and Canada, similar cultural problems are common.

The relationships examined in this chapter are primarily individual-to-individual interactions (how two people from differing cultures may relate better to each other) and organization-to-individual interactions (what the organization can do to improve the human relations between the organization and its members of one culture and those of other cultures). A new relationship component may thus be added to those in Figure 14.1: culture-to-culture interactions. The addition of culture to the model changes the ground rules of much of what has been stated previously in this text. Communication, leadership, motivation, group relations, and organizational relations often take different forms in foreign countries from those to which we are accustomed in the United States and Canada. The international cross-cultural relation demands a contingency approach to leadership and motivation.

AN INTERDEPENDENT WORLD

In November 1973 the Western industrialized nations came to a shocking conclusion. They were extremely dependent on forces outside of their control. The OPEC oil embargo revealed all too quickly the **interdependence** of the economies of the world's nations. Many nations found that they were much more dependent on others than they wanted to be. Since the 1960s, the names of places in remote corners of the world have become all too familiar to Americans and Canadians: Vietnam, Cambodia, South Africa, Nicaragua, Afghanistan, Pakistan, Iran, and Yemen, among others, have become household words. You see these faraway places on the evening news. You buy products from some of these remote corners of the world, products that just a few years ago you might not have had. Many of the products manufactured on the North American continent require raw materials from remote places. Trade with foreign countries has increased tremendously in recent years. The United States now conducts a brisk trade with China, but just a few short years ago no one would have considered such a development possible. Of critical importance to the U.S. economy is the fact that the United States imports much more than it exports. Its trade deficit with Japan alone amounted to $50 billion in 1985.

Business plays an important role in international human relations, and indeed is responsible for most of them. The **multinational corporations (MNCs)** link many cultures. MNCs are found in virtually every major country, although the United States probably has more of them than any other nation. The Japanese clearly function as an exporting nation, and the MNC is the dominant form of Japanese big business. Many European countries' larger businesses export within Europe as well as to the rest of the world, although most tend to be smaller than American MNCs. So many foreign companies

FIGURE 14.1

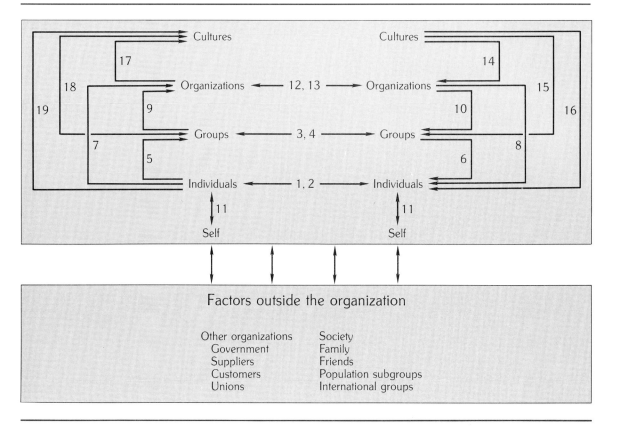

have invested so much money in the United States and Canada that Americans are now for the first time employed in large numbers by foreign MNCs, and thousands of Europeans are lured to the United States and Canada for vacations. The impacts of MNCs on income and consumption are tremendous.

For the society, for the organization, for the group, and for the individual, the problems of multinational business are complex and not easily solved. Host countries have learned that multinationals are often not responsive to their needs or to the needs of their people. Multinationals have learned all too well many lessons that they would just as soon forget. They and their employees have been subjected to terrorism, to expropriation of assets by host governments, to the vagaries of often unstable governments, and to the vagaries of international monetary exchange, to name just a few problems. Work groups within MNCs often are composed of people of different nationalities, with resultant problems of custom and language. Individuals may encounter different value orientations, different customs and habits, and numerous other problems. How can they overcome these problems? By practicing sound human relations—after they have redefined *sound.*

THE HUMAN RELATIONS BARRIERS FACED BY MULTINATIONALS AND THEIR MEMBERS

Regardless of their parent country, all multinationals face approximately the same problems. Since most of the readers of this text will be from the United States or Canada, these countries will usually be considered the parent countries in the examples we shall examine; occasionally other countries will be seen as parent countries. The following paragraphs examine some of the major difficulties that confront MNCs and discuss some of the strategies they have used to cope with these problems.

COLONIALIST AND POWER IMAGES

Western nations dominated much of the underdeveloped world in the early twentieth century. Great Britain built quite an empire, an empire on whose flag "the sun never set." There is no blatant colonialism evident among Western countries today, although other countries, such as the Soviet Union, do engage in blatant colonialist activities. The **colonialist image**, however, still taints the relations between many Western countries, their MNCs, and host countries. Unfortunately, this situation poses problems for the MNCs of Western nations. And some MNCs use their economic power in rather colonialist fashion, so that control by foreigners is not always just a memory for host countries. Economic colonialism sometimes still flourishes. IBM controls 70 percent of the European mainframe computer market and protects its interests so staunchly that European mainframe manufacturers sued to open up the market.[1] Western nations' MNCs are not the only ones to be seen as colonialist. In Southeast Asia, the Japanese, because of their tremendous economic influence, have come to be known as "the yellow Yankees." Japan's MNCs frequently "dump" products on the U.S. market at or below cost, and it has been argued that such practices amount to economic colonization of the United States.

The United States' effort to rebuild Europe after World War II and its foreign policy effort to be the world's policeman have for years provided its antagonists in the Eastern bloc and the Third World with political ammunition. Americans are routinely characterized as "capitalist imperialist warmongers," and Yankees are urged to go home. Such verbal attacks have posed many problems for U.S. companies that have tried to operate in Third World countries. Most citizens of those countries have little income and little education, but they have long memories. Anti-American sentiments born in the colonial period still flourish, fed by leftist propaganda, and some inappropriate human relations by MNC personnel. As a result, many U.S. multinationals have found their operations in these countries to have been very poor investments indeed.

According to Hal Mason, **host-country complaints** about MNCs focus on the restrictions placed on the development of the host country. Among their major complaints are limitations on the development of the host country's export market, monopolistic profits and fees, failure to develop new firms while taking over old ones, financing through local debt and retaining control, restrictions on access to modern technology, and failure to train local personnel (so that the host country remains dependent on foreigners).[2]

As a result, host countries impose certain **restrictive policies** on the actions of MNCs. Hal Mason suggests that the more important of such policies require shared ownership with the host country or with its nationals, reservation of certain management and technical jobs for local people, profit and fee ceilings, contract renegotiations, external debt capital, development of the host country's personnel and of its export market, and a preponderance of technology-based industries over extractive industries.[3]

When Walt Disney Companies negotiated with French officials to place a Disney amusement park in France, for example, the French required that at least 60 percent of all rides be manufactured in France, even though no manufacturers of such high-tech rides existed in France. Similarly, the French demanded that all 900 vehicles to be used at the park be made in France, though several types had never been made there before. Virtually all labor had to be French, whether workers with the necessary skills were available or not. The French seemed to be saying that if you want to do business in France, you do it the French way.[4]

These are human relations problems. Host countries have their rights. They also have something, sometimes many things, that MNCs want. This type of exchange is, after all, what business is all about. But doing business internationally is different from doing business in several states or cities, as MNCs have learned. Most have stopped investing in unstable nations. They try to sell services only. They front-load their payment schedules to cover possible expropriations. They have changed their human relations approaches, along with their other management processes—planning, organizing, staffing, influencing and leading, controlling, decision making, communicating, and all the rest.

CULTURAL BARRIERS

Communication skills are critical to the success of human relations. Chapters 5 and 6 stressed individual communication skills that could be used to improve human relations. Yet many of the skills noted in those chapters are culture-bound. Outside of the United States and Canada—and often even within them—the words and body language and approaches to self-image to which most of us are accustomed have differing meanings and results. Customs vary.

More fundamentally, the underlying cultural assumptions of any country cause many communication skills to be inappropriate beyond the national border. As we saw in Table 14.1, all cultures have rules governing courtship and hospitality, for instance, but the rules vary from culture to culture. MNCs and their employees must cope with local behavior and rules with which they are unfamiliar. Stefan Robock and Kenneth Simmonds suggest that **cultural differences** occur in these areas: assumptions and attitudes; personal beliefs, aspirations, and motivations; interpersonal relations; and social structure.[5]

Assumptions and Attitudes   U.S. and Canadian management systems have been significantly influenced by the belief in self-determination. Hard work, careful planning, and a positive attitude are commonly accepted as key determinants of the future, both the individual's and the organization's. In many other cultures the dominant belief is more fatalistic: human beings cannot determine their own future. As a result, planning is regarded as useless, and almost as a way of tempting fate: "What will be, will be."

Other problems arise as a result of other differences in underlying attitudes. Some of the most common problems arise in connection with the concept of time. Few people on earth are so concerned with time as North Americans. North American managers expect everybody to be "on time," to have their assignments completed "on time," and to "manage their time." In many foreign countries, such concerns are often unheard of. In fact, punctuality may be a liability. For example, the Orient is famous for unpunctuality. Americans working with the Chinese have found, for example, that being late is really of little consequence, since minutes or hours make little difference in the eternal cycle of human events. This is a very broad generalization, of course, and many exceptions can be found.

Personal Beliefs, Aspirations, and Motivations Intertwined with the dominant religious, economic, and political philosophies, personal beliefs, aspirations, and motivations lead to differing cultural and communication practices, especially as they relate to business. As we saw in Chapter 3, achievement motivation is not a worldwide phenomenon. Indeed, the term does not even exist in many languages. Yet, fortunately, the desire to be rich is strong nearly everywhere. Believe it or not, there are millionaires in China. And with the advent of American–Chinese economic relationships, these millionaires, most of whom are capitalists, have become an important part of the Chinese effort to modernize.[6]

Economic achievement motivation is dominant in countries that have a strong Judeo-Christian tradition. Protestant countries have historically been the most achievement-oriented of the Christian countries. Thus when U.S. and Canadian firms enter countries dominated by less achievement-oriented societies—Mexico, say, or Peru—or countries dominated by non-achievement-oriented religions, such as Hinduism in India, the amount of achievement orientation will be considerably less than they are accustomed to. The result is often a different attitude toward wealth. Wealth is often desired not for oneself, but for one's family (including one's third cousin's brother-in-law's aunt) and for one's village or town. Some societies almost glorify poverty—"Your reward will come in heaven." The consequences include difficulty in marketing consumer products, in obtaining managerial and professional talent in the host country, and in obtaining capital; lack of government support for economic achievement; and the need for more and often differing efforts to motivate employees.

Underlying beliefs about authority also affect human relations in other countries. In many other nations, a participative approach is totally unacceptable. Leaders lead and followers follow. Senior executives are seldom questioned. And in many other countries—Japan, for example—group and family orientations are common. In Japan, executives are promoted almost entirely on seniority, not on performance, a practice that would be unacceptable to many people in the United States and Canada.

> *Developing cultural empathy is the single most important prerequisite for the successful conduct of business in the world.*
> M. K. BADAWY

In South America it is not uncommon for promoted line personnel to retire "on the job." In many of these countries, managers are viewed in much the same way as the *patrones* of the plantations and ranches. Thus, when line people are promoted, they often do not expect to work longer and harder, as their counterparts in Canada and the United States would, but to work less, because they are now in a position of authority and power. South Americans also like to engage in long conversations. North Americans usually do not; they want to "get down to business." Again, the value of time is more important to North Americans than to South Americans. And this generalization too, like all generalizations, has its exceptions.

Rank and social status play a much more important role outside of the United States and Canada than they do in these countries. India is a classic example of this situation, with its caste system, which lingers on despite the government's efforts to outlaw it. But even in Europe, social status may play an important role in negotiations that otherwise would be strictly business. Philosophizing is common among Europeans, and Americans are usually not prepared to engage in lengthy mental matches over sociopolitical issues.

But for all of their differences, there are similarities as well. David Sirota and J. Michael Greenwood surveyed employees of large MNCs in twenty-five countries. Employees in sales, service, and technical areas were asked to rank fourteen goals—training, challenge, autonomy, earnings, advancement, recognition, physical conditions, and so forth—in the order of their importance. They found that the most important goals of these workers, pretty much regardless of type of job and nationality, were those related to personal achievement and success. The least important goals were also relatively similar in that they seemed to consist mostly of Herzberg's hygiene-factor items. Some differences were noted between the three types of jobs and between certain groups of countries. For example, the Japanese replies indicated high desire for earnings but low concern for advancement, two items that we would not expect to find together. The Japanese also expressed little concern for autonomy, but wanted challenge. It seems appropriate to assume that the group orientation of the Japanese may be responsible for both of these seeming contradictions; they would be contradictory in the United States and Canada, but not in a group-oriented society.[7]

Interpersonal Relations   We have already noted many aspects of interpersonal relations. Robock and Simmonds suggest that the nature of interpersonal relations in any society is revealed in its authority and family patterns.[8] We noted some differences in authority patterns above, and different approaches to participation were discussed in Chapter 8.

The family is extremely important in Japan. Japanese men play a much more dominant family role than most men in America. The family approach to society and business is common in Japan, less so in the United States.

Women are very subservient in most countries of the Middle East, but there are ranges of subservience. The Kuwaiti woman, for example, has many more rights and privileges than most other women in the Middle East. She drives her own car, she doesn't have to wear a veil, she can have a career in business. Thus the stereotypic image of the veiled figure in black is true more often than not, but it is not true everywhere.

Probably nowhere do women play so active a role in positions of leadership and management as in the United States. In the Soviet Union, women have for many years been active participants in the professions and in highly skilled labor fields, but not in the dominant force, the Communist party. In China, women have at least been high-ranking members of the Communist party, although their actual power is not known. Canadian and U.S. women, especially businesswomen, still find pockets of stubborn resistance to their functioning in the business role in their own countries as well as others. European families have traditionally been closer knit than those in the United States, but there, too, the situation seems to be changing with industrialization.

Interpersonal relations may also assume a different character in certain foreign countries, sometimes a violent one. Terrorism is common in many foreign countries and foreigners are often singled out for punishment, with emphasis on leading business representatives. Sometimes business negotiations take on an air of violence. One international lawyer, negotiating for an American client in Argentina, reports that the Argentinian placed a .44-caliber revolver on the desk between them during the negotiations for the sale of his firm. The gun was never mentioned, nor was it ever touched, but the communication was clear.[9] This sort of thing is not an everyday occurrence, but the story points up the fact that one must be prepared to cope with the unexpected in dealings with people in other countries.

Social Structure   Relative social status and interclass mobility play important roles in human relations in other countries. In the United States and Canada, one's abilities and to some extent one's opportunities and what one makes of them determine one's status and one's movement from one social class to another. But in most other countries, mobility is more restricted, and class structures tend to perpetuate themselves. In Great Britain, for example, speech, dress style, education, and employment are all a function of social class.[10] Again, this situation is changing, but social status and class structure must be recognized as important determinants of international human relations.

In many Latin American countries, landowners are extremely powerful. The middle class is small compared to the mass of peasants. This situation has changed somewhat with industrialization, but the dominant social structures often have not. In the Soviet Union and many other communist nations, the members of the Communist party are the dominant social group, with the privileges that go with elite status. The remaining 97 percent of the population fare less well. Such party dominance is less characteristic of Poland and Yugoslavia than of the Soviet Union and China. And because every detail of every decision must be approved by every major and minor official even remotely involved, decisions seem to take forever in communist countries.

In India, the caste system survives. Social mobility is no longer prohibited by law, but it is still discouraged by social custom. In England, educational opportunities are still partially a function of social class—as they are to some degree in the United States. But in the United States, scholarships and student loans make such elite schools as Harvard, Stanford, and the University of Chicago available to anyone, regardless of income or social class.

The Japanese focus much of their energy on group-oriented, patriarchically structured organizational activities. The work group is the center of the individual's work life. Teamwork is valued above individualism, and the company has a very parental attitude toward its employees. Employees often live in company housing, shop in company stores, and vacation at company resorts (the men often go without their wives). However, the winds of change seem to blow in Japan as they do elsewhere. Discontent with "the system" seems to be increasing among the Japanese.

In Summary   C. Wickham Skinner has analyzed how each of these four major cultural factors may affect a production organization (Table 14.2). If you will look at his analysis, you will see that many of our assumptions about the way people will act and react to managerial efforts are incorrect; and if

TABLE 14.2   The Cultural System as It Affects Production Management

DIFFERENCES IN THESE CULTURAL FACTORS—	. . . AFFECT A PEOPLE'S VALUES AND HABITS RELATING TO—	FOR EXAMPLE, THE LOCAL EMPLOYEE MIGHT FEEL THAT—	. . . AND THIS WOULD TEND TO AFFECT APPROACHES IN THESE (AND OTHER) AREAS OF MANUFACTURING MANAGEMENT—
I. Assumptions and attitudes	Time	Time is not measured in minutes, but in days and years.	Production control, scheduling, purchasing
	One's proper purpose in life	The only purpose which makes sense is to enjoy each day.	Management development
	The future	The future is not in man's hands.	Short- and long-range planning
	This life vs. the hereafter	Life and death are completely ordained and predetermined.	Safety programs
	Duty, responsibility	Your job is completed when you give an order to a subordinate.	Executive techniques of delegation and follow-up
II. Personal beliefs and aspirations	Right and wrong	I give the boss inventory counts which please him.	Inventory control system
	Sources of pride	A college degree places one higher in society for life.	Selection of supervisors
	Sources of fear and concern	Jobs are hard to get for a man laid off, regardless of the cause of layoff.	Layoff policy

TABLE 14.2 The Cultural System as It Affects Production Management (*Continued*)

DIFFERENCES IN THESE CULTURAL FACTORS—	. . . AFFECT A PEOPLE'S VALUES AND HABITS RELATING TO—	FOR EXAMPLE, THE LOCAL EMPLOYEE MIGHT FEEL THAT—	. . . AND THIS WOULD TEND TO AFFECT APPROACHES IN THESE (AND OTHER) AREAS OF MANUFACTURING MANAGEMENT—
	Extent of one's hopes	Without the right education and social class, advancement is limited.	Incentives, motivation
	The individual vs. society	The individual's wants and needs must be subordinated to the whole group.	Labor relations
III. Interpersonal relationships	The source of authority	My men don't like the new process. It won't work.	Quality control
	Care or empathy for others	I'd rather give my salary raise to my foreman than have to tell him he is not to receive one.	Merit reviews
	Importance of family obligations	I had to stay home because my father was sick.	Absenteeism
	Objects of loyalty	Friendship is more important than business.	Work-group relationships
	Tolerance for personal differences	If you don't agree with your boss, he will be insulted.	The decision-making process
IV. Social structure	Interclass mobility	I'd refuse to work for a man without a trade school certificate.	Promotion from within
	Class or caste systems	Men with my standing don't move heavy objects such as typewriters.	Job descriptions—flexibility of job assignments
	Urban-village-farm origins	The company must take the place of the village in caring for its people.	Fringe-benefit programs
	Determinants of status	Elderly people have wisdom. They deserve the most important jobs on big machines.	Equipment selection

they are not totally incorrect, other actions and reactions must at least be considered. As a manager, you cannot assume that all people will react the same way.

COMMUNICATION PROBLEMS

"The perpetual obstacle to human advancement is custom."
JOHN STUART MILL

How might each of the major communication techniques, systems, and practices discussed in Chapters 5 and 6 be affected by the cultural phenomena noted above? **Cross-cultural communication problems** are evident in all forms of verbal and nonverbal communications.

Verbal Communications   Simple language barriers can be almost insurmountable. First, one must learn the language. To assume that everyone should speak your language is shortsighted.

The complexities of not speaking the language are well illustrated in a story by Frank Ching. The growing number of Western business representatives in Beijing and other parts of China often face numerous cultural problems. One foreigner who could speak no Chinese wanted to be taken to a restaurant known as the Peking Duck. The taxi driver, of course, spoke only Chinese. The problem was how to communicate the destination. The foreigner began flapping his arms. The taxi driver nodded knowingly, and proceeded to the airport.[11] Learning Chinese is certainly very difficult, as few schools outside of China teach this language (which has several hundred dialects, further complicating matters). But somehow one must manage. The question always arises as to whether or not one should learn the language of the country when one is just visiting. Some say it's arrogant not to. But as a Tupperware executive commented to me, "It would be impossible. I visit twenty-five different countries every year. I learn the few words that are critical. Business has to be conducted in English."

Even if one learns the basic language of the host country, one still faces problems because nuances are hard to catch without much practice. In the English language, *like* and *desire* may be almost synonymous, but when they are applied to a member of the opposite sex, they have quite different meanings. The same sort of thing occurs in other languages, and when you consult your foreign dictionary, you do not want to trust the second or third words given if you do not know for sure what they mean. You may end up indicating that you "desire" Madame Lebrun when you would only "like" to see her.

Social rituals and pastimes and psychological games (see Chapters 6 and 17) are greatly affected by culture. Many high officials in foreign countries go through numerous exhausting rituals before they are ready to do business. Seemingly simple titles of address that have little meaning in America mean a lot to bureaucrats and professionals in most foreign lands. What constitutes intimate, open communication and who is allowed to be intimate with whom also are functions of the culture. If women and men are not equal in a society, they cannot communicate as American men and women do. It would be unwise, for example, to send a saleswoman to a Middle Eastern nation. But if you want to sell cosmetics and perfume in Latin America, a woman would be a good choice.

Within the social rituals what is proper? The English really want to know how you are when they ask you, and they expect the same in return. But Americans are usually only being polite when they ask about your health, and really do not expect anything more than "Fine, how are you?"

Body Language   A Greek who nods at something you say may be disagreeing with you. That signal does not have the same meaning in Greece as it does in the United States. A nod down means no, a nod up yes. In Japan, should you shake hands or bow, and who should have the last bow? If you do not understand the Italian system of hand gestures, your communications will be inefficient, and perhaps ineffective as well. If you are an active listener in some Asian circles, you may be considered to be impolite because of your constant eye contact. These are just a few minor incidental differences, but they can all lead to serious misunderstandings if meanings are not properly interpreted, if host-country customs are not followed. Accidentally insulting an Arab, a Mexican, or a Chinese could cause you and your organization many difficulties. There are any number of good books on the customs of most countries, and the U.S. State Department has a substantial amount of information to disseminate in this regard. So if you are ever assigned to a foreign country, you need to investigate these sources in order to become familiar with its customs. Several consulting firms now offer cross-cultural training.

Space, Time, and Touching   Americans stand farther apart than people in the Middle East. American conversational social distance is about two feet, whereas Arabs stand about one foot apart. People in positions of authority in countries where relative authority is more important than it is in English-speaking North America expect a greater distance to be maintained, both organizationally and socially, than is normal in the United States and Canada. Italians stand much closer than Americans and northern Europeans. American women stand closer to other women and men than American men stand to each other. Americans also stand closer to each other when they are side by side than they do face to face. Sometimes a curious thing happens when people accustomed to different social distances interact. If, for example, an American and a Saudi are talking, they may do a little dance as the American steps back and the Saudi follows, until each tires of the other's infringement on custom, or until a compromise distance is reached.

We have already examined differing concerns for and uses of time. Few other people are so concerned with time as Americans, but that situation is changing as American business practices become more acceptable internationally. Time marches on.

Touching is less common in America than it is in much of the rest of the world. In Europe it is not uncommon for men to embrace, even kiss, but such actions are not commonly acceptable in the United States, except perhaps in times of grief, as at a funeral. Even within the same country, different touching rituals may be practiced. U.S. football players, for example, may hold hands in the huddle to show solidarity, but to do so off the field would be totally unacceptable.

Dress and Appearance   Not everyone conforms to the Western style of dress. A Hart, Schaffner & Marx suit hardly seems as appropriate in a hot and humid climate as an open-necked shirt and Bermuda shorts. But clothing does indicate your interest in yourself and others, and personal grooming habits are extremely important, whatever the country.

In Summary   Styles of communication differ across cultural boundaries. Verbal and nonverbal forms, while tied to certain cultural universals, nevertheless vary widely, with widely varying results. If you are not aware of these differences, if you are not prepared to accommodate yourself to other people's ways, you may find yourself losing a client, losing a friend, or alienating an ally.

LEADERSHIP AND MOTIVATIONAL PROBLEMS

Without going into exhaustive detail, we may appropriately note some of the major leadership and motivational factors that may be affected by cultural differences. If you reexamine the TRRAP model of leadership in Chapter 8, you will note that the leader has choices of ways to treat people and that these choices should be based on six key factors: the leader's personality and needs, the subordinate's personality and needs, group dynamics, the nature of the task, the organization's structure and climate, and other relevant factors. Let us see how what might work in the United States or Canada may not work in other countries.

Manager's and Subordinate's Personalities and Needs   Managers are more authoritarian in the Middle East than in the Western world. Their subordinates expect this behavior and their personalities are geared to it. It would be difficult to practice significant participative management in these countries. A similar statement could be made about much of South America. On the other hand, many Western European countries have work forces that expect considerably more participation than ordinarily occurs in North America. Swedish and German workers, among others, expect to participate in decisions. Individual needs vary significantly, but they tend to be much lower in most developing countries than in the United States.

Group Dynamics   If you offered a Japanese manager a raise, he might not be willing to accept it unless all of his work group, his team (only occasionally her team), received one. Individual merit pay is not so important as group solidarity, although, yes, most people in Japan, too, want to be promoted and to make more money. In Israel one would also find many decisions being made by and for the group rather than the individual. Rewards might be distributed individually, however.

The Nature of the Task   Because of their emphasis on the group and on productivity, the Japanese, the Swedes, and the Germans often redesign tasks to include job-enrichment factors built around the group. Teams of workers perform jobs that individuals did singly before. Workers would probably require less supervision than most American managers feel comfortable with.

On the other hand, in many other places in the world, closer and more authoritarian supervision would be necessary.

Organizational Structure and Climate   If you examine foreign organization structures, you will find that many of them differ from their U.S. counterparts. Broad participation by workers is mandated by law in many European countries. Decision making is much more participative, even at the strategic level. And not all foreign organizations are structured according to products. As organizational climate is highly related to job design and participation, many of the differences we have noted apply here and need not be repeated. Many foreign organizations are much more bureaucratic than U.S. firms. And many, particularly in South America and the Middle East, stress the ties of kinship and friendship in doing business.

Other Factors   In many European countries, a manager is forbidden to terminate an employee, so don't try. In England workers expect never to be replaced, and the union will call a strike if you fire one. One American manager did not know this. When the union struck, he replaced all of the workers, and broke the hold the union had had on the firm for years. (So maybe we don't always have to abide by the local rules.)

In Argentina and elsewhere in South America, a worker would never question a manager's decisions, even if they were obviously wrong. In Japan, part of the reason for group decision making is that individuals do not want to have the responsibility for a bad decision. The person responsible would lose face. In a group, the loss of face can be shared with others.

You will find that the motivation/performance cycle model (Figure 3.2) functions very much the same way everywhere, so blocks 4 through 10 remain much the same. The difference is that needs are usually at a lower level among first-line workers in less developed countries than they are in the United States and Canada. This is not always true, especially in the rapidly industrializing nations, but it is true in much of the world. The implications are complex. Workers are routinely much less concerned with self-actualization or esteem needs than with physical and safety needs. Hence need satisfiers tend to be more basic. Leaders have to take such things into consideration when they choose the need satisfiers they will offer. Briefly, American methods can be introduced, but only once local customs, needs, and techniques have been considered and probably accommodated first. Change takes a long time.

People suffering from culture shock tend to wish they were home. This is as discouraging for the organization as it is for the homesick manager, because "he did so well in the United States."

David Noer describes the selection, preparation, and compensation of the **expatriate** employee (one who lives and works in a foreign country) by even the largest and most sophisticated of the multinationals as often "woefully inadequate."[12] And indeed, the evidence supports this contention. Not only are such employees often ill prepared for the cultural and communication

INTERNAL ORGANIZATIONAL PROBLEMS

problems they must face, but their organizations are unprepared for the consequences of these problems. Even worse, organizations are often unprepared to compensate employees adequately, educate their children, and accommodate other needs that are easily satisfied "back home."

James C. Baker examined training for overseas assignments by 74 of the largest U.S. MNCs and found that surprisingly few firms engaged in proper training.[13] Only 24 percent of the firms surveyed engaged in training programs for overseas assignments. These are low percentages indeed, considering the importance of such actions. What is also alarming is that the greatest cause of failure of employees overseas is the inability of the spouse to adapt, and yet only some of these firms conducted family-related training. Equally alarming, the courses were often only one or two days in length—not much time to absorb a new culture.

Examine the case "But He Did OK in the United States." What do you think might have been wrong?

"But He Did OK in the United States"

When it is late afternoon in Central Europe, it is morning in the Midwest, and Harvey, the worldwide sales manager for a multinational consumer goods company, was still staring at the telephone, haunted by the echoes of his first telephone call of the morning. Bill, his European sales manager, had just announced in no uncertain terms that he was coming home.

What had gone wrong? Bill was a superstar back in the United States. He had all the right ingredients for a successful sales manager: aggressive personality, total dedication to the job, willingness always to go the extra mile. When the company recognized the potential for business in Europe, there was no doubt in Harvey's mind as to who should get the job. It was Bill. Harvey would send him over there for a few years, let him shape up the local marketing organization, put local management on a sound business basis, then bring him back to the United States, where his future would be unlimited.

What had gone wrong? Harvey thought back to the telephone call.

> "Got that organization turned around yet?" Harvey began. His voice was filled with optimism.
> "Not exactly." Bill's voice was flat, tentative. "I'm having some problems."
> "Nothing good old Bill can't handle, eh?" responded Harvey.
> "Well . . . not really. These are more like personal problems."

Something really was wrong; this was not like Bill at all. He always kept personal problems inside. Harvey never could get him to open up. He had tried a few times, but it never happened.

> "What's wrong—family sickness, problems with the kids?"
> "No, not really . . . I . . . well, I just have to come back! Things don't seem to be working out over here."

"What! Come back?"

"Yeah, just have to. I've already booked the tickets and we leave tomorrow. Harvey, I know this will probably cost me my job, but I can't live here. It just isn't working."

When the conversation ended, Harvey studied the telephone in stunned silence. What really had gone wrong?

Reprinted by permission from David Noer, *Multinational People Management: A Guide for Organizations and Employees,* copyright 1975 by The Bureau of National Affairs, Inc., Washington, D.C.

Is it possible that some cultural problems were involved in Bill's decision? Could there also have been some communication problems involved, resulting from the differences in culture?

Do you suppose that Bill's aggressive personality was not such a virtue in Europe as it was in the United States?

Do you suppose Bill was unable to order a meal in a restaurant in a foreign language?

Do you suppose that Bill's wife missed her close family ties and the Sunday get-togethers?

Do you suppose that when Bill tried to use the threat of firing as a motivation technique, his employees laughed at him because the labor courts would not allow it?

Do you suppose that Bill, a product of a fast-food environment, lacked the social graces to conduct business in Europe?

Do you suppose that in cocktail-party chatter, Bill was inept when it came to economic and political philosophies, favorite subjects of the Europeans?

The answers are all yes. But the real tragedy is that Bill's career could have been saved. He should never have been sent to Europe in the first place.

Organizations must learn to select employees with proper qualifications for overseas assignments. What are those qualifications? Certainly the list must include:

1. A sincere willingness, even an interest, in an overseas assignment.
2. A spouse and family who are not only willing to live in a foreign country, but interested in and even enthusiastic about an overseas assignment.
3. An appreciation of the differing business environment, its rapid change, and the significance of the politics, history, and philosophy of the foreign country.
4. Flexibility of lifestyle and managerial style, with a willingness to learn the necessary foreign language, customs, habits, and nonverbal communications.

Next the organization must provide the selected individual and his or her family with the necessary training in the language, customs, business environment, political situation, and so forth. For example, as M. K. Badawy reports, *most* Middle Eastern executives prefer to have intercompany arrangements made with acquaintances and friends. The typical U.S. salesperson

"Nice work, Farnsworth . . . that snappy Japanese name you came up with for our new automobile means "guzzler" in English!"

Dunagin's People by Ralph Dunagin. By permission of News America Syndicate.

swoops down, makes a quick pitch, maybe with an extensive media presentation, and then attempts to close a deal. That simply will not work in the Middle East. Becoming friends with a potential client is much more important. It simply takes time and hard effort, and sales managers should not expect the same immediate results in the Middle East that they would in North America.[14]

But U.S. and Canadian organizations are not forced to send a large force of **parent-country nationals (PCNs)** to host countries. They may also employ **host-country nationals (HCNs)** or **third-country nationals (TCNs)** to manage or to fill important staff roles. Most jobs in foreign subsidiaries are held by HCNs. Usually only a few top management or staff positions are held by PCNs or TCNs. Some organizations employ only HCNs, and there are definite advantages to this course. Most firms, however, employ at least some PCNs to maintain consistency of management approaches. What are some of the advantages and disadvantages of each course? PCNs in key positions help to ensure consistency of management approach and control, and help to ensure that the parent company's interests are furthered. But some problems may arise. PCNs are usually paid more than HCNs, and HCNs resent the disparity.

Employment of HCNs improves relations with the host country's government and with HCNs themselves. Labor-management relations can generally be expected to be better, and obviously little adaptation is necessary, since the HCN is already adapted to the local situation. The negatives are generally the inverses of the positives for the PCNs, and some problems may also be associated with communication between headquarters and top management of the foreign office.

TCNs seem to offer at best only a limited solution to the problems of PCNs and HCNs. TCNs are most commonly used in lower-level jobs when the HCN labor supply is inadequate, or at the top management or staff level when no qualified PCNs or HCNs are available. As a result of these considerations, most MNCs have a mixture of PCNs and HCNs in top positions.

Once a PCN has been selected, he or she must be trained in the ways of the host country. Training is routinely provided by many organizations, but the individual is also expected to make an effort to achieve certain training objectives—to learn the language, for example. Next, an advance trip for the selected employee, his or her spouse, and if possible the rest of the family is highly advisable. Despite careful selection and training, an advance trip is necessary to help them cope with the culture shock that is all but unavoidable. Differences in housing, in lifestyle, even in traveling are difficult to prepare for. There is no substitute for being there. If you are ever asked to go overseas, you should request such an advance trip. Some international managers insist on such trips. The employee's performance during the trip should be evaluated and feedback provided.

Once all of these preparations have been made, the matter of compensation and other support become critical. Americans and Canadians find their dollars are often undervalued in relation to certain European and Japanese currencies today but often of greater value in relation to other European currencies—those of England and Italy, for example. Exchange rates fluctuate—another problem for PCNs. The expatriate needs to be compensated at least as well as counterparts at home, and a higher salary may be necessary to maintain the employee's accustomed lifestyle in a foreign country. Compensation must cover taxes, housing, living expenses, educational expenses, and even an occasional visit to the parent country. Educational expenses are vital to virtually all PCNs. Many Japanese, for example, are reluctant to accept positions in the United States for fear their children will fall behind their mainland competitors in educational level. Most expatriates are paid bonuses for overseas duty, and bonuses are usually increased for service in countries where living is difficult or hazardous. Some companies even help to find someone to rent the PCN's home during the foreign assignment. A very critical phase of the process consists of the advance payments and arrangements made to ease the relocation process. There is nothing worse than not having enough funds to make it through the first few months, the most difficult period both personally and professionally.

Upon the newcomers' arrival in the new country, someone from personnel should be assigned to guide them through the maze of immigration and customs procedures, secure any necessary permits, locate housing, and so forth. Since most transferred employees are men, their wives must often cope with many bewildering household arrangements. Allison Lanier recommends that a wives' committee be appointed to provide helpful information about schools, housing, shopping, and so forth.[15] Terrorism is a growing concern that must be addressed.

Repatriation of the employee—that is, bringing him or her back to the home country—is also an important consideration. How is the repatriated employee's lifestyle affected by the return? How does the employee's career continue from this point forward? Who will be the employee's new boss and what will the job assignment be? David Noer has suggested a system for resolving many of these issues, the **godfather system**.[16] As many such questions as possible are resolved in advance of the original placement in the foreign country through the assistance of an assigned "godfather," usually the individual's boss. A godfather, or sponsor, can eliminate many of the expatriate's problems simply by being there at home to look after one's interests, to communicate with, and to keep one informed.

Noer indicates that a **repatriation agreement**, spelling out in advance the details of the assignment, its duration, and so forth, is highly desirable. *Business Week* suggests that **repatriation committees** are becoming a popular way to provide an individual with assistance in the expatriation/repatriation process.[17]

The costs of placing PCNs in a host country are considerable. Allison Lanier reports that a factor of 2.5 or 3.0 should be applied to the PCN's home-country base salary to determine the comparative cost of placing this individual overseas.[18] Thus a $40,000-a-year person quickly becomes a $120,000-a-year person. But a premature return is estimated to cost an additional $80,000. Thus a system of screening applicants for overseas operations must be developed if the operation is to be cost-effective. *Business Week* reports that successful programs of applicant screening have reduced failure rates from 40 percent to 5 percent.[19]

LEARNING FROM OTHERS

There is much we can learn from other cultures. In fact, we are learning that the Japanese have developed a management system that is in many ways, at least for their people, superior to our own. In 1978, Dr. William G. Ouchi suggested that successful U.S. and Japanese business firms had similar characteristics; he identified such firms as **Theory Z** organizations. Table 14.3 indicates the basic characteristics that he found for Japanese firms, labeled Type J; U.S. firms, labeled Type A; and Theory Z firms. Theory Z firms in the United States include IBM, Delta Airlines, and Hewlett-Packard.[20]

Japan's domination of several major industries and generally increasing competition caused U.S. managers to seek ways to improve productivity. Ouchi's research and that of several others caused many U.S. managers to adopt selected Japanese management techniques.[21] Participative management techniques, especially the quality circle, have become increasingly popular among U.S. managers. Many employees have also begun to press for longer-term employment, a broadening of employee skills, and employee welfare projects. But not all Japanese management techniques are easily adaptable to the U.S. culture. This is especially true of collective responsibility. And many people argue that factors other than its management approach contribute to Japan's economic success story. Self-discipline and peer pressure, as well

TABLE 14.3   Characteristics of Japanese (Type J), American (Type A), and Theory Z Firms

TYPE J FIRMS	TYPE A FIRMS	THEORY Z FIRMS
Lifetime employment (for men)	Short-term employment	Long-term employment
Slow process of evaluation and promotion	Rapid evaluation and promotion	Slow evaluation and promotion
Nonspecialized career	Specialized career planning	Moderate career planning
Consensual decision making	Individual decision making	Consensual decision making
Collective responsibility	Individual responsibility	Individual responsibility
Implicit/subtle control	Explicit/formal control	Informal, implicit control with explicit measures available
Holistic concern for employees	Segmented concern for employees	Holistic concern for employees

SOURCE: William G. Ouchi, *Theory Z: How American Business Can Meet the Japanese Challenge* (Reading, Mass.: Addison-Wesley, 1981).

as a great concern for the work group and company as a whole, are major factors in Japan's success. A strongly authoritarian corporate culture takes advantage of these pressures. By calling for substantial amounts of free overtime by managers and professionals, the Japanese work ethic clearly raises their productivity levels. And the female population is clearly exploited, kept in low-paying, menial, and often short-term jobs. On the other hand, when Japanese firms have acquired U.S. firms, they have individually raised productivity levels substantially. Much of this increase in productivity has been attributed to changes in management techniques. When Quasar, a Japanese firm, took over a Motorola plant in the United States, for example, it slowly introduced its own methods of management, including quality-control circles, highly participative self-analysis units. Within months the plant was highly productive and making money, where before it had failed in both areas.[22]

> *If Japan had manufactured the Columbia, the tiles would never have fallen off.*
> YOSHIHIDE HIRAIWA

Japan's work ethic may be eroding. And as the Japanese adopt more and more Western ideas, such concerns as leisure and equal employment opportunity for women (see the Human Relations Happening on p. 364) are bound to be felt. As increasing numbers of Japanese women seek paid employment and many enter management and the professions, traditional Japanese values are coming under attack.[23] Japan suffers also from its emphasis on seniority. Young Japanese do not think much of this system and for the first time in history are beginning to think like entrepreneurs.

So while we may learn from the Japanese, they have also learned from us. So have the peoples of other countries. Many European managers seek to emulate U.S. managers and management systems.[24] We can certainly learn that we as Americans may not always know the best way of doing everything. We have learned from the Europeans that workers can actively participate in major decisions without hurting the productivity of the organization. We have also learned that in some countries, it may be more appropriate to be more authoritarian than one might be in North America. We are learning all of the time that others can show us ways to improve our productivity, our organizational climate, our communication, our leadership, and our motivation.

International business is an exchange process.

HUMAN RELATIONS HAPPENING

Japan Considers Equal-Employment Rights for Women

NEW YORK TIMES

TOKYO—The prospect of equal-employment rights for women has arrived in Japan. It had taken its time, and when it finally arrived some people wondered whether this resolutely male-oriented society would even notice.

Of the major industrial countries, Japan has been among the more resolute in keeping its men on the job and its women within reasonable proximity of the kitchen.

After seven years of public debate and behind-the-scenes compromise, the Japanese Parliament gave final approval Friday to a bill encouraging employers, beginning next April, to end discrimination on the basis of sex in their hiring, assignment and promotion policies.

Severe restrictions now placed on overtime and late-night work by women would be ended. These limitations were sometimes characterized as "privileges" by people who wanted to retain them. But they have had the effect of keeping women out of many jobs.

From now on, to cite one possibility, more women may wind up driving taxi cabs because they will be permitted to work lucrative post-10 P.M. shifts theoretically denied them thus far. Other beneficiaries should be women in executive positions that demand long hours.

Perhaps the most notable aspect of Japan's Equal Employment Bill, however, is that it has managed to please almost no one.

Women's groups are unhappy because, they say, the law is toothless. It merely requires employers to "endeavor" to

achieve equality, with no penalties provided if they do not bother.

Business groups are unhappy because, they say, the law threatens employment practices that they regard as part of the Japanese way of life. The changes, they contend, have come too fast.

Women make up 35 percent of the Japanese work force, but only 6 percent of the managers. Overall, their salaries are slightly less than 50 percent of those paid to men. The government says at least 80 percent of all companies have one or more job categories for which women may not apply.

In that regard, the government does little better. Women are all but invisible in the upper echelons of the bureaucracy. They hold only 27 seats among the 763 available in the two houses of Parliament.

SOURCE: Clyde Haberman, "Japan's Women Win Scuffle in Equality War," *The New York Times*, May 18, 1985. Reprinted in *The Orlando Sentinel*, May 19, 1985, p. A-19. Copyright © 1985 by The New York Times Company. Reprinted by permission.

TIP FOR SUCCESS

When you go to a foreign country, you can forget the specifics of what you have learned thus far in this book. The principles apply, but not the specifics. You must learn each country's specific behavioral norms.

SUMMARY

1. Because of the interdependence of the world's economies, it is becoming increasingly necessary to understand the major cultural variables and the resulting communication problems.

2. Host countries often make demands of MNCs,

and these demands must be studied carefully. The vagaries of unstable governments and international monetary exchange add to the problems of MNCs.

3. The host country's basic assumptions, attitudes, beliefs, aspirations, motivations, interpersonal relations, and social structures must all become familiar to expatriates if they are to be successful overseas.

4. Expatriates must develop skills in verbal and nonverbal communications.

5. Organizations should carefully select the individuals they send overseas, and carefully balance PCNs, HCNs, and TCNs. Preparation, training, compensation, lifestyle management, and repatriation are critical issues that must be addressed.

6. In the rapidly changing societies of the United States and Canada it is becoming increasingly important to learn cross-cultural skills.

7. Japanese management approaches can be applied in the United States, but certain cultural factors limit their usefulness.

8. Leadership and motivation techniques often have to be adapted to the cultural orientation of a host country. We can learn from the ways of others.

DISCUSSION QUESTIONS

1. Have you ever worked overseas? If so, describe to the class your major impressions of the differences between the host country and the parent country, the problems those differences posed for you, and the assistance your employer gave you in solving those problems.

2. Imagine that you have been assigned to work in West Germany. What steps would you take to prepare for this transfer? What different steps would be necessary if you were assigned to Japan, England, South Africa, Yugoslavia? Assume a three-year assignment.

3. Suppose you were charged with developing an international marketing campaign for the electric toothbrush. What factors would you need to take into account in developing this campaign?

4. If the country in which you are now living is not the one in which you grew up, perhaps you could share with the class some of your observations about the difficulties of living, working, and going to school in a foreign country.

5. Discuss the applicability of Japanese management styles to U.S. organizations.

APPLYING HUMAN RELATIONS SKILLS

How Would You Like Some Polish Hams?*   CASE

Julian Hartford had just closed a big deal with a Czechoslovakian firm. The Czechs desperately wanted his orange juice and he had needed to sell his surplus crop. Everything looked perfect. Three hundred thousand dollars would be his final profit. He sat back in his leather chair and contemplated how he would spend his money.

Ten weeks later, Julian was not quite so happy. His accountant had received payment and begun negotiations for currency conversion, but found that Iron Curtain currencies were traded openly only behind the Iron Curtain. His payment

*I thank Chappies Stearns for this incident.

was basically worthless—a few cents on the dollar were all that he could get. The orange juice had been shipped to Czechoslovakia. No one in his firm knew what to do.

Julian called around town and finally located an international management consultant. The consultant told him that his only hope was to buy some commodity in Czechoslovakia or another Soviet-bloc country that could be sold in the United States. Such a transaction would dispose of the Czech currency and allow Julian to receive his profits in American dollars. After three weeks of phone calls and negotiations, the consultant located another foreign seller who had a product that Julian's firm could sell in the United States. In fact, Julian knew just the company that would buy it. After expenses, he stood to make $75,000 profit. He called Howard Dunberg in Philadelphia. Howard was president of a large regional food chain. Julian's opening comment was: "How would you like some Polish hams?"

(This is a true story. The names and numbers have been changed.)

1. What cross-cultural mistakes did Julian make?
2. What should he have done in the beginning to prevent the complications he encountered?

EXERCISES

A Japanese Bank Training Program

The Japanese group orientation has already been mentioned in this and earlier chapters, but a discussion of a Japanese employee training program may give you additional insight into Japan's social structure. Ravi Sarathy tells us of a Japanese bank's training program, based on Zen Buddhist and Samurai traditions character development. Three main tenets were professed: social cooperation and responsibility, an acceptance of reality, and perseverance. The goal of the training program was to motivate employees to serve the interests of the firm: "the moral man works hard for the company." As part of the program, the trainees spent several days at a Zen temple. They were taught meditation, and selflessness was stressed. The trainees participated in military close-order drills, thereby seeing that groups could function well together. The trainees had to offer to work for nothing for strangers, in a ritual known as *rotoo*. The trainees spent time working with farmers, gaining, it was believed, insight into social interdependence and service. The capstone course was a twenty-five-mile walk, the first nine miles in a group, the next nine miles in smaller squads (for teamwork), and the final seven miles alone (for contemplation). Throughout, teamwork, persistence, and the relationships between mental and physical conditioning were stressed. Such programs are not uncommon in Japan, and in various forms may last from one concentrated month to six months of periodic training. In virtually all Japanese corporations, physical and mental preparedness are stressed through the disciplines of Zen and various martial arts.

The class will break into groups of five to seven students and discuss the following questions:

1. How could such a program benefit an American business organization?
2. What problems would arise in efforts to elicit employee participation in such a program? How would you overcome these problems?
3. Could any parts of the program be adopted in North America, and if so, which ones would have the highest probability of success? Why?
4. Design a program that would accomplish some of the same results but that might be more acceptable in the United States and Canada.

After these questions have been addressed, students should reassemble as a class and discuss their findings.

Culture Shock

Volunteers, using the role-play technique, will demonstrate the following:

1. How to order shrimp in a French restaurant when you do not speak French and the waiter speaks only French.
2. How to insult someone by using the wrong word in a foreign language. (You may need to consult with a language teacher.)
3. How to insult someone by disobeying a local custom. Research may be necessary.

REFERENCES

1. "The Road Is Clear for IBM's Drive into Europe," *Business Week*, August 20, 1984, pp. 44–45.
2. R. Hal Mason, "Conflicts between Host Countries and the Multinationals Enterprise," *California Management Review*, Fall 1974, pp. 5–14.
3. Ibid., pp. 7–9.
4. As reported to the author by Disney personnel.
5. Stefan H. Robock and Kenneth Simmonds, *International Business and Multinational Enterprises* (Homewood, Ill.: Richard D. Irwin, 1973), pp. 243–49.
6. Frank Ching, "Wooing the West, a Chinese Millionaire Leads Peking's Search for Investors," *Wall Street Journal*, November 14, 1979, pp. 1, 39.
7. David Sirota and J. Michael Greenwood, "Understand Your Overseas Work Force," *Harvard Business Review*, January–February 1971, pp. 53–60.
8. Robock and Simmonds, *International Business.*
9. As related to the author by the attorney's daughter.
10. Barry Newman, "Structured Society: A Briton Needn't Pay Much Heed to Class: He Knows His Place," *Wall Street Journal*, May 6, 1985, pp. 1, 26.
11. Frank Ching, "If You're Simulating a Duck, Don't Look Like an Airplane," *Wall Street Journal*, May 23, 1980, pp. 1, 35.
12. David Noer, *Multinational People Management: A Guide for Organizations and Employees* (Washington, D.C.: BNA, 1975), pp. 4–5.
13. James C. Baker, "Foreign Language and Predeparture Training in U.S. Multinational Firms," *Personnel Administrator*, July 1984, pp. 68–72.
14. M. K. Badawy, "Styles of Mideastern Managers," *California Management Review*, Spring 1980, pp. 57–58.
15. Allison R. Lanier, "Selecting and Preparing Personnel for Overseas Transfers," *Personnel Journal*, March 1979, pp. 160–63.
16. Noer, *Multinational People Management*, pp. 29–36.
17. Ibid., p. 42; "How to Ease Reentry after Overseas Duty," *Business Week*, June 11, 1979, pp. 82–84.
18. Lanier, "Selecting and Preparing Personnel."
19. "Gauging a Family's Suitability for a Stint

Overseas," *Business Week*, April 16, 1979, pp. 82–84.

20. William G. Ouchi, *Theory Z: How American Business Can Meet the Japanese Challenge* (Reading, Mass.: Addison-Wesley, 1981).

21. Richard T. Pascale and Anthony G. Athos, *The Art of Japanese Management* (New York: Simon & Schuster, 1981).

22. David P. Garino, "When Twain Meet: Takeover by Japanese Hasn't Hurt after All, Quasar Workers Find," *Wall Street Journal*, October 10, 1978, pp. 1, 41.

23. Masayoshi Kanabayashi, "Changing Roles: More Women in Japan Get Jobs, Shaking Up Traditional Marriages," *Wall Street Journal*, May 14, 1985, pp. 1, 24; Lee Smith, "Cracks in the Japanese Work Ethic," *Fortune*, May 14, 1984, pp. 162–68; "Japan's Secret Economic Weapon: Exploited Women," *Business Week*, March 4, 1985, p. 54.

24. George Anders, "Executive Style: German Bosses Stress Consensus Decisions, Technical Know-How," *Wall Street Journal*, September 25, 1984, pp. 1, 24; "Europe's New Managers: Going Global with a U.S. Style," *Business Week*, May 24, 1982, pp. 116–22.

6

UNDERSTANDING AND IMPROVING YOURSELF

15 CREATIVITY

LEARNING OBJECTIVES

When you have completed this chapter, you should be able to:

1. Describe the major reasons that individuals and organizations must become more creative.
2. Define the four *P*'s of creativity.
3. Determine whether or not a particular idea or physical entity is a creative product.
4. Examine a situation and ascertain whether or not the possibility of creativity exists.
5. Describe the steps involved in the creativity process and ways in which the process can be improved.
6. Identify the characteristics of a highly creative person.

CREATIVE POTATO CHIPS

A few years ago a manufacturer of potato chips was faced with a problem often encountered in his business: potato chips took up too much space on the shelf when they were packed loosely, but they crumbled when they were put in smaller packages.

The solution, according to creativity legend, was to use a creative process known as direct analogy—taking knowledge gained in one field and applying it to another. Forget about potato chips; think about biology. What in nature is similar to a potato chip? How about dried leaves? But decision makers realized that dried leaves crumble very easily. Furthermore, the leaves you rake in your yard are bulky. The analogy was too good. But wait, what about pressed leaves? They're flat. Could potato chips somehow be shipped flat, or nearly flat? Unfortunately, the crumbling problem remained. Continuing the creativity process, the decision makers realized that leaves are not pressed dry, they are pressed moist. They determined that if they packed potato chips in a stack, moist enough not to crumble but dry enough to be flat, or nearly flat, they might just have the problem solved.

The result, as you may by now have guessed, was Pringles. This was a landmark product, but perhaps more relevant, the result of creativity training. If creativity training can help one company, why can't it help others? Why can't it help you?

We are frequently exhorted to increase the levels of creativity in our society, especially in our organizations. We're told time and time again that innovation is vital to our future well-being. Many people say, for example, that it is the key to the revival of industry, the means by which we can maintain our technological competitive advantage, the wellspring of our future economy.[1] But we really don't seem to be doing very much about responding to these exhortations, as individuals or as organizations. There are too few examples like Pringles. We seem to depend on "naturally" creative people instead of developing creativity in all of us.

Most of us spend our time focusing on the rational decision process, not the creative one. And while a limited number of organizations do have crea-

> *Just as we can throttle our imagination, we can likewise accelerate it. As in any other art, individual creativity can be implemented by certain techniques.*
>
> ALEX F. OSBORN

tivity-enhancement programs, more stifle creativity with excessive rules, regulations, and procedures. In fact, while our society expresses a desire for more creativity in its members and its organizations, its socialization processes tend to discourage it. The family, for example, suppresses the infant's natural behavioral activities, most of which are creative for that little person, but few of which are socially useful. The child is made to "fit in," to "adjust" to society. Our educational systems are worse: they generally manage to stifle our creative talents almost totally. In the past ten years, for example, it is unlikely that you have been formally exposed to the subconscious decision process. Rather, you've been taught how to think logically. You've been taught how to follow decision rules and how to "crunch numbers." We've all been taught in that way. Now we have computers in our offices, our schools, our homes. We have ingenious software. Both allow us to approach decision making in an even more analytical manner. We know very well how to predict the bottom line, but we often can't get there because we don't understand creativity. Numerous studies suggest that creativity levels drop when a child enters grammar school.

Rational decision making is of course essential to individual and organizational success. But rational processes are not the only ones involved in making decisions or solving problems. Decision making involves both rational and intuitive/creative processes, but all too often people focus on the first and ignore the second. The best decision making combines the rational and the nonrational, subconscious, creative processes. It isn't that creativity is not being employed; subconscious processes are at work to some extent in any decision making. But creativity is clearly underemployed. The purpose of this chapter is to help you make fuller use of your own creative processes. We shall review four major reasons for being creative and define the concept of creativity. The four *P*'s of creativity—product, person, process, possibility—are reviewed, with a focus on the creative process and the creative person. When you complete this chapter and its exercises, you will have begun to understand creativity and to raise your own level of creativity.

CREATIVE PROBLEM SOLVING

"Capital isn't so important in business. Experience isn't so important. You can get both those things. What is important is ideas. If you have ideas, you have the main asset you need, and there isn't any limit to what you can do with your business and your life. They are any man's greatest asset—ideas."

HARVEY FIRESTONE

It's often difficult to believe, but that three-pound glob of gray matter that rests between your ears—your brain—controls your destiny. At its best, your brain is capable of the highest works known to humankind, but at its worst, it can screw up royally. High levels of mental performance are vital to your success. Mental development is a necessity, not a luxury. The brain works in still mysterious ways, but scientists are finally beginning to unravel its complex biochemical and electrical processes.

Life is a series of decisions, of choices among alternatives. Every time you choose a sweater to buy, a snack to keep you going, a movie to see, you have made a decision. Every time a leader directs people in battle, in producing a product, in assessing performance, a decision process is involved. The more effective you are at making decisions, at being rational and creative, the more successful you will be. Creativity gives you an edge—the creative edge.

Successful individuals and organizations have a creative edge. They design more new products and concepts, they market them more effectively and efficiently, they use information more judiciously, they manage their resources more efficiently, they finance their ventures more profitably, and they manage more creatively than their competitors do. It is creativity in marketing, operations, finance, human resources, and information management that separates the truly successful companies from the less successful companies.[2]

How can you as an individual, how can your organization obtain and maintain the creative edge? A three-pronged attack aimed at improving organizational characteristics, putting certain processes and techniques into practice, and improving individual use of the subconscious can achieve the creative edge. But before we examine this three-pronged attack, let's first review the reasons why individuals and organizations should be concerned about creativity.

Creativity is a misunderstood phenomenon. It is not solely the province of artists, scientists, engineers, and advertisers, nor are all who engage in creativity social nonconformists, as many people believe. Quite the contrary, thousands of men and women are creative in their jobs every day. They find more efficient ways to develop a compensation program, or they find a new way to manufacture a product for half a cent less per unit. Or the work group may develop a way of cutting scrap by 10 percent. They determine new ways of achieving a tax break, and they may in fact invent new products and ways to advertise them. Creativity is much more common than it has been thought to be, but it is still not so common as it needs to be. There are four key reasons why you should become creative. These are listed below.

Accelerated Pace of Change   If you study history—social, political, economic, and especially technological history—you will discover that the pace of change has accelerated over the centuries.[3] Alvin Tofler refers to the consequences of the rapid changes we are undergoing today as "future shock."[4] Just five years ago such products as the Commodore Amiga PC, the wine cooler, the suite hotel, low air fares caused by deregulation of airlines, and a myriad of others did not exist or certainly were not prominent in the marketplace. Tax laws and monetary and fiscal policies have all changed in this time period. The space shuttle, the information society, megatrends, all tell us that the future holds still more shocks in store for us. Many people find the pace of change too great to cope with. Adaptation to change requires creativity.

Increased Competition   Robert H. Hayes and William J. Abernathy warned us in 1980 that we were losing our competitive edge in international markets— that we were, as they put it, "managing our way into an economic decline." Their concern was that the firms in the United States were too little concerned with innovation; in other words, creativity. Their analysis indicated that we simply were not investing enough in research and development. Our economy had come to be based on the transfer of income rather than on its creation.

European and Japanese firms, they pointed out, were much more concerned about their ability to compete than U.S. firms were, and so were more interested in innovation. Though U.S. firms are currently showing more interest in creativity than they once were, they still lag behind the Japanese. Hayes and Abernathy believe that U.S. firms have become too concerned with such short-term objectives as return on investment. They avoid risk, and so are unwilling to invest in untried ideas.[5]

The accelerated pace of change, increasing competition by foreign innovators, deregulation at home, and rapidly expanding technology are forcing many companies to seek to develop new products and more efficient ways of producing them. Such innovations require creative decision making.

The Information Society   With the proliferation of computers, the task of the decision maker is changing. "What if" statements are much more important than they were even five years ago because we now have software that allows us to ask such questions and memory units that can process them. If you can't generate alternatives, if you can't see relationships between decision variables, then your role as a decision maker is going to be extremely limited. Numbers can be crunched for you; easily modeled decisions can be made by the computer. People won't have to make those kinds of decisions. People will increasingly be required to make decisions that are unstructured, unprecedented, different from all the decisions that have been made before—the kind that require creative processes.

The Intuitive Edge   Equally important, a growing body of research indicates that the creative manager is a superior manager. Studies by Arthur Reber have shown that when chief executives are rated by their peers for their ability and are tested for their rational and intuitive skills, it becomes quite clear that those executives with highly developed intuitive as well as rational skills are the most effective.[6] Additional efforts by Daniel J. Isenberg indicate that managers seem to perform better if they have highly developed intuitive skills, and that such skills become increasingly important as they rise in the organizational hierarchy.[7] In a related vein, a study by Siegfried Streufert reveals that successful upper-level managers are able to envision the effects of their actions and so are better prepared to implement their decisions. Such vision demands the same sort of creative skill that goes into the generation of alternatives.[8]

> ". . . the key managerial processes are enormously complex and mysterious . . . , drawing on the vaguest of information and using the least articulated of mental processes. These processes seem to be more relational and holistic than ordered and sequential, and more intuitive than intellectual. . . ."
>
> HENRY MINTZBERG

WHAT IS CREATIVITY?

The word *creativity* derives from the Latin *creare*, to make. **Creativity** is the skill of originating, inventing, or conceptualizing something new that has value for someone. The three key words are *skill*, *new*, and *value*. Creativity is a skill, and it can be learned. It results in a product that is new and has value—to the creator, to others, or to both. The thing created, the product, need not be a physical object; it may be an idea, an application of an existing idea to a new situation, a synthesis of old ideas that produces an idea that has not existed before—anything that, when fully developed, has value.

THE FOUR *P*'s
OF CREATIVITY

Creativity depends on four conditions, which we may call the **four P's of creativity**: product, person, process, and possibility.[9] If we are to recognize any behavior as creative, it must result in (1) a product that is new and has value, developed by (2) a person who has a certain amount of intelligence and experience in the subject at hand, who engages in (3) the creative process, involving the subconscious, right-brain function in tandem with the logical, left-brain function, using creative processes; in an environment where (4) the possibility of creative thought exists.[10]

The Creative Product   The creative product (an object, an idea, whatever) has at least potential value, not mere originality. The new is not necessarily of value to anyone. Determining what has value and what does not is not a simple task. Value is relative—to the value system of the evaluator and to the time at which the discovery is made. The inventors of the Xerox photo-copying process, for example, offered to sell their new idea to IBM, General Motors, and several other major firms, and were turned down by all of them. Finally in desperation they decided to make and market the product themselves. The Aztecs of Mexico invented the wheel, but with no horses or other beasts of burden before the arrival of the Spaniards, they had no use for it except on toys for children. Mozart died in poverty, yet his music has enriched the world.

The Creative Person   We know several specific factors that enter into creativity. A certain amount of intelligence is required, but not necessarily a great deal. This is the intelligence that's measured by one's ability to solve problems rather than by the standard IQ test. IQ test scores are only slightly correlated with creativity.[11] In fact, one study of successful architects found zero correlation between this type of intelligence and creativity.[12] On the other hand, if intelligence is defined as the ability to adapt to one's environment, to be a problem solver, then creativity and intelligence may be more highly interrelated.

Intelligence as it is commonly measured is probably a left-brain function. It is in the left side of the brain that the logical and analytical processes take place. The mental processes of memory and the associated skills are found there. Conversely, it is believed that the right hemisphere of the brain is the site of creativity and the related processes of fantasizing, dreaming, and spontaneity of ideas.[13] Studies now suggest that the right brain tends to be dominant in women, the left brain in men. Whether these findings are attributable to physiological or sociological factors, or a combination of the two, is still undetermined. It is likely that both sets of factors are at work.[14]

The Androgynous Brain   The creative individual has what we might call an **androgynous brain**—one that is characterized by both male and female thought processes. The androgynous brain is superior to one dominated by either the right or the left hemisphere. The right and left hemispheres of the human brain are believed to perform somewhat distinct and probably opposite functions. Apparently women possess a large corpus callosum, that part of the brain which connects the two hemispheres. As a consequence, women are believed to use both sides of their brains more frequently than men, who

> *"The best of all possible business worlds could be realized if traditional male and female behavior were somehow blended together."*
> ALICE SARGEANT

tend to make predominant use of the left side, the analytical hemisphere of the brain.[15]

Some of the management literature suggests that the average woman may ultimately be a more appropriate candidate for the management decision-making role than the average man, as women are likely to engage in both rational and creative thinking, whereas men tend to neglect the right brain functions in their emphasis on logical thinking.[16] We have far to go before we really understand the brain and its functioning. There are far too many men who are right-brain dominant and women who are left-brain dominant to permit us to generalize in this way. Freud to the contrary notwithstanding, biology is not necessarily destiny. The optimum choice for a position that involves decision making is someone who is androgynous, whose thought processes are dominated by neither the right nor the left hemisphere; someone who not only is capable of using both hemispheres, but routinely does so. As we move toward the twenty-first century, as the management of our organizations becomes more participative, it is apparent that more and more androgynous persons are needed, as more and more persons will be involved in decision making.

Experience and Knowledge   To be creative, one must have a certain amount of experience with and knowledge about the topic at hand. The person must understand how the problem environment functions in order to solve the problem. She must also understand the primary relationships between variables and how they interact with one another. For example, most of you reading this paragraph have not yet been exposed to enough coursework in computer programming to write a VisiCalc or Lotus 1-2-3 program. But if you had been, you could write those programs. And once you had enough experience, you could make the very ingenious programming decisions that save the machine time, and therefore the customer time and money. No one can say how much knowledge and how much experience are necessary. Some people can make creative leaps with only a very minimal amount of knowledge and experience; others require much higher levels of both to make similar strides.

Age, Sex, and Educational Level   Creativity apparently does not decline significantly with age. In fact, some evidence suggests just the opposite, that age may enhance imagination (socialization held constant). This finding may be partly a function of knowledge and experience. A number of older studies show no significant difference in the creative abilities of men and women. However, these studies do support the concept of the androgynous brain, and some more recent studies suggest that there may be some differences.[17] Some of these studies also suggest, in the words of Donald W. MacKinnon, that "the more creative a person is, the more he reveals an openness to his own feelings and emotions, a sensitive intellect and understanding, self-awareness, and wide-ranging interests including many which in American culture are thought of as feminine."[18] Educational level is not a significant factor in creativity either. Studies show no significant correlation between the two factors.[19] Note, though, that a certain amount of task-specific knowledge and experience are necessary before creativity can occur.

Socialization   It seems biologically likely that all persons have the capacity for creativity to some degree, some admittedly more than others. There are, after all, few Platos and Picassos. But there are millions of people functioning in various capacities in our society, each of whom has the opportunity and, perhaps more important, the need to function more creatively. So why don't they? The biggest single reason is what is known as socialization. Socialization is the process by which one learns the behavioral norms and standards of the society of which one is a member. The major instruments of socialization for most of us are our parents. The schools also play a large role in the development of the individual. The work organization takes a mature individual and issues further guidance with respect to acceptable behavior. Within all of these organizations—the family, the educational system, the work organization— friendship groups make important contributions to our understanding of our role in the society. Finally, the society as a whole, through its government agencies, religious bodies, and other institutions, teaches its expectations of behavior.

All of these groups and organizations require adherence to a preconceived set of behaviors—their norms and standards. We thus are discouraged from engaging in original, creative behavior that deviates from the preconceived norms. Rather, we are rewarded for conforming behavior. Unless our creativity is exercised within the bounds of conforming behavior, it is likely to be stifled. The parent who praises ingenious solutions to problems, who spends time with the child fantasizing and encouraging the free play of ideas, is providing the type of environment that leads to creativity. The teacher who encourages questions and rewards the inquisitive mind is contributing more to students' creativity than the teacher who insists on the "correct" answer. The organization whose managers delegate responsibility and the manager who provides for participation is encouraging creativity. Insistence on strict adherence to authority deters creativity. All societies demand conformance to certain rules, some much more than others. Fortunately, we live in a society that is generally receptive to creativity. We can change organizations; we can change ourselves. We can become what we want to be, if we set our minds to it. We first must recognize where we are creatively and how socialization has affected and does affect us, and then strive to take action to raise the level of our creativity.

Finally, creative people behave somewhat differently from the less creative. They use the creative process while the less creative do not.

> *It is not enough to have a good mind. The main thing is to use it well.*
> RENÉ DESCARTES

The Creative Process   Creativity is a two-faceted process: first small increments of progress, one step building upon another, then a great leap into insight that seems to transcend reality. Most of us have never entered into what athletes refer to as the "Zone," that region of performance that is beyond our normal capabilities.[20] The highly creative individual seems to make that leap into another dimension. Five major steps seem to enter into the process: preparation, concentration, incubation, illumination, and verification.[21]

Preparation and Concentration   Preparation consists of recognition that a problem or opportunity exists. The problem solver then gathers as much relevant information as possible. Creative people ask questions, read, gather data and analyze them, look for the abnormal, the reasons why. For example, Roger von Oech, a creativity consultant, tells of a situation in which he asked employees of client Applied Materials why they "always etched semiconductor wafers horizontally," and why they couldn't be made some other way. The firm had been suffering difficulties in arriving at a new engraving methodology and seemed destined to fail at the new endeavor. The project came in ahead of schedule and Applied Materials indicates that von Oech's questioning was the turning point. The answer was, of course, that wafers could be made in other ways than those that had always prevailed, but no one had questioned the fact "that it is always done that way," except von Oech.[22] The creative person questions the obvious. If you ask the right questions, you're already halfway to the answer. Creative people concentrate so intensely on the subject that they seem to be in another world, oblivious of what is going on around them. Interpersonal relations often suffer during such periods of intense concentration.

Incubation and Illumination   After a time, when the answers being sought remain elusive, the creative person wearies of the quest and puts the problem out of his mind (he thinks). He has entered the period of **incubation**, when the mind organizes information into new patterns. This stage of the process is not very well understood. The problem, having been thoroughly analyzed by conscious, rational processes, is somehow transferred to and processed by the subconscious part of the problem solver's mind. It is this ability to give the subconscious free rein while retaining control of rational processes that seems to separate the creative thinker from the rest of us. Incubation is much like a smoldering fire waiting to burst into flame. During incubation the creative person is not actively, rationally working on the problem, but the subconscious mind is.[23]

And one day while he is shaving or she is washing her car, the pieces of the problem suddenly (so it seems) click together and the answer rises full-formed into consciousness. This is the moment when the light bulb appears above the cartoon character's head: illumination at last. This is the "ah-ha" experience.

The exact processes of illumination, sometimes referred to as inspiration and intuition, have not been identified. Intuitive reasoning apparently takes place, but exactly how it works we do not know. Memory and observation apparently play important roles in this process, and one can only surmise that when the right neurological connections are made, illumination follows.[24] After preparation, concentration, and incubation, illumination comes without warning, and it may occur at any time—at any time, that is, when the individual is consciously thinking of something else altogether, or of nothing at all.

The incubation period may last from hours to days or months or even years. Many of the world's greatest inventions have been described by their creators as the products of overnight incubation periods. Thomas Edison, for example, went through a lengthy period of rational analysis in his efforts to invent the electric light bulb, but all of his experiments failed. One night, after working especially hard on the project, he finally put it out of his mind and fell asleep on the couch in his laboratory. When he awoke the next morning, he had the solution to the problem. Numerous others of his inventions were the products

"Every great improvement has come after repeated failures. Virtually nothing comes out right the first time. Failures, repeated failures, are fingerposts on the road to achievement."
CHARLES F. KETTERING

of similar incubation periods.[25] On a less lofty level, parts of several of the models in this book, including the TRRAP model and the motivation/performance cycle model, came to me during the middle of the night as I was sleeping, or in the morning when I first woke up. Many of my students and friends—managers, engineers, accountants, nurses, law-enforcement officers, counselors, professors—report similar experiences. The good news is that if we can learn how to use this capacity of our subconscious, we can all be more creative.

Verification   It's one thing to say that "it's an idea whose time has come"; it's another to demonstrate that the statement is true. The idea that comes in a burst of illumination must be verified: we must confirm that it fits the facts, that it works. Then we must confirm that it has value, at least to the person who has conceived it, ideally to others as well.

Verification is usually a lengthy process; years may be required to test an idea's validity, to refine it and win acceptance for it. The idea of microsurgery on spinal discs, for example, was subjected to lengthy experimentation on animals before it was tried on human beings.

Another concern relative to process are those creative techniques or processes which can be learned. These are discussed later in the chapter in the section entitled, "Increasing Your Creativity."

The Possibility of Creative Thought   If you are etching silicon wafers under a microscope, wafer after wafer, according to strict technical procedures; if you are following generally accepted accounting principles as you audit a firm's books; if you are playing basketball for a dogmatic coach; if you are locked into any of millions of confining situations, then the probability that you will engage in creative thought is low because the possibility of creativity is foreclosed. Regardless of your creative talents, despite your knowledge or skill, despite your concentration, you will not be able to create a new product, service, or concept that has value if you are not functioning in a favorable situation—if the possibility of creativity is not present. What you need, then, is a favorable situation.

> *Man's body is faulty; his mind is untrustworthy; but his imagination has made him remarkable.*
> JOHN MASEFIELD

What factors enter into a situation that encourages or at least permits the creative process to unfold? First, the people in charge of the situation, whether they be parents, coaches, teachers, or managers of an organization in which you find yourself, must provide an organizational climate that does not discourage creativity. Your associates, your peers, must also be supportive of your creativity. The organization must be supportive of creative endeavors. The society, at least the society of that segment of the organization in which you find yourself, must be supportive of creativity.

> *Management's basic dedication is usually to the continuance of the organization, while creativity usually leads to change in the organization.*
> RICHARD E. DUTTON

The crux of the matter is that you must be able to express yourself. Your family, your friends, your employer must be willing and able to provide an opportunity *for you* to create.

HOW CREATIVE ARE YOU?

Three primary means may be employed to assess someone's degree of creativity: a personality test designed specifically to reveal creativity, a general personality test followed by an assessment of the relationship between the

"Big ideas are so hard to recognize, so fragile, so easy to kill. Don't forget that, all of you who don't have them."
JOHN ELLIOTT, JR.

personality traits indicated and creativity, and finally an assessment of the products of the individual's activity. While creativity is readily defined conceptually, an operational definition that permits measurement by a personality test is much more difficult to arrive at. Authorities often disagree about the relationship of creativity and personality. One test that covers the traits and behaviors most generally associated with creativity may be seen in "Test Yourself: How Creative Are You?" Why not try it and see for yourself? Another predictor of future creative performance is past creative performance. Thus, typically, a biographical inventory instrument that tests for past creative achievements will provide information about both the strength and the direction of one's creative capabilities.[26] Think of your five most creative accomplishments or actions. But even this approach is inadequate, because there always has to be a first time. Lack of creative accomplishments in the past does not necessarily mean that the individual will not be creative in the future. Creativity levels can be raised through developmental exercises.[27] Testing for creativity, then, becomes a matter of identifying several indicators, recognizing that none will be totally predictive.

TEST YOURSELF

HOW CREATIVE ARE YOU?
By Eugene Raudsepp

How creative are you? The following test helps you determine if you have the personality traits, attitudes, values, motivations and interests that make up creativity. It is based on several years' study of attributes possessed by men and women in a variety of fields and occupations who think and act creatively.

For each statement write in the appropriate letter:
A = agree; B = in between or don't know;
C = disagree
Be as frank as possible. Try not to second-guess how a creative person might respond.

_____ 1. I always work with a great deal of certainty that I am following the correct procedure for solving a particular problem.

_____ 2. It would be a waste of time for me to ask questions if I had no hope of obtaining answers.

_____ 3. I concentrate harder on whatever interests me than do most people.

_____ 4. I feel that a logical step-by-step method is best for solving problems.

_____ 5. In groups I occasionally voice opinions that seem to turn some people off.

_____ 6. I spend a great deal of time thinking about what others think of me.

_____ 7. It is more important for me to do what I believe to be right than to try to win the approval of others.

_____ 8. People who seem uncertain about things lose my respect.

_____ 9. More than other people, I need to have things interesting and exciting.

_____ 10. I know how to keep my inner impulses in check.

_____ 11. I am able to stick with difficult problems over extended periods of time.

_____ 12. On occasion I get overly enthusiastic.

_____ 13. I often get my best ideas when doing nothing in particular.

_____ 14. I rely on intuitive hunches and the feeling of "rightness" or "wrongness" when moving toward the solution of a problem.

_____ 15. When problem solving, I work faster when analyzing the problem and slower when synthesizing the information I have gathered.

_____ 16. I sometimes get a kick out of breaking the rules and doing things I am not supposed to do.

_____ 17. I like hobbies that involve collecting things.

_____ 18. Daydreaming has provided the impetus for many of my more important projects.

_____ 19. I like people who are objective and rational.

_____ 20. If I had to choose from two occupations other than the one I now have, I would rather be a physician than an explorer.

_____ 21. I can get along more easily with people if they belong to about the same social and business class as myself.

_____ 22. I have a high degree of aesthetic sensitivity.

_____ 23. I am driven to achieve high status and power in life.

_____ 24. I like people who are most sure of their conclusions.

_____ 25. Inspiration has nothing to do with the successful solution of problems.

_____ 26. When I am in an argument, my greatest pleasure would be for the person who disagrees with me to become a friend, even at the price of sacrificing my point of view.

_____ 27. I am much more interested in coming up with new ideas than in trying to sell them to others.

_____ 28. I would enjoy spending an entire day alone, just "chewing the mental cud."

_____ 29. I tend to avoid situations in which I might feel inferior.

_____ 30. In evaluating information, the source is more important to me than the content.

_____ 31. I resent things being uncertain and unpredictable.

_____ 32. I like people who follow the rule, "business before pleasure."

_____ 33. Self-respect is much more important than the respect of others.

_____ 34. I feel that people who strive for perfection are unwise.

_____ 35. I prefer to work with others in a team effort rather than solo.

_____ 36. I like work in which I must influence others.

_____ 37. Many problems that I encounter in life cannot be resolved in terms of right or wrong solutions.

_____ 38. It is important for me to have a place for everything and everything in its place.

_____ 39. Writers who use strange and unusual words merely want to show off.

_____ 40. On page 382 is a list of terms that describe people.

(Continued on page 382)

Choose 10 words that best characterize you.

☐ energetic	☐ formal	☐ curious	☐ thorough
☐ persuasive	☐ informal	☐ organized	☐ impulsive
☐ observant	☐ dedicated	☐ unemotional	☐ determined
☐ fashionable	☐ forward-looking	☐ clear-thinking	☐ realistic
☐ self-confident	☐ factual	☐ understanding	☐ modest
☐ persevering	☐ open-minded	☐ dynamic	☐ involved
☐ original	☐ tactful	☐ self-demanding	☐ absent-minded
☐ cautious	☐ inhibited	☐ polished	☐ flexible
☐ habit-bound	☐ enthusiastic	☐ courageous	☐ sociable
☐ resourceful	☐ innovative	☐ efficient	☐ well-liked
☐ egotistical	☐ poised	☐ helpful	☐ restless
☐ independent	☐ acquisitive	☐ perceptive	☐ retiring
☐ stern	☐ practical	☐ quick	
☐ predictable	☐ alert	☐ good-natured	

How do you rate? See next page.

Scoring

To compute your score, circle and add up the values assigned to each item. The values are as follows:

	A Agree	B In between or don't know	C Disagree		A Agree	B In between or don't know	C Disagree
1.	0	1	2	23.	0	1	2
2.	0	1	2	24.	−1	0	2
3.	4	1	0	25.	0	1	3
4.	−2	0	3	26.	−1	0	2
5.	2	1	0	27.	2	1	0
6.	−1	0	3	28.	2	0	−1
7.	3	0	−1	29.	0	1	2
8.	0	1	2	30.	−2	0	3
9.	3	0	−1	31.	0	1	2
10.	1	0	3	32.	0	1	2
11.	4	1	0	33.	3	0	−1
12.	3	0	−1	34.	−1	0	2
13.	2	1	0	35.	0	1	2
14.	4	0	−2	36.	1	2	3
15.	−1	0	2	37.	2	1	0
16.	2	1	0	38.	0	1	2
17.	0	1	2	39.	−1	0	2
18.	3	0	−1				
19.	0	1	2				
20.	0	1	2				
21.	0	1	2				
22.	3	0	−1				

40. The following have values of 2:

energetic	enthusiastic	observant
resourceful	dynamic	independent
original	flexible	perceptive

innovative   dedicated   curious
self-demanding courageous   involved
persevering

The following have values of 1:
self-confident   informal
thorough   alert
determined   forward-looking
restless   open-minded

The rest have values of 0.

95–116	Exceptionally creative
65– 94	Very creative
40– 64	Above average
20– 39	Average
10– 19	Below average
Below 10	Noncreative

Ways to Become More Creative

If you scored below your expectations, don't despair. By learning new attitudes, values and ways of approaching and solving problems, you can considerably enhance your creative powers. Here are some ways to increase your creative ability:

- **Keep track of your ideas at all times.** Carry a notebook wherever you go, and keep it at your bedside. Ideas come at strange times, frequently when we least expect them, and they may never come again. Listen to your hunches and intuitions, particularly during moments of relaxation, before going to sleep or upon awakening.

- **Pose new questions every day.** An inquiring mind is a creatively active mind. It is also a mind that constantly enlarges the area of its awareness.

- **Learn about things outside of your specialty.** Seemingly unrelated pieces of knowledge can often be brought together to solve problems or create new products and services.

- **Avoid rigid, set patterns of doing things.** Overcome fixed ideas and look for new viewpoints; try new ways. Attempt to find several solutions to each problem and develop the ability to drop one idea in favor of another.

- **Be open and receptive to ideas, others' as well as yours.** New ideas are fragile—listen positively to them. Seize on tentative, half-formed concepts and possibilities: A new idea seldom arrives as a complete ready-made package. Freely entertain apparently wild, farfetched or even silly ideas.

- **Be alert in observation.** Look for similarities, differences, and unique and distinguishing features in objects, situations, processes and ideas. The more new associations and relationships you can form, the greater are your chances of coming up with really creative and original combinations and solutions.

- **Engage in hobbies.** Try ones that allow you to construct or produce something with your hands. This allows you to relax and enhances the creative problem-solving abilities so useful in your work. Also, keep your brain trim by playing games and doing puzzles and exercises.

- **Improve your sense of humor and laugh easily.** This helps you to put yourself and your problems into proper perspective. Humor relieves tension, and you are more creative when you are relaxed.

- **Adopt a risk-taking attitude.** Nothing is more fatal to creativity than fear of failure. Heed management consultant Chester Barnard's advice: "To try and fail is at least to learn. To fail to try is to suffer the inestimable loss of what might have been."

Abraham Maslow tells us of an important discovery he made: anyone can be creative.

> I soon discovered that I had, like most other people, been thinking of creativeness in terms of products, and secondly, I had unconsciously confined creativeness to certain conventional areas only of human endeavor, unconsciously assuming that *any* painter, *any* poet, *any* composer was leading a creative life. Theorists, artists, scientists, inventors, writers could be creative. Nobody else could be. Unconsciously I had assumed that creativeness was the prerogative solely of certain professionals.
>
> But these expectations were broken up by various of my subjects. For instance, one woman, uneducated, poor, a full-time housewife and mother, did none of these conventionally creative things and yet was a marvelous cook, mother, wife and homemaker. With little money, her home was somehow always beautiful. She was a perfect hostess. Her meals were banquets. Her taste in linens, silver, glass, crockery, and furniture was impeccable. She was in all these areas original, novel, ingenious, unexpected, inventive. I just *had* to call her creative. I learned from her and others like her that a first-rate soup is more creative than a second-rate painting, and that, generally, cooking or parenthood or making a home could be creative while poetry need not be; it could be uncreative.[28]

So even though you may not paint as imaginatively as Van Gogh or display the inventive imagination of Edison, you can increase your creativity in what you do.

INCREASING YOUR CREATIVITY

To begin to increase your intuition and your creativity, you must first get more in tune with your subconscious. It may be almost as simple as saying to yourself, "I want to be more creative." You have to put yourself in the right frame of mind; you have to say "I am creative" and "I'm going to come up with a lot of new ideas." You have to stop censuring new ideas, you have to go for quantity rather than quality. You have to relearn creativity. You need to become childlike again. You have to allow as many new ideas to pop into your brain as you possibly can, and suspend judgment as you do so. Evaluation comes later.

PROCESSES

There are three major means through which we can develop and stimulate creative output: (1) Improve the possibilities, (2) discover and use processes that promote creative thinking, (3) discover and use probes to stimulate and strengthen the subconscious. There are over 50 processes you can learn. Two primary ones are reviewed below.

Brainstorming   The brainstorming process as we know it was devised by Alex F. Osborn (then of the advertising firm of Batten, Barton, Durstine & Osborn) to increase the quantity and quality of advertising ideas within the firm. The process became known as **brainstorming** because the participants' brains were used to storm a problem. A version of the process was used by

Hindu religious teachers as early as the sixteenth century, "The Indian name for this method is *prai barshana*. *Prai* means outside yourself and *barshana* means question. In such a session there is no discussion or criticism. Evaluation of ideas takes place at later meetings of the same group."

Brainstorming is probably the best-known and most widely used method of raising the level of creativity in a group. The brainstorming process involves a group of six to twelve people, a moderator, and a secretary. The group needs to have at least six people so that enough ideas may be generated, but no more than twelve so that the ideas generated will not be too numerous to be absorbed by the group members. The moderator has indicated to the group, sometimes in advance of their meeting, that a given topic will be discussed. Once the brainstorming session opens, the moderator functions primarily to recognize contributors, to stimulate group members to offer new ideas, to keep the group on the subject at hand, and to make sure the rules are followed. The secretary records the ideas brought forth by the group. The list of ideas is later distributed to group members. There are four basic rules in a brainstorming session:

1. No judgments about any suggestion are made.
2. All ideas, even absurd or impractical ones, are welcome.
3. Quantity of ideas is a major objective, since it leads to quality.
4. Ideas may be combined, refined, and piggy-backed.[29]

It has been found that brainstorming dramatically increases the number of ideas generated. Its features of spontaneity, suspended judgment, and absence of criticism all lead to an increase not only in quantity but in quality of new ideas. A typical session should last no more than 30 to 40 minutes. These sessions are highly intense, and the brain and body have a difficult time coping with longer sessions.[30] Evaluation of these ideas comes after the session, and is preferably undertaken by the same group that originated the ideas. Topics should be narrow, and no more than one is covered in a session. Don't try to name a product and figure out a distribution system in half an hour. If writing is required, the process may be self-defeating. Writing is best done by oneself.

Because the process seems simple—and it is—you may be tempted to reject it out of hand. Don't. Give brainstorming a chance. Thousands of organizations have used it successfully. I can personally attest to its worth, but must confess that I was a doubting Thomas before I tried it. The synergism of this type of group is greater than you can imagine.

Synectics Synectics, too, is a group process, and it has some of the same dynamics as brainstorming. There is a leader, there is a secretary, and the group discusses ideas in response to the topic or problem presented. But there are significant differences between the two techniques. **Synectics** is defined by the developer of the process, William J. J. Gordon, as "the joining together of different and apparently irrelevant elements."[31] Synectics differs operationally from brainstorming in four primary respects: the emotional contents of interactions during problem-solving sessions, the underlying philosophical processes, the mechanisms used to stimulate creativity, and the guidelines for determining the composition of the group.

In a brainstorming session the group interactions are kept positive, pleasant, and low-keyed. Synectics encourages more intense emotions. Joy, anger, sarcasm, aggression, enthusiasm, and hostility may be expressed. The ventilation of intense emotions requires strong skills in the handling of group dynamics, as the group may easily get sidetracked by the emotions aroused. Not everyone who practices synectics insists on such intense emotions. Some proponents of synectics, headed by George Prince, encourage the expression of emotions more intense than those released in brainstorming sessions but less so than the ones encouraged by Gordon.[32] The advantage of the release of intense emotions is that it may result in more open thinking and expression. The major negative aspect is that just the opposite may occur: people may stop making suggestions for fear of criticism.

Gordon bases his approach on four psychological constructs: detachment and involvement, deferment, speculation, and autonomy of the object. *Detachment and involvement* he defines as the feeling of being removed from the object, then pretending you are the object and thinking about how the object would feel. *Deferment* refers to disciplining oneself against premature solution. *Speculation* is described as the mind's ability to run free. Finally, *autonomy of the object* refers to the belief that the solution has "an entity and demand quality of its own." Recognition of this quality is described as "the pleasurable sensation that accompanies the feeling of being right about a hypothesis or solution before it has been proven correct."[33]

Gordon seeks to make the strange familiar and the familiar strange. He feels that past experiences give meaning to the strange and thus provide an opportunity to piggy-back thoughts and improve creative output. Similarly, when the familiar is put into a new context, creative insights increase. To induce detachment and involvement, deferment, speculation, and autonomy of the object, synectics employs four mechanisms: personal analogy, direct analogy, symbolic analogy, and fantasy analogy.

Analogies can serve to identify problems and make them more understandable. They may also be used to generate alternatives. Analogies are pairings of two things that are essentially dissimilar but that can be seen to have some similarity when they are paired. "He came charging in like a bull into the arena": immediately we sense a situation of rage, danger, and some confusion.

Members of synectics sessions are encouraged to think of personal analogies—to see themselves as personally involved in the situation under discussion. The technique may be usefully employed by anyone. A major paper company found new uses for pulp and other tree parts and significantly raised profits when top managers role-played the part of a tree going through the paper production process.

Direct analogies apply to one field the knowledge, facts, or techniques that belong to another. As we have seen, Pringles potato chips were conceived when their makers developed an analogy between potato chips and pressed leaves.

By means of symbolic analogy, members of synectics groups use objective

"Reason can answer many questions, but imagination has to ask them."

Ralph W. Gerard

and impersonal images to describe the project and formulate solutions. They attempt to link the problem or the project to something familiar. A key word is associated with two or three analogous terms to pinpoint the nature of the problem. If a company is bankrupt, for instance, analogous terms might be "no cash" and "too high debt." These terms give the group members the essence of the problem, and they then know where to focus their efforts.

Finally, they turn to fantasy analogy to envision what the ideal solution should look like. This technique helps its users to find a workable solution.[34]

The selection of the group members is very important. According to Gordon, a broad spectrum of the organization should be represented. Members should be between 25 and 40 years old, with high energy levels. They should have administrative potential, should have the lean and hungry look of the entrepreneur, should have changed fields of interest and had varying job experiences. Some members should also be chosen from the "almost" group—people who are almost productive, who could be highly successful. Synectics may unleash their potential.[35]

Synectics has many supports and many detractors. It certainly has great potential, but it is shunned by people who fear the negative effects of unleashing strong emotions.

A number of actions may be taken by the individual to improve right-brain functioning. Among them are meditation, sleeping on it, hypnotic tapes, music, and visualization.

INDIVIDUAL ACTIONS TO IMPROVE CREATIVITY

Meditation **Meditation** is believed to encourage creativity by helping the individual to become aware of subconscious processes, so that they may be put to effective use. Its proponents also believe that meditation increases the productivity of creativity efforts, but as little research has been done on the effects of meditation, only limited data can be found to support this contention. Meditation induces an altered state of consciousness and modifies typical brain-wave patterns. Alpha waves, typical of the pre-sleep state, become much more pronounced.[36] Meditation is believed to transfer control of the brain from the rational left hemisphere to the right hemisphere, seat of the more creative brain functions.

The relaxation response (to be discussed in Chapter 17) is a form of meditation that was originally designed to reduce stress, but it also serves to give its practitioners access to their subconscious. You are encouraged to try this technique for yourself. Once you have performed the response four or five times and feel that you have gained sufficient mastery of the technique, try to do something creative either immediately after a response session or within a few hours afterward. Compare your creativity performance with your past experience. While this is hardly a scientific experiment, it will give you the flavor of what you are striving for.

If creativity seems slow in coming, remember the importance of the incubation period. After struggling with a problem till no more ideas will come, let it go and sleep on it.

Sleeping on It   Thousands of people have reported that they can think rationally for some time on a problem without finding an answer, then fall asleep and mysteriously awake with a solution. Little scientific evidence is available to indicate how the process works, or why, but it works. Going to bed at night and sleeping on it simply allows your subconscious processes to work for you.

Hypnotic Tapes   Listening to relaxation tapes or self-hypnosis tapes on the theme of creativity can heighten your creative experience. Such tapes help to establish the proper brain waves, a version of meditation. Some of these tapes ask you to "build" creative retreats in your mind—places to go when you want to be creative.

Music   Music helps, too. Classical music, especially in the key of D, seems to move the mind in creative directions. Listening to music is a right-brain function and apparently generates the appropriate brain conditions to induce incubation and illumination.

Visualization   Forming mental images trains the brain to visualize the problem. If you can see the problem in all its aspects, you are likely to see the solution too. The more imaging you are capable of, the more likely you are to be creative.

CREATIVE THINKING, CREATIVE DECISION MAKING

Our concern now is to raise the level of our creative thinking and creative decision making within our own environment. We can all increase our creative potential by employing the creativity stimulators discussed in this chapter. Most of us will never be Einsteins or Edisons, but we can be more creative at whatever we do if we try. We can all learn to combine old elements in new ways. We can all learn to use our childlike qualities to expand our horizons. We can combine rational and intuitive thought processes to produce creative thinking and creative decision making. We can practice being more open, more receptive to new ideas, more in tune with our subconscious, and we can put our subconscious to work for us. In fact, the rational decision-making process works best in combination with creative thinking. The new ideas, the new alternatives, the better solutions occur when the two work together.

TIPS FOR SUCCESS

1. Work on your personal creativity with meditation, with dreaming, with visualization, with hypnotic tapes, by sleeping on it.
2. Try the group techniques of brainstorming and synectics.
3. If you want to be creative in an organization, pick an organization that encourages creativity.
4. Understand that creative behavior is within your power. Never tell yourself that you are not creative.

SUMMARY

1. The accelerated pace of change, increasing competition by foreign innovators, deregulation, and rapidly expanding technology are forcing many companies to seek to develop new products and more efficient ways to produce them. Such innovations require creative decision making.
2. Everyone is creative to some degree, and our creative abilities can be enhanced by training.
3. Creativity is the skill of inventing or conceptualizing something new that has value for someone.
4. Creativity depends on the four *P*'s: product, person, process, and possibility.
5. The creative product may be a physical object or an idea, an application of an existing idea to a new situation, or a synthesis of old ideas that produces an idea that has not existed before.
6. The creative person has an androgynous brain— one that is characterized by both the analyti-

cal, left-brain thought processes associated with the male and the intuitive, right-brain thought processes associated with the female.

7. Sex, educational level, and IQ seem to have little effect on creative ability, though experience does contribute to the potential for creativity.
8. The creative process has four major stages: preparation, concentration, incubation, illumination, and verification.
9. Regardless of one's creative talents, one will be unable to exercise them unless the possibility of creativity is present in the situation. The situation must support and encourage creativity before the creative process can unfold.
10. Two techniques that stimulate creative output in groups are brainstorming and synectics.
11. Each individual can improve right-brain functioning by means of meditation, sleeping on it, hypnotic tapes, music, and visualization.

DISCUSSION QUESTIONS

1. Describe a creative project or a creative act in which you have engaged in terms of the four *P*'s of creativity.
2. Discuss the importance of creativity to you and to organizations in our modern society.
3. Name an organization that you perceive as being extremely creative and indicate why. Now name

one that you feel is not creative and indicate why.

Describe your plan to become more personally creative.

Describe how an organization might go about becoming more creative.

APPLYING HUMAN RELATIONS SKILLS

Boston Bank

Bruce Meyers, Boston Bank's vice-president for strategic planning, wondered how to make the bank's strategic planning more creative. It would soon be time for the bank's annual strategic planning retreat in Vermont, and he did not want a repeat of last year's efforts. Everyone focused on operational issues. They seemed most comfortable with such issues. And they rehashed the same things

CASE

that had been addressed over and over and over. Even the high-priced facilitators they had hired seemed to get mired in the present and neglected the future. Planning, after all, is supposed to focus on the future.

And whatever the focus, the results needed improvement. He wanted to try some new ideas, to open up the ranks to the strategic planning process, to reduce some of the bureaucracy, to lower some of the barriers to creative thinking that had long been a hallmark of what some people called a "stodgy old company." He wanted to try some new activities among the thirty or so senior officers who would assemble in Vermont in order to spur them toward new and better planning. He wasn't sure how to go about it.

What actions would you take if you were Bruce?

EXERCISE | **Making a Presentation**
Anne Sachs had been asked to give a speech on creativity in business. She knew the topic well, having taught several courses in it, but she was concerned that the speech itself be creative. She didn't want to just talk about creativity; she wanted to be creative.

How would you make such a speech creative? Your audience will be managers and staff from a cross-section of firms in various industries.

REFERENCES

1. See, for example, Roger von Oech, "How to Get Great Ideas," *Success*, November 1983, pp. 29–32, 59–60; Berkeley Rice, "Imagination to Go," *Psychology Today*, May 1984, pp. 48–56; R. Thomas Powers, "Tomorrow's Jobs Will Go to Creative Thinkers," *Florida Trend*, June 1984, pp. 51–53; Isaac Asimov, "Work in the 21st Century," *Personnel Administrator*, November 1983, pp. 42–46; *Creativity Development at the Center for Creative Leadership* (Greensboro, N.C., 1983); "Every Employee an Entrepreneur: An Interview with Allan Kennedy," *Inc.*, April 1984, pp. 108–17; Robert L. Lattimer and Marvin L. Winitsky, "Unleashing Creativity," *Management World*, April/May 1984, pp. 22–24; Walter Kiechel III, "Getting Creative," *Fortune*, July 25, 1983, pp. 109–14; David R. Wheeler, "Creative Decision Making and the Organization," *Personnel Journal*, June 1979, pp. 374–75, 379; Steve Lohr, "Overhauling America's Business Management," *New York Times*, January 4, 1981; "Productivity," special issue of *Business Week*, June 30, 1980; John Naisbitt, *Megatrends* (New York: Warner, 1982), chaps. 1, 2, 7; and Thomas J. Peters and Robert H. Waterman, Jr., *In Search of Excellence* (New York: Harper & Row, 1982), chaps. 1, 2, 4–7.

2. See n. 1.

3. Carl E. Gregory, *The Management of Intelligence* (New York: McGraw-Hill, 1967), pp. 3–5.

4. Alvin Toffler, *Future Shock* (New York: Bantam, 1970), pp. 7–48.

5. Robert H. Hayes and William J. Abernathy, "Managing Our Way to Economic Decline," *Harvard Business Review*, July–August 1980, pp. 67–77.

6. Michael A. Guillen, "The Intuitive Edge," *Psychology Today*, August 1984, pp. 68, 69.

7. Daniel J. Isenberg, "How Senior Managers Think," *Harvard Business Review*, November–December 1984, pp. 81–90.

8. Dina Ingher, "Inside the Executive Mind," *Success*, pp. 33–37.

9. Person, process, product, and conditions are believed to have been first identified as critical components of creativity by E. Paul Torrance in

"Scientific Views of Creativity and Factors Affecting Its Growth," *Daedalus: Journal of the Academy of Arts and Sciences*, 1965, p. 664. I have changed *conditions* to *possibilities* in order to strengthen the memory hook, that is, to make it four *P*'s rather than three *P*'s and a *C*.

10. Several writers have pointed to these factors. See, for example, Albert Rothenberg and Carl R. Hausman, eds., *The Creativity Question* (Durham, N.C.: Duke University Press, 1976); D. N. Perkins, *The Mind's Best Work* (Cambridge: Harvard University Press, 1981), p. 257; Carol Johnman, "Sex and the Split Brain," *Omni*, 1983 or 1984, pp. 26, 113; "What Makes Creative People Different?" *Psychology Today*, July 1975, pp. 46–49.

11. J. P. Guilford, *The Nature of Human Intelligence* (New York: McGraw-Hill, 1967), pp. 25, 60–64, 169–70; Donald W. MacKinnon, "The Nature and Nurture of Creative Talent," in *Readings in Managerial Psychology*, ed. Harold J. Leavitt and Louis R. Pondy (Chicago: University of Chicago Press, 1964), p. 96; Perkins, *Mind's Best Work*, p. 253; Donald W. MacKinnon, "Characteristics of the Creative Person," *Current Issues in Higher Education*, 1961, pp. 92–98; J. W. Getzels and P. W. Jackson, *Creativity and Intelligence* (New York: Wiley, 1962), p. 37.

12. MacKinnon, "Nature and Nurture," p. 96.

13. Recent evidence suggests, however, that the functions of the right brain may not be so totally divorced from those of the left brain as they have been thought to be. We now have evidence that each hemisphere performs some of the functions formerly believed to be the domain of the other. See "How the Brain Works," *Newsweek*, February 7, 1983, pp. 40–46; David Stipp, "Mysteries of the Brain Slowly Yield to Science, and Medicine Benefits," *Wall Street Journal*, December 19, 1983, pp. 1, 15.

14. Johnman, "Sex and the Split Brain," pp. 26, 113.

15. Ibid., p. 26; Alice Sargent, *The Androgynous Manager* (New York: Amacom, 1983).

16. Johnman, "Sex and the Split Brain," p. 26.

17. Alex F. Osborn, *Applied Imagination*, 3d ed. (New York: Scribner, 1963), pp. 18, 22; Johnman, "Sex and the Split Brain"; Sargeant, *Androgynous Manager*.

18. MacKinnon, "Nature and Nurture," p. 96.

19. Osborn, *Applied Imagination*, p. 22.

20. Richard M. Guinn, "Psychology for Olympic Champs," *Psychology Today*, July 1976, pp. 38–42.

21. Graham Wallas, "Stages of Control," in *The Art of Thought* (New York: Harcourt Brace Jovanovich, 1954), reprinted in *The Creativity Question*, ed. Albert Rothenberg and Carl R. Hausman (Durham, N.C.: Duke University Press, 1976), pp. 69–73.

22. Gregory, *Management of Intelligence* (New York: McGraw-Hill, 1967), chap. 10.

23. Ibid., pp. 10–11, 19–20, chaps. 9 and 10.

24. Ibid.

25. As told to the author by a tourguide while on a tour of the Edison home in Fort Myers, Florida.

26. Gary A. Davis, "In Furious Pursuit of the Creative Person," in *Assessing Creative Growth: Measured Changes*, bk. 2, eds. Angelo M. Bondi and Sidney J. Parnes (Great Neck, N.Y.: Creative Synergetics, 1976), pp. 243–57.

27. Gregory, *Managing Intelligence*, chap. 17.

28. Abraham H. Maslow, "Creativity in Self-Actualizing People," in *Toward a Psychology of Being*, 2d ed. (New York: Van Nostrand Reinhold, 1968), p. 135.

29. Osborn, *Applied Imagination*, pp. 300–301.

30. Ibid., pp. 302–306.

31. William J. J. Gordon, *Synectics: The Development of Creative Capacity* (New York: Macmillan, 1961), p. 8.

32. Morris Stein, *Stimulating Creativity*, vol. 2 (New York: Academic Press, 1975), p. 27.

33. Gordon, *Synectics*, p. 18.

34. Stein, *Stimulating Creativity*, pp. 186–91.

35. Gordon, *Synectics*, pp. 58–70.

36. Jacquelyn Wonder and Priscilla Donovan, *Whole Brain Thinking* (New York: Ballantine Books), 1984; Philip Goldberg, *The Intuitive Edge* (Los Angeles: Jeremy P. Tarcher, 1983).

16 MANAGING STRESS AND TIME

LEARNING OBJECTIVES

When you have completed this chapter, you should be able to:
1. Explain the stress reaction process.
2. Identify stress, its causes, and its impacts.
3. Determine whether stress results from stressors or from an individual's personality.
4. Describe how individuals and organizations can manage stress.
5. Explain the causes of poor time management.
6. Manage your time better.

ONE MORE DROP OF WATER

John Christian was studying for a master's degree at a large, well-known graduate school of business. He had never really tried very hard at academics before, and had been admitted to this prestigious school almost totally on the basis of the potential indicated by his test scores and his recent work record. It had been four years since he had been in school and he was determined to do well this time. He worked very hard. He became

engrossed in his studies, but he also pursued his hobbies, and he fell in love with a young woman. When he ran short of funds, he became a graduate teaching assistant. His day began at 7:00 A.M. and ended at midnight. One day as he stood in the shower, his head began to throb. He began to panic. Thousands of droplets of water were spraying him. And, as he told his counselor, "I felt like if one more drop of water hit me, I'd go crazy."

Have you ever had an experience like that of John Christian? If you have not, you may soon. The college years are stressful for most students. The number of new experiences and the importance of these experiences can become almost overwhelming. Business, too, has its stressors, and while executive and managerial stress receive considerably more attention, the stressors with which first-line and staff employees are confronted are also substantial. Homemakers are also subject to numerous stressors. Virtually everyone is subject to stressors, and hence most of us suffer to some degree from the effects of stress.

Stress management is vital not only to success but to health and happiness. Michael Matteson and John Ivancevich report that from 60 to 80 percent of all doctors' patients have stress-related health problems.[1] The symptoms are real, and the person actually is ill. But these are problems that would not exist if the individual were not attempting subconsciously to relieve a psychological problem—stress.

Solving the problems created by stress is vital to the organization because stress robs the organization of its employees' services in their prime performance years. Ulcers, heart attacks, and cancer, as well as less serious health problems such as colds and flu, have been attributed to stress and one of its more acute forms, burnout; or perhaps more accurately, to the individual's

Complete freedom from stress is death.
HANS SELYE

393

inability to cope with stressors. Many tragedies could be prevented if stress were managed.

Each of us needs to learn how to avoid stress when we can and how to cope with it when we can't avoid it. Stressors affect some people more than others. Some people are more vulnerable to stress than others. But every individual is exposed to many stressors and so will have some stress. Every individual needs to learn how to manage his or her stress. This chapter discusses stress, its causes, some of its effects, and some ways to relieve it. Burnout is also examined. The chapter concludes with a brief discussion of a critical element in overcoming stress: time management. The relationships examined are organization-to-individual interactions (the organizational causes of stress and what the organization can do to help the individual manage stress) and individual-to-self interactions (the personal causes of stress and what the individual can do to manage it).

WHAT IS STRESS?

Stress is a physical and psychological condition resulting from attempts to adapt to one's environment. Our perception of our ability to cope with perceived stressors is more important than the reality of either our ability to cope or the stressors. Stress affects the total human being. Stress is a function partly of personality and partly of stressors in the environment. Generally, the more changes we undergo in our lives, the more likely we are to suffer stress, and the more likely we are to have poor health. Stress results when we feel we cannot adequately cope with external stressors. Figure 16.1 shows the major variables involved in stress.

FIGURE 16.1   *The causes and results of stress*

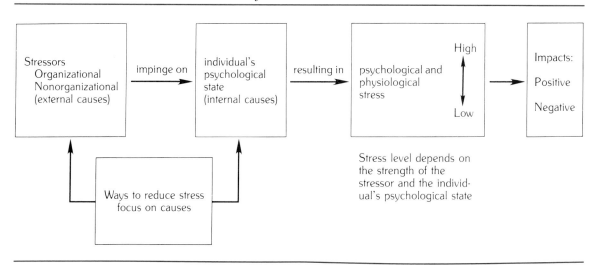

From *The Wall Street Journal*—Permission, Cartoon Features Syndicate.

Stress is a normal part of life. Since we cannot live without it, we must learn to live with it. Hans Selye, a leading authority on stress, has said:

> No one can live without experiencing some degree of stress all the time . . . crossing a busy intersection, exposure to a draft, or even sheer joy are enough to activate the body's stress-mechanism. . . . The secret of health and happiness lies in the successful adjustment to the ever-changing conditions on this globe; the penalties for failure in this great process of adaptation are disease and unhappiness.[2]

> *I am an old man, and have known a great many troubles, but most of them never happened.*
>
> MARK TWAIN

THE GENERAL ADAPTATION SYNDROME

The **general adaptation syndrome (GAS)**, first described by Hans Selye, encompasses the reactions of the body to external stressors.[3] There are three stages in this adaptation process: (1) the alarm reaction, (2) resistance, and (3) exhaustion. We must understand what happens during these stages if we are to learn how to manage stress.

During the **alarm reaction** the body prepares for fight or flight, our primitive ancestors' responses to threats. Our own responses are similar, although the fight may be more verbal than physical. During this stage, several physiological events occur. The hypothalamus, in the center of the brain, assumes control of the body and mind. It stimulates the autonomic nervous system and the pituitary glands. Hormones are released from the endocrine gland. The heart beats more quickly and more strongly in order to increase the supply of energy to the body. Blood pressure rises, causing the blood vessels to dilate and the flow of blood to the muscles to increase. Breathing becomes more rapid and deep, increasing the supply of oxygen to the body. Blood vessels near the surface of the skin dilate and in combination with perspiration cool the body, which is tensed for action. And finally, digestion and certain other body functions slow down in order not to divert energy from muscles that will be needed in fight or flight.

If the perceived stressor continues, the body enters the **resistance** stage. The body is in a heightened state of activity but the alarm reaction dissipates. If the perceived stressor still remains, the body continues in a heightened state of vigilance and readiness until it collapses in **exhaustion**. The price paid for combating a perceived stressor over a long period of time is usually poor health, both physical and mental. If the stressor is perceived to go away, then the body returns to normal functioning.

WHAT CAUSES STRESS?

Stress is caused by a combination of environmental and psychological factors. When we perceive that we cannot cope with these stressors as well as we would like, the physical/mental condition known as stress results. Each person reacts differently to each particular stressor. Each person has his or her own level of tolerance to stressors. Even if there were no external stressors, it is likely that many individuals would still suffer from stress because they would create their own stressors. They would imagine them. There are usually several causes of stress for any one individual at any point in time.

INTERNAL FACTORS

The major **internal causes of stress** include self-image (self-image has a direct impact on virtually every facet of human relations we have examined), personality type with respect to nonspecific fears, ability to adapt to the environment (to cope with change), motivation and success orientation, and the "hot reactor" personality.

Self-Image   People who have not coped successfully with life, who do not have an "I'm OK" attitude, are believed to be particularly vulnerable to stressors. The "I'm not OK" person lacks the self-confidence to meet challenges head on. Studies suggest that the pawn,[4] the vulnerable child,[5] the "not-OK" person,[6] and the person lacking in self-esteem[7] seem to share this susceptibility to stress. Do you feel that you are OK? What impact does your answer have on your ability to cope with stress?

Nonspecific Fears   Many people who lack self-esteem tend to function in a self-destructive manner. They continually worry about and exaggerate their problems, their situation, their disabilities, and their enemies' strengths, beyond reason. Most such people are remembering strong learned experiences and using them as reference points. Like many personality traits, this tendency toward exaggeration and worry seems to be passed from generation to generation. Such people naturally submit to stressors because they are not able to sort reality from their exaggerations. They do not function as rationally as they should, and react rather than reason. Similar stress problems result for people who suffer from fear of failure, fear of low performance, and fear of success. The emotional state is dominant in such people, but in many cases it is observed examples that cause them to react so emotionally.

Adaptability   Some people have learned to cope with change. Others have not. Since change is definitely related to stress and since change is a part of life, people must learn to adapt, to manage their experiences with change. Apparently, like much of personality development, this particular trait is a function of past opportunities, past successes, and past rewards. Adaptability to change is both a cause and a function of self-image.

Motivation Level and Success Orientation   The cardiologists Meyer A. Friedman and Ray H. Rosenman have identified two major personality types, one prone to heart disease, the other less so. According to their findings, the Type A personality is highly subject to coronary artery and heart disease, while the other type of personality, Type B, is much less so. The Type A personality is best described as one who is always in a hurry. The Type A strives to accomplish too much, too soon, too often. The Type A is usually aggressive, ambitious, restless, and a workaholic. These are characteristics generally admired in the business world. The Type B personality is the opposite of Type A. Type B's take their time, they realize their limitations, they relax.[8] Are you a Type A personality? Test yourself and find out.

The Hot Reactor Personality   More recently the research of cardiovascular surgeon Robert S. Eliot has uncovered a personality type that does not handle stress well, and consequently is subject to a high rate of cardiovascular failure. Dr. Eliot, himself a heart attack victim, observed that many Type B individuals

THE WALL STREET JOURNAL

"I'm trying to learn to delegate stress."

From *The Wall Street Journal*—Permission, Cartoon Features Syndicate.

suffered heart attacks and pulmonary artery disease, just as though they were Type A's. Through exhaustive research and clinical efforts, the "hot reactor" was discovered. A hot reactor is a person who exhibits "extreme cardiovascular reactions to standardized stress tests."[9] Hot reactors exhibit strong biological (though not always behavioral) reactions to virtually any external stressor. Their bodies are continually pounded by chemicals released in response to stress and by elevated blood pressure. These reactions, especially when combined with other elements in the bloodstream detrimental to health (such as cholesterol), weaken the walls of the heart and arteries. Thus only that last straw is needed to break the camel's back, or more to the point, cause that heart attack. A hot reactor's blood pressure will increase twofold in just a few minutes after exposure to continuous stressors. Hot reactors are twice as likely to be Type A's as Type B's.

Interestingly, Dr. Eliot has discovered a very cheap, valid, and reliable method for finding out if you are a hot reactor. Go to a shopping mall that has a blood pressure tester and some video games. Take your blood pressure at rest. Now play a highly competitive video game for five minutes, singly or against someone. Now take your blood pressure again. If you are a hot reactor, it will have risen sharply.[10]

TEST YOURSELF

THE TYPE A PERSONALITY

Check off each item in the list below that describes you most or much of the time.

1. You explosively accentuate key words in normal conversation.
2. You utter the last few words of your conversation very rapidly.
3. You always move, walk, and eat rapidly.
4. You are extremely impatient, especially with slow talkers (you may finish their sentences for them) or when someone pulls in front of you on the highway or when you have to wait in line.
5. You read summaries, not articles. You read only for business, not for pleasure.
6. You tend to do or *think* of more than one thing at a time.
7. You continually move conversation to subjects that interest you.
8. You feel somewhat guilty when you relax.
9. You tend to ignore your surroundings and things of beauty.
10. You are preoccupied with having rather than doing.
11. You often challenge other Type A's quite aggressively.
12. You have nervous habits, such as finger tapping, clenching your fist, banging your hand on the table, rapidly blinking your eyes.
13. You get things done faster and faster. You crowd more and more into your day.
14. You evaluate life strictly in terms of numbers—salary, number of clients met, number of pages read, etc.
15. You always play to win, even with children.

Scoring: The more of these items you checked, the more likely you are a Type A.

EXTERNAL FACTORS

The *external causes of stress* are known as **stressors**. (*External* here refers to external to the mind.) A stressor is primarily some form of blockage to individual need satisfaction. What is a stressor to one person may not be one to another. External factors may be classified according to three major types: those that are related to the work organization; those that are not, such as family, friends, hobbies, physical condition, and diet; and change.

Work-Related Factors   Among the **work-related causes of stress** are management and leadership style, organization climate and structure, organization and work demands, boredom or tedium, job pressures, game playing, continual crisis management, conflicts between one's role and one's values or between various roles one must play, decision control, changes created by technology, and other factors that interfere with the satisfaction of needs.

One of the major causes of internal conflict for the individual employee, and hence a major cause of stress, is incongruence between the treatment she wants and needs and the treatment she seems to be getting from the manager. Far too often the management style found in today's organizations is based on personal experience and observation rather than on sound management principles. There are far too many negative, authoritarian managers in all types of organizations today. Far too few managers attempt to build or maintain the self-images of their subordinates. The result is stress, because the employee must attempt to cope with an image-damaging situation. How is your relationship with your manager? How does it affect your stress level?

As we saw in Chapter 13, the perceived actions of management result in the organization's climate. The portion of the organization's structure that specifies the distribution of authority has a great effect on whether or not the organization will be supportive of employees' self-images. If the overall structure is not supportive, then individual leadership is not likely to be supportive either. What is the climate in your organization?

Increased demands for profits coupled with the changing nature of the worker (and the values of society) provide managers with stress. As the economy matures and as inflation increases, the push for profits intensifies. In any organization today, the values held by subordinates often differ from those held by managers. The result is stress, often for manager and subordinate alike. Hospitals, for example, are currently undergoing tremendous budget crunching and reorganization. The stressors are tremendous.

Think of a recent job you have held. Was it boring or tedious? Did you suffer stress as a result? Most people do. Boredom makes homemaking one of the most stressful of occupations. The effect of boredom and tedium on self-image contributes substantially to this stress.

Now think of a job you have had in which the pressures were great, where the demands made on you were almost inhuman. Did you have stress then? Or worse yet, does this describe your job now? The pressures on people in certain occupations are tremendous. And in any occupation the high achiever (Type A) will be involved in more stressful relations than the low achiever (Type B). Job pressures are felt in such organizational procedures as those governing communication, discipline, performance appraisal, and decision making, and in perceived bureaucratic red tape.

The deceitful communications that constitute psychological games can only add to stress. Organizations whose climates foster such games are bound to be less productive than they might otherwise be.

Is there always a crisis in your organization? Does your organization react, overreact, or plan ahead? Are you and others in your organization always putting out fires? If so, then you know one sure cause of stress.

Have you ever been placed in a position in which what your employer wanted you to do conflicted with your system of values? It happens every day to thousands of employees. Some such situations involve serious problems of ethics or morals. Most involve less potentially serious problems, such as the treatment of customers or subordinates. People who have a store of learned reactions related to proper conduct or have developed a strong code of ethical values are vulnerable to stress when they are required to violate those values. A great potential for stress exists if one of a person's roles conflicts with another. Conflicts may occur, for example, between one's roles in a bowling league and in one's family, between the roles of teacher and friend, between political and religious roles. Has the boss ever asked you to work late when your spouse had other plans? Talk about stress!

All of these external factors have involved situations that leave needs unsatisfied. Virtually every other work situation that prevents us from satisfying our needs or that involves change contains stressors and hence may lead to stress. Can you think of some additional such situations? Put yourself in the place of the workers on the ill-fated *Challenger* space shuttle, described in the Human Relations Happening on page 401.

Figure 16.2 indicates occupations that appear to be associated with great

FIGURE 16.2 *Stress at work*

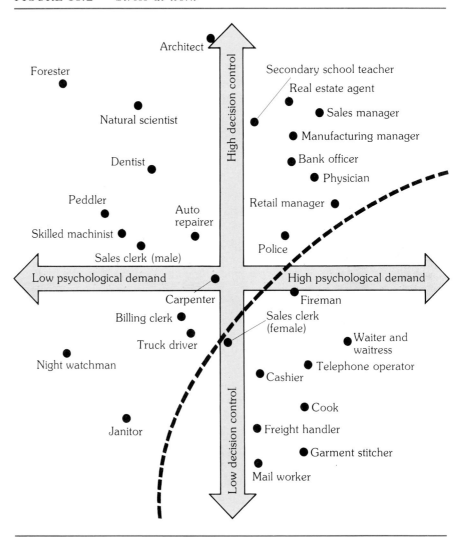

Jobs to the right of the dashed line are associated with increased incidence of heart disease.

SOURCE: Bryce Nelson, "Bosses Face Less Risk than Bossed," *New York Times*, April 3, 1983, section 4. Copyright © 1983 by The New York Times Company. Reprinted by permission.

HUMAN RELATIONS HAPPENING

GUILT, ANXIETY, AND FEAR OVER THE SPACE SHUTTLE DISASTER

When the space shuttle *Challenger* was destroyed in 1986 by the malfunctioning of the protective O rings in one of the rocket boosters, the nation was stunned. It was a national tragedy. It was also a very personal tragedy to those who worked directly on the project. In the days and months after the explosion, thousands of people were afraid that they had in some way contributed to the accident. They felt guilt even though all but a few were never actually guilty of any mistakes. They feared that they had somehow not done enough to prevent the accident, or that what they had done might result in tragedy to themselves—they might lose their jobs.

One Lockheed engineer was so upset by the fate of the shuttle and its seven-person crew that he drew a big black X over the picture of the shuttle that he had always proudly displayed in his office. One of the managers for Morton Thiokol, the firm that made the *Challenger*'s rocket boosters, says, "I'll never feel quite the same again." He describes a knot in his stomach that he can't seem to get rid of. "There'll always be the specter of this flight hanging over this operation." Employees of Rockwell International, who built the *Challenger*, angrily blame subcontractors as they discuss the incident at a bar in Downey, California.

Psychiatrist Peter Brill observes, "For people who are meticulous and very concerned about the quality of their work, having a failure like this . . . is a major psychological insult." One consequence has been that many have sought professional counseling to help them overcome their problems. Several of the organizations involved set up hot lines or counseling services to help their employees get through the crisis.

In addition to the immediate effects on the families of the shuttle's crew and the people who will eventually be found responsible for incorrect decisions in regard to the design, construction, and launching of the shuttle, the explosion resulted in the loss of many jobs, as the project was put on hold until an investigation could be completed and the faults corrected. The loss of a job is cause for severe anxiety.

But for those who continued to work on the shuttle project, this comment by the Morton Thiokol manager cited earlier sums up the situation well: "For most people, time will go on, and other crises will occur, and this will be forgotten. But for me and my people, every time we come to work, we produce more of the same vehicle that will someday again send astronauts into space. We can't help thinking about it."

SOURCE: Adapted from Francine Schwadel, Matt Moffett, Roy Harris Jr., and Roger Lowenstein, "Thousands Who Work on Shuttle Now Feel Guilt, Anxiety, and Fear," *The Wall Street Journal*, February 6, 1986, p. 27.

and little amounts of potential stress based on levels of psychological demand and perceived decision control—control over decisions on the job. Psychological demand results from the numerous factors discussed previously. Decision control apparently has a great effect on whether or not these psychological demands will result in heart disease. Jobs that have high psychological demand and low decision control lead to increased incidence of heart disease, according to research led by Robert A. Karasek.[11] This type of problem has been identified as part of **technostress**—"the feeling, often physical, of being overwhelmed and immobilized as computers transform the basic organization of work."[12] Technology induces stress by changing job designs.

Non-Work-Related Factors   Among the **non-work-related causes of stress** are family, friends, recreational activities, personal finances, the economy, lack of spiritual support, physical condition and diet, and the physical environment.

The family is one of the greatest sources of stress for all of its members. Any time that people must live together, sharing problems and good times alike, there will be stress. Close quarters have always made for stress, "getting on each other's nerves." Children, especially teenagers, suffer more from stress than any other age group. Children are expected to accomplish much, and the pressures for grades and social success are great. Parents, too, suffer from their family roles. They must cope with the changes through which their children go, and they must cope with the changes in each other.[13] In addition, the roles assigned to various family members place heavy demands on them. They are expected to provide a comfortable home and to provide for the family's needs, to be interesting companions, great lovers, and perfect parents. Two-career families and single parents are subjected to considerable stress as they juggle the responsibilities of both job and child care. How much stress is there in your family? Why?

Friendship, too, often causes stress. Just ask yourself about some of your own friendships. What types of stress have you had in your friendships?

Hobbies, sports, competition of any kind, vacations (vacations mean change and all change is stressful), mowing the yard, and so forth, cause stress.

Have you ever been hungry? Have you ever missed a payment on your car, the rent, your TV, stereo, credit cards? Have you ever overextended your credit—has it been difficult to "make ends meet"? These are very stressful situations for most people. Financial difficulties probably figure in the dissolution of more marriages than any other single cause. Unemployment, changing work situations, lack of high-paying skills, loss of promotion, and sickness can all contribute to stress.

Man has a limited biological capacity for change. When this capacity is overwhelmed, the capacity is in future shock.

ALVIN TOFFLER

People jumped out of windows in 1929 because of the collapse of the economy. Dramatic effects of the economy can still be seen today, most notably among farmers who borrowed operating capital when interest rates were high, then were unable to repay the loans when farm prices sagged. One admittedly speculative study by M. Harvey Brenner attributes increases in suicides, admissions to mental hospitals, and deaths from alcoholism and heart disease to the 1970 recession and the stress of unemployment during that period.[14] Thomas Petzinger, Jr., reports that most therapists agree that inflation leads to mental health problems.[15] Money motivates most people and we all need money to satisfy all kinds of needs. Concern about satisfying the very lowest level of needs—food, clothing, and shelter—will result in stress in most people. When the economy is down, a society's stress level increases greatly.

Have you ever been unemployed when you would have preferred to be working? How did you feel? Brenner has concluded that a 1 percent rise in unemployment would result in an extra 37,000 total deaths over a six-year period. Twenty thousand of these deaths would result from cardiovascular diseases, 920 from suicide, 648 from homicide. He estimates that first admissions to mental hospitals would increase by 4,200 and admissions to state prisons would increase by 3,300. The costs of economically induced stress are high.[16]

Many authorities point to the lack of spiritual support in Western civilization as one cause of stress. In the past, religion provided a port in the storm. As religious faith has declined, the number of people who seek relief from stress through religion has also declined. (Religion can also cause stress, however, especially when it is very rigid.)

The relationship between stress and physical condition is complex. Physical condition can be both a partial cause and a result of stress. When our physical condition and diet prevent us from meeting the demands placed on our bodies by all three stages of the GAS, our bodies are unable to react to stressors properly. People who are in poor health might do well to consider how stress could be reduced.

The body must be ready for fight or flight, and if it is not, the consequences may be serious. Conversely, prolonged stress weakens the body. Such stress may be fatal. Daily exercise accompanied by proper diet is essential if we are to be prepared for the GAS and maintain a positive self-image. Have you ever had a cold, a bad back, a heart condition? What stress resulted?

An unpleasant physical environment, such as extreme heat or cold, usually leads to stress. Overcrowded cities, the fast pace of urban life, and traffic congestion also contribute greatly to stress.

Change   Interacting with all of the previously mentioned factors is change, primarily external change, but change within the individual as well. Alvin Toffler describes in *Future Shock* the changing world in which we live.[17] As Toffler predicted, future shock is more of a reality today than it was when his book was written in 1970. The rate of change increases every day. If you cannot cope with these changes, you are going to have stress.

One series of studies involving a large sample of people has revealed quite clearly the **impact of change on health**. As the result of these and other studies, Thomas H. Holmes and Richard H. Rahe have developed a test that you can take to determine whether or not you may expect to encounter illness within the next year. This test is reproduced in the next Test Yourself. This self-administered test is a simple checklist of major life events. Points are assigned to each of these events. You simply skim the page, checking those major life events that you have had within the past six months. You then total the points associated with all of these events and compare your scores to ranges of scores with which certain probabilities of illness have been correlated. Another test is presented on page 405. This test provides a ready checklist of symptoms or signs of stress. If you check three or more boxes in this test, you may be under stress. You can look for some of the causes in the test on stressful life events.

STRESSFUL LIFE EVENTS

Life Event	Value	Your Score	Life Event	Value	Your Score
1. Death of spouse	100	____	24. Trouble with in-laws	29	____
2. Divorce	73	____	25. Outstanding personal achievement	28	____
3. Marital separation	65	____	26. Spouse begins or stops work	26	____
4. Jail term	63	____	27. Starting or finishing school	26	____
5. Death of close family member	63	____	28. Change in living conditions	25	____
6. Personal injury or illness	53	____	29. Revision of personal habits	24	____
7. Marriage	50	____	30. Trouble with boss	23	____
8. Fired at work	47	____	31. Change in work hours, conditions	20	____
9. Marital reconciliation	45	____	32. Change in residence	20	____
10. Retirement	45	____	33. Change in schools	20	____
11. Change in family member's health	44	____	34. Change in recreation	19	____
12. Pregnancy	40	____	35. Change in church activities	19	____
13. Sex difficulties	39	____	36. Change in social activities	18	____
14. Addition to family	39	____	37. Mortgage or loan under $10,000*	17	____
15. Business readjustment	39	____	38. Change in sleeping habits	16	____
16. Change in financial state	38	____	39. Change in number of family get-togethers	15	____
17. Death of close friend	37	____	40. Change in eating habits	15	____
18. Change to different line of work	36	____	41. Vacation	13	____
19. Change in number of arguments with spouse	35	____	42. Christmas	12	____
20. Mortgage over $10,000*	31	____	43. Minor violation of law	11	____
21. Foreclosure of mortgage or loan	30	____		Total	____
22. Change in work responsibilities	29	____			
23. Son or daughter leaving home	29	____			

What It Means

Check each event which occurred to you in the last year. Then total your scores for all events. A total of 0–150 indicates a 37% likelihood of developing an illness in the next two years. A score of 150–300 indicates a 51% probability of illness. A score over 300 and you are running an 80% chance of developing an illness in the next two years. These are major illnesses and include cancer, heart attacks, and psychosis.

*I suggest you substitute $50,000 for $10,000 in order to bring these figures up to more current amounts.

SOURCE: Thomas H. Holmes and Richard H. Rahe, "The Social Readjustment Rating Scale," *Journal of Psychosomatic Research* 11:213–218. Reprinted with permission from Pergamon Press, Ltd., copyright 1967.

THE IMPACTS OF STRESS

The tone of this chapter to this point may have suggested to you that the results of stress are always negative. And while the preponderance of **impacts of stress** are negative, there are some positive impacts as well, both for the individual and for the organization, especially when stress has been managed.

Most authorities on stress, most managers, and most people in general would agree that a limited amount of stress increases productivity. It is when too much stress occurs, when the resistance and exhaustion stages are reached, that stress becomes most detrimental (although, as noted earlier, if the individual encounters a major life change, stress can be fatal). A study by Bruce M. Meglino reveals that these beliefs regarding the relationship between stress and productivity are true. Up to some point, job stress increased job performance, but as stress continued to increase above that point, performance decreased[18] (see Figure 16.3). Off the job, the effects of a limited amount of stress may also be expected to increase performance to some point. If you have ever engaged in athletic competition, you know that many coaches use fear to motivate their players. Fear usually causes stress, and fear often motivates. In that sense, stress has caused performance.

POSITIVE IMPACTS OF STRESS

"New proponents of stress believe that a measure of it gives some executives the energy to be the achievers they must be. It makes them 'Adrenalin Freaks.'"
BUSINESS WEEK

TEST YOURSELF

SYMPTOMS AND SIGNS OF STRESS

Check each box that applies to you.

- ☐ Use of alcohol increasing
- ☐ Taking tranquilizers
- ☐ Elevated blood pressure
- ☐ Headaches
- ☐ Back pain
- ☐ Hot and cold spells
- ☐ Insomnia
- ☐ Chest pains
- ☐ Palpitations
- ☐ Choking sensations
- ☐ Using more antacids
- ☐ Waking up at night
- ☐ Fatigue

- ☐ Loss of appetite
- ☐ Too much/too little sleep
- ☐ Sense of dread
- ☐ Short-tempered
- ☐ Withdrawal
- ☐ More missed workdays
- ☐ Feeling of plunging from crisis to crisis
- ☐ Feeling you are overwhelmed with work
- ☐ Accident prone
- ☐ Loss of confidence
- ☐ Boredom
- ☐ Mistrust of associates

What It Means
If you checked three or more boxes, it's likely that stress is causing turmoil in your daily life.

SOURCE: Reprinted by permission of *Sales & Marketing Management* Magazine. Copyright © June 18, 1979, p. 59.

FIGURE 16.3   *Relationship between job stress and job performance*

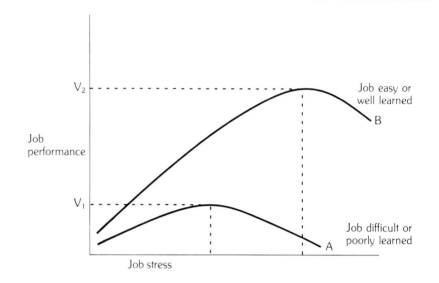

The determination of the point at which stress does not cause increased productivity is not an exact science. This point varies with personality, the stressors, and the situation.

NEGATIVE IMPACTS OF STRESS

The negative impacts of stress occur in two primary areas for the individual: physical and psychological consequences; and in one primary area for the organization: lowered profits.

Individual Physical Consequences   There is no longer any doubt as to whether or not stress causes physical illness. The question now is exactly how. There are two integral variables in the stress/health process: stressors and personality. There is thus a relationship between the physical and the psychological consequences of stress. The common belief is that for people who are psychologically susceptible, moderate stress will lead to physical consequences; and that for virtually everyone, prolonged stress will have some physical consequences. The most obvious consequence is physical exhaustion, but little doubt exists that ulcers, heart disease, coronary artery disease, cancer, asthma, bronchitis, diabetes, degenerative diseases of the vital organs, eyeball hemorrhages, and such minor problems as dizziness, susceptibility to colds, headaches, and numerous sexual difficulties are commonly caused by stress.[19] The evidence clearly indicates that stress must be managed if individual health tragedies are to be avoided. One result of stress is that some of the means used to cope with it contribute heavily to negative physical effects. Drugs including alcohol, smoking of tobacco, smoking of marijuana, overdoses of prescribed relaxers (downers), even eating too much or too little can lead to serious, even fatal health problems. Who do you know that is under considerable stress? How is their health? What about yourself—are you under considerable stress? How is your health? How do you cope?

Individual Psychological Consequences   Psychosomatic disorders abound. As noted earlier, 60 to 80 percent of the average doctor's practice is devoted to curing illnesses with a psychological component. Roy W. Menninger believes that most of these problems are attributable to "problems of living."[20] Many people who are subjected to prolonged stress enter into a state of depression from which they cannot move. The constant battering of stress can cause the person's self-image to plummet dramatically. No one emerges from prolonged stress altogether unscathed.

Another consequence might best be described as rigidity of behavior. The individual under prolonged stress often reacts in ways that, while not rational, are patterns that the individual feels comfortable with, patterns that do not require thinking, that do not add immediately to the level of stress (but do in the long run). Among such rigid behavior patterns are the yes-man syndrome, antagonism, uncooperativeness, and constant worrying. The person under constant and considerable stress may appear angry, thoughtless, inconsiderate, absentminded, unable to concentrate, defensive, anxious, inadequate, compulsive, obsessed, and irritable. Sometimes the consequences are even worse, as the Human Relations Happening on college students suggests.

HUMAN RELATIONS HAPPENING

STUDENT SHOCK

Stress poses many problems for college students, and the level of stressors that students are exposed to seems to be greater today than at any time previously. Bulimia (a pattern of food binges followed by self-induced vomiting), suicides, and depression all seem to be on the rise among college students. Rates of drug use are also quite high. Less dramatic results include the switching of majors and of schools. Students seem to be taking longer to finish school today than they did a few years ago, and counselors are booked solid on some campuses, often for a month in advance. One clinical psychologist, Mary Ann Rust, notes,

"The pressures of growing up have increased enormously, and neither students nor parents fully realize it." She has labeled the phenomenon "student shock."

College students are often faced by a bewildering array of course choices, by job prospects that fail to meet their expectations, and by weakening family support. Such traditional problems as the maturation process, dating, and social relationships are made more complex by these stressors. Parents and society in general often expect too much of the maturing college student, and they expect it too soon.

SOURCE: Adapted from Earl C. Gottschalk, Jr., "Student Shock: Stress Is More Severe for Collegians Today; Counselors Keep Busy," *Wall Street Journal*, June 1, 1983, pp. 1, 22.

Organizational Consequences   A major consequence of stress to the organization is reduced profits, caused by reduced productivity and the costs of paying for the consequences of individual stress. The estimates of the annual costs of stress to business firms in the United States (not including the large number of nonprofit organizations) range from $17 billion to $75 billion.[21] The variations in such estimates reveal that the problem is not yet well appreciated or its consequences well understood. But even the lower figure is so large that efforts must be made to manage stress.

Another major concern of organizations is their increasing legal liability for the stressful effects of various employment situations. Courts have increasingly ruled in favor of plaintiffs (often surviving spouses) when job-related stress has been the subject of lawsuits. Companies are especially vulnerable when the stress has been of concern to the employee for an extended period and can be documented. Companies now need to take preventive actions to lessen stress and encourage stress management.[22]

STRESS MANAGEMENT

Many techniques for **stress management** are available to both the individual and the organization. When the organization fails to initiate stress-reduction efforts that it alone can make, employees may simply have to do the best they can to relieve their own stress. One of the most important actions is identifying stressors and their causes. One consulting group suggests listing symptoms and causes, with their frequency, intensity, and duration. Then you can arrange them in order of importance and work on your worst situations first, identifying coping skills for each major cause and problem.[23]

ORGANIZATIONAL PROGRAMS FOR REDUCING STRESS

In the past, most corporate stress-management programs focused on reducing stressors. This approach is still viable. Today, however, most corporate programs center on means of coping with the stressors encountered, as well as on attempts to eliminate some of them. Such organizations as IBM, Xerox, Chase Manhattan, and Connecticut General have programs designed to help employees cope with stress. Most such programs are voluntary. It is one thing to teach people how to meditate; it is another to force them to do so.

Leadership   If the organization's leaders practice proper leadership techniques, the situation should be less stressful. The organization needs to formulate and implement a leadership strategy. Management-development programs are critical to successful implementation of any leadership strategy. Remember that most leaders learn by example, and unfortunately, most examples are bad. If you are a leader and you practice proper techniques and use the correct skills, then your stress situation should improve.

Management by Objectives, Results, and Rewards (MBORR)   If the individual has an ill-defined role in the organization, or an ill-defined objective for that role, considerable confusion, unhappiness, and unsatisfactory work performance usually result. Stress must naturally accompany such consequences. The solution is MBORR. Establish what needs to be accomplished, by whom, by when, and how; then much of this problem will be solved. Stress will be reduced. MBORR involves much more than has been described here. Chapter 11 addresses this process in more detail.

Organization Structure If the organization's structure is causing a problem, restructure it. Either redefine jobs and objectives (MBORR), redesign the work itself (enrichment, enlargement), or redistribute authority. Again, if you as an individual are suffering from problems of organization structure, you must resort to individual solutions.

Stress Training or Counseling Many corporations today encourage their employees to attend seminars, to consult counselors provided by the organization, to engage in physical exercise (some firms even provide facilities or club memberships), to participate actively in non-work-related activities, to take longer vacations. Much of this stress training involves the teaching of individual stress-relief techniques for example, variations of meditation.

Fitness Programs Many firms promote fitness through active exercise programs. Such programs appear to be effective. A survey taken at Johnson & Johnson one year after it began its fitness program showed fewer sick days, better stress handling, and increased job satisfaction.[24] Company gymnasiums, tennis courts, and training rooms or health club memberships were uncommon just a few years ago, but no longer. The Hospital Corporation of America, in Nashville, Tennessee, pays up to $2,833 per person in fitness bonuses for exercising in the company fitness program—4 cents a mile for bicycling, 16 cents a mile for running or walking, 64 cents a mile for swimming. Total health-care costs have declined since the program began.[25] Remember that it takes a long time to train a top executive, a key scientist, a skilled worker, and significant time to train any manager and many workers. Untold millions in training costs and experience are lost when valuable employees become incapacitated or, worse, suffer fatal illnesses.

INDIVIDUAL STRESS-RELIEF TECHNIQUES

The means that individuals may use to relieve stress are aimed at solving physical and psychological problems. Since the two are so closely intertwined, each relief technique will probably help to alleviate the other type of problem. Both need to be addressed in some way, however, because the events of the GAS are both physical and psychological.

Physical Relief In the general adaptation syndrome, the body increases hormonal activity, increases energy supplies, and takes other actions to prepare for fight or flight. Since these chemical changes take place in the body, some actions must be taken to return the body to equilibrium. Physical exercise will help the body to return to normal. Jogging, karate, weight lifting, golf, handball, tennis, racketball, and even walking are forms of exercise that help millions of people to return to equilibrium.

The average body needs approximately twenty to thirty minutes of strenuous heart, muscle, and lung activity each day to maintain its vigor and to protect vital organs from deterioration. A fit and trim body also enhances one's self-image. Thus for overall physical and mental health, exercise is imperative. Naturally, exercise can be overdone. Too much, too soon, and the effort may be self-defeating. The heart may fail more quickly than it would if you had not exercised. And for some people with certain physical incapacities, exercise is inappropriate.

Psychological Relief A number of techniques are available for relieving the mental aspects of the GAS. Among them are avoidance, defense mechanisms, acquiring greater control over stressors, and individual stress management—relaxation techniques, prolonged vacations, visual imagery, time management, life planning, talking with significant others, building support groups, hobbies, changing your personality, and, unfortunately, drugs and other stuff.

One of the simplest and most effective means of reducing stress is to avoid the stressors. If certain people cause you to have an alarm reaction, reduce your interactions with them. Even when the stressor is your boss, it is possible to practice this technique. This is a highly recommended technique when stress results from an excess of stressors in the environment. Pick and choose those that you need and avoid the others.

Many individuals unfortunately resort to defense mechanisms for relief of stress. They may pretend that there is no problem. They may enter into a depressed mental state. They may project their problems onto someone else. They may blame others. They may rationalize irrational behavior. They may become rigid in their own behavior. Such defense mechanisms usually do no more than postpone the inevitable. The real problem must someday be faced. Most defense mechanisms are not positive attempts to relieve the long-run impacts of stress.

Acquiring great control over stressors is an appropriate solution if you are able to manage it. But when you are under stress from your boss, from organization climate, from relatively powerful external stressors, then there is little chance for success in this approach. There is an old saying that goes something like this: "If you don't like it here, you have three choices: You can quit. You can stay and take it. Or you can become boss and change it." There is a lot of truth in those words. Within the organization, subordinates, including high-level managers, have only a limited impact on their everyday work world. But the situation is not so bleak as these suggested alternatives may imply. First, you can learn how to manipulate others, how to play politics. (See Chapter 17.) This is not the most positive means of change you could take, however. There is a chance to make change within the organization in a more positive fashion, in keeping with the spirit of the positive approaches discussed throughout this book: TA, assertiveness, active listening, MBORR, and so forth.

Yoga, transcendental meditation, self-hypnosis, and other commonly recognized relaxation techniques have been found to share common ingredients. Dr. Herbert Benson of the Harvard Medical School has developed a technique known as the **relaxation response**.[26] The box on "The Relaxation Response

"The Relaxation Response can act as a built-in method of counteracting the stress of everyday living which bring forth the fight-or-flight response."

HERBERT BENSON

Technique" provides a brief description of how to use this technique. Research evidence from a number of sources indicates that this and other relaxation techniques can substantially lower stress, improve health, lower dependence on drugs, and increase energy and productivity.[27]

Biofeedback is a very useful approach to these techniques. Biofeedback involves techniques developed to make people consciously aware of the functioning of their biological systems. Most of this awareness is related to how the person feels internally, not how he or she appears externally. This information, when combined with knowledge of how the body functions, gives the individual greater control over his or her own biological functions than had been thought possible in the past. The results have been astounding. Biofeedback has been used not only to provide relief from stress, but to assist in controlling diseases as well.

THE RELAXATION RESPONSE TECHNIQUE

1 A Quiet Environment

One should choose a quiet, calm environment with as few distractions as possible. Sound, even background noise, may prevent the elicitation of the response. Choose a convenient, suitable place—for example, at an office desk in a quiet room.

2 A Mental Device

The meditator employs the constant stimulus of a single-syllable sound or word. The syllable is repeated silently or in a low, gentle tone. The purpose of the repetition is to free oneself from logical, externally oriented thought by focusing solely on the stimulus. Many different words and sounds have been used in traditional practices. Because of its simplicity and neutrality, the use of the syllable "one" is suggested.

3 A Passive Attitude

The purpose of the response is to help one rest and relax, and this requires a completely passive attitude. One should not scrutinize his performance or try to force the response, because this may well prevent the response from occurring. When distracting thoughts enter the mind, they should simply be disregarded.

4 A Comfortable Position

The meditator should sit in a comfortable chair in as restful a position as possible. The purpose is to reduce muscular effort to a minimum. The head may be supported; the arms should be balanced or supported as well. The shoes may be removed and the feet propped up several inches, if desired. Loosen all tight-fitting clothing.

Eliciting the Relaxation Response

Using these four basic elements, one can evoke the response by following the simple, mental, noncultic procedure that subjects have used in my laboratory:

- In a quiet environment, sit in a comfortable position.
- Close your eyes.
- Deeply relax all your muscles, beginning at your feet and progressing up to your face—feet, calves, thighs, lower torso, chest, shoulders, neck, head. Allow them to remain deeply relaxed.
- Breathe through your nose. Become aware of your breathing. As you breathe out, say the word "one" silently to yourself. Thus:

(Continued on page 412)

breathe in . . . breathe out, with "one." In . . . out, with "one" . . .

• Continue this practice for 20 minutes. You may open your eyes to check the time, but do not use an alarm. When you finish, sit quietly for several minutes, at first with your eyes closed and later with your eyes open.

Remember not to worry about whether you are successful in achieving a deep level of relaxation—maintain a passive attitude and permit relaxation to occur at its own pace. When distracting thoughts occur, ignore them and continue to repeat "one" as you breathe. The technique should be practiced once or twice daily, and not within two hours after any meal, since the digestive processes seem to interfere with the elicitation of the expected changes.

With practice, the response should come with little effort. Investigations have shown that only a small percentage of people do not experience the expected physiologic changes.

(However, it has been noted that people who are undergoing psychoanalysis for at least two sessions a week experience difficulty in eliciting the response.)

A person cannot be certain that the technique is eliciting these physiologic changes unless actual measurements are being made. However, the great majority of people report feelings of relaxation and freedom from anxiety during the elicitation of the relaxation response and during the rest of the day as well. These feelings of well-being are akin to those often noted after physical exercise, but without the attendant physical fatigue.

The practice of this technique evokes some of the same physiologic changes noted during the practice of other techniques. . . . These physiologic changes are significant decreases in body metabolism—oxygen consumption and carbon dioxide elimination—and rate of breathing. Decreased oxygen consumption is the most sensitive index of the elicitation of the relaxation response.

The basic concept of biofeedback is that if we know how we feel, in what condition we are, and how we got there, then we know what to do to feel the same way again. As biofeedback is used in conjunction with relaxation techniques, the usual method is to induce stress, then show the person electrical displays of muscle tension, skin temperature, and brain-wave activity. After a relaxation technique has been employed, the same measures are taken again for purposes of comparison. These measures provide the subjects—often data-oriented and skeptical managers—with dramatic visual evidence that indeed relaxation does lead to definite physiological and mental changes.

Executives have long been guilty of trying to combine business with vacations. The evidence now reveals that such practices are self-defeating. Very little meaningful rest occurs on such trips, and without a prolonged period of relaxation divorced from work activity, the body simply does not rest. Short vacations have very little positive effect. Most stress experts today recommend that vacations be at least two weeks long in order that complete rest may occur.

If you will sit quietly whenever you have a couple of minutes, close your eyes, and use your eyelids as if they were a movie screen, you can envision places, persons, or experiences that have a calming effect on you. By doing this frequently when time is available, you can relieve your stress.

Many people who have high levels of stress are under time pressure. They try to do too much in too little time. Much of this pressure is related to personality type and basic values. The suggested treatments for these problems will help get at the core problem. But for some people, time management is all that is necessary. If people can simply learn to make better use of available time, there is then no need to try to change the personality. This solution is discussed later in this chapter in more detail. By combining time management with life planning—setting objectives for your life and making plans to reach those objectives—you can relieve much of your stress.

Sidney Jourard is the leading proponent of "self-disclosure." By disclosing one's problems, fears, anxieties, concerns, experiences, and happiness to others, one can make great progress in improving human relations and relieving stress. Disclosure to one significant other is the easiest means of obtaining release. In the normal course of events, disclosure begins with less significant events and progresses to major events as trust and confidence are achieved. The disclosure process requires that each person make disclosures to the other. Thus, at least in the beginning, there is usually only one significant other. But many individuals are finding that support groups, either formal or informal, can and do help. Close friends can be a support group. So can your family, or your boss and peers. The group you turn to depends on the type of support you need. Formal groups, such as MADD (Mothers against Drunk Drivers) and AA (Alcoholics Anonymous), offer appropriate support in many situations.

> *"Life is just one damned thing after another."*
> MARK TWAIN

Activities that might be described as "mindless," which take your mind off work and require little effort, can be of great assistance.

If you are aggressive and become assertive, other people will be less likely to be aggressive with you. Both TA and assertiveness help you to understand the causes of behavior and how to go about changing them.

Unfortunately, many people attempt to solve their mental problems through drugs and other stuff. Alcohol, uppers, downers, marijuana, cocaine, and "crack" are all signs of the times. Stress is rampant, and these are common ways of attempting to cope with it. Unfortunately, they only increase stress. Approximately 10 million teenagers in the United States consume alcohol regularly.[28] At least 10 percent of employees in the United States either are alcoholics or are addicted to other drugs.[29] It is estimated that well over $30 billion a year in health-care expenses are charged to American business as a result of drug addiction.[30] The increasing popularity of cocaine made its importing and distribution a $50 billion industry in the United States in 1984.[31] But the fact remains that *drugs do not decrease stress in the long run.* Drugs and other stuff only add to the individual's problems.

> Where in the book of economics
> Does the rule apply, that the
> Cost of operation should
> Outdo the benefits derived?

> Robert's Rules of Order left
> One important matter aside.
> A pause for introspection and self-evaluation
> Must be observed by those
> Of a business mind, or the
> Cost of operation will cause
> The machine to override.
>
> DOUGLAS ERWIN

BURNOUT: A SPECIAL KIND OF STRESS

A report issued in January 1986 by the Washington Business Group, titled "Corporate Commentary," indicates that about 45 percent of employees examined showed signs of severe burnout. According to this study, personality has little to do with whether or not an individual will succumb to burnout; the single most important factor is the supervisor's management style. People at greatest risk are those whose jobs lack clear roles and goals but who are subjected to strong pressure to produce. This sort of situation is identified in Figure 16.2 as a combination of low decision control and high psychological demand.

Exactly what is burnout and why is it so pervasive in our society? **Burnout** has been defined as emotional exhaustion, as "a state of fatigue or frustration brought about by devotion to a cause, a way of life, a relationship that fails to produce the expected reward." A psychologist friend of mine defines it as not caring, and not caring that you don't care. When the reality of a situation consistently fails to correspond to our expectations, we become emotionally, physically, and mentally exhausted. We feel trapped, helpless, and our job performance plummets. Many people caught in such situations respond to their declining productivity by putting in more time on the job, thereby intensifying the symptoms of burnout.

What does a classic case of burnout look like? Take John Nelson, an employee relations director for a manufacturing firm with headquarters in Massachusetts. He had worked hard to boost morale and reduce the high absenteeism rate at one of the company's plants in Oklahoma, but absenteeism remained high. "I just felt like a failure, I began to think all the work wasn't worth it, I removed myself from dealing with what was my job—people. I became more interested in writing policy manuals." Of course his performance declined. Fortunately, Mr. Nelson and others are seeking help. Mr. Nelson, for example, has found renewed enthusiasm for his work after obtaining outside job counseling.[32] Are you subject to burnout? Test Yourself on burnout and find out.

What can you do if you experience burnout? As burnout is essentially long-term stress, the stress-management techniques are appropriate. As this form of stress is associated with frustrated role expectations, however, the soundest way to treat the problem is either to change your role or to readjust your expectations. You must reestablish your sense of self. Self-esteem, as always, is extremely important. Talk positively to yourself. Hobbies and outside interests that you find relaxing also help. Avoid taking on more responsibilities.

TEST YOURSELF

BURNOUT

How often do you have any of the following experiences? Complete the following questionnaire, using the scale:

1	2	3	4	5	6	7
Never	Once in a great while	Rarely	Sometimes	Often	Usually	Always

____ 1. Being tired.
____ 2. Feeling depressed.
____ 3. Having a good day.
____ 4. Being physically exhausted.
____ 5. Being emotionally exhausted.
____ 6. Being happy.
____ 7. Being "wiped out."
____ 8. Feeling "burned out."
____ 9. Being unhappy.
____ 10. Feeling rundown.
____ 11. Feeling trapped.
____ 12. Feeling worthless.
____ 13. Being weary.
____ 14. Being troubled.
____ 15. Feeling disillusioned and resentful about people.
____ 16. Feeling weak.
____ 17. Feeling hopeless.
____ 18. Feeling rejected.
____ 19. Feeling optimistic.
____ 20. Feeling energetic.
____ 21. Feeling anxious.

Computation of score:

- *A*. Add the values you wrote next to the following items: 1, 2, 4, 5, 7, 8, 9, 10, 11, 12, 13, 14, 15, 16, 17, 18, 21: _____ .
- *B*. Add the values you wrote next to the following items: 3, 6, 19, 20: _____ .
- *C*. Subtract *B* from 32: _____ .
- *D*. Add *A* and *C*: _____ .
- *E*. Divide *D* by 21: _____ . This is your burnout score.

Interpreting your score: Score between 2 and 3 and you are doing well. A score between 3 and 4 suggests you examine your priorities and consider possible changes. If you have a score higher than 4, you are experiencing burnout to the extent that it is mandatory that you take action. If your score is higher than 5, you need immediate help.

Of the thousands who responded to the questionnaire, no one scored 1 or 7. It is unlikely anyone could be in a total state of euphoria as a score of 1 would suggest, and a score of 7 would indicate an inability to cope with reality.

Source: Adapted from Elliot Aronson and Ayola M. Pines, *Burn-Out: From Tedium to Personal Growth* (New York: Free Press, 1980), pp. 37, 38.

TIME MANAGEMENT

One of the most important aspects of managing stress is managing your time. What do you do with your time? How much time do you waste in a day?

Time is a unique resource. It is finite for each and every individual. Time is what life consists of, and success is a product of time management. You cannot increase your total time on earth, but you can improve the way in which you use that time. **Time management** is the process of making your time more productive by managing what you do with your time. How we use our time is a function of two primary variables: the organizations to which we belong and the way in which we manage our own time. The two major organizations to which most people belong are the work organization and the family. In the student's case, there is a third, the school.

Why is time management important? An executive who is paid $62,000 a year and wastes an hour a week has wasted how much of the company's money in salary? Multiply this figure by the number of executives in that salary range. Now do this for the rest of the organization's members and add the results. You can be talking of millions of dollars in salaries, untold millions in productive decisions. How about your own time? If you played cards one hour less per week, would you make an A instead of a B in this course? Or a B instead of a C? Or achieve knowledge instead of just getting an A? And if you achieve knowledge, will you get a better job? Or if you achieve the A, will you get a better job? You just might . . . and that's important.

Time management is a relatively simple process, but one in which few of us engage. First, you need to find out what you do with your time. Second, you need to analyze this use of time to determine if you used your time productively. Third, you must change those uses of time that are not productive for you personally. (Relaxation can be productive.)

Figure 16.4 is a daily time chart to be used to determine the uses you have made of your time. Take this chart and reproduce it until you have seven copies. Each day for the next seven days, keep a record of what you do. Try to complete the chart at the end of each hour, but certainly at the end of each day. (We tend to forget, so the more often, the better.)

Second, set priorities for the uses of your time. If the item is essential, it should have top priority and be designated Type 1. If it is important but not essential, it should be designated Type 2. If you could do without it, if someone else could do it for you, it should be designated Type 3. It is the Type 3s that cost managers the most time.

Obviously, no one set of characteristics is demonstrated by all managers, but most managers feel the need to be in control. Unfortunately, the need to control others often leads to a very poor use of time. Managers typically prefer to "do it themselves—so a quality job gets done." Or they frequently can be tricked into assuming someone else's responsibilities because they want to make sure that everything runs smoothly. William Oncken, Jr., and Donald L. Wass have described the need for control in terms of "care and feeding of monkeys." The problem is described as a monkey. When the subordinate has the monkey, he or she owns the problem. But when the manager has the monkey, he or she owns the monkey. The monkey is said to be "on their backs." According to Oncken and Wass, subordinates like to have the monkeys hop from their backs to their bosses' backs, thus feeling their own time for more important matters. And all too often, managers are all too ready to accept the monkey. How does this happen? The manager accepts the responsibility and agrees to perform what are appropriately a subordinate's duties. This is

FIGURE 16.4   *Daily time analysis*

Date: _____

Objectives
for the
day

1. _____
2. _____
3. _____

4. _____
5. _____
6. _____

Time	Activity	No. & nature of interruptions during activity	What was accomplished in this activity with respect to objectives (% productive/nonproductive time)	Type of activity (1, 2, 3)
7:30				
8:00				
8:30				
9:00				
9:30				
10:00				
10:30				
11:00				
11:30				
12:00				
12:30				
1:00				
1:30				
2:00				
2:30				
3:00				
3:30				
4:00				
4:30				
5:00				
5:30				
Evening				

SOURCE: Used with permission of William Stratton, Idaho State University.

the classic case of a failure to delegate responsibility. For example, suppose a subordinate comes to the boss and says, "You know, Melissa, I just haven't been able to get that Simpson project to work out. Would you see what you can do?" If Melissa replies affirmatively, the monkey is now hers, not the subordinate's. The proper reply would be to set the subordinate to further pursuit of the right approach to the Simpson project. To make matters worse, the subordinate checks back from time to time to see if the boss has completed the project. (This is known as supervision.) "Melissa, have you had a chance to figure out that Simpson problem?" Active listening, TA, and assertiveness are all appropriate here.[33]

Other Type 3 activities include answering the phone, attending unimportant meetings, spending too much time worrying, spending too much time on politics and not enough in productive behavior, spending too much time defending yourself, or even simpler things like getting up from your work station too many times to get a drink of water.

Once you have noted whether or not you should have been engaging in the activities in which you did engage, then you need to cut out Type 3 activities, reduce the number of Type 2 activities, and change your behavior patterns appropriately. This is not as easy as it may seem, because we are all creatures of habit. But we must learn to "manage," we must learn to say no, we must learn to be assertive, we must learn to "let" others be responsible.

Wasting time is a relative matter. If you don't "waste" some, you may find yourself extremely mentally fatigued. But wasting all of your time is clearly nonproductive.

──────────── TIPS FOR SUCCESSFUL TIME MANAGEMENT ────────────

1. Do not allow the telephone to control your work life. Get a good secretary and let him or her handle most calls. Do not permit the telephone to intrude. Try to avoid receiving work-related calls at home.

2. Control visitors to your office. Ask unexpected visitors to leave if you are busy.

3. Attend as few meetings as possible. Make sure meetings are short, are started and stopped on time, and have an agenda with times allotted to subjects according to relative importance; include only the people who are really needed; and tell participants what is required in advance.

4. Plan each day. Have objectives and priorities assigned as well as completion deadlines. Work that must be accomplished should be done first.

5. Do the important things and the unpleasant things when your energy levels are highest. Do the easiest tasks last.

6. Leave some time each day for unplanned or unanticipated demands.

7. Delegate responsibility. Do not let the monkey hop onto your back. Train others to do what you do not have time to do.

8. Do not procrastinate. Make decisions now unless additional information is absolutely essential. You do not have to maximize every decision. Many times a decision need only satisfy certain minimal requirements.

9. Do not file paperwork for later. Do it now. If it is not important, file it in File 13 (the trash can).

10. Choose the course of action that uses the least time. Use dictation machines instead of manual dictation. Write a brief response on the bottom of a letter instead of writing a letter in reply, if appropriate.

11. Stop driving your own car if your commuting time is more than fifteen minutes. Take a bus

or even move closer to work. A half hour a day times 220 workdays a year is a lot of wasted time.

12. Learn to relax. Pushing yourself to the brink of fatigue decreases your productivity.
13. Have clear and precise objectives for yourself and your subordinates. Emphasize results, not activity.
14. Use your secretary wisely. If you develop your secretary by delegating responsibilities, you not only enrich the secretary's job, you save yourself time and trouble.
15. Socialize off the job—at lunch, at breaks, after work. Tell people who wander into your work area that you need to work.
16. Take the time to do it right the first time. This will often keep you from having to do it again, which of course means that you must take more time.
17. Let your secretary screen your mail, prepare routine responses, arrange your schedule, and so forth.
18. Unclutter your desk, get organized. If you spend half of your time searching for things on your desk, stop being so messy.
19. Use otherwise wasted time. For example, while waiting for something—to see a doctor or someone else, to board an airplane—work on a project or read.
20. Periodically review your time-management practices.

TIPS FOR SUCCESS

1. Know your stress levels.
2. Learn how to cope with stress, physically and psychologically.
3. Learn time management, and use it.

SUMMARY

1. Stress is a physical and psychological condition that results from attempts to control one's environment.
2. Stress is partly a function of personality and partly a function of stressors in the environment.
3. The general adaptation syndrome (GAS), encompassing the body's reactions to external stressors, has three stages: (1) the alarm reaction, (2) resistance, and (3) exhaustion.
4. The aggressive, restless Type A personality is highly subject to stress and hence to heart disease; the more relaxed Type B personality is less subject to both.
5. Management style and organizational climate are among the primary work-related causes of stress.
6. The family, friends, and personal finances are among the primary non-work-related causes of stress.
7. All change is stressful.
8. Limited amounts of stress increase productivity, but intense and prolonged stress has negative consequences for the individual and for the organization.
9. Organizational stress-management programs today focus on means of coping with stressors as well as on attempts to eliminate them.
10. Physical exercise and relaxation techniques are helpful in reducing stress.
11. Burnout is a state of emotional exhaustion experienced when the reality of a situation consistently fails to correspond to our expectations.
12. Time management is the process of making one's time more productive.

DISCUSSION QUESTIONS

1. What is stress? What are its primary internal and external causes? Its organization and individual causes?
2. What are the three stages of the general adaptation syndrome? Describe each stage.

3. How does change affect a person's health?
4. What are the positive and negative impacts of stress?

5. How can organizations and individuals manage stress?
6. How can you manage your time?

APPLYING HUMAN RELATIONS SKILLS

CASES

Systems Flex

Systems Flex was a computer software firm employing some 200 programmers, systems analysts, and staff assistants. Aubrey Daniels was one of the fifteen project managers. He sat one day pondering his situation. His boss had indicated only very generally what he wanted from this project. Then he had gone out of town. His boss's boss had then called Aubrey, wanting immediate attention to be given to some items that Aubrey and his boss had not even discussed. It looked like overtime tonight. But he and his wife had that party with the new neighbors. And Katrina Winslow, one of his best systems analysts, was demanding a raise far higher than the boss would ever approve. And he thought there might be more to it than that. She wanted more control over her work. He always seemed to be putting out fires. . . .

The phone rang. It was his wife. She had had to write a check for more than the balance in their account, and he would have to deposit some money to cover it. His sister had called and wanted them to come over Friday for dinner. Their daughter had a cold and had to stay home from school. He decided not to work overtime. He would get Bill to do the work.

He finished his call and dialed Bill's number. Bill said he had his own problems, but agreed to look into it. Five minutes later Bill reported back that he just could not get to it (even though it was his area of responsibility). Aubrey needed Bill's work badly, so rather than get Bill to look into this matter, he resolved to come in early the next morning and take up where he left off. Ed stopped by to chat for fifteen minutes.

When Aubrey went home that night, his desk was piled high, his head muddled, his briefcase full. He wondered where the day had gone.

The next morning he got to work at 6:00 A.M. By 8:00, when the others came to work, he had solved several problems, but the two most important still remained. Between 8:00 and 9:00 he received six phone calls. None of them was important. His secretary had been bothering him to give her something more interesting to do, yet she could not even handle her routine chores, he thought. Three calls later, at 10:00, Aubrey's boss's boss called to find out what actions had been taken. Aubrey reported that he had begun to investigate and would report back by 3:00 P.M. He then proceeded to investigate. He was not quite sure what to do, but he plunged ahead.

1. Find as many causes of stress as you can in this case.
2. How could Aubrey have alleviated his stress?
3. How could the organization have reduced Aubrey's stress?

Maria Sanchez

Maria Sanchez meandered through her house. She had gotten the kids off to school, she had washed all of the clothes and dishes, and by 9:45 her house was clean. It was more than clean, it was immaculate.

She turned on the tube, but she despised the soaps and was tired of the quiz shows. She called Isabel to play tennis, but she couldn't. She had to go to the doctor (for another imaginary illness, thought Maria).

Maria decided to go shopping. After a couple of hours she ate lunch. She came home. She attempted to sleep, but could not. She took a pill to help her relax. The kids came home. They talked for awhile. They went out to play. It was only 4:00 P.M., but what the heck, she fixed herself a drink. At 5:00 she fixed her husband one, and herself another. He came in promptly at 5:15. They chatted, mostly about his day.

"What did you do today?" he asked. But before she could say, "Nothing," he started on another story about his job. They had a couple more drinks and she fixed dinner. Then they went out to play bridge. The next day she waxed the kitchen floor; otherwise the day began and ended about the same way. So did the next day, and the next, and the next. . . .

1. Find as many indicators and causes of stress as you can in this case.
2. What could Maria have done to alleviate her stress?
3. How could her husband have helped her to alleviate her stress?

EXERCISES

Relaxation Response

The whole class will practice the relaxation response described in the text. Experience has shown that students usually will not practice the technique on their own, but that if directed to do so in class, they are likely to continue the practice.

After the class practices the technique, participants may wish to share with others their feelings during the process. If biofeedback devices are available, they may be used to monitor individual reactions to the process.

Stress Experiences

Students may wish to share with the class personal stressful experiences or observations of others' stressful experiences. Discussion should focus on the causes, the impacts, and what could have been done to manage the stress.

REFERENCES

1. Michael T. Matteson and John M. Ivancevich, "Straining under Too Much Stress?" *Management World*, July 1979, pp. 5–6.
2. Hans Selye, *The Stress of Life* (New York: McGraw-Hill, 1956), p. vii.
3. Hans Selye, "The General Adaptation Syndrome and the Diseases of Adaptation," *Journal of Clinical Endocrinology* 2 (1946): 117–30.
4. Richard deCharms, *Personal Causation* (Reading, Mass.: Addison-Wesley, 1968), pp. 6–8.

5. Joann S. Lublin, "Stress Research Seeks Clues to Why Children Can't Cope with Life," *Wall Street Journal*, April 10, 1979, p. 1, reporting on the work of Dr. E. James Anthony, professor of child psychiatry at Washington University. Vulnerable children have the type of personality that makes it difficult for them to cope with even ordinary life events.

6. See chap. 5.

7. Jerry E. Bishop, "Research Is Indicating that Stress Is Linked to Physical Illness," *Wall Street Journal*, April 5, 1979, pp. 1, 28; see especially the section on "hardy" executives.

8. Meyer A. Friedman and Ray H. Rosenman, *Type A Behavior and Your Heart* (New York: Knopf, 1974).

9. Robert S. Eliot and Dennis L. Breo, *Is It Worth Dying For?* (New York: Bantam, 1984).

10. Robert S. Eliot, address to Florida Cardiovascular Group, 1984.

11. Bryce Nelson, "Bosses Face Less Kick than Bossed," *New York Times*, April 3, 1983, sec. 4.

12. Michael Uhl, "Technostress," *Forbes*, July 2, 1984, p. 158.

13. Lublin, "Stress Research."

14. See Bishop, "Research," p. 1.

15. Thomas Petzinger, Jr., "Inflation Can Threaten Your Mental Health, Many Therapists Say," *Wall Street Journal*, May 15, 1980, pp. 1, 35.

16. "The Human Tragedy of Unemployment," *U.S. News & World Report*, June 23, 1980, pp. 68–69.

17. Alvin Toffler, *Future Shock* (New York: Bantam, 1971).

18. Bruce M. Meglino, "Stress and Performance, Are They Always Incompatible?" *Supervisory Management*, March 1977, p. 8.

19. Bishop, "Research"; Tom Cox, *Stress* (Baltimore: University Park Press, 1978), pp. 99–102; Friedman and Rosenman, *Type A Behavior*; and Terry A. Beehr and J. E. Newman, "Job Stress, Employee Health, and Organizational Effectiveness," *Personnel Psychology*, Winter 1978, pp. 667–78.

20. "Coping with Life's Strains: Interview with Dr. Roy W. Menninger, President, the Menninger Foundation," *U.S. News & World Report*, May 1, 1978, pp. 80–82.

21. Matteson and Ivancevich, "Straining under Too Much Stress," p. 6; Rose Mary Rummel and John W. Rader, "Coping with Executive Stress," *Personnel Journal*, June 1978, p. 305.

22. John M. Ivancevich, Michael T. Matteson, and Edward Richards III, "Who's Liable for Stress on the Job?" *Harvard Business Review*, March–April 1985; "Stress Claims Are Making Business Jumpy," *Business Week*, October 14, 1985, pp. 152–53.

23. Related to the author by Rod Waddell of Dynamics Resource Development.

24. "Pays to Be Healthy," *Wall Street Journal*, February 19, 1981, p. 29.

25. "Corporate Fitness Programs," *Personnel Journal*, June 1982, p. 398.

26. Herbert Benson, "Your Innate Asset for Combating Stress," *Harvard Business Review*, July–August 1974.

27. See, for example, ibid.; and virtually every major book on stress contains some reference to the proven impacts of such efforts.

28. Leon D. Sager, "The Corporation and the Alcoholic," *Across the Board*, June 1979, pp. 79–82.

29. "What Industry Is Doing about 10 Million Alcoholic Workers," *U.S. News & World Report*, January 12, 1976, p. 62.

30. Janice Castro, "Battling Drugs on the Job," *Time*, January 27, 1986, p. 43.

31. "Cocaine: America's $50 Billion Snort," *U.S. News & World Report*, December 10, 1984, p. 8.

32. Robert S. Greenberger, "Job Hazard: How Burnout Affects Corporate Managers and Their Performance," *Wall Street Journal*, April 23, 1981, p. 1.

33. William Oncken, Jr., and Donald L. Wass, "Management Time: Who's Got the Monkey?" *Harvard Business Review*, November–December 1974, pp. 75–80.

17 POWER, POLITICS, AND CONFLICT

KEY TERMS AND CONCEPTS

power
politics
psychological games
conversational politics
legitimate politics
illegitimate politics
vertical politics
horizontal politics
external politics
internal politics
sources of conflict
conflict management

LEARNING OBJECTIVES

When you have completed this chapter, you should be able to:

1. Determine when power is being sought by political means.
2. Recognize whether politics is legitimate or illegitimate, internal or external, vertical or lateral.
3. Describe, recognize, and stop—or use as necessary—many different nonpolitical and political actions to gain power.
4. Recognize and stop—or use as necessary—psychological game playing.
5. Recognize and stop—or use as necessary—conversational politics.
6. Identify sources of conflict.
7. Identify the positive and dysfunctional consequences of conflict.
8. Explain when each conflict management technique should be used.

LEE IACOCCA KNOWS ABOUT THE POWER OF POLITICS

When Henry Ford, Jr., fired Lee Iacocca, he used only four words to explain his decision: "I don't like you." Iacocca, who had for years played the power game with Ford, didn't like losing that game. Iacocca told his family, "That's something I won't forgive." He told his kids, "Don't get mad—get even."

And as Iacocca reports, he did get even. "I got even in the marketplace. I wounded him badly and it took me five years." In five years he took a bankrupt company, Chrysler, and turned it into a major contender that took much of its market share from Ford.

And he got even in other ways. In his best-selling autobiography, *Iacocca*, Iacocca portrayed Ford as an egotistical, bigoted snob who had no time for anyone outside of his small clique of rich friends. Henry Ford may have won the battle, but Iacocca won the war.

Source: James A. Newman and Roy Alexander, "How to Guard Against Office Intrigue," *Success*, December 1984, p. 50.

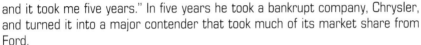

People who expect to be successful in an organization have to be sensitive to its power structure. They have to be aware of who will take what position on any major issue. They have to know the power other people possess and their positions relative to one another. They have to know who plays politics and who doesn't, who bases decisions on merit and who doesn't.

Successful people recognize that performance or merit alone is not enough in most organizations. They know that in any organization politics will influence many decisions, certainly the most important ones. If you want to get ahead in the organization, you must learn to work within the power structure. Power often derives from sources unrelated to the formal organization structure, and their name is politics. Lee Iacocca understood the political game and he played it well. But the man he worked for, Henry Ford, Jr., had more power, so despite Iacocca's political astuteness, he was bound to lose. "I don't like you" is a good enough reason to fire somebody when you own the company. Thus no matter how astute you may be at politics, there will be times when

> *"If power is for sale, sell your mother to buy it. You can always buy her back again."*
> 19th-century Ashanti proverb, quoted by James Morris

you will lose. Even if you own the company. But you can get even as Iacocca did, and there are steps you can take to avoid many such situations and to minimize the damage when they can't be avoided.

POWER AND POLITICS

Power is the ability to influence other people and to gain access to things of value. **Politics** is one means by which power is acquired.

THE DISTRIBUTION OF POWER

"The fundamental concept in social science is power, in the same sense in which energy is the fundamental concept in physics."

BERTRAND RUSSELL

Because the needs of organizations differ from those of their members, and because of the legitimate authority structure of the organization, the need does indeed arise to distribute power both formally and informally. Leaders can distribute power in certain ways (Chapter 8) and organizations in others (Chapter 13). When individuals' needs for power are not satisfied, when other needs are not satisfied because of the lack of power, formal power will be redistributed informally. There's only so much power to go around, and if you don't want someone else to get your share, you may have to play politics.

Five kinds of power and hence of influence have been identified by John French and Bertram Raven.[1] As they have been discussed in detail in Chapter 8, they will be reviewed here only briefly.

1. Legitimate power: power derived from a position in an organization. Also known as authority.
2. Reward power: power based on ability to control rewards given to others.
3. Coercive power: power based on the ability to punish others.
4. Expert power: power based on special skill or knowledge.
5. Referent power: power based on personal appeal, magnetism, charisma.

Any of these kinds of power can be used to satisfy your personal need for power within the organization if you take certain actions. Each can be viewed as appropriate or inappropriate by an organization or by any of its members.

POLITICS

The word *politics* seems to carry a negative connotation, but there are various types of politics, and not all are negative. Dan Farrell and James C. Petersen have suggested that most organizations develop Marquis of Queensbury–style rules to govern their internal politics. If you play by those rules, which are understood by everyone, your politicking is **legitimate**. It's **illegitimate** if you don't play by the rules. Political maneuvering in violation of the rules is illegitimate.[2] It's legitimate to learn to play golf because your boss likes to play golf; it's illegitimate to spread gossip about an office competitor in order to win a promotion your competitor expects to get.

Politics is a part of organizational life. In many organizations, politics is an important determinant of promotions, raises, transfers, termination, important assignments, career successes and failures. Much of what has been discussed so far in this text can be used by anyone to manipulate others. Strokes, games, listening or refusing to listen, problem solving, motivation, rewards, leadership, communication, body language, friendship—all may be used to satisfy personal needs at the expense of others. By playing on people's need for affiliation, you can manipulate them into agreeing with you. By playing on their need for power, you can get what you want by supporting them (thus increasing their power). By helping people to solve their problems, you can win their support and enhance your own power. You can ignore people who deserve recognition in order to reduce their self-image—perhaps to cause them to look elsewhere for a job. The examples are infinite and they occur every day, in just about every organization.

Playing politics is a learned behavior. People have been taught how to engage in these practices. You need to be alert to them and learn them for yourself, if you don't already know them. You have to make choices as to their use, as to which political games fit your value system. Some of these practices are simply part of playing the organizational game. Your concern should be primarily to recognize them and learn how to cope with them. You should be alert to both legitimate and illegitimate politics and be wary of the divisive factionalism that hinders the organization from achieving its objectives. More often, fortunately office politics is a process that has evolved simply as a means to distribute power. Power struggles are inevitable among strong-willed people with high need for power—the kind of people who inhabit the upper levels of organizations. You must be prepared.

Why does politics play such a prominent role in organizations? Some people say politics is part of human nature. Certainly some men and women are inveterate politicos. But politics also exists because of the nature of organizations. Alan Schoonmaker, an executive counselor, describes politics as part of the natural distribution of power in the organization.[3] Certainly this is one plausible explanation. Politics also arises from competition. Some people have lower performance levels than their competitors and they want to get ahead without raising their level of performance. Finally, people learn psychological games very early in life, and continue to play them in the organization. The basis of politics is psychological game playing.

WHY POLITICS EXISTS

Robert N. McMurray, a consulting psychologist, depicts the political process in organizations as resulting primarily from the insecurities of the type of person who is attracted to organizational life.[4] The apparent insecurities of many managers certainly seem to support this contention. Remember that while most managers appear to operate from a positive self-image, many secretly are insecure. These feelings lead them to engage in politics. McMurray depicts the majority of managers as being tremendously insecure and unable to let other people have the positive self-images they lack themselves.

THE INHERENT POLITICAL NATURE OF HUMAN BEINGS

One university branch president, a silent and very authoritative type, was reported to have screamed, "If that damn Student Government Association thinks it's going to use my new tearoom, I'll just rip up the carpet and then see how they like that! I don't care if the room is in the student center. I don't care if it was built by a federal grant. It's my room, and only I and my friends are going to use it."

Such persons often flip-flop between aggressiveness and docility. Their kingdoms are replete with political intrigue. This particular man unfortunately was soon promoted to the presidency of the entire university system because he had played the political role well with the governor, not because of any demonstrated ability. It wasn't too long, however, before the faculty and students at his new school, through exhaustive protesting and politicking, had him removed.

THE NATURE OF ORGANIZATIONS

Management practices have historically tended to reflect the family authority situations of the managers. Many male managers are authoritative, as their fathers and perhaps mothers were. The subordinate is expected to be childlike and submissive, as the manager was required to be as a child. The insecure manager who attempts to pattern his behavior on that of a stern parent is particularly prone to politicking. He tends to feel that he has gotten where he is by trickery; if he ever stopped, the real adults would find him out.

The Need to Politic   Politicking is inevitable because of the nature of competition for resources and power and because of the differences in ability of individuals who seek power. The world is becoming increasingly complex and competitive. Authority is extremely diffused throughout the organization. Many organizations lack a definitive chain of command through which you can count on rising on your way to the top. The ability to manipulate power

"For the present, Ashland, you'll have to take it, and perhaps someday, if you play your cards right, you'll be in a position to dish it out."

is especially important in large organizations with numerous locations and facilities, where the career path to the top is not always clear. Moreover, individual-to-individual relationships are changing as groups become more important in the organization. One must learn to work with groups. The experience of Harvey Coleman, a consultant to such firms as AT&T, indicates that in highly competitive organizations, long-term career success depends 10 percent on performance, 30 percent on image, and 60 percent on exposure. Since practically everybody is doing an excellent job, someone who is more visible than you may get that big promotion you wanted. Coleman observes that advancement often depends on who you know and how high up they are. Some managers feel that if you do your job, you will be noticed. Arthur Brown, director of employment at General Mills, comments: "You're going to be noticed if your performance is good."[5] But a lot of people don't feel that way, and some companies are taking action to try to help the less visible employee. They single out people to make presentations to top managers, assign someone they think has good potential to a project, assign someone else to a project team in the hope that the other team members will coach him. Politically astute managers at higher levels of the hierarchy can help these people by giving them visibility in the organization.[6] Finally, networking can be extremely helpful.

Psychological games are series of ulterior transactions that lead to predetermined, usually negative conclusions. We learn such games when we are children and carry them with us into adult life. Transactions of this sort (see Chapter 6) are not games unless they are repeated often, with the same or similar players, and have the same results. Each party participates in the game in order to interact with the other. The object of the game is to get and give strokes, or recognition. A negative stroke is called a kick. Both parties, at least subconsciously, know that they are playing a game.

Games vary in degree of seriousness. A few games are almost fun, but most can lead to problems for the individual's self-image and for the company's productivity. The person who initiates the game makes an opening statement that sounds innocent but is designed to hook some weakness in the other person—his quick temper, for example, or her insecurity. The hook is the statement's hidden meaning, one that both parties know. The receiver gives an equally plausible-sounding response, but one that has a hidden meaning that indicates that the game is on. These complementary transactions continue until the original sender eventually delivers the true message—the kick. Both players then collect some kind of emotional satisfaction and go their separate ways, until they meet and play the game again.

All games are versions of two fundamental games: "NIGYSOB" and "Kick Me." In NIGYSOB, Now I've Got You, You Son-of-a-Bitch, the person who initiates the game does so in an attempt to trap the receiver into letting the sender give the receiver a strong negative stroke. In Kick Me, the original sender attempts to manipulate the receiver into giving the sender a strong negative stroke known in this case as the kick. A typical NIGYSOB game might go like this:

PSYCHOLOGICAL GAMES

Boss to secretary: Have you seen the Johnson report? [holding it behind his back].

Secretary: No.

Boss (knowingly): By any chance did you take it to coffee break with you?

Secretary: Well, you know, I think I did. I bet I left it on the table.

Boss: Yes, I know you did. I just happened to find it on the floor in the lunchroom. [He brings the report from behind his back and throws it on her desk.] My signature goes where the coffee stains are. You'll have to redo it. [Now I've got you.]

In Kick Me, the game might go like this:

Husband: How was your day?

Wife: Horrible. First I . . . Then I . . . Why do these things always happen to me?

Husband (confirming her low self-image): Poor dear.

A common game in organizations is "Tardiness." In this game the boss tells the subordinate, over and over again, that the next time he comes in late, he's in trouble—but nothing is ever done. The employee continues to come to work late.

If you find yourself repeatedly engaged in conversations that seem to have the same dynamics, that leave the essential problem unsolved, that always leave someone with a lowered self-image, then you are involved in a game. Entire books have been devoted to psychological games; the best known is Eric Berne's *Games People Play.*[7] I suggest you read it. You'll enjoy it, and it will help you to recognize the moves in a game and learn now to stop them. Meanwhile, you can refuse to play. Don't give the originator what he wants—either the chance to kick you or the kick he invites from you.

CONVERSATIONAL POLITICS

> **"** *It used to be 'Go stand in the corner.' Then it got to be 'Could you go stand in the corner?' Then it was 'Is there a possibility we could discuss your going over and standing in the corner?' Now it's 'Why don't I go stand in the corner for you?'* **"**
>
> JOHN MACKOVIC
> *Kansas City Chiefs
> coach*

Have you ever felt that a conversation wasn't going exactly as you would like but couldn't explain why? Have you ever felt frustrated because the other person didn't really seem to be listening or care about what you had to say? You were probably witnessing **conversational politics**—"the violation of normal rules of conversation in order to assert power."[8] People who are engaging in conversational politics interrupt you constantly, give only perfunctory recognition of your comments, pay no attention.

Various research projects suggest that speech patterns and power plays vary with the situation. In a typical situation, the person who perceives himself to be more powerful than the other will engage in conversational politics. If the other agrees, she permits the power play. Doctors, for example, interrupt their patients more frequently than patients interrupt their doctors. The same is true of professors and students, husbands and wives, men and women.

In fact, the existence of conversational politics was little recognized until the ways in which women and men interrelate was studied. Linguist Robin Lakoff has identified a "women's language"—a language that is used most often by women, but may be used by anyone in an inferior power position, such as a subordinate in relation to a superior. This language may be recognized by the use of words that are rarely used by men (*mauve*, for example); the use of "empty" adjectives that have no precise meaning in the context (*divine, lovely*); the use of hedges (*sort of, a little, I guess*); a questioning intonation at the end of a sentence (suggesting uncertainty or subservience); the frequent use of *so* before an adjective (*so many people*); and the use of hypercorrect grammar and excessively polite speech.[9]

Research on the way people take turns speaking reveals the pervasiveness of conversational politics. Ordinarily speakers signal their intention to yield the floor, the next speaker follows certain rules of self-selection, or the current speaker may select the next speaker. But when conversational politics is being played, people violate these rules, and often. They interrupt, they jump ahead of the appointed next speaker. They hold the floor longer than they should. They attempt to dominate.[10] The way to counter such behavior is to be assertive.

There are many ways in which you can increase your power. Some ways are appropriate in managerial positions: some are appropriate in any position you may have. Some involve politics; some do not. Some are legitimate; some are not.

STRATEGIES TO INCREASE YOUR POWER

Political Strategies Dan Farrell and James C. Petersen have suggested that politics may be seen as either vertical or horizontal and as either external or internal.[11] **Vertical politics** is engaged in by superiors and subordinates. The subordinate complains to the supervisor about someone else in the work group, for example; the supervisor bypasses the next person in the chain of command. **Horizontal politics** is played by peers: they exchange favors, one offers help to another, they form a coalition or a network.

People who seek to gain power over the organization by involving outsiders are engaging in **external politics.** Whistleblowers, people who leak news to the media, employees who sue the firm—all are involving people outside of the organization in their efforts and so are engaging in external politics. **Internal politics** consists of political actions within the organization: trading favors, trading agreements, obstruction, symbolic protest gestures, "touching bases," forming alliances, even riots and mutinies.

Many legitimate strategies—those governed by informal rules that everyone understands—are commonly employed in most organizations:

1. Organized protest may be absorbed or seduced.
   (*a*) Management may absorb protest by denying the legitimacy of an issue, by transferring dissidents to other jobs, by isolating dissidents, and by suppressing information.
   (*b*) A manager may seduce protesters by engaging them in endless meetings and discussions of the issues, by instituting token reforms, and by bargaining with no intention of satisfying the group's demands.[12]
2. Find yourself a sponsor—a mentor. Cultivation of some important individual on an upper rung of the corporate ladder will advance your career. Conversely, be wary of close association with someone out of favor with top management.

> *"Corporate leaders often tell their charges that hard work will lead to success. Indeed this theory of reward being commensurate with effort has been an enduring belief in our society, one central to our self-image as a people where the 'main chance is available to anyone of ability who has the gumption and persistence to seize it."*
> ROBERT JACKALL

3. Learn to like your boss's and clients' hobbies. A lot of valuable contacts are made and friendships consolidated on the tennis court and especially on the golf courses, as the Human Relations Happening suggests.
4. Learn to like what your boss likes. It only makes sense that if your enthusiasms coincide with your boss's, you're more likely to be promoted than if your likes differ.
5. Be a yes person. This works only if your boss likes yes people. Some bosses do. Most realize that such people are not really contributing to the

HUMAN RELATIONS HAPPENING

WHY GOLF?

Charles McCabe, senior vice-president and director of marketing for Manufacturers Hanover Trust, found out early in his career that golf and business are a good mix. Virtually deluged by invitations to play golf with clients and associates, McCabe took lessons and began to play regularly as a way of doing business. "I decided that if I didn't want to be an office wallflower, I'd better learn how to play this game," he reflects. "Golf seems to be the sport of the vendors. I wouldn't say that it has gotten me where I am—I'd like to think that I'd be here if I did nothing more than play marbles. But I think golf has helped me tremendously in expanding my range of contacts."

"I call it linking," says Robin Schlueter, president of Links for Women, a California-based organization to help women break into golfing as a networking technique. "I tell my members, 'Even if you go out and get thrown into a game with three total strangers, by the time you've played a few holes, they've found out what you do, you find out what they do, and you've made a contact that could someday be important.'" The golf vine may be stronger than the grapevine.

Golf writer Charles Price observes, "This game is the greatest incubator for business deals. There are only four of you out there at the most. You have the guy's attention for at least five hours. It's such a slow-moving game that you have to socialize, so you dissolve any communication barrier that existed at the office."

There are some strict rules you should follow in business golf. For example, you should never bring up business—that is considered gauche by most people. Why ruin the aesthetics with talk of business? But after the game is over, then it's fine to make an appointment to get together. And if your guest brings up business, then certainly discuss it, but don't go for the deal then. The sales pitch should be made later, at a better time for both of you. Finally, keep your eyes and ears open. Even though you are not discussing business, you may learn a lot about your potential clients during those few hours, including whether or not you really want to do business with them.

SOURCE: Adapted from Jolee Edmondson, "Foreplay, Some of the Best Business Deals Begin on the Golf Course," *Success*, April 1985, pp. 28–31.

HUMAN RELATIONS HAPPENING

ETERNAL CONFLICT AT EASTERN AIRLINES

Less than three months after Eastern Airlines was celebrating its profitability after a long period of drought, Eastern appeared to be headed for bankruptcy. The outcome of its battle for survival hinged on the willingness of its unionized employees once again to take substantial pay cuts and eliminate certain positions. This had been chairman Frank Borman's strategy three times before when Eastern had faced bankruptcy.

Eastern's problems stemmed principally from the industry-wide price cutting that had followed deregulation of the airlines. When the airlines were deregulated, large numbers of new carriers entered the market, carriers staffed by nonunion personnel who were willing to work for considerably less than the unionized work force of the firms that had once dominated the airline industry. Established firms tried various strategies to meet the competition. Continental declared bankruptcy, terminated its union employees, then rehired many of them at substantially lower wages as nonunion workers. American Airlines instituted a two-tier wage scale, paying new employees substantially less than more senior ones doing the same work. Eastern's solution was to ask all of its employees for wage concessions—in the late 1970s, in 1983, and again

in 1985. Some of the concessions involved an exchange of stock; as of January 1986, employees owned 25 percent of the outstanding shares.

But in past years the stakes had been lower than they appeared to be in February 1986. This time Borman and the unions seemed to be determined to break each other. Eastern's employees even retained the services of takeover specialists in an attempt to turn their 25 percent into control of the company so that they could oust Borman.

Fare wars were rapidly eroding Eastern's financial position. Eastern's major creditors were becoming concerned. As one banker put it, "No bank wants to run an airline. What are we going to do with all those planes?" No one wanted bankruptcy, but it seemed to be inevitable when Eastern failed to win the concessionary labor agreements it required in order to extend the terms of its bank loans.

Deliverance of a sort came in the form of a takeover offer by Texas Air Corporation, headed by Frank Lorenzo. Borman accepted the offer. In the end, it was Borman's inability to come to terms with Charles Burgess, head of the International Association of Machinists, that threw Eastern into Lorenzo's grasp. Less than four months later, Borman resigned.

SOURCE: Gary Cohn and Roger Lowenstein, "Dangerous Game: Eastern Airlines Is in Yet Another Crisis It Should Survive," *Wall Street Journal*, January 24, 1986; "Frank Lorenzo, High Flyer," *Business Week*, March 10, 1986, pp. 104–6; Robert Cuttner, "Sharing Power at Eastern Airlines," *Harvard Business Review*, November—December 1985, pp. 91–101.

Several **sources of conflict** have been identified: the aggressive or conflict-prone personality, ambiguous roles, conflicting roles, differences in objectives, differences in values, differences in perceptions, inadequate authority, oppressive management, status incongruence, interdependence, inadequate re-

SOURCES OF
CONFLICT

sources and unsatisfactory communication. Let us quickly examine how each of these factors may contribute to conflict:

1. Aggressive or conflict-prone personality. Some people are just more prone to engage in conflict than others. They like a good fight, they overreact to even mild threats in their environment.
2. Ambiguous roles. If you do not know what you are supposed to do, conflict may result. If no one knows what to do, everyone will try to shift responsibility to everyone else, because "it's not my job."
3. Conflicting roles. If a man is required to work overtime the night his daughter is performing in a play, his role as employee conflicts with his role as father. One of his roles will have to be sacrificed.
4. Differences in objectives. The accounting department wants small inventories to keep costs down; the marketing department wants large inventories to keep customers happy. Their different objectives bring them into conflict.
5. Differences in values. The engineering department values perfection; the production department wants a product it can sell at a reasonable price for a profit. Perfection costs more and is usually difficult to manufacture. Somebody has to give.
6. Differences in perceptions. The personnel manager may see equal employment opportunity laws as a challenge; the operating manager may see them as another government nuisance.
7. Inadequate authority. You have been given an assignment. You try to carry it out. Someone refuses to do what you ask because "you don't have the authority." Conflict results.
8. Oppressive management. Dictators usually arouse resistance. Many organizations are run by virtual dictators. Informal groups form and conflict ensues, as the Human Relations Happening on Robert Abboud indicates.
9. Status incongruence. If you receive glowing performance appraisals and no raise, trouble is bound to follow. If you have very high status on one scale (a graduate degree) and very low status on another (your boss is interested only in your typing skills), the potential for conflict is obvious.
10. Interdependence. Farrah used to be a well-known brand of men's clothing. But Willie Farrah and the union had a major disagreement. A long strike ensued. Farrah is no longer an important element in the market. The union lost thousands of jobs. Both sides thought that if one side lost, the other must win. But they were wrong. Both sides lost.[15]
11. Inadequate resources. Much organizational conflict results from competition between groups for scarce resources. The budget stretches only so far.
12. Unsatisfactory communication. When understanding is lacking, conflict may result. That's why many companies have a "hot line": so that organizational members may talk to someone to clear up misunderstandings.

"In frank expression of conflicting opinion lies the greatest promise of wisdom in governmental action; and in suppression lies ordinarily the greatest peril."
Louis D. Brandeis

THE CONSEQUENCES OF CONFLICT

Conflict can have positive as well as negative consequences. While many people would like to eliminate all conflict, it seems more realistic to try to keep it within bounds and make use of it.

Positive Consequences   Much of change depends on conflict. Competition tends to enhance the general welfare, if the conflict level is not too high. The offensive unit and the defensive unit of a football team may compete to see who does its job better, and in so doing overcome the common opponent.

HUMAN RELATIONS HAPPENING

THE AUTOCRATIC MR. ABBOUD

In April 1980, *Fortune* described Robert Abboud, then chairman of First Chicago Corporation, as one of the country's ten toughest bosses. Abboud, who declined to be interviewed by *Fortune*, was described by associates and subordinates as "bright, abrasive, aggressive, extremely ambitious . . . very tough on people . . . used to dress down his peers as well as subordinates . . . likes to make decisions solo."

Shortly after he was fired later that month, an article in the *Wall Street Journal* indicated that many people at First Chicago blamed Abboud, his management style, and his decisions for the precipitous decline in the bank's fortunes. During his five years at First Chicago, some 200 vice-presidents departed, often by choice. The bank, then the nation's ninth largest, seemed mired in internal squabbling between Abboud's supporters and those who wanted him gone. The feelings against Abboud were extremely strong. As news of his departure spread through the bank, many employees gleefully sang, "Ding-dong, the witch is gone." One senior vice-president chortled, "It's steak and champagne at our house tonight."

Abboud's style was autocratic in the extreme. And he apparently engaged in highly political actions in attempts to destroy all opposition. He played one executive against another, usurped power for himself, chewed out subordinates in public, and came down harshly on anyone who had the misfortune to tell him something he didn't want to hear. One senior executive commented, "There has been a history of the messenger being shot for bringing bad news, so people tend not to bring bad news."

Still, bad management has not always resulted in the firing of bad managers. Abboud committed the cardinal sin: he presided over a sharp decline in the bank's profits. Outsiders characterized the firm as nonaggressive, not given to "chasing after business." The rapid turnover, apparently due in large part to Abboud's style, was believed to have hurt the bank's ability to compete in the loan markets, where long-standing relationships are critical. Other operating problems persisted, and Abboud apparently failed to confront them. The bank continued to make fixed-rate loans, for instance, long after rising interest rates made such loans unprofitable.

Morale and performance began to rise after Abboud's departure. As one would suspect, the board sought to replace Abboud with someone who had a very different management style. Barry F. Sullivan, Abboud's replacement, set the tone for the change by encouraging participation in decision making at virtually all levels. Employees have responded.

SOURCES: Hugh D. Menzies, "The Ten Toughest Bosses," *Fortune*, April 21, 1980, pp. 62–72; Lawrence Rout, "First Chicago, with or without Abboud, Is a Place of Tension," *Wall Street Journal*, May 13, 1980, pp. 1, 23; Paul A. Gigot and Laurel Sorenson, "Bank on the Mend: Morale and Earnings Rise at First Chicago under New Chairman," *Wall Street Journal*, May 27, 1981, pp. 1, 25.

Branch *A* and branch *B* may compete, and in so doing may cause the whole bank to grow at a much faster rate than it would have done otherwise. Conflict in the form of competition ordinarily increases group cohesiveness, which in turn usually increases the group's productivity. Loyalty normally increases when people unite against a common foe. If problems are recognized, solutions may be forthcoming. Change results. The organization survives and prospers.

Negative Consequences   People stop talking to each other. Activities, not results, become important. Biased perceptions of "the other guys" are reinforced. Communication that does not support such stereotypes is blocked. Strong leaders are sought—and strong leaders often turn autocratic in conflict situations. The overall objectives of the organization are forgotten. Bitterness turns to hatred. The conflict may become a test of wills, a test of egos, a test of who can outlast the other person, group, or organization. At the very least, inappropriate types or levels of conflict have been shown to be counterproductive. Some of the very negative results of conflict occur because people attack the individual rather than the problem.

RESOLVING CONFLICT

The manager's role is to choose the correct **conflict management** techniques and to keep conflict at an appropriate level. Unnecessary conflict is counterproductive. Many of the twelve sources of conflict identified earlier give rise to difficulties that could be avoided if appropriate steps were taken in time.

The common technique of simple dominance of the opponent will not suffice as a long-run method of conflict resolution, at least not in the business organization. The conflict situation should be viewed as a problem that should be solved in a rational manner, like any other problem.

In managing conflict, the manager needs to recognize that any of four outcomes is possible, depending on what happens to each of the two participants in the conflict, as shown in Figure 17.1. In the lose–lose scenario, one individual wants both parties to lose. A terrorist squad is a good example.

FIGURE 17.1   *Conflict outcomes*

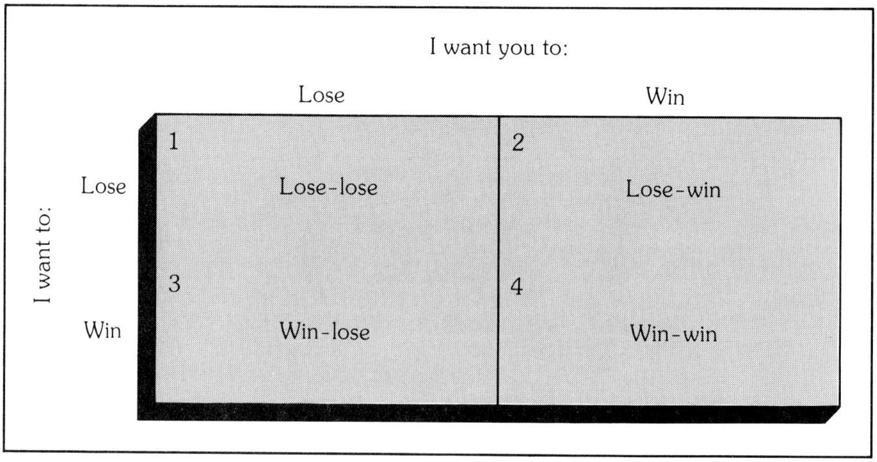

In the second situation, lose–win, the decision maker sees an advantage in losing, perhaps on a minor issue, in order to gain future leverage on a major issue. In the win–lose scenario, you want to defeat your opponent, perhaps a competitor in the marketplace. Finally, in win–win situations, both parties achieve their objectives. The modern view of labor relations is win–win, not win–lose, as it used to be.[16]

Eliminating Unnecessary Conflict   Many unnecessary role-related conflicts can be prevented by proper rules, procedures, policies, and an MBORR program.

Authority can be delegated in accordance with responsibility. The aggressive personality and the oppressive manager can be isolated, trained to be different, or removed. Status incongruencies can be moderated through rational understanding of the situation. Communication can improve perceptions and reduce stereotyping. Exchanges of ideas are of critical importance. So are proper organizational structures. For example, Edward Telling, former chairman of Sears, found upon taking over the company that twenty-two people reported to him. He spent all of his time managing unnecessary internal conflict. One of his first actions as chairman was to change the structure and reduce his span of control, so that his time and energy could be devoted to more important matters.[17] In short, a lot of conflict can be eliminated simply by the exercise of basic management practices.

Managing Conflict   As not all conflict can be eliminated and some is even desirable, managers must learn to manage conflict. Several conflict management methods have been suggested. Kenneth W. Thomas has suggested that these approaches may be explained in terms of the degrees of cooperativeness and assertiveness of one of the contending parties with respect to intentions concerning the conflict. Figure 17.2 modifies his approach to include aggression.[18] Thomas' approach can be used as a vehicle for discussing virtually all of the major conflict-resolution techniques:

> *The first major problem of groups in organizations is how to make them effective in fulfilling both organizational goals and the needs of their members. The second major problem is how to establish conditions between groups which will enhance the productivity of each without destroying intergroup relations and coordination.*
> EDGAR H. SCHEIN

1. Avoidance: no assertiveness, no cooperation. Most unpleasant realities can be avoided. The problem is not solved, it is only postponed, but in the short run this technique may work. It is not uncommon, for example, for people who do not have the strength to oppose their bosses on an issue to avoid them, perhaps in the hope of delaying a decision until they do gain strength.
2. Accommodation: no assertiveness, cooperation. One may also give in. Some people give in to others all the time. The win–lose situation must have a loser. Sometimes one must accommodate other people. Many people say that the U.S. auto manufacturers have for years accommodated most union demands in the interest of labor harmony, to the detriment of their ability to compete effectively with foreign firms. In the economy of the 1980s, however, labor is more ready to accommodate management.
3. Smoothing: low assertion, low cooperation. Smoothing is a mild attempt at problem solving. It focuses on similarities, not differences, and seeks resolution. The intent is to move the parties toward a common goal. Political parties must smooth over differences after a primary campaign.
4. Competition: assertiveness, no cooperation. This is a win–lose approach, but the competition must adhere to certain rules. The assertive person does

FIGURE 17.2   *A two-dimensional model of conflict intentions*

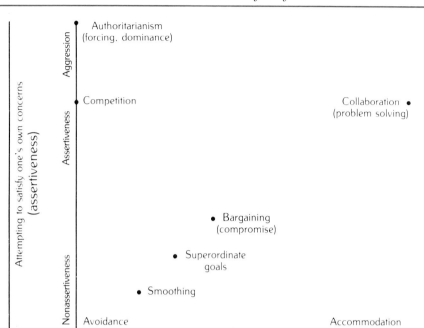

SOURCE: Adapted from Kenneth W. Thomas, "Introduction" (to a series on conflict management entitled, "Conflict and the Collaborative Ethic"), *California Management Review*, Winter 1978, Vol. XXI, No. 2, p. 57. © 1978 by the Regents of the University of California. By permission of the Regents.

not seek to harm the other's self-image, but competition does serve to change and improve the organization. Change and success are based on competition in a free-market economy.

5. Bargaining (compromise): moderate assertiveness, moderate cooperation. This is a give-and-take position. Negotiations between labor and management usually follow this pattern. Both parties satisfy some of their needs.

6. Superordinate goals: increasing assertiveness, increasing cooperation. The parties attempt to find a common set of objectives that will cause them to forget their differences. Superordinate goals may be imposed from above, in which case authoritarian forcing is the technique employed. Superordinate goals do not solve the underlying problem but provide more focus than smoothing. Members of the football team may fight among themselves during the week, but on Friday, Saturday, or Sunday, those differences should be forgotten because of a superordinate goal.

7. Authoritarianism (forcing, dominance): aggression, no cooperation. A party that feels it must win at any cost is using aggression. The unfriendly business

takeover in which all of the previous managers are terminated by the new management is an example of this approach.

8. Collaboration: assertiveness and cooperation. This approach is characterized by a genuine attempt to find solutions that satisfy all of the needs of both parties. It differs from compromise in the participants' attitudes: while trying to obtain their own objectives (assertiveness), they become increasingly cooperative.

Choosing a Conflict-Resolution Technique   In deciding how to resolve a conflict, each party must assess the other's willingness to cooperate and assertion level and factor the implications into the solution. A great deal has been written about the need to collaborate, as if it were the preferred mechanism to resolve all conflicts. The truth is that each conflict-resolution method is most appropriate in certain circumstances. Our task is to base our decision on the critical factors in each situation, beginning with the cooperativeness and assertiveness of both parties. Sometimes the conflict will be between equals; at other times one party will be dominant and the other subordinate. The same factors that should be considered in leadership decisions seem to apply here: the personality of the decision maker, the personalities of those involved, the nature of the groups involved, the organization's climate, the task, and other factors.

"I've heard this group has had some trouble reaching agreement."

Reprinted with the permission of *Industry Week*, March 20, 1978, p. 18. Cartoon for *Industry Week* by George F. Kocar.

TIPS FOR SUCCESS

1. Learn as much as you can about the power structure in your organization or any that you are considering going to work for.
2. Learn how the people around you use power and politics.
3. Be prepared for the various political strategies that others may use.
4. Confine your strategies to those that are ethical. In the long term, unethical tactics are unsound.
5. Perform at a high level, but pay attention to politics.
6. Manage conflict; don't be managed by it.
7. Remember: nobody said life was fair.

SUMMARY

1. Power is the ability to influence other people and to gain access to things of value; politics is one means by which power is acquired.
2. There are five kinds of power: legitimate power, reward power, coercive power, expert power, and referent power.
3. Politics is a part of organizational life. It exists because of the nature of people, the nature of organizations, and competition.
4. Psychological games are the basis of politics. You must learn to recognize games and be able to stop them.
5. Conversational politics is a violation of normal rules of conversation for the purpose of asserting power. People who perceive themselves as having more power than those with whom they are conversing often interrupt, ignore what others say, and show a lack of interest.
6. Vertical politics is engaged in by superiors and subordinates; horizontal politics is played by peers.
7. External politics consists of political actions involving people outside of the organization; internal politics consists of political actions within the organization.
8. Legitimate political actions are those governed by informal rules that everyone understands. Such strategies include absorption or seduction of protestors; finding a mentor; taking up your boss's and clients' hobbies; sharing your boss's enthusiasms; being a yes person; using flattery; making alliances; making friends of secretaries; playing conversational politics; and cultivating strength in your competitors' areas of weakness.

9. Illegitimate political actions are those not in accordance with the informal rules. Such strategies include giving subordinates tasks at which they will fail; giving subordinates too much to do; screwing up intentionally in a way that hurts one's enemies; getting nasty; using sex; ending protest by destroying the protestors; taking credit for someone else's work; shooting down all of your opponent's ideas; playing hard psychological games; and using creative political machinations.
10. Effective nonpolitical strategies to increase one's power include making good decisions; doing what's right; being somebody they can't do without; helping others to achieve their objectives; volunteering for tough assignments; showing concern and dedication; getting promoted; building a network; performing; being sensitive to others' territorial rights; and bluffing.
11. Conflict cannot always be avoided, but it can be managed.
12. There are twelve major sources of conflict: aggressive or conflict-prone personality, ambiguous roles, conflicting roles, differences in objectives, differences in values, differences in perceptions, inadequate authority, oppressive management, status incongruence, interdependence, inadequate resources, and unsatisfactory communications.
13. Conflict can have positive as well as negative consequences.
14. A conflict may have any of four outcomes: win–win, win–lose, lose–win, lose–lose.
15. Any of eight major strategies may be used to

manage conflict: avoidance, accommodation, smoothing, competition, bargaining, superordinate goals, authoritarianism, and collaboration.

16. The choice of a conflict-resolution technique depends on the desired outcome and the degree of cooperativeness and assertion expressed.

DISCUSSION QUESTIONS

1. Discuss the ethics of playing politics.
2. Describe a political action you have seen in an organization to which you have belonged.
3. Distinguish between legitimate and illegitimate strategies in the situation you have just described.

4. Give examples of the various legitimate, illegitimate, and nonpolitical ways in which you can gain power.
5. Describe various organizational conflicts you have witnessed, their causes, and how they were resolved.

APPLYING HUMAN RELATIONS SKILLS

Politics and Communication

CASE

Philip Shrewsbury peered out the window from the 38th floor into the snowy sky above New York City. It was really coming down. He could barely make out the offices across the street. Funny, he thought, that blur is a lot like the way we deal with each other around here. Philip was a product manager in a manufacturing subsidiary of a large conglomerate. In the smaller firm where he had worked before, people had been much more congenial and helpful. Here the politics was fierce. There was no communication that you could count on. If you wanted to know anything, you had to go outside normal channels and consult the rumor mill.

Much of Philip's work effort was spent in justifying, convincing, and negotiating with his boss and other managers about the future of his product list. His products were selling well, and he felt that it was wrong to be cutting back on product investment in growth markets. His sentiments were understandably shared by the other product managers. But the financial types in top management wanted a lean staff throughout. Philip was constantly battling for office space, marketing dollars, and staff to support the 25 percent growth of his product list, to no avail. And his personal travel budget, so vital for selling at trade shows and for learning the market's needs through customer visits, had not grown in four years. All of his problems seemed to stem from the style of top management and from the firm's related communication problems.

Much of his concern revolved around the boot-licking that he constantly saw at all levels of management. Most of his associates felt as though someone were always looking over their shoulders. Top management did nothing to lessen their anxiety; if anything, they encouraged it. They seemed to enjoy the ferment in the lower ranks.

Philip had always believed that as long as he did the job right, he would do fine. He was no longer sure that that was true. It was obvious that becoming part of the old-boy network was essential to success in this organization. He had begun to wonder whether he really wanted to be promoted in this firm.

1. Can Philip do anything to manage the politics in this firm? How can he best cope with this situation?
2. How are the politics and communication patterns of this firm related to its management style?

EXERCISE Test your political acumen by placing a check mark beneath the option you most agree with. I believe:

	agree	disagree
1. the boss is usually right, even if he or she really isn't.		
2. it is wise to compliment those in power on their performances as a part of my daily regimen.		
3. networking and visibility are every bit as important to getting ahead as performance.		
4. in doing favors for people so that I can cash in on them later.		
5. in playing golf if my boss plays golf, in playing tennis if he or she likes tennis, in handball if it's handball, etc.		
6. that you should build alliances in order to ensure your long-term survival in the organization.		
7. that the boss's secretary is the second most important person in my work group.		
8. it's a good strategy to screw up if it will rid you of a boss you don't like.		
9. whistleblowing is appropriate if it's a tough enough situation.		
10. power is the key to my future.		

SCORING: If you agreed to all of these statements, you are well on your way to organizational survivability. This is not to say that all of these behaviors are condoned, but rather that you recognize that politics are important. If you agreed 3 or fewer times, then you need to pay more serious attention to this chapter.

REFERENCES

1. John R. P. French and Bertram H. Raven, "The Bases of Social Power," in *Studies in Social Power*, ed. Dorwin Cartwright (Ann Harbor: University of Michigan Press, 1959).
2. Dan Farrell and James C. Petersen, "Patterns of Political Behavior in Organizations," *Academy of Management Review*, Fall 1982, pp. 403–12.
3. Quoted in Peter Chew, "Politicking, Inc.," *National Observer*, January 26, 1974, p. 18.
4. Quoted in ibid.
5. Quoted in Walter Kiechel III, "The Importance of Being Visible," *Fortune*, June 24, 1985, p. 141.
6. Ibid., p. 142.
7. Eric Berne, *Games People Play* (New York: Ballantine, 1973).
8. Mary Brown Parlee, "Conversational Politics," *Psychology Today*, May 1979, pp. 48–56.
9. Ibid., p. 51.
10. Ibid., p. 56.
11. Farrell and Petersen, "Patterns of Political Behavior," p. 407.
12. Rory O'Day, "Rituals of Intimidation," *Journal of Applied Behavioral Science*, December 1974, pp. 373–86.
13. O'Day, "Rituals of Intimidation," p. 378.
14. Barbara Buell and Alison Leigh Cowan, "Learning How to Play the Corporate Power Game," *Business Week*, August 26, 1985, p. 54.
15. D. D. Madley, "How the Union Beat Willie Farrah," *Fortune*, August 1974, pp. 164–67.
16. Keith Davis and John W. Newstrom, *Human Behavior at Work: Organizational Behavior*, 7 ed. (New York: McGraw-Hill, 1985), pp. 210, 211, 384.
17. Edward Telling, "A View from the Top," *Success*, February 1986, pp. 64–65.
18. Kenneth W. Thomas, "Introduction" (to a series on conflict management), in *California Management Review*, Winter 1978, pp. 56–60. Dr. Thomas does not conceptually agree with my modifications but has generously permitted me to make them.

18 LIFE AND CAREER PLANNING

LEARNING OBJECTIVES

When you have completed this chapter, you should be able to:
1. Plan your life.
2. Analyze your situation, including your strengths, weaknesses, and opportunities.
3. Plan your career, given your current situation.
4. Establish objectives and plans for ten major life areas.

LIFE AND CAREER PLANNING AT AT&T

Kathy listened intently as the program director announced, "When this week is over, you may decide that you would like some other career than the one you have now. You may even decide that you and AT&T should part ways. If you do, we'll both be the better for it."

Kathy had never expected a company program to take such a straightforward approach to a very tough issue: What if I find out I don't really match well with my current employer? Attending the AT&T life and career planning seminar turned out to be extremely beneficial to Kathy, a middle-level manager in AT&T's data systems division. After filling out numerous questionnaires, listening to speakers, and engaging in many group discussions, she learned that she had several strengths that she had not realized she had. She also discovered a few weaknesses. She reaffirmed some objectives that she had established for herself earlier, and she determined some new ones. She found that she really hadn't formulated plans to reach those objectives except in a very general way. She therefore appreciated the opportunity provided by the program to plan how to reach her objectives.

AT&T, like many employers, feels that life and career planning is critical not only to the individual but to the organization. AT&T is very concerned that the individual and the organization match. If they don't, then a parting of ways is probably best for both parties. When the week was over, Kathy and most of the other people who attended the seminar chose to remain with AT&T; a couple weren't sure they would. All who participated felt that they had grown and were better able than before to contribute to organizational success, wherever they might eventually be.

SOURCE: Courtesy of AT&T.

Have you established objectives and plans for your life, as Kathy has now done? Or are you in need of attending a seminar such as that sponsored by AT&T for its middle- and upper-level managers?

Perhaps you already have a career in mind. Perhaps you already know what you want in life. But you probably do not, even if you are now employed.

"Of all knowledge, the wise and good seek most to know themselves."
WILLIAM SHAKESPEARE

This chapter focuses on a management system to which you have already been exposed—management by objectives, results, and rewards—within your own personal framework to show you how you may become self-actualized and how you may manage your own career. Even if you have life and career objectives in mind, you may not have formulated them clearly, as you must if you are to reach them, and you may not have established plans to reach those objectives. This chapter shows you how to use some of what you have learned about management in your own life. While many enlightened employers, such as AT&T, provide career-planning assistance, most do not. Few provide any kind of help in life planning. Most people are on their own. Thus mastering the subjects of this chapter will be of great benefit to you in the coming years.

Throughout this book, self-analysis has been stressed. You have often been asked to determine your own strengths and weaknesses with regard to the skills being taught. Now is the time to incorporate all of this learning in a self-improvement program. Much of what this chapter asks you to do will be done outside the classroom because of the time involved (filling out forms, for example), but these activities will be discussed in class.

The relationships examined are individual–self interactions (self-analysis of your career and your life), individual–organization interactions (how you plan your career within an organization), and organization-to-individual interactions (how the organization plans individual careers).

LIVING BY OBJECTIVES, RESULTS, AND REWARDS

Biographies of successful people have revealed that virtually all of them shared three characteristics: they all had certain objectives that for them became burning desires; they were all persistent; and most of them had a positive self-image or were trying very hard to achieve one.[1] Examinations of successful leaders and managers also reveal their concern for objectives, their plans to reach those objectives, their persistence, and their positive views of themselves.[2] Most successful organizations have been shown to plan. So why can't you?

Most of us spend our most important asset, the time that we have to live our lives, without giving much thought to what we are going to do with that time. Did you stop this morning or last night and think about what you were going to accomplish today? Did you assign priorities to your activities? Was there some purpose to those activities? Do you know where you are going in life?

Human beings are by nature goal-seeking animals. Maslow's and Alderfer's hierarchies of needs (Chapter 3) are hierarchies of objectives. The needs are expressed as objectives to be achieved, goals to be attained. We have learned that when retirees have no more objectives to achieve, they wither and die. If retired people do not have a second career, if they do not have some type of endeavor in which to engage, an objective to achieve, their bodies become old very rapidly. The average retired IBM manager, for example, dies within two years after retirement.[3] Objectives are important, then, not just for success but for survival, and not just for retirees. Numerous reports stress the importance of objectives to success in getting out of the ghetto, in surviving illnesses, even in surviving a Nazi concentration camp.[4]

Planning your life is essentially a time-management process. Time management was discussed in Chapter 16 as a means of coping with stress and of accomplishing more each day. This chapter expands those time-planning horizons to longer periods.

This chapter introduces a systematic life-planning philosophy/system known as **living by objectives, results, and rewards (LBORR)**. LBORR enables you to combine your reasoning ability with visual imagery to achieve far greater objectives than you may have thought possible. LBORR, like MBORR, is not just a system, it is a philosophy. But as with MBORR, even if you use only the system aspects—that is, the mechanics of establishing objectives, plans to reach those objectives, controlling for results, and rewarding yourself for performance—you will be pleased with the results. But if you add the philosophic ingredients, the belief that you can achieve, then the results and rewards may be even more dramatic.

Richard DeCharms proposed that people may be classified as either origins or pawns (see Chapter 4).[5] The origins feel that they are able to control their own destiny. The pawns feel that they are victims of life's circumstances. You can probably see that a lot of your friends fall into one or the other of these categories. Into which do you fall? If you perceive yourself as an origin, this chapter will help you to achieve. If you perceive yourself as a pawn, this chapter may help you to change from a pawn into an origin. Critical to such change is the belief that you can question old learned and emotional reactions. Your rational self must be in command.

A PERSONAL PLANNING EXERCISE

This exercise is designed to show you how to actualize yourself—how to become all that you are capable of becoming. To broaden the definition of self-actualization, ten major life areas—areas that would appear to have meaning in terms of self-fulfillment—are presented. Later in the chapter, one of those life areas, the career, is examined in more detail. This area has been chosen for further study because most of you are preparing to embark on that journey for the first time. Indeed, most of you, whatever your age, may be making career decisions.

In using the LBORR model, you will be assessing your environment, assessing your own strengths and weaknesses, setting objectives, establishing plans to reach those objectives, controlling for results, and rewarding your own performance or receiving rewards from your environment, in such forms as promotions or pay raises or happy children.

To begin this exercise, read each of the ten **major life areas** listed below, and their definitions:

Discovering yourself can be a lifelong adventure.
MURIEL JAMES AND
LOUIS SAVARY

1. Aesthetic interests — An appreciation of the finer things in life: art, literature, nature.
2. Career and economic status — The occupational area of your life. How successful do you wish to be? How much money do you want to make?

3. Family life	Improving relationships with your family.
4. Leisure activities	Time spent not working or sleeping, which is or could be spent in enjoyment.
5. Mental development	What you do to develop your mind and raise your educational and intellectual level.
6. Physical exercise	What you do to develop your body, to stay physically fit.
7. Psychological well-being	Obtaining peace of mind.
8. Religious life	Pursuit of ultimate meaning.
9. Social life	Improving relationships with others.
10. Societal concerns	Contributing to the welfare of the society.

Are there any other major life objectives that you feel should be pursued? If so, list them.

11. _____   _____
12. _____   _____

In the LBORR system, self-actualization is perceived as requiring an attempt to become all that you are capable of becoming. If you do not set objectives and then reach them in each of these ten areas, according to the LBORR philosophy, you are not self-actualizing. Naturally, some life areas must take precedence over others. But throughout your life, each must be addressed. Maslow's self-actualization appears to be more concerned with social, psychological, and career success than the definition employed here.[6] Certainly one must give these life areas considerable attention, but one must philosophically question just what it means "to become all that one is capable of becoming." It surely includes more than these three areas of one's life. Self-fulfillment would seem to demand that each of these ten areas be part of your life.

Plans for these ten life areas, plus any others you may have listed, are the components of your life's strategy. These life areas are not mutually exclusive, and neither are the objectives you establish for the various areas. For example, many people will seek psychological well-being through their religion. Education and social skills often lead to career/economic success. (Why would most of you be taking this course if you did not believe that?) Physical health is directly related to psychological health. And so forth.

Your objectives in each of these life areas and your plans to reach those objectives will reflect your personality and the demands of the particular situation. Again, your personality is a function both of the people with whom you have interacted and of your biological makeup.

In LBORR, your intent should be to consider rationally what you are truly capable of becoming. You must consider realistic objectives, but you must also stretch your potentials. By definition, once you have become more, you are capable of becoming more.

One thing is certain: if you think you can't, you never will, because you just said so. You get what you expect. A lot of people will tell you that you can't do something. The truth is *they* can't, and they therefore think you can't.

So when they say, "You can't," they mean, "I can't." But the truth is, you can do anything you want to within the limits of your mind and body. Few of us will ever play professional football—and for good reason. We do not weigh 230 pounds, run the 40-yard dash in 4.4 seconds, bench-press 400 pounds, or take that joy in violence which seems to be necessary. But within your abilities, you should be able to accomplish whatever you set out to accomplish. With the exception of the mentally retarded, the capabilities of most people's minds appear to be endless. Even the extremely under-educated can achieve, if they are willing to work for it. So it is only the body that seems to constrain most of us. And if you believe in yourself, you might just make it even without the best body.

Think carefully, now. What would you like to accomplish before your life is completed in each of these ten areas? What do you want to become? Write your answers here.

1. Aesthetic interests _____
2. Career/economic status _____
3. Family life _____
4. Leisure activities _____
5. Mental development _____
6. Physical condition _____
7. Psychological well-being _____
8. Religious life _____
9. Social life _____
10. Societal concerns _____

Would you consider yourself to be self-actualized if you could accomplish all of these objectives?

THE LBORR PROCESS

In the LBORR process, you will follow a series of actions not unlike those that organizations follow when they plan their futures. This process requires, first of all, establishing long-term objectives (which you have just done) and establishing the plans to reach those objectives. Second, it involves establishing short-term objectives, which typically involve a period of from one day to one year forward in time, and the plans to reach those objectives. (See Figure 18.1.)

To establish these objectives and plans of action to achieve them, it is first necessary to perform a self-analysis and an environmental analysis. In performing the self-analysis, you are interested in discovering what your personal strengths and weaknesses are relative to achieving each of your objectives. In performing the environmental analysis, you are interested in determining the major obstacles or the major facilitating factors that will hinder or help your efforts to achieve your objectives in each major life area. After considering the results of your analysis, you should be able to establish the necessary objectives. In examining your strengths and weaknesses, you should be primarily concerned with their relationship to the environment in which you must

FIGURE 18.1   *The LBORR process*

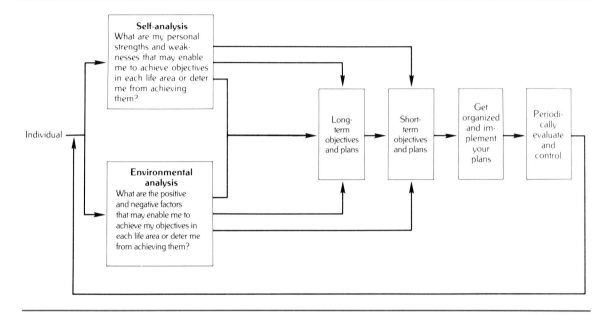

seek to achieve your objectives. For example, if you wish to become a successful top-level business manager, unless you own your own corporation, you will probably need to earn a master's degree in business administration (MBA). This is just the nature of the business environment today. Thus, if you do not have an MBA (weakness), then you should acquire one, which would give you a strength in that environment. This process is necessary for each objective that you establish in each major life area.

As you grow, as you actualize yourself, by definition, your objectives should change. As you become more of what you are capable of becoming, you are capable of becoming even more. Your potentials simply expand. Over time, you can increase your potential, increase your accomplishments, expand your objectives.

The "life strategy determination" form at the end of this chapter provides space for you to consider one life area and its various objectives. You can make copies of this form in order to consider all major life areas. Space is also provided for you to review your strengths and weaknesses and the environmental positives and negatives. As you move from long-term to short-term planning horizons, your plans of action should become more specific. For example, if your ultimate economic objective were to have a net worth of $1 million and your ultimate plan were to enter into the real estate business, then your short-term objective might be simply to qualify for a real estate agent's license and your plan might be to take a course in real estate at your local university or college.

"Nothing will ever be attempted if all possible objections must be first overcome."

SAMUEL JOHNSON

CAREER PLANNING

Now that you are familiar with the basic LBORR process, it seems appropriate to examine in detail an area of interest to most of you: **career planning**. Career planning is certainly one of the most important undertakings you will ever engage in. After all, in much of the Western Hemisphere, it is a career that determines your economic success, your familial success (divorce rates are extremely high among lower economic groups), and to some extent even your psychological happiness. It is difficult to be happy in our society when you cannot have all the things you would like to have.

The objectives and plans you establish now must remain flexible. Most of us change jobs three or four times, especially when we are young. But many people are now changing their careers in midlife, partly because they have come to question the appropriateness of their earlier decisions.

Career decisions may be quite appropriate at the time they are made, but may not be appropriate later in life. Why? At least partly because people change. A number of authorities on the individual life-cycle process, including Erik Erikson,[7] Roger Gould,[8] and Gail Sheehy,[9] have reported that people pass through various stages in their lives, what Sheehy refers to as "passages." Each of these stages has a significant potential impact on the individual's career and career choices. Each stage revolves around a crisis—not a catastrophe, but a turning point. Sheehy's "passages" are defined briefly below. Her stages are similar to those identified by others who have studied the life cycle, though the unrepresentativeness of her sample group, composed mostly of professionals, somewhat limits the applicability of her findings to the general population.

- Pulling up roots: After age 18, the message is clear. We must get away from our parents' domination. Sometimes attachment to a strong "other" results. Usually this is not a good solution, and divorce is not infrequent in such cases.

- The trying twenties: During these years we work things out. We see if we can come to grips with the reality of the social and work worlds. These years are dominated by "doing what we should." Life patterns are established here, and career choices are an important part of these patterns.

- Catch-30: In the late twenties and early thirties, people begin to question the decisions they made earlier. Not infrequently, the result is a destruction of the life made in the early twenties. Reflection is the watchword. New choices are made and divorce is common. Career choices are questioned.

- Rooting and extending: The early to mid-thirties are characterized by a turning inward to the family and by career commitment—commitment to "making it."

- The deadline decade: The mid-thirties to mid-forties foretell the end. Time squeezes us. We realize that we are getting older. Values, careers, life objectives are all reexamined. The push to make it may become too intense. Many people start second careers. Women seem to begin this stage earlier than men.

- Renewal or resignation: The last crisis comes from the mid-forties onward. Most people experience a mellowing, an acceptance of their situation. For others, the crisis may last forever. Life's cycle must be accepted. Some people never do accept it. (This is not to say that we must surrender physically or mentally. Quite the contrary. We can still get some exercise and we can still expand our minds.)

We all go through these stages, not always at the same times, but generally within the time spans indicated. Some people may reach stages later than others because of the time that career choices take. Some elements of one stage may overlap those of another. But we are all faced with these basic situations. And career planning must be sufficiently flexible to accommodate these changes. What are some of the major career issues that you must decide?

MAJOR CAREER CHOICES

Below are some of the major issues with which you will be confronted during your career. At this point you may not be able to answer or even relate to all of these areas. Your experience base may be too small. But look at them now, and again later in your career. Use those that are applicable now and the others later.

- Career field: What skill area are you going to enter, remain in, or change to? A typical progression seems to be from a skilled area into management. Upward movement occasionally involves a change in skill area, though not necessarily a radical change. For example, an auditor might become a cost specialist, or a personnel specialist might switch from selection to training.
- Industry: What industry do you wish to enter, remain in, or change to? Not all industries pay the same. Since a lower-level employee's pay is usually a percentage of top management's pay, you may wish to pick an industry, all else being equal, on the basis of potential pay. Industries become obsolescent, as do individuals. Do not remain in an obsolescing industry unless you are ready for retirement.
- Obsolescence: Are you obsolete? What skills do you need—technical, human relations, conceptual—that will make you more marketable?
- Life stage: In what life stage do you find yourself, and what is the impact of this stage on your career decisions?
- Management: Do you want to move into management? What are the pluses and minuses? Are you ready for the responsibilities?
- Mobility: Are you mobile? If not, why not? Have you been in your current job three years or more without a raise or promotion? If the answer is yes, maybe you should move on.
- Match: What is the match between yourself and your current and proposed future organization? Does it have the proper climate? How do they treat people? How do you want to be treated? Can you adjust to this climate?
- Impacts: What are the impacts of a career decision on family and friends? Will relocation be necessary? Where? Is this location acceptable?

Drawing by W. Miller; © 1979 The New Yorker Magazine, Inc. Used with permission.

- Value: Of what value are you to this organization? What indications do you have of this value? Are you likely to be promoted soon? What are your strengths and weaknesses?
- Experience: What kinds of work experience have you liked and disliked?
- Motivation: Do you have the burning desire that it takes to improve your career position?
- Organization: Do you need to leave your organization and find another? Why, or why not?

These and other major issues seem to crop up just about every time a career decision is made.

The self-analysis and environmental analysis portions of the LBORR process for the career life area might appear as they do in Table 18.1.

The items to be examined in both personal and environmental areas remain relatively stable whether long-term or short-term objectives and plans are being established. Major career skill areas are changed only rarely, but changes do occur. Industry is changed fairly frequently. Life stage changes only periodically. But the rest of the items could occur on any planning horizon, long-term or short-term.

TABLE 18.1 Self- and Environmental Analyses of a Hypothetical Senior Majoring in Accounting

SELF-ANALYSIS

Personal Strengths	Personal Weaknesses
Self-concept	Lack of direction
Need to be successful	No master's degree
Like business subjects	Little experience
Ambition	Not sure what firm to go with
Bachelor's degree	Not sure how to lead others
Good communication skills	Sometimes let others make decisions
Father has contacts	
Quick learner	
Good at planning	

ENVIRONMENTAL ANALYSIS

Opportunities	Threats or Obstacles
Employers seeking my degree area	They want experience, if possible
High salaries in my degree area	Travel about 50% of the time
Rapid turnover, quick advancement	Entry-level positions are often boring
Two companies have good climates	Job skills obsolesce quickly
Highly respected profession	
Demand outweighs supply	
Best jobs in urban areas	

ORGANIZATIONAL CAREER-DEVELOPMENT PROGRAMS

Many organizations have career-development programs for their employees. Unfortunately, most such programs are rather loosely defined and disorganized attempts at career management. In virtually all organizations, you, the individual, must take responsibility for developing your career. This means that you must take advantage of existing organizational programs, or if there is none—and unfortunately, most organizations have no career-development program—you must seize the bull by the horns and develop your own career.

Those organizations that have career-development programs seem to focus primarily on two facets of career development: career pathing (determining probable career paths through the organization) and management development and training (providing seminars in technical, human relations, and conceptual management skills areas).

Vern Walter has developed one of the more sophisticated employment-planning systems, "self-motivated personal career planning."[10] Organizational managers facilitate an employee career analysis process. A process not unlike the LBORR process is employed. Employees engage in self-analysis. This process includes several personality tests. Strengths and weaknesses are identified. Past accomplishments are inventoried, and career interests are tested against those accomplishments. The results are then matched against the organization's needs and opportunities. Specific action plans aimed at overcoming weaknesses and negative environmental factors and taking advantage of strengths and positive environmental factors (opportunities) are then formulated.

The benefits of this program are substantial, and we can expect to see more organizations adopting similar programs in the future. The benefits to the organization include:

- Discovery of people with career potential.
- Increased organizational effectivenss and efficiency through optimum use of people.
- Improved work-force motivation because individual goals are matched with the organization's.
- Improvement in commitment and cooperation.
- Help in affirmative action efforts.

The benefits to employees include:

- Identifying strengths and weaknesses so that a career may be based on strengths.
- Improvement in match of personality, individual goal, and organization.
- Knowing where one is headed (planning).
- Visibility.
- Reduction of confusion with respect to career path.
- Perceived greater self-control.

Before you enter into a career-development program, whether organizational or your own, there are several questions that might help you to determine your career decisions:

1. What are the most satisfying work experiences you can recall?
2. What are the least satisfying work experiences you can recall?
3. How do the answers to the two questions above relate to your current or proposed job?
4. What factors seem important to you in your job—for example, the chance for individual growth?
5. What type of job will provide you with these factors?
6. Where do you want to be a year from now in your career, and what do you have to do right now to get there?
7. Are your aspirations compatible with your probable career path in your current organization?
8. How are you viewed by management in your current organization—positively, negatively?
9. What are your priorities for your career with respect to the other twelve life areas?

If you ask yourself these questions and examine the issues noted earlier which seem to appear in career decisions, then you should be well on your way to improving your career.

QUESTIONS TO ASK YOURSELF

"One measure of a man is the questions he raises, and another is the goals for which he uses his powers and talents."
SIDNEY JOURARD

LAURA MEYERS:
AN EXAMPLE OF
CAREER
PLANNING

Laura Meyers is a personnel manager for a college with 120 faculty and 5,000 students. She observed her situation and determined that she might be becoming obsolete. She entered a master's degree program in personnel administration. Some time later, nearing completion of this program, she began to review her own career situation.

Tables 18.2 and 18.3 show her completed life planning form for her career life area. Laura is white, 32, divorced, and has one child, a daughter, aged 5. She has considerable experience in personnel, and intends to stay in that field for some time. But she is considering obtaining her Ph.D. and entering the college teaching profession. As you can see by her completed form, it is not necessary to do every phase in complete detail. In fact, that is the ideal, the exception rather than the rule. But she had made some important specific notations as to what she needs to be doing. And two months after completing this form, she revealed to me that because of this exercise, she had begun to take specific steps (i.e., a job search) to bring this program of action to fruition.

TABLE 18.2   Life Strategy Determination Form of Laura Meyers, Career/Economic Life Area, Part 1

| | ENVIRONMENTAL ANALYSIS | |
OBJECTIVES	OPPORTUNITIES	THREATS/OBSTACLES
Long Term		
1. Teaching in university, in human relations or personnel management area 2. Rank of assistant professor by 1990	1. Positive growth, limited entry	1. Job market could be affected by economic problems in 1990s 2. Relocation may be necessary—could be affected by housing market (economy)
Medium Term		
1. Personnel manager for large company in private industry 2. Goal of salary of $40,000 or more by January 1988	1. Market receptive to women in business; should continue 2. Am a generalist in the field; however, do have more training in certain areas that could prove useful if job opportunities indicate more needs exist for training, affirmative action, employment and benefits administration, or compensation as opposed to a general function	1. MBA market tending to become glutted 2. South does not tend to accept women in business as readily as other areas 3. Relocation necessary; housing market may slide downward
Short Term		
1. Seek new position in city that will allow me to work on Ph.D.	1. Current opportunities in personnel look good, judging from advertisement	1. Must be able to keep up with continuing changes in personnel field (could be long term)

TABLE 18.3   Life Strategy Determination Form of Laura Meyers, Career/Economic Life Area, Part 2

SELF-ANALYSIS		
STRENGTHS	WEAKNESSES	FINAL PLANS OF ACTION
Long Term		
1. Have good self-image	1. Must attain Ph.D.	1. Attain teaching situation
2. Original background was	2. Must support daughter, and all	shortly before finishing, to
teaching before business, so	plans must be worked out to	allow time to complete
am motivated to combine the	ensure she is not neglected	dissertation
two		2. Full-time teaching following
3. Have personal need to achieve		attainment of degree
and receive feedback		
4. Strong need for affiliation		
Medium Term		
1. Experience: have had	1. Impact on family and self to	1. Narrow choice of schools so
experience in private and	my move—do not enjoy	that can aid in job selection,
public sectors (8 yrs.)	being uprooted	if more than one offer occurs
2. Education: recent MBA	2. Could not afford to wait too	2. Select firm on basis of offers
3. Enjoy responsibility; do not	many years to make a move	and also previous interest in
particularly like to work for	into private industry as age	area
others	would hurt	3. Enroll in school and continue
4. Age a plus at this point		working as long as possible
Short Term		
1. Strongly motivated to succeed		1. Prepare résumé geared to
and be independent		private industry
2. Am mobile; can make moves		2. Select firms in cities with
and career changes, as am		schools that offer Ph.D.
single		3. Begin job search immediately

Her really long-term objectives include being a full professor, author of two books, a consultant earning $80,000 per year, and so forth. The ones on her form are more immediately obtainable objectives and they help her plan her future. Once she attains these objectives, she can then expand toward her long-term objectives. You'll note that she has decided to include some medium-range objectives and plans. This step is not required but it may prove beneficial for you as well.

As you can see from her objectives (which partially become plans—the how as well as the what), she intends to seek employment with a private employer in a large city where she can attend school, presumably at night. (Some Ph.D. programs do not require full course loads until the last year. Some also have basic courses that can be taken at the master's level in the beginning, and thus can be taken at night.) She apparently intends to pursue her program in a southern state.

Reviewing positive and negative environmental factors, she views teaching in the long run as positive. Her immediate concerns also reflect perceived

> *"People see things and say Why; I dream of things and say Why Not?"*
> GEORGE BERNARD SHAW

potential difficulties in the housing market. She expresses concern that relocation could be a problem. We do not know her thinking here, but perhaps she may postpone her move for a year as a result.

Among her personal strengths and weaknesses, her positives are all real pluses given her career motivations, except the high need for affiliation. This could be a negative and certainly should not be stressed in job interviews. This need is not highly correlated with successful business managers and might suggest inability to discipline in the classroom (long-term objective of teaching).

Her final plans of action are generally appropriate. With respect to résumé construction for the private industry position, she needs to make certain that she slants it correctly. But since she reviews many résumés a month, she should have no problem in this area. Her search for Ph.D. programs could be more specific in terms of identifying quality programs that meet her criteria.

Given what she knows about what she wants to do and where she might do it, this career plan is appropriate for now and can be modified as each objective or facet of her plan becomes more detailed. She could have made her comments more specific, and she could have addressed more of the basic career decision issues and questions than she did. You may choose to do so when you examine your career. This has been a simple but true and truly helpful career-planning exercise. Laura is progressing rapidly toward the completion of her plans. It is not so much the thinking through the process that makes it effective. That is largely a function of the time you have to do it. It is going through the process that makes it effective. The process itself is motivating. The process is not new. In one form or another, it has existed for a long time. But going through the process makes you realize what you need to be doing. That's why career and life planning are important. Of course you could do it on your own—but would you? Here, as part of this course, you must do it, and structure is provided to help you plan your career, and indeed your life. Now, fill in the forms that appear at the end of the chapter to plan your career.

PSYCHO-CYBERNETICS AND THE PYGMALION EFFECT

66The rung of a ladder was never meant to rest upon, but only to hold a man's foot long enough to enable him to put the other somewhat higher.99
THOMAS HUXLEY

The power of expectation is a powerful influence over one's own future. Your expectations of others also have a way of becoming self-fulfilling prophecies. Most people live up to their own expectations or the expectations of the people who are important to them—parents, bosses, spouses, children, and the like.

For many years people suggested that the way you felt about yourself—that is, your self-image—had a major impact on whether or not you were successful. It was generally believed that if you had experienced success, you would develop a positive self-image and would continue to be successful. Furthermore, you would perceive yourself as competent and would accept challenges head-on. It was not until Maxwell Maltz, a plastic surgeon, proposed the concept of **psycho-cybernetics** that a plausible explanation of this phenomenon was offered. Maltz, in examining the postoperative behavior of patients whose physical appearance he had markedly improved, found that most still perceived themselves as ugly and could not adjust their behaviors to their new beauty. It was only through conditioning that they could accept their new faces as real. Exploring his discovery, he found that the mind could not tell the difference between what actually, objectively happened and what the mind imagined had happened. It followed, then, that visualizing success, seeing oneself as successful, would result in success. It also followed that belief in one's inability to succeed led ultimately to failure.

Maltz tells about two groups of basketball players. One group sat and envisioned shooting the ball perfectly. The other group actually shot baskets. After a period of time, both groups shot baskets for scores. The group that envisioned shooting perfectly outscored those who had actually shot baskets.[11] Maltz's work has been substantiated by several additional research efforts.[12] The correlation is not perfect, but substantial evidence does suggest that the way you feel about your own abilities, whether those perceptions are true or not, affects your true ability to be successful in virtually every endeavor. Your objectives and plans are going to be formulated within your perceptions. You therefore must consider their validity. Psycho-cybernetics at least partially tells us why a burning desire is necessary. A burning desire may force you to overcome your perceived limitations. Maltz found that if you examine what makes for success, see yourself taking those actions, and then actually take those actions, you are more likely to be successful than if you do not. Now read about Franklin Chang, the Chinese immigrant from Costa Rica who

---

HUMAN RELATIONS HAPPENING

Costa Rican Fulfills Dream, Becomes Astronaut

BY DANIEL Q. HANEY

Associated Press Writer

CAMBRIDGE, Mass.—Franklin Chang left home with a dream, to become an astronaut.

When the 18-year-old high school boy got off a plane from Costa Rica 12 years ago, he had $50 in his pocket and spoke only Spanish. But he had his dream.

Today, at age 30, Dr. Franklin Chang is a nuclear physicist, and an American citizen. On July 7, he starts training to fly on the space shuttle, one of 19 men and women chosen in the latest group of astronauts.

Chang, grandson of a Chinese emigrant, son of a Costa Rican gas station owner, says the secret of his success is simple. He owns it, he says, to the traditional American ideals: ambition and tenacity and hard work, things his folks told him make people prosper and get ahead in the United States.

"You have a dream, and if you really work at it, you can make it happen," he said.

Ever since he was a little boy, Chang wanted to be a spaceman. As best he can remember, the dream began in 1957, the day the Soviets launched Sputnik I and the space age began.

"When I was 7 years old, my mother told me one day that the Russians had put up an artificial satellite around the earth, and if I went out in the yard in the evening and climbed up a tree, I could see it go by," he recalled. "Well, I went out and climbed a tree, but I didn't see anything. But I remember that day vividly."

Chang became a space fan. He kept a scrapbook of the American and Russian space feats. He knew the names of all the rockets and capsules and astronauts.

(Continued on page 462)

"My high school classmates were into it as well," he said. "We had little teams of space cadets who were going to go into space. Slowly, my friends began to get interested in other things, and by the time I graduated from high school, I was the only one who still wanted to be an astronaut. I was the only one who hadn't grown up yet."

So he went seeking his dream. His father bought him a plane ticket to Hartford, Conn., where he lived with distant relatives and repeated his senior year in high school. He stayed with them for four months, then boarded with other local families.

Teacher Allan Winter took it upon himself to teach Chang English. He started the teen-ager on Bertrand Russell's "History of Western Civilization."

"That was my first book in English," he said. "It took me about a year, but after I read it, I had pretty much learned English."

He finished at the top of his class, got a scholarship to the University of Connecticut and earned an engineering degree. Then he went to the Massachusetts Institute of Technology, where he spent four years earning a doctorate in nuclear physics.

By then an expert in nuclear fusion, he got a job at the Draper Laboratory, a private research organization in Cambridge, designing controls for atomic power plants.

Last September, he took the step for which everything else had been preparation. He applied to the National Aeronautics and Space Administration for the job of astronaut. He got it.

After a year of training, Chang will be a flight specialist, the scientist who conducts experiments, takes charge of the food supply and builds structures outside the spaceship.

The first experimental shuttle flight is scheduled for next March, and NASA hopes the crafts will be making 40 or 50 flights a year by late in the decade.

Chang seems delighted, but not really surprised, that he got his wish. His grandfather once lived in Boston, and he prepared him for America.

"He said it was a place where everybody worked, and everybody had a chance to do something meaningful with their lives. And if you had something you really wanted to pursue, some kind of dream, this was the place to be."

But Chang said this vision is dying in America, and it worries him.

"Nobody has a mission anymore," he said. "We're trying to get as much out of the government as we can. We all feel that we are owed something. And that's a very counterproductive attitude, because we're defeating the very system that is feeding us."

Chang, with a half-Chinese father and a Hispanic mother, said people ask him where his allegiances lie.

"It's hard to say. I'm such a mongrel by now," he said with a laugh. "I was born in Costa Rica. I'm a little Chinese. But now I'm an American."

From the Associated Press, June 12, 1980.

became an astronaut. He overcame seemingly insurmountable obstacles. He believed he could, he envisioned what was necessary, and he succeeded.

Pygmalion was a king of Cyprus who also happened to be a sculptor. According to the legend, he fell in love with a statue of a woman that he himself had carved. He called her Galatea. Because of Pygmalion's prayers to the gods, Venus granted Galatea life. The power of belief can give substance to our imaginings. The power of belief is an extension of psycho-cybernetics and is strongly related to the effects of positive stroking (and negative stroking) on personality development associated with transactional analysis. If you project to others through stroking that you expect them to be lazy and no good, they will be. Thus the assumptions of the Theory X manager usually turn out to be correct. So do the assumptions of the Theory Y manager. The **Pygmalion effect** is an important behavioral concept that is often overlooked, but we must now become aware of its relationship to success and failure in the organization.

Remember, prophecies tend to be self-fulfilling.

THE INTERVIEW AND YOU

When you graduate, most of you will be involved in employment interviews during which you will converse with representatives of potential employers, including your prospective immediate supervisor. Most companies still place great weight on the interview in making their selection decisions, even though the interview has questionable scientific validity. It does not necessarily do what it is supposed to, which is to predict the future job success of the people interviewed. There are two basic types of interviews that you will encounter—a preliminary screening interview and one or more comprehensive interviews. The ground rules are essentially the same, but the comprehensive interviews are the more significant hurdles.

The **interview** is a much-studied phenomenon and you should gain personally from what we know about it. Below are some suggested aids for improving your performance in the interview.

1. The interview is an exercise in human relations, usually between two people but occasionally involving a group of interviewers and one interviewee. The interview is therefore a process that involves much of what you have learned thus far in this course, and you should apply what you have learned.

2. Study after study has shown that the single most important action you can take with respect to the interview is to make certain that your appearance is flawless. Hair, clothing, shoes should all be appropriate to the job for which you are applying. Conservative fashion is recommended. I am reminded of one student who did not follow recommended practices. He came to me to complain after just completing a job interview, one that he was told he failed. His appearance was abhorrent. His hair was so greasy you could have lubricated your car with the excess. His jacket was plaid, his pants were striped, and he wore a string tie that had been out of style for twenty years. His body odor was unpleasant. He had clearly not brushed his teeth recently. He smoked constantly, and I suspect he blew smoke in the interviewer's face, as he did in everyone else's. Numerous studies indicate that interviewers form an immediate, though usually subconscious, first impression of you on the basis of your appearance and your actions in the first five minutes of the interview. They seek information throughout the interview to confirm this first impression, be it good or bad. Be neat and dress appropriately. Be positive and friendly.

3. Verbal (and obviously nonverbal) communication has been shown to be particularly important. Researchers report that the appropriateness of the content of your responses to the interviewer's questions (conciseness, cooperation, complete but not too verbose answers, keeping to the subject, stating your opinions when relevant, fluency of speech) and your manner of speaking (spontaneity, word use, and articulation) are the two most critical factors in interviewer decisions. Other important factors are maintaining eye contact, a clear and appropriately loud voice, an erect posture, nonverbal communications corresponding to verbal messages, personal appearance, and composure.[13]

4. Your perceived personality will play an important role in your interviews. Presumably they have read your résumé. They know what you have accomplished; now they want to know what you are like. Most interviewers follow a pattern. They ask the same basic questions of everyone (a sample of these questions is presented in Figure 18.2). Sometimes they are probing for confirmation of weaknesses that appear on your résumé. Sometimes they are gathering information. Sometimes they may want to test your composure by berating, badgering, or startling you.

5. Role playing is important. Sit down with a friend and practice the interview. Practice answering and asking questions. Practice on common interview problems. For example, the badgering tactic is fairly common, so you need to practice handling it.

6. Studies show clearly that honesty is the best policy. If you lie to get a job, your stay is likely to be shorter than if you found an organization you were really happy with. Honesty is the best policy for the employer, as well, although some still paint too rosy a picture.

7. You want to appear enthusiastic, intelligent, rational, motivated, and interested in the organization and what it has to offer. You do not want to deceive, but show genuine interest.

8. You should be knowledgeable about the potential employing organization. Do your basic homework—read company reports, analyze its position in the market, and so forth. A study by John D. Shingleton and L. Patrick Scheetz indicates that knowledge about the job and company or business is an extremely important selection criterion.[14]

9. Be on time. In fact, be early. This will allow you to adjust to the situation. Sometimes you will have to wait. Take something to read or study. It saves your time and may just impress the interviewer.

10. Ask questions. You should be prepared to find out what you need to know. Figure 18.2 also lists common questions you might want to ask. Don't be afraid to ask questions, but do not monopolize the conversation.

11. The interview characteristically begins with polite conversation—rituals. The interviewer usually will give a brief presentation about the organization, and then begin asking you questions. You can expect the interviewer's talk to consume most of the opening portions of the interview and anywhere from 60 to 80 percent of the total interview. Once the interviewer's questions have been asked and answered, the interview is usually thrown open for questions from the interviewee.

12. Listen attentively to the interviewer, and pick up on nonverbal messages. Is the interviewer leading you? If so, where? Does the interviewer seem interested in hiring you, or not? How should you respond in either case?

13. Always be polite and courteous. One Ph.D. in psychology with a strong résumé failed to be selected for a faculty position in a school of business because of his rude, almost hostile behavior. If anyone should have known how to behave, it was he. But he did not act appropriately.

14. Show your strong points. Not all interviewers are skilled at interviewing. Make sure the interviewer knows just how good you are.

15. All interviews come to an end. The interviewer is on a schedule and ordinarily must conclude the interview at a certain point. When the end draws near, you do not want to appear overly anxious. Ordinarily, a decision is not made until all candidates have been interviewed. So you will have to wait for a decision. Close on as positive a note as you can.

FIGURE 18.2   *Preparing for an interview: Have you thought about these questions?*

Questions Employers Often Ask

1. What was your overall grade-point average all through college?

2. What was your grade-point average in your major field of study?

3. What courses did you enjoy while in college? What courses did you enjoy least?

4. What do you know about our organization?

5. What qualifications do you have that make you feel that you will be successful in your field?

6. How did you happen to apply for this position with our organization?

7. Have you had any part-time or summer employment?

8. What have you learned from some of the jobs you have held?

9. Have you participated in any volunteer or community work?

10. How did previous employers treat you?

11. Do you like routine work?

12. What are your future vocational plans?

13. In what type of position are you most interested?

14. Are you willing to travel?

15. If you could write your ticket, what kind of job would you like to have?

16. What have you done that shows initiative and willingness to work?

17. Tell me about your extracurricular activities.

18. Did you hold any positions of leadership while at school?

19. Do you have any special skills, and where did you acquire them?

20. Have you had any special accomplishments in your lifetime that you would like to speak of?

21. Why did you leave a given job?

22. Do you have any geographical restrictions? (or preferences?)

23. How do you spend your spare time? What are your hobbies?

24. What are your salary requirements?

25. Do you have a girlfriend (or boyfriend)? Is it serious?

26. Why do you think you would like this particular company?

27. Tell me about your home life during the time you were growing up.

28. Have you ever changed your major field of interest while in college? Why?

29. Why did you choose your particular major?

30. What percentage of your college expenses did you earn? How?

31. Do you feel you did the best scholastic work you could?

32. What do you consider your strengths and weaknesses?

33. Is it an effort for you to be tolerant of persons with backgrounds and interests different from your own?

34. What types of people seem to "rub you the wrong way"?

35. Were you in the armed services? If so, what did you do?

36. What have you been doing since your last job (or since you got out of school)?

37. What books have you read recently?

38. If you were fired, what was the reason?

39. If you went to graduate school, what were your purposes and reasons for going?

40. When can you start work?

41. When can you visit our headquarters for further interviews?

Questions You May Want to Ask the Employer

1. Who was the last person on this job and what is he or she doing now?

2. Why was someone not promoted from within the organization to this vacancy?

3. Who will be my immediate supervisor and will I have a chance to speak to that person personally before being hired?

4. What is the growth potential of your organization?

5. What is the organizational pattern, and where do I fit into it?

6. What is the nature of the job?

7. Is there a job description of my job?

8. How long can I expect to be at the location in which I start?

9. Is it anticipated that I will have extended travel?

10. How much time will be spent away from home?

11. What is the normal progression of salary increases? (This should not be an early question.)

12. What are the housing arrangements and conditions in the general area?

SOURCE: From *Business Today*, second edition, by David J. Rachman and Michael H. Mescon. Copyright © 1976, 1979, 1982, 1985 by Random House, Inc. Reprinted by permission.

THE SELF-ACTUALIZED INDIVIDUAL

Now that you have knowledge of life planning, now that you have knowledge of career planning and the interview, it is time to turn your thoughts to the ultimate objective of the LBORR philosophy: self-actualization. How will you know when you have reached self-actualization?

Maslow himself describes the self-actualized person in *Motivation and Personality*.[15] And while I have expanded somewhat on his definition of this process, his descriptions are still relevant. Below is a brief synopsis of his views of the self-actualized person from a psychological and interpersonal viewpoint.

1. More efficient perception of reality and more comfortable relations with it. Secure people are more accurate judges of others' personalities than those who are less secure. A positive self-image is part of these people's personalities. They are able to detect fakery and phoniness in others.
2. Acceptance (of self, others, nature). These people accept themselves, others, and life for what it is. They are not crippled by shame, guilt, or anxiety.
3. Spontaneity, simplicity, naturalness. These are "real" people. They say what they think, they show their emotions, they are not deceitful.
4. Problem centering. They are concerned with tasks and objectives. They accomplish. They show less concern for themselves than for others, in contrast to an insecure person's continual introspection.
5. The quality of detachment, the need for privacy. They are able to remove themselves from the situation. They are able to contemplate. They seek solitude occasionally.
6. Autonomy, independence of culture and environment, will, active agents. They are relatively independent of events, circumstances around them, their physical and social environment. They are concerned with growth, not with deficiency motivation. They depend on the world less and themselves more than the average person.
7. Continued freshness of appreciation. Self-actualizing people have the wonderful capacity to appreciate again and again, freshly and naively, the basic goods of life, with awe, pleasure, wonder, and even ectasy, however familiar these experiences may have become.
8. The mystic experience; the peak experience. These people have feelings of limitless horizons opening up to them. They are subject to feelings of great ecstasy, wonder, and awe. This is not to be construed as a religious experience.
9. *Gemeinschaftsgefühl*. Maslow used this word, first coined by Alfred Adler and meaning "community feeling," to describe the deep feelings of concern that the self-actualized have for humankind. The self-actualized have a deep feeling of identification, sympathy, and affection for the human condition, but also may be angry or disgusted with it.
10. Interpersonal relations. Self-actualized people are more intimate than others. Their relations are deeper and more personal. They are also selective in their friendships and relations with others. They seek out other self-actualized persons. Their circle of friends is small.
11. The democratic character structure. Maslow found most self-actualized people to be democratic and unprejudiced. They seem to have no interest

in irrelevant, superficial personal characteristics of others, such as skin color.

12. Discrimination between means and ends, good and evil. Self-actualized people are usually certain of right and wrong. They have little conflict or chaos in their own lives over moral issues. They are ethical. They have strong moral standards, but not always the conventional ones.

13. Philosophical, unhostile sense of humor. These people poke fun only at humanity in general and at people's smallness. They are not hostile in their humor, nor do they like ethnic or superiority/inferiority jokes.

14. Creativeness. This was the single characteristic that Maslow found in all the self-actualizers he studied. There were no exceptions.

15. Resistance to enculturation; the transcendence of any particular culture. Self-actualizers do not adjust well to the dictates of the culture. They get along, but they have an inner detachment from it.

16. The imperfections of self-actualizing people. They suffer from the same problems as others, but usually not so many or so deeply. They, too, may be silly, thoughtless, wasteful. They may be surprisingly ruthless. They are often surgically cold when necessary. They may be boring, quick-tempered, so rational as to appear unkind, so deep in concentration as to appear unthoughtful. They may recover from someone's death so quickly as to appear heartless. They may be absent-minded, they may be rude, they are quite independent, they may marry out of pity, they may be taken advantage of. They may experience the range of emotions from euphoria to despair. They are usually powerful in human relations.

17. Values and self-actualization. Their value orientations stem from their positive views of people and life. They accept themselves, humankind, and nature.

18. The resolution of dichotomies in self-actualization. Maslow argues that healthy people, self-actualizing people, need to be examined so that a sound theory of psychology can be established. He argues that healthy people, too, have their personality dichotomies, but that they differ from those of less healthy people, on whom most of psychological theory is based.

Are you self-actualized? Do these descriptions sound like you? It is not likely that all of the descriptions would fit any one person, but if most of them fit you, you are probably self-actualized in these areas. It is very difficult to find job situations that are self-actualizing. As you know, most jobs do not have the decision latitude or the job content to allow for self-actualization. But by working through the ten life areas, one can be self-actualized without having a self-actualizing job.

RESULTS AND REWARDS

Periodically, once every few months or perhaps once a year, you need to look back at your objectives and plans and determine how they are progressing. You need to take corrective actions for any objectives you have not achieved, for any plans that are not working out. Occasionally you may wish to refor-mulate your life plans for certain areas.

You also need to reward yourself for high performance levels. Buy that car you've been wanting—if you deserve it and can afford it. For lesser achievements, treat yourself to a good dinner, new clothes, or whatever makes you happy. Take a vacation. You may not only deserve it, but if you are working hard, you may need it. Give yourself a pat on the back. Go ahead, be assertive. Agree with someone that, yes, you did do a good job.

TIPS FOR SUCCESS

1. Live for more than work.
2. Plan your life.
3. Believe in yourself.
4. Practice LBORR.
5. Become all you are capable of becoming.

SUMMARY

1. Living by objectives, results, and rewards (LBORR) is both a system and a philosophy for planning your life.
2. Ten major life areas can be pursued if you are seeking self-actualization—seeking to become what you are capable of becoming.
3. Techniques for planning these ten areas from LBORR.
4. If you choose to treat LBORR as a philosophy, then you must believe that you are capable of accomplishing whatever you set out to accomplish.
5. The fact is that if you think you can, you can. If you think you can't, you never will.

DISCUSSION QUESTIONS

1. What are the advantages of creating a life plan?
2. Which of the ten life areas pose the most difficulty for you?
3. Just what are you going to do when you get your degree?
4. What are your major personal strengths? weaknesses?
5. Are you self-actualized? Do you want to be?

APPLYING HUMAN RELATIONS SKILLS

CASE | **Allison Wentworth**

Allison Wentworth completed her bachelor's degree in education and moved automatically into a teaching position in a large city. She taught high school mathematics for ten years. Her teaching gave her great pleasure, but one day— her thirty-second birthday, as a matter of fact—she felt very tired, very bored, and very sick of having constantly to discipline what she perceived to be increasingly unruly children. The fun had gone out of her teaching. A large, well-known state university happened to be located in her city, and as she pondered her future, she began to think about getting a master's degree, maybe in business.

1. How would you advise Ms. Wentworth to apply the concepts presented in this chapter?

Take the ten life areas and plan your life in these areas. You may need to do some reading in order to determine what you wish to do in each area. List what you have learned about yourself from this book and how it applies to this exercise.

EXERCISE

LIFE STRATEGY DETERMINATION FORM

Short Term	Long Term
Objectives (destinations)	Objectives (destinations)
1.	1.
2.	2.
3.	3.
Strengths (internal)	Strengths (internal)
1.	1.
2.	2.
3.	3.
Weaknesses (internal)	Weaknesses (internal)
1.	1.
2.	2.
3.	3.
Opportunities (external)	Opportunities (external)
1.	1.
2.	2.
3.	3.
Threats (external)	Threats (external)
1.	1.
2.	2.
3.	3.
Final plans of action (roads)	Final plans of action (roads)
1.	1.
2.	2.
3.	3.

REFERENCES

1. Earl Nightingale, *What Makes Successful People Tick* and *The Common Denominator of Success* (Chicago: Nightingale-Connant Corp., n.d.), cassette tapes.
2. Dennis E. Waitley, *The Psychology of Winning* (Chicago: Nightingale-Connant Corp., 1978), cassette tape; Daniel Goleman, "1528 Little Geniuses and How They Grew," *Psychology Today*, February 1980, pp. 28–55.
3. As told by a company representative of the development program division to a group of new sales recruits, Fall 1985.

4. Waitley, *Psychology of Winning.*

5. Richard DeCharms, *Personal Causation* (Reading, Mass.: Addison-Wesley, 1968), pp. 6–10.

6. Abraham Maslow, *Motivation and Personality* (New York: Harper & Row, 1970), pp. 149–80.

7. Erik H. Erikson, *Childhood and Society* (New York: W. W. Norton, 1950).

8. Roger Gould, "The Phases of Adult Life: A Study in Developmental Psychology," *American Journal of Psychiatry*, November 1972, pp. 521–31.

9. Gail Sheehy, *Passages* (New York: Bantam, 1977).

10. Vern Walter, "Self-Motivated Personal Career Planning—A Breakthrough in Human Resource Management," *Personnel Journal*, March 1976, pp. 112–15, 136, 137, and April 1976, pp. 162–67, 185, 186.

11. Maxwell Maltz, *Psycho-cybernetics* (New York: Pocket Books, 1970), p. 35. Jack Nicklaus, unquestionably the most successful golfer ever, envisions every shot before he hits it.

12. Maggie Scarf, "Images That Heal," *Psychology Today*, September 1980, pp. 32–46; DeCharms, *Personal Causation*; Abraham K. Korman, "Toward an Hypothesis of Work Behavior," *Journal of Applied Psychology*, January 1970, pp. 31–41; Richard M. Suinn, "Psychology for Olympic Champs," *Psychology Today*, July 1976, pp. 38–42; Napoleon Hill, *Think and Grow Rich* (New York: Hawthorn, 1966).

13. James G. Hollandsworth, Jr., Richard Kazelskis, Joanne Stevens, and Mary Edith Dressel, "Relative Contributions of Verbal, Articulative, and Nonverbal Communication to Employment Decisions in the Job Interview Setting," *Personnel Psychology*, Summer 1979, pp. 359–67.

14. John D. Shingleton and L. Patrick Scheetz, "Recruiting Trends," Michigan State University, 1977.

15. Maslow, *Motivation and Personality*, pp. 149–80.

NAME INDEX

SUBJECT INDEX

About the author

JAMES M. HIGGINS is Professor of Management in the Roy E. Crummer Graduate School of Business of Rollins College in Winter Park, Florida. His primary research interests are in the areas of creative problem solving, creative strategic management, and the impact of self-image on motivation. Higgins graduated from the Emory University School of Business in 1965 and received his Masters of Professional Accountancy from Georgia State University in 1967. He completed his doctorate in management in 1974 at Georgia State University. Dr. Higgins is active in consulting and management development and the related experiences are incorporated in much of his writing. He has published numerous articles, papers and cases. His articles have appeared in: *Business Horizons, Personnel Journal, Human Resources Management, Managerial Planning, Business,* and *The Internal Auditor.* He is coauthor of *Strategic Management and Organizational Policy: Text and Cases, third edition,* Dryden Press, 1986; and author of *Strategy Formulation, Implementation and Control,* Dryden Press, 1985; *Cases in Contemporary Business,* Dryden Press, 1982; and, *A Manual of Student Activities in Human Relations,* Random House, 1982. Dr. Higgins is also working on two additional books, one on creativity, the other an introduction to management.